THE NEW ANNALS OF STATEN ISLAND

Cleve Overton

Diaspora Voices Press
Washington, DC

Unless otherwise indicated, all photographs and illustrations are from the author's personal collection.

Cover design by Cleve Overton and Signature Book Printing, Inc.

First Edition
 June 2014

Library of Congress Cataloguing-in-Publication Data.

ISBN 978-0-9772393-2-0

Printed by Signature Book Printing, Inc.
www.sbpbooks.com

This book is dedicated to my patron saint, Jude.

11-24-2014

Joyce:

Enjoy this voyage

Bless n cheers

ACKNOWLEDGEMENTS

How successfully one gets through depends a lot on others. I could not continue if I did not recognize certain people, alive and dead, who have assisted me in many ways, over many years.

I am a recipient of luck to have these few people in my life. They are mostly opposites, of each other and my own smugness to imagine that I understood the absurdity of the task, and unaware of the mental fissures between thinking and writing.

I want to express my deep gratitude to Marion Granigan, for her patience and editing skills, for hours and days and weeks of wordsmithing. Thanks to David Crawford who assisted in physical lugging and hauling, to Bill Brown, for providing antiquarian books to find sources; to Michael Janis, Rhodes Scholar, for his quiet wisdom and suggestions. Thanks to Janet Grace Rispoli, a constant voice of support for many years.

Thanks to my sister, Inez Black, for many years of food for my mind and body; Ross Cowey, for thoughtful critique, Moctar Toumbou, for holding my hand through Islam and Africa; Mickey "ole Sarge" Bell, for keeping the military memories intact; Mimi Wolford, a trusted buddy, confidant.

The supportive voices of Johnny "Honey" Jones and Henry Elliott remain alive after they have passed. And my extended families, especially the Shaws of Ithaca, New York, Barbara, Jim and Dennis, who remain intact, who give substance to longevity, and hope.

If anyone feels left out, at vespers they are with me.

Cleve

Contents

Introduction

1. The Dutch in New York   1

2. The 1741 Conspiracy   90

3. Cops   145

4. I Took a Man Down Tonight   207

5. Black History Month   219

6. Sandy Ground   234

7. Cemeteries   311

8. Murals   317

9. Skin, Hair, and Color   343

10. Black Special Agent   357

11. Reflections on Blacks in the Military   371

12. NASCAR Mocumentary   397

13. My Story of God   414

INTRODUCTION

My purpose was to try to write a story based on the lack of education and historical knowledge, to gather the facts, as best I can, in an historic proportion by avoiding unimportant and confusing details, omitting the dry and uninteresting statistics, and telling a simple, straightforward story, one that may add to the lives of young and old alike, and for the contemporary dude on the street.

It is important, before going further, to give a scope and geographical location on which these essays, stories, and maps are based. One method would be to divide the work into epochs, time and place fitting into each other, back and forth, working into details and events of interest. There is no way to tell the story from the beginning to the present without flashbacks, and hopefully they will be inconspicuous.

The island was written about by many people who have vanished into insignificance. My late father left few memories and his library was sparse, but I have his book, "The Annals of Staten Island," by J.J. Clute, who said of Staten Island, "If we look for a spot which is forever blest by nature with her perennial smile, we would never leave our own green isle." The book is now yellow, soft, brittle and crumbly. The only other legacy my father left is an oil painting of the red-caped guards at the palace gates of the Senegalese President in Dakar. Both have played a significantly large part in my life and have survived over these long eight decades.

There were people living on Staten Island before the beginning of recorded history. The inhabitants were called Indians. These people developed a society through commerce with other tribes and navigation around the other islands, subsisting on hunting, fishing. They did not leave a written language. However, archeologists have found their use of inscriptions, funeral mounds, implements, and weapons to be a reliable basis of history. There may be many secrets, and it is not too difficult to believe that these were the earliest people living on this mysterious land. Little by little, the story of this extraordinary people is unfolding as science and research progresses. To date, all the writings have been produced by Whites and Europeans. It is the Eurocentric point of view. Being a Black man of African descent, I believe these books and the lives of the authors are not much like mine or my ancestors. I do not doubt that historic places and people can be used in a school curriculum. It is only that there is something called a larger culture. The ethnicity of a culture is documented by those who possess the ability to publish history. This is a marvelous story, a marvelous land, and it was a marvelous island with people whose history we know so little of, except that they were conquered by a farflung race of European people and they perished.

There are also a number of other disciplines, studies and pursuits like anthropology and anatomy, etc. that extend the simple history and education by adding confusing statistics, numbers and verbal verbosity along with hieroglyphics and bewildering details. My purpose is specific. I am a Black man and an American born and raised in New York City, on Staten Island, the sister island of Manhattan, The Big Apple, the City of New York, the biggest, wealthiest, most populous city in the United States.

George Curtis said, "God may have made a more beautiful place than Staten Island, but He never did." That was the first micro-cut I swallowed when I began to find my way through the silent dilemma that surrounds most people who ask themselves, why am I here, and who am I? I needed a more accurate voice about this island than that of George Curtis, who has a high school on Staten Island named after him. My quote from Bob Marley is more accurate, when he said, "If you think education is expensive, being illiterate is more expensive."

However, it turns out that despite the books I have read, articles I have filed, short stories I have written from oral interviews, research I have done and the roads and countries traveled, to find my way home, I have come up short of my destination, and all this has developed into this compendium of essays.

The volume of photos, maps, ship logs, and tapes is so extensive that I found it difficult to know how or where to begin. It has become increasingly apparent that there is little historic depth in literature on the Blacks in New York and the surrounding areas since the arrival of slave ships from Europe and Africa. It appears there is a willingness to disregard the contribution of Blacks and the original inhabitants, the Indians, as irrelevant to written history. Like so many others trying to locate my place of origin on this globe, I have submitted oral swabs, hair samples, blood DNA to labs around the globe, only to realize they knew nothing more than I, and I found the money and time invested would be better spent at my desk to do this. It is also there among the detritus material that I would find my ancestors.

I had reached of needing to begin my own files, and investigate the truths attached to basic questions. Black Americans have not had the luxury of having long-range family genealogy, keeping files and creating a broad network to house them, except in the churches they attend for baptisms and marriages. I found that on Staten Island from the early 1900's no archives survive for scholars to read, examine or write about. There being no historical inquiry from other Blacks, and Whites use the conveniently available public libraries. There have been attempts at newsletters and bulletins, notices posted in various Black establishments, abandoned after a few years, with continuous historical readings done by Whites and Blacks which appeared on the margins with a Eurocentric voice. Black voices are found to contain needed color and amusement for White subtext. I found it rare to find Black people mentioned as Mr. or Mrs. Frank Jones, usually mentioned is "a negro," the "Black" or servant, meaning Black, never any reference to his or her life or work in the community.

Having completed reading and researching papers on Staten Island's early development, S.I. History on the web, a timeline of Staten Island History, the Historical Research Guide, items in the Local History Collections, Historical Organizations and Museums, the Genealogy Resources, Cemeteries, Census Directories, Church, Legal Records, and Military Records, I found nothing to tell me any more about my being a Black person in terms of my ancestors, or any Black families for that matter, or evidence that Black people lived here and made contributions. When historical documents mentioned Black slaves in the colony of New Amsterdam in 1629, I wanted to know more.

The nearest library was located in Port Richmond, one of the oldest communities on Staten Island. The most often quoted twin books are the "bibles" used to teach about the island history. The two huge volumes are titled, **Staten Island and its People, a History,**

1609 – 1929 written by Charles W. Leng, B. Sc. and William T. Davis, also referred to as **The Annals of Staten Island**. I found nothing in the Annals except that Blacks were there. The two massive tomes, contain stories about a farmer who sent his Negroes to notify his neighbors because his dog had cornered a suspicious person in a tree, who had in his possession three fresh beef tongues and a long knife. The suspicious person was quoted as saying, "Don't shoot massa, I'll come down." After descending they seized him, pinioned his arms. He was a stranger to all. Questions were asked and he remained silent. Growing impatient of the fellow's stubbornness, a noose was slipped over his head and in a very brief space he was dangling from one of the limbs of the tree. These are the only kinds of references one can find in these books, and they constitute an incomplete and Eurocentric view of the reality of the time.

Some numbers and figures relating to population are fairly accurate, while others are wide of the reality mark, guesswork at best. In order to know a person's actual age you must have his birth date. But census takers or colonial numbers keepers contain nothing more than estimates and guesses. Figures from the Leng and Davis Staten Island History books have been used extensively for generations of loyal followers. Unfortunately, many of the figures reported have been published without any clear indication of how they were arrived at, based on estimates and guesses and hearsay.

The new world was occupied by inhabitants who lived in huts, but there was no way of knowing the exact number of huts or the actual density of the native colony in various regions. Figures for males and females were often lumped together and no attempt made to distinguish their numbers, simply stated as "adult male" and "adult female," with the figures for children without value. The numbers for "child" were extremely vague.

The first colonies counted and classified the population by race. And every student of history and the colonies would like to know the number of Whites, the number if natives, in addition to the numbers of Blacks. But many colonial reports which distinguish the population by race do not convey this information.

Other classifications note religion, occupation or literacy. Birth and death registrations were nearly compulsory, however exact dates were difficult to come by in the 1600's during the occupation of the new world. This information was not recorded for slaves or natives and not enforced. The vital statistics data on the colonial population as a whole is in an unsatisfactory state, and utterly inadequate. The reasons for this chaotic state are manifold, but what is certain is that, whenever there is racial inequality, numbers are determined by those who consider themselves the superior one, a situation with which not only the colonial counts are confronted.

In the early 1900's, census takers, known as enumerators, in poor locations used a different form for persons who were not visibly "European." In these cases, census takers were instructed to refrain from giving any offence with any comment or question in the presence of the parties concerned, but to make a private note on the completed forms next to the names of any persons he considered not to be classifies as European. After which, the particulars with respect to the persons in question should be transferred to forms applicable to their skin color, to their race.

Staten Island history is filled with the notations and voices of confusion; Notations for "Colored" and "Creole" stated for the record, "These people through physical degeneration appear to lack the necessary stamina to withstand diseases affecting their respiratory organs, and fall easy prey to the pneumonia form of influenza." And also, "A considerable number of Staten Island-born Negroes insist on calling themselves Creoles, either through false pride or ignorance." The authors of census reports noted, "Many persons of mixed blood have improperly and ridiculously termed themselves as White." Interestingly enough, And as to the Dutch, in the Netherlands where a great majority of the colonists originated, these distinctions between European and native servants of color belonging to them were not maintained, and those assimilated with them were simply considered Europeans.

I had nothing to read about this island and why I was here. I had no memories other than scraps of overheard conversations of family and friends. My mother was an Eastern Star lady, their fancy dress occasions and commemorations faded by the time I was a teenager and she dropped any mention of it to me. My father was a Prince Hall Mason, and the males in our family had to join. That tradition faded for me when he was injured on his job, then separated from us and moved to California, then Mexico. There were no other special family rituals except the usual American holidays, which were special only because they gave me time off from whatever I was doing. We were fully assimilated Americans. At one time I had to relinquish my bed to make space for Gramma, my mother;s mother, who was old and very sick. She lived in Florida, they said, in "Okifunoki." When we giggled about her birthplace, we were told to HUSH-UP and behave. After she died on Staten Island in my bed, I found that her name was simply Gramma Sawyer, that she was born in a swamp, and she had been over 100 years old. She had no other family or friends, so she was quietly buried on Staten Island. I never had any more conversations about her, and that was the extent of what I knew about my family's history.

My life followed the strict regimens of the system for more than eight decades, and I found that I have not been accorded the knowledge that would allow me to live as a fully educated and useful member of society. The lack of education has left me with a hundred million micro-cuts that have crippled me, as it has great numbers of Black men on this island and in the United States. While I have no attaché brief case filled with charts and graphs, trust me, this is true. Education and the knowledge of history in the 21st century are overwhelmingly sought after in a shrinking globe and a rising world population and the total submersion in a technological electronic world. Their importance cannot be denied. And it is here among the detritus material collected that I would find my ancestors.

My friend said, "You have a story to tell and you will need to get it out there, otherwise other people will tell your story, and it's going to be wrong. So tell your own story in whatever manner is comfortable for you."

ON VULNERABILITY

Brene Brown wrote an essay on the power of vulnerability. What follows is a condensation of that essay, including some direct reproduction because it resonates with me and says it more eloquently than I could.

"My entire research career has been fueled by a commitment to bring to light the emotions, thoughts and behaviors that we all experience but never discuss – to find patterns and connections in our experiences so that we can learn more about the journey from fear and scarcity to love, belonging and worthiness."

"The most difficult and rewarding challenge of my work is how to be both a mapmaker and a traveler. For better or for worse, there have been tough lessons on finding balance, asking for help, and seeking out constructive, respectful debate and feedback without letting in too much of the downright mean-spiritedness that's rampant in our culture."

"But as hard and frankly, as weird as it's been at times, I didn't trade in my mantra nor did I give up on what I learned from the research. Vulnerability is not weakness, or is it optional. We can't opt out of the uncertainty, exposure and emotional risks through our daily experiences."

"The only choice we have is how we're going to respond to feeling vulnerable. And contrary to popular belief, our shields don't protect us. They simply keep us from being seen, heard, and known."

"Even if letting ourselves be seen and opening ourselves up to judgment or disappointment feels terrifying, the alternatives are worse: Choosing to feel nothing - numbing. Choosing to perfect, perform, and please our way out of vulnerability. Choosing rage, cruelty or criticism. Choosing shame or blame. They all lead to the same thing: disengagement and disconnection."

"Theologian Howard Thurman writes: "Don't ask what the world needs, ask what makes you come alive, and go do it. Because what the world needs is more people who have come alive."

This may help the reader to understand or to explain some of this book's recurring and perhaps disturbing, peculiarities, so at the outset I want to say this particular book has grown out of a chance discovery while researching a foundation for what I knew, but did not know. This comes after many years and attempts at assembling essential pieces of a puzzle, bit by bit.

This grew out of a chance discovery when boredom and curiosity led me to a stately building in Washington D.C. facing the nation's capitol across the well-scrubbed wide roadway. The Jefferson Building, a solid bulk, is the main building of the Library of Congress, the world's largest library. The stately building with its neoclassical exterior, copper-plated dome and marble halls, is named after Jefferson, one of the nation's founding fathers, and as president, he enshrined the institution into law in 1814. After British troops destroyed the first library's vast collection, he gave his extensive collection to the new library.

I moved into a prescient mode, with an inner feeling that I was where I was supposed to be. I entered and pass through the guard's inspection table and asked for a library card, showed my home address, had a photo taken, and was escorted with my plastic membership card into the caverns with an aide who talked incessantly while I mumbled answers because I had not gotten beyond the feeling that I should quite simply be here. I do not have a specific agenda or purpose, because I have been told that I am blessed, which is enough of a need for me, and besides, it was cold outside.

This was the older section of the library; there are two sections connected by an underground walkway. My focus would be about my island, Staten Island, what person or organization that has published information I might find here, the history of my birthplace, New

York City. I was told to go to the second floor. For an hour I read from magazines and booklets, old and interesting stories from the Civil War, newspaper articles and other interesting but meaningless words that seemed to have no connection for me. In the history of America, Blacks and Whites are entirely intertwined, and slavery was the most important institution in the early Dutch and British expansionist movement in the centuries that followed the first voyages of Christopher Columbus. As a Black man, that African bondage was essential for me as a guide to place my life and time somewhere in the framework of the history of New York, and it most logical that I should become concerned with the African background of the American Black man to order these thoughts with reference to time and sequence of the puzzle, and to think in terms of history and origins.

Today, the African Diaspora is the focal point of publications and interdisciplinary studies in anthropology, archaeology, history, material culture, and heritage dynamics concerning African descendant populations and cultures across the globe. The broad range of topics includes the historical processes of culture, gender, power, and racialization operating within and upon African descendent communities. The process reaches all corners of the continent and the world and engages scholarly, professional, and community perspectives on the social dynamics and the historical legacies of African decent and communities worldwide. Many interdisciplinary studies and fields are now attempting to coordinate studies of manuscripts, illustrations, essays, and research articles. Black slaves from the African continent were not culturally blank when they were brought to the new world territories. The men and women carried with them the physical and mental strengths to survive in conditions the world has never known, the first human holocaust.

I also wanted to find the depth of the African heritage that has been retained if any, that has an influence on life in America today, and what has been lost before bending to the will for survival to the White man. What are the social scientists learning of the convergence of cultures?

And there at the Library of Congress, I did find a book title that looked interesting. It was **The Great New York Conspiracy, a History of the Negro Plot of 1741.**

I filled out a reading room request and waited for the book to be delivered to the desk clerk. Little did I know at that time that I had one of the very few original printed books about this incident in New York in my hands, a well worn red leather, gold-embossed copy I would find later that there were very few printed, and that the topic and the issues were not read by or available to the general public. There was no historical research about this New York conspiracy. I would find reading the old English font printing difficult, but I also found reading into the story it was much more difficult to put down, inviting me to get inside, encouraging me not to abandon it, to keep at it, which I did. I will never be able to explain why, but this was a book that made me unable to concentrate on anything else. It gave me a contact high to be feeling, holding this venerable copy in my hands. I spent the rest of the day reading it and from time to time feeding coins into a machine to make copies. When the library closed, I put a hold on the book until I could return.

When I did return a few days later, I was told the book was in the process of being converted to an electronic file. I was frustrated but there was nothing I could do but follow the written instructions the clerk gave me. Electronic File Info.: gemic 1st0063 htt;//hdl.loc.gov/loc.gdc/gcmisc.1st0063. The clerk wrote "hot link to American Memory citation" and printed out 4 additional pages and passed them across the table to me. I thanked her before dressing again for the cold outdoors. I had no idea how I would ever again have access to that book, and I did not have access at that time to a computer to get into the electronic file. I would stuff them away until some inner need surfaced to move again. That was November 6th 2003.

That book and the subject matter, the year and the voice would not leave me. From the copies that I made I taped the cover of the book to my desk. The subject and the type in old English were difficult to read. It was first printed in New York by James Parker at the new Printing Office in 1744. The first text was:

"A Journal of the Proceedings in The Detection of the Conspiracy, formed by some White people in conjunction with Negro and other Slaves, for Burning the city of New York in America, And Murdering the Inhabitants. Which Conspiracy was partly put in Execution, by Burning His Majesty's House in Fort George, within said City, on Wednesday the Eighteenth of March 1741. And setting fire to several Dwellings and other Houses there, within a few Days succeeding, And by another Attempt made in the Perfection of the same infernal Scheme, by putting fire between two other Dwelling Houses within said City on the Fifteenth Day of February 1742 which was accidentally and timely discovered and extinguished."

The following translations from the book itself are difficult because of the old English word usage, print font, and speech patterns.

"I. a NARRATIVE of the Trials, Condemnations, Executions, and behavior of the several Criminals. At the Gallows and Stake, with their speeches and confessions, with Notes, Observations and Reflections occasionally interpreter throughout the Whole.

2. An APPENDIX, wherein it is set forth some additional Evidence concerning the said Conspiracy and Conspirators, which has come to Light since their Trials and Executions .

3. List of several persons (Whites and Blacks) committed on Account of the Conspiracy, and the several Criminals executed, and of those transported with the Places whereto."

THE SUMMER OF ORAL HISTORY

In 2006, I bought a new pick-up truck and a used trailer and lived on Staten Island, in a friend's vacant lot, while I conducted interviews of Black Staten Islanders. I called them oral histories, but the topics covered included the individuals' current situation, political views, and other current topics. Many of the people opened up to me in a way they would not have if I were younger, or White. Still, in reviewing the tapes, and other tapes I had made in earlier years, I came to the conclusion that I did not have the right to air those people's thoughts and words in this book. I would donate the tapes to the archives at the College of Staten Island, so that future generations would know what Black people thought in this century.

What the interviews told me was there is still an insidious residue of slavery and white domination, and latent racism still permeated the island. Geography, economics, politics, religion, and race relations contribute to this particular regional history, and this story uncomfortably represents larger national and international trends.

Racism is less visible but it has not been eradicated. The idea of representing some of the story at historical intersections avoids some of the pitfalls that result from isolating singular identifying factors from the mosaic that comprises the human experience. Language consistently intersects with and amplifies these factors. Various terms describe populations in this account and inevitably these terms are fraught with political and social meaning.

Current scholars, activists and others have engaged in rich and heated debates over significant issues. While it is hoped that this book may contribute to these important dialogues, it is hoped that these reinterpretations provoke thought rather than create new barriers.

When some documentation was initially presented, historians did not preserve that information if they deemed it not important or relevant. Considerable data from previous decades and centuries has already been lost to historians and more recent documents continue to be destroyed. Even when historians can access information, limitations abound, logs show a narrow, impersonal view. When historians contemplate a project, they long for personal artifacts like diaries, letters or drawings, items that reveal interpretations rather than experiences. When artifacts do exist, they are often the property of the institution, or their archives. Institutions have little or no motivation to release these artifacts to historians, especially if they shine light on policies or practices that are now considered shameful.

In order to address some of the gaps, I had to rely on my own oral history interviews. And even these close contacts were problematic. Many people shared their memories, offering detail and humanity that rarely filters through institutional reports.

Although there were attempts to contact individuals, many declined to participate. This work cannot be a traditional biography. While any work of history can be seen as projection of the authors' perceptions and interpretations, this history is especially complicated.

We are often painfully reminded that our lived experiences differ fundamentally from those of the early settlers and Indians. At the same time we are equally painfully reminded that this story is our story as both activist researchers and as people living in America at this time felt appalled and heartbroken while researching this story. The kinds of oppression, invasion, and injustice simply defy words. That is the trying narrative of this story. It has stretched my ability as well as my concepts of what a history or biography should be. In spite of the limitations, I hope that there is much to learn and remember from those who, on both sides, lived through unspeakable histories. Nor are those injustices completely insurmountable.

Being a minority in both caste and class, we moved about anyway on the hem of life, struggling to consolidate our weaknesses and hang on, or to creep gingerly up the folds of the garment. There were times of racial terror and brutal violence. They were the inheritors of a complicated legacy of freedom and horror.

Food was scarce and sanitation inadequate. In spite of the daily chaos there was a time of freedom and to come together. Plans of economic survival and growth were charted. Political leaders began to emerge, Churches and schools were established. There were times when they effectively removed all savages from areas with police and militias that made sure the savages followed those rules.

Members of the Black Staten Island community became barbers, restaurateurs, artisans, educators, preachers, lawyers, and physicians. As years passed, it became clear to Blacks that significant change in the racial dynamics of the Island would be a long battle with many setbacks and disappointments. The gerrymandering significantly dampened the Black political voice. But there was a strong infrastructure in the Black homesteads, based on the churches, schools and professional achievements. There were some interracial alliances that emphasized their common concerns and political power. Interracial democracy seemed to be the way of the future.

The film adaptation of Thomas Dixon's novel in 1915, "THE KLANSMAN" was a nation wide hit. The movie was grist for the mill to keep slavery alive, and it was well attended. But the event was not newsworthy due to the quiet resistance of many church ministers. Dixon was born on Staten Island and in an interview he said many of his characters were taken from his hometown. It was also shown at the theater on Richmond Terrace at the foot of Harbor Road in Mariners Harbor, where a number of shows, such as "Annie Get Your Gun" were preformed live.

The film was welcomed from the halls of the United States Congress and it gave a clarion call to halt Black legislators' clout. Black brutes were violating white women, miscegenation would run rampant and a savior was needed to halt this, namely the Ku Klux Klan. A way had to be found to assist the all White police forces, and the all White judges, and the all White juries. And case after case followed hanging after hanging, and castration to such an extent that Blacks followed the letter of intent, your lives are in danger, do not trespass.

■■

CHAPTER 1

THE DUTCH IN NEW YORK

I hope readers will forgive me for not entertaining other locations across borders.

My sole concentration is and has been Staten Island, which is the climate and breeding ground for the frustration and sheer relentlessness for so many in the shadow of the "big apple" who confront it each and every day. There are many big questions, and I have no easy answers, no easy breakthroughs. Like others, I have taken years of trial and error reinforcement of some behaviors to become a civilized adult human being.

There have been people living on Staten Island before the beginning of recorded history. The inhabitants were called Indians. These people developed a high degree through commerce, with other tribes and navigation around the other islands, subsisting on hunting, fishing, they did not leave a written language. However, archeologists have found a great number of instances of their use of inscriptions, funeral mounds, implements, and weapons and so forth, that have been considered a reliable ground of history. We suspect that there are many secrets, and it is not too difficult to believe that these were the earlier people living on this mysterious land. Little by little this story of this extraordinary people is unfolding as science and research progresses. It has always been written and the new writings are more impressive than the last. To date, all the writings are and have been produced by Whites and Europeans. It is the

Eurocentric point of view. Being a Black man of African descent, I believe these books and the lives of the authors are not much like mine or my ancestors. I don't doubt that historic places and people can be used in a school curriculum. It is only that there is something called a larger culture. The ethnicity of a culture must be advanced on the level equal to those that possess the ability to publish history. This gets quickly complicated when we have to learn history. This is a marvelous story, a marvelous land and it was a marvelous island when people whose history we know so little of, almost nothing, except that they were conquered by a nether race of people that were Europeans and they perished.

There are also a number of other disciplines, studies and pursuits like anthropology and anatomy etc that extend the simple history and education work by adding confusing statistics, numbers and verbal verbosity along with hieroglyphics and bewildering details. It was important for me to simply try to do this for very specific reasons. I am a Black man and an American born and raised in New York City, on Staten Island, the sister island of Manhattan, The Big Apple, the City of New York. the biggest wealthiest most populous city in the United States.
It was George Curtis that said, 'God may have made a more beautiful place than Staten Island, but he never did". That was the first micro cut I swallowed when I began to find my way through the silent dilemma that surrounds most people that ask themselves, why am I here, and who am I. I needed a more accurate voice about this island than George Curtis who has a high school on Staten Island named after him. My quote from Bob Marley is more accurate, when he said, "If you think education is expensive, being illiterate is more expensive."

I wanted to write a story based on the lack of education and historical knowledge, up to 2011, and the New York City Staten Island as best I can. To gather the facts in a historic proportion as best I can by avoiding unimportant and confusing details, omit the dry and uninteresting stats and tell a simple straightforward story, one in which I hope will add to the lives to the old and young alike. And for me high school and a smattering of a college education, the contemporary dude on the street, my concentration is Staten Island.
However it turns out that the books I have read, articles I have filled, short stories I have written from oral voices I have listened to, research I have done and the roads and countries traveled, to find my way home, I have come up short of my destination, and all this has developed into this compendium of essays.
The volume of photos, maps, and tapes are extensive, so large that I found it difficult to know how or where to begin. It has become increasingly apparent and continues to be little historic depth in literature of the blacks in New York and the surrounding areas since the arrival of ships from Europe that brought slaves with them. Reading the ship logs and shipping data it appears that a willingness to disregard the entire black and the original inhabitants the Indians people as irrelevant to written historical history. Like so many others trying to locate some place of origin on this globe I have submitted oral swabs. Hair samples, blood DNA to labs around the globe, only to realize they knew nothing more than I, and I found the money and time invested would be better spent at my desk to do this.

2

It is also there among the detritus material that I would find my ancestors. "Memory is a powerful force in human society, but the repression of memory is even stronger, especially when the past is upsetting or morally difficult to confront. In the early decades of the 19th century, America held two political values we now see as contradictory but which – we tend to forget – then coexist comfortably side by side. The first is egalitarianism, and the second is white racial supremacy."

"Many Americans after the founding decades of the republic espoused a fervent belief in the cause of Anglo-Saxon racial dominance, and in both spirit and practice, the United States was a nation of and for white Americans, a nation of black slavery and Indian removal and genocide."

"The evolution of American society, of all human societies, is a narrative that proceeds at different speeds, moving slowly in some eras, in others undergoing a rapid transformation. Time is routine, passing steadily in regular degrees, minute by minute, day by day; history is spasmodic. The trials discussed all took place during a period of swift change, a pivotal era in American civic life marked by the implacable approach of the Civil War, its unimaginable bloodletting and the painful, long lingering aftermath. Over the course of 20 years, hundreds of thousands of Americans would lose their lives; the nation would emancipate its vast slave population; and the federal government would undertake the ambitious plan to assist those who had been held in bondage – only to retreat from that effort, ushering in the era of Jim Crow. The black trials that took place during this volatile time were motivated by a series of persistent jurisprudential questions, whose answers we are only just beginning to understand today."

I had reached a point that I need to begin my own files, and the truths attached to basic questions. Black Americans have not had the luxury of having long range family planning and keeping files and creating a broad network to house them except the churches they attend for baptisms and marriages, I found that on Staten Island that has been recently from the early 1900's No archives survive for scholars to read examine or write about. There being no historical inquiry from other blacks, and white s use the conveniently available public libraries. There have been attempts at newsletters and bulletins notices posted in various black establishments, abandoned after a few years, continuous historical readings were done by whites and blacks appeared on the margins with a Eurocentric voice. Black voices are found to contain needed color and amusement for white sub text. I found it rare to fine black people mentioned as Mr., or Mrs. Frank Jones, usually mentioned is 'a negro' the 'black' or servant meaning (black") never any relevance to his life or work in the community.

Having completed reading and researching papers on Staten Island's early development, S.I. History on the web, a timeline of S.I, History, Staten Island History, the Historical Research Guide, Items in the Local History Collections, Historical Organizations and Museums, the Genealogy Resources, Cemeteries, Census Directories, Churches, Legal Records, Military Records, I found nothing to tell me any more about my being a Black person in terms of my ancestors, or any Black families for that matter, or evidence that Black people lived here and made contributions. When historical documents record Black slaves in the colony of New Amsterdam in 1629, I wanted to know more.

My thirst to know who I was and how my ancestors and I came to be residents of Staten Island prodded me to explore the history of the area, but the narrative I was taught in grammar school did not satisfy the thirst for the truth, neither its breadth nor depth ringing true. The fact that many of Staten Island's streets had Dutch names was a testament to the early settlers' proliferation, but their legacy was otherwise obscured. The part my own ancestors played in the development of New York and Staten Island has been even more obscured, and I was determined to bring it to light. I took on this responsibility because Americans can be reluctant to accept the messy details that lie beneath the country's official historical narrative, the one intended to make everyone proud of their heritage. Yes, we're an amazing country and have much of which to be proud. But let's be honest about the humanity of our founders and forefathers, of their sins, wickedness, and weaknesses as well as their strengths, honor, and bravery.

The Dutch were the first colonizers in New York, and for a relatively tiny country, they sent explorers and entrepreneurs to every corner of the globe. As the passage below describes, however, they would find that maintaining the far-reaching empires of colonialism would require too many resources, too many calculations of personal bodies, knowledge, and experience. The English coveted the port at the foot of Manhattan Island. The Dutch immigrants were less motivated to migrate to America than the English, and were not fond of their "dictator" of 17 years, Peter Stuyvesant.

He was the governor, all pomp and majesty, wearing a decorated peg leg, and ruled by stern decrees that won him many enemies. When the English fleet appeared in the harbor and demanded surrender of Manhattan, Stuyvesant's resistance was overruled by New Amsterdam's leading citizens, who were unwilling and unable to fight the well-armed British. These were the major reasons the Dutch would finally consent to giving land to King Charles of England. James, the Duke of York, renamed the colony New York, but his rule was equally dismissive of the needs of the colonists and lawlessness resulted. The following excerpt from [*book citation*] illustrates this further: "The English cast covetous eyes on the Dutch colony of New Netherland, especially the attractive port at the foot of Manhattan Island where the Hudson River ran into the ocean. The Dutch had not been as successful as the English in establishing colonies since its citizens lacked the impetus of English settlers in migrating to America. The people in New Amsterdam, for example, had little regard for the Dutch West India Company and its autocratic governors. The most recent dictator, Peter Stuyvesant, arrived as governor in the colony on May 11, 1647, looking "like a peacock." He was all pomp and majesty. He wore a decorated peg leg, having lost his own in a pitched battle several years earlier. Determined to bring order and one-man control to the colony, he ruled for seventeen years by stern decrees that won him few friends and many enemies.

Since England and Holland were commercial rivals, it did not take long for Charles II to initiate a war by granting to his brother James all the land between the Connecticut and Delaware rivers. Then a British fleet appeared in the harbor of New Amsterdam and demanded the surrender of Manhattan Island. The governor, Peter Stuyvesant, swore he would never surrender, but the leading citizens overruled him. They knew they could not fight off the well-armed and determined British, so they persuaded Stuyvesant to surrender the colony. And not a shot was fired. James, now the proprietor, renamed the colony New York. He blithely assumed he could rule the

Dutch settlers through his chosen governor without any consultation whatsoever with the residents. He soon learned that such an approach from across thousands of miles of ocean guaranteed disobedience and lawlessness."

The Dutch West India Company was composed of wealthy aristocrats and businessmen, usually numbering 28. Their likenesses grace the walls of museums all over the world, representing the seventeenth century Dutch "Golden Age." Often they were big men, had double chins, flabby cheeks, and puffy eyes, suggesting much time in ale houses and overindulgence in the products of their farms and breweries. They were often politicians and powerful dignitaries, and members of Amsterdam's three militia companies. In 2012, the Netherlands loaned many such paintings to the National Gallery of Art in Washington, DC. The group portrait, which grew out of the tradition of militia portraits such as Rembrandt's "Night Watch," memorialized and aggrandized important public figures and leaders.

Peter Stuyvesant had to report on the surrender of property to England when he returned to the Netherlands in 1665. A transcription of his report [book citation] follows.

REPORT ON THE SURRENDER OF NEW NETHERLAND, BY PETER STUYVESANT, 1665

Report of the Honble Peter Stuyvesant, late Director-General of New Netherland, on the Causes which led to the Surrender of that Country to the English, 1665.

Illustrious, High and Mighty Lords:

Whilst I, your Illustrious High Mightinesses' humble servant, was still in New Netherland I was informed, verbally and in writing, that the unfortunate loss and reduction of New Netherland were, in consequence of ignorance of the facts, spoken of and judged in this country by many variously, and by most people not consistently with the truth, according to the appetite and leaning of each. Therefore your Illustrious High Mightinesses' servant, sustained by the tranquillity of an upright and loyal heart, was moved to abandon all, even his most beloved wife, to inform you, Illustrious, High and Mighty, of the true state of the case, that you, when so informed, may decide according to your profound wisdom;

Not doubting that you, Illustrious, High and Mighty, will judge therefrom that this loss could not be avoided by human means, nor be imputed to me, your Illustrious High Mightinesses' humble servant.

I dare not interrupt your Illustrious High Mightinesses' most important business by a lengthy narrative of the poor condition in which I found New Netherland on my assuming its government. Which was caused, first, (in default of a settlement of the boundary so repeatedly requested) by the troublesome neighbors of New England.

Secondly, by the exceedingly detrimental, land-destroying and people-expelling wars with the cruel barbarians.

Less dare I, to avoid self-glorification, encumber your weighty occupations, Illustrious, High and Mighty, with the trouble, care, solicitude and continual zeal with which I have endeavored to promote the increase of population, agriculture and commerce; the flourishing condition whereunto they were brought, not through any wisdom of mine, but through God's special blessing, Illustrious, High and Mighty,

Not protected by a suitable garrison, as necessity demanded, against the deplorable and tragical massacres by the barbarians, whereby we were plunged three times into perilous wars,[2] through want of sufficient garrisons; in default thereof had they been seconded with the oft besought reinforcement of men and ships against the continual troubles, threats, encroachments and invasions of the English neighbors and government of Hartford Colony, our too powerful enemies.

That our abovementioned too powerful neighbors and enemies found themselves reinforced by four royal ships, crammed full with an extraordinary amount of men and warlike stores. Our ancient enemies throughout the whole of Long Island, both from the east end and from the villages belonging to us united with them, hemmed us by water and by land, and cut off all supplies. Powder and provisions failing, and no relief nor reinforcement being expected, we were necessitated to come to terms with the enemy, not through neglect of duty or cowardice, as many, more from passion than knowledge of the facts, have decided, but in consequence of an absolute impossibility to defend the fort, much less the city of New Amsterdam, and still less the country. As you, Illustrious, High and Mighty, in your more profound and more discreet wisdom, will be able to judge.

First, in regard to want of powder: it appears that there were not 2000 pounds in store in the city and fort; of that quantity there were not 600 pounds good and fit for muskets; the remainder damaged by age, so that when used for artillery, the cannon required a double charge or weight.

If necessary and you, Illustrious High and Mighty, demand it, the truth hereof can be sought from the gunner, who accompanies me hither, and who will not deny having said in the presence of divers persons and at various times: "What can my lord do? he knows well that there is no powder, and that the most of it is good for nothing; there is powder enough to do harm to the enemy, but 'tis no good; were I to commence firing in the morning, I should have all used up by noon."

In regard to provisions: Although our stores were reasonably well supplied with them the whole fore part of the summer, even more than ever heretofore, the falling off being commonly caused by the want of credit or ready money to lay up an abundant stock of provisions;

This scarcity being caused by the exportation of a large quantity of provisions to the island of Curaçao, in the little craft *De Musch*, dispatched thither three weeks previous to the arrival of the frigates, without any apprehension or suspicion of experiencing a want of provisions, as the good wheat harvest was not only at hand, but between the barn and the field.

In addition to this favorable prospect, we were relieved from all fear of any approaching enemy or imminent danger from Old England, by the last letters from the Honble Directors, dated 21 April, and received one month before the arrival of the frigates.

Placed by the aforesaid advices beyond all apprehension, we felt no difficulty in letting the aforesaid little vessel, *De Musch*, go with the loaded provisions; indeed we would have sent off more if we could have procured them anywhere.

The asserted scarcity of provisions is proved by the annexed declaration of the commissary himself, and of Sergeant Harmen Martensen, and moreover by the efforts we employed to obtain a greater quantity of these, were that possible.

Provisions were likewise so few and scarce in the city, in consequence of the approaching harvest, for the inhabitants are not in the habit of laying up more provisions than they have need of, that about eight days after the surrender of the place, there was not in the city of New Amsterdam enough of provisions, beef, pork and peas, to be obtained for the transportation of the military, about ninety strong, and the new grain had to be thrashed.

In addition to the want of the abovementioned necessaries, and many other minor articles, a general discontent and unwillingness to assist in defending the place became manifest among the people…

…appears from the fact that in the following year, 1664, Governor Winthrop himself came with two commissioners from Hartford, and one from the east end of Long Island, with a considerable number of people on foot and on horseback, to the reduced English towns, in order to get the inhabitants to take the oath of allegiance in the King's name.

Owing to the very serious war with the Esopus Indians and their confederates, in consequence of a third deplorable massacre perpetrated there on the good inhabitants, we could not at the time do anything against such violent attempts and encroachments, except to protest against them verbally and in writing.

All this, recorded fully in the form of a journal, was, on November 10, 1663, and last of February, 1664, transmitted to the Honorable Directors, together with our, and the entire commonalty's grievances, remonstrances and humble petitions for redress, either by means of a settlement of the boundary, or else by an effective reinforcement of men and ships.

On that account, therefore, in verification of what is set forth, are most humbly submitted to you, Illustrious, High and Mighty,

No. 1. An humble remonstrance of the Dutch country people on Long Island, whereof the original was sent on the last of February to the Honorable Directors, setting forth the threats and importunity made use of towards them by the English troop aforesaid, with a request for redress; otherwise, in default thereof, they shall be under the necessity of abandoning their lands or submitting to another government.

No. 2 is a copy of a letter sent to all the Dutch villages for a reinforcement, whence can be inferred our good inclination to defend the city and fort as long as possible. The answer thereto intimates their refusal, as they, living in the open country unprotected, could not abandon their lands, wives and children.

No. 3. The burghers' petition and protest exhibits their uneasiness; wherein they set forth at length the very urgent necessity to which they were reduced in consequence of the overwhelming power of the enemy; would be ruined and plundered, and themselves, with wives and children, more than 1,500 in number, reduced to the direst poverty.

This dissatisfaction and unwillingness on the part of burgher and farmer were called forth by the abovementioned and other frequently bruited threats, by the hostile invasions and encroachments that had been experienced and the inability to oppose them for want of power and reinforcements.

Besides the abovementioned reasons for dissatisfaction and unwillingness, the former as well as the ruling burgomasters and schepens, and principal citizens, complained that their iterated remonstrances, letters and petitions, especially the last, of the 10th of November, wherein they had informed the Honble Directors of the dire extremity of the country both in regard to the war with the barbarians and to the hostile attacks of the English, had not been deemed worthy of any answer; publicly declaring, "If the Honble Company give themselves so little concern about the safety of the country and its inhabitants as not to be willing to send a ship of war to its succor in such pressing necessity, nor even a letter of advice as to what we may depend on and what succor we have to expect, we are utterly powerless, and, therefore, not bound to defend the city, to imperil our lives, property, wives and children without hope of any succor or relief, and to lose all after two or three days' resistance."

Your patience would fail you, Illustrious, High and Mighty, if I should continue to relate all the disrespectful speeches and treatment which, Illustrious, High and Mighty, your servants of the Superior Government have been obliged to listen to and patiently to bear, during the approach of the frigates, whenever they sought to encourage the burghers and inhabitants to their duty, as could be verified by credible witnesses.

This further difficulty was made by the burghers that they were not certain of their lives and properties on account of the threats of plundering heard from some of the soldiers, who had their minds fixed more on plunder than on defence; giving utterance, among other things, to the following: We now hope to find an opportunity to pepper the devilish Chinese, who have made us smart so much; we know well where booty is to be got and where the young ladies reside who wear chains of gold. In verification whereof, it was alleged and proved, that a troop of soldiers had collected in front of one Nicolaus Meyer's house in order to plunder it, which was prevented by the burghers.

In addition to the preceding, many verbal warnings came from divers country people on Long Island, who daily noticed the growing and increasing strength of the English, and gathered from their talk that their business was not only with New Netherland but with the booty and plunder, and for these were they called out and enrolled. Which was afterwards confirmed not only by the dissolute English soldiery, but even by the most steady officers and by a striking example exhibited to the colonists of New Amstel on the South River,[1] who, notwithstanding they had offered no resistance, but requested good terms, could not obtain them, but were invaded, stripped, utterly plundered and many of them sold as slaves to Virginia.

To prevent these and many other misfortunes, calamities and mischiefs overtaking evidently and assuredly the honest inhabitants, owing to the aforesaid untenableness of the place and fort without assistance from Fatherland, which was not to be expected for six months, we and the Council, on the presentation of so many remonstrances, complaints and warnings, were under the necessity, God and the entire community know without any other object than the welfare of the public and the Company, to come to terms with the enemy and neighbors whose previous hostile invasions and encroachments neither we nor our predecessors have been able to oppose or prevent.

And, even if the good God had, for the moment, been pleased to avert the misfortune from us, to delay or prevent the arrival of those frigates, yet had we, through want of the reinforcements of men and ships from Fatherland so repeatedly demanded but not come, shortly after fallen, by this war with England, into a worse state and condition, in consequence of the overpowering might of the neighbors. This is sufficiently evident and plain from their hostile acts and encroachments against the inhabitants in a season of profound peace; being, as already stated, fifty to our one, they would afterwards, *jure belli*, have attacked, overwhelmed, plundered us and the good inhabitants whom they would have utterly expelled out of the country.

Many more reasons and circumstances could be adduced, Illustrious, High and Mighty, for your greater satisfaction and my vindication, if your occupations, Illustrious, High and Mighty, permitted you to cast your eyes over, or allow others to take cognizance of, the continual remonstrances, applications and petitions for a settlement of the boundary or a reinforcement, particularly of the latest of the years 1663 and 1664, and of the daily entries in the minutes bearing thereupon.

But fearing that your patience, Illustrious, High and Mighty, will be exhausted by this too long and unpalatable relation, I shall break off here and submit myself, Illustrious, High and Mighty, to your most wise and discreet opinion, command and order—with this prayer, that you, Illustrious, High and Mighty, would please to dispatch me, your humble servant, as quickly as your more important occupations will possibly allow; meanwhile praying that God will temper this loss with other more notable successes and prosper your government.

Illustrious, High and Mighty,

Your most humble servant,

Exhibited 16th October, 1665.

P. Stuyvesant.

The point of view of the town council about the situation Peter Stuyvesant described is presented below.

Letter of the Town Council of New Amsterdam, 1664

Right Honorable Prudent Lords, the Lords Directors of the Honorable West India Company, Department of Amsterdam:

Right Honorable Lords:

We, your Honors' loyal, sorrowful and desolate subjects, cannot neglect nor keep from relating the event, which through God's pleasure thus unexpectedly happened to us in consequence of your Honors' neglect and forgetfulness of your promise—to wit, the arrival here, of late, of four King's frigates from England, sent hither by His Majesty and his brother, the Duke of York, with commission to reduce not only this place, but also the whole New Netherland under His Majesty's authority, whereunto they brought with them a large body of soldiers, provided with considerable ammunition. On board one of the frigates were about four hundred and fifty as well soldiers as seamen, and the others in proportion.

The frigates being come together in front of Najac in the Bay, Richard Nicolls, the admiral, who is ruling here at present as Governor, sent a letter to our Director General, communicating therein the cause of his coming and his wish. On this unexpected letter the General sent for us to determine what was to be done herein. Whereupon it was resolved and decided to send some commissioners thither, to argue the matter with the General and his three commissioners, who were so sent for this purpose twice, but received no answer, than that they were not come here to dispute about it, but to execute their order and commission without fail, either peaceably or by force, and if they had anything to dispute about it, it must be done with His Majesty of England, as we could do nothing here in the premises. Three days' delay was demanded for consultation; that was duly allowed. But meanwhile they were not idle; they approached with their four frigates, two of which passed in front of the fort, the other anchored about Nooten Island and with five companies of soldiers encamped themselves at the ferry, opposite this place, together with a newly raised company of horse and a party of new soldiers, both from the North and from Long Island, mostly our deadly enemies, who expected nothing else than pillage, plunder and bloodshed, as men could perceive by their cursing and talking, when mention was made of a capitulation.

Finally, being then surrounded, we saw little means of deliverance; we resolved what ought to be here done, and after we had well enquired into our strength and had found it to be full fifteen hundred souls strong in this place, but of whom not two hundred and fifty men are capable of bearing arms exclusive of the soldiers, who were about one hundred and fifty strong, wholly unprovided with powder both in the city and in the fort; yea, not more than six hundred pounds were found in the fort besides seven hundred pounds unserviceable; also because the farmers, the third man of whom was called out, refused, we with the greater portion of the inhabitants considered it necessary to remonstrate with our Director General and Council, that their Honors might consent to a capitulation, whereunto we labored according to our duty and had much trouble; and laid down and considered all the difficulties, which should arise from our not being able to resist such an enemy, as they besides could receive a much greater force than they had under their command.

The Director General and Council at length consented thereunto, whereto commissioners were sent to the admiral, who notified him that it was resolved to come to terms in order to prevent the shedding of blood, if a good agreement could be concluded.

Six persons were commissioned on each side for this purpose to treat on this matter, as they have done and concluded in manner as appears by the articles annexed.[2] How that will result, time shall tell.

Meanwhile since we have no longer to depend on your Honors' promises of protection, we, with all the poor, sorrowing and abandoned commonalty here, must fly for refuge to Almighty God, not doubting but He will stand by us in this sorely afflicting conjuncture and no more depart from us: And we remain

Your sorrowful and abandoned subjects

Pieter Tonneman,
Paulus Leenderzen van der Grift,
Cornelis Steenwyck,
Jacob Backer,
Tymotheus Gabry,
Isaack Grevenraat,
Nicolaas de Meyer.

Done in Jorck [York] heretofore named Amsterdam in New Netherland Anno 1664 the 16th September.

During all this time, slaves were being transported to New Netherland to perform the labor needed to till and farm the land and build and develop the towns. The following are excerpts of entries in the logs of a ship, an account of what transpired on board a slave trader, the St. John, taken from "Sins of the Fathers."

"This has been a deliberately selective study of the Atlantic slave-traders, for a mere catalogue of horrors can prove as repetitious and ineffectual as any other from of mass information. The slave-traders of all countries were individuals. They showed the variations of character which you would find in men engaged in any form of commerce. Their motive, like that of all traders, was to make money. It was the means they coldly chose that condemn them to the execration of posterity."

"No writer can foretell the effect his book will have on any reader, but the one certainty he knows is the effect that writing it has had upon himself. Instigated, as I have already said, by the sight of the slave-vaults at Elima and Cape Coast, as well as by a wish to delve down into the origins of a racial problem that had puzzled me since a happy childhood spent in Washington, DC, I found that my researches and my travels were gradually making me as obsessional as Thomas Clarkson himself. The dimensions of everyday things seemed altered. One was becoming conscious of the evil realities of history which like behind the façade of much one used to take for granted."

Journal of the Slaver St. John.

We Weighed anchor, by order of the Honorable (1659. Mar. 4.)

Director, Johan Valckenborch, and the Hononarble Director, Jasper Van Heuffen, to proceed on our Voyage from Elmina to Rio Reael, to trade for Slaves for the Honorable Company.

(1659. July. 27) Our Surgeon, named Martin de Lanoy, died of the Bloody Flux.

(Aug. 10.) Arrived the Company's Ship Raven from Castle St. George d'el Mina, homeward bound.

Again resolved to pursue our Voyage towards the Island of Annebo, in order to purchase there Supplies for the Slaves. We have lain Sixty days at Cabo de Loop hauling wood and water. Among the Water barrels, forty were taken to pieces to be refitted, as our Cooper died at Rio Cammerones, and we had no other person capable of repairing them.

(1659. Sept. 24.) Friday. Arrived at the Island of Tobago and shipped Water there, also purchased some Bread, as our hands had no ration for three weeks.

Again set sail on our Voyage to the Island of Curacao, as before.

(Nov. 2.) Lost our ship on the Rifts of Rocus, and all hands immediately took to the Boat, as there was no prospect of saving the Slaves, for we must abandon the Ship in consequence of the heavy Surf.

On the first of November, (1659, Nov.1) two hours before day, have we lost the Ship St. John, upon the Reef of Rocus and fled with the Boat to the Island of Curacao, and left in the Ship eighty five Slaves, including Men, Women, Boys and Girls, and arrived on the fourth of this instant at Curacao.

Taken by Order of the Honorable Director Matthias Beck respecting the Capture of the Company's Negroes abandoned on board the Ship St. John on the Island of Rocus, and of the Company's Sloop which was sent to save them by the Honorable Director M. Beck aforesaid.

Appeared San Van Gaelen who was sent by the Hon. Director in the Company's Sloop, with the Skipper Hans Marcussen Stuyve.

..........in Denmark, to whom the men belonged who mastered and captured the Company's Vessel aforesaid, and transferred the Slaves to the Ship. In the meanwhile, the aforesaid

Vessel remained at Rocus with the Deponent's boat, in order, as they gave out, to save by their means, more Property, and they, indeed, brought off two more Slaves, some Elephants' teeth and other trifles, so that altogether they took 84 Slaves and ....

Two fucking Children, They also took and carried off the aforesaid Company's Vessel whereof Hans Marcussen Stuyve was Skipper, and told me, the Deponent, that even had I had said Slaves on board the Bark on their arrival at Rocus, they should have taken them away by force, and declared them good prize, because I had no Commission, but only a Sea brief. And the Deponent says, that they offered him money for the service they had received from his Bark and Crew; this he refused to take, as such service was rendered ....

.... saved and brought on board the aforesaid Bark of Skipper San Ryckertsen, Eighty two Slaves and two Sucklings and steered away with them to David's island, where said Rover lay at anchor with his Vessel named the Castle frigate, the Captain whereof was San Pietersen of Denmark, and compelled us to remain with our Bark at Rocus, with the little Sloop of San Ryckertsen aforesaid, to save as they said, some other Articles, which they did, namely, eight or nine little elephants' Teeth, two cooking Kettles some tin Ware and ......

Two hundred and nineteen Slaves big and little, were actually traded and purchased, wherewith we sailed in order to prosecute our Voyage and carry out Instructions. Not obtaining at the Calabari such sufficiency of provisions as this Voyage demanded for the sustenance of the aforesaid Slaves, we resolved to go to the Highland of Ambosius where we were unable to procure any Provisions, as was our desire. We therefore went to the River Camerones, where we obtained a few Articles, but not as much as we wanted.

Nevertheless, we pursued our Voyage towards Capo de Lopo Gonsalves, at which place we took in Wood and Water, and thence stood across although experiencing great misery and want of food, to Anabo, where we got some Provisions and went on our Voyage and made land in the month of October last at the Island of Tobago the greater portion of the Slaves having died from Want and Sickness, in consequence of such a very long so that we saved only Ninety slaves, out of the whole Cargo. Having taken in wood and ....

Then the Deponent was conveyed by them with the aforesaid Bark and Negroes, to David's island, where the Rover lay at anchor waiting for us, leaving behind them the Vessel whereof San Marcuffen Stuyve is Skipper, to save two Negroes whom the Deponent had left on board when he quit the Ship. That Vessel joined them the next day at David's island, bringing along the two aforesaid Slaves, some Kettles, Rope and about 700 pounds of Elephants' teeth, also some Flags, Compasses and other articles.

(Signed)

Adriaen Blaes.

Witnesses: Ghysbert de Rosa, Peter de Leeuw, Nicolaes Haek, Secretary.

PROCLAMATION

Matthias Beck, in the service of their High Mightinesses the Lords States General of the Free United Netherlands and of the Honorable General Incorporated West India Company, Governor over the Curacao Islands, Greeting:

Be it known, that one San Pietersen of Coling in Denmark, styling himself Commander of a Ship called The Castle Frigate, having with him some Englishmen, Frenchmen and Dutchmen, who are cruising with him on this Coast in the Ship aforesaid, hath dared to attack the Company's Vessels near Bonayre and Rocus, and forcibly to take possession thereof, and with them and the Company's Men to take by force, among others, eighty four healthy Negroes out of the Company's Ship, called the St. John, coming from the Coast of Guinea, which was wrecked on the Rifts of Rocus, where one of the aforesaid Company's Ships was already engaged in saving said Negroes for the Company, whose Property they were, with all that was in the Ship, to bring them here to Curacao, for which purpose they were expressly sent hence thither; Regardless whereof, the aforesaid San Pietersen hath not only prevented the Company's Vessels executing their Instructions and Orders, but hath made himself Master of said Vessles, and with them and Boats, stole not only the said Negroes and everything else, but in addition thereto carried off one of the Company's best failing Vessels called the Young Ostrich, to the great damage of the Honorable Company, and appropriated the same to himself in good booty, so as all is to be seen by the Informations, Relations, Reports and Delarations of the Skipper and Crews of the Vessels aforesaid.

And Whereas the aforesaid San Pietersen and his Men have heretofore committed similar acts under irregular Commission and persist in the same course, especially as public Pirates, by the seizure of the Company's Vessel and Negroes, and have threatened to continue to do; And Whereas among others, one of the Company's Matrosses named San Pietersen of Belacom, a Frieslander, being in our actual service, having sailed as Matrofs on board the Company's styger schuit, The Young Brindled Cow, hath voluntarily gone over to this Pirate, disregarding the Allegiance, Plight and Oath, whereby he was bound to the Company, but on the contrary as appears by Information, hath acted and is still acting, as a Spy for these Pirates; All which and what precedes are matters of very ill consequence, of serious damage and moment to the Honorable General Incorporated West India Company, who will not sail to express their highest Indignation on this subject, and endeavor by all ways and means, not only to make good and to procure indemnity for their damages and losses already suffered by the stealing of their Vessel and Negroes, so illegally purloined from them, but above all, to procure that such Rovers shall be punished as Pirates and Robbers, according to their deserts, as an Example to others.

To this end, therefore, with the advice of Our Council, upon the certain Proofs and Reports to Us rendered, We, being unwilling to lose any time in overhauling the said Sea Robbers, have Resolved and concluded, in the Name and on the Behalf of the Lords Principals, their High Mightinesses the Lords States General, and the Honorable General Incorporated West India Company, for their protection and the Public Good, hereby to warn all the Company's Captains, and Ships as well as Private Skippers and Ships and Vessels at present lying or about to come, within this Harbor, who owe allegiance to their High Mightinesses the Lords States General and are in the service of the Honorable General Incorporated West India Company not only to be on their guard against the aforesaid Pirates and Sea Robbers, but should they meet them at Sea, them to attack, openly and with force and arms, and bring them in here to Curacao, or if they fall in with them at any of the Leeward Islands, to complain of them to the Governors and Magistrates at such place where they happen to find them, according to the Proofs thereof in existence, and to procure that such Justice may be inflicted upon them as the Informations shall justify. Requesting all Generals, Governors and Commanders both on Sea and on Land, to whom these Our Letters for the execution of the premises shall be shown, to administer good Law and Justice to them. Such will We reciprocate on like Occasion. Thus done and enacted on the Island Curacao in Fort Amsterdam the 5th December, A° 1659.

At the Meeting of the Director General and Council of New Netherland, and made known and declared as followeth:

That they, the Deponents, set sail from the Castle del Mina on the 21st February last in the service and for the account of the Honorable Incorporated West India Company, Chamber at Amsterdam, in the Ship the Arms of Amsterdam, at which time Jan Gerritsen Nuchteren, who died on the passage, was Skipper, which orders and command from the Honorable General San Valckenburgh to repair to Loango in Angola, to take in a cargo of Slaves there, and convey them to the Island of Curacao.

April 15. Having arrived at Loango and taken on board 101 head of Slaves there, for account of the abovementioned Company, on the 28th of said month, again set sail for Curacao.

June 20. Sighted Curacao, but could not reach said Island in consequence of the strong Current and stiff East wind. Having vainly endeavored, during three days and three nights, to laveer, and Water beginning to get very low, we were necessitated to change of course, and thus, July 2, came to the Salt ground of Cayman, which is one of the Cayman Islands, where, whilst engaged in taking Water and some Turtle on board.

July 6, about noon, five Ships came to anchor there; four with English flags and one under Portuguese colors, which last, called the Maria of London, whereof one Robert Douwneman was Captain, after she had taken some hands on board from the other Ships, immediately weighed anchor again, and came down on the Deponent's Ship, calling out, "Strike for the King of Portugal;" and at once, without giving time to strike, fired a shotted Cannon and a discharge of Musketry killing two Negroes dead, and wounding one Dutchman. After having thus fired, came straight on board, seized the Ship and Negroes, forced the crew to go to the Ship aforesaid and plundered every thing. The Captains of the four English Ships abovementioned, one of whom was called Captain Gey, and another, Captain Bromert, got some of the Negroes because they had furnished him men, but the Deponents do not know how many. After they had lain there some days, said Captain having first dismantled his on Frigate set her on fire.

July 18, failed thence with the aforesaid Ship, The Arms of Amsterdam, having enlisted some of the Sailors, giving out that he intended to sail to Montserrat in the Caribbean Islands, but as the Ship was a poor Sailer, and Water was short, he set sail for Virginia and arrived September 10, in the Bay there.

September 19, arrived in Elizabeth's river, whence the Deponent went to Nancimon.

October 6, departed thence for this place in Mr. Foscom's Bark and arrived here yesterday.

All which they declared to be true and truthful. In testimony whereof these presents are signed by them in Fort Amsterdam in New Netherland, the 13th October A° 1663. FINIS.

Bill of Sale of a Negro

It has been documented that Blacks have been bought and sold in NY since 1646. This is the first evidence we have uncovered documenting a sale.

Before me Cornelis Van Tienhoven, Secretary of New Netherland, appeared Fredrick Lubersen, who declared to have fold unto Richard Lord, a Negro named Anthony, which Negro, he the Grantor hereby conveys and transports in right ownership to the abovenamed Richard Lord, who shall be at liberty to use the said Negro during his life, at all such work, as he, Richard Lord, shall think proper. He Frederick Lubbersen declares from this day forward to desist from all property in the said Negro. In testimony whereof these presents are signed by Frederick Lubbersen and witness hereunto invited, 28th 9 October 1646.

Frederick Lubbersten.

To my knowledge,

> Cornelis Van Tienhoven, Secretary.
>
> Adrian van Tienhoven, Witness.   FINIS.

Resolution of the Amsterdam Chamber of the West India Company.

Thursday, the 19th November, 1654.

Mr. San De Sweerts and Dirck Pietersen Wittepaert appeared before the Assembly, and requested permission to proceed hence with their Ship to Witte paert, to the Coast of Africa for Slaves, and dispose of these in New Netherland, on payment of the ordinary Tonnage, or the Duty fixed therefor. Question being put, considerable discussion ensued, and as it was understood that such would tend to increase of Population and advancement of said Place, the same was consented to, on condition that the Company shall have the option, on the arrival of said Ship, which must come in here to collect the proper Duties of the Goods which she is to bring with her, or the ordinary Tonnage duty, according to the Regulation enacted on the Coast of Africa, with which the abovementioned Messrs. San de Sweerts and Dirck Pietersen Wittepaert are satisfied.

Ordinance imposing a Duty on Exported Slaves.

Friday, 6. August, 1655.

Whereas the Director General and Council of New Netherland find that the Negroes lately arrived here from the Bight of Guinea in the Ship Witte Paert, have been transported and carried hence without the Honorable Company of the Inhabitants of this Province having derived any Revenue or benefit therefrom, the Director General and Council have resolved and concluded that there shall be paid at the General Treasury 10 per cent of the value or purchase money of the Negroes who shall be carried away or exported from here elsewhere beyond the Jurisdiction of New Netherland. Dated as above.

P. Stuyvesant, Nicasius de Sille, La Montagne.

Resolution of the Director General and Council of New Netherland.

Tuesday, 24th August, 1655.

The Petition of Edmund Scharburgh being read, requesting permission to depart from this place to Virginia with his Vessel and some Negroes he has purchased, this Apostile was given:

The request is granted, on condition that the Petitioner give bail in the sum of five thousand Pounds sterling, not to enter the South Bay or River, and that his Crew promise under Oath not go there, nor communicate any intelligence by Sea or Land to any person whomsoever. *

*Referring the Expedition against the Swedes, on the Delaware River, then about to fail.

Resolution of the Chamber at Amsterdam.

Monday, 3d. April, 1656

It being represented that a Ship, with the content of the Directors of Mendenblick, depending on the Chamber of Weft Frieland and the North Quarter, has failed to the Coast of Africa for Slaves, with intention to sell them at the Island of Curacao, * or to trade them on the Main, it is resolved to oppose the aforesaid sale or barter, and to write to Vice Director Beck there, to detain the aforesaid Ship and Slaves and to proceed therewith so and in Curacao was exclusively under the Direction of the Chamber at

Amsterdam, and it may be inferred from the above that the exclusive Control of Dutch Slave Trade was also vested in that Chamber.

Vice Director Beck to the Directors at Amsterdam.

Curacao, 11. June, 1657.

Honorable, Respected, Wife Prudent and most Discreet Gentlemen.

Gentlemen,

My last to your Honors was by way of the Caribbean Islands, which I hope has been received long ere this. Since then safely arrived here the Freight-boat with those who were commissioned and sent for purposes explained in our previous dispatch, form this place to the Caraquas, the principal Capital, wrote a Letter to me with his own hand, the original whereof is annexed, to purchase the Company's Negroes, that is, all that are here at present, on the following conditions, to wit; That the Company shall have a Ship with their own Crew here ready for the Negroes to embark in, and when resolved to accept his offer, to let him know, by those recently with him, at the place designated by him, when he will without loss of time, repair in person to this harbor, and enter into an Agreement and terms for what articles and at what price the Negroes shall be delivered at the place where he hopes to bring them in safety and without danger; and that he will not receive any Negroes before payment for them shall be made on board the Ship, and he or his partner shall remain on board the Ship, with the Negroes until the Conditions and Agreement which will be made here, shall be fully carried out.

He reports that the place to which he says he will convey them is on the North side of Cuba, where the (Spanish) Nation has no Fortress nor means to prevent the project or to disturb them; also the he will leave his own Cousin, who is likewise related to the friends to whom he will convey the Negroes, here at Curacao as a Hostage and security, until it be manifest that he shall have performed in good faith all he has promised; as more fully appears by the annexed Relation and report of Cornet Balthazar Van Ess and Johan Rombouts on the subject. He has requested an answer to this, for his information. I therefore with your Honors' early instructions hereupon, as to what I shall do, or omit in this matter, and that in the meanwhile I may receive a supply of provisions sufficient for the Negroes to enable me to wait for him.

I have received the Agreement and Condition your Honors have concluded with Mr. Henricus Matthias, merchant of Amsterdam, respecting the Negroes. On looking and reading it over, I find it very favorable for that gentleman, wherefore my impression is that your Honors' intention in concluding it is to begin and introduce the trade here. I shall not be wanting, God willing, in obeying and executing your Honors' orders and Instructions in this regard faithfully and to my best ability. Meanwhile, should it happen that

Mr. Henricus Matthias's expected Ship did not arrive here, as it has not yet done, I shall expect your further order and answer whether we shall dare to proceed or not with the Negroes on the aforesaid Biscayan's presented proposals extended as above. In the strong hope and expectation that we shall be able to open a trade with our nearest neighbors, I shall purchase on your Honors' account a small cargo from Skipper Simon Cornelissen Gilde, so that they may at least find something on coming here; and our Vessels on passing near Bonayre may advise the Biscayan and the other Inhabitant already mentioned, what goods can be purchased here on arriving, taking a sample along to show them, should occasion present, and, at the same time, inform the Biscayan that I have not received any orders to allow Negroes to leave the Island until payment for them has been made, and that I shall let him have, within four months after date, a fuller and more explicit answer which I hope I shall receive from your Honors in the meantime.

I am confident that on these Conditions he would readily give two hundred pieces of Eight for a merchantable Negro or Negress, one with another, whilst he gave us to understand, that the price of Hides would be Eighteen shillings.

Vice Director Beck to the Directors of Amsterdam

Curacao, 28, July, 1657.

Gentlemen

As I advised your Honors in my last, I dispatched the Freightboat to the appointed and prefixed place—a certain small Island near the Main—to the Biscayan and sent him word on the subject of his trading for Negroes, as I had informed your Honors more at large in my last. Whereupon he resolved to visit this place in person, in our aforesaid Freight-boat (Stygerschuit). He was accompanied by a certain Padre, named Friar Francis to purchase a few parcels of merchandize with one or two little Negro Girls.

I also sold to the above named Biscayan, a small Negro Boy with a few goods, for which he had brought with him some Hides and Tobacco in our aforesaid Boat; these are sent herewith as a specimen by the Ship Ostrich, the price of the Hides being Fifteen shillings each and of the Tobacco Six pieces of Eight the Arobe of Twenty five Pounds. I have sold to the aforesaid Padre Friar Francis, goods to the amount of Four hundred pieces of Eight and two little Negro Girls, all at a fair and reasonable price, in order to encourage and stimulate them to come to these Ports to trade, which I think is greatly for the Company's interest. Wherefore, I let the Padre have the two little Negro Girls @ One hundred and fifty pieces of Eight each, which together amounts to Three hundred pieces of Eight, and to the aforesaid Biscayan a little Boy at One hundred and twenty pieces of Eight. The Merchandizes which I sold them were purchased from the bearer hereof, Simon Cornelissen Gilde, Skipper of the Ship Ostrich, expressly for this purpose of your Honors' account before their arrival, in order that our nearest Neighbors on coming here may at least on such occasion find something for the asking, until your Honors might send such cargoes as the café requires, as I have partly explained in my last.

Although the abovementioned Padre, Friar Francis, did not bring with him any payment for what he purchased, yet could I not let him go away empty handed, as it was the first time, in consequence of the conversation and verbal Agreement entered into with our Commissary and Skipper of Freight-boat before his arrival here—that is to let them return to the appointed place with what they had purchased, on condition that they should not land, much less receive possession of what has not been paid for here, until they have made payment therefore to the Commissary and Skipper of the aforesaid freight Boat, in good sufficient Hides.

With regard to the trade in Negroes, aforesaid Biscayan, now here, hath given me such explanations and further information on that point, that we can come to no other conclusion than that a good and favorable result is to be expected from it. He hath communicated to me the most direct shortest route, how and in what manner not only a shipload of Negroes, but successively a cargo of good saleable Merchandize besides could be traded off. Were a Ship with necessaries in the harbor here, he is willing on receiving notice thereof at the appointed place, to come here and enter into such agreement with the Company from which as he firmly believes, he and the Company would derive great advantage.

The place the Negroes should be conveyed to is called Porto Velo, the staple place of trade. Permission can be obtained to dispose of the cargo freely there on paying One hundred and thirteen pieces of Eight for each Negro, which is the Royalty. But such permission is not given except to persons of their own Nation; but it can be obtained under the pretext that they had chartered a Dutch Ship and Crew to fetch and bring over the Negroes, and that the Negroes and Merchandize in the Ship are the property of their Nation.

Such is the manner in which the aforesaid Biscayan would contract for and purchase Negroes from the Company on the following Conditions: That he, or his companion, with five or six more of their Nation, shall embark at their own expense with the Company's Skipper, Commissary, Crew and Matrosses in the Ship lying ready to sail and prosecute with them their Voyage to Porto Velo, and after receiving a permit there from the Governor, sell the Negroes which they know they can sell immediately after their arrival at such a high price that the outlay of the aforesaid Royalty in order to obtain the Permit, may be easily repaid. Therefore, they will undertake this themselves, and pay to the Company, after safe arrival there, for each Negro and Negress between Eighteen and thirty years of age, Two hundred Reals or Pieces of Eight, in Silver bars or pieces of Eight; further they will be able to obtain there a proper permit to trade then to other places, to load the Ship with such cargo and freight as the countries supply and are most profitable to the country. In like manner, the price for the Goods being agreed upon and arranged here, the payment there for them shall be made in the same manner as for the Negroes, but the risk of the Sea and the expenses of the Negroes, until they arrive at the above place, must be borne by the Company, but when arrived there, they will be responsible for them. For the full performance of the Conditions which shall be made here on the part of the Company, the aforesaid Biscayan offers to stake his life, and even to remain here in person in the Fort, or to leave another responsible person here in custody of the Company at the risk of his life, if any fraud is or has been intended or designed. And it is further conditioned that the Negroes in their minority, as well as old and deformed ones, must be disposed of at a special and lower price. On these terms he is resolved, at all times from now henceforth, whenever a Ship with Negroes will be ready here, at the time and place to be named where advice is to be sent him, to come hither and with God's merciful help faithfully to perform whatever is abovementioned.

The other plan or proposal mentioned in my last, to run the Negroes in at the north side of Cuba, is not, he says, so feasible as this.

Charter of the Ship Eyckenboom for a
Voyage to Africa and New Netherland.

In the Name of the Lord, Amen. In the year of the birth of our Lord and Saviour Jesus Christ, 1659, the 25th of January, before me Henrick Schaeff, admitted by the Court of Holland a Notary Public residing in Amsterdam, and the undersigned witnesses, in their own persons came and appeared Messieurs Edward Man and Abraham Wilmerdoncx, Directors of the Incorporated West India Company at the Chamber here in Amsterdam hereunto authorized by the Board of their Associates, as charterers on the one part, and Skipper Fan Fansen Eyckenboom of Hoorn, Master under God, of his Ship named the Eyckenboom, with a half deck and forecastle on either side, and the aforesaid parties declared and do hereby declare to have made and concluded together a certain Contract for a charter of said Ship, in the form and manner hereinafter described, To wit:

That the aforesaid Skipper shall be bound immediately to deliver his aforesaid Ship here in the City fitted out, tight, well caulked, and provided with good and sufficient anchors, cordage, tackle, fails, running and standing rigging and all other necessaries and appurtenances thereunto belonging, and the same to mount with Ten good pieces of Cannon, with the requisite powder and shot and other ammunition in proportion, but the necessary consumption of powder and shot aforesaid shall be made good by the Company, which shall also put on board said Ship in addition to the Ten pieces aforesaid as many other guns as they please and can conveniently place, and shall provide and pay the expense of the powder and shot therefore, on condition that in the necessary consumption thereof, the aforesaid Skipper shall bear the contingent of his Ship aforesaid; that further, said Company shall man said Ship with such and so many hands an provide them with such stores as said Company will please and think proper. Which being done on the one side and the other, the aforesaid Ship shall on the part of said Company, be laden with a full and suitable cargo, or to such extent as said Company shall think proper; being laden with all such goods, wares and merchandizes as they will determine, the aforesaid Ship shall, with the first fair wind and weather that God will grant, be dispatched and sail from this country direct to the Coast of Africa and run along said Coast from above downward, or the Cape Verd down, and touch, trade, lie and remain at all trading posts and ports, according to the pleasure of said Company and their Commissary, unto the Castle St. George d' el Mina, where they shall receive or find orders form the Company's Director General and Council or shall be furnished with them on failing hence; And sail towards the Bight of Guinea and touch and trade at all other places lying therein according to the order which shall be given him by the Director General or here; from thence proceed further to the Island of Curacao, Bonaire, and Aruba in the West Indies, and also to New Netherland, and all round every where else the Company, or its Ministers, shall determine and order, and likewise at all said quarters and places trade and traffic Goods, Wares and Merchandizes and also take in people, load and unload at the pleasure of the aforesaid Company or its Ministers; And to that end sail to and from, run hither and thither, anchor, lie, load and unload at said Coasts, Quarters and Places as often and as frequently so long as the service of the Company such shall demand; Furthermore, return and come thence to this city Amsterdam or the destined port of discharge, and on her safe return and arrival, there discharge and deliver to the aforesaid Company her laden return cargo and goods. Which done, there shall be paid to him the Skipper for the contracted freight, every month, the sum of Eight hundred guilders of xx ftivers each, on condition that the Company is bound for the term of Six successive months or longer, to be calculated according to the length of time, all current months according to the Almanac, to run and commence when the Ship shall, in the prosecution of the Voyage, reach the Sea outside the last buoy of the Texel, and to expire when she shall arrive and cast anchor before this city of Amsterdam or her destined port of discharge, payable xiiii days ar three weeks after the aforesaid discharge here, besides average and pilotage according to the custom of the Sea, and over and above also Hat money for the abovenamed Skipper at the Company's discretion. And said Skipper, with and besides the Company's Crew, shall also make the Voyage with the aforeasaid Ship in order to look said Ship, her appurtenances, &c., making use of the Company's stores, but the monthly pay or wages not being at its charge; And he shall be, over and above, subject to the orders and instructions, articles and other rules of the Company during the Voyage, no more no less than if he had been sworn to observe the same, they being taken as inserted herein, and especially also in regard to particular or private forbidden trading, in shipping or conveyance of particular or private goods, merchandizes or private goods, merchandizes or wares, on pain according to the aforesaid Articles, Ordrs and Instruction of the said Company. The abovementioned Directors, parties hereunto, pledging for the payment of the aforesaid contracted monthly or freight moneys, average and pilotage, their private persons and property, real and personal, present and to come without any exception, submitting the same to the Court of Holland and all laws and judges, all aboveboard. Done at Amsterdam in the presence of Cryn van Seventer and Marten Hegervelt, free citizens (porters) here, witnesses hereunto invited.

Bill of Lading of Negroes.

I San Pietersen of Dockum, Skipper under God of my Ship named the Spera Mundi, now lying ready before Curacao, with the first fair wind which God shall vouchsafe, to fail to New Netherland, where my correct unloading shall take place, acknowledge that I have received under the deck of my aforesaid Ship, from you Frans Bryun to wit, Five Negroes, whereof one is a Negress, all dry and well conditioned, and marked with the annexed mark. All which I promise to deliver (if God grant me a safe Voyage) with my aforesaid Ship at N. Neterhland aforesaid, to the Honorable Director General Petrus Stuyvesant, or his Factor or Deputies, on payment for the freight of the above described goods, at the discretion of the said Director General, and for the performance hereof, I bind myself and all my goods and my aforesaid Ship and appurtenances. In witness of the truth, I have signed three Copies hereof with my name, all of the same tenor, the one being satisfied, the others to be void. Written at Curacao the 24th day of August, Anno 1659.

Jan Pieters Gros of Dockum

Vice Director Beck to Director Stuyvesant

Curacao, Augusts, 1659

Honorable, Valiant, Wife, Prudent and most Discreet Sir.

Sir,

I NOW transmit to your Honor duplicates of what I have already sent by the Galiot New Amstel, Skipper Augustinus Heermans, and it will be very agreeable to me if I may be informed by the earliest opportunity of their speedy and safe arrival. I would not forego the present favorable occasion and opportunity of the Ship Spera Mundi, Jan Pietersen Skipper, to acquaint you of the circumstances of this Island up to the present time (God be praised!) in regard to the Commerce with our nearest Neighbors. Hitherto there have not been imported as many goods as the demand requires, and especially the trade in Negroes at this place which the Company hath referred to itself or else all are sold.

There are lying here, at present, two Ships ready to sail hence for Fatherland, which occupy my whole time, so that I have not much leisure to write your Honor at length. The one is the Company's Ship called the King Solomon, which arrived here on the 2d of July from Guinea, with Three hundred and thirty one Slaves. Of these I have sold 300 at one hundred and fifty pieces of Eight each, to a certain Spanish trader whom I am daily expecting to here and receive them, which I wish may occur before the departure of the aforesaid two Ships in order to be able to transmit the proceeds to the Lords Masters.

Franck Bruyn purchased out of aforesaid lot of Negroes for your Honor, Two Boys and a Girl who go over in this Ship. I have done everything possible to protect them against the cold. Franck Bruyn hath also purchased Two for Commissary Van Brugh, who like wife go by this conveyance on said Commissary's account. Your honor will please to have such payment collected therefor from said Van Brugh for the Company, as you will consider just. Commissary Laurens van Ruyven hath also purchased Two young Negroes here for account of his brother the Secretary of your Province, at the same price as the lot sold for here.

ADDITIONAL PAPERS Relative to
THE SLAVE TRADE UNDER THE DUTCH.

Directors at Amsterdam to Director Stuyvesant.

[1646.] Having observed that more Negroes could be profitably traded off there than were carried thither in the Ship Tamandare, we shall pay attention that for the future more Negroes shall be conveyed thither.

Journal of the Slaves on The Arms of Amsterdam and Her Capture.

Paulus Heyn Ridder from Staden, aged about 51 years, Pilot of the Ship the Arms of Amsterdam, and Leendert Jacques van Cuelen, born at Amsterdam, aged about 26 years, Assistant Commissary, who arrived here yesterday from Virginia, in Mr. Foscom's Bark.

Introduction

In the Tract now published, we have collected and translated Papers in the Secretary of State's Office, illustrative of Slavery and the Slave Trade under the Dutch. As the Documents are authentic, they furnish reliable Material for a Chapter in the early History of our State at present unwritten, and hitherto but partially known.

Introduction.

(Smith's General History of Virginia, Ed. 1627, P. 126, Richmond Ed., II, 39.)

To the Dutch undoubtedly belongs the questionable Distinction of having introduced Negro Slavery into the Colonies, now the United States of America. "About the last of August" (1619), says John Rolfe, the celebrated Husband of Pocahontas, writing from Virginia, "came in a Dutch man of warre, that fold vs twenty Negars."

*This Event is generally stated to have occurred in 1620; but a careful Perusal of Smith shows that it took place in 1619. Mr. Bancroft, Hist. U. S., 1st Ed., I, 189, quotes Beverley as the original Authority for this Fact. Beverley only copied Capt. Smith, without acknowledging the Source of his Information; of which Circumstance Mr. Bancroft does not appear to have been aware.

Introduction xiii

Angola with Articles of Commerce; got Slaves in Exchange, which they carried to Brazil, and returned to Holland with Sugar and other Produce of that Country.

We now propose to trace the introduction of Slavery into New Netherland.

In 1625 or 1626, six or seven Years after the Dutch had discharged the small Lot of Slaves in Virginia, the first Negroes were brought to Manhattan. Among them were Paul d' Angola, Simon Congo, Anthony Portuguese, John Francisco, and seven other Africans, who were

Introduction xiv

...... probably captured at Sea. Their names denote the Country to which they originally belonged. Two years afterwards three Negro Women arrived at New Amsterdam and there are the only Instances on Record of the Introduction of Slaves in New Netherland prior to the Erection of Patroonships and Colonies in 1629, when the West India Company publicly promised to "use their Endeavors to supply the Colonists with as many Blacks as they conveniently can."

For causes, already noted, these "endeavors" were not followed as far as we have been able to ascertain, by any immediate Increase of Negroes here and it was not until after the Reduction of Loanado that the Current of Slavery set northward to any great Amount.

By an Edict issued in 1645, no private Dutch Vessel was allowed to trade farther North than Cape Florida, nor on any Account to the Virginias, New Netherland, New France, the Coast of Africa pr Brazil. (N.Y. Colonial Dec., I 223.)

Slavery existed in the Limits of the present State of New Jersey as early as 1628- N.Y. Col. MSS., I, 41.

In the Summer of 1646, the first Slave Ship of whose Name we have a Record, arrived in New Netherland. She was called the Amandare. This Vessel touched at Barbados, where "three Negro Wenches" were spirited away. The Remainder arrived at New Amsterdam in June, where "the Negroes were sold for Pork and Peas. Something wonderful was to be performed with them, but they just dropped through the Fingers." What Number of Slaves were brought in probably were brought from Brazil.

The Ventures and Vessels in this nefarious Commerce, belonged either to private Parties in Holland, or to the West India Company. "We have resolved, " write the Directors at Amsterdam in 1661, "not only that Slaves shall be kept in New Netherland, as we have been heretofore ordered, but that they shall moreover be exported to the English and other Neighbours." The Spirit of Avarice and Greed deadened Conscience and smothered all Feeling of Humanity.

 Horrors of the Middle Passage. One hundred and ninety-five human Beings were crammed into the Hold of that Vessel. Bad food, short Allowance, Want of Water, foul Air, and Bloody Flux, were the Attendants on the Passage; and as a Consequence, fifty-six per cent of the wretched Beings perished on the Voyage. Of the Balance, only one Negro eventually accrued to the Benefit of the Dutch; for, as a retributive Fate willed it, a Privateer, or Pirate, swooped down in the Vicinity of Curacao, plundered every thing, and carried off the surviving Negroes "towards the Main."

No better Fortune awaited the slaver, the Arms of Amsterdam. This Vessel brought one hundred and one slaves from Angola, but on her Voyage to Curacao, was overhauled by some English Privateers among the West India Islands, captured and carried into Virginia.

Curacao was, under the Dutch, what Barbados was subsequently to the English- the Slave Emporium to which Gunieamen brought their Cargoes of human Flesh.

The following accounts are from a translation of the "Narratives of New Netherland," written by David De Vries, who bought Staten Island from the resident Indians.

Narratives of New Netherland

Introduction

The author, David Pieterszoon De Vries, born in 1593 or 1594 in Rochelle, France, was a voyager who, after retiring from active life to his native city in Holland, occupied his leisure by writing and printing an account of his adventures. This very curious and rare little book was published in 1655, and its title may be translated: "Short Historical and Journal-Notes of various Voyages by David Pieterszoon de Vries, Artillery-Master to the Noble and Mighty Lords the Council of West Friesland and the Northern Quarter [of the Province of Holland]…

The voyages which the quaint little book chronicles began in 1618. His attempt to go to Canada for furs, in 1624, was frustrated by the new Dutch West India Company.

The fourth, fifth and sixth voyages were made to America. Samuel Godyn, a director in the West India Company, engaged his interest in a patroonship. In 1631 an expedition sent out by them founded a small settlement which they called Swanendael, on the west side of Delaware Bay—the first settlement in Delaware; but it was soon destroyed by the Indians. In 1632 De Vries went out as patroon and commander of a ship and yacht. De Vries came up along the coast of Manhattan. At this point our extracts begin, and the story of De Vries, and of New Netherland as he saw it, to June, 1644, the last period being occupied with attempts to plant settlements on Staten Island frustrated by the outbreak of Kieft's war.

His bias is that of a patroon, critical of the Company's management. But in the main the narrative is of original value, the observations those of a capable and energetic trader and a good manager, expressing himself in a homely style but vividly. We owe to him many interesting pictures of life in the young colony, and especially of the ill-advised and exceedingly disastrous warfare waged by Kieft against the Indians.

All the parts of De Vries's book relating to Newfoundland, New Netherland and Virginia are presented, in translation. The present issue is confined to the portions relating to New Netherland.

FROM THE "KORTE HISTORIAEL ENDE JOURNAELS AENTEYCKENINGE," BY DAVID PIETERSZ. DE VRIES, 1633-1643 (1655)

The fifteenth in the morning it was so foggy that we could not see our large ship. We heard the ground-swell and surf; threw the lead, and found it eight fathoms deep. Let the anchor fall. It was shelly ground. Fished with a drop line, and caught in a couple of hours, eighty-four codfish, very good-flavored sweet fish, better than those in Newfoundland. It began to blow from the southwest, and to be bright and clear again. So we weighed anchor and made sail. Found ourselves before Barende-gat, where the coast began to stretch to the northeast by north, and southwest by south. Towards evening we saw the high mountains, which make a high point running along the sea, for the most part east-southeast, and west-southwest. This is the first mountainous land which you meet when you come from the south. We sailed that evening to the Sandy Hook, which forms a large bay close by the point, and is also called Godyn's Point, where we anchored that evening in seven-fathom water.

The 16th, weighed anchor, and ran over to Staten Island, all along the shore of which runs a great sand-bank, entirely flat. Arrived at noon before Fort Amsterdam, and, found a Company's ship there, called the *Soutbergh*, with a prize taken on the way, laden with sugar. She had brought a new governor, Wouter Van Twiller of Nieuw-Kercke. He had been a clerk in the West India House at Amsterdam. I went ashore to the fort, out of which he came to welcome me, and inquired of me also, how the whale-fishery succeeded. I answered him that I had a sample; but that they were foolish who undertook the whale-fishery here at such great expense, when they could have readily ascertained with one, two, or three sloops in New Netherland. Godyn had been a manager of the Company as long as the Company had been in existence. While we stood thus discoursing, our sloop came to anchor at Sandy Hook, and would remain there until I gave other orders.

The 18th, arrived here an Englishman, who came from New England to trade in the river, having on board a trader named Jacob Elks, who had, during the time of the private association, navigated and commanded on the river, but whom the Company would not employ, seeking out unfit persons like this governor, whom they had made out of a clerk into a governor, who was the sport of the people. This Englishman invited the governor to come and see him. I went with him, in company with a number of people, who became intoxicated, and got into such high words, that the Englishman could not understand how it was that there should be such unruliness among the officers of the Company, and that a governor should have no more control over them; he was not accustomed to it among his countrymen. The Englishman remained six or seven days lying before the fort,

…but they separated afterwards good friends, when Cornelis van Vorst, wishing to give the commander a parting salute, fired a pederero which stood upon a palisade before his house, when a spark flew upon the house, which was thatched with rushes, and in half an hour it was entirely consumed, Whilst we were engaged in shipping our goods, two prizes, taken by the English, arrived. They had first, with a sloop and eighteen men of them, taken, near Carthagena a fine new and fast sailing frigate of about thirty lasts, laden with tobacco and hides, and then with it took a small bark, having hides aboard. They brought them to New Netherland, and ran into the South river, where they found one of our trading sloops, which brought them to Fort Amsterdam. They sold their prizes here at our fort, and shipped their goods in the West India Company's ship and put ten of the Englishmen in mine. As to which the captain maintained that he was ill-treated, as he wished to have his men with his goods; and wanted to have his goods in my ship, as I would have taken all his men with me also; but the commander Wouter van Twiller compelled him to ship all his goods in the Company's ship, and compelled me to carry over ten of the Englishmen, all which trading by force was very unreasonable.

The 8th of August, the gunner of the fort gave a parting feast, and had a tent erected on one bastion of the fort, where a table and benches were set and many guests bidden. When the banquet was at its highest, the trumpeter began to blow, as to which some words were passed; when the keeper of the store, Heyndrick Hudden, and keeper of the merchandize, Corelaer, railed at the trumpeter, who gave each of them *santer quanter*, whereupon they ran home, and brought out a sword, and wished to have revenge upon the trumpeter. They went to the house of the commander and used much foolish language, one calling out, "I am the same man who took the life of Count Floris." But when they had slept upon it, their soldiership was all over, and they rather feared the trumpeter than sought him; and thus the matter passed over.

The 13th, I requested Wouter Van Twilliger to register Staten Island for me, as I wished to return and plant a colony upon it, which he consented to do. I took my leave of him and went aboard. Weighed anchor, and by evening came to anchor at Sandy Hook, in company with the Company's ship, *The Seven Stars*.

The 15th, weighed anchor, as did also the Company's ship, and set sail for Fatherland, to which may Almighty God conduct us.

Here I make my Third Voyage to America and New Netherland, in order to plant a Colony upon Staten Island for myself and Frederick de Vries, Secretary of the City of Amsterdam, and a Manager of the West India Company: undertaken at his Request

I leased out the plantation of Staten Island, as no people had been sent me from Holland, as was promised me in the contract which I had made with Frederick de Vries, a director of the West India Company.

The 16th July, Cornelis van Thienhoven, secretary of New Netherland, departed with a commission from the head men and council of New Netherland, with a hundred armed men, to the Raritanghe, a nation of savages who live where a little stream runs up about five leagues behind Staten Island, for the purpose of obtaining satisfaction from the Indians for the hostilities committed by them upon Staten Island, in killing my swine and those of the Company, which a negro watched—whom I had been solicited to place there—in robbing the swineherds, and in attempting (unsuccessfully) to run off with the yacht *Peace*, of which Cornelis Pietersz. was master, and for other acts of insolence. Van Thienhoven having arrived there with the said troop, demanded satisfaction according to his orders. The troop wished to kill and plunder, which could not be permitted, as Van Thienhoven said he had no orders to do so. Finally, on account of the pertinacity of the troop, the said Van Thienhoven went away, protesting against any injury which should happen by reason of their disobedience and violation of orders; and, when he had gone about a quarter of a league, the troop killed several of the savages, and brought the brother of the chief a prisoner, for whom Van Thienhoven had been surety before in eighty fathoms of *zeewan*, otherwise he, too, must have been put to death. Whereupon the Indians, as will hereafter be related, killed four of my men, and burned my house, in revenge. I learned also from Thienhoven that one Loockmans, standing at the mast, had tortured the chief's brother in his private parts with a piece of split wood, and that such acts of tyranny were perpetrated by the servants of the Company as were far from making friends with the inhabitants.

The 20th of October, I went with my sloop to Tapaen in order to trade for maize or Indian corn. I found the Company's sloop there for the purpose of levying a contribution from the Indian Christians, of a quantity of corn. The Indians called to me and inquired what I wanted. I answered that I desired to exchange cloth for corn. They said they could not help me. I must go somewhat up the river, and, should the Company's sloop in the mean time get away, they would then trade with me; that they were very much surprised that the Sachem [*white people*], who was now at the Fort, dare exact it; and he must be a very mean fellow to come to live in this country without being invited by them, and now wish to compel them to give him their corn for nothing; that they had not raised it in great abundance, as one chief had generally but two women who planted corn, and that they had calculated only for their own necessities. So this affair began to cause much dissatisfaction among the savages.

Anno 1641. The 20th August, the ship *Oak Tree*[1] arrived here, in which came a person named Melyn, who said that Staten Island belonged to him, that it was given by the directors to him and to Heer vander Horst, which I could not believe, as I had sailed in the year thirty-eight to take possession of said island, and had settled my men upon it. I thought better things of the directors than this, as the sixth article of the Privileges mentions that the first occupant shall not be prejudiced in his right of possession.

The 1st of September, my men on Staten Island were killed by the Indians and the Raritans; and they told an Indian, who worked for our people, that we would now come to fight them on account of our men; that we had before come and treated them badly on account of the swine, that there had been laid to their charge what they were not guilty of, and what had been done by the Company's men when they were on their way to the South River, who came ashore on Staten Island to cut wood and haul water, and then at the same time stole the hogs, and charged the act upon the innocent Indians, who, although they are bad enough, will do you no harm if you do them none. Thus I lost the beginning of my colony on Staten Island, through the conduct of Commander Kieft, who wished to charge upon the savages what his own people had done.

The 2d of November, there came a chief of the savages of Tankitekes, named Pacham, who was great with the governor of the fort. He came in great triumph, bringing a dead hand hanging on a stick, and saying that it was the hand of the chief who had killed or shot with arrows our men on Staten Island, and that he had taken revenge for our sake, because he loved the Swannekens (as they call the Dutch), who were his best friends.

The same day Commander Kieft asked me whether I would permit Melyn to go upon the point of Staten Island, where the maize-land lay, saying that he wished to let him plant it, and that he would place soldiers there, who would make a signal by displaying a flag, to make known at the fort whenever ships were in the bay, to which I consented—but did not wish to be prejudiced thereby—and to let him have twelve to fourteen or fifteen morgens of land, without abridging my right, as he intended only to distil some brandy there and make goat's leather.

As I was daily with Commander Kieft, generally dining with him when I went to the fort, he told me that he had now had a fine inn built and of stone, in order to accommodate the English who daily passed with their vessels from New England to Virginia, from whom he suffered great annoyance, and who might now lodge in the tavern. I replied that it happened well for the travellers, but there was great want of a church, and that it

---

[1] Cornelis Melyn, next spoken of, afterward led the opposition to Kieft, and was persecuted and banished by Stuyvesant.

was a scandal to us when the English passed there, and saw only a mean barn in which we preached…

Thus were the walls of the church speedily begun to be laid up with quarry-stone, and to be covered by the English carpenters with overlapping shingles cleft from oak, which, by exposure to the wind and rain, turn blue, and look as if they were slate.

About the same time a harmless Dutchman, named Claes Rademaker, was murdered by a savage. He lived a short league from the fort by the Densel-bay, where he had built a small house, and had set up the trade of wheelwright. It was on the Wickquasgeck road over which the Indians passed daily. It happened that a savage came to this Claes Rademaker for the purpose of trading beavers with him for duffels cloth, which goods were in a chest. This chest he had locked up, and had stooped down in order to take his goods out, when this murderer, the savage, seeing that the man had his head bent over into the chest, and observing an axe standing behind him, seized the axe, and struck Claes Rademaker on the neck therewith, so that he fell down dead by the chest. The murderer then stole all the goods and ran off. The Commander sent to them and made inquiry in Wickquasgeck why this Dutchman had been so shamefully murdered. The murderer answered that, while the fort was being built, he came with his uncle and another savage to the freshwater, bringing beavers, in order to trade with the Dutchmen, that some Swannekes (as they call the Netherlanders) came there, took away from his uncle his beavers, and then killed him. He was then a small boy, and resolved that, when he should grow up, he would revenge that deed upon the Dutch, and since then he had seen no better chance to do so than with this Claes Rademaker. Thus these savages resemble the Italians, being very revengeful. Commander Kieft afterwards tried to attack, sending some soldiers there, of whom Van Dyck, the ensign-bearer, had the command, but in consequence of the darkness of the night the guides missed the way, and arrived there too late in the day, so that the attempt failed, and they returned again without effecting anything. Another expedition against these savages was subsequently sent, which also miscarried. When Commander Kieft saw that these attempts against the savages miscarried, and that trouble would follow, and found that the people began to reproach him with being himself protected in a good fort, out of which he had not slept a single night during all the years he had been there, and with seeking the war in order to make a bad reckoning with the Company, and began to feel that the war would be laid to his charge, he called the people together to choose twelve men to aid him in the direction of the affairs of the country, of which number I was, as a patroon, chosen one. Commander Kieft then submitted the proposition whether or not we should avenge the murder of Claes Rademaker and make war upon the savages. We answered that time and opportunity must be taken, as our cattle were running at pasture in the woods, and we were living far and wide, east, west, south, and north of each other; that it was not expedient to carry on a war with the savages until we had more people, like the English, who make towns and villages. I told Commander Kieft that no profit was to be derived from a war with the savages; that he was the means of my people being murdered at the colony which I had commenced on Staten Island in the year forty; and that I well knew that the directors did not desire a war waged against the savages, for when we made our colony in the year 1630, in the

South River at Swanendael, otherwise called Hoere-kil, and our people were all murdered through some trifling acts of the commander whom we had stationed there, named Gilles Oset, as I have already mentioned in the beginning of my journal, it was then proposed to the Company to make war upon the savages, but the Company would not permit it, and replied that we must keep at peace with the savages. This I related to Commander Kieft, but he would not listen to it, so it becomes the managers to take care what persons they appoint as Directors, for thereon depends the welfare of the country. Were it the case that the East India Company had gone to work in the East Indies, as the West India Company here, they would soon have to leave there like the West India Company; but in the East Indies they make no person commander of a fort, if he be not well acquainted with the country, and [they] have knowledge of the person's competence. But commanders are sent here whether they be fit or not.

About this time also I walked to Ackingh-sack, taking a gun with me, in order to see how far the colony of Heer vander Horst had advanced, as it was only a short hour's journey behind my house. On approaching Ackinsack, about five or six hundred paces from where the colony was started, a savage met me who was very drunk. He came up to me and stroked my arms, which is a token of friendship among them, and said that I was a good chief; that when they came to my house, I let them have milk and everything for nothing; that he had just come from this house, where they had sold him brandy, into which they had put half water; that he could scoop up the water himself from the river, and had no need of buying it; that they had also stolen his beaver-coat, and he would go home and get his bow and arrows, and would kill some one of the villainous Swannekens who had stolen his goods. I told him he must not do so. I then proceeded on to the house of Heer vander Horst, and I told some soldiers and others who were there, that they must not treat the savages in that manner, as they were a very revengeful people, and resembled the Italians in that particular. I then returned home. I was not long home, when there came some chiefs from Ackinsack, and from Reckawanck, which was close by me, and informed me that one of their Indians, who was drunk, had shot a Dutchman dead, who was sitting on a barn thatching it. They asked me what they should do; they said they durst not go to the fort; that they would give one or two hundred fathom of *zeewan* to the widow if thereby they would be at peace. I told them that they must go with me to the fort, and speak to the commander; but they were afraid that, on going to the fort, he would not permit them to return home. I made them of good heart, by telling them that I would deliver them safe home. They went with me, at length, to the fort; and, going to Commander Willem Kieft, told him the misfortune which had happened to them. He answered the chief of the savages that he wanted the savage who had done the act to be brought to him. They said they could not do so, as he had run away a two day's journey to Tanditekes; but if the commander would listen to them, they desired in a friendly way to make the widow contented, and to pay for the man's death with *zeewan*, which is their money; it being a custom with them, if any misfortune befel them, to reconcile the parties with money. They laid the blame upon our people, saying that it was because we sold the young Indians brandy or wine, making them crazy, as they were unaccustomed to drink; that they had even seen our people, who were habituated to strong drink, frequently intoxicated, and fight with knives. They therefore desired that no liquor should be sold to the Indians, in order to prevent all accident for the future. It seemed as if they had some fear that the governor would detain them, so they answered him, that they would do their best to get the savage, and bring him to the fort. They then took their departure; but on the way they told me that they could not deliver up the savage to him, as he was a *sackemaker's* son—that is to say, as above, a chief's son. And thus the matter passed off.

As I have related the manner of living, and the appearance, of the savages at Fort Orange, I will state something of the nations about Fort Amsterdam; as the Hackinsack, Tapaen, and Wicquas-geck Indians; and these are located at some two, three, or four leagues from the entrance of the river. Their manner of living is for the most part like that of those at Fort Orange; who, however, are a stronger, and a more martial nation of Indians—especially the Maquas, as before mentioned, who hold most of the others along the river to Fort Amsterdam under tribute. The Indians below here are also tolerably stout, have black hair, with a long lock, which they braid and let hang on one side of the head. The hair is shorn on the top of the head like a cock's-comb, as is shown in the plate. Their disposition is bad. They are very revengeful; resembling the Italians. Their clothing is a coat of beaver-skins over the body, with the fur inside in winter, and outside in summer; they have, also, sometimes a bear's hide, or a coat of the skins of wild cats, or *hesspanen*, which is an animal almost as hairy as a wild cat, and is also very good to eat. I have frequently eaten it, and found it very tender. They also wear coats of turkey's feathers, which they know how to plait together; but since our Netherland nation has traded here, they trade their beavers for duffels cloth, which we give for them, and which they find more suitable than the beavers, as they consider it better for the rain; and take two and a half in length of duffels, which is nine and a half quarters wide. Their pride is to paint their faces strangely with red or black lead, so that they look like fiends. They are then valiant; yea, they say they are *Mannette*, the Devil himself. Some of the women are very well-featured, and of tall stature. Their hair hangs loose from their head; they are very foul and dirty; they sometimes paint their faces, and sometimes draw a black ring around their eyes. When they wish to cleanse themselves of their foulness, they go in the autumn, when it begins to grow cold, and make, away off, near a running brook, a small oven, large enough for three or four men to lie in it. In making it they first take twigs of trees, and then cover them tight with clay, so that smoke cannot escape. This being done, they take a parcel of stones, which they heat in a fire, and then put in the oven, and when they think that it is sufficiently hot, they take the stones out again, and go and lie in it, men and women, boys and girls, and come out so perspiring, that every hair has a drop of sweat on it. In this state they plunge into the cold water; saying that it is healthy, but I let its healthfulness pass; they then become entirely clean, and are more attractive than before. The girls consider themselves to have arrived at womanhood when they begin to have their monthly terms, and as soon as they have them, they go and disguise themselves with a garment, which they throw over their body drawing it over the head so that one can barely see their eyes, and run off for two or three months, lamenting that they must lose their virginity; but for all that they do not omit their diversions at night, or other unseasonable time. This period being over, they throw away their disguise, and deck themselves with a quantity of *zeewan* upon the body, head and neck; they then go and sit in some place, in company with some squaws, showing that they are up for a bargain. Whoever courts best and gives the most *zeewan* takes her home with him, and remains with her sometimes three or four months, and then goes with another; sometimes a single month, according as they are inclined to each other. The men are not jealous, and even lend their wives to a friend. They are fond of meetings, frolic and dance much; but the women are compelled to work like asses, and when they travel, to carry the baggage on their backs, together with their infants, if they have any, bound to a board.

Insert: How the Indians of the North arm themselves when they go to war. When they dance they stand two and two beside each other, which I have seen at the north. They dance in two, three, and four pairs. The first pair carry a tortoise in their hands, as this nation say that they have descended from a tortoise father, at which I laughed. They then asked me where our father came from. I said he was called Adam, and was made of earth. They said I was a fool to say that he was made of a thing that had no life. I replied that it was full of life, for it produced all the fruits upon which they lived. They answered that the sun, which they looked upon as a God, produced it, for in summer he drew the leaves from the trees, and all the fruits from the ground.

ANNO 1643. The 22d February, there broke out a war among the Mayekander savages, who came from Fort Orange and wanted to levy a contribution upon the savages of Wick-quas-geck and Tapaen, and of the adjacent villages. There were eighty to ninety of those from Fort Orange, each with a gun on his shoulder. There came flying to my house, four to five hundred savages, desiring that I would protect them. I answered then that I could not do it, as the Indians from Fort Orange were also our friends, and that we did not interfere in their wars; that I now saw that they were children, that they were flying on all sides from eighty or ninety men, when they were themselves so many hundred strong, and had been wont to boast to me that they were such soldiers, yea, Mannetoe himself – that is to say, the Devil; but that I saw now that they were only children. As my house was so full of savages, and I had only five men with me, I thought best to go to the fort to obtain some soldiers for the purpose of having more force in my house. So I took a canoe, as my boat was frozen up in the kill, and went in the canoe, or hollow tree, which is their boat, as before related, between the cakes of ice, down the river to Fort Amsterdam, where I requested Governor Willem Kieft to assist me with some soldiers, as I was not master of my own house, because it was so full of savages, although I was not afraid that they would do any harm; but it was proper that I should be master of my own house. The Governor said he had no soldiers; that I must see how it would be in the morning, and stop at night with him, which I did. The next day the Indians came in troops on foot from my house to Pavonia, by the Oysterbank, where the great body of them encamped, and some of them came over the river from Pavonia to the fort. I spoke to some of them, and they said that they had all left my house. These Indians went to Correlaer's bouwery, where there were some Indians from Reckeweck (Rockaway), opposite the fort, on Long Island, who were under a chief, named Nummerus, whom I well knew.

The 24th of February, sitting at a table with the Governor, he began to state his intentions, that he had a mind to *wipe the mouths* of the savages; that he had been dining at the house of Jan Claesz. Damen, where Maryn Adriaensz. and Jan Claesz.

Damen, together with Jacob Planck, had presented a petition to him to begin this work. I answered him that they were not wise to request this; that such work could not be done without the approbation of the *Twelve Men*; that it could not take place without my assent, who was one of the Twelve Men; that moreover I was the first patroon, and no one else hitherto had risked there so many thousands, and also his person, as I was the first to come from Holland or Zeeland to plant a colony; and that he should consider what profit he could derive from this business, as he well knew that on account of trifling with the Indians we had lost our colony in the South River at Swanendael, in the Hoere-kil, with thirty-two men, who were murdered in the year 1630; and that in the year 1640, the cause of my people being murdered on Staten Island was a difficulty which he had brought on with the Raritan Indians, where his soldiers had for some trifling thing killed some savages, and brought the brother of the chief a prisoner to the Mannates, who was ransomed there, as I have before more particularly related. But it appeared that my speaking was of no avail. He had, with his co-murderers, determined to commit the murder, deeming it a Roman deed, and to do it without warning the inhabitants in the open lands, that each one might take care of himself against the retaliation of the savages, for he could not kill all the Indians. When I had expressed all these things in full, sitting at the table, and the meal was over, he told me he wished me to go to the large hall, which he had been lately adding to his house. Coming to it, there stood all his soldiers ready to cross the river to Pavonia to commit the murder. Then spoke I again to Governor Willem Kieft: "Let this work alone; you wish to break the mouths of the Indians, but you will also murder our own nation, for there are none of the settlers in the open country who are aware of it. My own dwelling, my people, cattle, corn, and tobacco will be lost." He answered me, assuring me that there would be no danger; that some soldiers should go to my house to protect it. But that was not done. So was this business begun between the 25th and 26th of February in the year 1643. I remained that night at the Governor's, sitting up. I went and sat by the kitchen fire, when about midnight I heard a great shrieking, and I ran to the ramparts of the fort, and looked over to Pavonia. Saw nothing but firing, and heard the shrieks of the savages murdered in their sleep. I returned again to the house by the fire. Having sat there awhile, there came an Indian with his squaw, whom I knew well, and who lived about an hour's walk from my house, and told me that they two had fled in a small skiff, which they had taken from the shore at Pavonia; that the Indians from Fort Orange had surprised them; and that they had come to conceal themselves in the fort. I told them that they must go away immediately; that this was no time for them to come to the fort to conceal themselves; that they who had killed their people at Pavonia were not Indians, but the Swannekens, as they call the Dutch, had done it. They then asked me how they should get out of the fort. I took them to the door, and there was no sentry there, and so they betook themselves to the woods. When it was day the soldiers returned to the fort, having massacred or murdered eighty Indians, and considering they had done a deed of Roman valor, in murdering so many in their sleep; where infants were torn from their mother's breasts, and hacked to pieces in the presence of the parents, and the pieces thrown into the fire and in the water, and other sucklings, being bound to small boards, were cut, stuck, and pierced, and miserably massacred in a manner to move a heart of stone. Some were thrown into the river, and when the fathers and mothers endeavored to save them, the soldiers would not let them come on land but made both parents and children drown—children from five to six years of age, and also some old and decrepit persons. Those who fled from this onslaught, and concealed themselves in the neighboring sedge, and when it was morning, came out to beg a piece of bread, and to be permitted to warm themselves, were murdered in cold blood and tossed into the fire or the water. Some came to our people in the country with their hands, some with their legs cut off, and some holding their entrails in their arms, and others had such horrible cuts and gashes, that worse than they were could never happen. And these poor simple creatures, as also many of our own people, did not know any better than that they had been attacked by a party of other Indians -- the Maquas. After this exploit, the soldiers were rewarded for their services, and Director Kieft thanked them by taking them by the hand and congratulating them. At another place, on the same night, on Corler's Hook near Corler's plantation, forty Indians were in the same manner attacked in their sleep, and massacred there in the same manner. Did the Duke of Alva in the Netherlands ever do anything more cruel? This is indeed a disgrace to our nation, who have so generous a governor in our Fatherland as the Prince of Orange, who has always endeavored in his wars to spill as little blood as possible. As soon as the savages understood that the Swannekens had so treated them, all the men whom they could surprise on the farm-lands, they killed; but we have never heard that they have ever permitted women or children to be killed. They burned all the houses, farms, barns, grain, haystacks, and destroyed everything they could get hold of. So there was an open destructive war begun. They also burnt my farm, cattle, corn, barn, tobacco-house, and all the tobacco. My people saved themselves in the house where I alone lived, which was made with embrasures, through which they defended themselves. Whilst my people were in alarm the savage whom I had aided to escape from the fort in the night came there, and told the other Indians that I was a good chief, that I had helped him out of the fort, and that the killing of the Indians took place contrary to my wish. Then they all cried out together to my people that they would not shoot them; that if they had not destroyed my cattle they would not do it, nor burn my house; that they would let my little brewery stand, though they wished to get the copper kettle, in order to make darts for their arrows; but hearing now that it had been done contrary to my wish, they all went away, and left my house unbesieged. When now the Indians had destroyed so many farms and men in revenge for their people, I went to Governor Willem Kieft, and asked him if it was not as I had said it would be, that he would only effect the spilling of Christian blood. Who would now compensate us for our losses? But he gave me no answer. He said he wondered that no Indians came to the fort. I told him that I did not wonder at it; "why should the Indians come here where you have so treated them?"

The 4th of March, there came three savages upon Long Island, with a small white flag, and called out to the fort. Then Governor Willem Kieft asked who would go over to them. There was no one who was willing to do so, among all of them, except Jacob Olfersz. and I, David Pietersz. De Vries. We went to the three savages. They told us that they came from their chief, who had sent them to know the cause why some of his Indians had been killed, who had never laid a straw in our way, and who had done us nothing but favors? We answered them that we did not know that any of their Indians were among them. They then said we must go and speak with their chief, who had fled seven leagues from there on the seacoast. We resolved to go with the Indians, for we believed that they were well disposed towards us two.

At evening we arrived at Rechqua Akie where we found the chief, who had only one eye, with two or three hundred Indians, and about thirty houses. They led us into his house, and treated us to what they had, as oysters, and fish, which they catch there; told us we were tired, and must rest a little; they would early in the morning speak to us about the business upon which we had come there. During the night, I went out of the house, when there came an Indian to me, as the moon was shining, and told me I must come into his hut. I then went into his hut, and by the light saw he was an Indian, who lived half a league from my farm-house at Vriessendael, with his squaws, who lived there with him, at which I was alarmed. But he assured me, saying, that I was a good chief, and that I came to make *Rancontyn Marinit*; that is, in their language, to make a peace. I asked them how they came so far from their dwelling. They answered that they were out a-hunting with these Indians, and had friends among them. I then returned to my comrade in the house of the chief. When the day began to dawn, we were awakened, and taken by a savage, who led us into the woods about four hundred paces from the houses, and when we came there, sixteen chiefs were there of this Long Island, which is thirty leagues long. They placed us two by ourselves, and seated themselves around us, so that we sat within a ring. There was one among them who had a small bundle of sticks, and was the best speaker, who began his oration in Indian. He told how we first came upon their coast; that we sometimes had no victuals; they gave us their Turkish beans and Turkish wheat, they helped us with oysters and fish to eat, and now for a reward we had killed their people. Then he laid down one of the sticks, which was one point. He related also that at the beginning of our voyaging there, we left our people behind with the goods to trade, until the ships should come back; they had preserved these people like the apple of their eye; yea, they had given them their daughters to sleep with, by whom they had begotten children, and there roved many an Indian who was begotten by a Swanneken, but our people had become so villainous as to kill their own blood. He then laid down another stick. This laying down of sticks began to be tedious to me, as I saw that he had many still in his hand. I told him that I knew all these things which he said had happened to the savages of Long Island; they had been done unwittingly; if any of them had been with the other savages, they should go with us to the fort, where the Governor would give them presents for a peace. The speaking now ceased and they gave to each of us ten fathoms of *zeewan*—which is their money, each fathom being worth four guilders. Then they all rose up and said that they would go with us to the fort, and speak with our governor Willem Kieft. We went to the canoes to go by water, and to make the journey shorter than when we came, for it made full three hours difference. When we reached the canoes, we found that the tide had not yet begun to make, and that we must wait some time before it would be flood. In the mean time, an Indian came running up with a bow and arrow, who had come on a run six leagues on behalf of a chief who had not been with us, and asked the chiefs who were going with us to the fort if they were so foolish as to go to the fort where there was such a villain, who had caused their friends to be so foully murdered; and who, when so many of the chiefs were together at the fort, would keep them there, and thus all the Indians would be in distress, being without heads or chiefs, and said the chief from whom he came thought it entirely inadvisable. They asked us two if we understood what he said. We answered that this was a crazy Indian, that they would find it otherwise, and would return home with good presents. Then one of the chiefs who knew me well said, "we will go on the faith of your word, for the Indians have never found you to lie as they have the other Swannekens." Finally, twenty of us went sitting in a canoe or hollow-tree, which is their boat, and the edge was not more than a hand's-breadth above the water. Arrived at the fort about three o'clock in the afternoon, and went to Willem Kieft, who made peace with the Indians, and gave them some presents. He requested them to bring those chiefs to the fort who had lost so many Indians, as he wished also to make a peace with them, and to give them presents. Then some of them went and brought the Indians of Ackin-sack and Tapaen and the vicinity, and the chiefs came with them, to whom he made presents; but they were not well content with them. They told me that he could have made it, by his presents, that as long as he lived the massacre would never again be spoken of; but now it might fall out that the infant upon the small board would remember it. They then went away grumbling with their presents.

The 20th of July, a chief of the savages came to me, and told me that he was very sad. I asked him wherefor. He said that there were many of the Indian youths, who were constantly wishing for a war against us, as one had lost his father, another his mother, a third his uncle, and also their friends, and that the presents or recompense were not worth taking up; and that he would much rather have made presents out of his own purse to quiet them; but he could no longer keep them still, and that I must be careful in going alone in the woods; that those who knew me would do me no harm, but I might meet Indians who did not know me, who would shoot me. I told him that he ought to go to Commander Kieft at the fort, and tell the same things to him. We went to the fort, and coming to the commander, the chief of these Indians told the same things to him. Commander Kieft told this savage he was a chief of the Indians and must kill these young madcaps who wished to engage in a war with the Swannekens, and he would give him two hundred fathoms of *zeewan*. I then laughed within myself, that the Indian should kill his friends for two hundred fathoms of *zeewan*—that is eight hundred guilders—to gratify us. It is true that they do so towards each other, when they are at enmity with each other, but not at the will of foreigners. Then the Indian said this could not be done by him; that there were many malcontents. Had he (the Governor) paid richly for the murder, it would have been entirely forgotten. He himself would do his best to keep them quiet, but he was afraid he could not, for they were continually calling for vengeance.

The 28th of September, arrived a herring buss from Rotterdam; the master was named Jacob Blenck. He was laden with a hundred pipes of Madeira wine, and had come by the way of the West Indies, wishing to go to the Virginias, but could not find them, and had sailed quite to New England. He could not sell his wine there, because the English there live soberly. He was compelled to return, and came along the coast inside of Long Island, through Hellgate to Fort Amsterdam; and coming here he could not dispose of his wines here either, because here was a prize laden with wines which the Company had captured. He sold his wines to an Englishman to be taken to the Virginias. As he could find no one who could pilot him to the Virginias, he asked me if I would take him there, as he understood that I wished to go there in order to take a well-mounted ship for the Fatherland, because my farms, where I had begun my colonies, were lying in ashes; and the Indians were discontented and desired to go to war again, or to have satisfaction. I promised the skipper that I would take him there out of friendship, and told him that he must provide himself with bread here if needed, for it was difficult to obtain it in the Virginias, because every one there only produced for himself.

The 1st of October, nine savages came to Pavonia opposite the fort, where there were three or four soldiers stationed to protect the farmer who lived there, named Jacob Stoffelsz., towards whom they were so well disposed that they did not wish to kill him. So they made a pretended errand, and persuaded him to go over to the fort (Amsterdam), and he came over accordingly; then they went under the guise of friendship, when the soldiers had no arms in their hands, and killed them all, except the young son of his wife by a former marriage, whom they took with them captive to Tapaen. They set fire to the farm-house and all the other houses at Pavonia; and thus began a new war. The next day the Governor came to me with the step-father of the little boy that was made prisoner by the Indians. He was the son of Cornelis van Vorst. The Governor asked me if I would go to the savages to obtain the release of the boy, as nobody dared go to the Indians except me. I said I would send them one or two Indians; but if I brought them to the fort, they must not be misused, for they would come with me upon my word. So I went over to Long Island and brought with me two Indians to go to Tapaen to obtain the release of the boy. When I brought the Indians over, every one wanted to kill them, and I had enough to do to save them. I took them to a privateer which was lying there, which carried them away, and they released the boy.

The 8th of the same month I took my leave of Commander Kieft, and left in the Rotterdammer buss for the English Virginias; and, in taking leave of Willem Kieft, I told him that this murder which he had committed on so much innocent blood would yet be avenged upon him, and thus I left him. Sailed past Staten Island through the Narrows to Sandy Hook, where we were detained two days by contrary winds. Picked each day some blue-plums, which are abundant there, and grow there naturally wild.

The 11th, weighed anchor to sail from Sandy Hook to the Virginias, with a northwest wind and a weather shore.

Author's Notes on Henry Hudson

Education and history go hand in hand, independently they are naked, and together they are dynamite I had to learn that independently. In the 1500's Verrazano blundered into the Narrows. Many Americans know the story of Henry Hudson sailing into the narrows, seeing Staten Island and claiming the area for the Dutch and calling it New Amsterdam. This is what our grammar school textbooks told us. We know Henry Hudson sailed in and called it Staaten Eylant, the Island of the States. The native Indians he encountered called it Egquahous, the place of bad woods. The story goes that while at anchor, a number of canoes surrounded the ship, and a "savage" climbed up the stern window and stole a number of articles. As he left the ship with his plunder, a shipmate saw him, killing him instantly. This was the first Indian blood shed by the Whites. When a boat was sent to recover the stolen items, an Indian swimming to the boat, apparently to overturn it, when a shipmate aboard the boat drew his cutlass and cut off the hands of the Indian and he was drowned. The Indians attacked the ship with arrows, causing no injuries, but the ship retaliated with cannon fire and small arms, killing many of them. Aboard Hudson's ship, no one was injured and there were no casualties. This initial bloodshed would never end.

A man named Robert Juet, an officer on the half Moon boat that began the chronicles in 1609. Juet was aboard the Half Moon, Henry Hudson's third voyage up through the narrows and into the lower bay. His day to day log books were written in Dutch, and omissions were noted when Juet did not mention the disillusionment and insubordinations of the crew, and any written chronicle of the mutiny aboard the vessel remains lost. Robert Juet also did not survive the voyage, he died aboard the ship before it returned to England. The many official and unofficial readings, editings and translations by "elebrated cosmographers."

Over many years I came to realize that no editing of or abstracts of historical materials can convey the intimacy of an authors original handwritings and personal on site images to be whole truth. It was a puzzle, and I began to understand the early diarists whose academic or personal positions were reflected in their coverage of early historic events. The eventual writings are intended for mass public consumption, with the constantly shifting sands and juxtapositions, to satisfy the advanced literacy of current populations.

An entry into the ship's chronicles of September 6,1609: the ship master sent John Coleman with four men to sound the depth of the river ahead. On their return to the ship they were attacked by Indians in two canoes, one canoe had 12 men and another longer canoe with 14 men. John Coleman was killed by an arrow shot into his throat and fell overboard. Two others were wounded. The Indians returned at ten the next day with the body of John Coleman, who was now dressed in the red coat that was given to them a day or so earlier.   This gesture was misunderstood by the crew of the ship. There had been a battle and there was killing. The affair had ended.   The next day Coleman was buried on a point of land which they named "Coleman's Point." They were now "savages" who watched the burial proceedings from a distance. The burial of Coleman in the sand was very brief. The seamen returned to the ship in their barge.

The Indians from the Hackensack's and Raritan's lived on the Island shore overlooking Coleman's Point. Many years later, Chief Redbone recounted the oral history of the event and the story of the burial on Coleman's point. It wasn't until some days later that savages ventured into the area and dug up and removed the body that was sewn in sailcloth and cremated it to purify the ground, return it to its sacred status and release the white man's soul to rejoin his ancestors. This story was recorded by Island settlers and can be found in the archives.

The ship now located in the narrow Kill Van Kull waters was approached again by the Indians, who came aboard and offered to trade tobacco and wheat and corn in exchange for knives beads, kettles, and metal objects, and did not offer any reason for violence to the ship men. They did not show any malice about the deaths, the tense situation as eased, however, the ship was then returned to wider lower bay, and anchored there all night. The chronicles read that day later the crew made a landing in a small boat to the house of an old savage and made them ''good cheer' .The next day the people of the country came aboard with fruits and pumpkins melons and traded for 'trifles', many others brought beaver skins, otter skins which were exchanged for knives, beads and hatchets, and the ship remained there again all night. There were so many Indians now on board the ship that the master and the mate took some chiefs down into the cabins to determine if there was any treachery in them. They drank a lot of wine and became "merrie" on of the savages brought one of his wives with him which sat modestly as any of our women would do in a strange place. One Indian became drunk and could not make of his situation, and he could not make of this strange feeling. They have nothing with which they can become intoxicated. On several occasions the ship stopped for wood and water and many Indians again came aboard,. One canoe had very loving people and a chief who gave the ship master more straps of beads for the master, who said he would show them the entire country that were at his command, two old men and their wives and two young maidens who were about sixteen or seventeen with them and they behaved very modestly. They were given a knife and presented the master with tobacco. At one o'clock they departed and made signs that we should come down to them, for they were two leagues of where they dwelt. There were gestures to come to their lands and eat with them. They refused and the old chief went away very disconsolate.

On the eight day they caught fish, mullets, and more to fill the ship stores. On this river there were many wild animals, beavers, otters, foxes, bears, wild cats and minks. The land is excellent and fertile, full of tall noble trees, nothing is wanted there but the labor and industry of man to render it the finest and most fruitful in the world, but the savages who inhabit this land are indolent, and some of them are evil thieves and wicked people.

ESSAY ON HENRY HUDSON

These translations from the Dutch language original manuscript at the Hague.

Henry Hudson, describes the manner and appearance of the people that he found dwelling immediately along the bay, in the following terms:

"When I came on shore, the swarthy natives all stood and sang in their fashion. Their clothing consists of the skin of foxes and other animals which they dress, and make the garments from the skins of various sorts. Their food is Turkish wheat, which they cook by baking and is excellent eating. They soon came on board, one after another, in their canoes, which are made of a single piece of wood. Their weapons are bows and arrows pointed with sharp stones which they harden and fasten with resin. They have no houses but sleep under the blue heavens, as on mats of bulrushes interwoven and some of the leaves of trees. They also carried with them all of their goods as well as their food and green tobacco, which is strong and good for use. They appear to be a friendly people but are much inclined to steal, and are adroit at carrying away anything they take fancy to."

"As they care nothing for the spiritual, they direct their study to the physical, closely observing the seasons. The women there are most skillful stargazers. But as of God, of Him who dwells above us, they knoweth not, affording all our Christians an argument to thank Him, that He hath so beneficially granted us knowledge of Him, leaving these savages in darkness so that what the apostle says is found to be true. It is not of him that willeth, not of him that runneth, but of God that showeth mercy. There is little authority among these nations. They live almost all equally free. In each village, indeed, is found a person who is somewhat above the others and commands absolutely when there is no war and when they are gathered from all the villages to go to war. But the fight once ended, his authority ceases. They are very much afraid of death; but when they perceive that they must die, they are very brave and more ferocious than beasts. When a lad desires a wife, he buys her generally in a neighboring village, and she, being a maiden, is then delivered to him by two or three other women, carrying on the head meal, roots, corn and other articles, to the young man's hut, and he receives her. The dwellings are commonly circular, with a vent hole above to let out the smoke, closed with four doors, and made mostly of the bark of trees which are very abundant there. They sleep on the ground covered with leaves and skins. At their meals they sit on the ground. Each highly esteems his own children, bringing them up very much spoiled. The women sew skins into clothing, prepare bread, cook the meat which the men hunt and kill with arrows, especially in the winter when all is bare in the fields and but scantly forage is to be picked off the snow; then the animals approach the villages and are shot."

"It is very common among them for one man to buy and to have many wives, but not in one place; when he journeys five or six leagues he finds another wife who also takes care of him; five or ten leagues further, he again finds another wife who keeps house and so on to several, constantly buying up peltries through the country. But as those inland find that furs sold too cheap among them, they come down themselves to the rivers and trade with the nations as best they can. Also those who will trade with them must furnish them food an at inhabitant's in the village – let them cook their meat and fish there, as much as they like, and then they thank the trader. In other respects, they are extremely hospitable."

"They live in summer mostly on fish. The men repair to the river and catch a great quantity in a short time, as it is full and furnishes various sorts. The arrows they use are pointed with little bones, iron or copper, with which they, being good marksmen, shoot deer, fawns, hares, and foxes and all such. The country is full of game: hogs, bears, leopards, yea lions, as appears by the skins which were brought on board. Oxen and horses there are none."

"In the woods are found all sorts of fruits: plums, wild cherries, peaches; yea fruits in great profusion. Tobacco is planted in abundance, but much better grows in the wild parts of Brazil; it is called Virginian. Vines grow wild there; were there wine-growers who understood the pressing, good wine could be brought hither in great quantity, and even as must, the voyage thence being often made in thirty days."

"Their trade consists mostly in peltries, (pelt skins) which they measure by the hand or by the finger. It happened that a woman who had seen a skipper's lace shirt, fell sick; finding she should die she gave her husband three fine peltry skins to present to the skipper for the shirt, which he willingly gave her, for she wished to be buried in it; imitating the Christians in the sumptuousness of their burials. In exchange for peltries, they receive beads, with which they decorate their persons; knives, adzes, axes, chopping knives, kettles and all sorts of iron which they require for housekeeping."

"They are so clever that they make use of the best for that purpose; what is poor of substance they deem unsuitable for their clothing. When they bring their commodities to the traders and find they are desirous to buy them, they make so very little matter of it, that they at once rip up the skins they are clothed with and sell them as being the best. They use the beaver skins mostly for the sleeves, as they are not so expensive; and they frequently come several days' journey from the interior, to exchange their goods with the tribes."

"The same course id followed in New Netherland. It is very pleasant, all products being in abundance, though wild. Grapes are of very good flavor, but will be henceforward better cultivated by our people. Cherries are not found there. There are all sorts of fowls, both in the water and in the air. Swans, geese, ducks, bitterns, abound. The men never labor, except to provide some game, either fowl or other wild sort, for cooking, and then they have provided everything. The women must attend t the remainder, tilling the soil, etc. As soon as our people arrived there, they proceeded to clear and plant. Before this vessel had left, the harvest was far advanced. It excites little attention if any one of the Indians abandon his wife; in case she have children, they usually follow her. Their summers are fine, but the days there are shorter than with us here. The winters are severe, but there is plenty of fuel, as the country is well wooded and it is at the service of whoever wants it."

"There is some respect paid to those in authority amongst them; but these are no wise richer than others. There is always so much in it that the chief is feared and obeyed as long as he is near; but he must shirt for himself like others. There is nothing seen in his house more than in those of the rest. But our people must pay their respects to him with a kettle or an axe, and he comes forward to beg a draught of brandy along with the rest."

"Since it is a marshy country, spoon-bills, ravens, eagles, sparrow-hawks, vultures are numerous and are quickly shot or knocked down by the natives."

"The science of foretelling or interpreting of events is altogether undeveloped and unknown to them; delivering no oracles or revelations of the one or the other sort, as they have very little knowledge of future or past things."

"It is somewhat strange that among these most barbarous people, there are few or none cross-eyed, blind, crippled, lame, hunch-backed, or limping men; all are well fashioned people, strong and sound of body, well fed, without blemish."

"In some places they have abundant means, with herbs and leaves or roots, to cure their ailments. There is not an ailment they have not a remedy for; but in other localities they are altogether devoid of succor, leaving the people to perish like cattle."
"Chastity appears to be of some repute among them, for the women are not all equally loose. There are some who would not cohabit with ours for any compensation. Others hold it in small esteem; especially as they are free, living without law." "They are not, by nature, the most gentle. Were there no weapons, especially muskets, near, they would frequently kill the traders for the sake of the plunder; but whole troops run before five or six muskets. At the first coming of the whites they were accustomed to fall prostrate on the report of the gun; but now they stand still from habit, so that the first colonists will stand in need of protection." The savages watch the prowess of the Whites fire sticks. They saw the instant death from a great distance. They were at times allowed to hold the weapons. Eventually they would give enough beaver pelts to the White traders to have killing sticks." [rifles]

HOW THE COLONIES WERE CREATED

The Sneewuil, 130 tons (lasts) a ship was fitted out under a commission from the West India Company, and freighted with families, to plant a colony among these people. But to go forward safely, it is first of all necessary that they be placed in a good defensive position and well provided with forts and arms, since the Spaniard, who claims all the country, will never allow any one to gain a possession there; and as the Spaniards have made many incursions as well above as below, in Florida, Virginia .and thereabouts, I deem it not uncalled-for to tell something thereof, being a mirror in which every one can see and defend himself, and how the Spaniards always aim as well in general as in particular at monarchy. Such description shall be presented in the commencement of Part the Seventh, as this book cannot contain it."

April, 1624

Found on the overleaf of Reverand Richard Hakluyt:
"*Homo est. animal sociable*, is in some sense a definition, in some sense a description, of man. Men's sociability led them to congregate and to live peaceably together, from which arose hamlets, villages, and cities, and afterwards chiefs were chosen among them; these, observing that the collected mass frequently so increased that they could with difficulty support themselves, separated a number of their people, who took up and settled the neighboring places. The patriarchs of the Old Testament, finding themselves altogether too many in their countries, sent some of theirs into the uninhabited valleys, and cultivated these. The Assyrians wishing to enlarge their monarchy caused the ir subjects to inhabit the invaded countries in great numbers. Those of the Persian monarchy did the same. But the Greeks extended their limits very far; for they by navigation peopled entire islands, as appears by the highly learned Petrus Cluverius, who furnishes us correct information on all points in his published *Italy*. The Romans domineering over the western world, spread colonies all over it, as is proved by the carved stones found everywhere; but what order they observed herein is well known to

us. Those sent thither, must acknowledge the senders as their lords, pay them homage, and remain under their sovereignty; they were also protected by these by suitable weapons furnished also to them. And whereas, God be praised, it hath come about that the Honorable Messrs. Directors of the West India Company have, with the consent of the Noble High and Mighty Lords States General, undertaken to plant some colonies, I shall give the particulars of them, as follows. We treated in our preceding discourse of the discovery of some rivers in Virginia; the studious reader will learn how affairs proceeded."

"Respecting this colony, it has already a prosperous beginning; and the hope that is will not fall through provided it to be zealously sustained, not only in that place but in the South River. For their increase and prosperous advancement, it is highly necessary that those sent out be first of all well provided with means both of support and defense, and that being freemen, they be settled there on a free tenure; that all they work for and gain be theirs to dispose of and to transfer it according to their pleasure; that whoever is placed over them as commander act as their father not as their executioner, leading them with a gentle hand; for whoever rules them as a friend and associate will be beloved by them, while he who will order them as a superior will subvert everything and bring it to naught; yea, they will excite against him the neighboring provinces to which they will fly. 'Tis better to rule by love and friendship than by force."

The ship Maeckereel would maintain constant contact with several colonies delivering supplies,tools, oxen, and horses, new families signed with the Company as they grew larger. In some cases families declined because of sickness or death, The ship often returned with pelts, beaver skins,martins, and foxes etc,. Often there were soldiers in chains returning for prison for insubordination or other crimes or had completed their tours of duty at the solitary outposts. Some military men, fled their posts never to be seen again, often joining Indian tribes, some became traders, one Belgian soldier learned the language so well that he became a chief.

April 1625

Though good care was taken by the directors of the West India Company in the Spring to provide everything for the colony of Virginia, by us called New Netherland, on the river Mauritius, near the Maykas, an extraordinary shipment was sent thither this month to strengthen it with what was needful, as follows:

As the country is well adapted for agriculture and the raising of everything that is produced here, the aforesaid gentlemen resolved to take advantage of the circumstance, and to provide the place with many necessaries, through the worthy Pieter Eversten Hulfrt, who undertook to ship thither, at his risk, whatever was asked of him, to wit; one hundred and three head of live stock – stallions, mares, bulls and cows – for breeding and multiplying, besides all the hogs and sheep that they thought expedient to send thither; and to distribute these in two ships of one hundred and forty lasts, in such a manner that they should be well foddered and attended to. Each animal has its own stall, with a floor of three feet of sand, arranged as comfortably as any stall here. Each animal has its respective servant who attends to it and knows what he is to get if he delivers it there alive. All suitable forage is there, such as oats, hay, and straw, and what else is useful. Country people have also joined the expedition, who take with them all furniture proper for the dairy; all sorts of seed, ploughs and agricultural implements are also present, so that nothing is wanting. What is most remarkable is, that nobody in the two ships can discover where the water is stowed for these cattle. In order to use the same plan another time if needful, I shall here add it: the above named manager caused a desk to be constructed in the ship. Beneath this were stowed in each ship three hundred tons of fresh water, which was pumped up and this distributed among the cattle. On this deck lay the ballast and thereupon stood the horses and bulls, and this there was nothing wanting. He added the third ship as an extra, so that, should the voyage, which is ordinarily made in six weeks, continue longer, nothing should be wanting and he should be able to fulfill his contract. So, in the eyes of the farseeing, this colony, which lies right beside the Spanish passage from the West Indies, has great prospects.

In company with these, goes a fast sailing yacht at the risk of the Directors. In those aforesaid vessels also go six completely equipped families, with some single persons, so that forty-five new comers or inhabitants are taken out, to remain there. The natives of New Netherland are found to be very well disposed as long as no injury is done them. But if any wrong be committed against them they remember it long, and should any one against whom they have a grudge be peaceably walking in the woods or hunting, even after a long lapse of time, they will slay him, though they are sure it will cost them their lives on the spot, so highly prized is vengeance among them ….

In our previous discourses, mention is made of New Netherland. Here is additional information: On further inquiry it is found, that they have a chief in time of war, named a *Sacjama*, but above him is a greater *Sacjama* (pointing to heaven) who rules the sun and moon. When they wage war against each other, they fortify their tribe or nation with palisades, serving then for a fort, and sally out the one against the other. They have a tree in the center, on which they place sentinels to observe the enemy and discharge arrows. None are exempt in war, but the popes or priests, and the women, who carry their husbands' arrows and food. The meat they eat consists of game and fish; but the bread is cakes baked forefather's fashion, in the ashes; they almost all eat that, even in war. They are a wicked, bad people, very fierce in arms. Their dogs are small. When the worthy Lambrecht van Twenhuyzen had once give the skipper a big dog, and it was brought to them on ship-board, they were very much afraid of it; calling it also a sachem of dogs, as being one of the biggest. The dog, tied with a rope on board, was very furious against them, they being clad like beasts with skins, for he thought they were wild animals; but when they gave him some of their bread made of Indian corn, which grows there, he learned to distinguish them, that they were men.

There are oaks of very close grain; yea, harder than any in this country, as thick as three or four men. There is a red wood which, being burned, smells very agreeably; when men sit by the fire on benches fade from it, the whole house is perfumed by it. When they keep watch by night against their enemies, then they place it (the fire) in the center of their huts, to warm their feet by it; they do not sit, then, up in the tree, but make a hold in the roof, and keep watch there, to prevent attacks.

Poisonous plants have been found there, which those who cultivate the land should look out for. Hendrick Christiaensen carried thither, by order of his employers, bucks and goats, also rabbits, but they were found to be poisoned by the herbs. The

Directors intended to send thither this spring voyage (1625) a quantity of hogs which will be of great service to the colony; and cows, with young calves, as shall follow.

Very large oysters, sea fish and river fish are in such great abundance there, and they cannot be sold; and in rivers so deep as to be navigated upwards with large ships.

The two lads brought hither by Adriaen Block were named Orson and Valentine. This Orson was a thoroughly wicked fellow, and after his return to his own country was the cause of Hendrick Christiaensen's death. But he was paid in like coin; he got a bullet as his recompense.

Chastity appears, on further enquiry, to hold a place among them, they being unwilling to cohabitate with ours, through fear of their husbands. But those who are single, evidence only too friendly a disposition. The common people fish everywhere. Whatever else is of value in the country, such as mines and other ores, shall by time and further exploration be made known to us. Much profit is to be expected from good management.

By the mid 1625 more French speaking Walloons applied to the West India Company for transportation to New Amsterdam to receive grants and supplies to become colonists, and freemen. Some few narratives survive. However one documentation survived in a deposition made in 1685 by a woman named Catelina Trico . One of a family that came out of the very first settlers voyage, living in Albany for three years. She gives interesting details respecting the distribution of the immigrants to Manhattan. And the remainder of her family numbered about 18 remained in Albany, she said that the Indians "were as quiet as lambs'.

The other narratives written by Catalina Trico have not survived documentation, in the Documentary History of New York. But in many details she differs from the contemporary account by Nicolaes Van Wassenaer, who's accounts sixty years after her were said to not to much reliance in her words after sixty years. It must be noted that Van Wassenaer had never crossed the Atlantic Ocean or had been to New Netherlands. It also must be noted that the captain of the ship Nieu Nederlandt was Cornelis Jacobsz May, and Cape May in southern New Jersey is named after him.

Subsequent accounts published in Amsterdam by Nicolaes Van Wassenaer the son of the Minister of The Reformed Church of Amsterdam. Van Wassenaer was called a learned scholar, who published a Greek poem on the siege of Haarlem, where he was then termed the "conrector" in the school. He then moved to Amsterdam to practice as a physician. He then wrote a history of the Turks, in 1624.

It was said that as a compiler of the "Historical Verhael' that the reader was not to expect too much of it's accuracy with respect to the statements coming from remote places when the means of information were so imperfect and casual. But Amsterdam was the best place to get any news from the New Netherland. Any surviving testimony is of value because there was so little information in any other source on a regular place. His papers were edited and translated by another person in 1850 Dr E,B, O'Callaghan for the "Documentary of the History of the State of New York. I must be understood that each translator has his biases, the Eurocentric patterns maintain the domination of the literature that would be printed.

The Chartered Dutch West India Company was given a monopoly of trade between Dutch ports and the west coast of Africa and all the coasts of America. Within these ample limits it could form alliances with native princes and tribes, appoint and discharge governors and other officers, administer justice and promote trade and colonization. Under the superior control of the States General, its government was vested in five federated chambers or boards of managers, the chief one at Amsterdam, others representing the investors of Zeeland, of the towns on the Maas, of North Holland and of the northern provinces of Friesland and Groningen. General executive powers were vested in the College of the Nineteen; and the government promised aid and protection. New Netherland was not specifically mentioned, and in all colonies the position and rights of colonists were left to be defined by a corporation formed for war and commerce. Throughout all the earlier part of the company's history, its interest in New Netherland was far less than in the conquest of Brazil from Spain, the maintenance of Brazil as a Dutch colony, and the war against the Portuguese for its retention, ending with its loss in 1654.

My interest was about the west coast of Africa. It was then I realized that the slave trade was also an ongoing business of the Dutch West India Company.

Sailing vessels from the colonies were returning to Amsterdam with enormous cargoes of furs. The Indians would bring their commodities to the traders who would buy them for little payment, thinking little of the transactions. Traders went deep into the country to trade with other tribes,and return to trade them for knives, bright beads, axes, metal tools. The colony began to advance bravely and to live in friendship with the Indians. Such was the friendship that a ship log noted that there were two sons of the principal Indian Sachem Chief, they were very dull men, they were expert enough in knavery. The trade was vigorous and the West India Company forbid any others to trade in their colonies. Some ships carried cargoes of black bear, otters, foxes and martins, beavers. The cargo sold in Amsterdam for twenty eight thousand, seven hundred guilders.

THE FOLLOWING ARE AUTHOR'S NOTES

Numbers and figures relating to population are fairly accurate, while others are wide of the reality mark. Making these numbers is like telling a persons age, guesswork. Any figure you suggest would be a wild guess. In order to know a persons actual age you must have his birth date. And I have not been certain that the census takers or colonial numbers keepers are nothing more than estimates and guesses. Figures from the Leng and Davis Staten Island History books are and have been used extensively for generations of loyal followers. Unfortunately many of the figures reported have been published without any clear indication of how they were arrived at, based in part by estimates and guesses and hearsay.

The new world was occupied by inhabitants that lived in huts and data was reasonably guesses at because there was no way of knowing that exact number of huts in various regions. There was no way of knowing the actual number of the density of the native colony. Separate figures for male or female were very often lumped together and no attempt to distinguish their numbers, simply stated as "adult 'male" and adult female" the figures for children as a rule were without value because there was no rule and without any value. The numbers for "child" were extremely vague.

The first colonies counted and classified the population by race. And every student of history and the colonies would like to know the number of whites, the number

The Dutch Arriving in the New World

Below: Shoes were handmade in the New World, and the cobbler's workbench was a necessary feature of every town. Free Blacks survived by learning crafts, such as shoemaking.

if natives, in addition to the numbers of blacks. But many colonial reports which distinguish the population by race do not convey this information.

Other classifications and numbers used note religion, occupation or literacy is made. Births and deaths registrations were nearly compulsory, however that date was difficult to come by in the 1600 during the occupation of the new world.

This information was not introduced for slaves or natives and not enforced. These vital statistics of the colonial population as a whole is in an unsatisfactory state, and utterly inadequate .The reasons or this chaotic state of the statistics are manifold, based in large part due to race. Whenever there is racial inequality among races, and some races are numbers, Numbers constitute who will be considered the superior one. This, of course, is a problem with which not only the colonial counts are confronted.

In the early 1900 census takers, (Enumerators) in poor locations will ask for a form the is used for persons that are not visibly "European." In these cases census takers were instructed to refrain from giving any offence by any comment or question in the presence of the parties concerned, but to make a private note on the completed forms against the names of any persons he considers not to be classifies as European. After which the particulars in respect of the persons in question should be transferred to a form or forms applicable to their skin color, to their race.

Staten Island history is filled with the notations and voices of confusion; Listings for 'Colored' increased and listings for ''Creole' Stated for the record' These people through physical degeneration appear to lack the necessary stamina to withstand diseases affecting there respiratory organs, and fall easy prey to the pneumonia form of influenza'.

"'A considerable number of Staten island born Negroes insist on calling themselves "Creoles" either through false pride or ignorance, the authors of consensus reports are legendary. And tell in detailed reports similar experiences.

"'many persons of mixed blood have improperly and ridiculously returned them selves as "white." Dutch slaves have denied any other classification. And as to the Dutch, it must be born in mind that, in the Netherlands where a great majority cam from, these distinctions between European and native servants of colors belonged to them the distinction is not maintained as we maintain it into the centuries, the two classes are grouped together as Europeans, and those assimilated with them are /were simply Europeans.

This statement applies with equal force to the present enumeration; and the white numbers when reduced will reduce by fifteen percent. And the "mixed" notations correspondently increased. The figures are dealt with as returned and being examined one could not help noticing with ambivalence that persons of undoubtedly mixed blood seemed to have undergone an alb scent re-incarnation.

The ridiculous aspect is evidenced by that fact that of the issue of the persons of mixed blood, one has returned as White while another has entered as "Mixed."

Privileges and Exemptions
[*March*, 1630.]

After the Right Honorable Directors of the Chartered West India Company in the United Netherlands had provided everything for the defence of New Netherland and put everything there in good order, they taking into consideration the advantages of said place, the favorable nature of the air and soil, and that considerable trade and goods and many commodities may be obtained from thence, sent some free emigrants thither with all sorts of cattle and implements necessary for agriculture, so that in the year 1628 there already resided on the island of the Manhattes two hundred and seventy souls, men, women and children, under Governor Minut, Verhulst's successor, and lived there in peace with the natives. But as the land, being extensive and in many places full of weeds and wild growth, could not be properly cultivated in consequence of the scantiness of the population, the said Directors of the West India Company, the better to people their lands, and to bring the country to produce more abundantly, resolved to grant divers Privileges, Freedoms and Exemptions to all patroons, masters or individuals who should plant any colonies and cattle in New Netherland, and they accordingly have constituted and published in print these following exemptions, to afford better encouragement and infuse greater zeal into whosoever should be inclined to reside and plant his colony in New Netherland.

In order to illustrate the conditions under which the Dutch expected to populate and develop their colony in New York, and the contracts made with the potential settlers, known as patroons, the following commentary and translation from the Dutch of the pamphlet printed by the Dutch West India Company in 1630 is provided below.

EXCERPT FROM NARRATIVES OF NEW NETHERLAND
WASSENAER'S HISTORISCH VERHAEL

(This was done on June 7, 1629. Although the issue of these privileges and exemptions made better provision than had hitherto existed for local government and for agricultural occupation of the province by small independent proprietors, it also, in its provision for large manorial grants, transferred to the New World some undesirable features of the (modified) feudalism of the Netherlands; and by opening very profitable opportunities to directors and other rich members of the Company, tempted them to assume interests opposed to those of the Company and paved the way for much dissension between patrons and directors general. Forthwith Samuel Godyn and Samuel Blommaert secured a patroonship on the west side of Delaware Bay, other associates another on the east side, Michiel Pauw one which he called Pavonia, extending along the west side of the North River from the Narrows to Hoboken and including Staten Island. All these proved temporary. Kiliaen van Rensselaer established a great and more permanent patroonship, Rensselaerswyck, by securing broad lands on the west side, later extended to both sides of the Hudson, above and below Fort Orange.)

By these means many persons have become inclined to repair thither and to plant their colonies there, so that it is hoped – since the land itself is fruitful, and adapted if well cultivated to bring forth rye, wheat and other grains, as has now been demonstrated on various voyages, and since also good traffic can be carried on there in all sorts of peltries, which are plentiful there and fine – that good profits may be expected thence for the Company and the colonists.

Privileges and Exemptions for Patroons, Masters and Private Individuals, who will Settle any Colonies and Cattle in New Netherland, resolved upon for the Service of the General West India Company in New Netherland, and for the Benefit of the Patroons, Masters and Individuals.

This document, so important in New Netherland history as the foundation of the system of patroonships, was printed in 1630 by the West India Company as a pamphlet. The document was also printed by Wassenaer, part xviii, pp. 94 recto-98 verso. Mr. van Laer prints the Dutch text and an excellent English translation in Van Rensslaer Bowier Manuscripts, pp.136-153. The present translation had been made by correcting, with the aid of the original Dutch, the version printed in N.Y. Col. Doc., II 553-557. Mr. van Laser's translation then arriving a few improvements were borrowed from it.

I. Such participants in the said Company as may be inclined to settle any colonies in New Netherland, shall be permitted to send in the ships of this Company going thither, three or four persons to inspect the situation of the country, provided that they, with the officers and ship's company, swear to the articles, so far as they relate to them, and pay for provisions and for passage, going and coming, six stivers per diem (and such as desire to eat in the cabin, twelve stivers); and undertake to be subordinate and give assistance like others, in cases offensive and defensive; and if any ships be taken from the enemy, they shall receive, *pro rata*, their proportions with the ship's company, each according to his quality; that is to say, the colonists eating out of the cabin shall be rated with the sailors, and those who eat in the cabin with those of the Company's people who eat at table and receive the lowest wages.

II. Nevertheless in this respect shall be preferred such persons as have first appeared and desired the same from the Company.

III. All such shall be acknowledged patroons of New Netherland who shall undertake, within the space of four years next after they have given notice to any of the chambers of the Company here, or to the commander or council there, to plant a colony there of fifty souls, upwards of fifteen years old; one-fourth part within one year, and within three years after the sending of the first, making together four years, the remainder, to the full number of fifty persons, to be shipped from hence, on pain, in case of manifest neglect, of being deprived of the privileges obtained; but it is to be observed that the Company reserve the island of the Manhattes to themselves.

IV. They shall, from the time they make known the situation of the places where they propose to settle colonies, have the preference over all others of the absolute property of such lands as they have there chosen; but in case the situation should not afterwards please them, or they should have been deceived in the selecting of the land, they may, after remonstrating concerning the same to the commander and council there, be at liberty to choose another place.

V. The patroons, by their agents, shall and may be permitted, at such places as they shall settle their colonies, to extend their limits four leagues along the shore, or on one side of a navigable river, or two leagues on each side of a river, and so far into the country as the situation of the occupiers shall permit; it being understood that the Company keep to themselves the lands lying and remaining between the limits of colonies, to dispose thereof, when and at such time as they shall think proper, in such manner, however, that no person shall be allowed to come within seven or eight leagues of them without their consent, unless the situation of the land thereabout be such that the commander and council, for good reasons, should order otherwise; always observing that the first occupiers are not to be prejudiced in the right they have obtained, except in case the service of the Company should require it, for the building of fortifications, or something of that sort; the command of each bay, river or island (apart from such exceptions), belonging to the first settled colony, under the supreme jurisdiction of their High Mightinesses the States General and the Company: but that the colonies subsequently settled on the same river or island may appoint one or more deputies to join with the first in considering what may be necessary for the prosperity of the colonies on the said river and island.

VI. They shall forever possess and enjoy all the lands lying within the aforesaid limits, together with the fruits, crops, minerals, rivers and fountains thereof; as also the high, middle and low jurisdictions, fisheries, fowling and grinding, to the exclusion of all others, to be holden from the Company as a perpetual inheritance, without its ever devolving again to the Company, and in case it should devolve, to be redeemed and repossessed with twenty guilders per colony, to be paid to this Company, at the chamber here or to their commander there, within a year and six weeks after the same occurs, each at the chamber where he originally sailed from; provided further, that no person or persons whatsoever shall be privileged to fish and hunt but the patroons and such as they shall permit. And in case any one should in time prosper so much as to found one or more towns, he shall have power and authority to establish officers and magistrates there, and to make use of the title of his colony, according to his pleasure and to the quality of the persons.

VII. There shall likewise be granted to all patroons who shall desire the same, *venia testandi*, or liberty to dispose of their aforesaid heritage by testament.

VIII. The patroons may make use of all lands, rivers and woods lying contiguous to their property, until this Company, or other patroons or private persons, shall take possession of them.

IX. Those who shall send persons over to settle colonies shall furnish them with proper instructions in order that they may be ruled and governed conformably to the rule of government made, or to be made, by the Board of the Nineteen, as well in the political as in the judicial government; which instructions they shall be obliged first to lay before the directors of the respective chambers.

X. The patroons and colonists shall be privileged to send all their people and effects thither in ships belonging to the Company, provided they take the oath, and pay the Company for bringing over the people, as mentioned in the first article; and for freight of the goods, five per cent ready money, to be reckoned on the prime cost of the goods here, in which are, however, not to be included such cattle and implements as are necessary for the cultivation and improvement of the lands, which the Company are to carry over for nothing, if there is room in their ships. But the patroons shall, at their own expense, provide and make places for them, together with everything necessary for the support of the cattle.

XI. But in case it should not suit the Company to send any ships, or there should be no room in those sailing thither, then in such case the said patroons, after having communicated their intentions, and after having obtained consent from the Company in writing, may send their own ships or vessels thither; provided that, in going or coming, they go not out of their ordinary course, giving security to the Company for the same and taking on board an assistant, to be victualled by the patroons, and paid his monthly wages by the Company, on pain, for doing the contrary, of forfeiting all the right and property they have obtained to the colony.

XII.　　And inasmuch as it is the intention of the Company to people the island of the Manhattes first, all fruits and wares that are produced on the North River and lands lying thereabout shall, for the present, be brought there before being sent elsewhere, excepting such as are, from their nature, unnecessary there, or such as cannot, without great loss to the owners thereof, be brought there; in which case the owners thereof shall be obliged to give timely notice in writing of the difficulty attending the same to the Company here, or the commander and council there, that provision may be made in respect to them as the necessity thereof shall be found to require.

XIII.　　All patroons of the colonies in New Netherland, and also colonies on the island of the Manhattes shall be at liberty to sail and traffic all along the coast, from Florida to Newfoundland, provided that they do again return with all such goods as they shall get in trade to the island of the Manhattes, and pay five per cent duty to the Company, in order that, if possible, after the necessary inventory of the goods shipped be taken, the same may be sent hither. And if it should so happen that they could not return, by reason of contrary currents or otherwise, in such case such goods shall not be brought to any other place but to these dominions, in order that, under the inspection of the directors, at the place where they may arrive, they may be unladen, an inventory made, and the aforesaid duty of five per cent paid to the Company here, on pain, if they do the contrary, of the forfeiture of their goods so trafficked for, or the true value thereof.

XIV.　　In case the ships of the patroons, in going to, or coming from, or sailing on the coast from Florida to Newfoundland, and no further, within the bounds of our grant, should overpower any prizes of the enemy, they shall be obliged to bring, or cause to be brought, such prize to the chamber of the place from whence they sailed out, in order that that chamber may obtain its profits from it; the Company shall keep the one-third part thereof, and the remaining two-thirds shall belong to them, in consideration of the cost and risk they have been at, all according to the orders of the Company.

XV.　　It shall be also free for the aforesaid patroons to traffic and trade all along the coast of New Netherland and places circumjacent, with such goods as they have acquired there, and receive in return for them all sorts of merchandise that may be had there, except beavers, otters, minks, and all sorts of peltry, which trade the Company reserve to themselves. But the same shall be permitted at such places where the Company have no factories, on condition that such traders shall be obliged to bring all the peltry they may obtain to the island of the Manhattes, if it is at all practicable, and there deliver to the Director, to be by him shipped hither with the ships and goods; or, if they should come here without going there, then to unload them with notice to the Company, and the making of a proper inventory, in order that they may pay to the Company one guilder for each merchantable beaver and otter skin; the retailing, risk and all other charges remaining on the account of the patroons or owners.

XVI.   All coarse wares that the colonists of the patroons there shall produce, such as pitch, tar, potash, wood, grain, fish, salt, limestone and such like things, shall be conveyed in the Company's ships, at the rate of eighteen guilders per last, four thousand weight to be accounted a last; and the Company's ship's crews shall be obliged to wheel and bring the salt on board, whereof ten lasts make a hundred. And, in case of the lack of ships, or of room in the ships, they may order it over, at their own cost, in ships of their own, and enjoy in these dominions such liberties and benefits as have been granted to the Company; but in either case they shall be obliged to pay, over and above the duty of five per cent, eighteen guilders for each hundred of salt that is carried over in the Company's ships.

XVII.   For all wares which are not mentioned in the foregoing article, and which are not carried by the last, there shall be paid one dollar for each hundred pounds weight; and for wines, brandies, verjuice and vinegar, there shall be paid eighteen guilders per cask.

XVIII.   The Company promises the colonists of the patroons that they shall be free from customs, tolls, excise, imposts or any other contributions for the space of ten years; and after the expiration of the said ten years, at the highest, such customs as the goods pay here at the present time.

XIX.   That they will not take from the service of the patroons any of their colonists, either man or woman, son or daughter, manservant or maid-servant; and, though any of these should desire the same, they will not receive them, much less permit them to leave their patroons, and enter into the service of another, unless on consent obtained from their patroons in writing, and this for and during so many years as they are bound to their patroons; after the expiration whereof, it shall be in the power of the patroons to send hither all such colonists as will not continue in their service, and not to set them at liberty until then. And any colonist who shall enter into the service of another patroon, or shall, contrary to his contract, betake himself to freedom, we promise to do everything in our power to deliver the same into the hands of his patroon or attorney, that he may be proceeded against according to the customs of this country, as occasion may require.

XX.   From all judgments given by the courts of the patroons for upwards of fifty guilders, there may be an appeal to the Company's commander and council in New Netherland.

XXI.   In regard to such private persons as on their own account, or others in the service of their masters here in less numbers than in case of patroons, shall be inclined to go thither and settle, they shall, with the approbation of the Director and Council there, be at liberty to take up and take possession of as much land as they shall be able properly to improve, and shall enjoy the same in full property either for themselves or masters.

XXII.   They shall have free liberty of hunting and fowling, as well by water as by land, generally, in public and private woods and rivers about their colonies, according to the orders of the Director and Council.

XXIII. Whosoever, whether colonists of patroons for their patroons, or free persons for themselves, or others for their masters, shall discover any shores, bays or other fit places for erecting fisheries, or the making of salt ponds, they may take possession thereof, and begin to work on them as their own absolute property, to the exclusion of all others. And it is permitted that the patroons of colonists may send ships along the coast of New Netherland, on the cod fishery, and with the fish they catch may trade direct to Italy or other neutral countries, paying in such cases to the Company a duty of six guilders per last; and if they should come with their lading hither, they shall be at liberty, though they shall not, under pretext of this consent, or leave from the Company, carry any other goods to Italy on pain of punishment, at discretion, the Company being furthermore at liberty to put a supercargo on board each ship, as in the eleventh article.

XXIV. In case any of the colonists shall, by his industry and diligence, discover any minerals, precious stones, crystals, marbles or such like, or any pearl fisheries, the same shall be and remain the property of the patroon or patroons of such colony, the discoverer being assigned such premium as the patroon shall beforehand have stipulated with his colonists by contract. And the patroons shall be exempt from the payment of duty to the Company for the term of eight years, and pay only for freight, to bring them over, two per cent, and after the expiration of the aforesaid eight years, for duty and freight, the one-eighth part of what the same may be worth here.

XXV. The Company shall take all the colonists, as well free as those that are in service, under their protection, and them defend against all foreign and domestic wars and violence, with the forces they have there, as much as lies in their power.

XXVI. Whosoever shall settle any colony out of the limits of the Manhattes island, shall be obliged to satisfy the Indians for the land they shall settle upon, and they may extend or enlarge the limits of their colonies if they settle a proportionate number of colonists thereon.

XXVII. The patroons and colonists shall in particular, and in the speediest manner, endeavor to find out ways and means whereby they may support a minister and schoolmaster, that the service of God and zeal for religion may not be neglected among them, and they shall, at the first, provide a comforter of the sick there.

XXVIII.   The colonies that shall happen to lie on the respective rivers or islands (that is to say, each river or island for itself), shall be at liberty to appoint a deputy, who shall give information to the commander and council of that region, and further the interests of his colony, of which deputies there shall be one changed in every two years; and all colonies shall be obliged, at least once in every twelve months, to make exact report of their condition and of the lands thereabout to the commander and council there.

XXIX. The colonists shall not be permitted to make any woollen, linen or cotton cloth, nor weave any other stuffs there, on pain of being banished, and as perjurers, to be punished, at discretion.

XXX. The Company shall use their endeavors to supply the colonists with as many blacks as they can, on conditions hereafter to be made, in such manner, however, that they shall not be bound or held to do it for a longer time than they shall think proper.

XXXI. The Company promise to finish the fort on the island of the Manhattes as soon as possible, and to put it in a posture of defence; and to cause these Privileges and Exemptions to be approved and confirmed by their High Mightinesses the Lords States General.

MELYN PAPERS

1640-1699

[Deed for Staten Island, July 1640]

We Willem Kieft, Director General and Councillors in behalf of the High Mighty Lords States General of the United Netherlands, His Highness of Orange and the Hon. Managers of the General Privileged West India Company residing in New Netherland: Make known that on this underwritten date we have given and granted as we are giving and granting by these presents (by virtue of a certain Act, dated July 1640, conceded by said Lords Managers), to Cornelius Melyn the entire Staten Island, situated on the Bay and North River of New Netherland, excepting so much land as appertains to a farm which by us Director and Councillors before mentioned had been granted and given— before the date of the before mentioned Act—to David Peterse De Vries of Hoorn, which land has also been occupied by him, David Peterse; all under express condition that he, Cornelius Melyn, or those by virtue of the present entering upon his rights, shall acknowledge the said Hon. Heeren Managers as their Lords, under the Sovereignty of the High Mighty Lords the States General; and hereto obey their Director and Councillors as good inhabitants are bound to do; providing he, Melyn, or those entering upon his right, submit in whole and in part to all such charges and requisitions as—in accordance with the exemptions of New Netherland—have been already levied or shall yet be levied by the Managers; consequently constituting in quality and by virtue as expressed before, said Cornelis Melyn, in our stead, real and actual possessor of the aforesaid parcel of land; granting him by these presents perfect power, authority and special order to take possession of cultivate, inhabit, use, the said Staten Island— except the said farm—as he may do with other his patrimonial lands and effects, without we, the grantors, in the aforesaid quality are reserving or retaining any the least share, claim or authority in the same, desisting of the same in behalf of as above.

The above is a true copy of the Part of a Patent as it is found in the Dutch book of Record in the Secry's office of the Province of New York.

Pr. M: Clarkson, Secry.

[Translated from the Dutch]

…In manner and on conditions acquired by Cornelis Melyn from the West India Company on Staten Island or elsewhere to be selected as well in regard to jurisdiction as to ownership of the lands, woods, and all other rights, appertaining to the said colony. Which one half said Melyn by these presents cedes to the Lord of Nederhorst; the other half as well as in regard to jurisdiction, lands, woods and rights appertaining to the same remaining to the said Cornelis Melyn; shall be divided in two equal parts, an exact map of which shall be made and sent over by the said Melyn, to be then drawn for by the said Lord of Nederhorst, and by the said Melyn.

…from the West India Company or their High Mightinesses, that said Lord of Nederhorst shall also exert himself as much as possible that said Melyn, in such case, shall also receive similar condition and privileges for his portion, without however being obliged to positively acquire the same. Said Melyn promising to act as superintendent and to take care that the people to be sent there by the Lord of Nederhorst (who will do so as soon as his Honor shall find an opportunity) shall be held to their duty, and to report on the same from time to time.

The said people to be sent there by the said Lord of Nederhorst are not to act in weighty matters unless with the advice of the said Cornelis Melyn.

Agrees with the minute of the deceased Notary Jan de Graeff, this 16th January Anno 1648.

By me

F. Steur, Notary Public

1648.

Endorsed:

Agremt with the Lord Nederhorst and Cornelis Melyen

[Translated from the Dutch]

MELYN PAPERS April 29, 1648

The States General of the United Netherlands, To the first Marshall or Messenger having power to serve when requested, Greeting: Make Known, that we, having received the humble supplication presented to us by and in behalf of Jochem Pietersz Cuyter and Cornelis Melyn, containing that they, petitioners, with permission and leave of the Assembly of the XIX of the General West India Company, with wife and children and with private means, besides a large herd of cattle, in the year one thousand six hundred and thirty nine, transported themselves from these countries to New Netherland, so that they, petitioners, after enormous expenses, difficulties and inexpressible labor, got into condition, in the year sixteen hundred forty three, their lands, houses and other undertakings which in the aforesaid year on account of the war (waged by Director Kieft unjustly and contrary to all international law, with the savages or natives of New Netherland) they have been obliged to abandon and as a consequence lost all their property. On account hereof the petitioners, besides the other six Selected Men took counsel and in the name of the joint Commonality in New Netherland in the year sixteen hundred forty four by the Blue Cock, sent two letters: to the said Assembly of the XIX, as also to the Directors in Amsterdam, containing their grievances regarding this matter, the disasters grown out of these actual murders, massacres and many other cruelties (which is appalling to every christian conscience having information hereof) which Director Kieft at the time, has caused to be perpetrated by his forces among the simple and innocent savages, as may be learned more at large from the original letter to the XIX; so that the Eight selected men did not know that they had transgressed in this matter, but had hoped that the same would have been taken in good part by the Lords Directors. But petitioners find on the contrary that their writings were taken in the worst part by the Lords, who consequently returned said letter with the New Director Pieter Stuyvesant to New Netherland to Director Kieft, from which subsequently followed that said Kieft began to proceed very vigorously against the Eight Select Men (especially against both petitioners) and has caused them to be prosecuted by the Fiscal. In such a manner that Director Stuyvesant (in order to please said Kieft in the matter) has banished petitioners for a number of years out of the country because they were not willing to repeal the truth, and adhered to their previous writings. Petitioners thereupon turned to us, requesting, imploring and praying for God's Sake, that we should be pleased to maintain them in their just cause, that they might again be able to join their poor, desolute wives and children, and to be reinstated in their former condition on their devastated lands. And in case petitioners have transgressed through any improper documents they submit to such punishment as we shall find to be proper. But on the contrary it will be shown that petitioners in their writings did not consider anything but that the common prosperity and the desire for peace in New Netherland might again be restored, and that the inhuman cruelties, tryanny and evil government (which in that country from time to time have been inflicted by the officers of the West India Company especially by Director Kieft upon the inhabitants of New Netherland) might be stopped. As a consequence of these barbaric proceedings the entire government of that country has been erupted the householders chased away, their lands laid waste, the farms and plantations to the number of fifty or sixty burnt and reduced to cinders. And then when the poor inhabitants complained about these and other harsh proceedings to the High Sovereign Government, they were, by the Director, chased out of the country, in such a manner that in course of time the country was denuded of the Dutch inhabitants, and it is to be feared that the English (who arrived some years after the Dutch, and within fifteen years increased to about fifty or sixty thousand souls in New England) and already now have had a taste of the fruitfulness and also of the convenient navigable rivers of our New Netherland, will in course of time attempt to become masters of the same. On account whereof petitioners again cordially pray that this aforesaid, and their humble petition may be considered by us, and they may be granted their reasonable and just request, which has even been promised by the Assembly of the XIX in their Freedoms of 1630 to all Patroons and Free Residents. Considering which we order and command you, commissioning you by these presents, that at the request of the said petitioners you summon in our behalf the aforesaid Director Stuyvesant and the members of the New Netherland government before mentioned, besides all others; if necessary to come and appear, or send attorneys, on an appropriate day, before us here at the Hague, to reply to such questioning as petitioners shall be inclined to put on the proper day, in order, parties heard, petitioners may be granted by us such remedies of Justice, that immediately and without delay they repair the same, putting it in its first and proper state. Leaving, in behalf of defendants, copy of the present and of your service, relating to us on the said day what you shall have done in this matter. Given at The Hague, on the twenty eighth of April, sixteen hundred and forty eight.

Hieron: Eyben

By order of the above named Lords States General

Corn. Musch1648.

Endorsed as follows: The States General of the United Netherlands, To all who shall see or hear read this present…

To the Hon. Very Respectable Lord Anthony Colve, Governor General and the Lords High Councillors of New Netherland.

Makes known with respectful humility Jacob Melyen, that his deceased father has been proprietor of the Staten Island and has inhabitated and possessed the same for many years, until he was surprised by a general war with the savages, many of his children and farmers murdered, their houses and goods burned and destroyed, on account of which great damage and ruin, and also owing to the temporary danger of the savages, he was forced to suffer the said island during some time to remain uninhabitated. Some little time afterward he went to Amsterdam and there entered with the Hon. Heeren of the West India Company into a contract, concerning the Patroonship and jurisdiction of the said Island, provided he retained to himself, his heirs and successors all his lands, according to the letter of the said contract, of which right your Honors' petitioner's deceased father and his heirs have been deprived, partly owing to lack of means, sickness and death of your Honors' petitioner's deceased father, partly owing to the scattered residences, smallness of means and immaturity of years and understanding of his heirs, and also partly owing to various changes of government. However your Honors' petitioner having made known his right to the aforesaid, to the first English Governor Colonel Nicholls, the latter, before his departure, consented—and had registered by his secretary in the minute book—that a considerable tract of land should be surveyed for the heirs of said Melyen. In expectation of Your Hon. Very Resp's favorable answer, remain Your Hon. Very Resp's subject and servant,

Jacob Melyen

New Orange 1674, April 12/2

But on the contrary the Director began by manifesting his old hatred and partisanship asserting first that at the Staten Island something should have been discharged which looked like contraband; second that I should have sold goods at the Red Island; third that one Casper Verlet, who said to be part owner of the ship should have been deprived of his claimed share in the ship and the merchandise; fourth, that I had too much encouraged the skipper in his evil intent and further several allegations not worth while enumerating here but which can be seen from the documents regarding the same. Owing to these before enumerated causes he begins, through the fiscal, to proceed very rigorously against ship and goods, attaches everything, arrests my person guarding me well with soldiers; as a consequence my newly arrived country people began to grumble, the desire for work, because I could not be present there, they began to loose to my great damage and expense; the crew were arrested, and thus were forced to make such declarations as pleased the authorities; (which arrest) caused me great expense to the crew, and for the ships repairs, up to the time when it pleased him to confiscate ship and goods and to appropriate the same to his own use. Not stopping at this, but for the purpose of absolutely ruining me, also my real estate being at the Menatans, consisting of some houses and lots, was attached and sold to my great damage under appearance of "rugrant" of the shipper and owners; so that owing to these before related acts I have clearly perceived that for me there was no security at the Menatans owing to these many arrests, citations, summonses and molestations and I have resolved to quit the Menatans and, thus Wronged and plundered, to join with wife and children my people in my colony on Staten Island. And I left the Director at the Menatans with all his proceedings to continue as he pleased without defending my just cause, as it would not have done me any good anyway, and further intending to repair my above mentioned losses, and attend to the support of my wife and children, which has again been assiduously undertaken by myself and my people, and commenced to cultivate the land which had been laying so long fallow to clear, plow, sow, mow, thresh, make a harbor to build houses, racks, barns for the purpose of lodging the people, and the cattle we were using, as an ornament of New Netherland and an honor and credit to the Hon. Company and further as an incentive and spur to all other country people as well villagers as detached farmers, and even to those arriving from the Menatans itself, who were surprised at the large crop of grain which had this year been produced through our diligence; and there had been commenced sixteen handsome farms as well by myself as by my children as also by the people taken along by me for the Lord Van der Capelle and sent over by His Honor; which farms were covered with twenty seven buildings; houses, racks and barns, each well provided with cattle as well beautiful plow oxen, milch cows, as calves for increase, so that every thing began to be abundant on Staten Island, and through God's blessing I again began to recover my losses. But Director Stuyvesant again became active, as if it appeared that my prosperity began to trouble him. For when, in the year 1655, in August, he had received some soldiers from Fatherland by the ship the Waech (Balance) Captain Frederick De Cooninck, to sail with them on an expedition to the South River, he dispatched said Cooninck with the Fiscal Cornelis Van Tienhoven and some soldiers to the Staten Island for the purpose of fetching me; but being ignorant of the same, about two or three hours before, I had gone in my boat to the Menatans in order to attend to some business concerning my colony. The Director Stuyvesant met me with some soldiers, and he immediately exclaimed Take hold of Melyn, conduct him to the guard house and secure him well. There I was incarcerated till the return from Staten Island of the boat with the said Capt. Coninck and Fiscal Tienhoven. He thereupon convened his council and the said Captain, has me brought before him, asks me "where are the letters you have received from the Swedes?" which sounded to me as strange as if I had been asked for letters from the great Turck, and gave for answer not to know of any letters from the Swedes, nor that I was expecting any. To this said Stuyvesant replied "you will soon be taught to speak differently," and ordered the fiscal to have me conducted to prison and to secure me well. I was there conducted and thrown in a dark hole, and I was not to see nor to converse with any one. This lasted twenty five days without a further hearing until the

16th of September when the Savages set fire to all buildings around the Menatans, and killed and murdered a large number of our people which at the Menatans and the whole country [here three quarters of a line obliterated] interceding and running to and fro of my wife and children as well as others, permitted me under certain conditions to leave the hole. I then immediately departed for the Staten Island to see whether I could save my people, houses and goods from the savages; but in vain; for a few days later the savages arrived there in great numbers and commenced to attack our people, to set fire to the houses, stacks, barns mostly full of grain, so that the people were obliged to seek safety in my house which they (the savages) also succeeded in setting afire. And when the cinders began to fall down on us we were forced to leave it and obliged to break through the savages to enable us to retire to another small house standing close to the shore. Here we held out for some time longer, hoping meanwhile to receive some assistance from the Menatans. But all in vain. At last the savages called out to us that if we desired quarter they would grant the same to us, whereupon we resolved as we saw no other refuge [here nearly an entire line obliterated] because from among our number already 15 or 16 persons, among whom my son 22 years old, my son in law and two nephews had been shot dead, besides some wounded; and thus fifty one in number went into captivity among the savages, where we remained during thirty one days until I had raised a ransom of about 1,400 guilders for myself, wife, son and son in law, which was to be paid if we did not want to be burnt alive in a fire which for this purpose had been already prepared and was burning. Subsequently arriving at the Menatans, as miserable as we well could be, we hoped to enjoy some quiet after our sad imprisonment. But the day following there arrived at my lodgings Secretary Van Reuven with a sergeant in command of soldiers armed with firearms and sword, saying "Melyn the Director sends us hither and lets you know that you must try to find more ransom, for the savages are not yet satisfied," and forced me immediately to go in search of 60 or 70 guilders additional payment, if I did not want to be put in the former prison. It appeared to me somewhat suspicious that the savages were so bold, and at the Menatans, through the servants of the Company, dared to vex me yet further; (it occurred to me) that the same might have been trumped up in order to at once ruin me. I submit to your Honour's judgment after all that had befallen me and I being in such a sorrowful and miserable condition, my children and people murdered by the savages, the houses, racks, barns to the number of 25, burnt, the people, cattle and farms destroyed, my goods stolen, and in place thereof debts incurred for my ransom, and retaining the bitter hatred of the Director, I have resolved to quit the Menatans, in order not to perish absolutely with wife and children and for the time being to put myself under the protection of the English; and consequently departed with my family for New Haven, until I shall have found opportunity and means to pay for the trip hither, Meanwhile making your Honors acquainted with my distress as related heretofore, with humble request to sustain me in my just cause against the aforesaid Petrus Stuyvesant regarding the evil acts and great damage unjustly inflicted on me, and to assist me in regaining my own, in order with the same means and your Honors' assistance to refound my ruined colony for the third time, and to restore the same to its former condition.

Endorsed in English

The Remonstrance & Petition of Cornelius Melyen to ye West India Company in Amsterdam Ano 1659.

[Translated from the Dutch]

Upon this thirteenth Day of June 1659—Mr. Cornelius Melyen (who untill this time hath been Patron, & hath had Jus Patronatus of ye Colony of Staten Island scituated in ye mouth of ye North River in New Netherland) for himself, his heirs & Successors acknowledgeth to have bargained & agreed with the Lords ye Directors of ye privileged West India Company at their chamber here in Amsterdam freely & most amicably by these presents (Vizt) That he consenteth to desist deliver over, transfer & Transport all ye Pow'r, Authority, Highness, Jurisdiction, preheminencies, prerogatives, Profitts, Emoluments, Liberties, & exemptions belonging to him in quality of Patroon & belonged to him until now in upon ye lands & Colony of ye sd. Staten Island with ye following dependencies & appendencies thereof none excepted by him procured, according to ye Resolutions, Acts, articles, freedoms & exemptions & other instruments as likewise by ye letters of conveyance made over especially unto him by Willm. Kieft Governor of New Netherland, are made to cease Expressly upon ye following conditions. Vizt. That ye abovementioned company & chamber shall in New Netherland make restitution of all such Sum or Sums of money, which were produced from certain his houseings & Lotts scituated & being upon ye Manhatans in New Amsterdam neer ye ffort (which were sold by Governor Stuyvesandt by Execution in behalf of Daniel Michiels master of ye Ship ye New Netherlands Fortune) shall be restored to him again in New Netherland by sd. Company & chamber for ye sd. Moneys or so much thereof as yet may be found to re-main with ye sd. company.

And moreover that ye Just Sume of fifteen hundred gilders shall be forthwith paid him, & likewise that he shall enjoy ye Freedome & exemption of ye Custome both here & in New Netherland of ye value of about one thousand gilders Stock of Merchandise, being necessary utensels for cultivating land & permitted, wch he should think fitt to carry with him into New Netherland.

As likewise that himself, his family & his people with him shall be transported over thither with their own ships or ships hired at ye charge of the company according to ye Prsent use. Also that he for ye future as a free Coloneer & inhabitant for himself & his Successors shall hold & possess as free & legal estate, ye lands houses & lots, which he hath there in ye sd. Colony, & hath hitherto made use of & which he yet shall be able to improve (& by others not possessed) they shall enjoy ye Succession thereof or by will, writings, donation or gift, agreemt. or otherwise may dispose thereof, as according to ye Articles of Privilege & Exemptions granted to Patroons & Coloneers. That likewise his eldest son being capable (& ye sd. Colony having need of a Schout, & one to be appointed thereupon) shall be preferred before any other by ye aforesaid. Company & Chamber. And Finally that by ye present Governor Steuyvesandt shall be shewed & maintained a perfect Amnestia of all Strifes, hatred & differences, which formerly may have risen between them; as well in respect of ye Company as their own private concerns; ye same hereby to remain forgiven & forgotten & for ye future they to be good friends & to respect & acknowledge each other in his quality & to demonstrate all resaonable Assistance. To ye performance of all ye premises He Cornelius Melyen bindeth himself & his estate movable and unmovable, present & future none excepted to ye Submission of ye Court of Holland & all laws & Judges as well in New Netherland as herein this Countrey

—In Witness whereof this is underwritten by ye undernamed Lords & Committe of ye West India Company thereunto authoriz'd by ye Lords their fellow brethren on ye behalf of ye aforementiond company & chamber by special Comission dated ye tenth of April last past, & by ye aforesaid. Cornelius Melyen at Amsterdam ye day & year aforesaid. was underwritten & signed. Edward Man as Direct. Abraham Wilmerdonck as Directr H: Bontemantel as Directr Cornelius Melyen late Patroon of Staten Island in ye presence of me as Notary, H: Schaef No. P.

It agreeth with ye original signed agreement being in my Custody

In Witness H: Schaef Noy Public

Examined this with ye Dutch agreemt. & find it to be a true translate to ye best of my understanding as Witness my hand Jacob Leisler

Also by me vera copia George Turfry

Endorsed: A Copy of ye Translate of ye Agreement of Melyen with ye West India Company Examd Pr Mr. Leisler

After this when I took out my Patent from Gover Willm Kieft pursuant to ye grant of ye aforesaid. Lords, I desired that ye Indians might once again be ask'd if they had yet any pretence to any Right upon Staten Island, or could pretend to make any, which was done by ye Secretary Cornelius Van Tienhooven, who could speak in ye Indian Dialect very well, whereupon they answered that they were well satisfied & well agreed with me, & they (ye sd. Indians), after that made no pretence till ye year 1649—at which time I was in ye mind to go with my wife, children & people to live upon sd. Island again. The Indians began then of to speak of buying ye Island again; I then demonstrated to them ye aforesd. Sale & agreement, which they acknowledged they knew very well, & that they did not speak of that, but they supposed that ye Island by reason of ye war, by killing, burning & driving us off, was become theirs again, and therefore thought that there must be a new bargain made, which I wholly refused them & would neither give, nor promise them any thing saying unto them, that which is sold, must remain sold & that ye Dutch will not pay twice for any thing, which they have once bought, but if they will once more have a small gift gratis to maintain good friendship as had been done before I would give it them, whereunto (after mature deliberation among themselves) they resolved; whereupon I gave them amongst them all two Coats of Duffles containing Six Ells four fathom of wampum, 5, or 6, little kittles, some awls & needles wherewith they were all well satisfied & cryed unanimously (Keene, Keene, Keene orit nietap) i.e. Thank you, Thank you, Thank you Good friend, and they were very well satisfied until Lubbert Vant Dincklagen began to speak with ye Indians of buying Staten Island again of them, who did it on purpose to find occasion to write to ye Lord Capell to try whether under that Covert he might bring about ye getting of some goods of ye sd. Lord into his hands to dispose thereof for himself & to give little thereof to ye Indians for there is indeed nothing at all due to them for by such means ye Indians would be induced often to make outrages, that they might ev'ry now & then be paid again & not only to play such Prancks upon Staten Island, but throout all New Netherland, where the Lords of ye

West India Company's Governmt. extendeth. I trust therefore that ye honour' d Lords will not approve (or allow) of such bargains, in order to ye preventing more mischiefs.

This is as much as I can write of Testifie of this matter

This done at Amsterdam ye 30th of Janry 1659—by me—the Indians in New-Netherland, & what they receiv'd

Two extracts of the resolution of the Hon. Heeren Managers dated 18th and 25th February, 1641, by which the afore said consent is renewed.

A groundbrief being the conveyance of Staten Island to Cornelis Melyn granted in consequence of the consent mentioned above, signed by the Heer General Willem Keift, dated June 19, 1642.

Agrees with the aforesaid Register,

C. V. Ruyven, Secretary.

Endorsed In the margin in English:

Govr Steuyvesant in Council, his Evil construction of ye agreemt of ye West India Company & Melyen.

[Translated from the Dutch]

Extract from a Letter of the Hon. Heeren, Managers to the Messrs. Director and Councillors of New Netherland, dated Jan. 27, 1662.

Concerning the contention of Cornelis Melyn, that he surely did sell and deliver to the Company the title and the right of patroonship of the Staten Island, but not the lands themselves, we can not observe that the same can be deduced from the contract entered into with him concerning the same, but assured by the opposite, as there is entered, as your Honors have justly remarked and argued against him, that from now on, as free colonist and inhabitant, he shall have and hold for himself and his descendants as a free, allodial possesion the lands, houses and lots he has in said colony

Upon the Petition & Request of Mr Jacob Melyen That his Fathers interest may be taken into consideration, upon ye settlement of Staten Island, The Governor ordered it to be Entered upon Record that Care should then be had of him, so farr, as that he shall be allotted a Convenient proportion of Land upon ye said Island, In lieu of what was reserved by his Father, & promised him by ye West India Company.

The petitioners are granted for each child of the deceased Cornelis Melyn, on the said land, a farm of thirty morgen [about 60 acres] amounting for the five children together to one hundred and fifty morgens, provided none of said lands, prior to this date have been granted [to others] and that thay shall be cultivated by the petitioners as per the orders of the government; In regard to the petitioners further request concerning said parcels of land, they are permitted to have the same measured by the sworn surveyor and further disposition shall be made after receipt of his report.

Agrees with the said Register, N. Bayard, Secretary.

Endorsed in English: A Grant of ye Dutch Govor Anthy Culve. In answer to ye Petition of Jacob Melyen whereby he grants 5 Farms with Medows sutable & comonages for ye same.

[Translated from the Dutch]

To his Excey Richard Earl of Bellomont, Capt. General & Governor in Chief of his Majties Provinces of the Massachusetts Bay, New York, &c and of the Territories thereon depending and Vice Admiral of the same.

The humble Petition of Jacob Melyen, most humbly sheweth

That yor Petitioners Father Cornelius Melyen by vertue of a Grant from the West India Company of Holland bearing date the Third of July 1640; was Governor & Proprietr of Staten Island in the Province of New York & was confirmed in the Governmt and Propriety thereof by Governor Kieft by a Patent bearing date the 19th of June 1642 and was in the quiet Possession & Enjoyment of the Governmt and Soyle of the sd Island as his rightfull inheritance, until he with his people [were] driven from thence by the Indians in the year 1643; and he was after that resettled thereon with diverse families, his servants, until another quarril was made at New-Amsterdam (now New York) with the Indians, Anno 1655 & were then cutt off upon Staten Island, having about twenty psons slain, who were of sd Melyen's Children, Nephews, Servants & Tenants. The Town consisting of about forty houses, which were burnt, & the Goods made plunder off, & yo petitioners sd father & mother & two sons with all those that survived were taken into a barbarous Captivity by the heathen; Your Excellcy's Petitir was one of the Sons who was much wounded, but recovered not wthout great difficulty. That his sd Father Cornelius Melyen upon some considerations did afterwards, vzt June 13, 1659, Resign his Right of Governmt back to the sd. West India Company of Holland upon sundry conditions, which were not all by then observed; But he never alienated or sold his Right to the Lands of the sd. Island or any part of his Estate there; but expressly reserved the same to himself And His heirs &c for ever as may appear by the sd agreement between the sd. West India Company & his sd Father, bearing date the 13th Day of June 1659, and that upon the Delivery of the Governt of New York to the English, One of the Articles of Agreement between the English & Dutch Commissioners expressly confirms unto all the Dutch Inhabitants, that continued there their freedome as Denizens and the Enjoyment of their Estates as before; Yet he the sd Jacob Melyen hath been ever since by fraud & Injustice denyed and hindred from the Enjoyment of his sd. Father's Inheritance he being the Rightfull heir, & this notwithstanding he hath made applica to ev'ry Governor that hath been sent thither by the Kings of England, by which means he hath suffered much Damage; All which will plainly appear to be true by the Records of New York, Copies of which have hitherto been denyed the Supplicant.

Your Petitior therefore being well assured of yor Excellcys great regard to Impartial Justice most humbly Prays that Your Excellcy will take his case into Yor serious Considera and permit him to take out of the Records copies of such Instruments & Papers as are necessary to prove ye Truth of what he hath before sett forth in order to Yor Lordship's more full Satisfac That Your Petitir hath a Right to the Soyle of the sd Island & that he may be better enabled to possess himself of the same.

And Your Petitir as in Duty bound will ever pray etc.

Endorsed: Jacob Melyen's Petition to his Excellcy Richard Earl of Bellomont etc.

Boston. Novembr 30th. 1698 [or 99]

THE VOICE OF GOD WILL PAVE THE WAY

OF CRIMES, AND FIRST OF SUCH AS DESERVE CAPITAL PUNISHMENT OR CUTTING OFF FROM A MAN'S PEOPLE WHETHER BY DEATH OR BANISHMENT.

1. Blasphemy, which is a cursing of God or wicked denying of God by Atheism or the like, to be punished with death. Lev. 24:15.

2. Idolatry to be punished with death. Deut. 13:1-11. 17:3 & 4.

3. Witchcraft, which is fellowship by covenant with a familiar spirit, to be punished with death. Ex. 22:18. Lev. 20:27.

4. Consulters with witches are not to be tolerated but either to be cut off by death or Banishment. Lev. 20:6.

5. Heresy, which is the maintenance of some wicked error overthrowing the foundation of Christian Religion with obstinacy if it be joined with endeavor to seduce others thereunto, to be punished with death. Because such a Heretic, no less than an Idolater, seeketh to thrust the souls of men from The Lord their God. Deut. 17:10.

6. To worship God in a molten or graven Image to be punished with death.

7. Whosoever shall revile the Religion and worship of God and the Government of the Church as it is now established to be cut off by Banishment.

8. Willful perjury, whether before the judgment seat or in private conference, to be punished with death. Rash perjury, whether it be in public or private, to be punished with Banishment. It is just that such a man's name should be cut off from his people who profanes so grossly the name of God before his people.

9. Profaning the Lords day with careless or scornful neglect or contempt thereof to be punished with death. Nu. 15: 30 & 36.

10. To plot or practice the betraying of the Country or any principal fort therein to the hand of any foreign State, Spanish, French, Dutch or the like, contrary to the Allegiance we profess & owe to our dread Sovereign Lord King Charles, his heirs and Successors whilst he is pleased to protect us as his Loyal Subjects, shall be punished with death.

11. Irreverent and dishonorable demeanor to Magistrates to be punished with banishment for a time, till they acknowledge their fault and profess Reformation.

12. Rebellion or Sedition or Insurrection by taking up of arms against the present Government established in the Country to be punished with death. Num. 16: 1, 2, 3, 31, 32, 33. Rebellious Children, whether they continue in Riot or Drunkenness, after due correction from their parents, or whether they curse or smite their parents are to be put to death. Deut. 21: 18. Lev. 20: 9. Ex. 21: 15 & 17.

13. Murder, which is a willful manslaughter, not in a man's necessary and just defence, nor casually committed, but out of Hatred or Cruelty to be punished by death. .

14. Adultery which is the defiling of the Marriage bed to be punished with, death. .

15. Defiling a woman espoused is a kind of Adultery, and punished by death of both parties. But if the woman be forced then by the death of the man only.

16. Incest, which is the defiling of any that are near of kin within the degrees prohibited in Leviticus, to be punished with death: unnatural filthiness to be punished with death, whether sodomy, which is carnal fellowship of man with man, or of woman with woman: or buggery which is carnal fellowship of man or woman with beasts or fowls.

17. Whoredom of a maid in her father's house kept secret till after her marriage with another, to be punished with death.

18. Man-stealing to be punished with death.

19. False witness against life to be punished with death.

OF CRIMES LESS HEINOUS SUCH AS ARE TO BE PUNISHED WITH SOME CORPORAL PUNISHMENT OR FINE.

1. Rash & profane swearing and cursing, to be punished

    a. With loss of honor or office if he be a magistrate or officer. It is fitting that their names should be dishonored who dishonor God's name.

    b. With loss of freedom.

    c. With disability to give Testimony.

    d. By Corporal punishment, either stripes or by branding them with a hot iron or boring them through the tongue as he hath bored and pierced God's name.

2. Drunkenness as transforming Gods Image into a Beast is to be punished with the punishment of a beast. A whip for the horse and a rod for the fool's back. Prov. 26:3

3. Forcing of a maid or a Rape is not to be punished with death by Gods Laws. But

    a. With a fine or penalty to the father of the maid. Deut. 22:28, 29.

    b. With the marriage of the maid defiled if she and her father consent.

    c. With Corporal punishment of stripes, for this wrong is a slander and it is worse to make a whore then to say one is a whore. Deut. 22:17, 18.

4. Fornication to be punished

    a. By marriage of the maid or giving her a sufficient dowry

    b. With stripes, though fewer than in the case of forcing of a maid.

Maiming or wounding of a freeman whether free burgess or free Inhabitant to be punished with a fine.

An Abstract of the Laws of Judgment as given to Moses for the Commonwealth of Israel, as they be of Moral value that is of perpetual and universal Equity among all Nations, especially such where the Church and Commonwealth are conjoined in Holy Covenant and fellowship with God in Jesus Christ, being jointly and unanimously Consented to as fundamental by the Inhabitants of this Colony of Southampton.

OR TRESPASSES.

1. If a man's swine or any other beast or a fire kindled by him break out into another man's field of corn, he shall make full restitution both of the damage done by them, and of the loss of time others have spent in carrying such swine or beasts to the owners or into the fold, (Exod. 12:5, 6) But if a man put his swine or beast into another man's field restitution is to be made of the best of his own though it were much better than that which was destroyed or hurt. (Levi. 34:18 Exod. 31:34)

2. If a man kills another man's beast, or dig or open a pit and leave it uncovered and a beast fall into it, he that kills the beast or the owner of the pit shall make restitution. (Exod. 21 :35 & 36)

3. If a man's beast kills the beast of another the owner of the beast shall make restitution. (Exod. 21:28 & 29)

1. If a man's ox or other beast gore or bite and kill a man or woman, whether child or of riper age, the beast shall be killed and no benefit of the dead beast reserved to the owner, But if the ox or other beast were wont to push or bite in former times and the owner had been told of it and had not kept him in, then the ox or beast shall be forfeited and killed and the owner also put to death, or else fined to pay what the Judges and persons indemnified shall lay upon him.

4. If a man deliver goods to his neighbor to keep and they be said to be lost or stolen from him, the keeper of the goods shall be put to his oath concerning his own innocence, which if he take said oath and no evidence appears to the contrary he shall be quit: But if he be found false unto his neighbor or unfaithful he shall pay double unto him.

   But if a man take hire for the goods committed unto him and they be stolen the keeper shall make restitution, but if the beast so kept for hire die or be hurt or be driven away unseen, an oath shall be taken of the keeper that it was without his default and it shall be accepted. Ex. 22:11, 13.

   But if the beast is torn in pieces and a piece be brought for witness it excuses the keeper. Exod. 22:13.

Answer to the Representation of New Netherland, By Cornelis Van Tienhoven, 1650

Presented to the High and Mighty Lords States General. Prepared by Cornelis van Tienhoven, Secretary of the Director an Council of New Netherland

In order to present the aforesaid answer succinctly, he, Van Tienhoven, will allege not only that it ill becomes the aforesaid Van der Donk and other private persons to assail and abuse the administration of the Managers in this country, and that of their Governors there,[2] in such harsh and general terms, but that they would much better discharge their duty if they were first to bring to the notice of their lords and patrons what they had to complain of. By passing by this point, and leaving the consideration thereof to the discretion of your High Mightinesses, they observe preliminarily and generally, that these persons say much and prove nothing, so that it could as easily and with more truth be denied, than by them it is odiously affirmed.

I will only touch upon those points as to which either the Managers or the Directors are arraigned. In regard to point No. 1, I deny, and it never will appear…

The policy of the Company to act on the defensive, since they had not the power to resist their pretended friends, and could only protect their rights by protest, was better and more prudent than to come to hostilities.

Trade has long been free to every one, and as profitable as ever. Nobody's goods were confiscated, except those who had violated their contract, or the order by which they were bound; and if anybody thinks that injustice has been done him by confiscation, he can speak for himself. At all events it does not concern these people.

Most of the remonstrants, being merchants or factors, are themselves the cause of this, since they are the persons who, for those articles which cost here one hundred guilders, charge there, over and above the first cost, including insurance, duties, laborer's wages, freight, etc., one and two hundred per cent. or more profit. Here can be seen at once how these people lay to the charge of the Managers and their officers the very fault which they themselves commit. They can never show this profit, cannot be prevented by the Director, the more so as the trade was thrown open to both those of small and those of large means.

It is a pure calumny, that the Company had ordered half a fault to be reckoned for a whole one.

And, as it does not concern the inhabitants what instructions or orders the patroon gives to his chief agent, the charge is made for the purpose of making trouble. For these people would like to live without being subject to any one's censure or discipline, which they stand doubly in need of.

That the inhabitants have had need of the Directors appears by the books of accounts, in which it can be seen that the Company has assisted the actual cost in the Fatherland, which is not yet paid. And they would gladly, by means of complaints, drive the Company from the land, and pay nothing.

It is ridiculous to suppose Director Kieft should have said that he was sovereign, like the Prince in the Fatherland.

The Directors have never had any management of, or meddled with, church property. And it is not known, nor can it be proven, that any one of the inhabitants of New Netherland has contributed or given, either voluntarily or upon solicitation, anything for the erection of an orphan asylum or an almshouse. It is true that the church standing in

---

[2] Van Tienhoven prepared this answer in Holland.

the fort was built in the time of William Kieft, and 1,800 guilders were subscribed for the purpose, for which most of the subscribers have been charged in their accounts, which have not yet been paid, but there is in New Netherland no instance of the kind, and the charge is spoken or written in anger. When the church which is in the fort was to be built, the churchwardens were content it should be put there. These persons complain because they considered the Company's fort not worthy of a church. Before the church was built, the grist-mill could not grind with a southeast wind, because the wind was shut off by the walls of the fort.

As the Director has never had the management of it, the deacons are responsible for it, and not the director. It is true Director Kieft being distressed for money, had a box hung in his house, of which the deacons had one key, and in which all the small fines and penalties which were incurred on court days were dropped. With the consent of the deacons he opened it, and took on interest the money, which amounted to a pretty sum.

It is admitted, that the beer excise was imposed by William Kieft, and the wine excise by Peter Stuyvesant, and that they continued to be collected up to the time of my leaving there; but it is to be observed here, that the memorialists have no reason to complain about it, for the merchant, burgher, farmer and all others, can lay in as much beer and wine as they please without paying any excise, being only bound to give an account of it in order that the quantity may be ascertained. Jacob Couwenhoven, who is one of the church-wardens, will be able to give an account.

In New England there are no taxes or duties imposed upon goods exported or imported; but every person's wealth is there appraised by the government, and he must pay for the following, according to his wealth and the assessment by the magistrates: for the building and repairing of churches, and the support of the ministers; for the building of schoolhouses, and the support of schoolmasters; for all city and village improvements, and the making and keeping in repair all public roads and paths, which are there made many miles into the country, so that they can be used by horses and carriages; for the building of inns for travellers, and for the maintenance of governors, magistrates, marshals and officers of justice, and of majors, captains and other officers of the militia.

…that it was as large by far as they say the people were compelled to pay. This is not the Company's fault, nor the Directors', but of those who charge one, two and three hundred per cent. profit, which the people are compelled to pay because there are few tradesmen.

It will not appear, either now or in the future, that 30,000 guilders were collected from the commonalty in Stuyvesant's time; for nothing is received besides the beer and wine excise, which amounts to about 4,000 guilders a year on the Manhatans. From the other villages situated around it there is little or nothing collected, because there are no tax collectors, except one at the Ferry, and one at Flushing.

The question is whether the Honorable Company or the Directors are bound to construct any works for the commonalty out of the recognition which the trader pays in New Netherland for goods exported, especially as those duties were allowed to the Company by Their High Mightinesses for the establishment of garrisons, and the expenses which they must thereby incur, and not for the construction of poor-houses, orphan asylums, or even churches and school-houses, for the commonalty.

The charge that the property of the Company is neglected in order to procure assistance from friends, cannot be sustained by proof.

The provisions obtained for the negroes from Tamandare were sent to Curaçao, except a portion consumed on the Manhatans, as the accounts will show; but all these are matters which do not concern these persons, especially as they are not accountable for them.

As to the freemen's contracts which the Director graciously granted the negroes who were the Company's slaves, in consequence of their long service: freedom was given to them on condition that their children should remain slaves, who are not treated otherwise than as Christians. At present there are only three of these children who do any service. One of them is at the House of Hope, one at the Company's bouwery, and one with Martin Crigier, who has brought the girl up well, as everybody knows.

That the Heer Stuyvesant should build up, alter and repair the Company's property was his duty. For the consequent loss or profit he will answer to the Company.

The burghers upon the island of Manhatans and thereabouts must know that nobody comes or is admitted to New Netherland (being a conquest) except upon this condition, that he shall have nothing to say, and shall acknowledge himself under the sovereignty of Their High Mightinesses the States General and the Lords Managers, as his lords and patrons, and shall be obedient to the Director and Council for the time being, as good subjects are bound to be.

Who are they who have complained about the haughtiness of Stuyvesant? I think they are such as seek to live without law or rule.

Nobody can prove that Director Stuyvesant has used foul language to, or railed at as clowns, any persons of respectability who have treated him decently. It may be that some profligate has given the Director, if he has used any bad words to him, cause to do so.

That the fort is not properly repaired does not concern the inhabitants. It is not their domain, but the Company's. They are willing to be protected by good forts and garrisons belonging to the Company without furnishing any aid or assistance by labor or money for the purpose; but it appears they are not willing to see a fort well fortified and properly garrisoned, from the apprehension that malevolent and seditious persons will be better punished, which they call cruelty.

Against whom has Director Stuyvesant personally made a question without reason or cause?

This I could prove also, were it not that the documents are in New Netherland and not here.

Stuyvesant has never contested anything in court, but as president has put proper interrogatories to the parties and with the court's advice has rendered decisions about which the malevolent complain; but it must be proven that anyone has been wronged by Stuyvesant in court.

The English minister Francis Doughty has never been in the service of the company, wherefore it was not indebted to him; but his English congregation are bound to pay him, as may be proven in New Netherland.

The Company has advanced the said minister, from time to time, goods and necessaries of life amounting to about 1100 guilders, as the Colony-Book can show, which he has not yet paid, and he is making complaints now, so that he may avoid paying it. Whether or not the Director has desired a compromise with Doughty, I do not know.

Director Stuyvesant, when he came to New Netherland, endeavored according to his orders to stop in a proper manner the contraband trade in guns, powder and lead. The people of the colony of Renselaerwyck understanding this, sent a letter and petition to the Director, requesting moderation, especially as they said if that trade were entirely abolished all the Christians in the colony would run great danger of being murdered.

It is here to be observed that the Director, fearing one of two [evils] and in order to keep the colony out of danger, has permitted some arms to be furnished at the fort. Nobody can prove that the Director has sold or permitted to be sold anything contraband, for his own private benefit.

It is true that a case of guns was brought over by Vastrick, by order of Director Stuyvesant, in which there were thirty guns, which the Director, with the knowledge of the Vice Director and *fiscaal*, permitted to be landed in the full light of day, which guns were delivered to Commissary Keyser with orders to sell them to the Netherlanders who had no arms, in order that in time of need they might defend themselves, which Keyser has done; and it will appear by his accounts where these guns are. If there were any more guns in the ship it was unknown to the Director. The *fiscaal*, whose business it was, should have seen to it and inspected the ship; and these accusers should have shown that the *fiscaal* had neglected to make the search as it ought to have been done.

The remonstrants say that we had relied upon the English, and by means of them sought to divert the college, (as they call it,) which is untrue. But it is here to be observed that the English, living under the protection of the Netherlanders, having taken the oath of allegiance and being domiciliated and settled in New Netherland, are to be considered citizens of the country. These persons have always been opposed to them, since the English, as well as they, had a right to say something in relation to the deputation, and would not consent to all their calumnies and slanders, but looked to the good of the commonalty and of the inhabitants.

It was not written on their petition, in the margin, that they might secretly go and speak to the commonalty. The intention of the Director was to cause them to be called together as opportunity should offer, at which time they might speak to the commonalty publicly about the deputation. The Director was not obliged, as they say, to call the commonalty immediately together. It was to be considered by him at what time each one could conveniently come from home without considerable loss, especially as some lived at a distance in the country, etc.

That they have not been willing to communicate, was because all whom they now paint in such black colors would have been able to provide themselves with weapons, and make the contrary appear, and in that case could have produced something [in accusation of] some of them. And since the Director and those connected with the administration in New Netherland are very much wronged and defamed, I desire time in order to wait for opposing documents from New Netherland, if it be necessary.

As to Vander Donk and his associates' report that the Director instituted suits against some persons: The Director going to the house of Michael Jansen, (one of the signers of the remonstrance,) was warned by the said Michael and Thomas Hall, saying, there was within it a scandalous journal of Adrian van der Donck; which journal the Director took with him, and on account of the slanders which were contained in it against Their High Mightinesses and private individuals, Van der Donck was arrested at his lodgings and proof of what he had written demanded, but he was released on the application and solicitation of others.

During the administration both of Kieft and of Stuyvesant, it was by a placard published and posted, that no attestations or other public writings should be valid before a court in New Netherland, unless they were written by the secretary. This was not done in order that there should be no testimony [against the Director] but upon this consideration, that most of the people living in Netherland are country and seafaring men, and summon each other frequently for small matters before the court, while many of them can neither read nor write, and neither testify intelligibly nor produce written evidence, and if some do produce it, sometimes it is written by some sailor or farmer, and often wholly indistinct and contrary to the meaning of those who had it written or who made the statement; consequently the Director and Council could not know the truth of matters as was proper and as justice demanded, etc. Nobody has been arrested except Van der Donk for writing the journal, and Augustyn Heermans, the agent of Gabri, because he refused to exhibit the writings drawn up by the Nine Men, which were promised to the Director, who had been for them many times like a boy.

Upon the first point of redress, as they call it, the remonstrants advise that the Company should abandon and transfer the country. What frivolous talk this is! The Company have at their own expense conveyed cattle and many persons thither, built forts, protected many people who were poor and needy emigrating from Holland, and provided them with provisions and clothing; and now when some of them have a little more than they can eat up in a day, they wish to be released from the authority of their benefactors, and without paying if they could; a sign of gross ingratitude.

… to which they are making an appeal.

Upon the second point they say that provision should be made for ecclesiastical and municipal property, church services, an orphan asylum and an almshouse. If they are such philanthropists as they appear, let them lead the way in generous contributions for such laudable objects, and not complain

We will only add some description of the persons who have signed the remonstrance and who are the following:

Adrian van der Donk.
Arnoldus van Hardenburgh
Augustyn Heermans

Jacob van Couwenhoven
Olof Stevensen
Michael Jansen
Thomas Hall
Elbert Elbertsen
Govert Loockmans
Hendrick Kip

In brief, these people, to give their doings a gloss, say that they are bound by oath and compelled by conscience; but if that were the case they would not assail their benefactors, the Company and others, and endeavor to deprive them of this noble country, by advising their removal, now that it begins to be like something, and now that there is a prospect of the Company getting its own again. And now that many of the inhabitants are themselves in a better condition than ever, this is evidently the cause of the ambition of many, etc.

At the Hague, 29*th November*, 1650.

The following footnote refers to a person NOT included in the above list: Hendrick Jansen the tailor was throughout Kieft's administration one of his bitterest and most abusive opponents, and was several times prosecuted for slander. In 1647 he sailed on the Princess with Kieft and was lost.

(Michael Paaw was given a patent of patroonship settlement of land on Pavonia on or about 1634 by the Dutch West India Company and he managed to prosper very well until he was unable to receive any additional workers promised him from Holland.

The war against the savages made him unable to defend the settlement and at times he was forced to escape to the Manhatans after his house and barns were burnt. He would take his complaint to the Honorable Company. Eventually the Company would purchase the Honorable heer Paaw property on Staten Island. He was paid 25,000 guilders for his colony.

On August 13 1636 the West India Company sold the land on which the farmstead was located to Captain David Pieter's de Vries. Heer de Vries would till the land and develop the many possibilities. As a result of animals theft from his settlement de Vries summoned Kieft to look into the matter. A large force of soldiers from the fort was sent to the island under the command o Cornelis Van Tienhoven the secretary of the director of the council of New Netherland, Kieft, who offered a bounty on each head killed and delivered. The Raritan Indians suffered badly, losing many men, women and children, the total number of 45 dead was never confirmed. This would ultimately lead to the first was with the Raritan Indians and an eventual loss of the patroonship of Pieter de Vries).

Author's Conclusions and Comments

These are the comments by way of introduction. I cannot remember a time when I was not in love with history. Many books, many hours, many years - decades, was captured and carried off by many of the books into myself. But still illiterate, these last few years I was ready for a new commitment. I committed to reading what I needed to know about history. I continue to wonder if I have the depth enough, have read enough, and have researched enough to convince anyone that the emotions here will in the future convince others to open the same pages. If I think about it, I was analyzing this literature for a long time. Literature that has preceded this - the historical record. History and race and theatre. Perhaps the book will help teachers who are still feeling a little uneasy about the topic of history and race. Perhaps it will help book club members in selecting this title, hopefully, the book will encourage journalists, historians, I don't know, to think more critically. If it accomplishes anything, if it will be worthwhile.

The narratives and stories have been narrowed down to deal more specifically with New York and Staten Island. The Dutch government has now added to the history of New Amsterdam under the Dutch rule and it also has become part of the English rule in New York. New technology, the electronic devices will help historians open the door of history of the United States. Behind the scenes, the attitudes and feelings of those convicted and doomed to face death or distant exile in the bowels of the basements of the home secretary's office at The Hague. In the near future it will become available. It also will show how the capital law worked. Year after year, the Home Secretary of Holland accumulated in its overcrowded and dark, dank rooms, a growing mountain of documents. Dust-covered, dirt-encrusted and tattered boxes told the tales of those who survived and those that have been barely noticed. It's difficult. You will find the petitions submitted by and on behalf of felons sentenced to death, sentenced to transportation or sentenced to rotting years in prison. There's a dismal flood of appeals among the papers; appeals occupy the center of much of the literature of the Dutch judicial system. Its very basis was the discretionary application or mitigation of penal pain. Along with those accompanying papers, sometimes extensive, sometimes brief, they have, for the most part. never been opened since they were first bundled away, tied in ribbons and twine over the centuries.

Of course, my research had to be narrowed down. I'm not a historian so I had to confine my reach into why the color of my skin was so indicative to the success or the failure; success of the countries that used slaves or the failure of the blacks to record this history.

The stories I've uncovered were from many different sources, many different nationalities, many different men: Scottish, Irish, English, American, African-American; who were forced by the whip to transport; the ship, the crimp and the slaver to cooperate on the gangway, in the hold, and in the rigging over the mortal dangers of the deep sea. The nature of this will be changed but the stories are there. Narratives are there. Peter Stuyvesant, who was the Governor General of the West India Company and the arrival of thousands and thousands of settlers came to this imaginary liberty, what they thought was a liberty, in a new and free country. It only seemed to have raised the level of irreligion, immorality and lawlessness in the colony of New Netherlands. There's a story well worth the historians to re-discover. It was an attempt to establish order and righteousness in a colony before it was too late. Stuyvesant was a very unusual, difficult, hated, venerated, feared, and loved man. He hated the Popish or the pagan roots, because they spilled over into riot and rebellion in his New Netherlands.

As the colonists moved, in many of the Indians drifted away or were forced away out of the area of what is now New Jersey, Pennsylvania, even Canada. Many of them fell victim to epidemics of smallpox. Less than 50 years after Peter Minuit purchased

Manhattan, virtually all of the modern-day Kings and Queens Counties around New Netherlands lay in European hands. It would continue into the 18th century. Wanton trickery and fraud continued unabated.

In 1652 Cornelius Van Werkhoven, a major shareholder in the West India Company, persuaded the two Nyack Indian chiefs to sell him the entire area - 1000 or more acres - for two shirts, two pairs of shoes, six pairs of socks, six axes, six hatchets, six knives, two scissors, and two combs. When the Indians realized that Van Werkhoven expected them to leave the land, they asked for a second payment: coats - kettles, axes, hatchets, knives, and combs - before leaving to Staten Island. After the deal was done Van Werkhoven died, but the project went ahead under the leadership of another man and others who received an official charter from Peter Stuyvesant. Stuyvesant came to New Netherlands…a troubled time. Its residents raised the Dutch flag, gave him a dinner and public entertainment in as good a style as the place could afford. In return he obligingly let them borrow some slaves to finish the palisades and sent half a dozen men shackled in irons to maintain law and order.

It must be mentioned that, before Peter Stuyvesant, war and the Indian Troubles, the land had become too valuable to ignore. To work the land, help bodies, were needed. Indians who became slaves were said to be poor miserable, lazy louts. They needed labor and they needed laborers. Peter Stuyvesant would see to it that slaves to work the land would be available. Peter Stuyvesant put into motion purchase or fiat…removing the negro plots, negro farms that the West India Company had previously set aside for former slaves. His brother-in-law, his son-in-law, combined with six others, combined all of this into a 200 farm nearby. Most privately owned slaves in the colony however, belonged to farm families and outlying villages like Flatbush where they and their masters worked and slept in the same houses, ate the same food, and worked side by side in the fields. Overall they were predominately male. The Dutch needed, the Dutch would work, the Dutch would own every man, woman, and child in their fields. Some Africans were free because the Company continued with its "half-freedom" policy, a condition of manumission. These slave women were liberated on condition that one of them do housework for the Director Stuyvesant general each week. Next year, Megan, an old sickly black woman, was granted outright freedom by the West India Company. She had served as a slave since the year 1628. She was almost certainly one of the original three females imported from Angola 35 years earlier. Under the Dutch men and women slaves began to form families against the great odds. There were many black marriages recorded in the Dutch Reform Church between 1641 and 1644, The dominies, or ministers, were increasingly reluctant to baptize either slaves or their children. They would ultimately stop the practice altogether. Due to their lack of knowledge and faith and because of worldly aims, this was the reason for denying baptism to anyone having black skin. In 1661 free blacks Emanuel Pietersen and his wife, Dorothy Angola, sought freedom for a lad, Anthony Angola, whom they adopted as an infant and reared and educated. Their petition to adopt was granted after they paid the West India Company 300 guilders, five times the original price paid for a slave in Manhattan.

The bottom rungs of society in New Amsterdam were occupied by Africans, though their lives and working conditions varied widely from every aspect of the building, makeup, and maintenance of New Amsterdam and most still belonged to the West India Company and worked on important agriculture, public, and military projects. Peter Stuyvesant requested additional slaves to be sent up from Curacao for Company use: "They ought to be stout and strong fellows," he explained, "fit for immediate employment on this fortress and other works; and also, if required, in war against the wild barbarians, either to pursue them when retreating, or else to carry some of the soldiers' baggage." Four years later he reported that he had utilized a recent shipment of slaves to harvest food, chop wood, repair oxcarts, and manufacture shoes. Time, because of the Company's chronic unwillingness to spend money, its slaves were also trained for more highly skilled tasks. Many Dutch would return to Holland unable to make meaningful success at their bouwerys, or farms, and deal with the heavy taxation appearing each year on their lands by the Dutch West India Company. Stuyvesant again appealed to the Directors in Amsterdam to send him some ships carpenters, only to be told that Dutch workmen were far too expensive and that carpentry, bricklaying, and other trades ought to be taught to the negroes as it was formerly done in Brazil. He appears to have followed orders and trained many negroes in as much as contemporary deeds began referring to negro caulkers, blacksmiths, coopers, carpenters, and so forth.

Other New Amsterdam slaves worked in private households, either as domestic servants or agricultural laborers. Stuyvesant himself acquired more than 40 or 50 slaves, far more than anyone else in the colony. Some were domestics, the rest labored in the fields and the orchards of his private bouwery or farm. It was a country estate lying between what is now 5th and 20th Streets in New Amsterdam.

The remainder of New Amsterdam's free white inhabitants comprised a diverse shifting lower class of laborers, cart-men, transient sailors, apprentices, soldiers, and minor West India Company functionaries. They were also farm hands and indentured white servants. Too many of the latter, Stuyvesant complained, were runaways, the same kind of people who until recently had made up the bulk of the colony's population. The popular culture in New Amsterdam centered on the town's always numerous taverns, grog shops, and pot houses, where noisy pipe-smoking crowds of men and women drank, gambled, and played games like backgammon, handball, and bowling, and women too, were particularly fond of a tobacco pipe. A favorite tavern, the Wooden Horse, a particular favorite of sailors and soldiers, was located in a thatched cottage on the corner of Whitehall and Stone Streets. Its small single room boasted only one window and reeking of smoke and stale beer, men sat at long wooden tables dimly lit by flickering candles, drinking West Indian rum, French brandy, and local brews. The owner was a Frenchman named Philippe Gerard who had once been sentenced to ride the wooden horse in his days as a soldier for the West India Company. Places like the Wooden Horse Tavern tended to treat the 9 o'clock closing hour casually, and their patrons often disturbed the peace with drunken brawls, sometimes involving knives, cutlasses, and pikes. One owner, a cantankerous old Indian trader, lost his license for entertaining disorderly people, and often disorderly Indian people in his taprooms near Smits Vly on the East River shore. His equally troublesome wife would be banished from New Amsterdam ten years later for openly selling liquor to the Indians.

By the end of Stuyvesant's first decade in office, the New Amsterdam folk were celebrating traditional Dutch holidays in full pleasure with gusto, just as in the

Netherlands. They would routinely commemorate the traditional bacchanal of eating and drinking while, as in Europe, young men dressed up like women and paraded about the streets.

Below the mercantile elite of New Amsterdam was a new hierarchy of white working people of modest means who were not exclusively Dutch, who provided the growing community with its basic goods and services. The backbone of this middling class consisted of skilled craftsmen and their families, a few dozen innkeepers, boardinghouse owners, surgeons, and notaries. These white working people would eventually make up the backbone for Stuyvesant's overwhelming colony payments for land. He would guarantee better services for thirty guilders per month. Some of them, like Abraham Willemsen, had joined this new generation of immigrant artisans representing the wide range of trades, made barrels, hogsheads, pipes, and kegs, in which the merchants exported flour, salted meats, and fish. The town's bakers by then ten of them, made bread, special cakes for festivals and weddings, and the hard biscuits that formed a large part of the diet of sailors at sea.

A Dutch wife wasn't her husband's peer. The law gave him extensive authority to control her actions and allowed him, among other things, to sell or bequeath their common property without her consent. Even so, culturally as well as legally, the husband's power was qualified by the conviction that a submissive wife was incompatible with a strong household. Members of this emerging municipal elite were unmistakably Dutch in taste, manner and outlook. Those who could afford to follow Stuyvesant's example in furnishing their houses, as did wealthy inhabitants of Amsterdam, with furniture, rare paintings, fine china, and heavy silver. Wives of wealthy merchants dressed in fashionable styles of Amsterdam and Paris. They surrounded themselves with servants and slaves. Many imported spinets and virginals to satisfy their love of music. They were highly sociable too. The Director, the councilmen, the burgomasters, and the orphan-masters frequently held meetings in taverns, except of course, during divine service.

I would call this next brief statement virtual reality, because I had to understand more about the Dutch and their paintings. Dutch paintings in The Hague in Holland and in the crunched houses are called their verisimilitude. These pictures were often considered uncommonly truthful and honest depictions of Dutch life. Was the status of realism for the 16th and 17th century artists and viewers by examining the pictorial means that suggest realities and the themes represented by them. Was always for many years a part of the Dutch life to have community members with black skin, usually they were young men and young women who came to Holland aboard the traders that made [inaudible] bounty of the African Trade, gold, ivory and produce, in unintended irony it always also represents a commercial staple for Holland. More slaves bound for America. Painters Franz Hals and Jan Steen have survived the decades of paintings from Holland that appear in museums and galleries. A close view of their work will provide the viewer with the black skins of unremarkable...Holland, where black members of households were frequent. To express it this way is to stand history on its head. Hals, Rembrandt and Steen produced exceptional portraits in a field of Dutch art more than any other noted for its conformity and its reality. For all of their apparent truthfulness, Dutch pictures show little of colonial working life. They were painted in…these Dutch painters worked mainly indoors and in Holland, concentrating rather on colonial benefits to trade, art and science. New Amsterdam. There are very few paintings by Dutch artists of landscapes outside of Holland, but for its incursion of Africans origin, there are a few paintings by Franz Post.

Dutch painters….paintings of verisimilitude was a suggestion that realism is always the term of their culture and genre. The Dutch artists seem to have been more concerned with this realism, this verisimilitude, than their colleagues in almost any other western culture. Several pictorial means signifying the real, clearly depend upon exquisite skill. Jan van Eyck and his patience already valued the finest differentiation of texture through the meticulous handling of paint that leaves no trace of the painter's hand, but realism values nevertheless.

Its primary purpose of painting was the imitation of nature that is reality in all its aspects which is very much why the black faces, figures, men and women, appear in Dutch pictures. They are bound by genre, conventions, and time. Pictures, paintings, images of the slave trade from Africa to the Americas suggests that these painters from Vermeer and Steen, whose works open a culture, only two of the numerous Catholic painters who successfully sold to middle-class Protestants and Catholics alike. Many surviving paintings of the commanding trading companies with monopolies on Dutch trade in the East and West Indies along the African coasts and in Japan. The West Indies Company gained similar privileges between Africa and South America. Politically diverse decentralization allowed the Dutch to enact locally sensible policies and the slaves were allowed Dutch titles and names, socially where tolerance and other religions and people were probably motivated more by business sense than by enlightened ideology as a record of the profitable Dutch genre.

But in other books, one would read about the arduous years in Surinam. The Dutch Sugar colony that was to become notorious for its unparalleled abuse of slaves, although these scientists were motivated by sincere and creative interest in knowledge of what could be revealed of God's design, with hindsight it is clear that their marvelous achievements depended on Dutch economic enterprises that entailed the systematic exploitation of other peoples and the lands that they inhabited. This practice, however mitigated individually by benevolent planters or isolated missionaries, was implicitly justified by a belief in the superiority of white Christians. Might makes right. A myth so self-evident at the time that it was articulated only obliquely.

The self-styled paintings of this registers the pride that the contemporaries took in the global trade and colonial endeavor.

What I wanted to do with the voice that I did before this, I really wanted to make a connection between the 13 murals in Borough Hall on Staten Island. Those murals, as you and I know, are inadequate, inaccurate, racist and insulting, and I was trying to make some connection with the primary purpose of the Dutch painters and how they wanted to do nature and reality in all of their painting respects, but we'll have to get this typed up and I'll try and re-do it to make it more literal, make it a little more, a lot more …What I realize is that those black faces have always been a part of the New York world and they were in every scene, rarely mentioned in the major text of any of the stories, just little jots and sentences. They remain just accomplices in….history of the New World…maybe history doesn't repeat itself but human nature really does.

I'm going to stop and perhaps get to something that I can articulate a little better because a lot of interesting things came up with stuff that was translated from the Dutch. One little page of land grants….let me read this one.

The Final Cornelius Melyn Papers Regarding Staten Island 1640 - 1699

The Deed for Staten Island is given to David De Vries of Horne, Holland and Cornelius Melyn by Willem Kieft, Director General and Councilors on behalf of the High and Mighty Lord States General of United Netherlands. Melyn was not given full title or control over all of Staten Island because William Kieft, the Director General of the West India Corporation, planned and pleaded making a still for whiskey on Staten Island. It was the first still that's mentioned in any of the documents. So there was property set aside to give Willem Kieft certain rods of land on which to build a still. The Melyn Papers are very long, much of it very difficult to read, but I will have to strike out much of it to shorten it to make it pertinent. Cornelius Melyn came to Staten Island three times to rebuild his colony and after the third time he was arrested after bringing a ship to Staten Island. Each time that Cornelius Melyn was burned out, he would leave Staten Island, live there for a time, and other times he would go to New Haven, CT to live with his family and the members that survived the Indian massacres on Staten Island. When leaving Staten Island after the Indians burned everything, the Indians resettled some portions of the island and when Cornelius Melyn returned he was told that he had to repay the Indians for the property again. The Indians did not agree with the one-time purchase of the island and they resettled and wanted to have, not money, but implements given to them. It should also be mentioned that Cornelis Melyn was given money by the Dutch West India Company for the land because Melyn asked Director Kieft, and later Director Peter Stuyvesant, he was given money to erect his colony again. He was going to tithe his people by cattle goods and other implements necessary for agriculture. There are several pages describing the houses and farms and everything that was burned, "my cattle besides some people were shot dead so that I was obligated to flee for sake of saving my life to sojourn with wife and children to Menatans" (Manhattan). Melyn was so angry at not being able to have Peter Stuyvesant put soldiers on Staten Island that he put eight men in the community together and made a pamphlet to be sent to The Hague requesting a meeting, which he did, and the Hague insisted that Stuyvesant come to the Hague to discuss the issues that were present and about the papers of the eight men. Cornelis van Tienhoven was the Director Stuyvesant's secretary. He eventually did go to Holland and that description is in some ….the former…..

Cornelis van Thienhoven could speak the Indian dialect very well and he was there at one time when Melyn came back to Staten Island and he was told by the Indians that he would have to give them coats, needles, ironware, wampum and small gifts to maintain good friendship.

At the final burning of Cornelius Melyn's property he left Staten Island for New England under the English domination where he died, but before he died he transferred all of his papers and documents to his son Jacob Melyn who took his father's interest in the settlement of Staten Island and the Governor ordered it to be entered on record and care should be then had of him and that he should be allotted a convenient portion of land on the island. By then the island had been parceled off bit by bit by Kieft, and Jacob Melyn, the son, could only get 60 acres for his brothers and sisters and was told that it was humbly and seriously expected that he be pleased to desire to obtain any land. The last time that Cornelius Melyn went to Staten Island and began his last colony, Peter Stuyvesant sent soldiers to arrest him. Cornelius Melyn was thrown into prison for three or four months and his son had to surrender all of his papers concerning his title to Staten Island to the West India Company. After his death, a petition by his children and heirs, Governor granted five farms on Staten Island to his children; that was rejected by Governor Dongen, but petitions Governor Bellmont to allow him to prove his claim to land on Staten Island. Jacob was also wounded in the last Indian raid. Finally a new Governor, Lovelace, gave Jacob Melyn title to 60 acres on Staten Island.

It's very difficult to read all of this from the Dutch translations, but the fraud, theft, the greed, the incompetence, the killings and torture, the lies and the massacres, the intrigue and the corruption were very hard to follow. I have to cut it down. The Dutch West India Company recalled Governor Kieft back to Holland. He sailed for Holland and was lost at sea in a shipwreck.

AUTHOR'S INTERIM CONCLUSIONS

18th May. This new work would normally be called the conclusions. Conclusions after months and years reading documentation - developed the following: it's not a scientific study; it's not really an attempt to ameliorate interracial black-white system in the world, 2012, but I needed, as I still do today, to find a place for my life, my work, my soul, to know who I am, what I am doing here, how I got here. Do I belong here? What does it mean that I'm here? There's no signpost or direction, there are no road signs, merely a very wonderful place that I find myself, the ability to delve into research, take the quiet times to do what I need to do to find out, as a black American male person, what it is that I have done, what I should do, what has brought me to this point.

I look back on many of the older documents that I have kept in my file and, I should say at this point that I am primarily and basically interested in focusing on the place of my birth. I think that would be a good part to narrow down what I've done, because it is really the only place, it's the only thing that I really know about, and that after travelling the globe looking for other bits and pieces of who I might have been or finding out Who AM I. Why am I.

There has been a great deal of literature coming out of my Staten Island/Richmond County New York. The genealogy resources, websites, books, cemeteries, census directories, churches, the immigration, the legal records, military newspapers, the obituaries, the organizations. After many years I am able now to glance very rapidly through the dozens of pages and know that there is very little that I would find in it that would be helpful to me, and it is published as the history of Staten Island in large black print. Most of it is very interesting historically when a student picks up these pages and tries to make some connection. I think it would be very difficult to come to any conclusion that this is a real historic document. I had to find a place to go to read about the real history of my island.

I've been very lucky to know antiquarian book dealers. For many years they have been supplying me with books, literature, papers, documents, narrations, about the area in which I was born, which was New York, an island New York. I found very interesting records from New York deeds, back to 1672. But in these documents, the books, like most literature that I have read, there is very little about black people being in, on, or transported to, New York. I found that most literature has been sanitized, edited, redacted, reframed, and revised. I mentioned the antiquarian book dealers, and it was a test of my patience to read and re-read the literature that I never knew, I didn't know, and I'm sure that most of the professors of history at the colleges on Staten Island wanted to hear my voice, but I was not at any time articulate enough to tell them that my education came to me very painfully.

My family have been home-owners, land-owners, and tax payers, and they have righteously marched into Borough Hall to pay their taxes on Stuyvesant Place. I found that Judith Stuyvesant gave to Francisco Bastiaensz a Lot of land, "free and unencumbered, without any charge resting on or originating from the same excepting the Lord's right" to Francisco Bastiaensz, the only proviso was "that the said Francisco is bound, with his neighbors to keep in repairs the fence of said land."

Appeared before us undersigned Schepens of the city of New Orange in New Netherlands the worthy Mrs. Judith Stuyvesant, widow and executrix of the deceased Mr. Petrus Stuyvesant, who declared to cede, transfer and convey in right, true and free ownership to and in behalf of Frans Bastiaensz, a free negro, certain parcel or piece of land situated across the Fresh Water about the Bouwery (farm) past the section or neighborhood called Crommessie along the public road running yada yada yada, and it goes on to say rods eight going west, has been possessed and occupied by grantor to this date, free and unencumbered, without any charge resting on or originating from the same excepting the Lord's right (with this proviso, however, that the said Francisco is bound, with his neighbors to keep in repairs the fence of said land). For which said piece of land said Mrs. Stuyvesant for conveyance and transfer acknowledged to have been satisfied and paid therefore she, grantor, desisting from any claims, ownershiprights and pretensions she or any one on her behalf should or might advance. Promising to firmly and irrevocably keep perform and carry out this conveyance. In testimony of the truth this has been personally subscribed to by the grantor besides the undersigned Schepens, at New Orange, September 24, 1674. Signed by the Secretary and her name Judith Stuyvesant.

It's interesting that Peter Stuyvesant had more than 40 slaves on his property or his farm, or his bowery, and after he died his wife gave a parcel of land to Francisco Bastiaensz, a free negro, which is also one of the things that make this reading all of this year in and year out very interesting.

Another one that I picked up out of the papers translated from the Dutch reads:

May 1, Anno Domini 1673. John Reay of this city, papermaker, for a value consideration to him in hand paid by Richard Tincker, also of this citty, transfer and make over unto said Richard Tincker and his heirs the assigned right and title to a certain lot of land lying and being within this city to the South Street called the Prince Street to ye west of Suzanna the negro. It points out to me, well it goes on to be that this is….it's a land grant, but it's one of these little things that I find by reading all of these papers is that, in the 1600s, there were blacks living in New York being given land, property, in New York City and much of it has been in the archives, and I've never heard any of this by reading the annals of Staten Island. I'll just put this aside for you to glance over.

We will find it is signed and this is translated from the Dutch and signed by the Schout and Schepens of New Orange, New York, of New England, September 24, 1674. But that is only one interesting thing out of many, out of dozens, out of perhaps hundreds of little bits of information that I had to find through research, re-reading. What does that tell me? It tells me that, upon further looking at the book of Deeds, that there were negros, blacks, living in New Amsterdam, but the strange thing that I would find would be in such documentation such as John Reay, a papermaker, in 1673, New Amsterdam, purchased the title to a certain Lott of ground "Lying and being with in this Citty to the south of the street called the Prince Street, to ye west of Susanna the negro".

I very often would find these interesting things that had to be documented in the historic files that were sent to The Hague. Very rarely would I find that find that some cases, like this: a negro women called Mathilda, which they were owners of a Lot of land, but there's no other information of the negro slave called Mathilda: if she had a last name, or if she was married, or if she had any children. But this phenomenon would appear over and over again. Dick was a negro, Cade, Elizabeth, and Armenie - negroes; A negro woman who was released called Fide. Another negro wench called Violet. A widow released a slave called London. Sylvester Dering makes affidavit of the birth of Achilles, a negro male child born of a slave, born to him in February. Very rarely would I find more than the first name. It was unusual that I would find a black who had anything other than his first name documented in any of the papers that were returned to me from Holland.

Continuing Conclusions

The connections of representative of the religious community, reverend Johannes Megapolensis, and many of the members of the religious community who were given land by first Director Kieft and Peter Stuyvesant. *Narratives of New England* is extensive, much of it dictated for publication by Father Buteux, Father Jacob Jogues, his recommendations to the West India Company about his life at Fort Amsterdam. The other extensive journals of New Netherlands: The history and management of New Netherlands, the causes of the Indian War, the Indian Reprisals, Director Kieft's vengeance on the Indians, the building of the churches, the building of the forts. The arrogance and the high pretensions caused many men, especially the nine farmers sent to The Hague; representatives to recall Governor Kieft were the nine men and their remonstrance. The Secretary in New Netherlands, Cornelis Van Tienhoven sent to the Hague to defend the Peter Stuyvesant administration and its conduct in judicial matters. Nine men went to The Hague to present their proposals. There are other letters of Johannes Bogert, Hans Bontemantel, letters of the Dutch ministers, letters of Dominie Minister Megapolensis, his view of the Jews who were now beginning to come to New Amsterdam. Minister Megapolensis and the Lutherans, Minister Megapolensis and the Jesuits on the conversion of the black slaves. This is interesting because I had never known or had an opportunity to find any of that literature in any of the history or school books that I had come in contact with.

The readings are extensive. Historical research of New Netherlands and the tribes, the customs, the progress of the colonies, disastrous accounts with the Mohawks, the letters of Isaac Rasiere and Samuel Blommaert the letters of Reverend Jonas Michaëius, his voyage and the death of his wife, the progress of the colony continues in letter after letter. There are two books that I had sent to me as two of the most important books and documents that would give me most in depth reading and information about the narratives and letters of New Amsterdam. There is the report on the surrender of New Netherlands by Peter Stuyvesant when he was summoned to The Hague to explain his surrender. The book, written by Melyn is important because it outlines much of what happened to him, his family, and his patroon killings by the Indians on Staten Island. The other book is the version of events on Staten Island in 1633 by David Peter De Vries.

The New York narratives in these two books that I have invested so much time in… Both men have tested the power and the misuse of law by those men who were given the authority to bring New Netherlands into a condition so that it would be profitable to the West India Company. But again, before I continue, I continually looked throughout the interesting narratives, and I would find very little about the slaves that were purchased along the coast of Africa and sent to New Netherlands. Very little about those black slaves. They were sent to New Netherlands after being purchased in Africa because the colonists could not make their bouwerys or farms, profitable without more labor. Peter Stuyvesant came to the rescue by having the West India Company buy slaves from Africa. Africans did not come without any history. They came with their own histories and uniqueness and were able to survive because of that willingness to survive under all the conditions that confronted them in New Netherlands.

Dutch culture had for many years before had interactions with Blacks from Africa, and had lived with Black people in Holland. I had only to look in my library to see that the Dutch artists would use what they called verisimilitude, which meant realism. They were concerned with documenting life as it was. Most painters, Rembrandt, Jan van Eyck, Pels, Van Munder, all of them used what was called verisimilitude, realism. My personal library documents the pictures of black faces in their paintings. It was not, as I would see it, unusual to have blacks used in New Netherlands. What happened was many documents leaving New Netherlands by people who wrote narratives about white women being whipped and sent to the gallows in New Netherlands, were forced to sit with a rope around their neck before being hung because the crime was being delivered with a negro child. There was an imbalance between black slaves on the farms who were used to produce, but the ratio of black men and black women was out of balance, and there became laws that forbade white women and black men of fornicating, being delivered to New Amsterdam midwives of black children. When the children were delivered the authorities were not notified; the children were given to ministers who housed them on Staten Island.

The Dutch Secretary under Peter Stuyvesant, Cornelis van Tienhoven had a reputation as a libertine and he was accused of giving birth to a baby conceived by an Indian woman. He was the Schout-Fiscal, the chief assistant, who worked under the leadership at the time in New Amsterdam for the West India Company. It was said that he played a skillful game and succeeded in delaying, in part averting hostile action of the part of the

States General. He was the doorman that kept peace for Peter Stuyvesant. Cornelis van Tienhoven had a brother who also worked for the West India Company who was accused of fraudulent delivery of goods in the province. He was the Reciever General, but he was able to abscond from the province before any action would be furthered to him.

Much of the correspondence was done by the ministers in the Dutch Reformed Churches that were in most of the European countries, and those extracts, the minutes, the classics, the correspondence of the ministers are printed in volumes and much of it was published by the State of New York under the title *Ecclesiastical Records of the State of New York* in 1901. Two men that I've read so much of, Cornelius Melyn and David de Vries, were exceptional in that, what these men realized was that their battles with the officials of New Netherlands, the number of minor officers, the clerks, the treasurers, the assessors, the overseers, the constables, the justices, the Schout and Scheppen, what you will read between the lines is that these forms and the accomplishments of a seemingly polite society, Dutch society of course, would, while to decipher, but the mere matters may be only boorishness and brutality refined or insipidly and little disguised. May read many times of the slave who sat beside the Dutch masters in the cold winters cracking nuts, drinking cider with the family, the Dutch having had blacks in their community in Holland realized that the vigorous specimens that they needed to work required not…a feeling that was not out of any extra humanitarian sentimentality, but their association was based simply on the bases of strict business - a happy and well contented, well developed black being considered twice as valuable and profitable as an ill-treated one.

David De Vries, finally, after three or four attempts to set up his colony on Staten Island, being burned continually by Indians, being obstructed in his safety by the Dutch West India Company heads in New Netherlands. Finally de Vries found that his best interests were to leave and return to Hoorn in Holland, where his ancestors lived for many generations. Cornelius Melyn moved to the English area of New England, where he died. His land and property on Staten Island was put under the direction of his surviving son Jacob, and Jacob finally was able to get a portion of their property returned and some of Melyn's family lived on Staten Island for a long period of time.

I'm frustrated, angry, because I know that the slaves were very vital to the continued success of the New Amsterdam community, but the reframed and revised papers make it very difficult to find whay black slaves meant to the growth, to the beginnings of New York, the place where I was born, the place that I know of.

I'm forced to return to the conclusions and I would hope that other people begin to investigate where the blacks were beyond the recent findings of the black graveyards in Manhattan. Hundreds of blacks were buried in lower Manhattan. A plaque marks the spot. Who they were, the names, their jobs, what they did. I'd like to know so much more about them, but we're left with bits and pieces such as this: 1641 A Dutch legal document notes that eight blacks were convicted of killing an African in a tavern brawl. But since punishing them all would have meant too much loss of their labor, lots were drawn to pick one man to be hanged. The rope broke under his weight and he was ultimately reprieved. These are some of the little bits and pieces that are placed in the pages. It was a peculiar institution and I would like to know more. Where are the papers and the information about New York's involvement in slavery? The scholars and the authors, where are they that would find the information that would free people like myself to understand who they are. The unearthing of the African burial ground in lower Manhattan in 1999 may have been the turning point, I thought, the remains of this graveyard of more than 400 black slaves from the 16th and 17th centuries discovered at a construction site. These remains made slavery all too vivid. The bones showed evidence of malnutrition and signs of injuries. I hope the scholarship from this discovery would come to the surface soon.

What I do realize is that black faces, men and women, have always been a part of this American world. I know that we have been in every scene, every adventure, every war. It's rarely mentioned fully in the major texts of our story, our history, we remain accomplices of omission to the history of the New World. Maybe history doesn't repeat itself, but human nature does. I can only say and express my personal utter frustration with the history of my island, Staten Island, that place, the home of my birth. The apathy and the incompetence still remains.

It is also my hope that some historian, some writer, will delve deeper, find more documents, narrations, that would bring any sordid details to the surface so that they would emerge and see that history perhaps does repeat itself. I would like to know more about the sub-dealings and the surreptitious dealings and the fact that Peter Stuyvesant's sister, Anna Bayard was a go-to person, if you had any difficulty with the law. Anyone accused or found guilty of corruption charges was usually able to buy his way out of anything. He could go to Curacao on the next ship. Very few or any were imprisoned, perhaps because there were no long-term prisons available.

So much of it needs to be investigated, brought to the surface. It's an albatross around the neck of white society until it uncovers the truth or brings some reality to democracy that many countries can believe in. I think that today it's more than necessary for historians to uncover much of what has been sanitized from the pages of our history. So much has been edited out, some of it simply left out - it didn't look good, it wouldn't feel good. It had no evil beginning, they thought it would finally come to the surface, cannot be held so long…

Eventually the ex-slaves, the Indians would become creatures of the past, the blacks, the negroes, the slaves. Very little any written historical data that can be found. It would mean that they were people who would have no past.

Conclusions and Comments Continued

Finishing up – the founders of New England, New Dorp. Oude (Old) Dorp or New Dorp was the first settlement by Europeans on Staten Island. In the summer of 1600 the Dutch commenced building in Oude Dorp, or New Dorp as it is now known. It was probably covered by huge, stout, tall, sturdy trees, and the Dutchmen cut them to build their odd-shaped houses. They were able to gather stone for the foundations and clamshells along the shore to make mortar. During the first year in New Dorp, there are some estimates that there were a dozen or so of these low Holland cottages. Acres of land had to be cleared nearby and agricultural pursuits were at once commenced and at the same time they traded in furs and pelts with the Indians. It was kept up and found to be very profitable by the Dutch of Staten Island.

This was, it reads, a rude little hamlet so it makes it necessary to study the Dutch people and the Dutch character. We know from tradition and fact that they were a religious people and that they came from the queerest part of the earth that the sun ever shone on, or the tide ever washed. Theirs was the oddest and funniest country that ever raised it head from the waves; the most amphibious spot in the Universe was Holland. Indeed it has been the chosen butt of jokes and good-naturedly the laughing stock of many people. The Dutch are the queerest and drollest of all nations, and yet so plucky, so wise, resolute and strong that "beating the Dutch" has become a familiar byword expressing the limits of their mortal performance. And yet little Holland, besides holding its own place, has managed to gain a foothold on almost every quarter of the globe. An account of its colonies is indeed a history in itself.

The East Indies at the time was under the authority of more than 40 million people. It is no wonder the Dutch have always been wise and plucky and strong, for they have had to struggle for a foothold upon every land of their birth. They have had to push back the ocean to prevent it from rolling in on them. They have had to wall in the rivers and lakes and keep them within bounds, to hold living in polders that they have been forced to decide which should be land and which should be given to water, forever digging, building, embanking and pumping for their very existence.

The Dutch history is no more terrible than their homeland. The heart-rending stories about the Siege of Harlem by the Spaniards in the 16th century, and whose success the Dutch rivals became the first settlers at Old Dorp on Staten Island. The Dutch are a branch of the German race - tough, stout, they are fierce, staunch and defiant, and taught their children only the law of might, and their children grew up to be mightier than they. Their votes at council were always given by a clashing of arms and often their wives and mothers stood by with shouts and encouraging them to fight in the thickest. Others go to battle, but these Dutch go to war.

It is said of them too that even the old conquering Romans with Julius Caesar at their head were glad to compromise with them. The Dutch cavalry could swim across the wide and deep rivers without breaking ranks, and their infantry was the best-drilled in the world. Sometimes defeated but never subdued, they were patient under subjection only until they were again ready to rise as a man and throw off the yoke. Treachery, oppression and breach of faith were sure, sooner or later, to arouse the Dutch pluck, and that Dutch pluck in the end has always won.

Besides risking the perils in crossing a wide and almost unknown ocean, the Dutch had a lot to face in this new continent. With the Indians in the best possible manner having to conciliate their favor and purchase their lands, to clear and cultivate a wilderness, to make the centurion oaks bend and fall before them, to build and to provide sustenance, to endure the changes of a rigorous climate, and to guard themselves from beasts of prey and reptiles, to spend their Sabbath without the privilege of public worship in lonely solitude.

And their slaves. Of the Negroes that helped cultivate this land very little has been mentioned. The Dutch negroes at Old Dorp, like most of the negroes, are famous for their risible powers. It is said these negroes, in fact, like the monks of the dark ages, engross all the knowledge of the place, and know infinitely more than their Dutch masters. They carry on all the foreign trade in pelts and skins, making frequent voyages to town in canoes loaded with oysters, buttermilk and cabbages. These negroes are great astrologers, predicting the different changes of the weather, almost as certainly as an almanac. They are, moreover, exquisite performers on three-string fiddles; in whistling they almost boast the far-famed powers of Orpheus's lyre, for not a horse nor an ox when in place at the plough or before a wagon will budge a foot until he hears the well-known whistle of his black driver and companion. And from their amazing skill at casting up accounts on their fingers they are regarded with as much veneration as disciples of yore. And to the honest burghers of Old Dorp, the negroes, like wise men and sound philosophers, never look beyond their pipes nor trouble their heads about any affairs out of their immediate neighborhood, so that they live in profound and enviable ignorance of all the troubles, anxieties, and revolutions of this distracted planet place. I am told that many of the negroes do verily believe that Holland, from which the masters come, is situated somewhere on Long Island, and their High and Mightiness is situated in New Netherlands or the city of New York that goes by the name of New Amsterdam. They also meet every Saturday afternoon at the only tavern in the place, where they smoke a silent pipe by way of promoting social conviviality, and invariably drink a mug of cider.

The province of New Amsterdam having passed from the Dutch to the English rule by James, Duke of York, who had this in his possession in America, there were practically three elements on Staten Island at the time - Dutch, French and English. The Dutch and French were united and on friendly terms, but from the start the Dutch looked upon the English with suspicion and dislike because of their aggressiveness and their success in gaining possession of the government and the confiscation of land which the Dutch had long claimed as their own. These rival elements soon created trouble for the rulers at New Amsterdam. Several plantations on Staten Island were claimed by both and neither would pay taxes until the authorities had definitely settled the question of proprietorship. There were ruptures among the people and in several instances the militia was ordered out to enforce the law and to preserve the peace. There is a tradition to the effect that some of the Dutch settlers absolutely refused to pay their taxes to English authorities, questioning their right to make levies. These Dutch were thrown into prison, their property confiscated for their pains.

It is rare, very rare, almost impossible, after reading many, many books about the beginnings of New Netherlands, that I ever was able to find actual voices of negroes, of slaves, of servants, in any of the narratives or stories. I would find bits and pieces such asthis by travellers: "There was a house. We went to it to see if we could find any one who would show us the way a little. There was no master in it, but an Englishwoman with negroes and servants. We first asked her as to the road, and then for something to drink, and also for some one to show us the road; but she refused the last, although we were willing to pay for it. She was a cross woman. She said she had never been in the village, and her folks must work, and we would certainly have to go away as wise as we came."

I would look at the records at the Court of Common Pleas in Richmond County, going through a number of the papers and would find no words, no voice of the blacks such as this: A negro named Anthony Neal was accused of breaking into and robbing a store by Colonel Aaron Cortelyou. The goods were valued at about twenty dollars and they were found in a wheat field nearby. The accused negro, after being imprisoned for about two months, was tried, convicted and hung. The scene of the execution was the site of the public school house in Richmond, the negro protesting with his dying breath that he was innocent, and it is said that on the day following his execution his wife confessed that she had committed the theft herself.

These are the stories, the bits and pieces that I have found after reading through all the books, all the narratives about the slaves and the negroes. I may have missed bits and pieces because there was only the reference to negroes' heavy eyebrows or eyelids, black eyes, thick tongues and all of them black hair. Never have I come by a story or stories of blacks. There was one interesting story that I would be remiss if I did not describe it.

I am angry because after reading so many books, going through so much – the narratives, the documents, the stories, the letters, I'm still trying to find out about my people, I guess, that is to say the blacks, the negroes, the slaves. I can find very little, if any, of it. So I will add one more story that I found which I think is not strictly from European structure, and get out of the 16th and into the 17th century. But I'm finding what I always knew, that the slaves didn't get here with a vacancy of mind and body. Slaves from Africa came with a language, with all of the human involvements in society, nature, politics, religion. They didn't arrive here empty, and I knew that I should find some stories that I think I should add when I know that the blacks, the slaves, could fuss, they could fight, they could fornicate with the best of the whites that they found here in New Netherlands, but I didn't find any words, but of course the Indians, they didn't leave a written record. The blacks could read a language, they could write a language, they had a language but they were looked upon as just that - chattels, slaves. They weren't important. They were transparent, they were invisible.

The story I think that would be interesting is the story about a man, an Indian named Ely S. Parker. General Parker was the military rank that he ultimately achieved. Ely Parker was born on an Indian reservation in Tonawanda, New York, in 1828. He was a full-blooded Iroquois of the Seneca or Wolf Tribe. He became the head chief, Grand Sachem, of the Tribes, but they're now scattered, difficult to locate. But the short notation of General Parker is worth noting. He received a good education and read and studies law, but was refused admittance to the Bar on the grounds that Indians in the State of New York were ineligible for citizenship, and none except citizens could be admitted to the Bar. Parker refused the license to practice law. He entered the Polytechnic Institute in Troy, New York, and studied civil engineering, graduating with high honors. Parker became a personal friend, somehow, of General Ulysses S. Grant, the General who was credited with winning the final battle in the Civil War. Parker was appointed to the position of engineering in the United States Army under another General, General Smith.

When the Civil War broke out, Parker entered the Union Army and received a commission as Captain of Engineers. He later became attached to General Grant's staff, and was commissioned a Colonel. He was also appointed a Military Secretary by General Grant, and went with Grant through all of his campaigns. When the Confederate General Lee surrendered, Colonel Parker, who had become General Parker, was a representative of the original owners of American soil, and he prepared the conditions of surrender at Appomattox Courthouse between General Grant and General Lee. After the war, General Parker returned to civil engineering. He was then a citizen because he had entered the military he was now a citizen of the country. He was given his citizenship because he had served in the Union Army which gave everyone the right of citizenship.

General Parker became a member of the Indian Commission of the United States and he negotiated the removal of his tribe from the State of New York to the fertile and pleasant green lands of Green Bay, Wisconsin. General Parker became an attaché of the New York Police Department, which title he retained until the day of his death. General Parker's family consisted of a wife and daughter. His widow was a white woman, a native of Washington, DC. His daughter was born in Washington. Writers have described General Parker as the "Mark Twain of Old Seneca." He was a member of the Grand Army of the Republic and of several secret societies. General Parker had in his possession the medal presented by Washington to Red Jacket the Indian Chief. He always wore the medal. His Indian name was Honondongekanee. He made his home at the Pavilion Hotel at New Brighton, Staten Island.

I had never heard this story or anything like this during my formal education on Staten Island or reading any literature about Staten Island. So I will add this to a number of the stories, bits and pieces, that I will find in the future. But I think we will get on the 17th century reading notebooks.

Before tossing the papers back in the files, I think it should be important to place some of my feelings about what I read into the book, being a Staten Islander.

At the Continental Hotel, just off or on Richmond Terrace, the famous Aaron Burr spent many of the closing days and months of his life. The Old Stone Jug on Richmond Terrace, part of the old Neville mansion group just outside of Sailors' Snug Harbor. The Old Stone Jug was originally a beautiful house built by Captain John Neville, retired officer of the US Navy, and it goes on and on, the house has been the scene of many gay receptions, given in the honor of representatives of the navies of our own and other countries.

The Fountain House still exists, partially already to be torn down. I remember the Church of the Ascension – Blacks were never allowed to purchase a pew seat there, they had to wait outside with the animals, and the horses and carriages for their masters. The Rose and Crown farm house, which became a tavern.

This brings me to the murals that still exist in Borough Hall. I fought like hell to have them removed or redone, or a caption added. Van Pelt's homestead. How many times have I walked, trod, on Van Pelt Avenue, again just minutes from my own street, which was Lockman Avenue, born on Lockman Avenue, ran Lockman Avenue as a kid for many years.

An Indian was convicted and imprisoned in the jail at Richmondtown. We know **what** he was, no name, nothing more. The French, the English, the Dutch, we can find the names of the husband, the wife, several of the children. What they leave out says a great deal, and what they add to these papers says a great deal about why the blacks that survived, that are still there, have been scarred. I guess you could say its PTSD, Post Traumatic Stress Disorder, we only recognize it now in the soldiers from Iraq and Afghanistan.

Colonel Ichabod Crane, a very unusual story to most of us on Staten Island who think the Crane family was seriously involved in permitting their home to become a ghost building. But Ichabod Crane had Juan, an Indian boy from the Umpqua tribe of Oregon as his brave, honest and faithful servant. He died on Staten Island and was buried on the Ichabod Crane property. Some say the ghost of Ichabod Crane or Juan the Indian boy come alive to anyone who dares to enter the property.

The names are not strange to me, Judge William Curtis - we have Curtis High School - he went to boarding school, became a clerk in a German importing firm on Exchange Place downtown. He owned Brook Farm in Concord, Staten Island.

Continuing to read about them, you will find that they were brilliant, noble old men with honorable careers. Most honored among American citizens, distinguished officers of the military, on and on and on, their stories, their families. We only know about how they managed to maintain the farms, the plantations on Staten Island when we read their wills, the documents that show how many slaves they had. John Freemont ordered the emancipation of his slaves and those in his district who took up arms against the United States. Bit by bit the pages say a lot by what they don't say, I suppose.

Many individuals, historians, have written books about this place in our history, New Amsterdam, New York, Staten Island. Depending upon who's doing the translating of a document, you can get widely different transcriptions, but I found few words, if any, that came from the mouths of the blacks, of the slaves.

But before I leave that I wanted to place a building, the Austin House, the house that was not originally owned by Alice Austin, but was eventually owned by Alice Austin the photographer, and it is an interesting building, beautiful architectural design. It is, I guess, as quaint inside as it is outside, but very few now would know that the huge ample fireplace that gapes into the cellar was surrounded in the evenings for many years by slaves who were locked there overnight in the old days. Locked until morning by the knocker, whose hammer was made of wrought iron fashioned into a griffin's head. I guess that was supposed to have been humorous, but of course someone had to hew the wood, draw the water.

Judge David Mersereau's mill was damaged, slight fires at his grist mill. Once it was really damaged and had to be rebuilt. According to the old records, several Indians and slaves helped build the mill and worked in it for a number of years. "Red Indian Pete" and "Black Sam" were paid for their services as laborers. Shortly after its completion a dispute arose among these two distinct races over some trivial matter and several attempts were made to take each other's lives. The Mill served as a fort for the negroes and the Indians kept up a siege until driven away by the militia. Several negroes and Indians were arrested and they were imprisoned in the Old Red Jail until their cases were disposed of. The Indians were made to work for the county as their punishment. The owners of the slaves were held responsible for their future conduct. The leaders, however, were to receive five and twenty lashes each at the whipping post. Guilt or innocence, you never really read that. Just these bits and pieces.

The old Bedell homestead at Green Ridge was a most dilapidated wreck. For the past few years it had been occupied by negroes and whenever they needed firewood, they pulled down a portion of the venerable structure. That's all. That's all. Who were these negroes, what were their names, were they family? I doubt if we will ever, ever, know.

I'm forced to make a decision, but this last bit must be entered. It is about freemasonry. Freemasonry on Staten Island was a provisional step that could be taken by white men – not women, just white men, it was an all-male world – but it was growing more and more popular, until at one point it had to be abandoned because of the cohesive nature of Masonry. But little did I know that looking at the pictures of many of the "prominent" men on Staten Island one would have to read "J Walter Wood, AM, MD" or "J Walter Wood", in another section, which read "Free and Accepted Mason". It would not mean very much to the contemporary farmer, worker on Staten Island, but I must add that, for most men to become whatever they needed on Staten Island, he would have to be a member of a Richmond Lodge, the largest, Richmond Lodge, No. 66, F.A.M., and various other organizations. The men gathered around the organizations; participated quietly and together. Dr. Wood is a Thirty second degree Mason, is a past Master of Richmond Lodge No. 66; past District Deputy Grand Master of the Twenty seventh District; past High Priest of Tyrian Chapter No. 219 R.A.M.; Eminent Commander of Empire Commandery, a Noble of Mecca Shrine, and for several years was President of the Staten Island Masonic Mutual Benefit Association; member of The Western Mutual Insurance Co; also the past Chancellor of Staten Island Lodge Knights of Pythias; Examining Physician for the Odd Fellows, Workingmen, Foresters; American Legion of Honor, Templars of Liberty and the New York Life Insurance Company, and visiting surgeon of the Smith Infirmary, which was only torn down in 2012, I might add. But there you have it. Blacks were not accepted in the Masonic organizations until they were given a Charter of their own which became the Prince Hall Masons of Staten Island.

It reads, "an incident occurred at that time which seems exceedingly ludicrous at the present. A rumor was started that the Masons were organizing on Staten Island for the purpose of controlling all the schools, offices, and churches, and that Masons were to be exempted from taxation. The feeling against Freemasonry became intense and at the general election handbills bearing coffins and red skulls were handed out to the general public."

There is one more organization that should be mentioned of the Masons on Staten Island. The Masonic Mutual Relief Association is said to be the fulfillment of one of the noblest principles which actuates the craft. The members were called in quorum Sir Knight; Eminent Commander Sir So-and-So; Sir Knight Generalissimo, Sir Knight Captain General; Sir Knight Judge Advocate; it goes on and on. The Swordbearer, the Standardbearer, the Warder, the Captain of the Guard, the Sentinel, the Trustees, all Free and Accepted Masons.

During the Civil War, in 1863, the battle of Gettysburg had been fought by General Grant. He had taken Memphis; he had taken Vicksburg; he had won the Battles of Lookout Mountain and Missionary Ridge; but more men were needed. Conscription became the word for Staten Island. The army needed men; it needed boots on the ground. Staten Island had no leadership. It was a universally popular uprising. It was directed against the blacks who were regarded as the cause of this war, and the events of 1864 on Staten Island were largely a repetition of the call that had been a year before. The recruiting office was offering $200 per man and $200 to the broker who would procure him. Little did I realize that my life could be read in the lists of the recruits credited to Richmond County under the call of March 14, 1864. Why do I make any connection to this? Because, in 1945, as a black person, I would experience this same measure of recruiting racism. The names are here, but looking closely one can see the names Richard Smith, William Smith-colored, Charles Cornell-colored, Robert Tappen-colored, James Jackson-colored, on and on, and I wondered if, after they were recruited, would they be subject to separation as I was and placed into a separate military unit, or were they allowed to fight for their dignity, their country, side by side with all of the other names on the list? There's no answer. I looked and read the papers; I found nothing.

But, of course, the people of Staten Island have always been very restless relative to their local governments under which they were living. There was always a conflict of authority and interests between the towns, the villages, and the various localities north of the island, south of the island, and it is but a simple truth to say that, with local jealousies this kept back the hand of progress, and it would draw a veil over one of the most beautiful and enticing spots on the earth. There has long been a plan to make a separate city of Staten Island, but most of all Staten Island lacked a proper leader and sufficient public interest to reach a tangible form. The hatreds, class, cultural…

A greater New York scheme would come to the surface time and time again when people were longing for a change. They wanted change, they wanted something different, but they did not exactly know what it should be.

Chapter 2

THE CONSPIRACY OF 1741

A quote by James Baldwin: "Re-examine everything. Go back to where you started, or as far back as you can, examine all of it. Travel your road again and tell the truth about it. Sing or shout or testify, or keep it to yourself, but know whence you came."

The following is an account compiled from various sources that briefly describes the events and judicial proceedings that became known as "The Conspiracy of 1741." Following this description is a longer translation from the Dutch of the undoubtedly biased account of the same events from the notes of one Daniel Horsemanden, a New York attorney of the time.

The six Negro oarsmen, their bodies covered with stiff waterproof sailcloth, pulled rhythmically at their poles as the barge moved silently through the waters toward the Fort Amsterdam turret reef light. Beyond the early night haze lay New York City, the path glitters in the moonbeams on the quivering water, while several schooners anchored lazily in silhouette, their aft-lighted stern candles marking their bulk to be avoided. In the distance the narrows inlet from the ocean, lighted rock beacons on either side, send their kindly beacons seaward awaited mariner's ships whose pilots ignore their warnings to steer carefully, lest their vessels and cargoes be lost on the rocks after months at sea.

No one spoke as the shore came nearer, the dozen passengers, huddled heads covered in the early night chill. The Negro at the tiller stood, and the oarsmen pulled inside their wooden poles to step ashore to bring the wooden craft silently to a floating dock to be made fast. There was no one at the dock as the oarsmen moved baggage from the barge using an oar held firmly from the boat to the dock to assist the several passengers. This quiet choreography had been preformed twice a day, and the Negro bargemen used a silent language to do their jobs while acknowledging with silent tips of their hats those who traveled more often, leaving small gifts at their seats.

Titus, a young mulatto slave, was excited; he would again see friends that he had not seen since the last year when he had used his leather belt to stop the flow of blood from the mangled arm of his master at the grist mill during their bagging time, one year ago. The arm was severed above the left elbow, and Mars John Chocheron became easily upset and angry, but never with Titus. Titus was now 14, stronger than and almost as tall as Mars Chocheron. He was assuming more and more duties because of the accident. Chocheron held the flat leather pouch across his shoulder at his side, always, never leaving it, Titus imagined it carried his money and other papers, Titus knew when to ask questions and when to be silent, and his huge right hand grabbed a sack and walked toward the cobblestone street away from the dock. The Negro bargemen, the last to leave the dock behind them, their cape-like coverings reaching the ground, each carried an oar, the tiller being under the arm of the unsmiling helmsman who offered a low "Good night, sir."

Titus came from this New York Island as a child of age two; his only memory of that time was that he was always cold. "Nanny," Mr. Chocheron's slave, was a dark-skinned Negro who became his mother and told him he was a Mullata, and he should always be a good slave and she would always take good care of him. His hair was reddish, his skin chocolate brown, and he had distinct Caucasian features. Titus learned how to read and write. He was always smiling and helpful, a favorite of the other White farmers on the road.

They walked down Pearl Street to the offices of the West India Company where the Negro watchman took Titus, with a small candle, to a place of housing for company slaves. It was a two-story stone building which was attached to a one-story wooden warehouse. A large empty room with large, well worn rough hewn tables and chairs, there were three windows facing the street, the shutters now closed for the night, and they were now covered with paper made of stiff walrus skin to keep out the cold. There was no one else in the room, the stone floor was cold, and while it left Titus isolated, he knew he was secure for the night. There was an occasional clip clop of horses and voices, there were bells striking nautical time from the sailing ships in the harbor. He made a bed on the bags on the cold floor; he hated the cold, blew out the candle and tried to sleep. He remember the tavern and the people there, it was closed now he thought, besides he was told by Mars Chocheron not to go to the tavern or any homes without him, he was told they would go outside in the morning, and Titus would see Mrs. Bradt's Tom, who was the same age as Titus.

What Titus heard next was the voice of Mars Chocheron nudging him. He pulled his boots on and stood quietly as Mars Chocheron sat at the table looking at papers from his satchel. Titus looked away through a hole in the paper windows at the harbor, the bay and the Narrows, he knew that Mars Chocheron was unhappy for some reason but he did not speak. He took a loaf of bread from the sack that was prepared by Mother Nanny and placed a section on the table in front of Mars Chocheron. There were many more voices outside now and voices coming from the ships that lay at anchor with White men and Negroes waiting to work unloading the cargoes. Giant horses were being pulled to their places in front of huge wooded carriages, a scene of constant motion; large wooden barrels rolling down the sides of the ship at the dock and ropes being slung to load them into balers. Titus wanted to go outside to be closer to this.

"I will be going to the Governors office this morning, and you will come with me," said Cocheron.
"Yes father."
"And I want you to address me as Mars Chocheron, do you understand?"
"Yes father," replied Titus.
"You can begin now, do you understand?"
"Yes."

There was no eye contact, as Chocheron pulled on his hard bread. Titus slipped his piece into his pocket, and went to the door to relieve himself.

John Chocheron spread the papers out on the wooden table, testing the effects of each word on his mind. The first was a statement of his count of people in his district. The second was to answer a request about his impression of any unrest, and the current feelings and attitudes of the Negroes and Indians and Mulattas in his area, and a report their state of mind in terms of potential insurrection and open disobedience. He would ask his second in command Lieutenant Thomas Dongan of his island district to do this.

John Chocheron, as Captain of the North Division of Staten Island in Richmond County, is ordered to deliver to the governor a list of Negro slaves, Indian and Mullata slaves in his north division of Staten Island. It was an order to deliver this list and present it to the Honorable James Delancee Esquire, his Majesties Lieutenant Governor and Commander in Chief In and over the province of New York and Territories thereon depending in America.

The document read as follows:

This is a true account of what has been brought in to me sir, your most humble and obedient servant. Lieutenant Thomas Dongan.

May it Please Your Honor
Where as there is Sundry free Negroes, Mulattas and Musteens under the age of fifteen Residing within ye township of Staten Island that may probably Be Likely In case of insurrections To Be as mischievous as ye slaves, Therefore I thought it my duty to acquaint Your Honor therewith; the following is a list of them residing in and about ye Village of Staten Island and I do expect the ye other Captains in other parts of ye township will acquaint your Honor of those residing in ye Township. From Your Very Humble Servant.
Thomas Dongan

The covering letter:

May it please your honor in compliance with an act of the assembly and in obedience to your Honors Command That I transmit and accompany of ye Negroes in that part of town that is Staten Island to me I wait your honors further command and shall in the utmost pleasure obey & I remain your Humble and Obedient Servant.
John Chocheron

Master's or Mistress' Name

John Androvet.......2 males Sensor and Jack   1 female Bet
Henry Butler...........female Jude
Paul Micheau........1 male Waterford
Daniel Winant......1 male Tew..............2 females Sarah 7 Bet
Josiah Smith..........1 male Harre............1 female Hanna
William Cornel.......2 males Gem & Sam....1 female...Gin
Aaron Cortileu.......2   males Jacob & Comfort...1 female... Gin
Christopher Billop...2 males...Cato & Mingo......3 females Cate & Bep
Peter Belew......1 male Cubit & Quack......2 females Sare & Luse
Jean Chocheron........3 males, Mink & Jack......2 females Nanne & Dyane
Joseph Bedell......1 male....Quack..........2 females. Grace & Lies
John Voorhees....1 Male... Herry............1 female... Isabel
Cornelius Van Den Veer....2 males... Claus & Isaac... 1 female...Jude
John Simonson.... 1 male. Sam...   2 females ...Emmy & Susan
Peter Van Pelt........2 males...Jafta & Ben....2...females   Roos & Bette
Jacobus Lott........ 1 male, Mink.........1 female, .Peg
Israel Dissoway....2 males, York & Cato...2 females, Gin & Rose
Richard Nesseraue....1 male, Charles &...1 female. ..Jemina
Jacob Corson..... 1 male, Seasor... & .3females, Ame...Gin...Dash
Benjamin Seaman...1 male, Cubit...&...2 females...Hanna. &..Gen
Isaac Butler... 1 male. Andrew......2 females...Ellie & Peg
Benjamin Prall...no male......1 female.... Agnes
Widow, Elizabeth Oostervout...2, females... San & Hester
Widow, Antie Shonmaker...2 males, Mingo, & Jack
Widow... Sarah Seamons, 1.....male, Jack...1 wench, Nancy

Widow...Tedoita Ashoonmaker...1 male, Herry... 1 wench Beg
Abraham Van Wegman...1 male, Segar...1 female...Cate
Jennke Van Eyck...2 males Tam & Jem... 1 female.
Lambert Brink. 2 males Quack & Tam…..   1 female...Mary
Widow... Isabel Van Wagnen...1 male…. Jack 2 wenches Eve & Sara
Widow. Jan Newkirk…1 male Jack…1 wench Susan
John Egbert... 1 male Ham… 1 female …Chat
Matthew Decker 2 males... Sam & Mingo. 1 female. Hester
Abraham Cole 1 male... Mink. .   1 Female. Dyane
Adrian Voorhees 1 male   Sam   & 2 females. Eva & Isabel
Englebart Voorhees 1 male…. & 1 female
John Beek.   1 male   Quack   2 females   Jude & Gin
Joseph Wood   2 females   Nancy & Sarah
Widow Evelyn Van Wagnenin   1 male Prince   1 wench Hester
Widow Johanna Van Leuven   I male Jack
Petrus Bogardus   3 males Sar, Mat, Titus 2 females, Bett & Gin
Evert Bogardus   1 male Tom
James Guyon   2 males Mose & Tom
John Totten   1 male Cuffe   2 females Ester & Gin
Widow, Gertrude Barnes 1 male Henry   1 female Agat
 Abraham Lackman   1 male Sambo   1 female Syne
Elizabeth Nichols   1 male Prince   1 female wench Isabel

The above account is a just account of Negroes, both male and female, above the age of fifteen to the best of my knowledge, belonging to the inhabitants of Staten Island at this time to every person belonging to name.

Mars Chocheron would leave Titus amid the activities at the dock. Hundreds of wretched, little White and Black slave children, recently redeemed from slavery, still hungry, malnourished, many barefoot in the still morning cold wetness, a training ground for hungry children. A new class of laborers, their forms bent already with rickets, their faces pale, most growth already stunted by premature births, unfit to be members of the society or the heads of families.

There would be no reform for generations, from this premature toil of sickness enslaved to labor for generations without proper education and weakened in bodily power. These children could be found in various parts of the city, begging, toiling in shops, at workbenches. Many would be taken aboard the sailing vessels and abused, often tossed overboard for any infraction.

The more fortunate White children may have access to a few years of a carefree and buoyant life, free from care and the burdens and responsibilities of life. The struggles for existence will come soon enough, for parents know how heavy the burden will be. But the parents of a poor child will have no time to indulge in such frivolity or sentiments. He is compelled to harness the little ones to an early cart of labor. He is struggling with poverty, and eager for every little hand to make an addition to his income. The child's wages are important to him, and he does not see the future in this environment to think much of any advantages in education, if he can put them to profitable labors. There is no law protection to minors.

At the docks some children threw stones at the Indian women at the dock trading items from their canoes, which are loaded with skins and fresh meat berries. The Indians wanted metal tools and pots, fishing hooks, Geneva gin and guns. This month ships came from the south carrying tobacco, the Indian women somehow knew the ships and the cargo, and when they would be here. The tobacco from the south was a prized possession.

The Negroes and White men with hooks and nets ropes and boards worked together to unload the coastal commercial, and sea schooners of many different types of cargoes, rum, sugar, bolts of cloth, and fabrics. Grains, iron ingots, glass, hardware. There were wooden cases marked that contained special European items for the rich, shoe buckles, pistols, razor strops, paint, buttons, spurs and stirrups, medical tools. The military and police waited patiently at dockside for their personal shipment. Lest there be items unaccounted for, or hogsheads "accidentally" dropped or broken open before the warehouse men could tabulate their items for storage. Longshoremen would later be sold or traded for drinks or gambling at Hughson's alehouse later in the evening.

His Majesty's Lieutenant Governor, The Honorable James Delancee Esquire was a portly man, with receding hairline, his frame covered by a dark gray worsted coat, a black necktie and a pearl button white shirt, his full beard was separated leaving his chin unshaven with outward pulled mutton chops, his lips seemed to be the only part of his face that moved. It was his eyes that John Chocheron saw. Questioning eyes, patient, questioning eyes. He didn't stand, waving a hand to his left and to his right. He said, "Mr. Horsmanden" and "Mr. Bradley" as he motioned Chocheron to a chair. The two men nodded but remained silent. Chocheron had never met the two men before. He heard about them and met the lieutenant Governor at his inauguration a few yearsp+

ago. "I take it you had a good trip over?" It sounded like an order. "And you have the reports?" /y5Chocheron opened his leather pouch and placed them on the table in front of him.

While he looked at them there was only the sound of metal cart wheels and voices on the streets. And your boy Titus. Yes he is here also, replied Chocheron. He has been mentioned, Mr. Chocheron, he said without taking his eyes from the papers given to him by Chocheron. A small hand movement.

Mr. Chocheron, I am sure you are aware of the recent rash of fires and we still have apprehensions concerning the dangers which still threaten us from conspirators remaining amongst us. We have called a grand jury to look into the most recent matter and I would like you to read of the information providentially discovered. He motioned, his hand barely moving toward the silent man on his right, Daniel Horsmanden, who gave Chocheron several sheets of paper.

"Colonel van der Kolk at the island garrison reports that you have a very peaceful island Mr. Chocheron," he said, "They are well supplied with firewood." Chocheron replied, "Yes, we have good relations with the soldiers and Colonel van der Kolk." There was no mention of the drunken and bored soldiers of the small contingent at the fort. Supplying the soldiers kept them from night raiding the community homesteads. There would be no complaints; a solution would simply add many more soldiers add to the already thin margin of civility.

Chocheron began to read the papers put into his hands by the full-bearded unsmiling man, Daniel Horsmanden, standing in front of him, his eyes forcing him to look at the sheath of papers.

About six o'clock, it was providentially discovered that some fire had been put into the gutter of a shed adjoining to the house where Walter Hyer lived, next the fence of the old Dutch churchyard the wind blowing very hard to north and the gutter laying south some of the coals were blown into the street, which were accidentally discovered by one Hendricks, a carpenter, who was opening the window shutter of a new house he was about to finishing, fronting the end of the street, in order to work; whereupon he immediately went to Hyer's house, and called him out of bed; and they found some live coals in the gutter next to the shed towards the churchyard, and likewise a brands end, or the bark of a brands end, on the other side of the house next to Ratsey's. The mayor being acquainted herewith, he summoned the magistrates to meet this morning at the City Hall, to consult what steps to take in order to discover the incendiaries; and the magistrates being accordingly met, it was proposed but one of them, as no person was suspected, that they should all go and view the house, and inquire what Negroes were in the neighborhood, and their characters, where by the most suspicious might be laid hold of and examined; it was thought most likely happened that the first persons Negro inquired after, was the widow Bradt's. She kept a bake-house nearby, and her yard ran along the rear of Hyer's and Ratset's houses, up to the churchyard fence, where were a heap of oyster shells lying so near Hyer's gutter, that a middle sized man might easily step up and put fire into the gutter, at the north end of it, and from the same yard as easily throw a brands end on the other side of the house next to Ratsey's; upon the inquiry, said that the widow Bradt had only one Negro, Tom, a sort of simple half-witted boy, but however he was ordered to be brought forth; and he appeared upon view to be a lusty well-set fellow, of man's growth, and was afterwards judged, by those who knew him best, and had brought him into the country, to be one or two of twenty years old; his natural countenance was none of the pleasantness, but his appearance on this occasion be up early, and have always have command of fire, which administered some color of suspicion, which, looks to the fellow very much heightened and he was therefore without ceremony committed, in order for the examination in the afternoon, and likewise some of the other Negroes in the neighborhood, who were afterwards discharged.

The magistrates met at three o'clock in the afternoon, and Tom was asked, how he came to put fire to Hyer's house, and who advised him in it and who had assisted him in it.

He directly owned that he put the fire in the gutter himself; and then being particularly examined, his confession was taken down in writing in the presence of the justices, and by them signed.

The Cryer was called and the scribe was summoned to record the confession at the goal.

THE CONFESSION FOLLOWETH

1. I Tom, confesseth and saith, that the Sunday before last, he being in the yard of Captain Jasper Farmer, a playing for pennies with Jack a Negro belonging to said farmer, a Negro belonging to Samuel Dunscombe, a Negro belonging to John Tudor called Peter, and a Negro belonging to Charles Crook (Rob) Jack told him (Tom) that his mistress was cross with him, he should take fire and throw it upon the shed or offdackye (Dutch for shed) and set them on fire; that if he the said Tom did not do it, he (Jack) would poison him; and that Jack told him in this hearing of Peter.

2. That jack told him if he fired the shed, that would fire the house of Captain Ratsey and his mistresses' house also too, and her in it; that Jack told him (Tom) that firing the shed, that would fire the whole town and then the Negroes in town with the Negro that would come from Long Island, would murder all the white people; and that he said this in the presence and hearing of all the Negroes above mentioned.

3. That all the Negroes above mentioned said. That when the Negroes came from Long Island they could do it all at once (that is murder) the white people; and they would help or assist murdering the whites and then they would be rich like the Backarara (Negro language that signifies white people.)

4. That Jack told him (Tom) to throw fire on the offdackye on Monday morning come week; and that he rose very early, about five o'clock, lit a candle, made a fire in the bake house, heated water to melt the sugar, then took a lighted coal of fire and threw it upon the roof of the shed.

5. That immediately after throwing the coal upon the roof, the coal in falling broke into several smaller coals; that the wind blew the sparks into the little street.

6. That soon after he heard the knocking, he was afraid to be discovered, and he ran into his mistress's bake house, and sat himself down at the fire side; that being afraid the he might be followed, he bolted the side door which leads into the yard.

With the finger thumb print on his X mark by Tom.

THIS CONFESSION WAS TAKEN BEFORE THE MAYOR AND SEVERAL ALDERMEN, BY THE RECORDER.

At a further meeting of the justices in the afternoon the Negro Tom (Mrs. Bradt's) further confession was had said:

1. That being at captain farmer's house on Sunday afternoon last with his Negro Jack, and going away, jack followed him Tom, to the gate and then told this Tom, that he should not forget tomorrow morning, (meaning to fire the offdackye or shed) and he should do it because the wind blows hard.

2. That on Monday morning last, about five o'clock, Tom being up, he heard a knocking at his mistress's gate, went and opened it,and found a Negro man there who's name he does not recall, unless it be Jack, who told him to fire the offdackye,immediately. That this Negro brought him a piece of walnut- wood bark which was on fire on one end and not the other end, and that this Negro man put that fire between the house of Captain Ratsey, and Walter Hyer's house; and that this Negro man then ran away when the knocking was at Hyer's house, over the church yard fence.

Taken before the Mayor, recorder and several Aldermen.

1. Tom being confronted with Framers Jack, charged him with what he has said against him in two former confessions, and says. That Michael (Dunscombs) Negro was afterwards proved to be nine miles out of

town Note; [which is no uncommon thing for Negroes to mistake in point of time]. And that Dunscombe Negro said thereupon, OH! fie, why do you put such a little boy upon setting fire? Oh! said jack he is big enough.

2. That his mistress called him up last Monday morning early, about five o'clock to make fire, to melt sugar to make cookies, and that he put fire, and that he put fire to the offdackye (shed) next to the church yard first; and that he had fire in the tongs in one hand, and bark of nut-wood on fire in the other. And the fire in the tongs he threw into the gutter next the church yard and threw the lighted bark afterward on the side of Hyer's house and next Ratsey's; house; and this he says between five and six in the morning; the coal he had in the tongs he got out of the bake house, the nut wood bark he had out of the par lour.

3.   That he put this fire all alone, and that no one was with him or helped him.

4. There was a Negro came for fire that morning. And took it, having knocked at the gate for that purpose, and then went out at the gate again, and he does not know who he was.

TAKEN BY THE RECORDER William Wright, THE FORMER [ONE WEEK LATER]

          The justices met for a fourth time, in order to endeavor to pry further into this mystery of inequity, by examining Tom once more; for as to what has been drawn from him hitherto one cannot give entire credit, as the reader may conclude, excepting as to the instrument of putting the fire ; and it being intimidated by one of the magistrates that Tom's mistress had a strong imagination, (one might say a strange one) that she and her son, if the magistrates would permit their attendance, could prevail on their Negro to speak the whole truth, As there are many of us, there was there was a difference in opinions upon this matter. However at length it was ruled that they should be permitted and were sent for accordingly concerning this matter; and he declared himself at first to the same purpose as to the Negroes he before accused, and as to the same matter and substance with his examination before set forth; but in the close; there was great doubt made of his veracity, being strenuously urged by some go the magistrates, and the master and mistress, to be sure that he spoke nothing but the truth, and being asked weather he was sure that what he had said as to those Negroes was the truth he thereby recanted, and declared what he had related concerning the Negroes he had accused were all lies; and took the whole up himself. And being asked why he did it, and how he came to do so. He answered that he could not help doing it.

Third justice Esquire Mr. D. Horsmanden:

This fellow having thus prevaricated, no use could be proposed to be made of him as evidence to convict others, however he might have chanced to change his note afterwards; and it was therefore determined to bring him upon this trial. But it may be proper to observe that in the interval between this Negroes Tom first and last examination, the Negroes accused by him, were several time closely examined, both separately and face to face, but they all along positively denied everything alleged against them by this Negro Tom concerning the fire.

          But owned their being together at Farmers playing at pennies though it could scarce be imagined the Negro Tom (who was really no fool, nor any of the wisest) had framed this scheme, and made an attempt merely on his own bottom, which should so correspond with the villainous confederacy of last year. His recantation was not taken down in writing, but what is above set forth contains the substance of it.

          At a meeting this day of the justices and five principal free holders of this city, pursuant to the summons and directions of an act of the general assembly of this colony, made in the forth year of his present majesty's reign. Entitled, an act for the more effectual preventing and punishing the conspiracy and the insurrection of Negro and other slaves; for the better regulating them, for the repealing of other acts therein mentioned relating thereto.

Present, Daniel Horsmanden, Esq. mayor, the recorder, justices of the quorum
James Murray, John Chambers, William Smith, James Alexander, Esqrs.
Mr. John Chocheron having been summoned upon this occasion appeared, and excused himself from serving;
Mr James Searle was summoned in his room, and appeared.

"Cryer, have the Negro slave Tom, brought to the bar."

And William Smith, Esq. having been appointed by the justices, council and prosecutor for the king, he delivered into the court articles of accusation against the prisoner.

By this act the owners of slaves have it in their choice to try them by jury, which is attended by some small charge' but on the question proposed, Mrs. Bradt declined. Before the articles were read, the freeholders were sworn, well and truly to try and judge as directed by the act of assembly; and the recorder warned the prisoner in favor of life, that he need not plead guilty to any of the articles, but, never the less, that his several confessions being read to the court, would amount to the full proof, so far as they affected himself.

[The articles were read, and were as followeth]

Tom, Negro man slave belonging to Divertie Bradt of the said city, widow, stands charged and accused.

First, for that said he the said Tom, on Sunday the seventh day of February last past, at the dock ward of this city, did conspire with Jack, a Negro man slave belonging to Jasper Farmer. Michael, a Negro man slave belonging to Samuel Dunscomb, Peter, a Negro man slave belonging to Charles Crooke, of this city, and diverse other Negro slaves unknown, to kill and murder the said Divertie Bradt, Baffie Vandewater, and other of his majesty's liege people within the city of New York.

Second, that he the said Tom, on Monday the fifteenth day of February day last, did willfully put fire to and burn the shed or outhouse of Baffie Vandewater, and the house of Andrew Bradford and Cornelia his wife, in the dock ward of the same city.

Thirdly, for that he said Tom, did on the fifteenth day of February last past
at the city and ward aforesaid, attempt to kill and murder Divertie Bradt and Baffie Vandewater, of this city by setting fire to their houses and burning them in same.

Fourthly, that he the said Tom, on the fifteenth day of February last past, at the city and ward aforesaid did attempt to burn the outhouse of the said Divertie Bradt and the dwelling houses, of Braffie Vandewater and Andrew Bradford and Cornelia his wife, situate in the same ward, and to burn the whole town and city of New York.

To the first article the prisoner pleaded not guilty. To the second, guilty, to the third, not guilty.

And here it may not be improper to observe, that the prisoner distinguished and pleaded to the three several articles directly, without hesitation, which seems to be further argument that he had more sense than some people were willing to allow him.

Crier: "Proclamations for silence and witnesses."

Witnesses for the king have sworn, Hendricks and Hyer.

Hendricks said, he discovered the fire to fall out of the gutter as he was looking from a window into the street; and that thereupon he went and knocked at Hyer's door, and called him out of bed, and they searched and found coals on each side of the house; some in the gutter next to the shed, towards the church yard, and some on the side next to Ratsey's house.

Hyer said, that the gutter next to the church yard was burnt black in the spot, or part of the gutter where the coals were lying.

The criminal's confessions read as before set forth.

And the judges further informed the court, that the criminal at his last examination, though at the beginning of it persisted in the same story as to the accusation of Negro Jack (Farmers Negro) prompting and proposing to him to put the fire.   and as to the other Negroes present at the two meetings at Farmers house, advising and threatening him if he did not. yet in the close he declared the truth, that all he said was related to them, were lies, and that he put the firs of his own head, and being asked by the court why he did it, and how he came to do so ? he answered; he could not help doing it. And being asked by the court weather he did not make such confessions as he had been just read? he answered yes. He was then bit to tell the same story over again as he had told to the justices at the first three examinations, and likewise at the first part of the forth and last; and he repeated the same over again, as it were in the same words; and when he had done, being asked weather what he had then said as to the other Negroes was true? He answered, no, it was all lies, and took all again upon himself, and owned his recantations to be the truth.

"Cryer, have the prisoner removed from the courtroom."

The audience being ordered to withdraw, the prisoner taken from the bar and the courtroom cleared; William Wright, the recorder advised the justices and freeholders, and having taken their opinions, which were unanimous upon that occasion, the doors were ordered to be opened, and the prisoner brought back, Clerk Wright proceeded to admonition and sentence, as followeth:

> You, Tom the criminal at the bar, hearken to what is now to be said to you. You stand convicted of willfully putting fire to and burning the shed or outhouse of Baffie Vandewater within this city. The evidence of your guilt has stood principally upon your own confession before your trial. Which you now confirm by your plea; and indeed this is of the strongest proof, the highest conviction that can be; for this single fact you deserve death; and though the court proceeds to give judgment aainst you upon this article, yet your offense is of a complicated nature, i.e. consists of many particulars, all tending to one and the same monstrous and execrable purpose; the murdering of inhabitants of this city.
>
> The hellish scheme you have engaged in, as you have confessed before the magistrates over and over again, I think no more than four several times was, to set Walter Hyer's house afire, and as you concluded and proposed that would consequently set the next house Ratsey's on fire, and that would set your mistress's house a fire, and burn your mistress in it; and then that would burn the whole town, then Long Island Negroes were to come over to the assistance of the Negroes here, and they in conjunction, were to murder all the white people of this city, and in order that your malicious, hellish purposes might effectually take place, the fire was to be put, as it actually was, when the wind blew hard that in all probability, any attempt to extinguish the flames, might be in vain.
>
> And such a trusty agent have you been in the devils service, that in the prosecution of this infernal conspiracy, you did actually take the first step proposed, in order to accomplish this diabolical purpose, by putting fire to Hyer's house on both sides of it.
>
> All this that I have said, you have confessed over and over again, and in this we must take your word. It was a merciful act of providence that your designs were timely prevented, that you were committed upon suspicion only, and that thereupon the truth was bolted out from you.
>
> It was rumored without doors, that you were an half-witted fellow, a boy I think they called you, though you are said to be two or three or twenty years old, and indeed one would think hardly anybody but arrant fools, or mad folks, would engage in such chimerical, wicked, villainous and dangerous projects, which must most probably end in the confusion and destruction of the wretches concerned, as you have found by woeful experiences in the many examples of these miserable creatures of your color that expired in flames and at the gallows, the last summer, for the like detestable offences, and yet so hardened and stupefied are ye in villainy, that no examples though ever so severe, no terrors of punishment can affright ye, but ye will even defy the gallows and commit your bodies to the flames, rather than not risk the chance of gratifying your savage, cruel, and insatiable thirst for blood.
>
> But, never the less, to convince one that you are not that half-witted fellow, as some would represent you, you showed some cunning, as it should seem you thought after your commitment, in providing for your own safety and preservation, by laying this scheme upon and accusing others, as having prompted you to this mischief, hoping thereby, as it must be supposed, to be admitted in evidence against them, and so save your own life. This was thought too deep for a fool, or a half witted fellow, and indeed, from my observation of you, during the course of your several examinations, I could

discover no reason for an insinuation, that you had less sense than those of the most common rank of Negroes, but that your qualifications for mischief are inferior to none of them, that you have sense enough to distinguish between good and evil, that your own conscious could direct you what was fit and proper to be done, and what not, you yourself, buy your own confessions, have given most convincing proofs, for when as you all along said till the last time, when you recanted and declared that what you had told concerning the other Negroes was all lies, I say as you told the story, your mistress was cross with you, and you must set fire to the house and the offdackye. And you upon Negroe Jack's proposal was, no my mistress no cross with me, my mistress good enough, what should I set fire for, you may do it yourself, or words to that effect, that thereupon Jack insisted that you should set fire, and the reason why you at last agreed to do it. Was it because, you said Jack threatened to poison you if you did not. That is what we call natural reason, and shows such a measure of it, or there is such a chain of consequence drawn by it, that supposing it is your own scheme, as you now take all upon yourself.

You can be no fool, or half-witted fellow, and if it was the shame of others proposed to yourself, your very repetition of it, your telling that story as you have done so often over and over again, almost in the same words, shows that you do not want understanding, but that you have made very bad use of it, and acted against that light which God almighty has given you to employ to better purposes, so that here, I say in these instances of the very proposal and answer, you give convincing proof that you were conscious for other words that you yourself was sensible and knew, that what you was going to attempt was wrong, was wicked, and what you ought not to do, weather Negro Jack was the person that proposed you to do we cannot tell, but that somebody did, and that you did not do it altogether of your own head, I am fully persuaded. But if no one but the Devil and you contrived it, then so much must be drawn from it as is sufficient to show that you acted against the light of your own conscience, your own reason, by your own way of arguing, and out of your own mouth you are judged. How you cam at last to withdraw your accusation against those Negroes, you for four examinations running, charged with advising you, and being concerned with you, in this villainous plot, I know not, nor can I account for it, without the devil had a mind to leave you in the lurch at last.

You Negroes are treated here with great humanity and tenderness, ye have no hard task masters, ye are not laden with too heavy burdens, but your work is moderate and easy, you say, your mistress no cross with you, she very good, or she good enough, and yet with small persuasion you were prevailed upon to destroy her in flames, such worthless, detestable wretches are many, it may be said most, of your complexion, that no kindness can oblige ye, there is no such untowardness, as it should seem, in the very nature and temper of ye, that ye grow cruel by too much indulgence. So much are ye degenerated and debased below the dignity of human species, that even the brute animals may upbraid you, for the ox knoweth his owner, and the ass his masters crib, even the very dogs will by their actions express gratitude to the hand that feeds them, their thankfulness, they will fawn and fondle upon their masters, nay, if anyone should attempt to assault them, they will defend them from injury, to the upmost of their power. Such is the fidelity of these dumb beasts, but ye, the beasts of the people, though ye are clothed and fed, and provided with all the necessities of life, without care, in requital of your benefactors, in return for blessings ye give curses, and would scatter firebrands, death and destruction around them, to destroy their estates and butcher their persons. Thus monstrous is your gratitude!! But thanks to almighty God, that his wondrous and merciful providence, your hellish devices are discovered, and now you are to receive the just reward for your labors.

And since justice has at last overtaken you, I shall in compassion to you poor soul, which is in the utmost, the greatest danger of being forever miserable, give you a word of advice, in order to prevail on you to make these last few moments you have to remain in this world, to the best advantage, for be not deceived, there is another world after this, and there is a God above who has a clear view of all your actions, and knows there very secrets of your hearts, and will require at your hands according to that degree of reason which he has given you, and though your body be consumed in the flames here on earth, this punishment of short continuance, yet your soul will never die, that must survive the body, either to be forever happy or forever miserable, according to your actions here.

What a horrible expectation must your then!! That you would murder and destroy without mercy, nay without provocation, what reasonable hopes can you entertain at the hands of the God of mercy and justice, who will reward every man according to his works, they that have done good shall be forever happy, they that have done evil shall be cast into a sea of fire and brimstone, to be forever tormented with the devil and his accursed spirits, from hence there will be no returning, no coming out again, but there will be bitter weeping and wailing, and gnashing of teeth, time without end.

Now to avoid this dreadful everlasting punishment, the only method you can take, is to make the best use of the time allowed you between this and your execution, by bringing yourself to a due sense of your guilt, your, heinous crying sins, truly repent you of, and be heartily sorry for your wickedness, and earnestly to pray to God almighty for forgiveness, and this is not all, but that your repentance may be sincere, you must make that little that amends which is in your power, towards us you have designed and conspired to murder and destroy, by discovering all those persons whom you know to be any ways engaged or concerned in this hellish plot, that you may thereby prevent all further mischief. Upon these conditions only can you have any reasonable or well-grounded hope or expectation of the salvation of your soul, and avoiding the dreadful eternal punishment against which I have forewarned you?

And now it were but just, that the same mischief which you have intended for others shall fall upon your own pate, but the court has had some regard to your confession, as you acknowledged your guilt on your first examination, they have adjudged you to be hanged, otherwise you would have been burnt. And therefore the sentence which I am to pronounce against you is that the court then ordered the execution to be on Friday next between the hours of ten and one. But his honour the lieutenant governor, by advice of his majesties' council, thought it proper to reprieve him to the Friday seven night.

The Negro Tom was executed. At the gallows he declared, that now he was sure he must die, he would tell the truth, and said that Farmers Negro Jack, Duyckink's Negro Philip, William Gilbert's Cuffee, and David Van Horns Negro Corah, were playing at pennies with the white boy Titus, these were the persons that put him upon setting the fire.

Recorder William Wright reported the execution to Judge Horsmanden who was not present at the hanging wanted to hear it concise and clear.

Negro Tom was executed at the gallows at the stroke of ten, a sturdy boy, sand weights at both ankles were helpfully located,he stepped off the wagon with no kicking, some urination was noticed after ten minutes. Immediately after Tom's execution, Cuffee, Corah and Philip, were apprehended and strictly apprehended and strictly examined by the mayor and the recorder, but nothing could be got out of them, and released.

John Chocheron and Titus were at the warehouse long room, with tellers and clerks, selecting provisions from a long list that would require an additional barge trip back to Richmond. He had hired a teamster and wagon to transport the goods to the dock and a watchman with a long pike, until there was a barge to transport it to Richmond, Staten Island. Titus was aware of the strange feeling he had since Mars Chocheron returned from the court house. He said little to Titus, and Titus asked no questions. Titus was aware that Mars Chocheron was upset; perhaps he was angry not to be able to work with his one arm, at hauling the bags to the wagon while directing the agent and discussing the current prices. There was a crushing taxation now for goods imported from Europe, the teamster a toothless, gruff leather creased face, holding a long stem pipe with this rubber lips, brushing his horse not wanting to assist loading said that "we are just falling into ruin" and that the government was working in league with Popists to get money. Chocheron did not answer, allowing the man to mutter under his breath. After the conspiracy trials last year, there was a pervasive sense of anxiety that the whole jerry-built system would break down and shatter.

The docks became alive at dawn with bodies and sounds, this coordinated intensity and chaos would not cease until the late afternoon bells and whistles signaled a halt to prevent privileged plunder after dark, the usual working time was from 6 am until 6 pm. The unloading of a ship required the coordinated labors of many men, black and white working together calling, signaling, pushing, heaving, and rigging cargo to be transported to the warehouses.

The slaves had no rights or liberty, or property at all, they were rented by their owners. Some slaves depended on the customs agents for money, and were used as infiltrators to watch for damages and spillages, which became income for workers. However their jobs were short, lived due to their being maimed, regularly by riggings that caused sever injuries below decks.

Most whites were Irish, Scottish, English, most were illiterate, exsailors, criminals, felons running from debt or prosecution, a floating human population that made their way at trades that required physical labors and freedom to move aboard a ship when under duress, they worked easily with and among the port slaves,

The tobacco hogsheads weighed from 300 pounds to more than one thousand pounds and loading them required a skill to stow them below deck for cargos were known to sink a ship when cargo was not chocked properly resulting from the rolling and pitching at sea. If wages were not paid on time, pilferages increased proportionately, this was considered their rights to remove cargo that would pay their bills at the local alehouse or barter it for sex, food or a bed.

"Socking" was an old custom and tobacco was high priority, it was a right to take because they wanted it not to fill their pipes but to fill their stomachs, to sell or to barter. The creation of this unspoken custom was for survival. Products of the transatlantic trade and commerce lead to accepted forms of behavior and customary appropriation tolerated.

The dock work was dangerous and hard, it took a tremendous toll on men and the ships that had to be prepared for open sea voyages that could last for three months, sails needed to be opened to repaired, rigging needed to be stabilized in the blocks, caulking at the waterlines had to be preformed at the docks, derricks put up for slinging timber aboard for new ship masts of hardwood stout chestnut and oak from the new world to the old had to be preformed by human cooperative manual labor at any costs. Broken bones, rope burns lacerations were common.

"I will have to leave you here, Titus, until I return," he said suddenly.

Examples of how poorly Black history has been reported and preserved can be found in every book that purports to present it. Each of these books begins with an introduction explaining that the human sources of the information may have been biased and that the story is only as reliable as the witness and the author. A 2003 publication, **The Great New York Conspiracy, a History of the Negro Plot of 1741**, by Peter Charles Hoffer, begins with an introduction that explains that the events described therein have not been elaborated in American history textbooks, yet it reflects an important part of New York City history saw racism and anti-Catholicism fuel popular hysteria and mass executions. When slave populations soared to 20% of the city's population in the early 1700's, a series of arsons and burglaries quickly became the basis for exaggerated fears and allegations of a conspiracy involving Blacks and Whites. Most of the accounts of the trial itself come from Daniel Horsmanden, a British attorney who recorded the testimony in his own hand, but who had his own agenda and biases throughout the conspiracy trial. As the book demonstrates, it is clear that conflicting testimony was ignored, crucial questions were ignored or unanswered, and pleas of innocence were dismissed. Hoffer appropriately asks whether we should consider Horsemanden's testimony as trustworthy or discard it as that of an hysterical partisan. His account is an attempt to justify the actions of the court, of which he was a leading member, by proving that some White people in conjunction with some Negroes and other slaves planned to burn the city of New York and murder its inhabitants. Similarly, all official accounts of slave rebellions are biased in favor of those writing them, the prosecuting slave owners. Nevertheless, Hoffer reminds us that "behind all the screens of bias and flawed perception, something actually happened. Hoffer includes the name of every slave who stood trial, gave evidence, or was found not culpable by a grand jury. He also gave slaves who only had a first name the names of their master rather than assigning ownership, such as, by saying "John Varick's Caesar." He concludes that much of what Horsemanden wrote was at least partially true, albeit tainted with his own prejudice and agenda, and lets the reader draw his own conclusions.

I went to the Library of Congress and filled out a reading room request, then waited for the book about the 1741 conspiracy to be delivered to the desk clerk.   (Little did I know at that time that I had one of the very few original printed books about this incident in New York in my hands). It was a well-worn, red leather, gold embossed copy. I would find later that there were very few printed, and that the topic and the issues were not read by or available to the general public. There was no historical research about this New York conspiracy. I would find reading the old English font difficult, but I also found that as I read the story, it was much more difficult to put down, inviting me to get inside, encouraging me not to abandon it, to keep at it, which I did. I will never be able to explain why, but this was one that rendered me unable to concentrate on anything else. This book gave me a contact high feeling, holding this venerable copy in my hands. I spent the rest of the day reading it and, from time to time, feeding coins into a machine to make page copies.

The library would be closed in a few minutes and I knew that I would return the next day to read and copy more, and I put a hold on the book until I could return. When I did return a few days later, I was told the book was now in the process of being made available in the electronic file. I was frustrated, there was nothing I could do but follow the written instructions the clerk gave me. Electronic File Info.: gemic 1st0063 http://hdl.loc.gov/loc.gdc/gcmisc.1st0063. The clerk wrote "hot link to American Memory citation," and printed out 4 additional pages and passed them across the table to me. "OK?" she said. I smiled and said, "Oh yes, thanks," before dressing again for the cold outdoors. I had no idea how I would ever again have access to that book, and I did not have access to a computer to get into the electronic file. I would stuff them away until some inner need surfaced to move again. That was November 6, 2003.

The subject matter and the year and the voice would not leave me.
I taped the cover of the book to my desk, although the old English font was difficult to read. It was first printed in New York by James Parker at the new Printing Office in 1744, entitled, **A Journal of the PROCEEDINGS in The Detection of the Conspiracy**, formed by some White people in conjunction with Negro and other Slaves, for Burning the city of New York in America, And Murdering the Inhabitants, Which Conspiracy was partly put in Execution, by Burning His Majesty's House in Fort George, within said City, on Wednesday the Eighteenth of March 1741. And setting fire to several Dwellings and other Houses there, within a few Days succeeding, and by another Attempt made in the Perfection of the same infernal Scheme, by putting fire between two other Dwelling Houses within said City on the Fifteenth Day of February 1742 which was accidentally and timely discovered and extinguished.

The following translation from the book itself is difficult because of the old English word usage, printed font, and speech patterns, and it is thus introduced by way of dialogue.

CONTAINING

I. a NARRATIVE OF THE Trials, Condemnations, Executions, and behavior of the several Criminals. At the Gallows and Stake, with their speeches and confessions, with Notes, Observations and Reflections occasionally interpreter throughout the Whole.

2. An APPENDIX, wherein it is set forth some additional Evidence concerning the said Conspiracy and Conspirators, which has come to Light since their Trials and Executions.

3. List of several persons (whites and blacks) committed on Account of the Conspiracy, and the several Criminals executed, and of those transported with the Places whereto.

By the Recorder of the City of New York

Quid facient, Domini, audent, cum talia Fures Virg. Ecl

NEW – YORK

Printed by James Parker, at the New printing Office 1744

THE

NEW- YORK CONSPIRACY

or a

HISTORY OF THE NEGRO PLOT,

with the

JOURNAL OF THE PROCEEDINGS

AGAINST THE

CONSPIRITORS AT NEW YORK IN THE YEARS

1741 – 2.

TOGETHER WITH

SEVERAL INTERESTING TABLES,

Containing the Names of the White and Black Persons arrested on the account of the Conspiracy- the times of their trials- their Sentences-their Executions by Burning and Hangings—Names of those Transported, and those Discharged.

With a variety of other useful and highly interesting matter

BY DANIEL HORSMANDEN, ESQ

NEW-YORK

PRINTED AND PUBLISHED BY SOUTHWICK & PELSUE,

No. 3 New- Street.

1810

I got a copy of this book with the notes written by Daniel Horsmanden. And what I read made me sick. I had to return to the 250 or more pages again and again to read it a second and a third time, and even a fourth time, before trying to write this. I gave a copy to white friends and to black friends to read, and later asked them what they thought, and how they felt afterward to discuss it with me. For years afterward, simply thinking of this book I would become ill, and unkind to friends and family around me. I read it as a slave and as a black man, as a white man, and as a white woman who owned slaves. I tried desperately to be in the mind and body and life of those that had gone to his or her death. I became a white woman slave owner and a white woman with a black slave. I wanted to be as close to this time frame as I possibly could get. I looked for and found other books and papers to bring the characters to life. The slaves had no voice, they answered to prepared questions, they could not cross examine anyone who spoke against them. A slave was chattel, bought and sold, property as horses and oxen. There is little else to find about them.

I wanted to know Daniel Horsmanden. His thunderous voice was heard through the long pages of the trial of conspirators; his writings are the only record that survives in such detail. The city could not afford a recording secretary.

Here I was, a black man in New York, marginally educated in reading, writing, and arithmetic, and I am fascinated in reading and researching the past.

I wanted for many years to know more about my family and how we came to be here on this island in a semi-segregated community of blacks and whites. The nearest library was in Port Richmond and after many visits I could only find any information regarding blacks on the island were in two huge volumes written by whites who's titles were 'historians' Charles W. Leng B.Sc. Director of The Staten Island Institute of Arts and Sciences; Local Historian for the Borough of Richmond; Research Associate, American Museum of Natural History, contributor to Various Historic and Scientific papers, etc. and William T. Davis President of the Staten Island Historical Society; Vice-President of the Staten Island Institute of Arts and Sciences ; Author of Days Afield on Staten Island, " Homestead Graves ", Staten Island Names, Ye Olde Names and Nicknames'; The Conference House or Billopp House"; Etc. These huge volumes No 1 and the other volume No 2 STATEN ISLAND AND ITS PEOPLE, A History 1609 – 1929 published in 1930. By the Lewis Historical Publishing Company In 1930.

These books have become the foremost bibles, words for historians and others researching the history of Staten Island. Ask a librarian or a curator of island history and you will be told to read these for a firm knowledge of Staten Island.

There have been very few historians or researchers or scholars of Staten Island history that have recorded much of the early history of New York City the island or any major case in the accounts of the colonial era. No textbooks have written about the case that I found as a neglected forgotten part history, what I did not know was that Staten Island has always found itself on the begging (Paupers) end of history, far into the 20th century when a wave of secession occurred politically, and now into the 21st century the recurring theme returns. Few Black or White American, historians have opened this primary source of information about the administration of the City of New York and the English Colonial law. Most formal dated state records have been lost to fire or destruction much had been returned to England after the Revolution.

There has been no interest it seems in the episode of 1741. Of slaves rising up demanding dignity, knowing if there was a failure they would be put to death, which by reading this document was usually the case. It was interesting to me that whites also lived here in the first recorded instance of 'diversity' in the face of inhuman conditions. This historic time frame in the building of what became the biggest metropolis in the new world New York City has become a neglected part of history. Diversity it would seem was equal at the bar of justice when more than one hundred and fifty slaves and twenty two whites were detected and prosecuted hanged, burned at the stake, in what the attorney general called the most heinous barbaric, crimes in the colony. And this book published in 1744 is more than a journal of those proceedings.

In the meantime I asked an antiquarian book dealer friend Bill Brown living in Kingston, New York to help me locate information to research the history of New York and the Conspiracy Trials of 1741. He was instrumental in providing me with impressive volume's and tapes, books and information so much that I was amazed at the mysterious transformation of knowledge that played such an important part of the early history of New York, and New York City.

My need to know, my need to understand who I am, and what I am, and where I belong in the sum total of these long decades of my life. And it's time to get specific. Working on the issues of this book has taken me to many countries, and many years to gather the pieces of the puzzle that all Black Americans deal with. Especially Black men. This makes me I believe obsessive in pursuit of the initial "who am I?"

And I realize that I am showing signs of wear and tear at the very seems of daily life, but I am lucky to have this time to set it down in words that are mine and mine alone, and I use this as delicately as a pair of old well worn slippers. I know there is a well used format for writers, and a well documented format for presentation, and a well used intellectual wording cosmetically wise.

Another summary of the events:

This monstrous conspiracy began on Saint Patrick's Day, 1741 this conspiracy was designed to destroy the city of New York by fire and massacre the inhabitants. It was a Sunday and most black men and women slaves were free to go to church or gather together to socialize. There were a number of fires that burned a great portion of the Fort George, the main government house of the royal governor.

Many of the buildings and houses were wooden structures and close together with split shingle wooden roofs three building were burned and some five days later more fires threatened the entire town and a week later there were more fires. And some slaves were seen removing the contents of the houses that were burned. A stable attached to a house burned the next day and a White woman Abigail Earle, was at her shutters when she overheard two slaves walking by say "" Fire, Fire, ""Scorch, Scorch and Burn "by and by. Abigail then told her neighbor Lydia George who said she knew one of the slave men named Quack. She then repeated that to one of the Alderman who instructed the magistrates to have a meeting. While the meeting was being arranged there was another fire at the home of Sergeant Burns near the fort. Another fire the same day at the house of Agnes Hilton and not far from the slave market on Wall Street. There was some still hot coals burning in a hemp rope and placed at the shingles of the Hilton house. This finding was now seen to be deliberate and it was thought to be set by one of the Spanish Negroes that Agnes Hilton purchased the week before. They were a group of seven Blacks taken as spoils of war and condemned to slavery. The Spanish blacks were taken into custody and remanded at the goal jail) and questioned. And as they were questioned there was another fire at the Phillips store house, as flames ran up the shingle roofs of the old wooden roofed building and extinguished. The next day there were four fires in different parts of the city. It was now expected that these fires were not accidental, even when some chimney were made of wood and dauber.

The rumor was these fires were part of a plot increased when a slave named Cuffee, who belonged to Adolph Phillips, was seen running from the scene of one of the fires. A frightened group gathered at the well for water with their slaves noticed there was an unusual silence, and there was no eye contact an indication now suspected that these were confirmations of something evil. A cry went up that the Negroes were rising! Some said they saw a Black man running from the store house and jumping over several fences, they said he was Cuffee, the Negro slave of Colonel Adolf Phillips. Cuffee was caught drawing water at the well and brought to the jail by the crowd.

Many others began to take their slaves to the jail for questioning by the magistrates. Many of the White citizens began to question their slaves and ordered them to be inside at nightfall or be subject to sale. The governor also ordered a night watch of soldiers from the fort who were armed and assigned to shoot any black on sight after dark. A slave found intoxicated at the pier was trundled off to jail and forced to say where he had consumed the Geneva, the Dutch gin liquor, he said he had taken a dram or two, but would go no further. Rewards were offered and pardons for anyone who could help capture the arsonists, 100 pounds for Whites and 20 pounds and manumission for slaves, and 20 pounds for their masters and 45 pounds for free blacks, mulattoes, and Indians. There were now printed warnings and posted that slaves were intending to revolt. And that this board will issue their warrant to the chamberlain, or treasurer of this corporation for payment of such sum as any person, by virtue of such proclamation, shall be entitled unto. And that the mayor of such city and recorder wait on his honor the lieutenant governor, and acquaint him with such resolution of this duly elected board. The mayor and the recorder/cryer William Wright waited on his honor accordingly, and a copy of the order was also delivered to him.

The fears of fires and fears of strangers lurking about the city and seamen from the ships were becoming targets of suspicion. The aldermen proposed a curfew and a strict watch on establishments serving slaves and indigenous 'others' not being recognized from the community. They also proposed and gained approval from the magistrates and councilmen and constables to search each ward on the south side of the water pond. The following Monday was fixed upon for making the experiment.

The scheme was communicated to the governor, and his honor thought fit to order the militia out that day in aid of the magistrates who were dispersed throughout the city, and sentries posted at each ends of the street to guard and exits and entries during the search, with orders to stop all suspected persons that shall be observed carrying bags or bundles, or removing goods from house to house in order for their examination. All this was to be kept secret until the plans were put into execution. On Saturday last the general search was made, but there were not any goods discovered which were said to have been lost, nor were there any strange lodger or suspicious person detected. But there were some things found in the possession of one slave Cuba and his wife Robin, slaves belonging to Mr. Chambers which the alderman thought improper for a slave, and unbecoming for a slave to possess, which made him suspect that they were not come honestly by, and therefore ordered the constable to take them in possession, and to be reserved for further inquiry, and these two Negroes were committed to the jail.

After the second week in prison Mr. Chambers was summoned to the magistrate's office where he was told about the night wailings of his slave in the jail. He was told that the recorder Mr. Simeon Johnson was unable to get to give him any information for the coming trial of theft. And as to her coming by such materials. She has refused food and at night she is said to be calling out to "him." "I am Christian," she said. As her body began to consume itself, Robin began to recite passages from "the book," over and over as her liver stored glucose used up her body fats and proteins. Cuba was not allowed to see her while begging Simeon Johnson the recorder that he would do anything he wished if he were allowed to go to her. Robin's full life as a fastidious house keeper, cleaner, and servant of Mr. Chambers and his second wife, Annabelle, was now a slovenly aggressive Negro slave refusing food which she said was poisonous and now in the grip of delusions. Cuba gave the recorder several coins to let him bring water to Robin who's famine was now beyond consuming any sustenance, she took the crockery jar of water from Cuba pouring it on her head she said that she was now being washed in the blood, as she reached under her long soiled dress to bring to her face a hand covered with her blood.

Her howl became a moan and the constable was instructed to enforce an order for her to be quiet, but he failed to do so. Mr. Chambers was taken to the jail by the constable and the recorder Mr. Johnson. He asked Robin where she had gotten the cloth and the clothing. She said she made it long time herself for her gong home clothes, and the doilies were made of coffee sacks and the way she was taught by Mrs. hambers, Annabelle, and she often gave them as gifts and sold some to get more money for colorful threads, from Mrs. Hogg shop, she said the tool she used was made by the cobbler at the Fly, and she gave him several dollies afterward, for payment. She said that she was baptized and she wanted only one thing for she was going "home," and that was to be dressed in her fine clothes she had made, for more than ten score years.

Recorder Wright carefully noted; the constable did not strike her head, nor use his lash, she did not ask for any treatment, she would be buried in her going home clothes Friday morning. Recorder Mr. William Wright recorded the death as self starvation.

Mr. Chambers, Robins master, and Cuba her husband who had been released from prison placed her needles threads, lies, and check linen cloth, buttons and carved shells, her church book into the casket. Slave women left their jobs stood silently on the gravel sidewalk, where they were joined by several other Negro men and women walked together behind the wagon to the Negro burying ground. The iron wheels the only sound on the main cobble stone road which ended at the tilled field of tall grass, and other marked graves and mounds with stones and crosses where they placed the wooden box carefully to the ground and began to dig silently, there was no other ceremony. Mr. Chambers turned the wagon about and returned to the city. Cuba would return and place a marker after ten required days. (It was reported by the Anglican Priests that 'heathenish rituals' were preformed at the burial grounds) very often the private Negro ceremonies became even more secretive and many Negroes did not know when to be present. Many graves were ordered dug up and opened by the magistrates to check for valuable items that may have been stolen and buried by slaves from their masters.

One week later, the lieutenant governor, by and with the advice of his majesties council, issues a proclamation, therein reciting the aforementioned order and resolution of the common council, promising the rewards agreeable thereto.

Between the sixth and seventeenth instant, a great deal of time had been spent at the magistrates in the examination of the Negroes in custody, upon account of the fires, but nothing could be got out of them. Cuff, Mr. Phillips Negro was closely interrogated, but he absolute denied knowing anything of the matter. He said that he had been at home all that afternoon, from the time he returned home from Hiltons fire, where he had been to assist to carry water buckets. And that he was at home when the bell rang for the fire at Colonel Phillip's warehouse. It appeared that at inquiry and the examination of witnesses, that he, at his masters orders, had been sawing wood that afternoon with a White boy, and that his master had come home from dinner, he took him off that work, and set him to sew on the vane aboard his sloop, and that he left him but little before the bell rang for the fire, and that the white boy Wilson stood by him to see him sew it, and when the alarm of the fire was, and it was supposed to at his masters storehouse it was said, Cuff asked weather he would go out with the buckets, and that he should answer, he had enough of being out, in the morning. Some of the neighbors also declared, that they had seen him looking over his masters door but a little before the bell rung, but an old man that had known Cuffee for several years, deposed that he had seen him at the fires at the storehouse, and that he had stood next to him, there seemed to be some objection against the mans evidence, it was thought that he had been mistaken, being very near sighted. Upon examination, it was found that he could distinguish colors, and he described the clothes he had on, and moreover he declared, he spoke to him, and asked him, why he did not hand the buckets, and that there-upon, he answered him, and did hand water, and that he knew his voice.

There was very strong proof that he was the Negro that leaped out of the window of one of the storehouses as the fire was extinguished, and most of the people drawn away on the new alarm of the fire, that he was seen to leap over several of the garden fences, and run home in great haste. Upon the whole it was thought proper that Cuff should remain in confinement, to await further discovery.

The city jail confinement was used to convince any inmate to confess. The jail was located in the dank earth beneath the city hall, the seat of the city council. The windowless spaces were was dug for the foundation of the building above, and now it's timbered wooden walls held spaces for men and women prisoners. The jailers were yeoman, tough large hands and bones, farmers, few words were need to control prisoners. They did not have firearms, their weapons were stout hand hewn oak clubs, and horsehide whips. The iron gate was made by a blacksmith, installed with huge hinges hammered into the timbers secured by chain and anchor bolt, with no lock. Food and bedding was supplied by family or friends, or pay to the jailers, or the prisoner went without. In winter many had frostbite, in summer it was sweltering. In winter if firewood was available they survived, they were at the mercy of the court. Many survived simply by confessing and accepting freedom to supply labor for the city until their day in court.

This book in my hands was very rare, and there have been no textbooks in the history of New York that have been printed for academic or historical study. It is I will find just one source of Historical Amnesia, that I would find again and again in my need to know more about that city in which I was born and the place of the black people in the building of the United States. This book was originally published in 1744, revised and printed again in 1745 by the author at that time by an English born lawyer Daniel Horsmanden. Horsmanden wore many hats at the time of this "trial" he was one of three judges and he became the recorder because there was no one on record to take the task. I would find his name in many accounts, official and unofficial. Written accounts of this trial were also taken by Justice Frederick Philipse, and delivered to the governors office.

Daniel Horsmanden was born in London in 1694 and managed to get his legal training at the Innes Court in London, he was born of little money, however he had many connections, and married into a wealthy family which records show he divorced because of his wife's adultery. He then came to America in 1732 or 1735.

He served several years in patronage political positions which advanced his political career and records of 1764 appears as Honorable Daniel Horsmanden Chief Justice of the Province of New York. He was described as a strange and mostly unattractive figure. He was also described by his fellow Jurist William Smith Esquire as a righteous man.

I would get to know Daniel Horsmanden personally after reading many books about his role in the proceedings.

The fires frightened everyone in the city; it created tension and created fights and swearing and accusations, and the removal of household belongings to safer places north of the city. This created more tensions because there were those that told of having belongings stolen and the need to have more slaves placed to guard homes. The entire city of New York would soon be more overwhelmed by a robbery reported on February 28th 1740.

Recorder notes from the constable's office reported a robbery committed at the home of one Mr. Robert Hogg a merchant with business on Marckvelt Straet

Where diverse pieces of linen, several silver coins, chiefly Spanish medals and other goods for a total of more than sixty pounds. The robbery and the persons involved will appear more fully in the flowing text and trials. A white young man of seventeen called Wilson was a sailor aboard the Man-O-War ship The Flamborough stationed in the harbor. Wilson became friendly with two White servants who lodged at Mr.

Hogg's house, Wilson became a regular visitor and that gave him access to the Hogg residence and store on Marckvelt Straet. Wilson became acquainted with Negroes from the city who were seemed to be suspicious characters. Caesar, a slave belonging to John Vaarck, a baker. Prince a slave belonging to Mr. John Auboyneau a merchant, And Cuffee a slave belonging to Mr. Adolph Phillips, Esq.

This reported robbery would eventually connect the fires and the conspiracy; it would be the basis for this journal and the narrative following for more than a full year afterward.

The following translations are from the original notes: **The New York Conspiracy** by Daniel Horsmanden. Sworn before recorders Simeon Johnson and William Wright.

The Thursday before this robbery was committed, Wilson came to Mr. Hogg's shop, with one of the man of war's people, to buy some check linen, and having bargained for some, part of the money offered in payment, was of Spanish coin, and Mrs. Hogg opening her bureau to change the money, pulled out a draw in the view of Wilson, wherein were a considerable quantity of milled Spanish pieces of eight: she soon reflected that she had done wrong in exposing the money to an idle boy in that manner, who came so frequently to her house, and immediately shut up the bureau again, and made a pretense of sending the money out to a neighbor's to be weighed.

Mrs. Hogg's apprehensions happened to be right; for this having a sight of the money, was charmed with it, and, as it seems, wanted to be fingering of it. He told his comrades the before named Caesar, Prince and Cuffee, where they might have a fine booty, if they could manage cleverly to come at it; he said it was at Hogg's house in the Broad street; his wife kept a shop of goods, and sold candles, rum, molasses, etc.

The Negroes cached at the proposal, and the scheme was communicated by them to John Hughson, who kept a public house by the North River, in this city, a place where numbers of Negroes used to resort, and be entertained privately (in defiance of the laws) at all hours, as appeared afterwards, and will be shewn at large in the ensuing sheets. Thither they used to bring such goods as they stole from their masters or others, and Hughson, his wife and family, received them; there they held a consultation with Hughson and his family, how they should act, in order to compass the attainment of this booty.

The boy (Wilson) told them the situation of the house and shop; that the front was towards Broad street, and there was a side door out of the shop into an alley, commonly called the Jews-Alley, and if they could make an errand thither to buy rum, they might get an opportunity to shove back the bolt of the door facing the alley, for there was no lock on it, and they could come in the night afterwards, and accomplish their designs. (At nights they usually let people in at the front door in another street, and went through the parlor into the kitchen, which Wilson well knew).

At Hughson's lodged one Margaret Sorubiero, alias Salingburgh, alias Kerry, commonly called Peggy, or the Newfoundland Irish beauty, a young woman about one or two and twenty; she pretended to be married, but no husband appeared; she was a person of infamous character, a notorious prostitute and also of the worst sort, a prostitute to Negroes, she was here lodged and supported by Caesar (Vaarck's slave, also known as John Gwin) before mentioned, and took share (in common with Hughson's family) of the spoils and plunder, the effects of Caesar's thefts, which he brought to Hughson's; and she may be supposed to have been in most of their wicked secrets; for she had lodged there the summer before, and removed from thence to a house by the new battery, near one John Romme's, a shoemaker, and was well acquainted with him and his wife: thither also Caesar used frequently to resort, with many other Negroes; thither he also conveyed stolen goods, and some part of Hogg's goods, of which John Romme had his choice, if what Caesar said, after his condemnation, be true; and by what will appear hereafter against Romme, and from his intimacy with Hughson, his merits may be concluded to fall little short of his companions.

With this Peggy, as she will be hereafter commonly called, Caesar Mr. Vaarck's Negro used frequently to sleep at Hughson's with the knowledge and permission of the family; and Caesar bargained with and paid Hughson for her board; she came there to lodge a second time in the fall, not long before Christmas, 1740, big with child by Caesar, as was supposed, and brought to bed there not many days before the robbery at Hogg's, of a baby largely partaking of dark complexion.

Here is laid the foundation of the characters of Hughson and his family, Peggy and John Romme, which will afford frequent occasion of enlarging upon; and from which a hopeful earnest the reader may well expect a plentiful harvest.

Wilson from the Flamborough ship coming to Mrs. Hogg's on Sunday morning, to see his acquaintance as usual, she complained to him, that she had been robbed the night before, that she had lost all the goods out of the shop, a great deal of silver Spanish coins, medals and other silver things, little suspecting that he had been the occasion of it, notwithstanding what she apprehended upon pulling out the drawer of money before him, as above, but as she knew he belonged to the man of war, and that several of those sailors frequented idle houses in the Jews-Alley, it happened that her suspicions inclined towards them; she imagined he might be able to give her some intelligence about it, and therefore described to him some things that she had missed, viz. snuff-boxes, silver medals, one a remarkable eight square piece, etc. Whereupon Wilson said, he had been the morning at Hughson's house, and there saw one John Gwin, who pulled out of his pocket a worsted cap full of pieces of coined silver; and that Mr. Philipse's Cuffee, who was there, seeing John Gwin have this money, he asked him to give him some, and John Gwin counted him out half a crown in pennies, and asked him if he would have any more; and then pulled out a handful of silver coin, amongst which, Wilson said, he saw the eight square piece described by Mrs. Hogg.

This morning search was made for John Gwin at Hughson's, supposing him to have been a soldier of that name, a fellow of suspicious character, as Mrs. Hogg conceived; and the officers making inquiry accordingly for a soldier, they were answered, there was no such soldier used that house; but it fell out, that Caesar, the real person wanted, was at the same time before their faces in the Chimney corner: the officer returned without suspecting him to be the person meant, but the mistake being discovered by the boy (Wilson) that the Negro Caesar before mentioned went by that name, he was apprehended in the afternoon, and being brought before Wilson, he declared that he was the person he meant by John Gwin. Caesar was committed to prison.

Caesar (Vaarck's Negro) was examined by the justices, and denied everything laid to his charge concerning Hogg's robbery, but was remanded.

Prince (Mr. Auboyneau Negro) was this day also apprehended upon account of the same felony: upon examination he denied knowing anything of it. He was also committed.

Upon information that Caesar had shewn a great deal of silver at Hughson's, it was much suspected that Hughson knew something of the matter, and therefore search was made several times at his house, yesterday and this day, but none of the goods or silver were discovered.

Hughson and his wife were sent for, and were present while the Negroes were examined by the justices, and were also examined themselves, touching the things stolen, but discovered nothing; and they were dismissed.

Hughson's house having been searched several times over by Mr. Mills, the under-sheriff, and several constables, in quest of Hogg's goods, without effect, it happened this evening, that the slave Negro wench Mary Burton came to the house of James Kannady, one of the searching constables, to fetch a pound of candles for her master; Kannady's wife knew the girl by sight, and who she belonged to, living in the neighborhood near them, and having heard of the robbery, and the several searches at Hughson's she took upon her to examine the wench Mary Burton, "whether she knew anything of those goods, and admonished her to discover if she did, lest she herself should be brought into trouble and gave her motherly good advice and said if she knew anything of it, and would tell, she would het her freed from her master." Whereupon at parting, the girl said, "she could not tell her then, she would tell her tomorrow; but that her husband was not cute enough, for that he had trod upon me." And so went away. This alarmed Kannady and his wife, and the same evening Ann Kannady went to Mr. Mills, the under-sheriff and told him what had passed between her and the wench Mary Burton. "Whereupon Mills and his wife, Mr. Hogg and his wife, and several constables, went with Ann Kannady and her husband, down to Hughson's house; and Ann Kannady desired the under-sheriff to go in first, and bring Mary Burton out to her; but he staying a long time, Ann Kannady went into Hughson's house, and found the undersheriff and his wife, and Mary Burton, in the parlor, and she then denied what she had before said to Ann Kannady, as above; then Ann Kannady charged her home with it; til at length, Mary Burton said she could not tell them anything there, she was afraid of her life; that they would kill her. Whereupon they took the girl out of the house, and when they had got a little way from thence, she put her hand in her pocket, and pulled out a piece of silver money, which she said was part of Hogg's money, which the Negro had given her if she would lay with him, she handily refused and they gave her a cut of the house,   They all went to Alderman Bancker's with her, and Ann Kannady informing the Alderman that she had promised John Hughson's wench slave Mary Burton to get her freed from her master; he directed that she should lodge that night with the undersheriff at the City Hall for safety; and she left there accordingly. For Mary Burton declared also, before the alderman, her apprehensions and fears, that she should be murdered or poisoned by the Hughson's and the Negroes, for what she should discover.

Deposition Sworn before recorder Simeon Johnson; Anne Kannady wife of James Kannady:

That some time after the said wench, Mary Burton was parted from Hughson. To the best of the deponents remembrance, it was after the house in the fort was burnt, she came to the deponents house and the deponent asked her to come in and warm herself, and if she would like to drink hot Geneva tea, thereupon the deponent took it upon herself to ask her several questions, first of all she asked her own name, which she told her as above, for the deponent did not know it, though she had been several times at her house upon the errands, she knew that she had lived at Hughson's then the deponent asked her weather that was a black child or a white child which that Irish beauty had, which lodged at their house ? and she made answer, that it was as white as any of her children, or any other child, the deponent, the deponent then told her that she heard that there was a Negro who kept company with her and was the father of the child.

The said Mary Burton answered there was a Negro came thither to her, but he was not the father of that child, she believed, then the deponent took upon her to give the said wench Mary Burton good advice. She told her she would give her a blessing as a mother would a child, as she Mary Burton was a stranger in the country, the, deponent advised her to have no dealings with Negroes, and to have no hand in thievery, for that would be a means of bringing her to the gallows.

The deponent again asked Mary Burton if she knew anything of the thievery of Mr. Hoggs goods and the deponent was talking about the robbery at Hogg's, and about butter, indigo and bee-wax which had lately been stolen from other persons, and Mary Burton said that John Hughson his wife and family had them all, it was plain enough, and that she knew enough to hang and burn them all, and then deponent Mrs. Kannady then advised her to tell that entire she knew, saying it was a pity that such people should go on in their wickedness unpunished.

The deponent then asked her if she had a mind to be freed from Hughson's, if she and would discover the goods from the Hughson's, the deponent would free her the deponent said tell me where the goods are, and I will take you away from him that night, she answered that she would not tell her anything to night, she would tell her tomorrow. The deponent let the said wench Mary Burton return home.

That after this conversation was over, the deponent Anne Kannady went the same evening to Mr. Wells, the undersheriff, and told him what had passed above, whereupon the said Mills, Mr. Hogg and his wife, and several constables, with the deponents husband and herself, went down to Hughson's house, and the deponent desired Mills to go into the house first, and bring wench Mary Burton out to her, but Mills staying a long time the deponent went into the house to him, and found him and his wife and Mary Burton in the parlour, and there she wench, Mary Burton denied all that she had said to the deponent, as above, then the deponent charged her home with it, until at last the said Mary Burton said she could not tell them anything there, that they would kill her, whereupon they took her from the house, and when they had gotten a little away from thence, she put her hand in her pocket, and pulled out a piece of silver money, which she said was part of Hogg's money which the Negro had given her, whereupon they an went with her to Alderman Banker's and the deponent informing him what she had promised the said wench,that is to say, to get her freed from her master, the alderman directed that she Mary Burton be night lodged with the under sheriff, at the City Hall for safety, and the deponent went with the said wench Mary Burton, and left her at Mr. Mills accordingly.

That some time after this, she said Mary Burton said to the deponent that she was better than ever her mother was to her, and that she was relieved to be away from the hands of her enemies, by being the means of taking her away from Hughson's and that if ever it was in her power, she would reward bet handsomely for it.

That the said wench Mary Burton further said to this deponent,that if they had not taken her the said Mary Burton from Hughson's the night that they did, she verily believed they (meaning the Hughson's) would either have murdered her, or sent her away in a boat the next morning.

The same day and time James Kannady and Mary Goddard (daughter of said James and Anne) wife of Christopher Goddard of New York, mariner, having severally heard the before mentioned deposition of Anne Kannady taken and read over in their presence, did severally make oath, that that part of the said deposition which relates to what discourse passed between the said Anne Kannady and Mary Burton, did so pass between them when they (the deponents) were respectively present; and that what therein is deposed is the substance and effect of what was so said between them.

Sworn before the recorder. William Wright.

Deposition. – Rebecca Hogg, wife of Robert Hogg of the city of New York, merchant, deposeth:
1. That one Wilson, a boy belonging to the Flamborough man of war, used to frequent her house, upon pretence of acquaintance with two white boys, servants to two gentlemen that lodged there.
2. That the Thursday before the robbery was committed, the said Wilson came to her house with a man belonging to the aforesaid ship, in order to buy some chequered linen; and the deponent shewed them into the shop, where he (Wilson) bought something of her, and gave her a Spanish nine-penny silver piece in pay, and the deponent unadvisedly opening her desk to weigh it, she pulled out a drawer in view of the said Wilson, wherein were a considerable number of Spanish pieces of eight, whereupon she immediately recollected herself and shut up the drawer and desk again in haste, thinking she had done imprudently in exposing her money to an idle boy who used to be so often backwards and forwards at her house, and thereupon made an excuse to send the piece of money aforesaid out of the house to be weighed. And on the Saturday night following her shop was robbed.
3. That the Sunday morning after, this boy (Wilson) came to the deponent's house, as usual, and she was telling him that she had been robbed, and that as she knew he belonged to the man of war, she thought he might be able to give her some intelligence; as there were several sailors who frequented vile houses that were near her; the deponent described some snuff boxes and coined silver pieces, one an eight square piece; whereupon he, the said Wilson, answered that he had been that morning at the house of one Hughson, by the North river, and there he saw one John Gwin [whom the deponent understood to have been a soldier of that name - a person of vile character, who lived at the deponent's back street; but it turned out to be Caesar, Vaarck's Negro] whom he saw pull out of his pocket, a worsted cap full of coined silver; and that Philipse's Cuffee came into Hughson's upon pretence of having his master's shoes mended, and seeing John Gwin have this money, he asked him to give him some, and he counted him out half-a-crown in pennies, and asked him if he would have any more, and pulled out a handful of silver in the presence of the boy, Wilson, amongst which he said he saw the eight square piece so described by the deponent as aforesaid; but the deponent did not then suspect Wilson to have had any hand in it.
4. That upon this information the deponent told her husband and he and Mr. Mills went the same Sunday morning to Hughson's, to inquire for one John Gwin, a soldier, and Hughson told them that he was not there, nor did he use the house, but Caesar, the Negro who went by that name (as he himself after he was apprehended, and after his conviction, confessed to this deponent) was at the same time standing in rite chimney corner, in the same room where Mr. Hogg and Mr. Mills came; whereupon Mr. Hogg returned to his house, and told the deponent that there was no such soldier as John Gwin that used that house, that the boy, Wilson, who was present, thereupon said, it was not a white man, but Caesar, a Negro belonging to one Vaarck, a baker, who went by that name.
5. Upon this Caesar was apprehended the same Sunday about 3 o'clock, and being brought to Wilson, to know if that was the right person he said it was.
6. That upon her examining the said Negro Caesar, in jail several times, as well as before his trial as after his conviction of this robbery. He confessed to her as followeth.
7. That the boy Wilson used to be frequently in company with him (Caesar), Philipse's Cuffee, and Auboyneau's Prince, Negroes, at Mr. Philipse's house and at Hughson's; and that he Wilson) came to Hughson's where were

112

present Hughson and his family, Caesar (himself), Cuffee and Prince, and there he told them where they might have a good booty, and described the deponent's house and shop to them, and told them what money he had seen in the drawer, as aforesaid, and said he believed there must be more by seeing that in one drawer. That Caesar and he did not know where Mr. Hogg lived, but he knew the house if it was where the widow Scott lived formerly; and that so said Hughson, that he did not know Mr. Hogg, nor where he lived: but Caesar further said upon this information they contrived it at Hughson's how to commit this robbery and that he (Caesar) going to see Peggy Kerry, who lodged at Hughson's on the Saturday evening following, he dropped asleep there, and about 10 o'clock John Hughson came to him and waked him, telling him that he had forgot what he had promised the boy (Wilson) Cuffee and Prince, to go to the house in Broad street to get that booty.

8. That thereupon he, (Caesar) went to Mr. Philipse's house (Cuffee's master) and finding nobody there he sat himself down in the cellar kitchen by the fire; and by and by, hearing his confederates coming, he feigned himself asleep and they came in with a large bundle, and hid it in a bran box in the stable or out house, in the yard, as he discovered by their talk, they thinking him asleep, for they did not attempt to wake him, but went out again in search of fresher prey.

9. That when they were gone, he went and took the bundle they had so hid, and carried it to John Rommes at the new-battery, who opened the door for him himself, and let him in, and he (Caesar) threw the bundle in a chair, which was tied up in a large table cloth, which Romme opened and took out a piece of cotton and linen cheque, and a pair of silver knee-buckles belonging to Mr. Hogg, and some other linen things which he could not particularly remember, and after this he (Caesar) carried the remainder of the bundle to Hughson's and left them in the room where Peggy was and went to bed; and in the morning when he awakened, he took the snuff-boxes, a child's whistle, and ring, and a pair of earrings, and a locket with four diamonds, and gave them to Peggy, with some money; and the linen and chequered shirt he left with Peggy, to distribute as she thought proper, but he bid her give an apron to the girl, meaning Mary Burton) and when he (Caesar) went down stairs he distributed money to Hughson, his wife and their children, and likewise to the servant girl.

10. That Caesar confessed to the deponent, that when he came to Hughson's with the things, the family was all a-bed,; but that they had left open a window, as was usual, and he climbed upon the shed and got into the house, and went to bed to Peggy, as Hughson and his family knew he used to do every night.

The recorder having been informed by Mary Burton, that she had several times talked to the wife of Daniel Masters, carman, concerning the conspiracy, and what she had heard the Negroes and the Hughsons often talk about it, whilst she lived at Hughson's and this before the fire at the fort; he spoke to Daniel Masters and desired him to send his wife to him, in order, as she told him, to enquire of her about it, within three or four days afterwards Susannah Masters came to the recorder (viz. this morning) and be examined her upon the matter, and took down what she said in the form of a deposition, consisting of twelve sections or paragraphs, which she signed and swore to, after hearing the same distinctly read over; the recorder being obliged to go out, and pressed in point of time, he did not examine her so fully as otherwise he would have done, but upon reading overt the deposition in the afternoon, several other questions occurred to him, which he thought might be proper to interrogate her upon; therefore he then sent for her again, and she came very readily, and freely answered the questions he proposed to her; notes were taken at large of the fresh information she gave which she was told were to be drawn out in proper order, and added to her deposition, and the whole be fair copied, ready to be read over to her the next morning, in order to be sworn and signed; and she promised to come the next morning for that purpose; but it may be presumed she had been otherwise advised, for though her husband had been several times afterwards ordered to send her again, yet she thought fit to decline coming; the recorder did not care to be over solicitous about it, for some trains, but has ventured to give the public her examination at large, as it was drawn from hi notes, which he does aver, he thinks is faithfully done, and to do the woman justice, she seemed to behave upon the occasion with the greatest sincerity and candor. For distinction, the particular paragraphs contained in her first disposition, which were read over to her, and by her sworn and signed, are enclosed between inverted commas.

Note: upon the fair copying, some of the paragraphs were transposed, and the words enclosed in the thus at the end of §10, were added upon her second examination.

The deposition and examination of Susannah Masters, wife of Daniel Masters, of the city of New York. She said:

1. "That Mary Burton, late servant to John Hughson, (executed for the conspiracy) soon after her removal from her said master (upon the discovery of Mr. Hogg's goods, the last year, which were stolen and lodged at the said Hughson's house) came to live with one Wilson, in the same street with this deponent, with whose family this deponent was well acquainted, they used to fetch water at this deponent's house, and to dry their clothes in her yard; and after Mary Burton came to live with Wilson, she used alien to come to the deponent's house upon the name errands, which gave the said Mary frequent opportunities of talking to this deponent, and said she was glad she was got from the Hughson's to the place she was now, for she was afraid there would be mischief in the town, for that site knew there used to be the cabals of heaters at Hughson's whilst she lived there, almost every night at supper, and they used to make her wait upon them; and at such meetings, Hughson and the Negroes used to talk of killing people and burning the town, that the governor's house would be first, and then they would begin at the Fly, and so go through the whole city, and the Hughson's wife said, that rather titan it should go undone, she would lend an hand herself; and when all this was done, it was agreed among them, that Hughson was to be king, his wife Queen, Vaarck's Caesar governor, and Peggy, his mistress, governess."

2. "That Mary said, that the Negroes and the Hughsons several times threatened her, that if she discovered anything, out of the house that she heard there, they would certainly make away with her."

3. "That the said Mary had discoursed in this manner to the deponent three several times before she spoke of it to her husband; but it had made the deponent very uneasy, though she could not know how to give credit to it."

4. "That at the times of this discourse, Mary Burton seemed very uneasy, and used to sit down and cry and bemoan herself and said she was but a young girl, a stranger in the country and no friends, and she was in danger of her life; the deponent they asked her why she did not go to a magistrate and make a discovery of all this? Mary answered that if she should tell them what she knew, they would not believe her, as she was but a poor girl and a stranger."

5. "That upon the girl's crying and bemoaning herself to her, the examinant (considering the circumstances she was under, from the manner of her relating her story) was very much affected, and could not but take great compassion of her, as she had no friends or relations in this country to advice with upon her case or to protect her; and yet the examinant says, she would at sometimes be cheerful and merry, and laughing at the folly of the conspirators, when she was telling the examinant of some particular odd passages which happened at such nightly meetings, and that she bore up against the difficulties she was under, much better than the examinant could have done in the like circumstances, and that she though she had very good spirits."

6. "That the said Mary used further to talk, that when Hughson and the Negroes had anything extraordinary to do at nights, the Hughson's would send her up to bed; and the nights that Hogg's goods came thither they had sent her up to bed; and she heard when the goods came and she got up and looked out of the window and saw the goods delivered in, but it being dark she could not discover who they were that brought them, for there were many of them, but she heard and knew the voices of Vaarck's Caesar, Auboyneau's Prince, and Philipse's Cuffee, Negroes."

7. "That Mary told the deponent, that the night Hogg's goods were stolen, Caesar was asleep upon the table, that he had been drinking very hard, and John Hughson came to him about 11 o'clock and waked him, and said to him you forgot your promise, don't you? Caesar answered no sir, I don't, and thereupon got up and went out; and then Hughson sent Mary to bed, and Mary said that upon this she suspected something extraordinary was to be done, she could not sleep; and she heard the noise when they brought the goods, which she took to be about 12 or 1 o'clock."

8. "That Mary Burton told the deponent, that she saw the goods the next morning, and that Caesar offered her as much speckled linen before Peggy, as would make her an apron, but she said she would not have it, and threw it down upon the floor, and told them she did not want it; that want it she did, but that she would not have it in that manner, that she told them she believed they did not come honestly by it; at which she said they were affronted, but she did not value it, she would not receive anything of them, if she could but get victuals, drink and clothes as long as she staid with them, that was all she cared for: that Caesar offered her a piece of silver, which she supposed was to engage her to look after Peggy in her lying in but she said no, she would not take care of her and her black child, but perhaps she might have submitted to have looked after white people's."

9. "That at last the deponent told her husband of what had passed between her and Mary, but at first he thought it was all idle talk in the girl, and could not give any credit to it, and rebuked the deponent for giving an ear to her."

10. "That the said Mary further said, that there were many white people, and some in ruffles that used to come to Hughson's, and go into a private room with Hughson; and if she, when she was bid, brought any wine or any thing to the door of the room where they were, Hughson used to stand ready at the door and receive it, and send her away again: that these white people in ruffles used to come seldom but they used to send letters and money in them to Hughson often" [for that she has received several letters brought thither, and has felt money in them, large round pieces, which she took to be milled Spanish pieces of eight.]"

11. "That the said Mary said, that Hughson had a large parcel of arms, which he hid under ground; but she did not know what became of them."

12. "That the said Mary told the examinant, that Kannady the constable's wife (at the time that he had been searching in Hughson's in quest of Hogg's goods that had been stolen) upon Mary's going to her shop upon an errand, advised her, if she knew anything of Hogg's goods to discover it, or else she told her she might be brought into trouble; and that Mary told her, Ah! said she, the constables in this place were not half cute enough, that they went over them several times, and had poked a stick (or cane she thought she said) into a place where some of them were (the examinant apprehended her, that there was some place in the stairs that was broken that they were so poking at) and Mary said that she could scarce forbear laughing to see how dumb they were, and yet she dared not tell them. [Hereupon Ann Kannady's preceding deposition being read over to the examinant, she declared.]"

13. "That Mary Burton told her what had passed between the said Ann Kannady and the said Mary, which to the best of the examiner's remembrance, was much to the same purpose as is related in the said Ann Kannady's deposition, and that soon after she came to live with Wilson as aforesaid, and before the fire at the fort."

14. "That all the conversation before related, passed between the deponent and the said Mary concerning the conspiracy before the fire at the fort, and before the proclamation issued, promising a reward to such as should make discovery of any person or persons concerned in setting fire to the houses."

15. "That Mrs. Waldron who is since married to - - Miller coming one day to the examiner's house, before the fire at the fort, Mary Burton being there, she related before her most of the particulars herein before set forth, much to the same purpose as before related: and the said Mrs. Waldron was much surprised at it."

16. "That the day the fort was fired, Mary Burton came to the deponent's house and said to her, now you see this is the beginning of it, Mrs. Masters; they said the governor's house should be the first; you did not seem to take much notice of what I said to you; and Mary seemed to be in a very great fright and much perplexed, and said, it was a thousand pities it should not be discovered; but says she, if I was to speak what I know of it, they would not believe me, and she said, when she looked upon the houses, she thought what a pity it was, that they must all come down."

17. "That after the fire at the fort, the said Mary used to come frequently to the examinant''s house, until the time that her master, Wilson, removed to live in the fly, which was at May day, 1741; and she would be talking about these matters and of her fears and apprehensions, that she should be murdered by the Negroes; and she told the examinant one day, after she had been first examined by the grand jury concerning Hogg's goods, that she met one of Vaarck's Negroes (Bastian) who was one of the conspirators (whose master lives near the examinant) and he asked her whether she had discovered anything about the fires? And Mary said she answered him, no; and the Negro replied, we shall soon take care that you shall not tell any more, or words to some such purpose: and Mary said, she came immediately into the examinant's house, before she went to her master's; and she seemed to be frightened almost out of her wits, when she told the examinant this story, and said, she looked behind her all the way, expecting she should be followed and knocked on the head."

18. "That after Wilson was removed into the fly, the said Mary told the examinant, that one Sunday morning her master and mistress being gone to church, a Negro who she believed did belong to old Hughson, father of John Hughson executed, came into her master Wilson's cellar-kitchen, and asked if there was a barber there? That Mary answered him no; that the said Negro made a pretence that he wanted to send the boy out, the only person in the house besides herself, in order to fetch him a barber to shave him; but Mary said she was afraid he had some ill design, and would not let the boy go; and at last, when church was near out, the Negro went away, and people beginning to come into the streets, the Negro took to his heels and run away; and she said she

thought to have got somebody to have laid hold of him, but he made too much haste out of reach; that afterwards she told her fears and apprehensions to a magistrate, and care was taken to remove her from her master Wilson's; and she was then lodged again at the under-sheriff's at the city hall, where she was to remain, and the corporation purchased her indentures of Wilson for that purpose."

19. " That this examinant was out upon the common at the execution of Quack and Cuffee where she met the said Mary Burton, and the examinant said to her, she wondered how she had the courage enough to be there; she answered, that she knew they had deserved it and that if half the Negroes in town were executed, she believed they had deserved it; that she knew a great many of them by sight, but did not know their names, nor who they belonged to.

20. That when the governor had ordered a military nightly watch to be kept in this city, that evening that Philipse's storehouse was burnt, Mary, having been talking to the examinant about the conspiracy and the several fires that has happened that day said, that was right, and the only way to prevent farther mischief.

21. That when several fires had thus happened, the examinant was then convinced of the truth of what the said Mary had often before related to her; and the examinant's husband resolved to inform, and did inform a magistrate of what Mary had told the examinant, or of the substance of it, as the examinant's husband informed her.

22. And lastly, the examinant saith, that from the beginning of these conversations with the said Mary Burton, about these plottings and caballings between the Hughsons and the Negroes the examinant had heard the said Mary Burton mention the names of several white persons of condition beyond the vulgar, who she said resorted sometimes to Hughson's and used to go into a room with him in private, whom she suspected; and others who used to be with the Negroes and the Hughsons in public, whom she said she know from what she had seen and heard at such meetings, were concerned in the conspiracy [whose names the examinant does not care to mention, without a promise not to insert them in her examination] but among several others, she had heard his name Corry, the dancing master, as one particularly, who used to be with the Hughsons and the Negroes when they were talking about burning the town and killing the people.

The following letter and dialogue were sent from Mr. Favieres, of the city of New York, merchant, directed to the recorder.

Sir – Having been interrogated concerning some discourse I had with the Negro Bastian, concerning the conspiracy, you were pleased to propose to me, that I should recollect myself as well as could, and set down the substance of it by way of dialogue, which I have done, according to the best of my remembrance, as followeth.

Being at New London with my sloop, the beginning of last September, Elias Rice, commander, having sixteen Negro men and one Negro woman on board, who were transported for having a hand in the late plot, and have since been delivered at Hispaniola, I about that time received a letter from my wife at New York, dated August 31, 1741, in which letter she informed me, that one John Ury had been executed the Saturday before, as one concerned with the conspiracy, and that it was the opinion of many people, that he was innocent of what had been alleged against him at court; this piece of news occasioned me to go on board, to try what I could learn from the Negroes, and I was relating this account of Ury to captain Rice, in French, and Bastian, one of the transported Negroes, who attended on captain Rice, being near the door of the cabin within hearing; at my saying a great many people thought him innocent, he seemed to smile and spoke as if somewhat surprised, he innocent! Says he, he was one of the worst of them all. Upon which I said to him, Bastian, you know all that was to have been done, and you must tell me all that you know of the matter, and he answered that if I would come on board in the afternoon, he would relate to me all that he knew concerning the plot, but was unwilling any of the Negroes should hear him. I according to his request returned on board in the afternoon, and taking him privately into the cabin, I put the following questions to him, which without scruple, he answered as I have here penned down, or to the same effect.

Note that most of the conversation was in French, Bastian having been bred from a boy in Mr. Fauconnier's family, where they chiefly talked that language.

Question: Bastian, seeing you are now to be transported, and that it hath pleased the governor to pardon you for a crime, wherein many of your associates have suffered death, you need not fear any dangerous consequences by giving me an impartial account of all you know concerning the Negro plot, tell me all you know if that affair from the beginning to the end, without amusing me with any falsehoods, and this you may depend on, it will be in a great measure obtain a pardon likewise from God, for your many and detestable sins.

Answer: Sir, you may depend upon it, that I shall declare to you nothing but what I am very certain of.

Q: Who was the first person that introduced you at Hughson's?

A: Caesar, belonging to my master.

Q: The first time you were at Hughson's, what did you do there?

A: Hughson himself filled me a bumper of liquor, and after having drank it, I found myself quite intoxicated, but I remember he brought me a book, and bid me lay my hand on it, and bid me to swear, and told me if I refused it he would kill me upon the spot, finding myself in so great a stress, to save my life I took the oath.

Q: What book was it that Hughson made you swear upon? Was it a bible?

A: I don't know what book it was, but by its make I thought it looked like those books you call bibles.

Q: What was it Hughson obliged you to stand to, and after what manner did you swear?

A: By lightening and thunder, and by hell flames, that I would set fire to whatever I came across and destroy as many whites as I could.

Q: What did you propose to do, if in case you had got the upper hand of the whites; did Hughson make you any promise?

A: He promised to make us all free.

Q: Did there generally use to resort many Negroes at Hughsons?

A: Yes, for I have been there many a time when I have told them fifteen, often twenty, and sometimes thirty Negroes.

Q: Did you used to eat and drink there, whenever you went to see Hughson?

A: We always had a good supper and never wanted for liquor.

Q: The night after the fort burnt, did you return to Hughson's?

A: No, the night after that we were a jolly company, and had a fine supper prepared for us, and seemed all of us to be well pleased with our late good success.

Q: Did you know any whites that were concerned with you? Did you ever see any at Hughson's at your meetings?

A: I have seen Will Kane there very often, and two or three soldiers whom I knew not, and another little man who was a stranger to me.

Q: Was the little man young or old? Of what make was he? And how did he employ his time among you?

A: He was far from being a tall man, but short, very lean, and a pale visage, nor was he old, his place was at the upper end of the table; he often encouraged us to remain firm like men in our designs, he read and wrote a great deal.

Q: Do you know what he wrote?

A: I have seen him take the names of the Negroes down, from time to time, by way of list.

Q: But how could Hughson, who was but a poor man, support so great an expense at his house? There were suppers every night for you all, candles and other things, the charge of which must have been very great; this goes beyond my comprehension; for you know the person who wrote so much must have had lights to see; I say I do not know how he did to support all that charge!

A: The Negroes brought what they could steal to him; the white man you speak of was short sighted, and never wrote or read without spectacles.

Q: They say he was a Romish priest, do you know anything about that?

A: I do not know that he was a priest; but he used to exhort us like a minister, to continue steadfast in our intentions, and used to throw his hands about like a preacher, and he said to us at the meeting at Hughson's the second night after the fort was burnt, now God has prospered us in the beginning in burning the fort, and we need not fear; we must be resolute and proceed in the work, and no doubt God will prosper us in all; that the town was too much alarmed at present, but they must go on when the fine weather came, that they (the Negroes) need not fear, he would forgive them their sins if they kept true to their engagements, and by and by the Spaniards would come, and they should be free.

Q: Have you been baptized by the little man, they called a priest?

A: No, but I have been told by some Negroes of our company. That the little man had baptized them.

Q: Is it true you were to burn the English church?

A: Yes, we agreed to burn it last winter, but the man whom you call priest opposed it, and advised us to stay till spring, when there would be a larger congregation.

Q: Your intentions then were to destroy all the whites while they were in the church; how were you to go about it? Had you arms? And could you think otherwise but that many would have made their escape through the doors and windows? Explain me these things as well as you can.

A: We had combustibles prepared by doctor Harry, made up into balls, which we were to set fire to and throw them upon the roof of the church, which sticking fast would set fire to the shingles; after which, guarding the doors, we were to let none pass, but destroy them all in the church with our fire arms, for we had a great number of them at Hughson's.

Q: Where did you use to keep your arms at Hughson's? for when the searchers were sent there they were not to be found.

A: I believe not, for the plot beginning to come to light, Hughson to secure himself, had them all thrown into the river, before they were hid in a hole in the cellar.

Slaves were routinely hanged for minor offenses.

Slaves and criminals were made to stand on the wheel while locked with head and hands in the stocks.

Bastian further declared that he had not seen the person they called a priest since he came into jail.

James Favieres

James Favieres, of New York, merchant, made oath before the recorder, that the aforegoing relation contained the substance of the discourse that passed between him and Bastian, a Negro, at the time and place above mentioned, according to the best of his remembrance.

Deposition – Elias Rice saith.

1. That in his passage with the seventeen Negroes, Burk's Sarah acknowledged that she was concerned in the plot; never was at Hughson's, but often at Comfort's amongst the Negroes, a forwarding the plot, and she had willfully set fire to her mistress' house several times.
2. That Ten Eyck's Dick was cooking the victuals for the ship in the passage, and the Negroes suspected he had a design of poisoning them, and saw him busy with yellow stuff in shells in a bag; which upon examination the Negroes looked upon to be poison which he had from Doctor Harry, the Negro. Some of the Negroes knew it to be poison, the same sort they saw in Guinea.
3. H. Rutgers' Jacob and Lush's Gill denied being at Hughson's, but all the rest owned it.
4. Bastian owned he had been a head-man there, was there very often, and saw a little man there they called a priest, but never saw him after he came to jail.
5. Tickle said he had killed fowls there: Kelly's London had carried a quarter of mutton there.
6. Myers Cohen's Windsor had carried a turkey there: and all (except as aforesaid) owned they had many a good feast and good liquor there.
7. That Bastian was always during the passage, very free in owning his being engaged in the plot, and kept to the same story; and said that he had often seen Kane at Hughson's, and that he was concerned in the plot, and many more soldiers that used to come there with him, whose names he knew not.
8. That Bastian declared, that all the Negroes that were executed he had often seen at Hughson's entertainments, and that they were concerned in the polot. Elias Rice. Sworn before the recorder.

Deposition. John Thurman, of the city of New York, baker, being duly sworn on the holy evangelists of Almighty God, deposeth, that after John Campbell came to live at the house where John Hughson formerly lived, by the North river, he applied to the deponent, to put his children to school to him, informing him that John Ury, who was a very good scholar, a Latinist, was to be a partner with him in keeping school; and that he the deponent would be sure to have his children well instructed, but the deponent having no good opinion either of Campbell or the other, gave no heed to his proposal. That soon after Ury came to live in that neighborhood, as the deponent was informed, he took upon him to preach, and went about inviting the people to come and hear him; and that some of the deponent's family, as they afterwards told him, did go to hear him; that before Ury came to live in that neighborhood, he knew his person by sight, having seen him several times. That the day John Hughson, his wife and Peggy were executed, the deponent went upon the commons to see the execution;nand as he was returning from the gallows, he saw the said Ury near spring-garden, returning with the crowd to town, and walked alongside of him till he and the deponent came to the market by Bogart's the baker, when the deponent turned down towards his own house; that the deponent did at that time, and still does think, that Ury was returning from the execution of the Hughsons.

Sworn before the recorder.

JOHN THURMAN

The information of John Williams of the city of New York, baker, touching the confessions made to him by Will (Wad's Negro) executed for the conspiracy.

1. That he (William) lived next door to Mr. Ward the clock maker in Duke Street, and knew his Negro man, Will, who was executed as a confederate in the conspiracy; that he always, had great suspicion of him, of being concerned with some mischief, having seen him at play in his master's back storehouse, with many Negroes at a time, of a Sunday afternoon, playing at dice or papa; and he had heard also that this fellow had been concerned in the conspiracy of Antigua, about four or five years ago, which made him keep a very watchful eye over him.

2. That the day Mr. Philipse's storehouse was fired, and there was an alarm that the Negroes were rising, he thereupon went home to get his arms in readiness, and to secure his house and family; and as he had conceived a great jealousy of Ward's Will, he called at his house, and asked him where this Negro was, in order that he might have him in sight, and secure him; Ward answered he was back in the kitchen; and he calling him several times, Will at last answered out of the garret; he was ordered down, and Williams commanded him to keep upon his master's stoop, within his sight, and told him if he offered to stir from the door, he would shoot him; Williams having at the same time a loaded gun in his hand; and there he accordingly remained until the hurry was over.

3. That some time afterwards, when the affairs of the plot broke out, and several persons had been executed for the same, and the proclamation was issued, promising pardon to such Negroes as should come in by the time therein limited; the day before the expiration of that term, he charged Will home with being concerned, and advised, if it was so, that he would go and confess to save his life; but he stiffly denied knowing anything of the matter, and said, think not, master, that I am such a fool; for the Negroes here live as well as the white people at Antigua; I was concerned in a plot there, and had been hanged (would have been hanged) only I turned king's evidence, and by that means got clear, I could not stay there on account of the other Negroes, being apprehensive of their intending to kill me. And the next day he was impeached, and taken into custody; soon after which Williams went to talk to Will in jail, in order to try what he could get out of him, and asked what he thought of it now? He answered, he thought he was in the wrong, that he had not taken his advice, but he thought they were all hanged or sent off, that knew he was concerned.

4. Then Williams asked him, what would become of him in case the plot had gone on, whether he had a greater antipathy against him than any other? He said no; but he would have fared as the rest; he should have killed all that came in his way; for he had taken the oath of the priest; and that there was a matter of twenty or thirty of them in all, that were sworn together by the priest, a little man, with a long gown on; but he did not know him, or ever had seen him before as he know of; Williams asked him to what were they sworn; he answered, to burn and destroy what they could; Williams asked him what would have become of his master? He answered, as he was sworn, he must have gone on to destroy what he could.

Examination of Ann Lyng, Jemina Ross her mother, and Jemmy; taken by the recorder and deputy town clerk.

Ann Lyng, wife of Harman Lyng of the city of New York, mariner, declared that some short time after John Ury the priest was executed, she was one Sunday morning boiling of chocolate, and Jemmy, a little boy of about six or seven years of age, who was boarded with her and her said mother, said to her, aunt Nancy, my mammy Campbell used to boil chocolate every morning, but used to give me suppan, and sometimes chocolate with it; whereupon Ann Lyng asked him, who used to eat the chocolate? He answered, his daddy Campbell and Mr. Ury used to eat the chocolate, then she asked him if he knew Ury? He answered yes, very well; for he used to be by, when his daddy Campbell and Hughson used to play upon a board with little pieces of wood upon it; she then asked him if he knew Hughson? He said, very well, he was a tall man, with a thin face, used to wear a red coat and a white cap; that he often came to his daddy Campbell's, but always at night; that he knew Ury well, he used to teach him his book sometimes, and was a very little man, and lodged sometimes at his daddy Campbell's

[Note (b): (b) So the child used to call him; he boarded, and went to school with him, before he came to Ann Lyng.]

Mrs. Ross declared, that upon her said daughter's telling her what Jemmy had said, as above, she asked him questions much to the above purpose; and the child declared over again to the same effect.

Then the boy was asked some questions by the recorder and town-clerk, tending to the same purpose, concerning the knowledge of Hughson and Ury; and he described them as above, and said, they used often to be together at his daddy Campbell's and his daddy Campbell and Hughson used to play at chequers or draughts, [as they understood, according to the child's description; for he was put in mind of it, it seems, by Ann Lyng's child having some beans given it, which it was playing with, and throwing about the floor,] and that Ury used to be by, and looking at them, and used to say, Now Campbell you will win, and now Hughson you will win.

The child also described the persons of Hughson and Ury very exactly, and said Ury used to wear spectacles, and made punch for Hughson and Campbell, whilst they were playing.

What follows is a recounting, from the same notes of Daniel Horsmanden, of the trial of John Ury, sometimes referred to as John Jury, a White man accused of conspiring with the Negroes in the conspiracy and of being a "popist" or Catholic, a follower of the Pope.

TRIAL OF JOHN URY, ALIAS JURY

SUPREME COURT

Wednesday, July 29.

Present, the chief justice, the second and third justices.

The King against John Ury alias Jury.

The prisoner was brought to the bar, and the court proceeded upon his trial, as followeth.

Clerk in court. Cryer, make proclamation for silence.

Cryer. O yes! Our sovereign lord the king does strictly charge and command all manner of persons to keep silence upon pain of imprisonment.

Cryer. If anyone can inform the king's justices, the king's Attorney General for this province, or the inquest now to be taken on behalf of our sovereign lord the king, of any treason, murder, felony, or any other misdemeanor committed or done by the prisoner at the bar, let them come forth and they shall be heard, for the prisoner now stands upon his deliverance.

Clerk. Cryer, make proclamation.

Cryer. O yes! You good men that are impanelled to inquire between our sovereign lord the king, and John Ury alias Jury, the prisoner at the bar, answer to your names.

Clerk. John Ury alias Jury, hold up thy hand.

These good men that are now called and here appear, are those which are to pass between you and our sovereign lord the king, upon your life or death; if you challenge any of them, you must speak as they come to the book to be sworn, and before they are sworn.

[The court apprised the prisoner of the nature and extent of that liberty the law allowed him for making his challenges to the jurors.] The prisoner challenging none, the court proceeded, and the jury were sworn, to wit: William Hamersley, Gerardus Beekman, John Shurmur, John Hastier, James Tucker, Brandt Schuyler.

Clerk. Cryer, make proclamation.

Cryer. O yes! Our sovereign lord the king does strictly charge and command all manner of persons to keep silence upon pain of imprisonment.

Clerk. You gentlemen of the jury, that are now sworn, look upon the prisoner, and hearken to his charge.

The prisoner stands indicted, for that, whereas a Negro man slave, called Quack, belonging to John Roosevelt of the city of New York, merchant, on the 18th day of March, in the 14th year of the reign of our sovereign lord, George II, by the grace of God, king of Great Britain, &c. at the city of New York, into a certain dwelling house of our said lord the king, which then was standing and being at the fort in the said city of New York, and was then in the possession of the hon. George Clarke, esq. his majesty's lieutenant governor of the province of New York, did enter, and of his malice afore-thought, lighted fire, then and there wickedly, maliciously, voluntarily, willfully, and feloniously did put, and with the said lighted fire, he the said Negro man slave called Quack, the dwelling house aforesaid, and then and there wickedly, &c. did set on fire, and burn, and wholly consume, and destroy, against the peace of our said sovereign lord the king, his crown and dignity: and that John Ury alias Jury, private schoolmaster, on the 22nd day of February, in the said 14th year of the reign of our said lord the king, and divers other days and times, before the felony and burning aforesaid, in form aforesaid, done and perpetuated at the city of New York, of his malice afore-thought, wickedly, maliciously, voluntarily, willfully, and feloniously did counsel, abet, procure and encourage the aforesaid Negro man slave called Quack, the felony and burning aforesaid, in form aforesaid committed and perpetrated, to commit and perpetrate, in most pernicious example of all others in like case offending, contrary to the form of the statutes in such case made and provided, and against the peace of our sovereign lord the king, his crown and dignity.

Upon this indictment he has been arraigned, and hath pleaded thereunto, *not guilty,* and for his trial hath put himself upon God and his country, which country you are.

Your charge is to inquire, whether he be guilty of the felony whereof he stands indicted, or not guilty. If you find him guilty, you are to inquire what good and chattels, lands and tenements he had at the time when the felony was committed, or at any time since. If you find him not guilty, you are to say so, and no more: and hear your evidence.

Of counsel for the king - - the Attorney General, Mr. Murray, Mr. Alexander, Mr. Smith, Mr. Chambers.

In order to maintain the charge against the prisoner, upon this indictment, we shall produce to you the following evidence, to wit:

That the prisoner was actually concerned in the plot to burn the king's house and this city, and murder the inhabitants.

That he has frequently been at Hughson's house, in company with Hughson, his wife and daughter, and Margaret Kerry, and with divers Negroes, talking with them about the plot, and counseling and encouraging them to burn the king;s house and the town, and to kill and destroy the inhabitants; that the Negro Quack, who burnt the king's house, was present at one or more of those times, when the prisoner counseled and encouraged the Negroes as aforesaid; that he advised them what would be the fittest time to set the English church on fire; and that the prisoner, as a popish priest, baptized Hughson, his wife and daughter, and Kerry, and also divers Negroes, and told them then, and at several other times, that he could forgive sins, and that he forgave them their sins relating to the plot.

That when he was with the Negroes at Hughson's house, he used to make a round ring on the floor with chalk, or some other thing, and stand in the middle of it with a cross in his hand, and swear the Negroes into the plot, and that they should not discover either the plot or him, or any other person concerned in it, thought they were to die for it.

That some time last winter, he (at Hughson's house) swore Hughson, his wife and daughter, and Kerry, and several Negroes into the plot.

That he went by several names, and that when he baptized the Negroes, or any of the conspirators, he used to tell them he forgave them all the sins they should commit about the plot.

We shall likewise produce to you, a letter from general Oglethorpe to this honor, our governor, whereby it appears that some time before the plot broke out here, the Spaniards had employed emissaries to burn all the magazines and considerable towns in the English North America, and that many priests were employed, under pretended appellations of physicians, dancing masters, and such like occupations, and under such pretences to get admittance into and confidence in families.

This, gentlemen, was their hellish device to set on foot and carry on the late dreadful conspiracy among us; and the prisoner, in conjunction with Hughson (as we now have reason to believe) drew in the rest of the conspirators.

Gentlemen, what I have alleged, and much more, you will hear fully proved against the prisoner, by the witnesses for the king on this trial: but before we enter upon their examination, give me leave to say a few words concerning the heinousness of this prisoner's offenses, and of the popish religion in general, which I shall speak but very briefly to, as there are several other gentlemen of counsel for the king on this trial, and as I have not had either health or leisure to prepare to say much on this occasion.

Gentlemen, the late dreadful conspiracy to burn the king's house, and this whole town, and to kill and destroy the inhabitants, which the prisoner, as well as Hughson advised and encouraged, and swore many of the conspirators to join and bear their parts in, are crimes of too black and inhuman a nature to need any aggravation, and no doubt, the prisoners engaging at the peril of his own life, in so destructive, so bloody and dangerous an enterprise, proceed from his being employed in it by other popish priests and emissaries, and his zeal for that murderous religion; for the popish religion is such that they hold it not only lawful but meritorious to kill and destroy all that differ in opinion from them, if it may any ways serve the interest of their detestable religion; the whole scheme of which seems to be a restless endeavor to extirpate all other religions whatsoever, but more especially the protestant religion, which they maliciously call the Northern heresy; and to attain this wicked end, their first trick is, by subtle arguments to persuade the laity out of their senses, by showing them a seeming necessity fof their believing as their church believes, if they tender their own salvation; and this, with many more frauds, the church of Rome has artfully devised to get an absolute dominion over the consciences, and they may the more easily pick the pockets of credulous people: witness the pretended pardons and indulgences of that crafty and deceitful church, and their masses to pray souls out of purgatory, which they quote (or rather wrest) scripture for, when no such thing is to be found there; but it is a mere invention and cheat of their own to gull the laity of their money.

Then they have the doctrine of transubstantiation, which is so big with absurdities that it is shocking to the common sense and reason of mankind; for were that doctrine true, their priests by a few words of their mouths, can make a God as often as they please; but then they eat him too, and this they have the impudence to call honoring and adoring him. Blasphemous wretches! For hereby they endeavor to exalt themselves above God himself, inasmuch as the creator must necessarily be greater than his creature.

These and many other juggling tricks they have in their hocus pocus, bloody religion, which have been stripped of all their wretched disguise, and fully exposed in their own colors by many eminent divines, but more particularly by the great Dr. Tillotson, whose extraordinary endowments of mind, his inimitable works, and exemplary piety and charity have gained him such universal esteem and applause throughout all the protestant world, as, no doubt, will endure as long as the protestant name and religion lasts, which I hope will be to the end of time.

Gentlemen, when you have heard the witnesses prove to you what I have alleged against the prisoner, I make no doubt but you will, for your oaths sake, and for your own country's peace and future safety, find him guilty.

Witness for the king - - George Joseph Moore, clerk in court, sworn.

He proved the arraignment and conviction of Quack, on the 28th and 29th days of May last, who set fire to the fort.

Mary Burton sworn.

Mr. Chambers. Mary, give the court and jury an account of what you know concerning this conspiracy to burn down the town and murder and destroy the inhabitants, and what part you know the prisoner at the bar to have acted in it: tell the whole story from the beginning, in your own method, but speak slow, not so hastily as you usually do, that the court and the jury may the better understand you.

Mary Burton. Why I have seen Ury very often at the Hughson's about Christmas and New Year, and then he stayed away for about a fortnight or three weeks, and returned again about the time that Hogg;s goods came to our house. I have often seen hi in company with Hughson, his wife and daughter, and Peggy, and several Negroes, talking about the plot, burning the fort first, they the fly, and then the dock; and upon some of the Negroes saying they were afraid of being damned for being concerned in the plot, I heard Ury tell them they need not fear doing of it, for that he could forgive them their sins as well as God Almighty and would forgive them. They were to burn the whole town and kill the people: Ury was to be captain of a company of Negroes and he was to begin the fire where he was lodged; that when they were once together above stairs, Ury, Hughson, his wife and Peggy, they called Mary, and I went up, but when I came upstairs Ury had a book in his hand, and bid me go away, and asked me what business I had there, and said they did not call me, they called Mary Hughson, and he was angry and shut the door again, and I looked under it, and there was a black ring on the floor, and things in it that seemed to look like rats, I don't know what they were. - - That another time I heard him talking with the Negroes, Quack and others, about the plot, and turned the Negroes out of the room, and asked me to swear? And I said I would swear if they would tell me what I was going to swear, but they would have me swear first; and Hughson and his wife went and fetched silks and gold rings, and offered them to me in case I would swear, but I would not, and they said I was a fool; and Ury told me he could forgive sins as well as God, I answered I thought if was out of his power. That one night, some time about new year, I was listening at the door of the room upon the stairs, where there was Ury, Hughson, his wife and daughter Sarah, Vaarck's Caesar, Auboyneau's Prince, Philipse's Cuff and other Negroes; and I looked through the door and saw up on the table a black thing like a child. And Ury had a book in his hand and was reading, but I did not understand the language; and having a spoon in my hand, I happened to let it drop upon the floor, and Ury came out of the room, running after me down stairs, and he fell in a tub of water which stood at the foot of the stairs, and I ran away. When they were doing anything extraordinary at night, they would send me to bed.

[Note (p): (p) At Croker's near the coffee house, by the long bridge.]

[Note (q): (q) See Sarah Hughson's examination, § 9, and note letter (f) thereon. What Mary saw was by looking under the door, which it may be supposed, afforded but an obscure view, and the Negroes perhaps pulling their black toes backwards and forwards. Mary might be puzzled what to make of them. But Sarah Hughson and

Kane agree with Burton, that there was a ceremony used with a ring or circle upon the floor, at swearing the confederates.]

Prisoner. You say you have seen me several times at Hughson's, what clothes did I usually wear?

Mary Burton. I cannot tell you what clothes you wore particularly.

Prisoner. That is strange, and know me so well.

M. Burton. I have seen you in several clothes, but you chiefly wore a riding coat, and often a brown coat trimmed with black.

Prisoner. I never wore any such coat. What time of the day did I used to come to Hughson's?

M. Burton. You used chiefly to come in the night time, and when I have been going to bed I have seen you undressing in Peggy's room, as if you were to lie there; but I cannot say that you did, for you were always gone before I was up in the morning.

Prisoner. What room was I in when I called Mary, and you came up, as you said

M. Burton. In the great room upstairs.

Prisoner. What answer did the Negroes make when I offered to forgive them their sins, as you said?

M. Burton. I don't remember.

William Kane, soldier, sworn.

Mr. Chambers. Kane, will you give the court and jury an account of what you know of the prisoner at the bar, and of his being concerned in the conspiracy for burning the fort, and the town, and murdering the inhabitants? Give the whole account at large.

Kane. I know the prisoner very well, I have seen him at Croker's at Coffins, and Hughson's; particularly with Daniel Fagan, Jerry Corker, and one Plummer, and several Negroes, at Hughson's. Jerry Corker was one of the first that brought me into the plot. One day before Christmas last, I was standing sentry at the governor's door, and Jerry Corker coming out, I being dry asked him for a beer; Jerry said he would get some, that he had rum in his pocket, and would make flip, and then he went in and made it in a copper p;ot, and told me it was with loaf sugar, I drank a draught of it; and when I was relieved at night, Corker came into the guard room and asked me if I would go to Croker's at the fighting cocks, where there was to be a christening by a Romish priest: we went thither and stayed till past ten o'clock, but the people did not come that night: the next night Corker and I went there again, but the people were not there: the third night we went to New Street, to the house of one Coffin, a peddler, there they had a child and Ury christened it, and read Latin; three acted as priests and handed the book about. Ury put salt into the child's mouth, sprinkled it thrice, and crossed it. That Ury and Corker there endeavored to ;persuade me to be a Roman Catholic; Ury said it was best to be a Roman, they could forgive sins for anything ever so bad; I told him I did not believe him, and Corker told me that Ury and all the priests could forgive sins. That Ury was present at Hughson's, when John Hughson swore me and his father and brothers into the plot, there was Quack and forty or fifty Negroes there at the same time; we were to burn the town and destroy the people. David Johnson was there, and Ury tapped him on the shoulder, and they went into a room together and stayed a quarter of an hour, and when they came back Johnson said d- - n me, but we will burn the Dutch and get their money. That by Ury's persuasions that he could forgive sins, many were brought to be concerned: Ury was near me when I was sworn, and the Hughsons and I took him to be on of the head; Ury wanted to christen me but I would not, and he would not speak to me nor before me for a long time, for he could not abide me because I refused to become a Roman, till after he knew that I was concerned in the plot, and even then he did not much care for me: Ury was by when Hughson swore eight Negroes into the plot in a ring, and it was then talked among them of burning the fort, and Quack, who was present, was at that time pitched upon to do it, in the presence of Ury, who he believed might and did hear it. Jerry Corker told me that the English church was intended to be burnt on Christmas day last, but Ury put it off, and said that when the weather was better, then there would be a fuller congregation.

Prisoner. You say you have seen me very often, you saw me at Coffin's, you saw me several times at Hughson's, pray what clothes did you see me in?

Kane. I have seen you in black, I have seen you in a yellowish great coat, and sometimes in a straight bodied coat, of much the same color.

Prisoner. What time of the day have you seen me at Hughson's, and what did I say to you?

Kane. I have seen you there chiefly at nights, and you told me you could forgive me my sins, and there would be no fear of damnation, and you wanted to christen me.

Prisoner. You say you saw me christen a child at New Street, how was the child dressed, and what ceremony did I use, and who was present there then?

Kane. The child was not naked, it was dressed as usual; and you put it on your left arm, and sprinkled it with water three times, and put salt in its mouth, and crossed it, as I said before; there were about nine persons present.

Prisoner. Did I use anything besides salt and water?

Kane. Not that I saw.

Prisoner. Who was present at the christening?

Kane. Eight or nine persons, I think; there was Jerry Croker, Daniel Fagan, Coffin, you, the mother of the child, myself, and two of three more.

Prisoner. You say you saw me at Hughson's several times, what room was I usually in?

Kane. Sometimes in one room, and sometimes in another.

Prisoner. At what time was I there?

Kane. At night.

Prisoner. What habit have you seen me wear?

Kane. A black coat, yellowish surtout, and sometimes a light colored close bodied cape coat.

Prisoner. What did I offer in order to induce you to become a Roman catholic?

Kane. Foregiveness of all my sins past, and what I should do in this case; and I said to you, whats a fine thing it is to be of such a religion, when a priest can forgive sins, and send one to heaven.

Mr. Chambers - - Call Sarah Hughson.

Prisoner. I except against her being sworn, for she has been convicted, and received sentence of death for being concerned in this conspiracy, and therefore cannot be a witness.

Attorney General - - But Mr. Ury, she has received his majesty's most gracious pardon, which she has pleaded in court this morning, and it has been allowed of, and therefore the law says, she is good evidence. H.Hawk title pardon. Chap. 37 § 48.

Court - - Her pardon has been pleaded and allowed, and be law she may be admitted.

S. Hughson sworn.

Mr. Chambers - - Sarah, do you give the court and jury an account of what you know of Ury's being concerned in this conspiracy.

S. Hughson. I know him, and have often seen him at my father's, late in last fall chiefly: I have seen there at nights in company with Negroes, when they have been talking of burning the town and killing the white people. I have seen him make a ring width chalk on the floor, which he made the Negroes stand round and put their left foot in, and he swore them with a cross in his hand, to burn and destroy the town, and to cut their master's and mistress's throats. He swore Bastian, Vaarck's Caesar, Auboyneau's Prince, and Walter's Quack: He swore them to keep secret, not to discover him or anybody else, if hey were to die for it. I have heard Ury, and the Negroes, talk of burning the fort; and he said, if that did not do they were to begin at the east end of the town, with a strong easterly wind, and that would go through the whole town. He asked me to swear to the plot, and said that I should have all my since forgiven, if I kept all secret; and he swore me on an English book and my parents and Peggy were by; and he swore Peggy too; and I heard him tell her, that all the sins which she had committed should be forgiven her; and he told her, that priests could forgive sins as well as God, if they would follow their directions. That he used to christen Negroes there; he christened Caesar, Quack and other Negroes, crossed them on the face, had water and other things; and he told them he would absolve them from all their sins.

Prisoner. How did I swear you?

S. Hughson. On a book. I believe it was an English book.

Prisoner. Who was present when I swore you?

S. Hughson. My parents, Peggy, Kane and others.

Prisoner. You say I baptized several people, pray what ceremony did I use at baptizing?

S. Hughson. When you baptized the Negroes, you made a cross upon their faces, and sprinkled water, and you used something else, but I cannot tell what; and you talked in a language which I did not understand.

Prisoner. Whom did I baptize?

S. Hughson. Cae, Prince, Bastian, Quack, Cuffee, and several other Negroes.

[Note (s): The behavior of this miserable wretch was, upon this occasion, beyond expectation, composed and decent. She seemed to be touched with remorse and compunction. What came from her, was delivered with all the visible marks and semblance of sincerity and truth; insomuch, that the court, jury, and many of the audience, looked upon her at this instant to be under real conviction of mind for her past offenses, which was somewhat surprising to those who were witnesses to the rest of her conduct, since her condemnation and several reprieves. Her evidence, as the reader may observe, was regular and uniform, and agreed with the account of the plot, as to the persons and things she spoke to, and was chiefly confirmed by many concurring evidences; and therefore, for once, it seems but reasonable and just to allow that she spoke the truth. She was brought this morning to plead her pardon out of the condemned hole, where she had been confined from the time of her condemnation; and when her pardon was pleaded, she was taken fro court into a room in custody of the under-sheriff, where she was to be near at hand for call upon this trial, and there she remained until wanted and was sent for; and the witnesses delivered their testimony in the order of the time they are here placed, out of the hearing of each other, till each respective person had given their evidence - - which is mentioned, that the reader may more particularly observe the correspondence and remarkable agreement between her evidence, Kane's and Mary Burton's, which must be seen by every one that will be at the pains to make the comparison: and Sarah was underground before and all the time Kane had been committed, so that there could have been no confabulation between them, nor could Mary Burton have intercourse with either, who was the first white evidence that impeached Kane, and Kane by his confession confirmed her evidence, and now all three confirm each other.

Court - - Mr. Ury, have you any witnesses; for now is your time to produce them?

Prisoner. May it pease the King's judges, and the gentlemen of the jury - - it is very incongruous to reason to think that I can have any hand or be any way concerned in this plot, if these things be duly weighed: that after the discovery of the conspiracy and the execution of many for it, that I should act in such a lunatic's part if I were guilty as to continue in this city, join with Mr. Campbell, and not only so, but publicly advertise myself for the teaching of grammar yea further, that I should still continue even after the caution Mr. Webb gave me a week and a few days before I was taken into custody he told me Mr. Chambers told him that the eyes of this city were fixed on me, and that I was suspected to be a Roman priest and thought to be in the plot I answered my innocency would protect me I valued not what the world said, again another instance that must free me from this plot is when Mr. Campbell went to take possession of Hughson's house his daughter refusing to go out and she swearing like a life guardian I took up the cause. Mr. Campbell not exerting himself as I thought was proper at that time and told her if she would not go out quietly I would take another method with her for I would have no such wicked person (as she was said to be) live where I was to dwell now reason must pronounce m einnocent for had I been engaged in their scheme, my guilt, my fears would have forced me to have acted in a very different manner rather to have soothed her and gave her liberty to stay till provided for instead of not showing her the least countenance and further what corroborates my non knowledge of this plot is that the Negro who confessed as it is said that he set fire to the fort did not mention me in all his confession doubtless he would not have neglected and passed over such a person as I am said to be, namely a priest and if he was bound by any oath or oaths a he confessed it showed he thought it or them of no value and therefore would have confessed and laid open the whole scheme and all the persons he knew concerned in it but more especially the priest as it is said I am and what is still more strong for my innocency is that neither Hughson his wife nor the creature that was hanged with them and all that have been put to death since did not once name me. Certainly, gentlemen, if I am a priest as you take me to be, I could not be so foolish as to engage myself in a contrivance as to blind myself with a cord for Negroes or what is worse profligate whites the scum of this earth, superior in villany to the knights of the post to make an halter for me gentlemen, as there is great unknown and tremendous being with whom we call God, I never knew or saw Hughson, his wife, or the creature that was hanged with them to my knowledge living, dying or dead or the Negro that is said to have fired the fort excepting in his last moments but put the case I had known Hughson's and had been at his house is it to be inferred from thence that I must be acquainted with his villany or knew his secrets and as he kept a public house which is open and free for all is it reasonable to think that all or any man being seen at Hughson's must make him or them culpable or chargeable with his villany surely not for if soad would be the case of many gentlemen who in traveling the countries in England who have used bad houses or inns and lit into the company of highwaymen who by their garb and conversation they took for some honest country gentlemen or tradesmen and yet these have not been in the least suspected but I fear all this trouble of mine springs from and is ground upon the apprehensions of my being a Roman priest. I believe no priest would hold a confederacy with Negroes; they are too wise, to cunning to trust, such sort of gentry, it is not men of good fortune, good sense, and learning they care to meddle with or entrust in such affairs as plots.

And further what is of great note is that Hughson was sworn to be the whole projector and carrier on of the plot and if these witnesses knew me so well as they pretend to, how came it about what reason can be assigned why they did not bring me out before?

Court. Mr. Ury, if you have any witnesses to examine, it is more proper you should do that now, and make your defence afterwards.

Prisoner. If that be the pleasure of the judges, I have several witnesses; I desire Mr. Croker may be called.

Prisoner. As I have lodged at your house for some time, you can best give an account of my manner of life and conversation; and pray inform the king's judges and the jury; if you ever saw any Negroes come after me.

Croker. No, I never saw any Negroes come after you.

Prisoner. Give me an account of what you know of me.

Croker. Mr. Ury came to my house the summer before last, and stayed a week; and then returned to Burlington, and came back last November, and said he was going further; but I prevailed upon him to stay, to teach my son Latin, for which I was to give him his lodging and diet. He taught Norwood's children, and Col. Beekman's daughter to write and cipher. Some time ago he went to Staten Island, and preached there, and said he was paid for it: he lodged at my house from November till a little before Campbell took Hughson's house; and while he was with me, he kept pretty good hours; sometimes he came home by eight, or nine, or ten o'clock, and sometimes stayed out till eleven or twelve at night. He once went to Brunswick this spring, before the fort was burnt, as I heard, or else I do not know that he lay out of my house; that once talking of Negroes, I heard him say, he did not think them proper objects of salvation. He used to go up stairs sometimes, light a candle in the daytime and lock himself up in a room alone.

Attorney General. Pray, Mr. Croker, was you in town all the time he lodged at your house?

Croker. No, I have been out for a day or so.

Attorney General. Pray, Mr. Croker, what hours did the prisoner usually come home at?

Croker. Sometimes sooner and sometimes later: I have known him stay out sometimes till eleven or twelve o'clock, once or twice later: I have known him stay out sometimes till eleven or twelve o'clock, once or twice later; I asked him why he stayed out so late, and where he had been? He commonly told me he had been at Mr. Webb's; and sometimes at some other private houses.

Attorney General. When did Ury come to lodge at your house, and when did he leave it?

Croker. He came to my house in November last, and left it a little before Campbell went to live at Hughson's house.

Attorney General. Have you ever heard him preach?

Croker. Yes, once, and he then said he was to preach again the next Sunday; and I his prayer before sermon, he prayed for his majesty king George, and all the royal family.

[Note (w): Which is beyond what any other witness says, and contrary to Ury's own pretended principles of a nonjuror.]

Joseph Webb called for the prisoner and sworn.

Prisoner. Mr. Webb, I desire you will give an account of what you know of me.

Webb. I have known Mr. Ury since November last, I was then at work at John Croker's, at the fighting cocks, and hearing him reading Latin and English, and thinking he ready well, enquired of Croker who he was? He told me he was a schoolmaster lately come from Philadelphia; and from this he became acquainted with him, and I asked him if he would teach a child of mine: and he said he would, if Croker would give him the liberty of coming to his house; which Croker agreed to; and I sent my child to him, and he taught him Latin; and after this I recommended him to Col. Beekman, to teach his daughter to write and cipher; and he and I growing more intimate, and observing a poor and mean appearance in his habit, I thought his pocket might be answerable to it; and I gave him an invitation to my house, and told hi he should be very welcome at my table noon and night, at any time, when he saw proper; and he frequently came to my house accordingly all the winter: that he used often to stay at my house late in discoursing, sometimes on one subject, sometimes on another; and has stayed there now and then till eleven or twelve o'clock at night, and I have often gone home with him to his lodging at those hours. Mr. Ury told me he was a non juring minister; having asked him who ordained him, he answered me, the senior non juror in England: I have heard him preach, and have heard him say, such a day is my sacrament day, and he must be at sacrament.

Attorney General. Did he say he must take the sacrament, or be at sacrament, or administer the sacrament.

Webb. I cannot be sure, but I remember he said it was his sacrament day.

Attorney General. Was it Sundays or working days he said were his sacrament days?

Webb. I cannot be sure, but I think I have heard him name both.

Attorney General. Do you know anything of his buying wafers, or going to a confectioner's?

Webb. He asked me for a confectioner's shop, and I showed him Mr. De Brosse's, where he went along with me; and after he asked for several sorts of sweetmeats, he asked for wafers; which being shown to him, he asked Mr. De Brosse if he made wafers for the Lutheran minister, and he was told he did, but I do not remember that he bought any of them: I have heard him pray and preach several times, but do not remember that ever I heard him pray for King George, but in general terms for the king. I am by trade a carpenter, and Ury applied to me to make him something in Hughson's house, which I have heard since called and altar; that Ury gave me directions for making it and said it was a place to lay books on to read, or to put a candle or a bottle and glass on, or other such like common uses; it was two pieces of board, which formed a triangle, and was raised against the wall, at the bottom of which was a shelf, on each side there was a place to hold a candle.

Attorney General. Do you think if a man wanted a shelf or other place to lay a book on to read, or set a bottle or glass on, he would have made it in that frorm?

Webb. I can't say; people may have odd humors, but I should not.

Attorney General. When you made it, what did you take it for?

Webb. I can't say: I followed his directions.

Attorney General. Do you know anything of Ury being imprisoned in England?

Webb. Ury did tell me he was imprisoned in England: for he said he had wrote a book there, and that the critics laid hold of it, picked a hole in it and construed it treason; but if it was, he said, it was contrary to his intentions.

Attorney General. Mr. Webb, in your conversations together, what have you heard him say about Negroes?

Webb. We were one day talking about Negroes, and I said I thought they had souls to be saved or last as well as other people: Ury said he thought they were not proper objects of salvation; I replied, what would you do with them then; what, would you damn them all? No, says he, leave them to that Great being that has made them, he knows best what to do with them; says he, they are of a slavish nature, it is the nature of them to be slaves, give them learning, do them all the good you can, and put them beyond the condition of slaves, and in return they will cut your throats.

Court. Mr. Ury, would you ask this witness any more questions?

Prisoner. No sir. I have more witnesses, John and Mrs. Campbell.

John Campbell and his wife sworn.

Prisoner. Mr. Campbell, did you ever see me at Hughson's house before I went there with you, and what passed there?

J. Campbell. I never saw him there till I went to take possession of the house at May day last, and then as we were going there together he said he did not know the way thither, and when we came down, he took Gerardus Comfort's house for it; as for anything else, I know nothing more of him, for I took him for a grave, sober, honest man.

Prisoner. Mrs. Campbell, will you please to give an account of what you know of me, and what passed between Sarah Hughson and me, when we went to take possession of the house.

A. Campbell. I went with my husband and Mr. Ury, on May day last, to Hughson's to take possession of the house, and when we came there Sarah Hughson the daughter was in possession, and we told her she must go out of the house, for that my husband had taken it: whereupon Sarah Hughson swore and cursed at me; Mr. Ury said to her, how dare you talk so impertinently and saucily to an old woman, you impudent hussy! Go out of the house, or I will turn you out; Sarah then swore miserably, and said you have a house now, but shall not have one long. I have often heard him pray and sing psalms, and he prayed by a sick woman; I never saw any harm by him; my husband and he were to keep school together.

Court: Will you ask them any more questions?

Prisoner. No sir, I have nothing more.

Attorney General. If your honors please, as the prisoner has been endeavoring to prove he is not a Romish priest, and has already insisted on it as a part of his defence; I shall beg leave to examine a witness or two to that point.

Joseph Hildreth, schoolmaster, and Richard Norwood, called and sworn.

Attorney General. Mr. Hildreth, will you give an account of what you know of the prisoner, how you came to be acquainted with him, and what has passed between him and you in conversation from time to time.

Hildreth. What I have to say, sir, I have committed to writing. [and produced a paper from his pocket.] I had a little business on board Captain Griffiths, where I met with him and Webb in company, which was the first time I ever spoke to him, then after our salutation of each other, he began to ask me some questions concerning my school and method of teaching; after which we stepped in at Baker's and took a serious glass together; at which time he took a small book from his pocket (English and Latin) and construed (I think) the 117th psalm; then laying the book on the table, I took it up, and was going to look on the title page, but he directly seized it out of my hands, and told me I must not look into it, and put it into his pocket.

Another time at my school, I had some discourse with him concerning Mr. Whitefield's letter in answer to Mr. Wesley's sermon on free-grace, which letter he did not approve of at all, and told me he believed it was through the great encouragement the Negroes had received from Mr. Whitefield, we had all the disturbance, and that he believed Mr. Whitefield was more of a Roman that anything else, and he believed he came abroad with no good design. Then I asked him what was the signification of a non-juror, as I understood he pretended to be? And he answered those that would take the oath of allegiance, as he did not; I asked him why? Says he can you swear one to be a bastard? No, no more can they say King J - - was one; and the difference between we non-jurors and others, in this; we in the prayers for the king and royal family, mention no names, as they do; I asked him if they prayed for the pretender? He said, for him, let him be who he will, that was the king, he mentioned no names.

At another time, says he, you talk so much against popery, I believe though you speak so much against it, you will find you have (or I think will have) a pope in your belly, for says he, the absolution of the church of Rome is not half so bad as that of the church of England at the visitation of the sick: but says I, I don't approve of their confessing to priests, etc. says I there is a deal of wickedness and deceit in it: says he, no, no, for when any person makes confessions the priest does not know who they be, for he does not so much as see them, but only hears and absolves them: then says I, I was mistaken. Oh! Says he, they speak against the church of Rome, but don't know them; their priests says he, are the most learned of men; the articles of the church of England were made in distracted times.

And I observed several times he said, we priests. Says he, your Roman priests will make you believe, and prove by the plain rules of grammar, that black is white, and white black, and that the wafer and wine is the real boy and blood of Christ.

We were often in company, but the best part of our discourse was upon salvation by faith alone, which he would not allow, nor predestination: and he told me he really believed the moon to be an inhabited planet, and all the stars were inhabited; or else says he, I would not repeat that part of the Nicene creed, begotten of his father before all worlds; and says he, many texts of scripture confirm it to be so.

I was several times since I his company, but do not remember anything in particular relating to priests, etc. but the last time I had anything of discourse was about two days before I heard him preach, and then in his room; I seeing the altar placed in the corner, I asked him what use that was for? First he said only to lay books on, or for a candle to sit and read by; but I told him I could not think it, for I supposed it for the sacrament by its form and odd color; I begged him to let me know what it was; so after some time he seriously told me it was for the sacrament; and he told me, I think, every saint's day it was exposed, only covered with a piece of white linen, and tht he administered on some proper days; and he told me they received the wafer instead of bread, and white instead of red win: I asked, why the wafer? Because says he, the wafer is more pure; and no bread he thought pure enough to represent the body of our Lord; then going to his small box, says he I will get a piece and you shall taste it if you will, and he brought me a piece, and I took and eat it.

I think he told me, that some time before he had baptized a child in the house, but they used more ceremonies than we; and he talked as if they anointed and washed one another's feet; he told me further, that at the time of the celebration, or at what time the sacrament was exposed, they had lighted candles burning to represent our Savior as the light of the world; and when I came in to hear him preach, I accordingly saw it as he told me; for he told me be before, that if I came on Sunday evening to hear him, I could see it, for the sacrament was on the altar, covered with a white linen cloth, and there were three candles burning, but not a minute after I came in, he put out the candles, and put his sacrament in his box, and locked them up.

Some time after I became thus acquainted with him, I was informed he kept a private meeting, and made use of the church form of prayer every Sunday evening, at the house of Mr. John Campbell, in his own hired room.

My curiosity led me the next Sunday evening to go and hear him preach, but when I came there he told me he did not make a practice of preaching to any others but those of his own society, and those of his society did not make any practice of running to any of our churches or meetings, for he did not approve of any such thing; and as he was a non-jured minister, so he had a society and members of his own.

Afterwards he told me he had some company from Philadelphia (I think) and desired to be excused; but next Sunday evening, if I would call, he would be glad to see me.

The next Sunday evening I accordingly went, and heard him discourse upon the second chapter of the second epistle of S. Peter, the 1st, 2nd, and 3rd verses; and before he dismissed us, he told us he would preach the next Wednesday following (being the day his majesty began his happy reign) upon the 16th chapter of Matthews, the 18th and 19th verses, adjoining to them the words of our Lord to his disciples, whosoever sins ye remit, they are remitted unto them, and whosoever sins ye retain, they are retained: which discourse I did not hear.

Council. Mr. Ury, would you ask this witness any question?

Prisoner. No sir, I have nothing to ask him.

Attorney General. Mr. Norwood, will you give the court and jury an account of what you know of the prisoner at the bar?

Norwood. I became acquainted with him last fall, and I agreed with him in December to teach my children to write and read; that several times in conversation with him, he talked in such a manner that I suspected him to be a popish priest. He used very often to miss coming to teach my children at the school time, and made frivolous excuses, and at last I was very angry with him and discharged him; that in the evening he used very often to pretend that he must go to pray by a sick person by the English church, that belonged to his society, or that he must go and pray with his society by the English church: whereupon I once asked him to let me go along with him, but he refused me, and said it was not proper for anyone to go there who were not of the society, which occasioned a jealousy in me, and I had often a mind to have dogged him, to have seen where he went, and do not know how it happened, but I never did; that one day I met Campbell, the schoolmaster, in the street, who said to me, what do you think? Webb has taken away his son from me, and has put him to a schoolmaster that lodges at Croker's; and Campbell said, d - -n him, he is a popish priest; and at last having a bad opinion of him, I discharged him, lest he should inveigle my children, and I told him I would have nothing more to say to him.

Court. Mr. Ury, would you ask this witness anything?

Prisoner. No sir.

Mr. Murray. May it please your honors, and you, gentlemen of the jury.

That the prisoner is a Romish emissary, sent according t the intimation in general Oglethorpe's letter, I think must be concluded from what has been given in evidence against him; and from the known principles of the Romish religion, it may be judged what inducement the prisoner had to undertake so wicked and diabolical a project. The letter of general Oglethorpe has been offered by way of inducement, and in aid of other evidence in general, to show that there was a plot, and herein I apprehend we are justified by the precedents and authorities in law before cited.

Mr. Smith, addressing himself to the court, proceeded as followeth.

Before the prisoner enters upon his defence, we conceive it will be proper to read to him some passages out of the sundry books that declare the customs and usages of the church of Rome, to which his practices among us, as declared by the witnesses, bear some conformity; and unless he can make it appear that his practices are warranted by the usage of any other church, we conceive they will convince everybody that he is a priest of the Roman church, and no other.

More court testimony:

Peggy had said several times, as well after her conviction as condemnation for the conspiracy, as the judges were informed by the under-sheriff, that she had sworn falsely against John Romme; which was so gross a prevarication, as discouraged them from taking any further pains with her, since there could be no dependence upon what she should say; the evening before her execution she sent a message to Mr. Justice Philipse, signifying her desire to speak with him; he accordingly went to her; she declared to him, that she had forsworn herself, for all that she had said about Romme and his wife was false, excepting as to their receiving the stolen goods of the Negroes. — From the scanty room in the jail for the reception of so many prisoners, this miserable wretch, upon her conviction with the Hughsons for the conspiracy, was put in the same cell with them; which perhaps was an unfortunate incident; for though she had to the time of their trial screened them from the charge of the conspiracy; yet there was reason to expect, that upon the last pinch, when she found there was no hopes of saving her own life if she persisted, the truth as to this particular would have come out; and indeed it was upon this expectation, that she was brought upon trial for the conspiracy; for her several examinations before set forth, and what Arthur Price had sworn to have dropt from her in accidental talk in the jail, had put it beyond doubt, that, that she was privy to many of the Hughson's secrets concerning this detestable confederacy; but when she was admitted to the Hughsons, under the circumstances of conviction and condemnation for the conspiracy, they most probably prevailed with her to persevere in her obstinacy, to the end to cover their own guilt, since they were determined to confess nothing themselves; and they might drive her to desperation by subtle insinuations, that the judges she saw after they had picked all they could out of her, whatever expectations she might have raised from her confessions, or hope she flattered herself with of saving her life upon the merit of them; yet after all, she was brought to trial and condemned for the conspiracy,

Thou vile wretch! how much does thy ingratitude enhance your guilt! and your hypocritical, canting behaviour upon your trial, your protestations of innocence, your dissimulation before God and man, will be no small article against you at the day of judgment, for ye have all souls to be saved or to be damned; your spirits are immortal, that is to say, they will live forever, be either eternally happy or eternally miserable in the other world; and be not deceived, God will not be mocked, he will not be baffled withal, he knows all your thoughts, and sees all your actions, and will reward every one according to their works; those that have done good shall go into everlasting res and happiness, that is to say into life eternal; and they that have done evil, and die hardy and impenitent, shall be thrown into the internal lake of fire and brimstone; together with the devil and his accursed spirits, where the worm never dieth, that is, the biting, gnawing worm of conscience will forever be upbraiding you, and fire will never be quenched, but in this torment you must remain under the most bitter weeping, wailing and gnashing of teeth, time without end.

If you would not have this your portion, then let us tell you and admonish you in compassion to your wretched miserable souls, immediately to confess your guilt, your horrid sins, before God and man, and discover your accomplices, that you may prevent all further mischief which may otherwise happen from this your hellish conspiracy; sincerely and heartily bewail your heinous and crying sins, and entreat forgiveness of God Almighty; for upon these considerations only, can you entertain any rational or well grounded hope of being received into the arms of his mercy.

And now what is the end of tall these your most wicked, detestable and horrible devises? why, you have succeeded so far as to put part of your accursed scheme in execution; you have burnt down and consumed the king's house and buildings in the fort; he house of Van Zant, and have made attempts to burn several others, which God Almighty in mercy and his wonderful and gracious good providence has prevented, by suffering the flames to be timely extinguished; the villainies of these diabolical confederates have been detected, many of them have already met with their deserts, and are gone to their long homes, whither you are in a few hours to follow them, for you are now also delivered into the hands of our laws, and in this world you must have justice, and you are left to the mercy of God in the next.

What has already been said, is applicable, most of it, to every one of you.

And in as a particular manner, Quash, may you be upbraided with the like reproaches for your ingratitude, for as we have been informed, you have likewise had a very indulgent master, who has put great trust and confidence in you, it may be presumed from your having better sense than the rest of his Negroes: how vilely then have you abused his indulgence! in return for kindnesses, you wretches would imbrue your hands in the blood of your masters and their families; you that would destroy without mercy, with what face can you expect mercy at the hands of God, unless you acknowledge every one his guilt and bewail it with hearty sorrow and sincere tears of repentance, and beseech his forgiveness, laying open the whole wicked scheme, and discovering your several confederates and accomplices, all the parties concerned, so that an effectual stop may be put to all further mischief: upon these conditions only can you expect mercy at the hands of God Almighty.

As to you two Catoes, and you Fortune. You appear indeed to have been inferior agents, but your hearts as corrupt and ripe for mischief as any of the rest; you have all alike taken that hellish, execrable oath, and equally bound yourselves in that villainous engagement, not only to burn and consume your master's substance, but to murder and destroy their persons and families; you were willing and ready as the ablest of them to act your parts in this bloody scheme.

It is s very irksome task to pronounce this sentence which the law requires of us, for we delight not in any man's blood; but the law adjudges you unfit to live.

Therefore the sentence against you is that you, each and every of you, be carried from hence to the place from whence you came, from thence to the place of execution, where you Ben and Quash, are to be each of you chained to a stake and burnt to death.

And you Cato (Mr. Provost's) you Cato (Mr. Cowley's) and you Fortune, are each and every of you to be hanged by the neck until you be severally dead. And the Lord of his infinite mercy, have compassion upon your poor wretched souls.

The one indictment is grounded upon an act of assembly of this province, supposing them to be slaves, by which act the testimony of one Negro slave shall be legal evidence against another.

But it has been made a question, whether these prisoners, now before us, are slaves or not; and the prisoners themselves pretend to be free subjects of the king of Spain, with whom we are now at war, from whom they have been taken and made prize, and have been condemned and adjudged as such in the court of admiralty there, without any plea being offered there, or so much as any claim or pretence of the prisoners being entitled to any privilege, as being free subjects of Spain; and surely there never could have been a more proper time and season for them to have set up such pretence, as when their case was depending before the court of admiralty, where they should have offered it by way of plea; especially considering, that by their neglect of that opportunity, they must well know the consequence would be, their being adjudged as part of the goods and chattels of the subjects of Spain, would be condemned as lawful prize, and would also be sold as slaves; but if this pretence had been offered there, (as it was not) and they could not have proved the truth of the plea, it would not have availed them, but they must have been adjudged to be slaves.

But they have made that pretense in this court, and what has been offered in support of it? Why, there has been several witnesses that have spoke to the point; and what is the amount of their testimony? Why, it is no more than the hearsay of an hearsay of a person, who imagined or believed, that they or most of the Spanish Negroes taken by Capt. Lush, were freemen; but which of them were, or were not, he could not say, nor does it appear that the prisoners at the bar, or any of them, are such of Capt. Lush's prize-prisoners, as that the said Spanish gentleman imagined were free; for it was no more than his imagination, as to any of them being such.

You have heard the adjudication and decree of the court of admiralty read, by which it appears, they were condemned as prize, and that they were sold as slaves, has been proved by the vendue-master; therefore for what appears now before the court, it should seem that they really are slaves; and as nothing appears; no sufficient or proper evidence appears to the contrary, then if you take them upon these considerations, to be slaves, all the Negro evidence which has been given upon this trial against them, is legal evidence, and so you are to consider of that testimony, and let it have its full force; and if you should have sufficient reasons in your own consciences to discredit them, and that notwithstanding the weight of that evidence, you can think them, or any of them, not guilty, you will then say so and acquit them, or such of them as you think innocent as to the charge of this indictment, upon the act of assembly.

Gentlemen, the prisoners having started this pretence, of being free subjects of the king of Spain, is case it should have happened upon this trial, as we think it has not, that there should be sufficient evidence to shew that the prisoners were freemen, if we could take them to be such, is it fit that persons guilty of so atrocious and enormous crimes (let them be free or bond) such execrable villains should miss of their deserved punishment and escape the justice of the law? surely that would be very unbecoming, that such wickedness should be suffered with impunity in any well regulated government or society: therefore be they freemen, or be they slaves, the main question before you is, whether they, or any, or which of them are guilty of the charge against them, in the second indictment, of conspiring with other slaves and persons to burn the house in the fort, to burn the town and murder and destroy the people.

To prove the charge in this indictment, there was the testimony of Mary Barton [Negro wench] : I must observe to you, that her testimony, as to the charge in this indictment, is single, there is no other witness; but nevertheless gentlemen, one witness is sufficient, and if you give credit to her testimony, you will no doubt discharge a good conscience, and find them guilty; if you should have sufficient reason in your own minds to discredit her testimony, if you can think so, you must then acquit them: the prisoners seem all to be equally involved by her testimony, in this unparalleled and hellish conspiracy, and there is no room to make any difference between them; therefore you will either acquit them all, or find them all guilty.

Then the jury withdrew, and in about half an hour returned, and found them all guilty.

The king against Sarah Hughson, and Jamaica, a Negro.

The judges having advised with his honour the lieutenant governor, ordered, the execution of Sarah Hughson and Jamaica, be further respited until next Friday seven-night; though with respect to Sarah this was a mere act of mercy, for she yet remained inflexible.

This day Duane's Prince, Latham's Tony, Shurmur's Cato, Kip's Harry, and Marschalk's York, Negroes, were executed at the gallows, according to sentence; and the body of York was afterwards hung in chains, upon the same gibbet with John Hughson.

Some few days after this the town was amused with a rumour, that Hughson was turned Negro, and Vaarck's Caesar a white; and when they came to put up York in chains by Hughson (who was hung upon the gibbet three weeks before) so much of him as was visible, viz. face, hands, neck, and feet, were of a deep shining black, rather blacker than the Negro placed by him, who was one of the darkest hue of his kind; and the hair of Hughson's beard and neck (his head could not be seen for he had a cap on) was curling like the wool of a Negro's beard and head, and the features of his face were of the symmetry of a Negro beauty; the nose broad and flat, the nostrils open and extended, the mouth wide, lips full and thick, his body (which when living was tall, by the view upwards of six feet, but very meager) swelled to a gigantic size; and as to Caesar (who, though executed for a robbery, was also one of the head Negro conspirators, had been hung up in chains a month before Hughson, and was also of the darkest complexion) his face was at the same time somewhat bleached or turned whitish, insomuch that it occasioned a remark, that Hughson and he had changed colours. The beholders were amazed at these appearances; the report of them engaged the attention of many, and drew numbers of all ranks, who had curiosity, to the gibbets, for several days running, in order to be convinced by their own eyes, of the reality of things so confidently reported to be, at least wondrous phenomenons, and upon the view they were found to be such as have been described; many of the spectators were ready to resolve them into miracles; however, others not so hasty, though surprised at the sights, were willing to account to them in a natural way, so that they administered matter for much speculation.

The sun at this time had great power, and the season as usual very hot, that Hughson's body dripped and distilled very much, as it needs must, from the great fermentation and abundance of matter within him, as could not but be supposed at that time, from the extraordinary bulk of his body; though considering the force of the sun, and the natural meagerness of his corpse, one would have been apt to imagine that long ere this it would have been disencumbered of all its juices. At length, about ten days or a fortnight after Hughson's mate, York, was hung by him, Hughson's corpse, unable longer to contain its load, burst and discharged pail fulls[d] of blood and corruption; this was testified by those who were near by, fishing upon the beach when the irruption happened, to whom the stench of it was very offensive.

[Note (d): (d) Which may be understood to mean a surprising quantity.]

Those who were inclined to account in a natural way, for what was by some esteemed almost miraculous, by all very surprising, observed, that by the written evidences of witnesses, both black and white, information was given of poison being distributed among the conspirators[e] and of the use their principals intended should have been made of it; Harry, a Negro doctor, was to bring the Negroes poison to use (if they were discovered and taken) before they were executed; Kane had seen him give poison, as they called it, to Walter's Quack for that purpose, in papers; Quack said he should not be suspected, he might go to the prison to carry victuals and so could give the poison to those that were condemned, to prevent their execution;[f] Kane saw doctor Harry give a large quantity of it to Hughson.

[Note (f): (f) This office we may suppose was to be administered by Quack, without the knowledge of the patients (and he speaks as if they had a confidence in him) in order to dispatch them, and prevent their telling tales: for when they found themselves in jeopardy, there might be danger of their speaking the truth, and discovering their principals, in hopes of saving their own lives by it.]

It has been related already that Hughson when he was brought out of jail to be carried to his execution, had a red spot in each cheek, about the bigness of a shilling, which at that time was by some thought very remarkable, because he was always pale of visage, and the sheriffs (who observed it) did not believe from the care that had been taken, he could have drank any strong liquor in jail, which was an additional reason why they took so much notice of it.

Upon the supposition that Hughson had taken poison, it has been made a question whether that might not have occasioned the swelling of his corpse to so amazing a bulk? Nay his arms, legs and thighs, were enlarged in proportion to the body; this is submitted to the consideration of the curious and connoisseur in physic.

As to the change of complexions in Hughson and Caesar, some imputed it to the influence of the sun, but to that it was objected, it would be strange indeed that the sun should have two such different effects as to turn Hughson [a white] black, and Caesar [a Negro] whitish.

As to Hughson's taking poison, that by some was thought very improbable, for as it is said in their account of his behaviour at, and going to his execution, his actions were observed to be such as betokened his expectation of being rescued, he held up his hand as high as his pinion would admit of, and seemed to beckon with his finger as one expecting deliverance, and if that was his persuasion he would not have taken poison, which was certain death; and besides if he had taken any, he would have taken a sufficient quantity, and time enough to have answered the design of it, which it must be supposed to be to destroy himself to prevent his execution.

To this it was answered, that though he might be determined to take poison to destroy himself, and did take some, yet he might do it with so much reluctance as not to take the quantity prescribed sufficient to answer the end, which though he might not be aware of, but expect certain death from it, yet the nearer he approached the gallows, the more his thoughts might be confused, and nature prevailed; as long as there is life, there is hopes, and his deliverance might be uppermost in his mind; he would willingly have avoided the infamy of hanging, and stand the chance of saving his life in the bargain.

Whatever were the causes of these changes, the facts are here related, that every one may make their own conjectures upon them.

But Hughson it seems let the worst happen to him in all events, declared as he was going to mount the cart which was to carry him to execution, that he did not doubt but some remarkable sign would happen to him, to shew [or signify] his innocence; and if his corpse becoming monstrous in size, and his complexion (for once to use a vulgar similitude) as black as the d—l, can be deemed remarkable signs or tokens of his innocence! then some may imagine it has happened according to his expectation.

Witnesses of the king – Mary Burton sworn.

Mary Burton said that she had seen captain Ben, Quash, Cato (Provoost's) and Cato (Cowley's) amongst the conspirators at the meeting at Hughson's, and that they were all four consenting, and as forward as the rest for burning the town and killing the white people. She did not remember that she had seen Fortune at those meetings, but thought she knew his face.

That Hughson, his wife, daughter Sarah, and Peggy and the said Ury, when this deponent has come into the room amongst them to bring what they wanted, have several times turned out all the Negroes present, and then have all joined in tempting this deponent to take an oath; but upon her asking them for what? they would not tell her, but said she must swear first, and then they would tell her, but this she absolutely denied over and over; at which refusal they were angry, and turned her out of the room, and Ury said to her, had not you better swear and go fine, than go as she did; for they all (the Hughsons, Peggy and Jury, had when they proposed to swear her) offered her silks, and a deal of fine things, if she would comply with their requests, and Peggy said she was a great fool if she did not.

That about a fortnight or three weeks before Hogg's goods were stolen, she has observed Campbell (with whom she has heard Jury used to keep school) come to Hughson's of a Sunday, sometimes one Garrit Van Emborough with him, and that Campbell used to go into the room below with the Hughsons, Peggy, and Caesar, Prince, and Cuffee (Negroes) and when these were met, the Hughsons used to turn the deponent up stairs; but she cannot say she ever heard them talking of the plot before Campbell, but she strongly suspected that he knew of it, from his keeping company with the Hughsons, and the said three Negroes, whom she looked upon to be the principal heads of the Negroes in the conspiracy.

That during the time there was snow upon the ground all last winter, she has often known Hughson to go out of town a-days, upon the pretence of fetching firewood from the commons, with his sleigh; and that he has not returned home till eight, nine, ten or eleven o'clock at night, at different times, and has brought Negroes to town to his house, and that he has carried them back again in his sleigh after midnight, one, two or three o'clock, and has not returned home again sometimes till seven or eight o'clock in the morning.

That she has several times seen Mr. Peter De Lancey's Spanish Negro Antonio at Hughson's when he (Hughson) has come home late out of the woods, and that she has seen him many times get into Hughson's sleigh late in the night, and that Hughson has not returned home till six, seven or eight the next morning; but at the time this deponent did not know where the said Spanish Negro lived, whether in town or country.

That one day at Hughson's, some of the Negroes had behaved rudely towards her, and being in a passion, she was provoked to swear at them, in the presence of Jury alias Ury, above mentioned, and upon recollecting herself she said, God forgive me; whereupon the said Jury answered her, that was a small matter; he could forgive her a great deal more sins than that; that was nothing.

That at another time when the Negroes had provoked her, she wished those black toads at the devil; oh, says Jury, let them be clack, or what they will, the devil has nothing to do with them; I can forgive them their sins, and you yours too

The five Spanish Negroes convicted of the conspiracy on the seventeenth of June last, were this day called up to judgment, viz, Mr. De Lancey's Antonio, Mesnard's Antonio, Becker's Pablo, Sarly's Juan or Wan, M'Mullen's Augustine; and having nothing to offer in arrest, but protestations of their innocence, Mr. Gomez[a] was directed to interpret what the court delivered.

[Note (a): (a) He had been interpreter upon the trial]

Then the third justice proceeded as followeth.

Mr. Gomez, pray tell the prisoners at the bar, that the court observes, 1st. That they were taken with some Spaniards by an English privateer, were brought into this port and condemned as lawful prize, being supposed to be slaves belonging to the subjects of the king of Spain; and nothing appeared to the court of admiralty (which is the court to which jurisdiction concerning things of this nature does properly belong) to shew that they were freemen, and they have made no pretence or claim in that court to be such, they were therefore adjudged to be slaves.

2ndly. That the court of admiralty having so adjudged them to be slaves, they had been severally sold and disposed of, by which means they were discharged from confinement in prison, and thereby have had the opportunity of caballing with other wicked, mischievous and evil disposed persons, as well white men as slaves, and have confederated themselves with them, in a most diabolical conspiracy, to lay this city in ashes, and to murder and destroy all the inhabitants; whereas had they appeared to have been freemen, they would have been prevented this opportunity of venting and gratifying the rancour of their hearts, by being closely confined as prisoners of war.

3dly. If notwithstanding they were freemen, they ought in all reason to have waited the event of the war, and suffered patiently under their misfortune; and when peace should have been concluded, they might have made the truth of their pretensions appear, and then justice would have been done them.

But now, as they are found guilty of this most horrid and villainous conspiracy, by the laws of our land, nothing remains but to pronounce sentence of death against them. Accordingly they were sentenced to be hanged.

The King against Duane's Prince, Latham's Tony, Shurmur's Cato, Marschalk's York, Kip's Harry, Negroes.

The prisoners having been convicted of the conspiracy, were brought to the bar, and having nothing to offer in arrest of judgment, the court passed sentence on them to be hanged: and ordered their execution to be on Friday the third instant, and that the body of York should be afterwards hung in chains on the same gibbet with John Hughson.

[DANIEL HORSMANDEN, ESQ. SPEAKS IN CONFERENCE]

A criminal confesses himself guilty at his own peril: it may be the only chance he has for saving his life; if he denies all, and the crime is proved upon him, his case becomes desperate; but when once he confesses his guilt, it will be standing evidence against him. — The remark upon Negro recantations once for all is, that one can scarce be thoroughly satisfied when it is that they do speak truth, unless what they say be confirmed by concurring circumstances; and the very sight only of their masters may make them change their notes at any time, if they give them not advice and instruction with respect to the their conduct, which there was too much reason to believe some of them did; and perhaps many of these wretches buoyed themselves up with the notion, that their masters would at all hazards save them from the gallows or transportation, if they could; especially such of the slaves as had been bred up to trades or handicrafts: they might flatter themselves that the want of them would be a great prejudice and damage to their owners: as if for their sakes, vile wretches, the whole town must ran the risk of their houses being fired about their ears, and having the inhabitants butchered; but their having once confessed their guilt, a recantation and denial of it afterwards, will scarce be thought an argument of sufficient force to prove their innocence. — The commissioners who tried the Negro conspirators upon the detection of the plot in Antigua, in the year 1736, in the report of their proceedings to their governor, have the following clause apropos to the aforegoing observations, § 20, say they, "there were some steps not of a common kind taken by us in the course of our inquiry, which possibly might have been excepted to; two particulars, one the trying the criminals privately, excluding all white persons (or particularly the masters of slaves) excepting the constables guarding the prisoners, and excepting twice or thrice where some gentlemen of figure (not masters of any slaves under trial) were accidentally present; (the other not being material to the present purpose is omitted.) It goes on — "As to the first, we had experienced the contrary method in the beginning, by trying some of the criminals openly; but the business being of a nature requiring the utmost despatch, we found our proceedings much retarded by the spectators asking many questions of the prisoners and witnesses, and some of them not proper; we soon discovered too (by some things that happened) how much masters were prone to countenance and excuse their slaves, and that slaves were emboldened by their master's presence, and witnesses intimidated; besides we found secrecy necessary, which even oaths of secrecy might not have effectually procured, considering human frailty and forgetfulness, and the common unguardedness of speech most persons are liable to; for sometimes a dangerous criminal might be mentioned by witnesses as parties accused in the course of the trial, and this might be talked of abroad, and occasion flights and concealments, and other inconveniences not to be foreseen.

In our own case, masters and owners of slaves were admitted as witnesses, which, all things considered, perhaps was too great an indulgence: for it is a known rule of law in civil cases, that a party interested in the event of a suit cannot be a witness; and by a parity of reason it may be concluded, that masters of slaves in criminal cases, should not be witnesses, especially in matters of so much consequence to the public; and if any such like case should hereafter happen, which God forbid, upon the reason of that rule, and the inconveniences which have happened from this indulgence, it may be judged necessary to vary from that practice.]

The sentence of Sarah Hughson the daughter, having been respited for upwards of three weeks since the execution of her father and mother, and she in that time often importuned to confess what she know if the conspiracy, did always peremptorily deny she knew any thing of the matter, and made use of many wicked imprecations in order to excite compassion in those that moved it to her, after the manner of her parents, whose constant practice it was, whenever spoke to about the plot: And this being the day appointed for Sarah's execution, she was this morning brought up to Mr. Pemberton, who came to pray by her, and after all his admonitions still denied her guilt, and being carried back to her dungeon where was the Negro wench Sarah, under sentence also to be executed this day; Sarah Hughson at last owned to her, that she had been sworn into the plot. This Negro wench (thinking as may be supposed to make a merit of it) soon after, told what had passed between them to the under sheriff, who acquainted the judges with it, and they sent for Sarah Hughson, who confessed before them her knowledge of the conspiracy, whereupon the execution of both criminals was further replied.

Examination of Sarah Hughson under condemnation, before the chief justice, second justice and others. — Sarah Hughson being examined said, She believes the first time she heard of the plot to burn the city and to murder master and mistress, and if they could not prevail to murder, then to burn them up, was when they lived at Ellis's dock, about a year ago; the Negroes said they had white people to help them; Kane was there often, and came with several Negroes.

- Said she had seen John Ury the priest often there when the Negroes were there, and speak to them; tell them to keep secrecy, and to be true, and not tell of one another if they were to die for it; that they should burn the town down, and in the night cut their master's and mistress's throats with knives they should get; told her not to discover what he said, if she did he would be the death of her.
- He christened Vaarck's Caesar, and others.
- She was sworn by Jury⁽ᶜ⁾ Kane and Sarah were confined in cells separate and distant from each other; but though her owning to the Negro wench that she was sworn into the conspiracy, was the occasion of the respite of her execution, and her being sent for and examined by the judges, yet she owned no such thing upon her first examination, but now she does it with such circumstances: concurring with other evidence, as puts the truth of the matter beyond doubt, and thereby adds credit to the rest of her confession.] when Kane was, of a Sunday night, as things were generally done on Sunday nights.

Desposition No. 5. — Mary Burton being duly sworn and produced before William Kane, soldier, said that she had seen the said Kane at Hughson's very often, talking with Hughson, his wife and daughter, Peggy Salingburgh alias Kerry, Caesar, Vaarck's; Galloway, Rutgers'; Prince, Auboyneau's, and Cuffee, Philipse's, Negroes; and the discourse amongst them was, that they would burn the town, the fort first, the governor and all his family in it, and kill all the white people, and that she heard the said William Kane say, that he would help them all that lay in his power.

Then Mary Burton was ordered to withdraw, and Kane was apprised of the danger he was in, and told he must not flatter himself with the least hopes of mercy, but by making a candid and ingenuous confession of all that he knew of the matter, or to this purpose: but he still denied what had been alleged against him by Mary Burton, till upon most solemn admonition, he began to be affected; his countenance changed, and being near fainting, desired to have a glass of water, which was brought him, and after some pause, he said he would tell the truths though at the same time he seemed very loth to do it; but after some hesitation began to open, and several hours were spent in taking down heads of his confession, which were afterwards drawn out at large, and distinctly read over to him, and being duly sworn, he made oath that the same was true, and (not knowing how to write) he put his mark to it.

The King against Sarah Hughson.

This criminal continuing inflexible, it was ordered she should be executed, according to her sentence, on Wednesday the eighth instant.

About noon this day, the under-sheriff informed the recorder, that John Hughson wanted to speak to the judges, and (as he had said) to open his heart to them, and they should know more, and was very urgent that somebody should go to them to acquaint them therewith. Pursuant to Hughson's desire, the recorder did go up to the City-Hall in the afternoon, expecting he would make some material discovery, and having sent for him, he was asked, what it was that he wanted with the judges? Whereupon Hughson asked if there was a bible, and desired that he might be sworn. He was told that no oath would be administered to him; if he had any thing to say, he had free liberty to speak, but he wanted very much to be sworn. The recorder thereupon reproached him with his wicked life and practices, debauching and corrupting of Negroes, and encouraging them to steal and pilfer from their masters and others, and for shewing his children so wicked an example, training them up in the highway to hell. He further observed to him, that he, his wife, and Peggy, then stood convicted of a felony for receiving stolen goods of Negroes; and that now nothing remained but to pass sentence of death upon them, and to appoint a day for their execution for that fact; but that it was now determined, that he, his wife and daughter, and Peggy, should also be tried for being confederated in this most horrible conspiracy; that the evidence would appear so strong and clear against them in this particular, that there was little doubt of their being all convicted upon that head also; that it would appear undeniably that he was a principal, and head agent in this detestable scheme of villainy; the chief abettor, together with the rest of his family, of this execrable and monstrous contrivance for shedding the blood of his neighbours, and laying the whole city in ashes, upon the expectation of enriching himself by such an inhuman and execrable undertaking. He therefore admonished him, if he would entertain the least hopes of recommending himself to the mercy of God Almighty, before whose tribunal he must soon appear, that he would ingenuously tell the truth, and lay open the whole scene of this dark tragedy, which had been brooding at his house, and discover the several parties he knew to have been engaged in it; in doing which he would make some atonement for his past villainies, by preventing that slaughter, bloodshed and devastation, which he and his confederates had intended; or the recorder expressed himself in words to this purpose. But hereupon Hughson put on a soft smiling air of innocence upon his countenance, again desiring that he might be sworn, which was refused him, and he then declared, he know nothing at all of any conspiracy and called to God to witness his protestations, that he was as innocent with respect to that charge as the child unborn, and also his wife, daughter and Peggy, for aught he knew.

Whereupon the Recorder remanded him to jail.

Whether the man was struck with a compunction, or flattered himself with making a merit by his discovery, and thereby recommend himself to mercy, and that he should so save his life; or whether he imagined that if he could be sworn, and then make the most solemn protestations with the sanction of an oath, that this would give such strong impressions of his innocence, as might make way for his escape; what his view was can only be guessed at; but several who were by him in the jail when he expressed his desire of having the opportunity of speaking with the judges, as above mentioned, concluded from his condition and behaviour at that instant, that he was then really in earnest to lay open this scene of villainy, but it was thought that in two or three hours afterwards, his wife or others had got the better of him, and prevailed with him to change his mind, and desist from his former resolution.

"*May it please your honours, and you gentlemen of the jury,*

"You have heard the charge against the prisoners at the bar contained in their several indictments, to which they have each of them pleaded *not guilty*. Mr. Attorney has opened the matter of the evidence on the part of the king, and the witnesses on both sides have been heard, and I cannot think that one among you is in any doubt concerning what verdict you ought to give upon the oath which you have taken.

"*Gentlemen*—Scarce any thing can be conceived more horrid than the crimes charged on the prisoners. A scheme so black and hellish, as the burning of this city, and the murdering of the inhabitants of it, one would hardly imagine, could enter into the thought, much less be harboured in the breast of any human creature; but more wonderful is it, that so great a number should unite and conspire in so detestable a piece of villainy. And yet, gentlemen, there seems nothing wanting to complete the evidence of so barbarous, unjust and cruel a design as has been set on foot; of which we have had in part occular demonstration, in the late fires that have been enkindled in divers parts of this city; several of which have been lighted up in one day, to the amazement and terror of the people.

"*Gentlemen*—Though the circumstances attending these fires convinced every body that the most of them did not proceed from accidental causes, but from a malicious and willful design; yet it was long before any considerable discovery could be made of the authors and abettors of this most wicked and destructive undertaking. Yet at length, by the blessing of heaven, and the uncommon diligence of the magistrates, we trust that some of the principal authors of this mischief, and the ringleader of it are now before you."

Upon this Mr. Smith proceeded to a district consideration of the charge, and in observing upon the evidence of the witnesses (which was in substance as before set forth) distinguished the proofs against each of the prisoners; which for brevity sake are here omitted. And then concluded,

"Thus, gentlemen, nothing remains to be considered of by you, but the credit of the witnesses, against which I can see no reasonable objection; if they are to be believed, then the prisoners are guilty; and you now behold, at this bar, the authors, abettors, and contrivers of those destructive fires which your eyes have seen; two of the immediate agents of those villainies, have already suffered a deserved punishment, and died confessing their crimes. The witnesses declare the principal contriver of those mischiefs to be that wicked man, John Hughson, whose crimes have made him blacker than a Negro; the scandal of his complexion, and the disgrace of human nature! whose name will descend with infamy to posterity! who could not be content to live by the gains of honest industry, but must be rich at the expense of the blood and ruin of his fellow citizens! miserable wretch! how has he plunged himself and family into that pit which he has dug for others, and brought down upon his own pate that violent dealing which he contrived, and in part executed against his neighbours! Gentlemen, though the crimes charged on the defendants are such as merit a just indignation, yet in matters that affect life, you ought to have the most convincing evidence: the trial of the fact is your province. In matters of judgment, to condemn the innocent, and acquit the guilty, is equally criminal. If you can, after what you have heard, think the prisoners innocent, you ought to acquit them; but if you find them guilty, you cannot acquit them without the greatest injustice and cruelty to your country and yourselves. Gentlemen, I shall add no more, but leave you to the direction of the court, and your own consciences."

Then the third justice charged the jury as followeth.

Mary Burton speaks of their having poison amongst them[g] she says she has seen three or four papers of poison in Hughson's drawers, which she understood he had of some Negro. [Note (g): (g) In her evidence upon trial of eight Negroes, 15th of this month, viz. her testimony against doctor Harry.]

Then he was confronted with Kane and Adam, who severally repeated the substance of what they had before declared in their examinations concerning him; but the doctor was stout, denied all, and was remanded.

The doctor was a smooth soft spoken fellow, and like other knaves affected the air of sincerity and innocence, but was of a suspicious character, well known to the magistrates of this city, had a few years before been forbid the town for mal-practice in physic, upon the penalty of being severely whipped if he was seen here again.

The prisoners having been indicted for the conspiracy, were arraigned, and Othello, Quack and Braveboy pleaded *guilty*, and Galloway and Harry, *not guilty*.

The prisoners having pleaded guilty, were set to the bar, and the court proceeded to pass sentence; which was, that Quack and Othello should be burnt, and Braveboy hanged.

Court adjourned till to-morning ten o'clock.

The jail being now thronged with Negroes committed as confederates in the conspiracy, many whereof had made confessions of their guilt, in hopes of pardon in consequence of the proclamation, and others who were pardoned and turned evidence; it was feared, considering the season of the year, that such numbers closely confined might be apt to breed an infection; therefore the judges thought it was proper to examine the list of them, and to mark out such as should be thought proper to recommend to his honour the lieutenant governor, to be pardoned, upon condition of transportation to be therein limited by a short time, and to distinguish which of them who had been made use of as witnesses, might be necessary to reserve for some time; and for this purpose they associated to them Mr. Nicholls and Mr. Lodge, by whose assistance the following list was accordingly settled, which the judges reported to his honour, and submitted to his consideration.

A list of Negroes recommended this day by the judges to his honour the lieutenant governor, for transportation.

Wednesday, July 8. A list of the Negroes recommended this day by the judges to his honour the lieutenant governor, to be pardoned in order for transportation--.

[John Chockem's(sp?) servant Titus]

English's Patrick, Vaarck's Will, Varian's Worcester, Ellison's Jamaica, Abraham's Scipio, Pintard's Caesar, Clarkson's Fortune, Wilkins's Fortune, Ben, Moore's Tom, Leffert's Pompey, Marschalk's London, Low's Wan, Latham's Fortune.

The Negro Tom was executed. At the gallows he declared that now he was sure he must die, he would tell the truth, and said that Farmar's Jack, Duyckink's Philip, William Gilbert's Cuffee, and David Van Horne's Corah, were the persons that put him upon setting the fire.

Immediately after Tom's execution, Cuffee, Corah and Philip, were apprehended and strictly examined by the mayor and recorder, but nothing could be got out of them.

Ordered, that the execution of Cowley's Cato, Fortune and Cato alias Toby, be on the morrow the 16th instant, between the hours of nine and one of the same day: and

That the execution of Ben and Quash be on the morrow the 16th instant.

This day Will, Ward's Negro, was executed according to sentence, and made the following confession at the stake.

An Anonymous Sermon

Before bringing forward upon the stage the characters who figure in the drama, I have endeavored to make the reader acquainted with the ground on which the different scenes were acted out. To the audience, everybody was in some way or other actively or passively sustaining slavery. Yet everybody disclaimed all responsibility for its existence, opposed all efforts for its extinction, and was as much anti-slavery as anybody else.

Truth, love, freedom. Hah! These are the difficulties of writing the history of the past. They are greatly enhanced by the scantiness of the materials. Our own contemporaneous history on the contrary seems clogged with their abundance. So many simultaneous events, seemingly of small consequence, yet all having an important bearing on each other and proving in reality the hinges on which the more conspicuous ones turn. So many threads which the insufficiency of narration at once to combine compels the writer to stop for a time although he must finally travel back to pick them up. Or the connections of things will but imperfectly appear. Yes again, truth, love, freedom, are ever the same. Truth, love, freedom will always be the same. But some signs of their presence and the manner of their workings on society at different times will be far unlike that. The problems we present may be wrought out of different processes, though the results are the same. The reflection on this will enlighten us as to the causes of the convulsive terror now manifest by the body of the ministry and their dupes, the clerical politicians. When such lose their confidence in the identity of the principles of freedom with those of order and Christianity they become disunited in soul from those who are pressing forward with diminished confidence, and to disguise their change of feelings they sacrifice their integrity. In our grief at their conduct, we undergo strong temptations to mitigate, to cloak, and to conceal when we ought to expose and condemn.

What is the church saying? What is the church doing? Selling indulgences for sin. The worst of sins is of man stealing. Yes, the sin of stealing and selling a brother in the church. What do they do? The hammer is lifted over the head of the Christian. Yes, he is a Christian; a child of God. And the cry is "Who bids?" Brother sells his brother and the church says "It is all right", while the watchmen on the walls of Zion pass the word "All is well". And the watchman on the walls of Jericho passed the word "All's well".

Though this auctioneer is a church member; the seller and the buyer and the poor slave are all members of the same church, yet the church does not censure this deed. It is all right. The church that does not pronounce slavery a sin and deal with its members who refuse to confess and forsake it in effect licenses slavery. It stands as a virtual endorser of the crime. If men are robbed of the bible and all knowledge of its letters, if parents are punished as felons for teaching their children the alphabet and the church does nothing, then the church by its silence endorses it and declares it is all right. Parents are robbed of their children, forced to see them dragged to the market on the block, and knocked off to the Negro speculator, and the church stands by and says it's all right. The church allows this, not only in its members, but in its elders and deacons and pastors and bishops, and hence it stands justly responsible for selling indulgences to license the sin of slavery.

And what have we seen here? Why don't he give the bible to his own slaves, this buyer, and teach them to read it? And by refusing to give it, or let us give it, to several hundred thousand immortal beings in his own State, why, what a hypocrite. Is there a being on the earth, the most degraded even of the miserable slaves whose souls are left to perish,

143

who cannot see this insistency? Can they not see the absurdity? Can they not listen and hear this hypocrisy? Is God a fool to be thus mocked?

Gentlemen, I will raise my voice against such hypocrisy as long as I live. It shall ring in the ears of every slaveholder who asks us to help him give bibles to the heathens across the seas thousands of miles off, while he withholds them from the slaves at his very door. Why his very bibles he sends with missionaries to Hindus or others are bought with the blood and souls of his slaves. It is dividing the gains of hell with God. If this is Christianity, well might the heathen say "God defend us from Christianity."

Chapter 3

COPS:
THE SILENCE
OF MY QUIET FEARS

Reading from my large dossier of police files brings to the surface my reality of a

fear that still rings clear in the voice of my mother as a kid when I was old enough to leave home alone for long periods like school or for errands. Her words still ring clear at middle or should I say old age.

"Be careful don't get into any trouble behave yourself'." There was never any racial meaning or tone in her voice about being careful of White police. The two-person police team that worked our part of the island consisted of friends that came round in a two seater Green Hornet. Plymouth automobiles with no outer decals or signs. One Irish and the other Italian Vince and Eddie. There was no evidence that they were even armed with pistols or handcuffs. They ambled slowly about the neighborhood visiting families for chit-chat cake and coffee. This was the entire Police force of the North shore of Staten Island.

Police later became "cops" when I returned to Staten Island after the war. They were younger faster even as they were weighed down with body armor and gear cruising the North Shore streets 24/7 round the clock in 4-door sedan squad cars with strong wire separators inside red and white with colored lights on the roof top and search lights. The door markings were simply P.D. I believe most if not all Black mothers shed tears for their sons' lives when they left home. To deal with their fears for their sons' safety they entered the quiet unspoken belief that to arm the children with racial fears of white police would somehow give birth to hatred. I am sure that there were quiet tears of joy when the young sons returned home. But there would always be fear that somehow sometime there would be a knock at the door. The truth was written in the Staten Island newspaper the Advance and the Daily News articles about Black men being arrested on Staten island and no single Black man was immune or safe. Who would be the first in our family? It never dawned on me how many nights my mother sat up waiting for me to walk inside.

It was well understood in the Black community that the best jobs were to work for the city government in either the fire or the sanitation department or a job with the post office. I do not remember being told to try to pass a civil service test for the Police Department somehow at that time the job of policeman never came up.

I have never spoken to my White friends about my fear of the police on Staten Island. Somehow I knew it would be difficult to tell White people because they have white skins. It would be difficult for them to comprehend. And of course my male macho would not enter into a conversation about fear being over 6 feet and weighing almost two hundred pounds and black. My fear of White policemen grew larger and stronger as I grew older living with this fear never goes away perhaps it never will only now in the 21st century I fear policemen. A confrontation with police and a black skin is a check mark for disaster bridges that have never been healed.

I was arrested in 1978 …. Driving alone in my car outside Procter & Gamble flagged down by a White guy I thought was looking for a ride. He put a pistol to my head there were two plainclothed men. I was handcuffed and slapped and taken to New York City and imprisoned for a day and a halfr. There was no trial and with the advice of my attorney Joseph Holzka I did not fight. I could not afford to sue. I was released. I was poor and I was Black.

I started the police files with newspaper clippings dating back to 1969 when I read that one of the Charles Manson killers had lived on Staten Island. Staten Islanders claim other newsworthy people that have lived on the island but never a Charles Manson creep killer.

At the time and for no particular reason I began to add stories and articles into my files that I had been collecting about police on Staten Island. I had to become aware of many things to find a basis for my inner fears and to understand the reasons for this.

The police have arms and training and the physical power. Their agenda is set by the political climate who are White and their power is constrained by the fact that they need the community to obey them and respect their authority. I must say that there are factors in the ever changing immigrant community on the island that have made a more aggressive police force and they are bad trends. Black youth have access to guns and have entered into a surge of killings of Blacks killing Blacks and Blacks killing Black police officers that have not been addressed the youth are armed and dangerous. Many Blacks have failed their children and many have looked the other way we have watched a sat quietly behind plywood covered doors and windows watching TV soaps we know the truth there is no excuse and there is no honest justification. These are bad trends and fear is the killer. The civil political authorities control the powers that monitor and control the police. There is evidence that suggests the Staten Island police have used judgments that are part of the DNA of the New York City myth that the northern part of the island community has been an area of rising crime. And more police is the way to stop it and if you are a police person and you hold these beliefs then they are ready to become a racial profiler. Everything has been set to smash people in this crisis in brutal ways. Ignorance breeds fear and this fear is difficult to understand for either side of the coin the police officer and the pedestrians on the street Black White Asian Latino.

My fears have grown enormously.

Some statistics; from the N.Y. Police Department data base of 2010 show that there are more Staten Islanders registered having gun permits. Many are retired police officers.

The south shore residents of Staten Island has more legally registered guns at 75 permits per 1000 residents. Tottenville Richmond Valley Huguenot Princes Bay area are the most well armed folks in the five borough's of the state of New York. The only place on Staten Island that has a gun shop is in Tottenville where guns are sold.

SUBTLE ENCOUNTERS

The following is a fictional account of true events, cobbled together with names changed to protect the innocent and the guilty, and me from a libel suit, that shows the degree of corruption on Staten Island and illustrates the reason why I am fearful, especially of the police. Just because I'm paranoid does not mean they are not after me.

Detective Kevin Murphy was tired; it was after 10 pm when he got to the Dog Pub. Looking around it was obvious to everybody that he was the man of the hour. He had just been made Lieutenant in the New York City Police Department. Kevin Murphy had been on the job for over 20 years. He smiles he waves he slaps palms and high fives with a number of the men here some still in uniform and some in plain clothes. He smiles turns around to the bar to order a beer only to find five already-filled glasses waiting.

Joey pops up from behind the bar smiling and says "Hi Chief!" Joey could be anywhere between 20 and 30. He has cerebral palsy and has a funny walk like hip-hop. He somehow manages to run the place. Joey knows everybody and everything. He's a Yankees fan. The owner of the Dog Pub is a Department of Corrections Officer a guy named Mario DeVincenzio.

Kevin is from Staten Island; he was born and raised here and lives in the family home in Westerly. His father was also a cop who lives now in Belmont NJ near the shore. Kevin's grandfather was a cop too; it was a tradition. They had called themselves the "Irish Blue". It was a job. After graduating from Port Richmond High School Kevin had a few jobs on the Island. He filled vending machines he loaded trucks at Proctor and

Gamble he sandblasted boat bottoms and hulls at Marine Power and Light on Richmond Terrace.

His father pressed a copy of *The Chief* into Kevin's hand after he came home with a bloody nose and a black eye after a fight on his first night working as a bartender. "Look at the city jobs" he said. With little conversation after that and a great deal of help Kevin zipped through the Police Academy training as a cadet. Kevin had not much contact outside of the Island but he began to like being a cop.

Kevin sat at the bar watching the clock; it's midnight and he's impatient. He put a dollar in the Cuss Jar on the bar. Joey looked up and said "Hey chief what was the word?" Kevin said "Shit!" as he slammed the top of the jar with the palm of his hand. Joey said "Shit is only 50 cents. Ah but you said it twice. You're right that's a buck chief."

Kevin had had a bad day. He had wanted this new Staten Island assignment because he didn't like the travel to Manhattan. He didn't like the traffic of Manhattan though he complained about the roads that screwed up the front end of his car. He didn't even like the trees of Manhattan not when compared to the trees on Staten Island. He liked his new space the office at the Teleport on South Avenue. He knew that Staten Island would be a less demanding place – so he thought.

His wife Connie was very happy that he was closer to home. Connie was Italian. She thought that perhaps she could bring him his lunch at the Teleport or they could even have lunch at the diner on Forest Avenue. She didn't like Kevin's being a police officer; she would have been contented with any job he had that was simply eight hours. He should call her to tell her that he couldn't be home at midnight but decided not to.

Kevin's last three weeks had been spent fighting problems and chasing down the Russian mobsters who have been quietly gaining a foothold on Staten Island.

He has found that the Russian mafia has been slowly trying to move into one of the larger markets which was now the OTB or Off Track Betting. It was obvious to him that they were testing the ground on Staten Island. These guys had a few numbers bookies they even printed money. Fake IDS used auto sales fake immigrant IDs. It's been growing on the Island and the Albanian gangs have been looking to get a foothold in the market to move out the Italian mafia.

Kevin has also found out recently through the meetings and intimations that the Russian mafia is not really a mafia yet. These men come from the Caucuses; they have been trained in the prisons trained to kill and make it look like the person died of a bad sneeze natural causes. These are serious men; they don't want half a loaf they want it all.

Downtown at One Police Plaza they call the Island precincts the Red Borough. These men are conservative they feel that the socialist policies here in the United States remind them too much of the oligarchy in their own native lands. They are buying into businesses clubs political organizations businesses diners trucking companies. He's seen them gotten to know some of their names: Mashikov Kalmanova and Omanova. He would be seeing much more of them in the coming weeks.

Other detectives in the other precincts in the Borough have been feeding him information. They've had to stake out and wire many of the cafes and bars where the

Russian corporations hold their meetings. These up and coming Russian/Israeli/Albanian gangs are bold and they are just that. They're simply known as "The Group." In many Island precincts they are known as "The Sixth Crime Family" not headed by Italian Americans but by Groups.

These men have no fear. The most powerful is the Solntsevo Group the Russian syndicate. Their Group Brigade leader is Andrei Skoch. He's based in Moscow Europe and many other places. Their activities are financial.

Anton Malevsky and Sergei Mikhailov were ordered out of Israel deported. Their Group about 1000 members have been slowly filtering into the United States their activities are extortion money laundering and trafficking in women and drugs. Many of these Groups are tied to other Groups. Mikhail Chernoy still lives in Israel. Here the word is that Mikhail is suspected of drug trafficking prostitution racketeering and theft.

Many of the Groups cooperate with other Groups. The ties are very difficult to find except through the names of many of the criminals. Out of the system of Russian prisons come names like Anton Malevsky Musa Talarov and Aslan Kasarov. Many of them operated in several countries especially in Europe. The Group's activities share similarities in extortion prostitution counterfeiting fraud kidnapping when necessary gambling and the smuggling of cars and drugs. These men follow a code of conduct developed by inmates of the Soviet penal system and they don't roll over.

Several Albanians wannabes have struck out on their own and they're raring to do battle with the Lucchesi and Gambino families for territory. At one time there was a quiet undercurrent for territory in Queens in the Bronx and in Westchester.

The information comes out daily weekly monthly of the activities which include the same underworld activities—racketeering attempted murder extortion loan sharking and gambling. They maintain their network of profitable gambling interests by sheer muscle and they would not only traffic in narcotics but in humans.

As the Groups become more sophisticated and daring they go on to become more profitable and violent. Many of them on the street level are simply enforcers for the established Groups. Some have even worked for La Cosa Nostra to learn the business and they go on to their own businesses. They have their own languages and their own skills. Many are said to be like the old Sicilians.

The heat of all of this comes out of One Police Plaza and few would speak on condition of anonymity because even they have not been authorized to speak to anyone below the rank of Captain and they know that these guys they don't roll and they don't cooperate. These guys and their Group associates would make John Gotti look like an errand boy.

One spat was with the old Mafia boss Arnold Squitieri from the Gambino family. There was a meeting of sorts with the Albanian Group headed by Alex Rudaj. Mr. Squitieri and about 30 of his men appeared carrying bats guns and other weapons but the Albanian guys were ready. One of Mr. Rudaj's men put a gun to Mr. Squitieri's head and another Albanian pointed a shotgun at a gas pump threatening to blow everyone up unless Mr. Squitieri's men put their guns down. According to the witnesses Mr. Squitieri and his boys backed down.

Kevin's been on the job for a long time for over 20 years and he could smell trouble coming down the 'pike. He's been meeting openly with a lot of these guys. He's been speaking to them at citizen's club meetings on the East Shore to inform them that he is aware of their activities and that he is aware of their expanding base on the Island.

Kevin likes the rush when he talks to these community men. They pounce on him to explain that they want to be involved and that they want to part of the Staten Island community. They tell him that they came from countries where they were unable to express themselves where they didn't have the right to organize or vote. They just want to become part of this community on Staten Island. They want to become a part of the

"We want to show you that we do feel patriotic" they said "and we know that if you work hard and you do the right thing you will get rewarded right? We want to show people that we are normal. We Russian and Jewish people here work together. We are the same people." Again and again men corner Kevin repeating again and again that they simply want to become part of this Staten Island community.

The verbal barrage came and Kevin excused himself and presented a few of his men street patrolmen and detectives to the organization. These middle-aged men with heavy accents stood and shook his hand before he moved to the exit. "We are simply looking to break the ethnic stereotype" they said. "We don't want Russians to be seen as just the stereotypical Serbian beer and vodka drinkers." After the meeting and Kevin's departure the other men in Kevin's NYPD street cruiser unit and the Russians shared smiles and hugs coffee beer and vodka sweetbreads and candies on long tables.

Years ago Kevin and a detachment from Manhattan South the Commissioner's office came to the Noor Al Islam Center on Richmond Terrace. Kevin watched other officers and removed his shoes off as mandated by the Imam while in the mosque as the Police Commissioner Bernard Kerik told the Muslims that he would play ball with them if they were straight with him and if they were straight with him there would be no trouble. But now Kevin realized that he is no Bernard Kerik. He had to use a different approach a different style a different voice.

He worried that he should just do his job. He had opened the door to communications but he was still worried about what would come down the 'pike next.

It's late. Kevin's partner Rosario Campanella "Rosie" hadn't arrived hadn't called. Kevin did make the call to his wife Connie who didn't seem to be too upset; she was watching TV; Letterman the Tonight Show and others. Kevin sat watching the group around him. He had a good pension coming. He and Connie were going to put a down payment on a nice house in New Jersey. His two boys were now in college. His daughter Terri also had been through college had married recently and had a 2-year-old child. Kevin thought of his two boys. He did not want them to be cops.

Kevin tried again to reach Rosie on his cell only to listen to it buzz. He drank another beer and he felt the acid reflux. He knew that if he were to sit in one of the over-stuffed chairs behind him he would soon fall asleep. He couldn't do that in a place like this. The Dog Pub had no class.

He knew that the young cops and the cop mixtures need the cop "flip switch." They need places like this before going home before going on the street.

The mood was relaxed and along the wall there were rows of plump worn sofas. Young men hunched over tables in conversations some watched the giant TV screens and others bent over the pool table. He had been on the job a long time and he knew that soon some of these new cadets would be weeded out.

A few days ago two men were arrested for buying steroids at a Brooklyn pharmacy that was already bugged to snare bigger prey. They wanted muscle they wanted heft. But at the precinct when they were called down they cried. They cried and cried when they were asked to turn in their tin and their Glock pistols.

Many of these young men would become bitter at some time when the rigid police tactics that they have been using don't necessarily translate into a bust or an arrest or a victory to help them move up the ladder. Some would use the NYPD to move on to private businesses while off duty but here the "flip-switch" is a camaraderie for most young unmarried and some married cops; a watering hole for those on the job. Cops firemen Department of Corrections off duty officers a couple of retirees come in for a few; some simply stop for a shot and a beer some become regulars hanging out watching either the scores on the large TVs or Alice's ass.

Alice is Mario's friend. She balances a full tray of glasses as she wiggles around the tables and sashays between the leather sofas. She knows the regulars and those that will hit on her and she will refuse anyone who has had too much to drink or touches her ass!

Alice van Rinker met Mario DeVincenzio on the Staten Island ferry last summer. Mario had been watching the tourists take photos of the Statue of Liberty and the lower bay. He was especially fixating on the tall blond. She was busy taking photos and left her handbag on the bench. A young perp sat next to her bag stuffed it under his coat left the bench and quickly walked away.

Mario watched all this. As the man came walking in front of him he stuck out a leg causing the perp to hit the deck hard. He held the man down calling for the deck hands calling for a cop. He identified himself holding up his DOC shield. He held the perp face-down with his leg and he also asked Alice if she left this bag unattended. She looked at him holding her bag up and said "Yes. Are you a policeman?"

"Yep but I'm off duty now." Mario had hit a homer.

The tall blond had been in New York for three weeks looking for a job while sharing a room with a friend from Minneapolis MN. She had a degree in theatre art but she was waitressing part-time. Mario would waste no time. "Can we have coffee when we dock?" He wouldn't leave an opening for her to refuse. He was now standing up smiling hitting on her hard. He was hitting on her to get her into bed before sundown. He was in love. Tall blond, big tits, nice ass.

He owned a private club he said and he could also use some waitressing on the weekends if she was interested. She said she might be.

"It's very safe place to work because all the members of our club are policemen some firemen and maybe a sanitation guy court officers" Mario told her. "Where are you from?"

"Hibbing Minnesota" Alice said.

"Are you Polish" he asked.

"No. I'm part Dutch. I believe my father was part Dutch. I don't know any more than that. We own a hardware store in Hibbing. That's where I worked."

"You gotta change that van Rinker."

"Why?"

"Sounds like a comic book."

The conversation was stilted but they seemed animated sparring merrily Mario simply wanted to get her into bed. Her mind he could not understand. Alice was fascinated by this man his easy camaraderie.

"Minnesota?'

"Yes."

"Bob Dylan?"

"Yes."

"I heard of him. He's a western singer. The western guy."

"Well not really."

The crosscurrents of conversation were a theme for comedy. They both seemed to be interested in what they were saying.

Before Mario met Alice it was a challenge to make enough money. Mario had hired chubby twin sisters as pole dancers for a few lunches. He hired them cheap paid them a few bucks made a few bucks enough to keep the lights on but when Alice came she was an attraction. She was responsible for the upturn in customers on Friday and Saturday. The plump twins had been hired to boost his attendance after he had the floor to ceiling pole installed but no one really watched the sisters and after one month Alice van Rinker was now Alice Smith. Mario said "Easier to remember right?" She didn't mind. Alice Smith.

Alice was always also being asked if she would work at the Fat Cat Saloon in New Dorp by another Department of Corrections guy who wanted to open up a place with a gang at mid-island but Alice enjoyed the attention here. She wore her bra up higher to enhance her cleavage in her low-cut tight tank top. She was learning fast! She was learning to separate the easy flatter from the direct call for sex. "You get enough tits here" she would say as she leaned down carefully to place a drink on a table "but leave the ass alone."

Mario, he's a Corrections Officer. He's married. Mario is now humping her. No one said much about that. Mind your business mind your business. Mario was "Knuckles" and he could take a joke about Corrections Officers being called "copstitutes" or "Meter Maids lacking intelligence." He'd heard all the jokes all the jokes about Corrections Officers and their supposed lack of intelligence. He's heard them all. The Corrections Officers test: How many eggs in a carton? How much water can you put in a gallon can? Mario has heard them all; it would be wise not to try to top him. When the copstitute poetry appeared pasted on the walls Mario removed them.

Mario is a big guy he runs about 240 lifts weights but he's losing his once-long black hair and facing his mortality. He's a no-nonsense Rikers Island cop and he is short tempered. Mario don't want any bookies in here or anybody smoking that other shit in here: it's the real thing or a cigar.

Mario has black friends at Rikers; he tells them to come down to the club but if you can't take a joke stay out of the heat. Mario knows a lot of black guys who would talk "the dozens." He heard it many times as they trashed their friends their mothers and their sisters and find it a laugh; they could laugh at these intimate exchanges. But here at the Dog Pub most of the men were Italians and their mothers were saints. You never make fun of a mother or a sister or women at all if you want to be safe. Many of the mothers were pain in the ass saints but you never talk about their mothers out of disrespect.

Some of the customers are friends and family of the cops here brothers and cousins. A lot of cement truck drivers come in that work for a neighborhood cement company. All Italians all ready to protect their turf and family. They're goodfellas goombahs but not guineas never guineas. They learn the wise-guy Italian traits before the age of 10. And Mario knows what to look for. He's been in corrections for a long time. He can spot them the wise guys and the wannabes and knows who makes a little money on the side while on the job. The Dog Pub is a nice place. They don't have many fights here.

Kevin didn't like the term "copstitute" either. The men joke with it back and forth corrections officers to cops cops to corrections officers. And Kevin knew there were many times when a little intoxication would cause some fists to fly and many of the men came here carrying their sidearm Glock pistols.

Kevin was soft-spoken; he was middle-aged now and he was calm. He wouldn't say the words but he'd put his coins in a pile on the bar smacking them into the glass jug with his hands. Kevin didn't like cussing or fighting among police officers and the corrections officers. Everyone knew it; you said a cuss word you put half a buck in the glass. Everyone could afford a few bucks. It was worth a great deal more now that Alice was here being who they are on this little island. Alice was the top. A few bucks here and there keep the lights on.

And Kevin was patient. He looked around him and wondered if there was ever any perfect saloon on Staten Island. He liked Big Nose Kate's out on the South Shore. But Kate's didn't have Alice.

He remembered the Upper East Side joint when he worked in the 114th precinct. He was a young cop then and he was moving up the ladder. He was classy; he liked the class up on the East Side.

Kevin and Rosie had become regulars at Elaine's. Elaine's was a watering hole owned by Elaine Kaufman. It was never a "cop bar" but Elaine got to like these two men who were pleasant soft-spoken and didn't appear to be cops on the beat. They were like her own boys she would say. She'd call them by their first names "Oh yes Kevin Rosario was here a while earlier. He'll probably be here later." Elaine had a special place for Kevin and Rosie.

That was years ago. Elaine's on Seventh Avenue was a high class joint. Kevin liked it he loved the place. He thought "This is my crowd." There were private eyes and FBI agents criminal defense lawyers and other detectives. There were daily newspapermen and Kevin would get to know them. There were Federal agents from the ATF; they'd be schmoozing here at Elaine's. They were smart fast thinkers in the NYPD. He wanted to be like them and he entered into conversations with the Federal drug enforcement agents. He could always be heard and seen mingling with them. This was their hang-out and Elaine's was known as a classy watering hole. It had a clientele mix of intellectuals celebrities.

At Elaine's customers carried guns but no one really thought about it much. Here at the Dog Pub Kevin always had his ear at his back listening. They would never make the cut at Elaine's; they were too rowdy and if they had come into Elaine's she'd have given them a table near the kitchen. Kevin looked around at the Dog Pub bar and thought what a shame it was that Elaine's was now closed.

Kevin was here on a mission. He was unable to reach Rosie on his cell and it was now after 1:00 am and Joey hopped over and placed another cup of black coffee next to him. Kevin closed his eyes stretched out on one of the over-stuffed chairs it felt good and he thought for a moment that he was being annoyed by this persistent buzzing at his waist.

"Yes."

"Murph. It's me Rosie. I'll be there in 15 minutes. We need to talk."

****

After a gentle tapping on his shoulder Kevin opens his eyes looks up and sees Rosie. Rosie's got that look in his eyes. After all these years together as partners Kevin has seen it before. "This better be good Rosie" Kevin says "or I will see to it that you get committed to Belleview and a rubber room for the abuse of a senior officer."

"Good" Rosie said. "That thought always cheers me up and I like to spread cheer wherever I go. But please Kevin come with me."

Rosie takes Kevin's arm and leads him to the door and outside to his van. He slides open the side panel and motions for Kevin to get in. Kevin looks inside and there is a black man about 23 skinny long bare legs with his knees almost up to his chin. He's holding a basketball between his legs nervously turning it. He has a baseball cap with a Yankees logo and a tee-shirt with a Jets logo. The young man looks at Kevin but says nothing. His face is smooth-shaven and his facial expression does not change. Rosie pulls down the seat facing the young black man as he slides in behind him.

Before Rosie can slide it shut there is a tapping on the door side and standing at the curb is Joey a smile on his face carrying a cup of black coffee. Kevin takes it and says "Thanks Joey." But his chest is hurting. He's now reminding himself not to drink because of this fierce burning. Kevin hasn't eaten since noon and has no desire to add to this discomfort.

Rosie says to the Black man "Bruce this is my partner Lt. Murphy." The young man says nothing and Kevin fills in the void by saying "You a Jets basketball fan?"

The youth Bruce McNeil says flatly "I work at the morgue with Mr. Santini and I know nothing about the ring. Besides the Jets are a football team."

Rosie looks at Kevin and says "I took a call at the precinct hospital security found a ring seems to have been stolen suspected thief works at the hospital. I spoke to Joe Perillo he's security chief retired NYPD security chief and they wanted to try to keep this in-house until there was a positive. And that's how I got to know Bruce Mc Neil. I got to know him about two weeks ago and I think what he has to say is very interesting."

Bruce without waiting says "I like my job I like what I do. When I first came here I saw my first dead body. I was 19 at the time and I wanted to be a pre-med undergrad and I had this opportunity to view an autopsy at the medical examiner's office. It was a car-accident victim. He was driving a souped-up Chevy Camaro and not wearing his seat belt. Going like crazy he hit a tree and had been propelled through the windshield. He died from multiple compound fractures and ruptured internal organs. The exposed anatomy of his body seemed like something a normal completely stable person would never want to see. But I loved the entire experience" Bruce continued. "I watched the whole procedure from exploring the bloody wounds to learning about the strange tools used during an evisceration.

So anyway I tried doing the usual volunteer thing the other pre-med students did— working at clinics with patients listening to their concerns. Sure I wanted to help people but I didn't have the patience to listen to them and I felt I didn't have the human interaction skills to continue with live people. To put it bluntly" he laughed "I preferred to help dead people. And my family is in the business—undertakers in Jersey City so I'm familiar with the dead.

"This job is never boring but it's just a job and it pays well though it's nothing like TV or CSI. Nope no crime scene investigation. I'm there every day 6-7 days a week if we have a summer rush. People like to kill better during hot weather. If we need help we can get it and Mr. Santini leaves a lot up to me now. He stays in his office and taps on the glass if he needs my attention."

Rosie elbows Kevin and says "Mr. Santini is the old guy who's head of the morgue."

"He may be retiring soon" says Bruce "and I hope he recommends me for the job. He likes papers and paperwork copying and filing everything. I keep a separate file also. There'll be no missing bodies or stuff on my watch.

"Never had a Black guy as head of the morgue here no Black people ever worked in this morgue said Bruce except me." He paused and looked at both of them. "The first thing I would do here is get those cardboard boxes about a dozen piled in alphabetical order on the floor out of the room. Get some fire-proof steel file cabinets. The old oak wooden file cabinets they're his. He's about 60 or so I guess He doesn't talk much if the paperwork is done and if the bodies are in the coolers and tagged. Nice man wants his Sundays off; go to church Catholic guy. Brings his own lunch in a cooler. Wants to share wine but the only thing is I simply can't eat there."

After a while Kevin is in a trance. He has listened to Bruce for more than a half-hour maybe an hour. His mind tells him one thing; his stomach reminds him of something else that he needs medical care. He moves the door slide and steps onto the curb. Rosie is speaking however and he cannot seem to grasp all of it that he's heard. Kevin looks back and says "Rosie is this about the body snatchers?"

****

It's been three days now since Kevin has responded to any phone calls. His wife called their doctor and removed all the clocks wristwatches and anything else that might make a noise that would awaken Kevin. The doctor came examined him and prescribed some sleep medication and another medication that he felt Kevin should use for his acid reflux.

It's now Sunday morning and Kevin and Connie decide that it's time for him to submit his retirement papers. Kevin makes a call to Rosie asking him to come to his home. He wants Rosie to know what he intends to do. Connie answers the door and gives Rosie a hug. Rosie bounds up the stairs to Kevin's bedroom enters and says "You look good.

"Liar" Kevin replies.

Rosie moves a chair closer to the bed. "Well you really need to stop visiting those Island saloons."

"Never mind Rosie I'm not a very good blusher" Kevin said.

Rosie immediately says "I got Captain Zimmerman to let you and me figure out this puzzle. I think the kid is not involved."

"Involved in what?"

"The ring some missing body parts the morgue."

"What are you talking about? Fill me in Rosie please."

Rosie says "I need your brain. This is about a ring and maybe much more. Yes or no?"

"You're not making a lot of sense Rosie but go on. You know Zimmerman knows I have this high profile meeting with the Russian American Council on Staten Island. What are you getting me into Partner? There'll be a lot of booths in this hall a lot of public relations (PE) to promote the Russian owned pharmacies restaurants builders and all the other businesses. They expect thousands from Brooklyn and New Jersey. This is an important meeting Rosie" I need to make contacts. Russian City Radio says "we come to raise children it is a nice quiet place."

But Rosie wasn't listening. If he did he dismissed it. "Zimmerman said he could put any number of men to do that."

"You always manage to cheer me up Rosie Always." Kevin said. "Well you're on and I'll have a box of your favorite doughnuts delivered to cushion the blow."

"I need you to read some of this" Rosie said "and I'll see you tomorrow morning. Someone has gone through a shitload of trouble to set this kid up frame him."

156

"Because of a ring?"

Kevin falls back on his pillows as Rosie leaves and thinks *Monday always comes and all of the honey bees return to their cubicles and perform the monotonous chores of a meaningless toil of life.* "*Retirement*" he thought "*How wonderful*" "He would learn to sail a boat. He would learn to plant tomatoes for sauce; Rosie's tomato sauce. Connie would like that.

But Connie is standing in the doorway with her hands on her hips. "What did he say?" Connie asks Kevin. She had come upstairs quietly and heard the entire exchange outside the bedroom door. She turns looks back at Kevin who is looking up at the ceiling and says "We have an appointment with Dr. Mazella on Wednesday."

****

It's been four days now since Kevin came into the office. The private room for privacy the door is open and Rosie is having coffee and doughnuts with Bruce. Bruce is drinking a huge chocolate malt from a bottle; he has cut the doughnuts into small bite-sized pieces as he speaks. Rosie motions Kevin to the chair and moves the large box of doughnuts within his reach. "Coffee?"

"No" says Kevin "I just had breakfast tea with milk and toast and eggs."

Bruce continues his voice low and strangely detached. "You know the morgue is the last stop for those who perhaps misunderstood the good advice and did not go gently. They drank too much or snorted and crashed their way into that good night."

Rosie is taking no notes and he has no tape recorder on the table. He seems to have gotten into an easy relationship with this young man. Kevin notices perhaps that a relationship has developed and Bruce continues relaxed. "A lot of bodies stay unclaimed because families can't afford the expense of burial. Many times people just leave Grandma or Grandpa Jones to rot on the city's bill. Mr. Santini usually has arrangements worked out with the Public Administrator. We find ways to bury them certain funeral homes donate their services but we get them buried. That's what we do.

"There's about 300 Staten Islanders a year who have no known family or who would otherwise go to an unmarked grave in the mass city burial ground on Hart Island. It's a sign of dignity. I know it's tragic for people who are suffering for those who are still alive but we can't forget the people who have passed.

"There are times" Bruce continues "that a family barely gets to say hello never mind goodbye. When a small wrapped bundle is brought down to us from Labor and Delivery I simply record it into the logbook and make copies for Mr. Santini and for my files. Every body that enters and exits the morgue is in the logbook. But these infants and fetuses make up a large majority of the morgue population I guess due to their fragility. The fetuses these are the children of moms who received no prenatal care moms who are drug abusers moms who have genetic diseases as well as moms who were perfectly healthy who received the best care and who followed every rule to the letter.

"Labor & Delivery is known for its quick removal of dead babies to the morgue. In fact it happens so fast that many times the mother does not even see the baby when it is born.

Dead babies have a gamey stench he says like wet dog fur. After a baby is fast forwarded to us the social worker contacts me so that the body can be re-released back to the parents if they want to see their child. Most do not. I keep them wrapped in the pink and blue blankets to give them some identity but most of them do not even have a name. Babies do not have to be cleaned up of the attachments or bracelets and stuff.

"Mr. Santini makes notes of any jewelry rings or bracelets on the body. We tag it for the undertaker."

"Yes the ring" said Kevin. "When would you let me know how the ring got into your pocket?

"The ring" says Rosie "is a gold plated piece of shit worth all of about $150 found in a lab coat that belongs to Bruce." Rosie reaches into his desk and shows Kevin a small ring in an evidence bag.

"OK what else do we have?"

We have a meeting at the hospital with the complainant a staff person at the hospital and we have these" Rosie says and gives Kevin a small package of notes. "Copies from Bruce's daily record."

Kevin is getting fidgety. He has heard enough and he didn't want to hear any more about the morgue. "Tell me about the body snatchers" says Kevin.

"Well let me put it this way" Bruce says "It's the only way I can. We had a reviewing room once a big glassed-in room for reviewing remains—same as upstairs where you view the newborns—where families could sit with their departed loved ones and grieve over their deaths. That room is no longer used. It was the room taken over by the hoodlums."

"You mean the body snatchers?" Kevin says.

"Yeah the body snatchers" Bruce replies.

"Anyway because of an increase in fainting accidents the hospital now has this no-viewing policy and the room was closed off tight. I thought it was the right thing to do" said Bruce "because many times family members fainted at the sight of a dead body. Fainting in a morgue is like taking a bath in a toilet; the morgue is cleaned with bleach but it's never quite sparkling clean. The room always has that unmentionable odor of death.

"And the general public does not realize that when people die in the hospital they do not die in a clean sterile manner. Most bodies are partially covered in blood feces vomit and all the other stuff inside us that can be smushed out and leaking. What can be more traumatic is that the medical staff does not take out the IVs triple-lumen catheters thoracotomy tubes gauze needles or endotracheal tubes after a person expires. They come with the body. Usually these devices and many others are left in place for the funeral home to remove.

158

"Anyway a lot of bereaved families and nurses find this no-viewing policy insensitive; think it's a bad rule to close the room off but there are good reasons for it. Many times family members would refuse to leave the body so it could be taken back into the cooler. These days I have to turn crying family members away from the morgue door. Some become hysterical and bang and kick on the morgue door. I tell them to have a last view and say goodbye one last time at the funeral home."

Kevin is now visibly upset. He has started a cup of coffee and is eating doughnuts. He has never heard this before.

"The body matures..." Bruce begins.

Kevin slams his hand on the table.

"But there are certain rules that I have to follow when trying to move the bodies—rules that I have unfortunately learned from mishaps when trying to place bodies on the shelves. Only one body can fit on a rack at a time though with cancer or a wasting disease patient we may put two on a shelf. We only have 25 cooler shelves and if the cooler is extremely full which can happen on holidays and long weekends we can make two of the smaller bodies share the same shelf. But the racks can't be trusted to hold overweight or bloated bodies at all. These get to stay on stretchers in their own corner of the cooler until they are released to funeral homes. The skinny wasted and small we can wrap them together on a cooler wrap.

"Sometimes we get bodies in the morgue right after death. Depending upon whether or not the family has seen the patient the fresher bodies are wheeled into the cooler on a stretcher provided by the operating room or emergency room where they must sit for a few hours to develop rigor mortis. Trying to move a body from the stretcher onto the rack too soon is pointless because a freshly dead body is wobbly and it will shift around like Jell-O when moved onto the shelf. And it's just too warm too close to the act of dying. The very idea that the person was breathing smiling and possibly talking just minutes before makes me feel my own mortality with a bit too much clarity he says so it's easier to wait until the body cools down a bit—then it seems as though I'm moving an object and not another person.

"Sometimes I just need to step outside breath in the air just to make sure I can feel it inside look up at the clouds or even just get wet in the rain you know? I need to step away from death and back into life.

"Bruce?"

"Yes?"

"Nothing. Go on." says Kevin.

"But then it happened."

"WHAT happened?" asked Kevin impatiently.

"I was doing my daily tasks like determining the size of body bags we needed to restock deciding what detergent is best and what disinfectants to buy. You know the blood and stomach contents can escape from cuts and rips in the body bags. We have to double-bag some to hide the body odor of piss shit or pot. Some are really bad.

"But I do remember when we took this kid's brains out. They took this kid's brains out and I remember because the kid was from the Island not far from where I had been staying. They took this kid's brain out; they put it into a jar name age date and other stuff. They signed the papers and passed them on for me to sign. They looked real official a bit unusual but I had no reason to believe there was anything wrong. I signed my name.

"The kid looked to be about 14. He died in an automobile accident. Yes he was really dead. But when the body came down to the morgue it had been opened from neck to crotch then sewn up. Then it began to leak. I let him sit on the stretcher for a while to have some stiffness so I could put him into the cooler. But I had to look at him for two hours double bag him up and slide him in.

Did the family know about the stuff that was missing taken out? What was protruding what were these objects? That's when I began to wonder what really happened until you told me about this organ donor network."

Kevin looks at Bruce.

"Bruce" he says.

"Yup!"

"It was unusual for them to ask me for one of the I-shaped headrests used to elevate the head while opening the skull in order to remove the brain. I hung around the room simply to get it back. They didn't seem to like that I was just hanging out in the room but I wanted my I-rest back for the morgue."

DON'T ROCK THE BOAT

An in-house attempt was made to keep the suspected theft quiet. A casual inquiry was made to ask Mr. Santini at his office in the morgue if his accounts of purchases accounts receivable and paperwork were in order and if he would make certain the morgue was in compliance with procedures and safety due to an upcoming inventory of the hospital.

"Yes…yes" Mr. Santini responded smiling as he waved at the cardboard boxes tagged piled and numbered sitting on the floor about the room. The sturdy oak file cabinets were locked secure he said we only throw out the dead. "Mr. Mc Neil makes copies of everything" he said as Bruce stood smiling behind the two men who did not ask him anything. Bruce was happy that Mr. Santini had referred to him as Mr. Mc Neil.

"Do you think we need to question the kid Rosie?" asked Kevin "No" Rosie said "But we do need to make and arrest. We need to close this low profile ring thing no? We need Dante. His arrest while at the autopsy room in broad daylight will prove that we have the perp. I can see it now: African American male arrested in hospital - accused of theft." Kevin said "Good headline. Think 'profile' Rosie. Profile. Dante is our theater Rosie we just need to protect him not to get his head blown off."

It's 7:00 am and Rosie is already sitting at a desk with a huge file marked "Confidential. Not for Distribution." He's in the office of the deputy inspector Sam Blanchard the head of the Island Borough Command in New Dorp; and the coffeepot sends off a relaxing aroma as Kevin walks in with a large container of orange juice. Kevin takes one of the several pastries and says "We must visit you more often Sam. We have to watch our weight limits. We're already violating police guidelines by looking at these files and eating these donuts."

Blanchard comes over and says "Yes you've already violated police guidelines but we have a special folder for these cases. Once we get an inquiry we have to put it into the system and once you put it into the system it stays there it's a very impressive system. However we don't have people to deal with all the inquiries and update them for additional content. It's a patchwork of events and police reports over the years but we have to keep it. It's a State Law Number yada yada yada dash yada" says Blanchard. "We need to keep them for some unknown reason and I expect you both to let me know if you turn up anything."

Rosie hands Kevin a special folder that has a last notation about a guy who died two years ago: an alcoholic who could put down a fifth of Jack Daniels in the guise of friendship before leaving the bar. "He died of a heart attack in a boardinghouse watching TV. He worked for the *Advance* newspaper here and drank his way out of a job before the new technology could take it from him. No next of kin born on July 4 1931. That might be why he was still celebrating with the bottle. Hmm. He was born in St. Vincent's never married; his VA payments and checks were gathered at the door. That and the smell brought the radio car and the EMS med-ambulance.

"The guy was 74 years old male with bad teeth bad feet and a drinking problem he'd keep for the rest of his life. He learned his trade of typesetting it seems on the GI Bill and worked at the *Advance* for some time. There's lots of smaller fill in the file but a morgue attendant at the hospital was fired because of violating this corpse. They fired the guy and they kept the entire affair closed. In-house quiet. Hospitals don't like that kind of PR. We didn't follow up but I had a bad feeling about this one. Nobody came nobody cared case closed. The guy who got fired -a necrophiliac maybe? I don't know.

"We need to visit that morgue attendant. His name is Martyn Tsyganov; they called him Marty. We have a picture of his ID card. He looks like a guy of 25 clean shaven a short hard intense look on his face. That's about it.

"We found that Tsyganov lives in Brooklyn and his last job was at a hospital in Bensonhurst. He worked in the Vascular Surgery Service as an assistant attendant. Everybody liked Marty. He never missed a day; always available on the ward. Most of the patients were diabetics with horrible feet and mean infections starting at their toes or their heels and climbing up their calves. Their flesh was rotting and they were obese depressed and usually alone.

"Most of them were Blacks from the project area here a lot of them. And when the doctors and the students made their morning rounds to each room they would unwind the pus-stained gauze and wince from the smell of decay and make notes. That was the signal that the necrosis was really bad. And that meant amputation; every day 2 or 3 amputations.

"Marty helped with the sawing and the cutting. Sometimes if it was really bad he had to saw off the leg at the thigh. You had to be strong and learn the strength to put into the bone. Marty had to hold back for the last minute before the blade went clear through so as not to fall on the operating table. Marty was aloof. He had to disassociate himself from the sad human beings to whom these diseased limbs were attached.

"I think Marty works in New Jersey now at the BioMed Tissue Service. Yes we also got an ID photo from them."

"Let's visit the hospital" Kevin says. "I have a hunch."

On the way to the hospital Kevin says "I have a hunch that Bruce is being set up. There's something that bothers me about all this. I just got a hunch."

Rosie knew the security guard a retired cop living on Staten Island in Great Kills Joe Parillo. Kevin told him that they were working on the Staten Island "Ring Case." They wanted to meet the complainant for the facts. They had the initial report from the station house which was much too slight to make an arrest much of it just hearsay.

Kevin did not like hospitals any more than morgues. His stomach made no distinction. When they parked Rosie gave him a sheaf of papers and at the top of each page was stamped "FYI." He scanned the papers and folded them placing them in his inner jacket pocket. Inside they walked to the desk and asked for Mr. Joe Parillo. Parillo was a heavy-set man with a round face; he was a retired former sergeant in the New York Police Department with an easygoing smile.

He made a call to Ms. Satuyev. They walked down the hall and met her in her room behind a desk surrounded by young men and women in scrubs. She wanted each room to have hand wipes and slippers for anyone wearing street shoes that was on the hospital staff. She was an unsmiling woman as she waved the workers away and then motioned for Joe Parillo to bring in the two men inside.

Her nametag read Reza Satuyev Infection Control and she was born in the Ukraine. She spoke Russian and English with an accent. She was about 5 foot 6 inches and her blonde hair that made her a few inches taller was held firm in mounds of what looked like a beehive with hair beneath. She was made up with eye shadow and pink-red lipstick. She wore gold earrings and bracelets a fine chain with a gold cross around her neck and her lab coat was a floral print of colors over a white dress. Her huge breasts were held up almost horizontal beneath her chin and her shoes were slip-on 3" heels with small bows attached. Her blue-grey eyes followed whomever she was speaking to in shifting commands bordering on direct orders.

Her immigration file was a five-page document that read that she was a medical doctor in her homeland before coming to the US but had been unable to obtain a license to practice medicine here. Her asylum application said that she and her family had been threatened and some were beaten. Her husband a former militia officer never returned after receiving orders from his regional commander to respond to the abuse of administrative and military resources. He had been simply listed as "disappeared." Her green card allows her to work to support her family of five.

It was Reza Satuyev that that informed the security staff that a ring had been found in the lab coat that Bruce McNeal left behind after watching the autopsies of the young victim's auto accident a week before on Highland Boulevard. As usual an in-house attempt was made to keep this suspected theft quiet; hospitals simply do not like this unwelcome press.

Ms. Satuyve said "The room was being quarantined for a full-scale cleaning and inspection before it could be used again. These people live like pigs" she said. "You have no idea of the problem we have in this hospital. My team work very hard."

"Would you tell us when you found that lab coat with the ring in the pocket please" said Kevin.

"Yes it was two weeks ago Saturday. An accident; one boy died two others badly injured. Was horrible. I remember that. That man left the room without his coat. He was seen carrying articles. He was seen removing articles from that room. I cannot understand why those people choose to do these things. There was only one coat in that room when my team entered to disinfect. That young man did not have a coat when he left. It was the only lab coat left in that room and in the pocket I found a ring."

"You found the ring?" Rosie said. "Did you find the ring in that lab coat?"

"Well it was one of my cleaning team" says Ms. Satuyve. "Julie did and she is one of my best workers and she is honest and she is African American."

"Well we want to thank you Ms. Satuyve. We wanted to get the facts ma'am just the facts."

Outside Rosie gets behind the wheel and Kevin returns to the papers while Rosie drives. Almost as an afterthought Rosie says looking straight ahead "We need to make an arrest. Dante"

"You took the words right out of my mouth" says Kevin. "Dante."

"Like I always said Rosie we no longer have to bring them down to the station house and grill 'em with a rubber hose threaten the shit out of them. Just let people talk and they'll tell you what you need to know. Just let 'em talk long enough."

****

Dante was a black undercover detective in the Organized Crime Control Bureau. At one time jobless he had been an off-Broadway actor working as a waiter before taking a job and becoming a cop. Now at 23 Dante was a member of a potent and extreme unit used when the built-in structural problems of the NYPD meant that departments did not talk to one another. It's a "you-against-me" mentality; a possessiveness of information. The Organized Crime Control unit remains purposely small and they are out-of-the-box thinkers.

Dante will not meet Kevin and Rosario at the precinct he avoids entering and exiting any island precinct. He has a shield which he carries inside his belt buckle and a glock which he refuses to carry. His street smarts have been developed over a number of years and his career spans Manhattan Brooklyn and Staten Island. His official work meetings are off site arrangements and never in a rod and gun club or bar or after hours joints to kick back or celebrate. Dante has a record of arrest assists are extensive he appears via closed circuit video if possible when testifying on any case. His casual street walk and his clothes are style of the neighborhood easy his daily workout it a small boxing gym in Brooklyn Heights where he is a member he changes locations after 6 months or so. He has learned Judo and Karate as a child he holds a black belt.

Kevin would let Dante know what he was thinking and what he expected and why the clandestine mode. Dante would of course apply the disguise. Kevin's relationship with Dante was an off and on again relationship. There were no official written standards. They both wanted to get the bad guys and their lives were in the hands of their back-up white supervisors.

After receiving the call Dante would meet with Kevin and Rosario at the precinct but Dante as usual would avoid entering and exiting any Island precinct. He has a shield which he carries inside his belt-buckle and a Glock pistol which he refuses to carry. His street smarts have been developed over a number of years and his career spans Manhattan Brooklyn and Staten Island. His official work meetings are off-site arrangements and never in a rod and gun club or a bar or any after-hours joint to kick back or celebrate.

Dante has a record of arrest assists and they are extensive. He appears via close-circuit video if possible when testifying on any case. His casual street walk and his clothes are the style of the neighborhood: easy and casual.

His life beyond the job is private and Dante would leave the New York police department if he could not use his skills. On occasion he has been a paralegal a park department worker a librarian a real estate broker. He also has been a belligerent drunk a pickpocket and a visibly obnoxious dysfunctional vagrant and drug pusher. His job is his theatre his art. He could actually be a twenty-something co-ed or student. He could also be a cold-eyed down pimp hustler.

At the gatehouse driving his own Honda Civic Dante stops at the gatehouse and tells the guard that he has an appointment with Lieutenant Murphy and he says "My name is Joe Friday" thinking that the man in the guardhouse would never have seen the black and white television show. Not showing any surprise at the name the guard simply picks up the phone and repeats the visitor's message.

"Yes you can go on but park in the Visitor Area over there" he says pointing to an area away from the main building. Some cars and police cruisers are parked in numbered asphalt spaces. "RHIP" Dante thinks "Rank Has It's Privileges."

There is no one else on the grounds and the buildings have magic marker numbers on papers attached to the glass doors. In front of the glass doors is a tall round green can with a small hole in the top. The sign reads DEPOSIT ALL SMOKING AND CHEWING ARTICLES HERE. With an arrow pointing down. Dante stops and reads the printed message he smiles and attaches his chewing gum on the rim of the receptacle.

Another sign printed with a magic marker above a brass plate with four buttons says "press ". One number is as good as another he thinks as he presses one of four buttons at the doorway. A microphone overhead says "Be down in a minute Joe."

A moment later Kevin comes to the huge glass doors opening one he says "Joe nice to see you how have you been. He smilingly fist-bumps Dante who says "Kevin you look unwell: are you sick? I was told you wanted this job because it was an easy run to get points before you retire" says Dante.

Touching his stomach as they reach the top of the stairs Kevin says "Gas Reflux. I'm off coffee and donuts now. I don't live far away from here and Connie wants me home at 6:00 now and she feeds me suppers; suppers Italian style. I'll gain back a little weight and I haven't had time to put in my papers yet."

He opens another door and inside the office there are dozens of screens and keyboards GPS-like devices with maps that show the east west north and south and where hundreds of cameras are located; on the bridges and ferryboats. There's an eerie white glow from overhead lighting and the wall-screen monitors with blinking red dots. Along the bottom of the monitors is a continually running text none of which Dante can understand.

"Looks like a movie set Kevin What's this all about. Star Trek right?"

Rosie looks from behind a bank of computer screens and says "Hi Dante." He points to a wall cabinet and says "Coffee and tea and crumpets. Hang on; I'll be with you in a minute."

Another man is sitting at a keyboard and Kevin asks him to leave for a while so they can talk. "We have civilians on contract to gather all this together" says Kevin. The man stands and looks at Dante who tries not to make eye-contact or need to recognize him.

"This is Island Ground Zero" says Kevin. "A bunker above ground you might say. It's a former satellite station; not complete yet. Not much walking the beat on Staten Island any more we can walk with mouse and finger." He walks across to the wall screen and slides the view down to a mosque enlarging it waiting for pedestrians to walk by. "Bus stops corners shopping malls and restaurants. If we don't have it we'll get it. This is the new NYPD Dante a 9/11 special."

"It's spooky" says Dante.

"Yeah Dante, spooky. Come over here look at this. See this? Little ICs. We can place them at eye level rather than the cameras embedded in the ceiling. These are new cameras that feed data here into facial recognition software like the kind used by the FBI. It logs the age gender and race of passers-by. Cool huh?"

"Instead of the bulky overhead security cameras these ICs provide better data because they are at eye-level. I can't elaborate Dante because I don't know much more but we have Wi-Fi iPads and video screens. We can profile but it raises legal and ethical issues. I guess the law department will figure that one out.

"OK Dante. We have already asked Zimmerman if we can use you on a detail and we will give you all that we have at this time. We need to bust a Black guy for theft at the hospital to cool tempers. We need a distraction."

"Pseudo profiling eh?" Dante says.

"Yea" Rosie says "racial profiling. The complainant is a white woman on staff at the hospital. She tells us she thinks a Black man in the morgue has been stealing gold from morgue victims. We have a gold-plated ring worth less than 150 bucks. We think she wants him removed because he was in the wrong place at the right time. The morgue worker has access to valuable equipment and inventory shows no purchases over the required items needed. Why would he rip off a cheap gold plated ring? We also need to keep our undercover work about the organ donor network on the back-burner for now."

"What's an organ donor network?" asks Dante.

"It's now a big business" says Kevin. Worldwide; big time; body parts. Legitimate organ donors provide a potential lifeline to patients with failing organs but there's a long waiting list. Problem is there are at times not enough livers hearts or kidneys and so forth and the niche can only be filled by hustlers ballsy and fast enough to take part before people are pronounced dead."

"Well where does this Black dude enter the picture?" asked Dante. "The morgue dude?"

"Squeaky clean" says Kevin. "We might ask him to wear a wire sometime later."

Dante is quiet for a long time then says, "White dude craziness all the way."

"It's not a Black stereotype at all."

"Black dude gets arrested for stabbing another Black because he's suspected of speaking to his girlfriend disrespecting him."

"Young Black male, right?"

"Guy walks into a 7-11 and kills 6 people and turns the gun on himself: White guy all the way."

"You know you've got to hand it to the brothers; at least they have a reason to shoot someone."

"It may be simplistic but at least Black guys offer some excuse, like, "He looked at me funny" or "I wanted his North Face coat" or "He's wearing too much bling!"

"If you ask a white guy why he killed and dismembered a body he'll say "I don't know. I just wanted to see what it's like." As a Black man I have to ask - What's up with that?"

****

The actors were in place the hospital theater was buzzing with worker bees no one noticed the young black man with a small goatee mustache and short dreadlocks in a white lab coat and green hospital pants and name tag intently checking his clipboard he moved casually around the gurneys and wheelchairs in the hallways and entered an elevator pushed the "down" button patiently waited until the doors opened.

He walked to the end of the long corridor noting a red ceiling sign that pointed to the exit doorway to check if the door were able to be opened from this floor. He held a cell phone to his ear and casually responding to a message "I am here thank you." No one has looked at Dante who nods smiling as he coolly walks the length of the corridor again checking offices and waiting rooms.

166

At the end of the long corridor Dante walks to the end door marked "Infection control" looks inside as five or six people are listening to a lady holding up a canister calmly saying "Excuse me" casually opening other doors in the corridor he enters a room marked "PRIVATE EMPLOYEES ONLY." There are two women sitting at a small round table having coffee. They say "Yes? Can we help you?" Dante looks around the room producing his best guilt-face excuse "Oh I was looking for a toilet" quickly turning around reentering the corridor purposely dropping and scattering small items and a handbag to the floor and walking quickly away.

A tall white male watching from a waiting room doorway shouts "Hey you stop!" Dante begins to walk fast toward the end of the corridor and the exit door. More voices shouting he stole this catch him there he is. Dante moves up a stairway leaving articles behind his lab coat now falling to the floor as voices call out to stop him. "Call 911 he's the thief!" The white male is now behind Dante followed by a dozen angry hospital workers yelling "Hold him…hold him. Get him!" Security men alerted by the noise volume now attempt to hit Dante who avoids the blows falls to the floor to cover his face. The white man is now holding a police shield and says "I'm off duty call 911." He pulls Dante's arms behind his back pressing his leg across Dante beneath him. Many hospital workers are now holding items for the security people to see "I didn't do it" shouts Dante. Immediately two NYPD patrolmen are holding Dante by his arms and rushing him to a police cruiser outside. They return to take notes and names of the hospital staff. Many workers said to have had missing items recently and they were glad to supply additional voices to the statements and stories.

The perp has been apprehended he will be taken to the 120 police precinct and tossed into a cage. Later he will be seen leaving the precinct by an Advance newspaper photographer with a hood over his head for a trip to the Tombs.

A dark moonless fall night. Kevin looks at the lighted alarm clock; it's one a.m. and the karaoke singer is calling out for suggestions.

No it's a dream; he's coming out of a long vivid dream about spending time at the shore he doesn't know exactly where but its New Jersey. He is still in that psychic space between waking and sleeping not sure if his eyes are open or not but his senses become aware of a deep grayness and it seems that an even darker gray shadow has formed; a figure silent moving as if on a stage singing with a mic but there is no sound calling for him to ask for a Sinatra tune.

It's the middle of the night and the two sleeping pills he took to fend off those recurring images have not kicked in. The figure the image seems to be someone he knows but it is somehow on another temporal plane; he can't focus on a face.

He is calm and yet angry. He can't seem to avoid or suck in the intense experiences. He will not mention them to Connie because he believes that they are dreams and everybody has dreams right? It's another rambling kind of night and he has been up for...how long? The wedding party and the singer that's it!! Or was it just his imagination once again; the holidays the wedding school kids college plus...

He doesn't really dream. OK he's sure that at some time everyone including him sees images and fragments of crap parading through the subconscious during normal sleep.

167

He's heard that it happens to everybody. He never seems to remember dreams when he wakes up. So he assumes he doesn't dream.

What's bothering him is that kid Bruce McNeil going on about the morgue and descriptions and details; he seems to need the job more than the job needs him. Kevin has a hunch McNeil has a full size rubber body at home to feel connected when he's away from the morgue. He has not seen anything strange for 4 months

Connie's side of the bed is empty. Connie must be downstairs sleeping on the couch. She has slept there on and off for a week watching late night talk shows; Conan O'Brian and that other guy. It sounds like rain maybe she's making oatmeal again or tea toast and scrambled. He hates tea

His rib-cage hurts while he's dressing. When he tries to take a deep breath his chest is tight; what's that about he wonders. Maybe he could use one of those colon–cleansing elixirs his mother used to make!

It's Thursday and they just got the message on Monday—important meeting. Three Bs One Police Plaza calls this one—Balls Brass and BS. "I don't want to be late for this" he thinks. "It's going to be a lopsided affair One Police Plaza brass vs. Rosie and me. I think I had a good night's sleep so I'm ready."

In the kitchen Connie says nothing at least nothing audible. She's not smiling much or talking about Terri or their grand kid. He's seen it before and it's not a good sign.

It's 6:30. Kevin heads out to the car and stops. He turns back and Connie is at the door holding an umbrella. They kiss; she's cold and smells like vanilla and he's already wet. The roads will be wet and bad; the leaves have started to turn colors. This rain is soothing; the wipers slamming down on each side a bit rare for this time of year.

At the gate he opens his window slows down and shows his badge. The guard waves him on and he parks in front of the building. He pushes out the umbrella and stands for a moment; there is no noticeable pain anyplace. He pushes the buzzer above the "No Smoking" sign.

The new private security man inside is sitting behind a desk watching a monitor. He stands up and when Kevin holds up his gold badge he comes to open the door. He is a heavy set black man in a blue uniform; his tag says Tim Martin. "I'm Lieutenant Murphy" I say. "You're new here?"

"Yep. We'll be here 24/7. I'm Tim. Detective Campinella said you would be along shortly. We have this list of regulars civilians and policemen maintenance and others."

"Who are the 'others'?" I ask.

"I have no idea" he says. "They have no uniforms and they have offices space in the main floor down there" he says pointing down the long hall.

Upstairs in the huge room there are two civilians with ID photo cards on chains around their necks working at tables and screens Kevin ignores them and says to Rosie "What's going on downstairs? Who the fuck are they?"

"FBI is my guess and 'others.' Don't you feel safe?" says Rosie.

"YES! It's the 'others' that bother me" says Kevin.

"Not only did they pull our boys out of their vans and off the street DOI from IG's office sends this." Rosie puts a folder on the table in front of Kevin.

Confidential not for distribution order. USA Patriot Act. Section 216 © "We're cops for God's sake not lawyers. I swear to God using trap and trace devices without a court order in emergency situations. Back to carrier pigeons we go with that."

The final subsection of this section modifies the definition of "court of competent jurisdiction" section 216 ©. "Good luck with that!!"

The purpose of the amendments is to issue orders for clarity concerning the continued validity of the pre-existing authority.

This threatens to be a serious practical problem when gathering information. 125(b) of this bill.

"Given how cranky I have been lately I got an appointment with an acupuncturist; maybe all her needles will make everything all right. Irritable Bowel Syndrome was the diagnosis giving up coffee donuts and cigarettes the remedy. The punishment fits the crime."

Rosie has put two tables and chairs together; in the center he has two large open boxes of donuts. Kevin examines them and asks "Rosie where did you get these?"

"I had Maria pick them up this morning at the bakery for our guests 18 dollars a dozen" he says pointing. "These are not your usual deep fried sweet rounds of dough. These are candy colored with sprinkles cinnamon and sugar crusted lemon-poppy glazed and bittersweet chocolate."

Rosie is lost in his selection. Picking one from a box he says "It has a ricotta center. I'm Italian!"

"And you're getting fat" says Kevin as he chooses one with a liberal dusting of powdered sugar. "Just one" he says removing a thermos of tea from his bag. "The new coffee machine dispenses coffee but has no tea bags."

"I will make a report" says Rosie smiling. "

"I hope the donuts make some points;" says Kevin "we may need them."

"Maybe we're making a colossal blunder waiting for another hit on the morgue bodies Kevin. It's been almost five months and we haven't had a bite."

"No I have a hunch. These guys aren't stupid Dumb yes; they function on a level lacking anything above what they have learned knowing only what they need to get by. There is a connection. The VCR'S on that monitor show familiar faces in Brighton Beach Café Kaskan the Uygher Restaurant and the Uzbek sauna. Our 75 hours of video show 'persons of interest.' We have seen the old Soviet black market skills returning; bootleg cigarettes car and truckloads up Interstate 95 small stuff we let slip. We need patience Rosie. The old esoteric rituals and skills are disconnected from the old country and sharpened by Barkar Malyukin. He's a consigliere and he will kill when he is told." Kevin moves to a large screen and begins a video "That's Marty Tsyganov the organ grinder.

169

Here he is going into the sauna. If you want to know faces watch the sauna. Can't beat the sauna eh?"

"That buzzer" says Rosie "is from the front door desk. We have our visitors."

Rosie asks the two men who are civilian technicians under oath of office and are not uniformed members of the force to take a long coffee break. "Better you should take in a movie" interrupts Kevin. "This might drag out."

****

Deputy Inspector Chris Cohen came up the career tracks; he was made deputy inspector by the police commissioner. He is a cop's cop acting as a political hack to watch the back of the commissioner from outside.

Captain Jeff Hammond of internal affairs; one of several command structure officers the eyes and ears of labor problems union disputes problem solving community voices and politically sensitive

Frank Castellano the S.I. Borough Police Chief made his career tracks and is about to retire He donned the white Tyvek and rubber boots working with Kevin on the Fresh Kills 911 recovery site.

Walter Bokowski is an attorney investigator supervisor with internal affairs.

Their shirt and tie plain clothes would not attract any attention if they were part of a funeral coffin detail or a church wedding. They were well fed middle aged men given to smiles and patience. None wore stylish double breasted pin stripe suits and none had noticeable bulges. If any carried a gun it would be a Smith and Wesson model 36 a .38 caliber Chief's special snub nosed 2 inch barrel revolver which is easy to conceal while wearing civilian clothes.

"Fresh coffee" says Rosie to the group as they began to choose chairs around the table. "Yes and help yourselves to the bon-bons. We no longer call them donuts!" There are smiles at Rosie's attempt at humor.

Frank Castellano says to Kevin "So this is why you haven't put in your papers. Nice place. I haven't been invited to this comfortable secret retreat close to home. Haven't seen you since Fresh Kills."

"I did not want to return to a precinct" says Kevin.

"We got your hospital perp at the precinct; he ended up at the 122." Castellano passes a sheet of official papers to Kevin; the top sheet is a copy of the police newspaper report about the incident at the hospital.

Convicted felon arrested after hospital chase

A twice convicted felon is accused of stealing hospital workers' bags and purses. The suspect was identified as Deshawn Ali. He appeared to be about 30 years old and had no fixed address. He was accused of theft from hospital staff rooms and closets. He is charged with fourth degree grand larceny petty larceny two counts of criminal possession of stolen property and possession of burglary tools.

Hospital security said Mr. Ali was spotted trying to enter locked rooms with burglar tools. Another employee witness said she saw him trying to sneak behind her station desk when she called security. After a chase an off duty police officer pinned him down until police arrived.

"We didn't know he was your undercover guy until after the pat-down; he later gave us your number from his shoe lace. Gutsy guy with no shield. I had to take him down to the detention center to get him out."

"Who are the undercover officers?" Castellano asks. Captain Hammond interrupts and says "They are hardworking minority men and women mostly Hispanic and Black. They grew up in a lot of the toughest streets and neighborhoods that we haven't been able to get into. We make a special effort to recruit them and give them special training and allowances to un-box them to get them into the NYPD to make a difference. The NYPD uses them.

"Well don't they depend upon a field team" says Castellano "back up?"

"I will admit that this hospital perp bust was more Dick Tracy than we would like we need to talk about it to Murphy and Campinella."

"But these guys are a small elite firearms unit they trained specially. They become experienced undercover officers most of whom intend to make a career out of that kind of work and there has been no white undercover officer in a lot of years that can make that cut as well.

"Dante is a specialist. A special line has been created for these guys detectives the lieutenants and they are typically found in specialized units because they possess a unique or esoteric skill that we need. We have to find them – sharp shooters bomb technicians scuba divers; you name it we're looking. It's a new world of police investigations."

Walter Bakowski is a lawyer investigating supervisor from internal affairs. "It's difficult" he says. "We have the Legal Aid Society and law firms breathing down our necks."

"Yes we're trying to make a difference. The black cops know that once you're in there's no way out of these units. They don't want to pound the pavement in a precinct in Tottenville. They are constantly at risk of being robbed and even killed. They may even face a risk of being shot by other officers by mistake. They are mistaken for the bad guys armed criminal punk street perpetrators. We had two African Americans from the firearms investigating unit who were executed on Staten Island by a black man they believed was going to bring them to a place to buy guns. Black on black

"I put it on the table so you'll know we're not underscoring the racial disparity between those who work undercover and their supervisors. The work is not glamorous and these guys their efforts are aimed at those who sell drugs guns you name it. They know that their jobs are inherently dangerous. We have back up teams."

"Did Dante have a backup field team at his hospital arrest?" Chris Cohen asks.

"No I'm afraid he didn't. He didn't have a transmitter. That stuff is unreliable and outdated. We don't have any equipment any longer like the hip worn beepers popular many decades ago. Those would be difficulties plaguing any undercover unit at this time.

"We had to pull the stake-out video team that Kevin and Rosie asked for. They worked for two weeks round the clock got nothing. The team had two cars and a van. In the back of the van there were seven shelves of equipment and tools including two television monitors divided into four video feeds so that the person inside the van could see what was going on to the left or the right or the front and back of the van. We had dust busters walking the streets posing as pedestrians people of the community alcoholics and hookers. Some wore bullet proof vests pepper spray Glocks batons.

"We went through a shitload of trouble to set that up. The bad guys are more intelligent today. Without pat downs they can spot a cop they can spot a ghost even with a backup team. The bad guys are smarter but they are still dumb. We have to find ways to bust them. Many of our techniques that we used years ago are no longer legal. The court says we can't make these set ups. We can't tape wires to a test man we can't make undetected wires on men like Dante. That would put their lives in danger and they know it. And we understand the difficulties plaguing undercover units in the NYPD. We will give them everything they need to do the job and protect themselves.

"I want to repeat that our pulling the team out of the vans with all of the equipment was because it no longer seems to work on the streets. We are dealing with much more intelligent killers and assassins; the sky is the limit. They are armed with everything to do their work. We have to keep up with them. We have to straddle both sides of the street. Sometimes we have to switch off between working as an undercover ghost and just hang out on the street wearing a police rain jacket."

Bokowski impatiently tapping his pencil on the table says "I like these cases of police malfeasance to go on for a long time. People forget they get scared they move and things get lost. The slow process is in our favor now but it will change with that electronic work" he says pointing to the huge wall sections.

"Legal Aid knows this and they are putting pressure on judges to accept plea bargains and lesser charges or no jail time. After you work on these cases for ten years and get a misdemeanor after that the case may disappear. I'm an attorney and we gotta work with the district attorneys. There is a problem reconnecting with the victims and witnesses. It pisses me off. And the police tend to lie to save their skins. Mistakes are made; the process is antediluvian so put it here on the table with your fantastic donuts."

Kevin remains quiet. Rosie takes notes says nothing. Captain Hammond stands and motions for Kevin to show him what they have now.

"They call this an I-lab system. The tech men need time to understand the rhythm and so do we. I get a print out of this" Kevin says pointing at the Brighton Beach cabaret on the screen. "We can see faces on our eyelevel drop cams to ID and follow up for more information. It's not like using the printer at home; we stop and search stop and enter what we found. It's a big and complex system. And it must be kept in-house. These tech savvy guys are stressed at the break downs and they sometimes get embarrassed at what they don't know."

Another touch brings faces into focus on another screen Walter Bowkoski says "WOW! Candid Camera!"

"That's Bakar Malykin the new consigliere high ranking driver collection man contact person; never been arrested since he came here but he will kill. He lives in a basement apartment with an arm candy model from Ukraine a farmer's daughter calls herself Tina. No arrests yet.

"This fellow is Martyn Tsganov likes to be called 'Marty.' He calls the Rasputin Café his seat when we find him in Brighton Beach Brooklyn. He's a surgeon without portfolio the 'parts' man. The case at his feet is a special cooler that can be plugged into a 120 outlet. In and out of hot spots buying and selling stolen gold jewelry. His reputation is raising red flags. There are many more we have listed as 'persons of interest'.

Kevin stops. His face is glued to a ghost-like figure on the screen in front of him. It's the man in his dream holding a mike asking him what he would like to hear.

Deputy Inspector Cohen taps Kevin on his shoulder and says "Go on" pointing to the screen.

"I wish our cameras had voices" Kevin says

"Are you waiting for a voice here?" says Cohen. "You look as though you've seen a ghost."

"No. No these computers break down Murphy's Law and we get mixed signals the tech guys here understand the difficulties undercover units have. We leave the stress to them."

Changing this uncomfortable line Kevin asks Inspector Cohen about the tenants the 'others' on the first floor here. Who are they?

"FBI CIA ICE. We don't communicate with one another. We have our army navy coast guard and air force right here in the big apple; the NYPD is fully staffed." The Commissioner and the Mayor agree on keeping our independence.

"We have lists of male and female figures; most eventually take American sounding names and frequent cafes and restaurants not to feel disconnected from their origins; not to lose that cultural sensitivity. We have our Russian speakers in the department but we need more ears on the ground."

"Do you have a time-line for this?" asks Chris Cohen.

"No but I do have a hunch."

"Right" Chris Cohen says. "I mean you're having one of your hunches right here now."

"Yep. We will have his ass. He fits that pattern.

"It sure does" says Rosie. "The price of parts is going up and he is the leader on the island and in Brooklyn. This Bay Ridge pharmacy supplies him with any drugs he wants. The 81st Precinct in Brooklyn has gathered this including the audio recordings."

The market prices are now high and the beasts are waiting. Lungs are 2500 each Liver 1300 to 3000 kidneys 3 to 4 thousand spleen 5 to 6 thousand ribs 1500 to 3000 each full brains are now 5 grand or more and a gall bladder is 5 grand. Bones like femurs are 2 thousand. The list is flat rate and changes with demand and location. And the private air costs are not part of the price list.

Chris Cohen is quiet; he senses a tenseness as Kevin looks at the screens and places his hand on his shoulder tapping gently like a physician searching for traces of arthritis. "There seems to be a bit of emotion that's involved in this assignment" he says close to Kevin's ear "it's part of the job. I spoke to Connie and she wants you to see Dr. Mazella. So do I."

Kevin does not respond continues looking at the dozen monitors. Pushing a screen of faces Kevin stops to bring a face into expanded focus. "A 30 year old island woman with one kid diagnosed with cystic fibrosis. The family opted for an organ transplant they had little time the other organs were getting messed up with mucus; she had difficulty breathing. She received a lung transplant. Ya know what?" Kevin says still looking at the screen. "She was diagnosed with lung cancer. Never been a smoker or even lived with one. Her life-saving lung transplant belonged to a heavy smoker. She's dead. The hospital accepts the lungs and other parts of a smoker's body for transplant if they are of 'good' quality. The hospital apologized for not notifying the family that they did have a choice not to accept."

"That's funny" he said still looking at the face on the screen. "My daughter Theresa is 30 and she has one kid."

"Yes I know. And you're a cop Kevin and not a personal crusader."

Chris Cohen wants a time line. Quietly pressing he asks Kevin "Another six months? A year?

"Yep about a year. If not I'll put in my papers" said Kevin.

"You have this routine this predictable schedule" said Cohen. "Another year will increase your pension equal to half your salary you do the math. This is a young mans game now. This new I-lab is the language of another generation computers break down under the stress and so do their owners. Murphy's Law."

Kevin does not respond. He is drawn to a shadowy figure on the screen he has no idea why. He squeezes his eyes for better focus.

"We are over burdened and under pressure from One Police Plaza. They want to clear the calendar of old cases. I hope this is not a catch and release effort."

Rosie made another pot of coffee and has been making small talk with Jeff Hammond and Frank Castellano while Bokowski is tapping the keyboard of the new integrated system computer screen making low "wow" noises as he sees the thousands of closed circuit Comstat camera's license plate readers and other surveillance devices as he gazes at the screens displaying the casual mundane nature of island life. There are no donuts left in the box.

Chris Cohen clears his throat in an attempt to take control "Are there any more questions for Kevin or Rosie?"

****

"I have to admit that was a surprise ending and it caught me off guard" Kevin says.

"I guess they liked the donuts best of all. I'm watching your back" says Rosie. "Good deal" says Kevin. "I got the front."

Leaving in late afternoon Kevin feels the fall weather chill even more. He reaches into the pockets of his coat and finds a carefully folded paper: Dr. Mazella appointment time and date. Connie has placed three copies into his clothes pockets.

Connie is happy to have Kevin home for dinner though she says little while Kevin awkwardly tries to respond to conversation. He will go to bed early but Connie will stay up late to watch Jay Leno or David Letterman. Kevin will not watch any TV screens; he wants to avoid the shadow entertainment figures.

****

Kevin was taking leave time to rearrange his life with Connie and to give Dr. Mazella's orders and medications time to work. He had had X-rays an EKG and a gastro insertion test - he had hated that. Connie will get the results from Mazella first. He knew Connie and Dr Mazella were in constant communication and the trip to New Jersey with a room at a hotel in Atlantic City would ease the tension. He loved Connie; she was the reason he took a city job and they had raised their three children on his police salary. And he liked being a cop.

They walked on the boardwalk in winter sweaters and long coats. They did not talk about the eventual move to Jersey but Kevin knew that life in New Jersey would not be perfect. New Jersey the most densely populated state in the entire country. Everyone wants a part of the beach a bit of the "shore" and Kevin knew he would be joined by other Staten Islanders that made the hop-skip-and-a-jump from Brooklyn to Staten Island and eventually to New Jersey.

He didn't like hunting for Jersey tomatoes at the farmers market on Saturdays or bird feeders walking a dog beehives or more mosquitoes than the island nor could he recognize a poison oak tree or a Jersey pine. He was born and raised on Staten Island; would he need a special travel pass to return to the island once they moved? Perhaps Connie recognized his ambivalence to discuss a move to New Jersey she never suggested they "look"; the retirement move conversation could wait.

They had dinner and walked late at night again in the cool evening cold and now they held hands again. It was after eleven when they returned. He took a small bottle of wine from the fridge pouring two glasses. Connie wore little makeup; she paused for a long time looking at her nude body in the tall mirror. Had she gained weight? Would he notice the new wrinkles? Did she shrink a little in height? She patted the belly bulge; but we did three kids here she said to herself. Kevin watched as she undressed casually. She was beautiful he told her before they cuddled and hugged. Connie would miss the Late-Late show tonight.

****

The first day after their return from New Jersey there were several messages from Rosie. Probably to invite them to his upcoming wedding Kevin thought. "One big wedding" he said.

"Italian big" said Connie. "Bay Ridge big. You the best man?" she asked.

"'Dunno" said Kevin. "It's all too sudden. This love thing is catching" he laughed as the phone began to ring. "It's six o'clock" Kevin says into the receiver. "No I did not take my cell phone. I'm taking some medical leave remember?"

Rosie continues. "The Odessa group. Kevin you need to get down here PDQ. Your hunch was right."

"You got something?"

"Yep."

"What is it? Rosie tell me?

"Santini has been wacked."

Kevin took the address hung up and dressed. He entered the kitchen and sat at the table Connie had made toast tea scrambled eggs and juice and she had left his medications for him in a small plastic cup. "Rosie?" she asked.

"Yep. It may be a late day" said Kevin.

"I'll pack a sandwich Connie said smiling.

****

Several cruisers were holding traffic and yellow tape had marked the perimeter. An ambulance was idling nearby as police officers talked casually in groups. There was no hurry; the person was obviously dead.

Church Lane just off Bay Street is a paved alley and dead ends at a wall. The body is definitely that of Mr. Santini dressed in a white shirt bow tie and suit. He seems to be resting. Why would he be here in the alley? He lived less than a block away on Bay Street; he went to Saint Mary's Church regularly. St Mary's a seven story red brick church with a cross at the top of the steeple. A popular church well attended; most Italians use this church for marriages baptisms and funerals.

The moody in-charge detective from the precinct says 'He's clean. No nothing not even a handkerchief. Fuckin' muggers." He has seen it all before. There were no outward signs or even any blood.

176

Staten Island residents under surveillance.

Teleport Police Entrance.

"The signature clean whack" says Kevin. "Dislocated shoulder dislocated mandible fibula break and sternum break. Very controlled anger.. It probably started in a rage but at some point it became methodical. There'll be no outward marks until the ME completes his job. One different kind of consigliore Rosie. In the old days the Italian consigliore would simply whack a guy with a .38 in the back of the head. The most grisly techniques would be to bury a guy alive in the sand under the boardwalk or maybe give him size 20 cement block swim shoes.

"Che peccato" says Rosie. " What a pity."

"I have a cruiser from the 120th sitting out front of his house" said Rosie. "We can walk down." The older two-family street homes on a long stretch of the street have been occupied by Italian families for decades the houses often changing hands to immediate family members or cousins. A solid middle class community: civil service workers police sanitation workers and longshoremen along with family owned storefront delicatessens.

The front porch has a few wicker chairs and a small round table with wind chimes and small metal angels hanging from the center. There are two huge flower pots with plants that seem to be well cared for. There are two doors and two bells indicating separate door entrances. Rosie decides to push the bell on the right to alert the owners. The crochet curtain moves to one side to check them and the door opens enough for an old woman to ask "Yes?"

"Mr. Santini lives here?"

'Yes."

"We are police officers and we need to tell you that he has had an accident." The woman lifts her hand to her throat and says "Yes?"

"He apparently had a bad fall or a mugging. He's is on his way to the hospital" says Rosie. "Are you Mr. Santini's landlord here?"

"Yes" says the lady. Her gray hair is covered with a shawl and she squints directly at each face.

"We would like to have a key to Mr. Santini's apartment" says Rosie showing his gold badge.

"Just a minute" says the woman and closes the door.

A moment later a man appears and asks 'What can I do for you?' He is a younger heavyset man wearing a checkered work shirt. He has large workman's hands and is unsmiling his face blank. He also has trouble looking at the two police.

"We think Mr. Santini either fell or was a mugging victim" says Rosie. "We need to have more identification. We know he lives alone and we will need to notify the next of kin." He asks no further questions.

"All right" says the man. He produces a ring of keys from his pocket and saying nothing more opens the door on the left. He does not climb the stairs.

Rosie and Kevin climb the stairs and open the door at the top. There are three rooms a large central room with an open kitchen a bedroom and a bathroom with another porch facing the street.

The main room is clean and seems to be cared for; it's separated by a huge square rug in the center of a linoleum tile floor in the center of which is a square wooden coffee table with a candy dish a couch with several small pillows and a footrest. Beside the couch is a small wooden table with a hand-made silk doily on which is a reading lamp. There is one well-used fully padded chair with a blue and white striped slip-cover and a foot rest and there are several pottery vases holding colorful artificial flowers.

There is no dust. There are no clothes lying about no magazines no newspapers or books no television and no ash trays. There is a religious crèche on the coffee table two more crèche's on the kitchen counter and on the window sill and another one in the bedroom which seems to have been freshly made. The clothes closet has three dark suits shoes that have been polished to a high shine a few hats and an umbrella.

Beside the bed is a black and white photo of Santini and his wife serious expressions in what seems to be an outdoor celebration that may have been taken in Italy; there is no inscription on the front or rear. The bathroom has clean towels hanging and the medicine cabinet has several boxes of band-aids aspirin shaving creams and lotions. There are no prescription medicine bottles. There is a comb and a brush; neither of which have hairs attached to the surface. A new roll of toilet tissue has been added to the holder. Rosie calls Kevin and points "So you got a hunch chief?

"Oh yes' Kevin says. " Santini doesn't live here. It's a really bad set-up."

There is absolutely no dust. The kitchen area is surgically clean. The few glasses cups bowls plates and other dishes are clean and tidy all piled neatly in an open front cupboard. The small canisters of salt sugar and pepper the bottles of oils the napkin holder and the jars of herbs are clean and spotless and there is no visible food on the hardwood counter.

A small round table with two bentwood chairs is scrupulously clean with two apples and two oranges holding center stage on the small round table. There is no odor of any recently cooked food. The fridge is spare and all it contains is milk juice some wrapped packages and bottled water. There is no leftover food inside. The fridge door is covered with magnets from the Statue of Liberty and the Empire State Building from Atlantic City and from Foxwoods Did he gamble? Play the slots? "The flowers aren't real" Kevin says. "Is any of this real?"

The obituary in the Staten Island Advance was brief:

Salvatore Santini 68 died Monday at the Staten Island University Hospital Ocean Breeze. Born in Bari Italy Mr. Santini moved to Rosebank and worked in the Staten Island Hospital.

In his leisure time Mr. Santini enjoyed watching the New York Jets and traveling to Atlantic City and Foxwoods Casino. He enjoyed tending his garden where he had fig trees grapes and tomatoes. "He was always happy and liked to make people laugh" said his friend Michael Sansone. Mr. Santini was preceded in death by his wife of 30 years the former Terri Manino. Funeral will be Saturday with a mass at 10:45 at St Mary's Church Rosebank. Cremation will be in the Rosehill Crematory Linden New Jersey. His ashes will be returned to Bari Italy.

"For Christ's sake Kevin let's set some bait. We know who's responsible; let's dig a ditch!!"

"Do you mean bait a hook plant some weed or set up a sting? I've never heard anything so stupid in my life" says Kevin. "We planted a drop-cam outside that house. For the last week we got nothing; the guy goes to work at a grunge job in Brooklyn the 81st precinct says he's clean. The woman goes shopping we tail her and she comes up clean. Like Santini's room clean. Why? No one has visited that house since we left; look at the cam recordings on the screen. They are methodical clean too clean. Professional killers until Santini.

****

X-cop Joe Perillo hospital security has caution-taped the morgue on Kevin's "crime scene" orders. Bruce McNeil is sitting at the door holding a folder. "Mr. Perillo said you'd be here. Can we go inside now please" Bruce said. "I need to tell you something."

"Christ! You're not going to explain the morgue and body system again are you?" asked Kevin.

"I'm sorry about Mr. Santini." Joe opened the doors and inside the morgue everything had been covered. The smell of disinfectant was strong; there was a cone of silence and the echo of voices he had not noticed before. "This is definitely a place for the dead "Rosie thought.

"Has anybody been in here since I called you to put up the tapes?" asked Kevin.

"Only the cleaning crew" said Joe. "Orders from upstairs I believe."

"Do you mean the infection control crew?"

"Yes said Joe. " On the 26th two weeks ago. 'Disinfect'" he said looking at his notepad. "They closed it down after the death and sent the bodies to a Brooklyn hospital. I'll be upstairs; call me if you need me. I'll lock up."

Kevin looks at Rosie who looks at him saying nothing the fragments were now being strung together like beads on a string. "Raisa Satuyev" Kevin says. "Infection CONTROL."

"The bitch" interrupted Bruce. "She had to get into his room but I know she didn't find anything."

"O.K. Bruce talk to us now!!"

"I wanted to help Mr. Santini by having him stay with me. He was scared I should have called you but we didn't trust you. I wanted him to recommend me for the job and he did look at these" Bruce said taking the rolled up folder of papers he held.

"Wait stop slow down and talk to us. Do you mean Mr. Santini confided in you?"

"Yes" said Bruce.

"About what?"

Bruce walked into the small office giving several keys to Kevin. "Try them" he said.

Kevin pushed the key into the round brass hole in the top draw to open it but pulling the small brass handles did nothing. The heavy wooden oak cabinet drawers would not open. Bruce slid the top surface back while pressing a small spring loaded vertical piece down and then pulled the top drawer open. It was empty. The second and the third and the fourth drawers were all empty. "He said these were in his family."

"So what was inside these drawers" asked Rosie

"Gold silver diamonds. Mr. Santini had been in this place a very long time" said Bruce. "He gave me a very nice job appraisal and recommendation rating; I wanted this job a lot."

"And the gold Bruce? Where is it?"

"It was sculpted and turned into golden crematory ash containers and sent to Italy legal funeral parlor official documents. No one asked questions. FEDEX is very efficient. I believe that gold is now $1700 an ounce. The foundry in Brooklyn melts the stuff down."

"I see you had a great deal to talk about Bruce he trusted you."

"And he could sleep at night at my place because he trusted me. But he wanted to go to his church. I dropped him off that Sunday so he could walk there. The other pieces like diamonds were bought by a jeweler named Anton Malevsky."

"Bruce?" asked Rosie. "Santini gave you all this information? Why?"

"He was frightened. He wanted to leave to go back to his place in Italy; he knew that he'd stayed here too long Scared shitless. He could take the dead ones at the morgue but it was the live ones that he feared" said Bruce. "He trusted me and I wanted to get that job."

"Did he give you anything?"

"Nothing. He didn't offer and I would have refused; I think he knew that. Like I said he trusted me. We were so different and so much the same; he wanted someone to tell all this if he was killed. He wanted to return to Italy."

"And he will Bruce" said Kevin. "How did you become so tight with him? I don't get it.

"Neither would anyone else" said Bruce. You didn't did you? And you're a cop."

"Fred Astaire and Ginger Rogers" said Rosie.

"No" said Bruce "Sammy and Sinatra." They all laughed.

"I need you to come with us to look at some faces and I need you to help us" said Kevin.

"Why?" asked Bruce.

"Because I trust you" said Kevin.

"But you're a cop and cops lie right?" says Bruce.

"Yep" says Kevin. "Some cops do lie."

At the teleport Rosie asked Bruce to look at the screens as he pointed out places and figures. Rosie asked Bruce if he recognized anyone.

"That's the jeweler Malevsky" he said pointing. "He also came to pick up bodies from the morgue driving a private ambulance. I began to understand and watch since you talked about the organ donors. He delivered the guy that rammed his car into a tree. The family called for an EMS ambulance but they got him the jeweler. He was taken to the Medical Center and pronounced dead on arrival. The body was claimed and released to a funeral home; the medical examiner's office didn't give any details. A twenty three year old do you want odds on survival?

"Formally pronounced brain dead" a hospital spokesperson said!! Someone gave that dude a shot" said Bruce. "The timing was critical; those organs begin to deteriorate fast and you gotta get that liver out and into a cooler. I bet 10 or 12 hours later it was a transplant. I've been with a lot of bodies and if you want proof that this guy was opened up by a specialist dig him up and see if the organs were lifted by a person who was an expert with a number ten blade knifed from front to back with anatomical precision along the heart the aortic arch and the pulmonary vein."

"I guess we had you wrong Bruce" said Kevin.

"Not me" said Rosie. "I always knew you were an imposter" he said laughing.

Rosie asks Bruce if he will agree to wear a 'wire'.

"What's in it for me?" asks Bruce.

"We will get your job back."

"Can I trust that?" asks Bruce.

"You can put that in the bank" says Kevin. "We only work with professionals.

The teleport office complex days always start with questions as the two civilian nerds are fussing about the turntables and gizmos placing stickers on some screens speaking in tongues. Rosie says aloud "Are you guys gonna fix all this so we can use it? We'd like you to bring in the drop-cams we've set up."

Kevin is here early his thermos of tea on the long table; he's quietly looking at the screens taking notes and not looking at Rosie says "They are on the move." The group has managed to elude exposure for a long time they've sidestepped scrutiny and now they need money. Parts prices are high and they are going into alternatives: diamonds and gold. "Rosie the whole thing just made sense to me."

"You have a hunch?"

"Yeah. We need to set some bait Rosie. I want to have a few ambulances coming into the Island and Brooklyn territory from New Jersey. We need Zimmerman to sign on; he can get the money and the drivers and we'll set up an office at the Fountains on Castleton Corners make a lot of advertisements and noise; doctors' offices inexpensive patient transportation.

Rosie says "The quintessential old time cop super nice guy hardworking do you think we need to talk about this a lot more Kevin?"

Their heads turn at a tapping on the door "Security Tim Martin" a voice says "A visitor wants to talk to Mr. Murphy. I didn't want to buzz you because this lady doesn't want to come inside. She showed me a shield; I think she is upset."

"O.K. I'll be right down" says Kevin who takes his jacket and follows the security man down the flight of stairs. Kevin looks at the black lady showing a police shield just outside the door. She motions for Kevin to come outside. The black woman does not take her eyes off Kevin as he opens the door and steps out into the chill air. Her face is round and when she is not speaking her full lips are pursed; she is no-nonsense and there is no makeup on her smooth unwrinkled brown skin. She could be about fifty years old her black hair is in carefully woven curls and she is not wearing any earrings. The woman is tall at least five or six inches taller than Kevin full bodied maybe 240 pounds.

"I'm Lieutenant Murphy" he says. Holding the door open for her to enter Kevin asks if she would like to come inside as he brings the jacket collar up around his neck aware of the coming winter chill now.

Not moving she says "Would you like to talk in my car?"

"No but let's make this brief" says Kevin. "Do you have some other ID?" he asks

She opens her collar and around her neck is an official photo ID with her rank.

"I'm Captain Henrietta Cunningham Corrections and I want to talk to you about your boy."

"My boy?" says Kevin. "I have no boys."

"Vincent Mezzacappa" she says "Vinnie."

"Vincent Mezzacappa is my son-in-law."

"Yeah well your son-*in-law* has been fucking my sister-in-law Isabel who is also a corrections officer at Rikers and she's pregnant. Pretty boy Vinnie has lap-dancing sessions in his station every night when their schedules click. Isabel needs to have an abortion and a doctor to get it done soon. My brother Fred Isabel's husband has been overseas with his National Guard Unit and he's due home at any time. Your boy Vinnie wants nothing to do with this. Isabel is just a kid from the Dominican Republic; we need a safe quiet doctor no back alley dude. I simply want you or pretty boy Vinnie to get a good doctor for her. I'll pay. Your boy wants nothing to do with this."

Kevin's expression has not changed his guts tell him to listen to this forceful woman. "Let's sit in your car and turn the heater on please" says Kevin.

"I guess you want to know who I am besides being a sister-in-law and a corrections officer. I am the baddest of the boldest mothers sister on Rikers. Behind my back they call me Henry but I don't allow anyone to call me Henrietta on the Island job. I will be called Captain Cunningham; matter of fact I insist on being called Captain Cunningham."

Her hands begin to chop the air between them to emphasize her meaning; she had momentarily re-entered Rikers to tell Kevin who she is. "I earned that title. I've been on this job for 16 years and I was on the floor as a CO before getting the grade rank. Patting down and putting up with a lot of shit; real shit called feces. I came in there God-fearing but when I got clocked by a perp waiting for trial God and the other CO's stood by waiting for me to get back up to get clocked again. That was a lesson to show me not to get too big being a nigger woman. Never forgot it; from out of nowhere I got smacked up side my head twice out of the corner of my eye I saw it comin' and down I went.

"I lay down because I saw the black brothers wanted to teach me a lesson without a classroom and no Academy instructor in front. They knew when to pull him off and escort him to his cell. They had canisters batons handcuffs and I had a busted mouth a busted eye and a busted tooth bridge. It was scary you don't have time to think; you don't know if the inmate has a shank or a pick or something; you're thinking of your life and I knew this would not be written up; it was an accident. My story of the injuries would be that I was injured restraining a 300-pound inmate."

"But I would get up and I would get rank. I had to learn to step on a sucker's neck and put a shoe up his ass when they came through those gates with an attitude. I would let them know that I was the new law and I owned them lock stock and barrel. Many have nothing to lose many have been there before and they can and will hurt you. You have to have a thick skin to work there because you may not leave at the end of the day if you let them slide or let them try to avoid a shakedown. I took this job to pay my mortgage. I count every roll call in there like I count my paycheck—properly. The boldest baddest Babylon is Rikers."

"Will you please tell me about my boy Vincent" Kevin asks quietly.

"That boy needs help" the captain says "First time he came on the floor we had a TSO (Tactical Search Operation). We have to go into the cells like gang busters we be raising hell just to shake them up open and rip up everything mess up their minds and their private stuff we just let them understand that we ain't gonna tolerate any shit from anyone. We gotta strip search all of them. Politely you might say "Please strip motherfucker!" Vinnie loved to look up asses embarrassing humiliating; he would crack some open with his rubber gloves checking. Getting stink all over his hands. I see this white boy smiling and know that I got a sicko on my hands sprung from some psycho seed; he could easily be a resident of Rikers if turned loose. On this job we get the strange and the weird I can understand how weird normal life can be it's predictable. Might be I'm viewing it from an entirely different standpoint I think that boy is dark inside."

Henrietta opens the console compartment between the seats and brings out a bottle of Courvoisier cognac. She twists the cork top and drinks she offers the bottle to Kevin who looks at it briefly and says "Thanks" taking a long slow drink.

"I hope you believe me. If not your boy had better be in a witness protection program after a paternity test is requested. Your boy Vincent is fucking my sister-in-law right there on the job."

"Isabel is my problem because I got her into the CO program when she needed a job a really bad choice I made. A simple virginal kid from the Dominican Republic shy and sex stupid falls for the Latino type good looking arrogant son-of-a-bitch. I am sure your daughter thinks he is a choirboy right? Hail Mary I bet he never wasted any time taking his pants off. Isabel will be out of the corrections job dammed fast."

"O.K." Kevin interrupts taking another drink "What about her? She's your sister-in-law. How do you see taking care of this pregnancy?"

"If it Vincent's we need to get her an abortion fast. I want you to find a safe dude on the Island. I will front the cash you will check with your boy Vinnie so he understands what his loose dick has done."

"I know Isabel very well I went to the D.R. with my brother Fred after he met her during a Dominican Day. She was exotic crazy beautiful and he was hooked. She was young at the time I think 16; she still had to finish high school. They dated and hooked up. She wanted to be married. I'm a bit more practical so I learned a lot about the language and the culture the customs. Fred and I went to meet her family to know who she was and I learned a lot about why her family got her out of the D.R.

They got a lot of hookers in the D.R. and she would be going into the part time trade of pussy for cash during the holidays. Her friends do it and it's quite normal to make money during the holidays when the tourists are in great numbers. She's a good kid and her family trusted her to be good or at least to remain a virgin. How she would remain a virgin in the DR was beyond me. I don't put too much on virginity because I lost mine at 14 but what I saw in the Dominican Republic was a pattern to sell sex part time. I was amazed; I saw that was a way to do it so frequently that it diminished the authentic sexual experience; they are conditioned to just do it fast hump—fuck for cash. She would be on her way to becoming a prostitute. Anyway they got married after high school."

The sharp tapping on the window was Rosie; he pointed to his watch and signaled to Kevin to return inside.

Henrietta puts her hand firmly on Kevin's arm eye locks him and says "Let me leave you with this. While New York City is paying 10 million in a class action suit we still strip search we have this Body Orifice Scanning chair to sit on but the power freak CO's like to feel pinch and squeeze. Women are sent to Rikers after being arrested for minor drunken crap shoplifting disorderly conduct some pot smoking. Misdemeanor charges not felonies we get 'em at Rikers simply because they can't make bail. The freak boys and women CO's at Rikers can inspect rectums and vaginas make 'em remove sanitary pads lift their boobs petty bullshit because the arresting cop wants an on-site blow job. Your pretty boy Vinnie loves this he's a sick puppy.

****

184

It was raining as Kevin headed home and everything looked grey; grey people grey cars. It was about 5 p.m. when he left Rosie and it was now after 10 p.m. as the colorless rain streaked back and forth on the windshield. Kevin was going south on the West Shore Expressway splashing through the sheets of silvery puddles. He would soon pass the Woodrow Road exit and was approaching the Goethals Bridge entrance to New Jersey. He recovered quickly driving onto the last exit road on Staten Island. He stopped and laughed at his situation finding he was actually still in the car drinking with a black Captain from the NYC – Department of Corrections (DOC).

His chest heaving with spasmodic laughter he kept the sound private in the closed vehicle. It was the kind of laughter that caught in his throat and his chest and felt very much like being struck violently. He stifled a spasm at thinking he might have driven off the bridge into the river below he was now laughing at his demons Jesus Christ!!

The release gave him time to call Connie to say he would be a bit late she said "Fine" hanging up. Kevin then called Rosie on his private cell phone. He needed to meet him at the Salty Dog.

Joey popped up beside him. "Where you been Cap?"

"Really busy Joey."

"Said you were going to pack it in Cap."

"Soon Joey real soon."

Alice seeing Kevin sashays across the room and bends to kiss him blocking Joey. Joey looks up at her and asks "Why are your boobs always looking like they are trying to escape?" Alice has now become the center of attention.

Sensing a rift Kevin says "Just milk please."

Joey says "I'll get it." Alice grimaces and waves a finger bye bye to Kevin while pointing to the door as Rosie enters upset.

"Kevin if this late night drinking keeps up I won't get married. I just left Maria and she wants me to put in my papers."

"Rosie do you have your van with you?" Kevin asks.

"Yes."

"We need to talk."

"Shit." says Rosie "Shit I came to have a few."

"That will be one dollar" Joey says "Two 'shit's right?" he says tapping the bar. "One buck!"

Inside the van Kevin tells Rosie about the encounter with the lady from DOC the pregnancy of Isabel and his son-in-law being involved. "You speak to Vinnie yet?"

"No" Kevin says.

"You may be getting set up" says Rosie. "If that's all you got break it down before you jump into any contusions."

"Set up for what Rosie?"

"The black lady might just dislike Vinnie maybe it's personal. She could just write him up for misconduct right?"

"Now you're improvising Rosie. She confronted Vinnie and he did admit to the fucking part. If she writes up Vinnie into a report for misconduct she has to write her family in the mix get a test or try to have an abortion on the quiet. She will front whatever money so she's not going into this for a spit of cash either. She wants me to find a good doctor."

"Yeah Kevin" says Rosie "The Patrol Guide and the rule number zip-zip-zip- and all parallel connections in the new orders dated zip-zip-zip. Confidential I might add not for distribution. But this is personal with you Kevin. Vinnie is a very egotistical person it comes through when you talk about him wanting to be the island's Sinatra smelling like Laura Biagiotti's Roma at fifty bucks a bottle. Your problem is you can't think of Vinnie as a fucking perp or a perp fucking another DOC officer; he's your son-in-law your daughter's husband and a father right?

"You're going to have to choose the regulations as a guide or some whistle blower to jam you up. The sub-sections cover everything piss in a bottle jump when your told we've been together for so long that I am going to be with you when you decide because detectives are required to be accompanied by a partner on everything. Police protocols right?"

"I have always tried to do the right thing" says Kevin "Except for a few criminal incidents improperly classified." The cold rain on the van roof is the only sound as the two men sit quietly exhausted.

"See you in the morning Kevin" Rosie says "Go home get some rest. We can go to Rikers in the morning."

****

Kevin has parked in the driveway. The entire house is dark and when he opens the rear kitchen door a small light illuminates the stove clock. It's 3:30 a.m. Connie has set the table with food covered with a napkin. There is a covered pot on the stove but Kevin has no appetite. Connie is sleeping on the living room couch the TV playing with the sound down. The male figure on the screen is a preacher who walks back and forth with a microphone in his hand and points to his audience. Kevin watches for a moment before turning on a lamp light. The preacher's well dressed well-coiffed hair in place Kevin wonders if he uses Laura Biagiotti Roma perfume also.

Kevin turns up the sound and the TV preacher is saying "Mary was proclaimed our mother by our dying savior. He who honors this sacred blood as it deserves to be honored he has such a deep and vivid faith and trust in its infinite power that he firmly believes and abides in hope then in view of his sorrow for his sins of impurity and sacrilege the blood of Jesus will wash them all away from his soul so absolutely that no trace of their guilt will be left as though they had never stained his soul at all."

Kevin stands quietly beside the sleeping Connie; he is drawn to the figure.

186

"The blood of Jesus exerts this effect through the holy sacrament of penance. As soon as the penitent candidly and contritely confesses his sins and receives absolution he at once belongs to the number of those who are come out of tribulation and have washed their robes and have made them white in the blood of the lamb."

Kevin turns off the TV and the screen becomes black. He stands waiting and then touches Connie's shoulder gently. Connie looks up and says "Hi."

Kevin says "I'm putting my papers in at the end of the month."

"O.K. O.K." says Connie rubbing her eyes "but let's go to bed before I wake up."

****

It would be several days before Kevin and Rosie could make arrangements for a visit to Rikers. It was not possible for the NYPD to make night prison visits unless the DOC Commissioner gave permission and the schedules for Captain Cunningham Vincent and Isabel were such that it would not be possible at all during the next few weeks for all to be available at the same time. And he knew Captain Cunningham would be calling him. She wanted to act on the abortion fast. It had been ten weeks and Isabel was not sure at all when she had her last period. Cunningham was not going to postpone any arguments about procedures she wanted to know if Kevin had spoken to Vincent "your boy" as she called him.

In the meantime Kevin would drag himself through another cold gray-lit day in a stupor. He has not spoken to Vincent; did he believe Vincent was responsible for the pregnancy? Did he believe Vincent was a sick motherfucker? The answer was yes. His attention was magnified he had to be careful nothing should be overlooked he had to find an abortionist. He would detach himself and consider the right and wrong in their abstracted and variable states disregarding the present laws and opinions and rise to the transcendental truths which will always be the same and content himself with man being a motherfucker.

Connie had sensed a mood change in Kevin who calmly explained that it was his leaving the job; he would have the official papers open for Connie to see to give credence to his decision to leave after more than 32 years as a New York City Police officer; that it was actually going to happen.

He asked Connie about Kristie their granddaughter who was born a day before Christmas and was given a name to remind everyone in the family that she was close to Christ. "And how are Theresa and Vinnie?" Kevin asked casually. "I haven't had time to visit with them lately"

Connie said "Theresa is not happy with Vincent and his band of angst-ridden fellow band mates who seem to be unemployed misfits. He has been spending a lot of money to buy clothes special haircuts and workout machines he put in the basement. She is very upset at his late night singing he may leave the DOC. I suggested she might want to seek some counseling so I asked Father Torres to come over for some suggestions."

"Father Torres? Where is father McEvoy?"

"He's retired Kevin. When was the last time you were at mass?"

****

Kevin was owed some chits long ago arrests that were quashed because he did not report a shipment of bootleg cigarettes. Kevin could make a call to Miami; would they remember him? Or he could call an island contractor who produced false documents after a building wall fell killing one man and injuring two other Mexican men. Others who became friends after he turned a blind eye on activities that would send them to prison owed him.

His past life as a cop on the street became a resource where friends and connections are all important step by step up the ladder of promotion perhaps to the topmost rung. In that kind of life it was much better to be seen as an aspirant and noble family man. Would it all rebound and make him an absolute pauper? He needed an abortionist.

****

Kevin received a call from Rosie. "Kevin I have what we need Maria went to a spa to get a winter spray tan we were asking the wrong sex Kevin! Let's tie up those loose ends and go to Rikers we need to meet the ladies."

"It's a prison Rosie not a strip club there's no rehabilitation it's all incarceration." Rosie laughs and says "See you tomorrow."

Rikers Island is New York City's jail. After a court sentence prisoners are sent to prisons upstate to do their long sentences. Rikers is big on an island in the East River. Not many New Yorkers know where it is unless they work there are awaiting trial or have visited. Rikers holds an inmate population of 15000 souls and an officer population of 9000. Rosie will drive his own private car instead of a police cruiser wanting a minimum of interference during the 25 mile trip over the Verrazzano and up through Queens. "Never been to Rikers but I have sent a lot of perps there" says Rosie. "I had to get this official trip through the Deputy Commissioner's office so it's business we will have to check our weapons at the arsenal." Finding the unmarked roadway and the toll free unmarked Francis Buono arching bridge is fairly easy and the lot at the south end of the island has several signs that leave no confusion.

YOU ARE ENTERING RIKERS ISLAND THE N.Y.C JAIL COMPLEX. ALL PERSONS AND THEIR POSSESSIONS ARE SUBJECT TO SEARCH UPON ENTERING WHILE ON OR UPON LEAVING THIS ESTABLISHMENT.

CAMERAS AND RECORDING DEVICES AS WELL AS OTHER ITEMS THAT MAY BE CONSIDERED CONTRABAND ARE PROHIBITED. VIOLATORS OF THESE RULES WILL BE SUBJECT TO DISCIPLINARY

ACTION OR PROSECUTED TO THE
FULLEST EXTENT OF THE LAW.

NO DISCHARGE OR PICKING UP
PASSENGERS IN THIS AREA.

VISITOR PARKING TO THE RIGHT.
DEPARTMENT OF CORRECTIONS OFFICER
PARKING TO THE LEFT.

Geographically located just ten miles from the Statue of Liberty Rikers Island is the world's largest penal colony. Ninety nine percent of the inmates at Rikers Island are black or Hispanic.

Before going through the metal detectors they turn in their firearms and receive a slip of paper to retrieve them later. The walls of the Control Building are covered with more posters and signs prohibiting cameras cell phones tape recorders beepers and weapons of any kind. Visitors are searched more than once and on command they are forced to stop and answer questions no one gets to visit an inmate unless they are a relative or have special passes from the commissioner's office. There are no surprise visits here on Rikers Island. And the officers men and women mostly black some white and Hispanic run the island where few smile easily. The world's boldest correction officers who operate Rikers hold people that are perceived to be threats to the peace and stability an amalgamation of sizes body types ages and colors.

Captain Cunningham managed to have Isabel temporarily relieved from her Officer's station post to meet with Kevin and Rosario. Isabel slowly walked into the room in her uniform a small boned light brown skinned woman about 5 foot 6 inches she would be all of 130 lbs. Her jet black hair is pulled tightly back into a pony tail she is wearing no makeup or jewelry; she could be 18 years of age. Seeing Rosie and Kevin seated on benches she smiles slightly. Without any change in facial expression Captain Cunningham hovers and points to a chair suggesting she sit.

She stands and asks their names and where they are from. After Kevin and Rosie stand and respond Isabel brings a chair closer; her eyes do not move from their faces. "I think we are into 18 weeks" says Captain Cunningham trying to break the formal spell.

"Have you seen Officer Mezzacappa lately" asks Kevin.

"No I have been moved to Mental Observation Houses" answers Isabel.

"I had her moved so there would be no contact. He has not been on the job for a week" says Captain Cunningham. "Have you managed to find a good doctor?"

"Yes" says Rosie "We have. Isabel do you want the abortion?" asks Rosie. "You're pregnant and do you think it was from your night sessions with Vincent Mezzacappa?"

"Yes."

"Any other sex except here?"

"His van in the parking lot yes we did."

Kevin says "Yep white Ford Econo Line Van.

"Did you know he was married?" asks Rosie.

"Yes he told me" she said looking beyond Rosie.

Kevin touches Rosie's arm cautioning him to go no further. "Isabel have you had any other sexual contact since Fred has been away we need to be sure." Cunningham is now standing her full height commanding an answer.

"No I did not only with Vincent."

"Why" Cunningham asks "Why?"

"I don't know why says Isabel "He was nice."

Her sheltered naïve child-like responses withheld nothing no emotion no fear the room became silent. "We are going to set it up for this Saturday she can return to work on Monday" said Rosie.

Captain Cunningham inhales loudly "No she will not return to this place. I will see to that."

****

Rosie is at the wheel driving south to the Verrazano Bridge. Kevin sits looking straight ahead saying nothing. "Fucking traffic can you imagine doing this every day?" says Rosie. Kevin is quiet. "Have you told Connie about any of this shit?"

"Nope haven't got the balls. I also didn't want to believe any of this shit. I did get the papers I thought it would tamp down her suspicions. I think she has a hunch something is out of whack. She has suggested that Terri see a marriage counselor and now I hear from Captain Cunningham that Vinnie hasn't returned to work at Rikers. I try not to bring the job home but this—Call it police domestic violence."

"You're still a cop Kevin and you're pissed more than that it's fucking up your head lieutenant" said Rosie "You're covering all the bases with Connie and Terrie. Vinnie is still out there singing or fucking some naive kid. So what would you like to do?"

"I would like to see him dragged with a hook up his ass with me as a mounted cop and dragged through the streets so people can kick his carcass before it's thrown into the Kill Van Kull. Rosie this doctor is he safe? Will he do some blood tests? Are we sure it is not a late term thing? How do we keep all this confidential?"

"Maria said he is the quintessential old time doctor a surgeon a super nice guy hardworking Islander kind to his patients and he's very straight forward. He's had his office in New Dorp for years the tanning ladies and the hair salon people are his steady customers Maria said. We will need Dante to play the role of her black husband Fred and we have to be there this Saturday evening. Get in touch with Dante give him all the details no phones or communication other than eye to eye. You might want to meet Dante at 'At-Da-Game' lounge on Van Duzer Street in Stapleton. Joey said. Vinnie is singing there."

"Not likely Rosie better to meet Dante at Home Depot he's shy."

After checking his cell phone messages Dante returned Kevin's call. He wanted Kevin to come to his apartment alone which was unusual because Kevin never knew where or even in what borough he lived. New Brighton was a mix of private houses and low apartment buildings. Finding the building Kevin pushed the third floor buzzer and after a moment the door clicked open and he walked into the lobby and took the wide stairway to the third floor.

Dante was waiting in the hallway for him to come inside. He is dressed in shorts and a tee shirt and Kevin notices his trim chocolate brown athlete's body. He is small about 5 foot 7 inches and his head has a covering of braided twists. Kevin thinks he seems school-boyish. Inside are small rooms a bedroom living room a narrow kitchen; spare with a number of books and a CD player a racing bicycle hung on a wall the narrow kitchen clean seemingly unused except Dante had opened a bottle of wine placing two glasses on a chrome-edged dinette table and two chairs. Two large windows faced a well-kept green courtyard below.

There was a small television and some photos. Kevin looked at them and Dante interrupted "That's my father he was forty three had a heart attack and died."

"Sorry to hear that" said Kevin.

"And that's my mother that's why I wanted to see you."

"Because of your mother" said Kevin.

"In a way yes" said Dante. "Have a seat please. My mother wants me to leave the NYPD job get married have kids and have a real job. I'm an only child and after last week's fiasco in Brooklyn more like a shootout on the OK Corral I have decided to leave. This cat no longer has nine lives. Your calling me says you have a problem and need a black face I will listen and make up my mind whether to help you okay?" He pours wine and they touch glasses. "Is red O.K.?"

"Fine" Kevin says. "Mind telling me about the shoot out over there?"

"ICE and the FBI are working the same morgue cases that you and Rosario have been living with" Dante says. Zimmerman says One Police Plaza will not play with them and they have set up their own ground rules. The body snatchers are working overtime and at many places and hospitals. My role was to set up drop cams and some recorders. All basement morgues are creepy those autopsy tables the sloping stainless steel that drain and the rickety refrigerator drawers; the dead don't mind a rickety ride though. Mister Bruce McNeil would be right at home there. That facility was a filthy dungeon.

Things went wrong; Their high-tech devices had found one of my recorders. From there everything went straight downhill. I went to remove the other recorders and they had bugged them and the alarms sounded. I heard one voice yelling "STOP MOTHERFUCKER STOP!!" I ran into three cruisers; I was clean but I ran. I had nothing; I didn't have my gun or badge with me so I ran. They yelled furiously at me I still ran up a few steps down another corridor out into an alley. I ran. I crouched waiting for a sniper to aim at my head for a clean shot; still I got up and I ran. I was a running black man with no back-up.

I got to a street and walked casually and I thought that every person was staring at me in fear and hatred I was waiting for the voices to begin again "There he is." I was a black person to be hunted down and destroyed. I decided then to give up the job. I have yet to make a report; this is the first time I've spoken about it. I can get a good safe job at Wal-Mart or Target."

"I need your talent Dante it's a very personal mission" Kevin says

Dante finishes a glass of wine pours another and looks at Kevin. "First I want to tell you how I got here Kevin.

"I was about ten when my mother was attacked inside our home. She was dressing for her class at the local school my father had gone moments before. The guy beat my mother around her head asking for money I saw most of it. She gave him her purse and he continued to beat her asking for more money I heard her screams and yelling for him to stop. Our friendly dog Romper a mixed border collie and cocker spaniel watched the man opening draws in the master bedroom he found nothing more. Angrily he repeatedly punched her before leaving.

At the hospital Mom was unrecognizable puffed into a purple mound of bandages and swelling. My father got another dog a pit bull and set up cameras. My mother was hospitalized for more than a month facial bones needed to heal some had to be reconstructed. Her emotional resilience was giving us hope that she would return home the same that was not to be. The scars were there but I never saw any emotional flashbacks of the incident from her. My illusion of safety was shattered and our new ferocious security dog did not make me comfortable to be at home alone. Then my father died of a heart attack. I have had flashbacks at my helplessness I replay her screams and decided to go after the bad guys become a cop. Wrong choice.

Dante listened to Kevin for an hour finishing the red wine together. He would be the black husband of the black Isabel.

****

Henrietta Cunningham Dante Kevin and Rosie are waiting for Isabel to come downstairs "Are you ready sweetheart?" Henrietta calls. She has placed a bottle of Chivas Regal on the coffee table along with glasses and a tray of ice. "Drink up" she commands her bold presence and authority ruling the room.

Dante says "I am a teetotaler never touch the stuff I'm on the job."

A small smile lifting the moment Rosie raises his glass "Cheers."

"Cheers" says Kevin. Henrietta never sits her huge frame moving she gives an envelope to Dante and says "Whatever you need." Dante looks inside and there are a number of large denomination bills he does not count and puts it in his jacket breast pocket. Rosie gives Dante a cell phone "Your back-up is Maria if you have any problems her number is programmed in. Don't use it for any other purposes.

192

Isabel quietly descends the stairs careful not to upset anyone at the base of the stairs she stops and looks at everyone saying nothing a slight nod to their presence. She is dressed in wide black pants and a white top reaching below her waist. She has no make up or jewelry and her shoes are simple black flats. Dante stands and introduces himself to Isabel almost whispering to her to say he will be with her all the way she looks up at Dante and smiles. Rosie thinks she looks like a teenage Peter Pan Kevin looks at her thinking of Vinnie fucking her in the back seat of a car in the safety booth at Rikers. How could this child have gotten a job at Rikers. Henrietta says "It's cold outside wear your winter coat." Her orders send Isabel to a closet returning holding a long tan-colored winter coat.

Dante wants some conversation he wants to hear her speak he stops at a deli to buy some chocolate bars and cokes. "Like chocolate?"

"Yes and I like Coke. Ms. Cunningham doesn't drink soda."

"Any special brand Isabel? What do you like to drink?" It was the first time he had used her name.

"Coconut water but they don't get it here."

"No I don't think so" he says laughing.

"We have it back home and orange soda is good."

"We could stop and get a slice of pizza if you like."

"O.K."

At the first pizza take out window Dante waits. It was then that Dante notices that he's being followed. He makes a right turn and another right turn to be sure; whoever it is he thinks they also know that he's made them. "You like pizza yes?" She smiles and responds by placing a napkin on Dante's lap.

At New Dorp Lane Dante makes a right turn follows the directions and pauses before reading the driveway sign and carefully moves to a parking space. An overhead light at the rear a freshly painted cream colored door the number is correct; it's locked. He pushes a buzzer.

"Yes may I help you?"

"Yes we have a 7:30 appointment."

"And your name is?"

"Mr. and Ms. Fred Cunningham."

"Would you spell that last name please?"

"C U N N I N G H A M."

"Are you two together?"

"Yes." Dante knows they are now on camera; looking about he sees that the entire area is under surveillance. The door clicks and he pushes it open for Isabel to enter before climbing the flight of stairs. The ten by ten room could be any dental or medical office except for a slight odor of ether. Dante hopes Isabel does not notice and freak out; she says nothing.

A heavy set woman behind a Plexiglas window motions them to come over. She gives Dante a clip board and some papers and asks how he intends to pay. Dante opens his jacket and says "Cash. How much?"

"That will be twelve hundred" she says dryly. Looking at Isabel standing behind Dante she asks "Is this your wife?"

"Yes" Dante says. There are five or six others in the waiting area. Dante gives Isabel the clipboard and watches as she begins the task of answering the questions she looks at Dante and he says "They have to protect themselves." Age time of last period weight height on the pill had an abortion before use contraceptives.

She finishes and walks to return the clipboard and questions. Isabel waits looking at the lady behind the glass who scans the page glances up and says "O.K." Other young women laugh and sip from soda cans. There is a television screen but there is little or no sound; a handwritten sign says "do not touch the television." Dante pops a candy into his mouth then notices all the candy wrappers on the floor with the soft drink and coffee containers. He puts his candy wrapper in his pocket.

He is aware of a girl staring at him. He lets his gaze wander to another woman reading a magazine and a urine sample on the chair beside her. Dante sees the gaze and feels uncomfortable wanting to dissolve into the chair. The middle aged woman behind the screen taps loudly on the glass telling them to pipe down. "Bitch" a man says loudly to a lady next to him who responds "She wouldn't know an orgasm if it bit her on her fat ass" They all laugh Dante looks at a magazine. They are the only black people here and Dante becomes aware of it he wants no problem. He has no ID and this reason for being here is important.

A young man with stringy long hair looks at Dante and asks if he rides a bike. "Yes" said Dante "I do a lot of miles every week."

"You got a Harley?"

"No can't afford one mine is a two wheeler" and they laugh and slap hands.

"Your wife is good looking" he says. "How long you been hooked up?"

"Three years" Dante says. "And you?"

The girl beside the young man has auburn colored hair rolled up into a bun. She is beautiful. "Long time" he says "a long time." The young guy seems friendly but has a dejected face and looks like he'd rather be elsewhere. "You been here before?" the young man asks. Dante says no. And the young man says "We been here twice before; she doesn't want to use anything and she forgets to take the pill." He says that he doesn't want to use a rubber 'cause it don't feel the same and she says she likes to feel him.

The walls advertise birth control and birth control methods HIV testing and condoms. The conversation is now engaging the other men in the room. There is a basket of free condoms on the shelf near the receptionist's office. The nurse comes out of a door at the end of the hall and asks Isabel to pee in a cup then to go into the back room to have her blood pressure and temperature taken as well as blood drawn to determine if she is anemic. "Are you a bleeder?" asks the nurse after taking out a needle. Isabel says no. Isabel's heart is pounding and she is amazed that the blood does not spurt across the room. She returns to the waiting area and finds a few more couples have come into the room. Another young woman is buzzed in as they wait. "May I help you? Name? Are you together?" The young woman pays in cash a handful of crumpled bills. Shakily she tries to smooth each one before handing it to the receptionist who rolls her eyes.

Isabel is prepared when they call her name again "Mrs. Cunningham?" Other women look at Isabel and the nurse says "First come first served." This time she is introduced to a woman counselor who takes her into another room with a big desk and nothing on the walls. On her desk is a life-sized plastic uterus and vagina. The counselor uses them to illustrate exactly what is going to happen during the procedure. Isabel thinks procedure is a better word. She doesn't know why but it sound better than some of the other words Mrs. Cunningham used. She finds herself searching almost obsessively for the right words to say and think. She doesn't want words to come back and haunt her.

The counselor tells her of the risks involved; incomplete evacuation infection perforation of the uterus hemorrhage. She is told that statistically the procedure is far less dangerous than giving birth. She is warned that the vacuum machine is very loud and alarming. She adds "With all of the advances in medical science isn't it terrible" says the counselor "that they can't find a more humane sounding machine for this sensitive purpose." The counselor asks if she wants some birth control pills to take home with her.

"No thank you" she says. "I didn't like the pill. I was on it for a short time but felt uncomfortable and it messed with my hormones."

"Of course" the counselor said "though whatever you do use has failed you miserably this time!"

Her heart has been going like mad ever since she read about in graphic detail the material required about the procedure.

The counselor informs her that the doctor who will perform the procedure on all women there today is wonderful and very experienced. "We're lucky to have him here today at the clinic." The counselor asks if there are any other questions. By the time the doctor is ready everyone is prepped counseled and waiting. He does procedure after procedure until 11 pm or later an assembly line method. It seems brutal but it is efficient and the counselor has a grim sad conviction in her explanation. Before Isabel leaves the room the counselor gives her two Advil in a paper cup for cramping later. The counselor says "We would like you and your husband to be here for 45 minutes after the procedure before leaving."

The buzzer sounds again. "Do you have an appointment? Can you please identify what you have in your hands." The receptionist's voice is strained and tense.

"Napkins pads a box – I'm gonna need them" said the voice through the intercom with some humor. The caller is finally buzzed in. She is a striking tall black woman and she is alone. She looks as though she may be 6 foot 5 inches with long black hair. Dante

195

thinks she may be a model of some kind. The receptionist asks her to leave the box on the counter. She does so. The receptionist asks the woman her name again. It is hard to decipher and everyone in the room looks up at this tall black woman who may be from another country. So a little clarifying is necessary with the receptionist. Finally the woman takes a place near the door standing. There are now no empty chairs. The woman looks at Isabel who returns the look with a nodding smile.

The woman with the dyed auburn hair and her skinny blond long-haired boyfriend smile one another. The room is filled with people beginning to adjust to their surroundings. The bathroom door opens and closes continually. Some are reading the information sheet intently and filling out forms others hold hands and smile at each other even laugh softly a few times. There is something reassuring in their affection and their intimacy their obvious respect for each other. In the middle of this crowded waiting room this camaraderie would not normally exist but everyone is here for the same purpose. Some look off into the distance occasionally sadness in their faces. Isabel cannot take her eyes off them.

Number 3 is called. Her heart leaps out of her chest and she wants to run. Before she can Dante squeezes her arm. She stands up and moves past the cramped row of chairs.

"Can my husband come?"

"No you are going in for the actual procedure now and he has to wait out here." She hands him her coat and goes through the door.

The nurse asks her to empty her bladder then comes up to her with a frank smile and as they enter the small room tells her that she will be with her throughout the whole procedure. She asks Isabel to undress from the waist down leaving her socks on. She is to sit on the examining table with a sheet over her lap to wait for the doctor.

There is a sink a table a cart of instruments not much to look at and it is very warm now. The walls are thin and she hears conversations. The nurses are talking about vacations about cruises somebody mentions the Bahamas. There are excited gasps and muted swell of laughter.

From next door through the thin walls she hears a loud machine switched on. It starts and stops a couple of times over a few minutes then is quiet. It sounds Isabel thinks like an industrial vacuum cleaner. She thinks her heart is going to give out.

From outside the door there is more casual conversation as the nurses continue to talk about vacations. A man's deep voice joins briefly in the levity. There is a rustling of papers then a brisk knock. The nurse enters first wheeling a machine and she is followed by a thickset man who introduces himself in a rich foreign accent. He is soft-spoken as he prepares.

She has been asked to recline and to shove her bottom right to the edge of the table "until it feels like you are going to fall off." The nurse stands at her right side and hands things expertly to the doctor as he seats himself on a low stool. The nurse looks at Isabel and says she may hold her hand if she wishes. She answers that she may take her up on that. The doctor assures her that the nurse may look petite but that she has very strong hands indeed. He says this as his own hands quickly examine her uterus.

She tries to relax as the speculum is inserted. The nurse tells her what the doctor is doing so she can prepare. He gives her a shot of anesthetic in her cervix. She bucks and apologizes when the doctor looks up and firmly tells her not to do that again. She then takes the nurse's hand and holds on tight to the protective latex glove. For hours afterwards her right hand will smell like latex.

Another shot in her cervix the pain is unexpected and nauseating. She feels like she is being stabbed. Apologizing for her moaning and her twitching away from the doctor until the nurse really had to get sharp with her. The doctor is now crouched between her legs asking questions and making comments as Isabel tries desperately to keep her mind on the questions or the vacation story he is asking about. But even she knows they are simply keeping her distracted in order that she be more pliant during the procedure.

The third and final shot is given and she cries out as quietly as she is able aware of the thin walls on the other side with women behind them. The doctor has to manually dilate the cervix. She cramps immediately and tries to breathe as the nurse coaches her. He goes in again with a large tube and she grips the latexed hand as tightly as she can. The cramping sensation is sickening and she slips into herself for a moment until the nurse tells her the worst is over and that they are almost done now.

She tries concentrating as the vacuum is switched on and starts to gurgle and hiss.

The machine is switched off. The doctor scrapes inside her uterus with a spoon-like instrument whose name she was told but cannot remember. There is a little more vacuuming like for crumbs. She vaguely thinks and it is done. The nurse leaves for a few moments and the doctor stands. He is at the small counter quietly filling in forms.

She lies on her back the fluorescent lights in her face. Her ears are ringing in the silence. Her heart has slowed. But she now fears it will slow too much and just stop. And at that moment she doesn't care. Her emptiness and horror are so deep that she cannot think. Silently she weeps she cannot imagine ever stopping.

The doctor finishes his paperwork and prepares to leave. He looks at Isabel as he opens the door and tells her softly to let it out to cry as hard as she can that it is healing. She nods but keeps crying silently after he leaves afraid of what might come out if she let go.

The nurse returns briskly to tidy up and see how her patient is doing. She is allowed to sit up then stand if she doesn't feel too woozy. The bleeding is determined not to be excessive and she is allowed to dress. Before she can get into her underwear with the sanitary napkin already in place a large drop of bright red blood falls on the floor. The nurse immediately sprays it with a massive dose of disinfectant and wipes it away.

As she puts on her shoes she says to the nurse that she thinks this must be one of the hardest jobs imaginable. The nurse is busy preparing the room for the next procedure and says this is what she believes in what she knows is the right thing for families children and women. She is worried about what the future holds for clinics like this. Her strength is contagious her conviction gratifying. The nurse has her sit in a reclining chair brings her a cup of hot tea and puts a heavy blanket over her. Although it is too hot in the clinic the weight of the blanket is comforting. A moment later the nurse looks at her and asks how it is going. She just nods and tries to look like she is pulling herself together. She is still weeping and cannot stop. The tears continue the warmth of the tea seeps into her body where the blood and tissue have left a hole. Another woman is led into the room and seated in a chair to the right. She does not want to see this other woman and thinks she would dissolve if she did. The nurse takes out 2 bottles of pills and explains what each one is for and how to take them. There is a drug to help the uterus clamp down and stem the flow of blood and there is an antibiotic to ward off infection. She is instructed to eat a yogurt a day to help prevent yeast infections and to rest as much as possible and look for any signs of trouble: infection hemorrhage or deep depression. The nurse asks her when she feels up to it to go into the bathroom and check the sanitary pads and places three of them in her hand. If the blood flow does not exceed the rate she experiences on the heaviest day of her period she can go.

Dante is waiting in the crowded waiting room. She feels all the faces on hers searching trying to read her experience. She feels her face must speak volumes. She reaches for Dante's hand and motions for him to follow her. At the Plexiglas she makes an appointment for a follow-up visit in two weeks. Dante notices as they leave the clinic that the car is still following them.

The bleeding slows to a weak spotting getting heavier if she is especially active but certainly fading dying dimming with each passing day. She never faints never bleeds more than a normal amount. She doesn't go mad or die. In fact she feels her body becoming her own again in a few days. Her nausea and exhaustion disappear almost without her knowing it.

Two weeks after the abortion she is steady and calm.

****

Kevin has found the black minister pacing across the TV screen. He looks at Kevin explaining in gestures and bible verses. "Do the best you can and tell your pastor or priest or minister all your sins as they occur after a close examination of conscience after renewing your act of perfect contrition and the firm purpose of amendment. Gawd will hear you! Speak directly sincerely and plainly yet reverently and delicately.

You need not describe in detail how you did this or that impure action or what was the particular trend of your impure thoughts. The ministers know what is the kind of your mortal sin and the numbers of times you have committed it. The Lord knows your pastor knows they have heard sin before. That is sufficient. Do not get upset because he asks you questions. He does it only for your benefit. Answer him respectfully and candidly. Tell him everything you feel you ought to tell him according to your capacity.

Once you have done your part all your sins will be forgiven by Gawd. You might unintentionally have forgotten a number of your mortal sins or failed to mention certain necessary circumstances. So do not worry but have trust in the Lord thy God whose tender mercies are over all his works.

The one in his innocence the other in his penitence. Maybe you are saying Gawd yes but to make my confession that is my difficulty. I am through with sin. I could not be more disgusted with impurity than I am now. I feel that with Gawd's help I will never return to such vileness again. I am not ashamed to tell what a terrible sinner I have been. I am glad and eager to humble myself before God's representative after having been so woefully wicked. The more this humiliation hurts me the more I will like it. I want to atone for my sins and I know I am going to enjoy this abasement of myself in a humble confession. The trouble is some of you do not know how to tell their sins of impurity. The preacher stops momentarily and looks straight at Kevin. I am afraid I may not tell them clearly enough. If only through this confession how relieved and happy I should be.

****

A new four-man crew is taking over the project at the teleport Rosie scoffs they send four NYPD personnel to do their work; under twenties one sergeant on the job less than four years. Three are young men and one woman a lieutenant; a straight laced no nonsense stringy short haired blonde from Brooklyn's 84th precinct; she wears pants and wants mid-week meetings on Wednesday mornings at 8 sharp. Kevin and Rosie give her the file keys and privacy reports all persons not department officials or NYPD are asked to leave her team will manage the electronic maze. She has set her stamp on the project and there are no questions.

****

Kevin will have a stent implanted next week. Connie's conversations begin with"Dr. Mazella and I." Kevin thinks Connie smiles much too often; she is waiting to pick them up for brunch today. She will help Maria with the arrangements. Rosie plans to be married both men seem to relax.

****

Kevin never really heard Vinnie singing he did know that Vinnie wanted to be the Staten Island Tony Bennet and appear at the Saint George Theater maybe as Sinatra or Vic Damon Elvis or Johnny Mathis.

****

Kevin wanted some help he asked Joey where Vinnie might be singing "Goldfingers" says Joey "and they got strippers. Lipsticks Hipps and maybe Curves on Arthur Kill. Or try The Black Garter out in Charleston."

"How do you know all this" Kevin asks. "Topless chief !! Follow the bouncing boobs. They got the "grunge" down there chief we got upscale gentleman's clubs on Midland Beach No grunge Scarlet's was nice they got busted and I don't know Scarlett's on Sand Lane they got topless top heavy island broads. Why do you want to know this stuff chief don't you like Alice?"

"Yes Joey I like you both but this is business. And if you know where I can find Vinnie or where he's singing call my cell O.K?" Joey salutes Kevin and hops away.

It was predictable Kevin thought as he adjusted to low light and the detail inside the bacterial grunge bar with the OPEN sign in the small window. This is Pleasant Plains or Princess Bay or Point Pleasant the names do not fit the night environment this was simply the south shore.

Kevin stepped inside and put his arm on the bar; the voice coming from behind the bar said "Wadleya have?" The voice is low coming from a face behind volumes of facial hair and sleep saddened eyes his arms and neck heavily tattooed.

"A beer please and by the way will there be singing tonight?" Kevin asks.

"I guess so not sure. Never seen you here before? You a cop?"

"Nah. I just want to hear Vinnie sing."

"O.K. Look take that gold off your finger some of them skanks here are disgusting O.K. but they got principles. The only entertainment tonight is coming from the island Guidettes some do a cool porn rapping. It's cold out there; just put your heater on just pick a good head job…be back home before the wife puts the kids to sleep." The flat voice behind the hairy face continued speaking he simply wanted this new guy to get what he came for; boy girl the singer or a clinger he would keep an eye on Kevin.

Everyone seemed to be in sync with the happenings this was going to be an "awesome" event which Kevin heard over and over a waitress asked Kevin if he wanted a seat at a small table with three giggling young women no he just wanted to hear Vinnie sing yea he's "awesome."

"She's setting you dude go for it" the bartender said. Julie over there down in front from Perth Amboy brings her own pillow covered Escalade. Look at that" he said pointing at a couple ready to have sex "I can't believe how these skells spend their waking hours they look disgusting and act disgusting foul disgusting mouths and they live around here in the Mac Mansions we gottem here buddy Guido's and Guidettes. Lots of older guys come down to pick up few skegs at 2–3 a.m. but not you. You're here to listen to a singer right?" Kevin finished his beer and placed a ten dollar bill on the counter and walked out into the cool refreshing night air.

Kevin would continue to visit other places Big Nose Kate's Night Gallery and finally the reason to stop is a group of men fighting outside Beer Goggles. He identified himself and asked what had happened; underage drinking firefighters and off-duty cops still fighting over 911 terrorist attacks loose Testosterone. There would be no arrests.

Connie and Terri are seated in the kitchen when Kevin walks in. "Where's Kristie" he asks.

"Daycare" says Terri. "You're just in time we have a date here with Father Torres. Mom told me you're leaving the police department we hope to use you as a sitter cause I'm getting a job we'll need some cash to cover counseling sessions."

Connie says nothing as she gives Kevin a kiss and places a glass of juice peeled fruit and oatmeal cookies in front of him.

"Vincent has been going batty with his clothes buying first it was the shoes Louis Vuitton then a Louis Vuitton jacket I called to find out what he paid for that eleven hundred bucks!! He's been dipping into our savings every month to buy Salvatore Ferragamo boots and clothes; the credit card shows only a few of his purchases and I think his kooky group make money for him to buy more Ralph Lauren stuff I mean did Tony Bennett start this way?" Terri begins to cry. "Papa I haven't wanted to bother you with this and we are going straighten it out once I get him to accept the fact that he needs help. First the late nights then the all-niters now the clothes and I know he loves me except this need to sing I can't go there because on the young girls he says they are his fans I refuse to see it. I hate that Laura Biagiotti he uses. The last straw is his hair he's losing it wants to have something done for replacements. We need counseling and prayer I know he loves Kristie and me. We can work it out."

Vinnie tries to remember where he left his van. It's still dark as he walks unsteady down the street. At the intersection on Forest Avenue he tries to remember which way right or left. He'd been drinking; after the three sets they got paid for his band had picked up a few late night strays stashed the gear in his van and taken off. The other bodies in the club were either stoned or drunk and he wanted to drink. Two not-so-bad-looking young women sat at a table they looked like sisters staring smiling. Could he separate them for sex? He could entertain both he thought finishing another beer and Chivas Regal. He was in no hurry as long as he made it home on time to meet Kevin the next morning.

They came to see him "Did you hear me sing?" he asks.

They spoke in unison "Yep. We want to take you home."

In the parking lot Vinnie opened the van doors and saw the interior; instruments clothes and junk. "Aw shit" he said.

"Shit happens" one twin said. "My brother married a girl from Italy and he called her his Piza-shit." Vinnie doubled over trying to laugh. Many people would be at a loss for a response he thought.

"You ride with him and show him the way. We don't live far."

Vinnie squints driving out of the parking lot listening to the young girl beside him giving directions. Minutes later "Park here" she orders "we can walk the rest of the way."

Inside an all-night store she chooses several items and as she opens her wallet for a credit card he sees a plasticized photo inside of a young man stripped to the waist pointing to his pecs

"A friend" she says.

"Your boyfriend?"

She laughs at him. "That's the Situation!" He did not recognize the popular home town hero.

After more drinks and beers the girls roll joints; the flat TV screen is now porn low voices and moans. "Would you like to take your coat and shirt off? We think it's fine in the confines of a person's room we think of it as being free of confining clothes and stuff inhibitions you ever been with two girls before?"

"Only like at one time."

"Don't be afraid inhibitions are a turn on once you overcome it."

"You're not ashamed are you?"

"You can do what you want to. We can spend the whole night if you want to."

"I don't like to be hurt; you don't like to hurt do you?"

"I get pins and needles when I'm fucked."

The bong passes Vinnie pulls long exhales the porno film sex is distant as the two young girls sit on his face masturbate him hoping to drive him to ecstasy He says "I love you."

"Don't ever say that unless you really mean it do you hear Mr.?"

"Of course I mean it I never meant anything more in my whole life."

"Do you want to go?"

"Yes."

His clothes are gathered and he dresses quickly the funk of booze and grass has settled into his clothes. They will need to be dry cleaned everything smells of skunk.

Vinnie has now realized that he has walked in the wrong direction and has not found the white van he will turn around and go back. Winter has begun to release its hold the morning chill is gone there is no wind. There is a fog coming off shore and the ship horns blow a sad steady safety warning the deep throat penetrating fog horn sound. The water traffic will slow and the early traffic auto lights appear from the fog slowly finding their way.

Vinnie has had time to regroup and clear his head did he use a condom? What were their names? Did he have an orgasm? He doesn't remember if he had an orgasm. Did he fuck them both? He had wanted to see them naked smiling at him fresh with morning allure and innocence begging him not to leave.

He's not far from Westerleigh. The traffic on Forest Avenue is light due to the fog crazy weather about 60 degrees. The left turn drive up a gentle slope is four blocks. Vinnie parks the van on the far side of the park; his house is located on Springfield Avenue and Kevin's house on Main Street also borders the park.

Westerleigh is a community of well-kept one- and two-family homes of many police sanitation workers firemen and other city employees mostly white. The attractive park once called Prohibition Park because the area founders were against alcohol. is a full city square block. The wide streets surrounding Westerleigh Park: Main Avenue Neal Dow Avenue Springfield Avenue and Willard Avenue are well maintained by the New York Parks Department. All dog walkers must pick up dog poop; a disagreement here could start a feud in this close-knit square.

The forty foot tall oaks and the well-trimmed grass lawns are gathering places for elderly and mothers with children; low fences and benches are placed along the asphalt walkways. The decades old lighting has remained to give an overall pleasant setting for surroundings the large conical roofed gazebo with a new red brick foundation and wide stair ways remains a place for performing orchestras and festivals.

Vinnie approaches the sitting figure he does not recognize Kevin who is wearing blue jeans a bulky woolen sweater and a baseball cap pulled down over his eyes. His head is slightly back .

"Is that you Kevin?"

"Yep."

"Are you feeling OK?"

"Yep. Just trying to remember the feeling of Kristie the first time I held her at the hospital. Our Christmas gift. You wanted to remember and call her Kristie born just two days before Christmas. She smelled like vanilla cookies and shampoo; she would squirm when I pushed my nose in her blond hair. Remember the hot day when she tried to wrestle with the water spigot in the yard and watered everything in sight naked? She would collect all the bugs worms and ants giving them names. Sit Vinnie take a load off your feet. Where have you been?

"Terrie said you wanted a boy. Girls are different don't you think? Special. She's going to kindergarten now.

"You missed the birthing. Remember the breathing exercises you both took? Shame you didn't feel the irregular inhale pause exhale pause sixteen seventeen seconds pause.

"Connie was upset when she was pregnant we had to oil those silver filigree stretch marks with coco butter How many years you married Vinnie I forget? Five? Six? Ah the women in our lives And we had that big goomba wedding at that big place on Hylan Boulevard cost what 30 or 40 grand? 350 plus guests. We told the families no pots and pans or toasters just put the cash in a "boost" get the kids started. Some cheapskates doubled up twenties and tens to make a fat envelope. Bad goombas.

And your father God bless his soul threatened not to feed the cheapskates. Boy did they eat trays of eggplant parmesan sausages and peppers baked clams meatballs and spaghetti the cocktails went by the gallon and don't talk about red wine. Remember that Vinnie?"

Kevin has not looked at Vinnie. He could smell him which was much too close.

"Yeh my father got into a fight and bloodied a guy's face for feeling up a wife. He was a goomba.

Yeh baked Alaska pies espresso Sambucca ice cream the whole nine yards steak veal and lobster. When I danced with my little girl the guy sang ""Daddy's Little Girl"" I did good right Vinnie? I had to dig deep for that honeymoon trip to Bermuda. Vinnie you took my little girl Vinnie. I didn't want to know about your first night she was a virgin. Connie cried the first night that we knew about "together the whole night." Connie's traditional. I imagined you had busted a few young pussies before Theresa she fell for you. You gotta test drive it before you go for the whole thing yes? That was before you started creeping like a pro.

I did some leapfrogging also Vinnie before I met Connie. Goombas are emotional they gotta cry weddings funerals you gotta cry.

"So tell me Vinnie what are you gonna do?"

"About what Kevin?"

"*Mala femina* the bad woman *dalla pelle color caffe* mocha skin or coffee? Afro Americano chicks Vinnie. Do you want to talk to me Vinnie? The black lady Isabel at Rikers. Captain Cunningham is too big and too loud to be wrong Vinnie. She said you wanted no part of it. We got rid of it. You're bad Vinnie very bad. Vinnie is silent he wants to close his eyes. He wants to close his ears as Kevin continues.

Kevin is standing now with his arm around Vinnie. He continues to talk while not allowing Vinnie to walk toward Springfield Avenue and his home. He stops at the sidewalk in front of the white van he kisses Vinnie and says "I will take care of everything. You were depressed. He kisses Vinnie again on both cheeks. "You know what you have to do."

The fog is lifting and the temperature is about 45 degrees. It's going to be a good day he says.

****

Vinnie drove carefully he didn't want to be stopped by the police. He was stone cold sober; he hadn't had a good nights sleep but he was wide awake. He even wanted to taste something sweet maybe stop and get some M&M's. He liked the chocolate coating on his tongue and his teeth. It's early and some convenience stores will be open on the terrace maybe a 7-Eleven. The fog is heavier along the shore he wanted something sweet some sugar and looking down he saw the empty wrappers he would stop and put all of them into a public garbage can. Hooked on sugar he laughed. Yes a 7-Eleven and a hot cup—Vinnie stop stalling. OK. He drove narrow crazy quilt streets turning right up the steep grade to stop in front of the Saint George Theater pausing for a moment to hear the applause. Yep the audience is clapping enthusiastically. "I coulda been a contender" Vinnie said. The applause continued.

Just drive carefully we don't want some asshole cop pulling you over wasting your time. A mile or so to the toll plaza no collections you don't have to stop for some asshole to question what you're doing you're just doing the right thing. The traffic is slow because of the fog and the fat fucks in reflective vests waving for who knows what "You can't see it's the fog!!" You should have gotten sweet chocolate M&M's for this dry mouth. No I didn't read the signs.

But I did a long time ago many times. LIFE IS WORTH LIVING. LIFENET-24 HOUR HOT LINE. PHONE AHEAD. CALL 1-800-LIFENEW. You gotta be kidding. Everyone has a right to make their own decisions. As a truly healthy person do you call ahead and reserve a space? No medical but you get a shot to postpone it you stay attached to a bed while they give you more tests. It's in my dick motherfuckers can you fix that. To describe the condition they will use some officious Latin terms because they don't have a term for this condition.

Put the flashers on and pull over to the side. My heart goes bumpity bump. I forgot to clean out that van cab. Grungy mothers they can do it—they messed it up. You really don't have to know all this but these clothes are really messed up too I should have gotten them cleaned and pressed. A car behind me blows it's horn "Pull around me bitch I'm busy can't you see?"

The guard rail is only waist high and a small lip at the bottom is just enough for a foot hold it's easy to just slip off this thing. Looking down at what should be water is only a gray wall flat no ripples that would be like jumping in to a cement wall at one hundred and ninety miles an hour

If you listen for a moment you can still hear the audience clapping enthusiastically. The people are yelling happy to have heard my voice grabbing at my sleeve wanting autographs...

All lanes have been reopened on the Staten Island bound lanes of the Verrazano Bridge as emergency crews continue to look for a man who jumped into the water shortly before the fog lifted and the rush hour traffic resumed.

Witnesses reported seeing a car stop in the right lane of the Brooklyn bound upper level the driver reportedly exited the vehicle before singing and immediately jumping said a spokesperson for the MTA. The driver's identity was not available at this time. NYPD Harbor Patrol and Emergency Services are continuing to search the waters off the Island shore.

****

For the last time Kevin is leaving One Police Plaza in Manhattan; the formalities were completed handshakes and hugs hi-fives from the old times and the young lions. Kevin relaxed and headed for the exit Captain Zimmerman placed his hand on his shoulder and said in a low voice "'In the interest of full disclosure I think I should say that at this moment they are executing a search warrant at your house and seizing any and all of your and phone messages and electronic devices."

****

We seldom value the true worth of what we have till it's discovered that we can have it no more.

Anonymous

205

Chapter 4

I TOOK A MAN DOWN TONIGHT

I do believe that most cops are decent. However, the oath to uphold the "Blue Wall of Silence" on training day, is simply a cover for the few rule-breaking, slimy cops in their midst, and a code for the Patrolman's Benevolent Association (PBA) to cover in-house crime. Like all unions, the PBA simply considers enabling members to evade just punishment at any cost. But sometime the rogues surface, smearing shit on the uniforms and faces of the entire police force in New York City, with stains reaching other police officers from Maine to California. The most morbid, inhuman and gruesome acts were committed by police officers that lived on Staten Island.

My files of the horrendous case have grown more than three inches thick. I have searched them for a title, and found only that they are best described as "White testosterone-charged policemen torture Black man." It describes little to most Whites but volumes to most Blacks. The two most articulate articles written about the case appeared in the S.I. Advance, written by two Blacks, one male, an attorney, and one female, Stevie Lacy-Pendleton, an editor for the Staten Island Advance.

The headline read:

NYC officer arrested in alleged sexual attack on suspect

NEW YORK (CNN) -- A police officer surrendered Wednesday night to face charges of sexually brutalizing a Haitian with a toilet plunger while the man was being held in custody.

The officer, Justin Volpe, 25, of Staten Island, turned himself into Internal Affairs just before 10 p.m. Wednesday, a police spokeswoman said.

Deputy Inspector Michael Collins said Volpe would be charged with aggravated sexual abuse and first-degree assault. Collins also said charges against Louima relating to the nightclub fight were being dropped.

Another officer involved in the case, identified by a police source as Thomas Bruder, 31, was assigned to desk duty. Collins said only Volpe faced charges Wednesday night.

But few things are ever explicit. The messy details, the lies, the fabrications the deceit and the shear hatred are mind blowing. Reading the files to write my essay continues to give the historical events of the past between the Black and White race new fuel in understanding how far the races have advanced in the 21st Century. Had the two White N .Y. City police officers, Justin Volpe and Charles Schwarz, simply taken the Black man, Abner Louima, behind the station house and shot him dead, the crime would appear on a single line on page 31 in most newspapers across the country. They would say Abner Louima, a Black man, was trying to escape. Period. Case closed. The PBA and the NPDF (National Police Defense Foundation) would be standing by to "Protect and Support Law Enforcement."

The events leading to the alleged torture began early Saturday morning in front of Club Rendez Vous, a Brooklyn dance club where many of New York's Haitian community gather to relax and unwind.

On August 9, 1997 in Brooklyn, N.Y., at the 70th Police precinct, two Black men had been arrested, Patrick Antoine and Abner Louima. The arresting officers were White, Justin Volpe and Charles Schwarz. They were charged with assaulting a police officer outside a night club. Patrick Antoine was a pedestrian caught up in the frenzy by officer Volpe, who smashed him with his flashlight, kicked and then cuffed the terrified man. Volpe had been struck in the melee outside the club and was angered. Abner Louima looked like the Black person who had struck him, and was also arrested and beaten in the squad car and at the station house, where the most severe beatings continued. They were Black men who were charged, convicted about to spend several years in the pen. But the events of that night in the 70th police precinct sank to the lowest level of human savagery. Abner Louima was taken to the restroom with his trousers at his ankles. Abner Louima, 5 feet 9 inches, 175 lbs, handcuffed and held down by Charles Schwarz, a solidly built 6 ft., 1 in, 235 lb. ex- marine with ten years on the police force, restrained him while Justin Volpe rammed a wooden toilet plunger up his rectum, puncturing his colon and his bladder. Not finding that brutal enough, Volpe removed the stick and shoved it into Louima's mouth, admonishing him, "If you tell anybody about this, I'll find you and kill you." Volpe and Schwarz, born into cop culture, did nothing to hide their deed. Volpe showed the bloody stick to other cops, announcing that, "I took a man down tonight, I broke a man." Other officers in the 70th precinct who were later questioned, stated that they did not hear Abner Louima's screams. Justin Volpe's brother is a cop, his father was a cop; he knew the "blue wall of silence" was on his side, and his fellow officers would protect him. But the vile nature of the acts revolted some of the other cops, and the blue wall began to crumble when some came forward to protest. The first officer from Stapleton, S.I., testified that he did not tell what he saw because he did not want to be viewed as a rat or a stoolie; eventually four officers would confess to the worst betrayal which is not to his sworn duty as a cop, but the betrayal of his false loyalty to his colleagues.

Before they were both convicted, the comedic theater and dance surrounding the events before the actual sentencing are worth mentioning, if only to gauge the pulse of an island of slumbering idiots unaware or openly unconscious of the messiness of their brains. Directing the chorus of reporters on the sidewalk immediately after the arrest of Justin Volpe was his defense lawyer Marvin M. Kornberg, who suggested, "Louima had engaged in gay anal sex, and despite the "egregious" charges against his client, Justin Volpe, he would be exonerated after a fair trial. I watched the unfolding theater of events for three years from the balcony, gathering the songs and scripts from the players on stage. The political muscle from a testy borough president, Guy Molinari, who sings an aria that will become his standard, "I am convinced that Chuck and John are innocent!...Schwarz is being railroaded!"

The newspaper article continued:

"There were four police officers beating, and there were two officers in the bathroom, and many police officers at the precinct seeing what was going on. Someone should have known and stopped this from happening," he said.

It was there that Louima says the officers pulled down his pants and led him to the bathroom, where they allegedly sodomized him with the plunger and then jammed the handle in his mouth.

Mayor Rudolph Guiliani and New York City Police Commissioner Howard Safir, usually quick to defend the police, are reacting differently in this case."

"This police commissioner and this mayor, I know, will tolerate no racism, no abuse, no undo force or unprofessionalism by any police officer and we're not going to tolerate it in this case," he said.

Family members said Louima, a security guard who moved to New York from Haiti six years ago, had no bruises or injuries at the time of his arrest.

The Rev. Al Sharpton, who is running for mayor, stood beside Louima's family offering up his opinion, part of a city-wide outcry, about the incident.

"The climate in this city has added to police feeling they could get away from such perverted acts. They need to be arrested. There is no reason, none, that you can justify torturing a human being in a civilized society," Sharpton said.

For his part Louima, says he used to like cops. That is, until this happened."

Guy Molinari, would convince large numbers of islanders to join him in a rally at the local Petrides Educational School with taxpayers' money for his "Free Chuck Schwarz" rally. A small chorus from the Staten Island African-American Political Association sans the large Liberian Community will call for an investigation onto the use of city funding for the rally. B.P. Molinari's song changes weekly. The "Rally for Justice" flyer states "An innocent man sent to prison for a crime he did not commit," yet officer Schwarz has been convicted twice. The testosterone-charged B.P. has convinced the U.S. Marine Corps League to host a Bar-B-Que fund raiser; during the cook-out, cheers, boo's and jeers went up whenever the names of the snitches, Eric Turetzy and Francisco Rosario were mentioned. Chuck Schwarz was an ex-Marine and the Marine Corps League presented his wife Andra with a large plaque, although it was unclear what the plaque read. More than 200 people attended; as usual, Catholic priests blessed these gathering, an attending young Priest volunteered the use of St, Peters Church Hall for another event. The PBA head, Patrick Lynch, said "Evidence at the last trial was being withheld from Chuck's attorney, Ronald Fischetti. From the Federal Medical Center in Devens, Massachusetts, convicted police officer Charles Schwarz said, "I'm being lynched." I resisted a call to the Black city hall reporter Reginald Patrick to find out if these were actually his words. "This is a modern day lynching! I am not going to take the rap myself and I will not apologize for a criminal act I did not commit," the ex-cop Schwarz said.

In January of 2000, I drove to Manhattan, to the Roth Horowitz Gallery on the uppereast side to see an exhibition called "Witness." There were about 50-60 photographs, postcards and other artifacts that chronicled lynching in the U.S. between 1883 and 1960. It was a cold day and the long drive aggravated my bum knee, and while I stood on the long line, I said to my self that this had better be worth my time. It was a small gallery and there were no more than 25 people allowed to go inside at one time. Once I got inside, there was a dead silence, Whites and Blacks stared blankly at the photographs depicting the graphic history of the country. The decapitations, castration, and hangings, the roasting of humans was more than I could take. For me there was no ignorance of the past; I had been researching the Black history of Staten Island and found it there, in the shadow of the Statue of Liberty. Just how much of our history remains buried, in Tulsa, Oklahoma, Rosewood, Florida, Elaine, Arkansas, the endless list of atrocities in Americas history. The tears from my eyes blurred the images and I left. I would purchase the book "Without Sanctuary" later.

I wondered if Charles Schwarz had seen the exhibit "Witness."

Guy Molinari's voice became louder, the song was the same. The justice system in the U.S. was corrupt. He vowed to sell "the farm." Molinari again repeated to a reporter from the S.I. Advance that we was planning to put his Bay Terrace townhouse up as bail, and he planned to be in court with the papers in hand. Both Charles Schwarz and his wife Andra said they were apprehensive. However the melody lingers on, and Molinari said, "I am angry as a hornet," because U.S. Attorney Alan Vinegrad was playing "hard ball," and called Vinegrad "a politically ambitious man" who is reeling from recent reversals two weeks before by losing the Yankel Rosembaum murder case. Guy Molinari is now out of office and has a law office in West Brighton - Russo,

Scamardella & D'Amato. "What kind of game is the prosecutor playing here?" Molinari's volume escalated as he said he looked for more heavy hitters to support the case of Charles Schwarz. "I'm free now, I will do more, I couldn't do that before as Borough President, it will be easier now that people know that I will put up my home as bail collateral." Having passed his seat at Borough Hall on to James Molinaro, Molinari could now call upon the Republican Party and it's chairman Carmine Ragucci for support. Carmine Ragucci was "a piece of work." New York waterfront tales have been a part of the "dock lore" in my family and the tales continue to be dinner table discussion in the 21st century. Some mob plots on the waterfront are worthy of Hollywood movies, and highly seasoned with Italian goombas and "Goodfellas." Until Carmine Ragucci was invited to change his political party from Democrat to Republican on the advice of M&M (Molinari and Molinaro), Ragucci was forced to be a back-stage goodfella, use the back door while Molinari was in the B.P.'s office. Carmine Ragucci, once president of the vast Howland Hook Container Terminal, did not have clean hands. He was often said to have been fired in a shakeup or to have left in a money shares dispute, but then nothing is ever explicit here. Ragucci's son Christopher was vice president and general manager when he made front page news. An unsealed indictment accused him of cheating iron workers who built the "Banana House" at the terminal out of proper union wages, to the tune of more than $ 300,000. The wage rate for iron workers in New York is $ 60.43 per hour. A construction company from Pennsylvania paid its workers at the "Banana House" job $ 15. per hour. Carmine Ragucci, who is now the Republican party Chairman on Staten Island, becomes a heavy hitter and an M&M team player.

With the top tier of the Republican Party in the bag, no one dares protest Guy Molinari, or James Molinaro or his in-your-face use of the Republican Party offices for his fund raising headquarters. I had to heed the call from Molinari, "For all Staten Islanders to show their support the fight for justice for Charles Schwarz," at a giant rally. I wanted to be there badly. Schwarz' lawyer used the "race card" when he suggested that there was some question of "German bias" that was added to the juror questionnaires. Reports of anti-Semitic or anti-German bias, he said, may have figured also.

It was a beautiful, warm day in June 2000 when I arrived at the rally with a White female friend I had persuaded to come with me. I knew the area well, having taught at the school when the campus was Staten Island Community College, and I had made huge paper maché sculptures for the very same quadrangle where the rally was taking place. The school was now called "The Michael Petrides School." I watched as a few Black people gathered in front of a Black woman, who I learned later was Janet Wilson, President of the S.I. African-American Political Association. Ms. Wilson was holding a pencil-printed cardboard sign which was difficult to read. Ed Josey, President of the Staten Island Chapter of the NAACP, was present. We didn't speak. He wore a large logo-printed NAACP tee shirt and ball cap; there seemed to be no other NAACP members at his side. Black attorney Todd Turner was silent, solemn faced. Todd Turner and Janet Wilson, President of the African- American Political Association, would later ask the N.Y.C. Department of Investigation to look into the use of funds for a "partisan" rally on public school grounds and denounce Molinari, who spent approximately $1,700 of public funds mailing flyers from his office and using staff time to support the event.

Payback! Molinari said he smelled a rat, and that rat was Jerome O'Donovan, a Democrat and Chairman of the City's Council for Economic Development. Molinari would then ask the DOI to investigate O'Donovan's one million dollar budget allocation to preserve as park land property next to his home. Jerome O'Donovan said he had no part of the African-American's calls for an investigation into Molinari's use of public funds for his "Free Charles Schwarz" rally. O'Donovan then called Molinari to assure him that he would attend the rally and that he believed Schwarz was innocent of holding Abner Louima down in the toilet while Officer Justin Volpe sodomized him with a wooden bathroom plunger. Molinari would have none of O'Donovans mea-culpa, and again stated his view to the press, saying O'Donovan was welcome at the rally but that, "O'Donovan's set-aside budget moneys for the property had the appearance of impropriety!" Jerome O"Donovan said others have done the same thing, including Molinari's ally, Councilman James Oddo. Guy Molinari became incensed at O"Donovan's arrogance and pointed to a provision in the city charter that states, "No public servant shall use his position to obtain any personal or private advantage, direct or indirect." It was payback time and O'Donovan had crossed him. Molinari said, "It was the right thing to do," stating that two of his staffers, Jennifer Nelson and Joanne Nuzzo had spent a small portion of their workdays preparing for the rally. Todd Turner said he did not discuss his decision with O'Donovan in calls for an investigation. Patrick Clark, a Department of Investigation spokesperson, said his agency had no record of requests for an investigation from the African-American Political Association.
I could find no newspaper story of the disposition of the charges if filed.

Kelvin Alexander, representing 100 Blacks in Law Enforcement, spoke in front of a group of reporters. Standing behind him were several White men and women showing their support. Kelvin Alexander, a N.Y.C. police sergeant, said, "I was taught to support the criminal justice system. But now I am being told not to support that system. I do not think borough president Molinari should be supporting Schwarz, a twice-convicted felon." I watched carefully as the young testosterone-laden white men seated a few yards away made catcalls and jeered at the smaller group. Guy Molinari was a folk hero to these men and it was well known that Guy would "stick up" for them. I guessed the number of people to have been at least 300 whites, and the odds for any winner in an altercation was a no-odds bet. I walked around, snapping photos, and I recognized the White police officer who was usually at the Borough Hall security desk, and remembered him as the officer that said I would get trouble if I was asking for it. He was wearing casual civilian clothes but I knew he would have a pistol in a leg holster and I backed off carefully. I had loaded my extra camera with film to record any disturbance that would erupt, and I knew if it did the Blacks and the Whites supporting them were in very bad trouble. I snapped as many photos as I could without attracting attention of the white men and women seated in the center of the quadrangle. On the fringe I noticed Ed Josey, alone, wearing his NAACP emblazoned cap and t-shirt. He seemed not to notice me and I saw that he had nothing protruding from his pockets and only a few papers in his hands. I watched him from a short distance but I was afraid

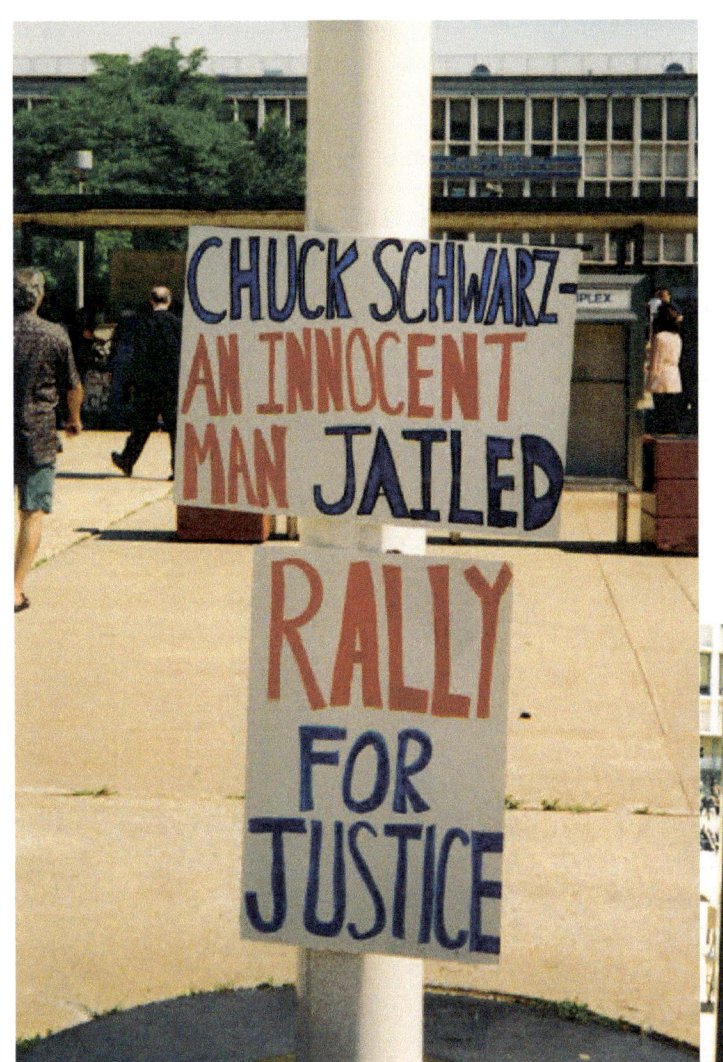

At the Petrides High School Quadrangle (1997), a rally to support one of the two White police officers (Swartz), who rammed a wooden bathroom plunger handle into the rectum of a Black man, Abner Louima, causing extensive internal damage.

LEFT: Television reporter interviews a former police officer disabled in a confrontation with a Black youth.

LEFT and BELOW:

At the "Free Swartz" rally, S.I. NAACP President Ed Josey (in yellow) puts his life in jeopardy by walking alone into the rally crowd.

The Borough President (BP) and church officials at the podium called on the crowd, consisting mostly of White police officers, firemen, corrections officers, and sanitation men and women to refrain from violence, and the BP promised to sell his farm to have the men vindicated and released.

that his life would be in danger if anything happened with this group. There were very few uniformed police here.

A large special van pulled to the curb and a cheer went up for the guest speaker, Steven McDonald, seated in a wheelchair because he was a paraplegic after being shot by a bicycle thief in Central Park. His message was a message of tolerance and non-violence. His cards read, "You are all very special." As I watched the large group in the quadrangle, seated in the hot sun, I wondered if his message would fall on open ears. My own ears closed to anything more Steven McDonald had to say after he said that he was convinced of Charles Schwarz' innocence. I moved closer to the podium while the Priest blessed the gathering in front of the American and N.Y.C. flags, draped limply on their staffs. I bowed my head and said a prayer. Molinari stepped in front of the podium, his eyes squinting into the sun behind large eyeglasses, his lips pursed as he waited for the applause to stop. Behind him were the dignitaries: Councilman Jerome O'Donovan, Assemblyman Vitaliano, Councilman Oddo and councilman Fiala. James Molinaro, standing silent, as other speakers waited patiently. The crowd clapped and cheered each speaker. There were few shouts from the Blacks, as returned shouts drowned them out. A few burly guys wanted more action, but they were held in check by Guy Molinari. It was his day; he said he was not a hero because he would put his house up for bail. It was the right thing to do. The applause lasted until he signaled. The cops, fireman and sanitation men knew he would fight city hall for them and the quid-pro-quo was to fight his fight. One had to give the little Guy credit.

As the tragic comedy ends and the curtain falls, the main characters, White ex-police officer Justin Volpe was convicted and is doing 30 years in prison. His father said he has found God and is studying religion. The other White, ex-police officer, Charles Schwarz, is doing five years in prison after copping a plea because a fourth trial and conviction would have returned to him his original 15-year sentence. Race had nothing to do with the 4 years of trials and sentencing. Skin color was not an issue and made no difference to the men and women gathered at the rallies solemnly blessed by Catholic Priests.

The Black victim, Abner Louima, received $8.7 million dollars in a settlement against the city and the police PBA. He moved his family out of New York to Florida and founded Babou's Enterprises. Abner Louima's soul has been seared, he will carry the scars for the rest of his life.

I waited for other island-wide voices, Asians, Whites, Liberians, Pakistanis and Pax Christi, witnesses to these four-year long events. Where were the voters, the indignant voices that followed the front page stories, those who read of the political noses that were thumbed at the constitution and the law? Where were the Blacks? The choral voices that sang, "We shall overcome." They don't mean a word of it. Where were those who talk up a good game and sing the hymns? Where are those Blacks who voice their opinions whenever the Advance calls on them to do so? Marching and protesting for fair play in Alabama or Georgia requires no effort. However, that indifference and ignorance and cynicism is alive and well on the island.

For the M&M team, they would salve their anger with continuous Staten Island Advance Op-Edit pieces. Block headlines, "For standing up for Charles Schwarz, Guy Molinari deserves respect and gratitude." Writers added quotes from Shakespeare and

Oscar Wilde. Others quoted Gilbert and Sullivan, and the bible, "God is not dead, he is asleep." To Guy Molinari, I offer our thanks and the nautical blessing, "May success always follow your flag." The Black editor, Stevie Lacy-Pendleton, was tongue lashed for her biased reporting again and again, for lies, anonymous sources, and her "hatchet job" on ex-police officer Charles Schwarz. I have no idea if Ms. Lacy-Pendleton reads the letters her attackers send to her newspaper; some have not only questioned her ability to write well, but also her qualifications for the job, and if she were assisted in obtaining her position because of her skin color.

Upset, unhappy, unapologetic, the M&M duo in Borough Hall remain undaunted and unashamed in their efforts to set aside irrational and rash judgments. Two weeks after ex- police officer Charles Schwarz was sent to prison for his part in the Abner Louima torture case, ex-borough president Guy Molinaro had a conference with Borough President Jim Molinaro, his long-time consigliere, about getting a job for Schwarz's wife Andra. Andra Schwarz was then hired as an aide at borough hall to the tune of $28,000 a year. No Civil Service exam, no qualifications, no advertisement, no questions asked. At the same time, staffers heard that there was a "doomsday" budget cut by Mayor Bloomberg coming from City Hall. Later, eleven staffers were notified as per union rules, of a two-week advance layoff notice. The water cooler and the outside smoker staff were furious at Molinaro's hiring of Andra Schwarz. Debbi Rose, the Black Staten Island activist, and two dozen others in the bitter cold, led a protest against the hiring in front of Borough Hall. Ms. Rose said with sarcasm, "It's heartening to know that no preferential treatment was extended to Andra Schwarz." Other political leaders on the island said they did not know of the hiring, another said he would not comment on it until he talks with Molinaro. B.P. James Molinaro said, "You can't go on continuously punishing people, she didn't do anything wrong. I am what I am, and I didn't do anything wrong." My phone calls to other lawmakers for comments about the unusual, sudden hiring of Mrs. Schwarz were never returned. The employment of Mrs. Schwarz lasted less than a month. A comment about the hiring from Vito G. Fossella did not sit well with the M&M duo.

Vito Fossella, White and Italian, black, wavy hair, big fellow, nice, even teeth smile, about 6 foot 2, weighing in at about 210. Calm and handsome, clean shaven, Vito never appears in a rumpled suit. The Staten Island Republican in the U.S. House of Representatives was young, brash and ambitious. Vito Fossella was considering a run for the office of mayor of New York City. Perhaps Vito Fossella did not know or ask the Republican Party about the sitting Mayor Bloomberg, who had announced his wishes to run again, and was a frequent visitor to Staten Island and a friend of former mayor Rudolph Giuliani and Guy Molinari. Staten Island was a safe bet for any candidate who knew of its Republican, Conservative, Right-to-Life philosophy and large Italian and Irish city worker base.

I will never understand how Vito could let such a story get out into the press. Rudy Giuliani, ex-mayor, is Italian, a friend of Mike Bloomberg, the Jewish Mayor, and Giuliani promised him his support for another term. Bloomberg and Rudy were also friends of ex-B.P. Molinari, and Rudy came through with more than $70,000 big ones tucked into his budget for a baseball stadium in front of Borough Hall. Bloomberg came religiously to Staten Island to dine on Pizza. Staten Island makes the best pizza, he joked about his new found taste and love for cannolis.

Guy Molinari is an intelligent person. Guy Molinari is a sensitive person. And Guy Molinari knew there were cracks in the family. His talents and abilities were being tested and it was time to re-assert authority. He wanted undisputed leadership, without internal squabbles. He was out of official office now, but was not going to entertain the idea that he would be forced into retirement like other political families, at least not just yet. He had just announced the formation of "The Molinari Group, LLC," a consulting and lobbying firm.   In the public relations newspaper photo with his partners, John D'Amato and Robert Scamardella, Guy Molinari looked good. He had changed the signature large, dark-rimmed glasses for new, thin wire glasses, red power tie, and looked fit in front of the required law library book cases.

It was time for the compulsory annual ritual, and he was ready for business. He did not like the previous few years. With the Bolsheviks at the door, new political groups had emerged, such as the American Muslim Alliance and the Chinese American Coalition. Guy had questions and he wanted answers. Signs had appeared to vote for Michael (Mustafa) Plinkovic. Guy was not worried; he simply wanted to know what they wanted, and why they had come to Staten Island. He wanted their names and addresses, he wanted to know how to pronounce the names, and he wanted to know if they were real doctors. Suhail Muzaffan and Dr. Saquib Kitan. He wanted them checked out, he wanted to know why they wanted to reach out to other ethnic groups on the island. He didn't need this; he had gotten along very well with the ethnic groups on the island. The Blacks had Michael McMahon on the North Shore, some played golf with him. He didn't want to disturb the Democratic section of the island. If he didn't act now, he felt the family would be left rudderless.

Would the fraternity hold for another 4 years? Would there be any defections? He had not been implicated in any crimes and there were no investigations that he knew of. He did worry about Jimmy Oddo, but like most of the others, Oddo was a Monsignor Farrell High School boy, Italian and a good Catholic. Fossella, Porzio, Lanza, Cusick. The Irish? McMahon, Devlin. They were all from good families, and grew as an impressive crop of lawyers, politicians and police, all of whom are White and continue in public office today.

On the North Shore, Saint Peter's High School, like most schools on the North Shore, declined in the late Sixties. The school principal at Monsignor Farrell, a priest, did not know if there were any Blacks enrolled.

Author's reflection:

I remembered leaving the U.S. aboard a flight to Mali and dwelling on the morass of Staten Island politics and the hopes for the future. Staten Island Blacks had recovered from an intense "crabs in a barrel" fight for a change in the Black school board seat, and forcing the eighth-term Black Board member into a coalition to work together. The Staten Island Political Action group and the Staten Island Ad-Hoc Committee spearheaded voters, younger, more educated. The signs were there for a change in Black lives. Education was the weapon, along with voter participation, weapons carried by the new, more-than-qualified, Clarence McGhie, Ed Bethel, James Frazier, Hank Pedro, to name a few. I felt they were the new core of badly-needed Black leadership on the island. My hopes soared as the plane rose over the Atlantic. Thirty years later, I look for traces of the Black power invested for better education; the public schools are underperforming and more segregated. The constant re-arrangement of the school system, with pressures from the public, the unions and the political machine. Borough President James Molinaro, whose education ended in the eighth grade, appointed a White woman, owner of a Victoria's Secret lingerie shop in New Dorp, with no college degree, to be his representative on the New York City Panel for Education. I found no response to this in the newspaper or from any Black organizations on the island.

The public bickering angered Guy Molinari when he heard Jim Molinaro discuss his growing up in Little Italy on the lower east side of N.Y. and his late wife being Irish. "That makes my two kids half Irish." Molinaro had pushed a button. Jay O'Donavan said his name is Irish, but his nose is a dead giveaway, and that he is actually part Italian. The hopeful candidates confessed their true identities. Joe Wein, a mid-island hopeful, said he was Jewish but his mother's maiden name was Funicella, and he would highlight that in his campaign literature. Republican Rep. Vito announced that he also had Irish lineage. Senator Vincent Gentile was asked if he was French. Republican maverick Robert Straniere, the only Jewish elected official (Judges aside), said his daughter-in-law was Irish and he was also Italian and Jewish. Assemblyman Bob Stranaire wanted the office of Borough President badly, but he knew Guy Molinari wanted his personal consigliere, Deputy Jim Molinaro, in his seat. In an action described as one part dog-and-pony show and two parts bully pulpit, Guy Molinari would oust Straniere a few months later and replace him with a 29-year old political novice, White Italian Vincent Ignazio. It ended Bob Straniere's bid to hold his 24-year long term South Shore seat. Republican Robert Straniere had pissed Guy Molinari off once too many times, and Guy set the stage for his removal, it was payback time. Italian Steve Fiala would become the new County Clerk and he revealed that he too had an Irish mother. During the run for genetic confessions, none confessed to having Chinese, Puerto Rican, or Korean blood ties. Most are Italian and Catholic, but there is no Anti-Semitism on Staten Island. Those legislators on the North Shore that have not been Italian or Catholic, being out of the loop they simply have not penetrated the domain of the remaining two thirds of the island to promote a Protestant agenda.

The family was called together over the next two weeks. Not in sports bars, social clubhouses or restaurants but in the crisp clean leather-backed chairs in legal boardrooms where no electronic wizardry could eavesdrop. Rudy Giuliani was under pressure to extricate himself from the Bernie Kerik fiasco and could not attend the opening session. The conferences were said to be "private" business affairs when the press inquired, or simply organizational structuring. The power players cut deals, and everybody got what he wanted, no questions asked. The only leaks were from members that wanted to explain Guy Molinari's new face to the changing ethnic community. The

Black woman reporter questioning a man who was seen leaving a meeting hit a raw nerve. When questioned about racism and why Guy Molinari did not send a delegation or phone his party members to appear at a Nelson Mandela function, the answer was telling. Some island councilmen who work right there in City Hall said they were much too busy with fiscal matters for the three days Mandela would be in town. Albany sent a delegation of 24 to New York City, no Staten Island legislator was in that group.

Most legislators perform double somersaults to be in attendance on the island's Saint Patrick's Day Parades, Irish or no. Their shoulder to shoulder attendance at charity luncheons and dinners are mandatory, and their absence would be noted and remembered in the press. For every politician, it was business-as-usual when Nelson Mandela, president of South Africa and civil and human rights leader came to town, unimportant perhaps but telling.

The Black island organization leaders were silent.

In December 2-12, another newspaper article reported:

Justin Volpe, cop who sodomized Abner Louima with broomstick inside Brooklyn police station, marries Staten Island woman in Florida prison

The 'I do's' came 13 years after Volpe admitted torturing Louima in a 70th Precinct bathroom, becoming a national symbol of police brutality and igniting racial tension across the city.

The wedding between Volpe, 40, and blushing bride was officiated by Devery, a priest formerly of Staten Island. Both Volpe's and the bride's families hail from Staten Island.

Their union will go unconsummated for a long time to come: Federal prisoners are banned from enjoying conjugal visits, according to Bureau of Prisons spokesman Chris Burke.

And Volpe's earliest release date on his 30-year prison term is Aug. 3, 2025.

Police Officer Justin Volpe

Mike McAlary, a *New York Daily News* journalist, won the 1998 Pulitzer Prize for distinguished commentary for his exposé of the brutalization of Louima by NYPD officers.

Louima's subsequent civil suit represented by attorney Sanford Rubenstein against the City of New York ended in a settlement of $8.75 million on July 30, 2001, the largest police brutality settlement in New York City history. After legal fees, Louima collected approximately $5.8 million.

Chapter 5

BLACK HISTORY MONTH

 **Dynasties and Dinosaurs**

Once upon a time, it was a dark and stormy night!

Where do I begin this screed? I will admit first off that I have had a lot of assistance from friends and enemies to do this; a lot of work and time goes into a treatise such as this. There are many voices, places, years, and people involved. And I have benefited from both support and criticism while speaking about my innermost feelings and attempts about doing this. For a long time I did not think I had the intelligence or ability to commit my life to words. There were no signposts or guidelines, nor any role models on Staten Island, which is where I will confine my story.

This book has taken me many miles to gather the wisdom, thoughts, and requirements needed to gain the insights to various subjects. I have gathered the materials in essays and notebooks, diaries and tapes for decades. I listened, I took notes; I remembered. There are folks that welcomed me into their lives in foreign countries and I am deeply indebted to them. I have the utmost respect for my best friend Jude, whose keen intellect for listening to my voice and realizing that for me to survive with my mind intact; I had to leave Staten Island.

And most of all, I am very lucky; during the months and years of my travels about the island I heard many times, "Cleve, you are blessed." I will not bore the reader with an intellectual trove of words, bunches of arcane facts, and dry figures. There is a great amount of fantasy in my life and it captures a reality that I can only use to express what

I witness in the contemporary plane of everyday life. There is no crystal ball, no tea leaves, but I have, over the years, done considerable research to hone my thoughts for the ideas expressed in this book.

Last but not least, this book is a thank you for the people in my life, regardless of race or color or cultural differences. The people I have met throughout my life have and still continue to occupy a significant part of my life, providing me with direction and support.

Being a Black person has been beneficial for me to understand the race issue facing Staten Island. Although it is nationwide, I will confine my words to the place and experiences that I know.

It was 2006 and I had just completed a talk at Richmond College before the library and historic archives and records department. I was not satisfied with my address; my thoughts and frame of reference about the scope of the problems on the Island were wide ranging and I was unable to cover topics that I thought were important. I felt constrained by time and place and uncomfortable lecturing to others.

Preparing the foundation for doing a book, I had an idea to do a one-on-one oral history of mostly Blacks and some Whites on Staten Island. I was still unsettled about how to work at uncovering whatever it was that I wanted to understand. My need to find a comfortable place to live while conducting the interviews was primary, making time for interaction with people I did not know was also necessary. We then decided to use the summer of 2006 for my oral history work. I would live and work on Staten Island for an entire summer. Reviewing the costs, travel, and housing, material needs to cover the island and the time frame to accomplish my grand mindscape and do a thorough job was overwhelming. There was no funding available, no time to write a proposal, wait for an answer, have meetings, and follow instructions to do what was developing in my mind. I did not ask for assistance from any agency, company, foundation or friends, and I knew that my lifestyle and work habits would not allow me to be confined in any way. I also knew that the subject matter of race on Staten Island was tenuous and I would need to walk on thin ice if I accepted any funding.

I was given a great deal of information and some books detailing the need to do a good oral history job by Dr. James Kaser at the College of Staten Island. What was I going to do? What was I going to ask other Black islanders? There was no Black institution on Staten Island that I could go to for research into the Black history. I did go to the Richmondtown Historical Society where I found only records and books, wills and documents by white islanders.

I worked in the archives of the Staten Island Museum in the small, cramped, basement space below the New York City Health Department building, next door to the Museum on Stuyvesant Place. There was always a blank wall. My schooling never taught me anything about Black people on the island. My father's Prince Hall Masonic fraternity had a private Negro week at the headquarters on Richmond Terrace in West Brighton, which was a quiet assembly of men gathered to remember former members that had passed away. There was no recorded information on who they were, what they did, or why it was important for members to know that they had lived and died here.

I was fortunate to be among a few Black and white Staten Islanders who worked and created a place that would eventually become The Sandy Ground Historical Society. Like many others, I hoped for it to become a place for actual documents and a bricks and mortar location to provide knowledge for students and teachers about Black history of Staten Island. The history archives of the Staten Island Museum were extensive, but were also white dominated, similar to Historic Richmondtown. Most writers of island history used these two sources for information and research. There was no other resource to gather any facts or information, except perhaps the filed documents in the Surrogate's Office in the basement at the County Courthouse.

Vetting resources and research took a great deal of time and patience. The published books from the Museum were most informative, but I received nothing historically about my people that lived on this island for centuries.

The answer to my continued probing about the scarcity of archival information on Black history with religious ministers was simple; that sort of academic research was apparently not God's work so they were not going to do it.

B. The Process

We found a camper in Baltimore on Craig's List. It was a special type of small camper that was placed on the bed of a pick-up truck. It had a stove, sink, water tank, and a fridge, a work table and a long bed that fit my six foot frame. The unit was actually quite compact, and I could use an electrical cord extension to allow me to recharge my cell phone and laptop computer from the camper wall outlets. We bought a new, heavy duty, Dodge pick-up truck, drove to Baltimore, bought the camper, and placed the camper on the truck. To outfit the camper, I needed to have the truck electrical system combined because the unit covered the rear truck lights and I would need to have turn signals and safety lights, yellow for the front section and red for the rear section. I would need bottled gas to cook with and the water tank added hundreds of pounds to the weight. The toilet was a dry chemical unit, a seat covered can. Anything that was not needed was removed; I would not have any guests or friends visiting. I would only take light summer clothes and food that could be heated by a small 6-inch round electric stove for tea and canned soups. I would use dry ice for refrigeration and a basket for soiled clothes. I would need a wind up alarm clock, radio, and batteries, files and cameras, flash lights, single cotton bed sheets, boxes of whole grain energy chocolate bars, toiletries and wash towels. Every space would have to be used efficiently.

Inside the truck cab were tools and rain gear, an assortment of ropes, a ladder to climb on top for use if needed. I did several dry runs and road checks, I believed I had covered all the bases, I was cool. But I would find out much later that I had a lot to learn about living in a camper on the road.

My first experience was at the toll gates at the Baltimore tunnel. I had eased through and parked on the roadside after being flagged by a police officer who came along side and asked if I had any HAZMATS. Being Black, I had to size up what this white police officer might be thinking, and it was a surprise question because I did not realize what a HAZMAT was. I replied that no, I did not have anything like a HAZMAT and what was it?

I told him, even before he asked me, that he was welcome to look inside. He asked if I had a cooking stove inside and when I said that I did; he asked where the gas was. I said it was inside the side panel, and showed it to him. He said it was a HAZMAT and that after 9/11 they had to ask campers about the canisters. I told him that it was empty and I was not going to use it anyway, and when he asked if I would take it out and disconnect it, I said yes. It then dawned on me that the signs that I had never understood or had to reason to check were HAZMAT signs. HAZMATS, Hazardous Materials.

He was courteous and asked where I was going and what I did. I did not think he would believe me if I told him I was going to Staten Island to live in this and what I planned to do, so I said I was a retired bird watcher and I was going up to the Catskills to watch the migrations. He seemed relaxed and I took a deep breath, hoping not to receive some sort of summons for breaking the law. I opened the rear door lock for him to look inside, and as I opened the door, a river of broken glasses and dishes, papers, books, overturned water, and food fell out onto the pavement. Everything that was not firmly held in place was in a pile on the camper floor at the rear door. The officer grabbed a few pieces of paper from the pavement and handed them to me as I stood dumbfounded, pissed, looking at my own negligence and stupidity. Not wanting to engage in any more conversation, I told him again I was retired and I was going to bird-watch in the Catskills. He said nothing more, while I began to remove stuff from the roadway, he walked away.

I turned around and returned to Washington DC to get rid of anything I thought were HAZMATs or dangerous items, and to spend more time preparing to live in this mess, then continued on my odyssey. I got permission from friends on Staten Island to park my camper on their vacant lot for a small fee and the use of one of their electric lines to hook up my camper to power, and then proceeded to spend the summer conducting interviews with many kind and knowledgeable individuals. Some weeks, it was so brutally hot in the camper, which had no protection or shade from the suns rays, that I would become dizzy and nearly faint from the heat. The noise from the bars nearby kept me up or woke me from sound sleep. But I soldiered on, bent on my mission. Those interviews are preserved on tape; many of them transcribed, and will be donated to the archivist at the College of Staten Island and the African American Museum in Washington DC.

I did have a plan to integrate myself back into the Staten Island community. I would use my time in barbershops to engage in small talk until I was an accepted stranger, I would attend Sunday church services, and I would find evening places that Black folks frequented, and I would make eye contact and speak to anyone. What I did not realize was the island hills and traffic would make moving around the island a bitch. Each evening I had to clean the inside of the camper as anything I had not attached securely had fallen. I was always tired running after folks all day to speak with, opening the huge gates in the parking area, and hooking up the electric so that I could recharge my phone and make tea or coffee before bed.

I decided to take the "Chinese bus" at Times Square in Manhattan, return to Washington and come back with my smaller old Toyota car. I waited to catch a bus to the New York ferry, but did not have a prepaid ticket. I told the driver I did not know about that and I wanted to go to the ferry terminal, and the driver nodded for me to stay on board to the South Ferry terminal. I crossed the lower bay to South Ferry in Manhattan, bought a ticket at a kiosk for the 7th Avenue subway line ride to Times Square, then went up to street level to ask passersby where the Chinese bus to DC was located. I never feel quite at ease stopping people on the street and asking questions. Was I dressed properly? Would they think I was a panhandler asking for loose change, a pickpocket, or a dope seller? At six feet three I think I was a bit intimidating, so I used an accent to approach people on the street, which seemed to work since New York City was Mecca for people from all over the world to come and live and work. Conversation was easy after a few moments, and folks would often talk to me about the weather, politics, or their personal lives, so that I would have to break off politely. I had to get back to Washington to bring my much smaller Toyota car to Staten Island. After that I realized that this was still "Struggle Island."

C. Entrepreneurs – 2010 – Preparations

On September 19, 2009, I received an e-mail from Diane Matyas, a friend who is one of the curators at the Staten Island Institute for Arts and Sciences, the museum on Staten Island. It reads:

> Dear Cleve:
>
> I wanted to ask you if you would be a part of a proposal and hopefully accept the project titled "Staten Island History as It Happens: Portraits in American Leadership." This project would be focused at identifying, interviewing, photographing, and finally podcasting five African American leaders on Staten Island. I was hoping that you might agree to help as a consultant to develop the questions, help identify prospects, and work with our folklorist and the community outreach administration to make the project a meaningful exercise with your guidance and knowledge.
>
> If this interests you, let me know
>
> Sincerely, Diane

Diane Matyas was developing this project that would be produced for the February 2011 Black History Month. I knew the Staten Island Institute of Arts and Sciences and would support and work with the museum as a first choice. When I published my book, *In the Shadow of the Statue of Liberty*, I sent letters to dozens of organizations on Staten Island, most of them Black; I would hear absolutely nothing. Diane Matyas arranged for me to have my 9/11 artwork shown in the museum and also assisted in organizing a book-reading at the museum. I would think very seriously because the museum is the place where I began a special part of my life, working in the archival section many years ago, to produce a project which became *The Black Man on Staten Island*.

Diane Matyas would give my name to the Project Director who was moving the *Portraits of Leadership* project forward, Ms. Janine Otis. We began an e-mail conversation; initially it was necessary for me to find out more about this project,

Portraits of Leadership. Before meeting Ms. Otis, I sat at my desk and Googled her, learning she was the Arts Education Director at the Staten Island Museum. I further learned through a friend that she was, indeed, a Black person, which made my acceptance to work with the project that much easier. The project described in the e-mails included consideration of Sandy Ground, and, this being an issue of great importance for 40 or perhaps 50 years of my life, I wanted to get to know Ms. Otis even more; I sent her a letter:

> Ms. Otis:
>
> Your name has been forwarded to me and I need to know more about you. I am in the process of tying together essays and research about my life on Staten Island and the time that I have lived there. I am not the head of any organization, committee, or foundation, and I represent no one. I do not have time to meet with you unless you have read my book and we would be on the same page for any research and understanding about Staten Island.
>
> I sincerely hope that you have done some legwork and are prepared to be open and honest with me about why you are using this venue for information. For me, that is the sole purpose for my life and times at this point in my life. I am an 82-year-old Black man. I am married and I live now in Washington, DC. Please let me know something about you and why you need to interact with me. Cleve

Our e-mail and phone conversations went back and forth, and Ms. Otis said she would come to Washington and meet with me in person. Ms. Otis came. She is a tall, slender, brown-skinned woman. I guessed her age to be about thirty-five to forty. We had a 3- or 4-hour conversation, and at that time I said that I would think very deeply about working with the project. I was about to enter the hospital for a foot operation on a painful neuroma. Although I was active at the gym every day, my body was acting weird; previously unnoticed little aches and pains began to surface, headaches and stomach upsets, but I dismissed all the telltale symptoms of my body's reaction to what I was about to commit myself to do.

Looking back, I realized that I was stressed and also short with Ms. Otis. She did, however, leave me with the material about the project that she was working on.

The project developed by Ms. Otis would produce a film of *Portraits of Leadership: The African American Entrepreneurs on Staten Island*. Great I thought, it would add another dimension to the island history. Ms. Otis, I thought, would bring a new dimension to a project of this magnitude. I told Ms. Otis that I would drive to Staten Island on December 16, 2010, to discuss further what the project should entail from my files. I also wanted to know who were the other folks that I would be working with, and I would bring along my suggestions, diaries, notebooks, some essays, papers, newspaper clippings, and whatever else I thought could perhaps make my presence helpful. There was always a need on Struggle Island for real progressive leadership in politics, education, and the arts; at the time I could find none. There were no Black men in the structural process to do this, while Black women would be in many roles and places. There was no balance, but I imagined that it was only my paranoia.

I knew in my heart, however, that to visit Staten Island for this 2011 participation in Black History Month would be, for me, a disaster. I really didn't want to fight the same old tired battles that have dominated presentations of Black history in life. I wanted to try something new.

We drove to Staten Island and met her at her office, a few hundred feet from Borough Hall. While Jude and Ms. Otis spoke together, I tried to set aside the micro-assaults, the micro-insults that I had witnessed and suffered on these very streets, these very sidewalks, as a result of the mural controversy. I felt uneasy, but my "method acting" personality would come to the surface.

We couldn't find a quiet place to have lunch; there was never a place in the midst of the court houses, police precincts, and administration offices buildings on the North Shore close enough to have any privacy.

Ms. Otis began to give me the names of the people to be on the program. Kevin Buford, described by the folklorist at the Council on the Arts as a social entrepreneur, was a Staten Island ferry vendor. Kevin Buford didn't have any display cases, or tables; somehow he was selected because attitude counted as much as fancy resumes. Other people were Delores Morris, an educator and TV producer, and Gerald Barclay, a writer, director, and producer, who came to Staten Island when his family was forced out of Liberia in a violent coup d'état. Gerald Barclay was an entrepreneur.

I never met first face to face any of the other people on the panel. I had their names and occupations etc, but never had an opportunity to sit and find out what each person would or could contribute to the "Portraits of Leadership" Black History Month program at the Staten Island Museum. I would ask again, "Why me?" I didn't really expect anything new or exciting, but I'm stubborn, I had to go on, go forward, in the hope that something would happen, hoping for that rebirth of wonder.

One of the reasons I moved further before deleting everything was that I was told that this Black lady, Ms. Otis, would be the primary engine to produce the series of events for 2011. The Staten Island Museum has always been primary for me while I lived on Staten Island. I worked in the Archives of the library, producing the documents that became the *History of the Black Man on Staten Island*. I worked very hard, for a very long time, with many white and Black people at the Museum, and many years later the Staten Island Museum would give me a book-reading at a time when I found it very difficult to find any Black person or organization that would give me one. Because the Staten Island Institute would sell my books at their Museum shop, and the Staten Island Museum would show my works of art when I had found it very difficult to find any Black organization to assist me, ever, I would think very carefully about supporting the events at the Staten Island Museum with their Black History Day 2011 events.

D. Entrepreneurs – 2010 – The Wagner Event

A few weeks later I received an invitation from the Wagner College History Department asking if I would participate in a program they were doing for African American History Month in the same year, 2011. Their dates were basically the same; Portraits in Leadership with the S.I. Museum on February 12, and African-American Entrepreneurs at Wagner College on February 15. Wagner College was a place where I had been invited before, and I had appeared with other Blacks at Wagner during the Civil Rights Era, and although I did not know the two professors at Wagner or the assistant chair of the History Department, their offer was interesting enough for me to consider.

I searched my diary, notebooks, files, essays, and paper clippings to prepare what would become another visit to Staten Island, with my patron saint of hopeless cases, Jude, because after decades of filing away my personal history of Staten Island, I was addicted. I did not want to have a simple photo-op, a 10-minute rant in front of a disinterested group on Staten Island. I knew that with the weight of my memory and the feelings that I have while looking through my files, doing anything at all would be very dangerous for me if I did not have Jude at my back. I was vacillating between high and low; I needed testing for bi-polar.

I knew Staten Island well from the perspective of a Black man. Still, I knew that what I would say would not sit well with any 10 or 15 minute presentation. After eight-plus decades, I cannot become a part of the contemporary dialogue which I knew would unfold with "I used to...," "When I was...," "We had...," "My family..." There would be no archival documentation of anything that would happen, and after Black History Month it would be as it always has been, like perhaps it didn't happen at all. We would leave no footprints. We do not have any archives in any Black organization on Staten Island; we have been unable to capture the sequences of our community's plight. It's simply just to survive.

Black History Month is clothed in so much religious, emotional reverence that I had to endure many days and weeks of sleeplessness before I would give any response to being a participant. The bipolar condition of the Black Staten Islanders will allow them to hold a "pity party" in which to sing, pray, and whine about white oppression, who we are, why we ain't, and a celebration of this kind of history that, we are to believe, has no downside whatever. Black history will not have a downside. We will not allow it. Could I advise or give advice?

The unpleasantries that I live with would be glossed over in this You-Know-What Month. We are very aware of what it is that we would want and why we are here, and why we come together each year in the month of February, but we would follow the annual which would not allow anyone to interrupt the events that are repeated and conducted every year. I always thought that, if our prayers, our songs, our dancing, and our speeches could break chains, we would be free.

I knew in my heart, after days and weeks of deliberation about a visit, that this visit to Struggle Island would not go very well for me, but for this 2011 Black History Month fête I would try. I would speak with the historians, curators, filmmakers, and promoters of the two major events, but I knew down deep that I did not want to fight the same tired battles that have dominated presentations of Black History life. I would go; it would be a final voyage, I thought, but it did not work out that way. At 80+ years on Staten Island I realized that of the old players, many of the Black men were dead,

Left: Entrepreneur Carl Jones and bartender Alfred Newcombe, both deceased, in front of the now defunct Jonesey's Tavern on Holland Avenue. Carl Jones was the last Black restaurant entrepreneur on Staten Island's North Shore.

Right: Singlelicious, owned by a Black woman, was on Forest Avenue, but is now a distant memory.

Left: Cleve's residence, a truck-mounted camper, for the summer of 2006.

Top: Books celebrating Staten Island history.

Below: Celebrating Black History Month.

Above: Black S.I. leaders accepting proclamations at Snug Harbor Cultural Center.

Above: NAACP leader Ed Josey honors S.I. Black policewomen.

Above: Debi Rose becomes first Black elected official on Staten Island.

Right: Debi Rose has her day in 2009.

This is the face of pervasive "White Power." Two White men have lived here for more than 30 years; they do not allow visitors inside the million dollar historic mansion. Public funds from Richmondtown and the NYC Parks Department are used to pay utilities, insurance, etc. to maintain the crumbling structure.

""She wants to know if this is section 8 housing""?

Stan Rayfield

QUICK! LET'S FORM A COMMITTEE!

Stan Rayfield

"CLEVE RECEIVES FINAL INSTRUCTIONS AND BECOMES A GRIOT."

hospitalized, and bedridden, and the Black women that I tried to contact, their numbers were dwindling.

Wagner College sits atop one of the highest hills from Maine to Florida with a fantastic view. New York City lights up the bay looking north, the Verrazano Bridge connects Staten Island to the east with the Atlantic Ocean to the south. I had visited Wagner numerous times during my life on the island, and a few faculty people I knew were still employed there. I had had a few art exhibits there and my most unforgettable visit was a huge CORE (Congress of Racial Equality) rally at which I was master of ceremonies with James Baldwin as the guest speaker and a group of entertainers. This was during the active civil rights days on Staten Island.

I had worked at other schools and campuses on the island and I liked the atmosphere. I accidently forgot to graduate from college, I meant to, 30 or 40 years ago, but things just got in the way for me.

I was well prepared to bring materials to the table from my files for the Museum and Wagner College events and the film for African American Entrepreneurs, but I was disturbed to realize that the Museum curators and personnel, and the Wagner College professors, assistant professors, and associate professors in the History Department, while they had exciting curators jobs and were receiving salaries, had not done their homework. There was no place to find the information they wanted, no organization to explain the too-often neglected accomplishments of Black islanders. It didn't amaze me, but a quiet rage existed inside.

I was in possession of my mental weight of history; I could rattle off places, businesses, and entrepreneurs, over and over again, that had once been popular for Black people on Staten Island. They would be forced to realize, as I realized, that it would simply be a blank place in their minds.

I wondered where the young Black upscale men and women gathered on Staten Island now. Where are the quality amenities that the Blacks patronize? Where is the coolest place on Staten Island to meet for conversation, or perhaps to listen to some jazz and socialize? At the Elks Club in Mariners Harbor I would need patience to have a conversation over the sounds of the air conditioner or the recorded music from several large speakers. As I learned in my talks and interviews, Blacks go to Elizabeth, New Jersey, or Brooklyn. Black retail business owners are rare. A labor of love that perhaps had potential for a real community revival, but somehow it never took.

Jude and I came over the bridge to Forest Avenue to find Singlelicious, the middle upscale restaurant operated by Sharon Singleton. In 2006, her delicious Southern fare was a palate for the soul. Sharon Singleton was the Executive Chef, a hostess, the occasional waiter and bartender at her restaurant. Five years later, Singlelicious and Sharon Singleton were no more.

The panel discussion at Wagner was scheduled from 6 to 9 pm, and the program began at Spiro Hall. The Spiro Hall auditorium theater was about half empty and the history students who sat in the upper seats appeared to be mostly white and bored, texting while waiting for the session to begin. I was soon joined by two friends from Manhattan and took a seat in the second row so that I could see and hear everything. I looked at the few papers and data that I had about Black Staten Island entrepreneurs; there was not very much. Seated at a table were five people, four Black women and one Black man, all of whom were over the age of sixty except for the Black man who may have been 35-40. He was described as a multi-media specialist who has acquired a great deal of knowledge about Staten Island. I came with my own sheet of papers published in the last 5 years by the Staten Island African American Chamber of Commerce that focused on Black Business. There was no one in the audience or on the panel from the organization. I had several pages from the Staten Island Economic Development Corporation Director who said there were statistics citing 700 woman- and minority-owned businesses on Staten Island. I had articles from the *Advance* newspaper about Black women who had started their own businesses, such as cleaning buildings, and teaching table manners and settings, etc. at etiquette school.

A Black female panel member, whom I had known for over forty years, and who has been in business since 1970, said nothing about business. Instead she regaled the audience about visiting the slave house island of Gorée and being ripped off during a visit to Senegal. Another panelist talked about the racism that forced many Black men and women 40 to 80 years ago to work in the vast horrific hospitals that were country wide seats of experimentation, such as the Seaview Tuberculosis Hospital, and about the notorious Willowbrook State School where research was conducted on mentally disabled children that led to the development of hepatitis B vaccine. Many high profile physicians felt this was a legitimate practice to experiment on people that did not have full rights in society. Black women and nurses knew of these past medical experimentations, but kept silent.

Those studies often involved making working men and women sick. There is no documentation of this by any Black organization on Staten Island where many of the men and women, now senior citizens, and their families still live. There has been no comprehensive study to follow up on employees that have died of unknown illness. My family also had worked in these notorious hospitals; this was a part of the basis for the study "The Black Man on Staten Island Project."

The multimedia specialist on the panel read from a packet of statistics, figures, and models of island entrepreneurs and said there were more than 7,000 Black business people he had counted as entrepreneurs. What bullshit! The use of U.S. Census figures about the minorities on the North Shore of Staten Island when it comes to keeping racial statistics is in transition, and I know that the northern part of Staten Island is and has been racially segregated. Diversity be damned.

Lumped together, Blacks, Asians, and Latinos all look the same from a data/numbers perspective. And the reality on this island is much different, by class, by economic status, and by race. And there are different kinds of discrimination experienced by each group. No amount of research will change the visual numbers that exist on Staten Island where a contemporary dude on the street can give more accurate information for statistics. There is a need for more and better and honest numbers information. It is time for us to stop lying to ourselves.

It was embarrassing to me to hear a Black man describe numbers of Blacks doing business undercover and off the books. 7,000!!! I thought again that was quite amazing.

He described shoe shiners, numbers collectors, barbers, and bookies, etc., he went on and on.

I waited for a few honest Black daily working entrepreneurs to appear from behind the curtain, but no. I realized that we were talking about a new meaning of the term "entrepreneur," that the Black people being interviewed were actually called "social entrepreneurs" by some dingbat folklorist.

I listened, amazed, to the comments of the Reverend Dr. Demetrius S. Carolina, Sr. who described the wonderful living, working, and business careers on Staten Island, but I found it lacking in completeness. I had a difficult time wrapping my head around those people who would be on the panel to speak about Black entrepreneurs. My history of Black entrepreneurship on Staten Island goes way, way back. How could I bring to the surface in a 10-15 minute talk the amazing places that once lived and breathed on Staten Island, all of which are now gone?

One of the panel members described how Staten Island, indeed, had many entrepreneurs, but they were "off the books." The numbers that they gave in the hundreds were for people who would sell "loosie" cigarettes on the sidewalk, or people that would shine shoes, but they would not remember the real Black entrepreneurs who would have a pickup truck to drive about picking up from the sidewalk metal or objects to salvage. They did not mention the Black entrepreneurs who ran barber shops, funeral parlors, retail stores, moving businesses on Staten Island. They did not mention the Black entrepreneurs who had recently tried and failed to establish restaurants on the island.

I wondered if the Black history of Staten Island would include the African American Africans or the African African Americans. While on Staten Island I would become familiar with the African shop owner Amadou Diallo, the owner of a sportswear store in Concord. Amadou Diallo came from Guinea and had been in business for several years, but was forced to close when the store was looted during an electrical Blackout. His store on Targee Street would lose over $115,000 to theft. Would he be considered an entrepreneur? Would any Black organization have this in its files? Would Amadou Diallo have been called to talk about his life on Staten Island as an entrepreneur?

The *Advance* Columnist Judy Randall had written a number of articles about Black entrepreneurs on Staten Island. Would Marcia Lloyd be called to speak about her entrepreneurship on the island? Marcia Lloyd had a cleaning business on Staten Island called Good and Clean. It was an offshoot of a company that she operates in midtown Manhattan. Marcia Lloyd grew up on Staten Island in Port Richmond, graduating from Curtis High School. Would anyone ask Ms. Lloyd to join the panel for Black History Month? My files produced many people who tried and discontinued their business opportunities on Staten Island.

A month earlier, an article in the *Staten Island Advance* mentioned Benjamin Carr, a living Black entrepreneur whose old pickup was his vehicle for supplementing his retirement pay. Benjamin Carr was a 58 or 59 year old resident of Port Richmond on a fixed income, social security, and his old 1983 GMC pickup truck was his lifeline. Benjamin Carr was given a $2,000 fine by the city Department of Sanitation officers. His truck was taken to the impound lot in Coney Island, Brooklyn. It's still there because

Benjamin Carr does not have the money to get it out. He didn't know the law. "I wouldn't break the law, I wouldn't take a chance," Mr. Carr said. He had been picking up an old water heater to take to a recycler where he could have made about $10. "I'm just trying to make a little dollar," said Mr. Carr. "My check income does not cover all my bills. What do they want a person to do? Get on Welfare?" But Mr. Carr was one of 32 people who had been arrested for taking newspapers, cardboard, salvageable material from the sidewalk. I wondered if anyone of these entrepreneurs would be remembered in the files or archives of any organization on Staten Island. Would he appear, had they tried to contact this person? He would not be on the program.

Another failed Black entrepreneurship was Hoppin' Johns restaurant on Beach Street, now shuttered and closed. These most recent Black entrepreneurs would not be on the panel.

One of the history professors at Wagner produced a booklet about the Port Richmond section of the North Shore community; there was nothing in it about Black folks. The photo images in her book did not show the Black entrepreneurial role on the main shopping street, Richmond Avenue, which was to wash windows and machine wax the floors of the movie theaters, jewelry stores, clothing, furniture, and food shops.

While sitting in the first row waiting patiently, listening patiently, I would pass Sajda Musawwir Ladner at the coffee container. She mentioned to me very quietly that they had received my packet of information asking her to be receptive to my exhibit which had closed in Georgetown, Washington, DC. She said, quietly, "We are going to take your proposal up at our next meeting." When you have a Black skin, getting angry and having a red face is not obvious. I had known Sajda for over 50 years and the bullshit that can cross her lips so easily with an accompanying smile would leave me disappointed and frustrated, as well as angry.

Several months earlier, I found the Universal Temple of the Arts on Jersey Street closed and I sent Sadja my packet of information, a carefully packaged 3 minute color video, photo images, text and newspaper reviews regarding my show, "UNDER SURVEILLANCE," a collaboration with Harriet Lesser in Georgetown at the Parish Gallery. I did not get a response until meeting her that evening at Spiro Hall at Wagner College. When she whispered to me that, "They were going to review it," I bit hard on my lip before leaving the auditorium.

I had also spoken to others, most were white people, some were friends, that had the space, the jobs, and the ability to have my exhibit shown on Staten Island, but I never heard from them either.

Most of the speakers mentioned in the program never showed. I had supposed that Kevin Buford would be on the panel. Kevin Buford sold trinkets at the ferry terminal. The Reverend Dr. Demetrius S. Carolina Sr. would speak on the video of how wonderful his entrepreneurship was, making itself felt on Staten Island.

I tried several times to purchase a copy of the film, and although it was promised to me, it never arrived.

E. Debi Rose – A First

I was visiting Sri Lanka when my friend Jude called me to say that Debi Rose was elected "the first Black" from Staten Island to the New York City Council. Whenever I read or hear that expression "first Black" and Staten Island in the same sentence, I feel elated that we have broken another link in the stereotype chain. There had never been any Black person from Staten Island elected to any public office in my lifetime. Clearly there were white people who had come to realize that there were Black people on the island worthy of their most cherished voice, the ballot box.

I had known Debi Rose for decades and she has a long list of achievements. A few years earlier, I received a notice from her that I had been selected by the Staten Island Black Political Action Group to receive a proclamation as a Griot. I was traveling out of the country and asked my sister Inez, who lived on the island, to attend the celebration and accept the award for me. I thought that was so cool because I had never received any award or proclamation. I had lived in several African countries and had met many of the village sages and mentors. I had attained the Senegalese Fida and Kersa of the Griots and I was nearing eighty, so I had the credentials to be a Griot with a heady dose of history and experience for my home community of Staten Island.

I had known Debi Rose for perhaps 30 or 40 years. I interviewed her for my oral history project before she was elected. We had long conversations at her home in St. George and at her office at the College of Staten Island. While still in Sri Lanka, Debi sent me an e-mail invitation to her inauguration, and I congratulated and embraced her by e-mail.

It has taken white folks over 300 years to find that Black folks could do just about anything that white people could do. I also believe that W.E.B. DuBois would have made a far better president than Woodrow Wilson, but that is another story. White people have had that narrative implanted in their heads that white skin was superior to darker skin. I believe that with the emerging developing nations around the globe since the last world war that narrative has begun to change. It was imperative for me to take this crucial personal visual voyage to Staten Island in 2011.

F. The Snug Harbor Gala

My last and final evening on Staten Island would be to attend a giant rally at the Music Hall at the Snug Harbor Cultural Center. Councilwoman Debi Rose was celebrating a special salute to trailblazers in the Black Staten Island community. At the event, sitting on stage, were a dozen Black men and women who would rise to be given enormously large proclamations. At the call to honor the Sandy Ground Historical Society, Sylvia D'Alessandro rose from her seat on the stage and Councilwoman Rose said that her committee was in the audience. Several women then stood and applauded Sylvia D'Alessandro. I wondered if any one of them would occupy any position on the Board of Sandy Ground Historical Society. Sylvia D'Alessandro had been the President of the organization for decades. Her daughter had been President for a short time; a very few others might Chair the organization briefly, but in the Sandy Ground Historical Society, like the NAACP, the Presidency had become a meritocracy. There were no Treasurers, no Secretaries, and no Vice Presidents. It was sad, so very sad, to see, to listen, to watch.

Ms. Jeanine Otis was the Master of Ceremonies before Debi Rose gave the presentations. Ms. Otis conducted an exchange with the audience on Black History trivia, throwing out questions and soliciting answers, and two white council members sitting in front of me immediately stood and slipped out the side door during one of the bursts of overwhelming applause from the audience.

During Black History Month, on that weekend of February 2011, I attended many of the seminars, the gospel extravaganzas, the award celebration, and the salutes to Black History Month at Wagner High School. The Staten Island branch of the National Association for the Advancement of Colored People, NAACP, would honor Black female police officers from the Staten Island precincts.

The aged doyenne of Black History Month, Evelyn King, was in the Silver Lake Nursing Home—she would die there a month later.

The celebration no longer had the factual journal that would be passed out each Black History Month day called *The Sojourner, Freedom's Journal*. The white man who has been a part of the Staten Island NAACP for decades, Richard Mudgett, would not be there. I asked about him; someone said that he had died. But I noticed that the NAACP Secretary was another Mudgett, Joseph Mudgett, whom I assumed was Dick Mudgett's son. Edward C. Josey, the President, had spent over 40 years at the helm. There were Betty Bellamy, Ella Mae Clark, and Helen Settles, long-term NAACP members. The Fellowship Baptist Church choir and Victorious Praise Dancers performed, as did the St. Phillip's Baptist Church Combined Choir and the Mount Sinai Youth Choir. The Keynote Speaker was Kathleen Barrett-Layne, the pastor of Reach Out and Touch Ministries.

It was sad for me to be there, to witness the slowly disintegrating performances started so many, many years ago. It seemed as though the coming together would be to salute someone, some organization, and to finally sing together, Lift Every Voice and Sing, the words by James Weldon Johnson. A sadness would come over me but I needed to leave finally this sad, sad, continuation of Black History Month.

The NAACP would give Image Awards at this annual gospel extravaganza to a dozen Black female police officers on Staten Island. It turned out afterward that the trip to Staten Island had lots of drama but not much substance. My friends would tease me about my visits, which seemed like a "home-sweet-home" obsession. How could I explain my moral ballast in returning time and time again? Few people understood the obsession and even I could not capture the puzzle for easy explanation. This Black History Month would be a finale. There are many people living there now with no memory of what came before, neither its history not its culture.

Having allowed three or four days to see the Black History Month activities, I went to the Silverlake Nursing Home on Castleton Avenue to visit an old friend, Bill Givens. Bill Givens was a friend of many, many, years, from the time of the Civil Rights struggles. Bill was in pretty bad shape; he had kidney trouble and was on dialysis. I felt he was someone that I should see; I had this prescient feeling that it would be my last visit with Bill. When I visited Bill at Silverlake, he suggested I go see Evelyn King. She was there, one floor below, he said. Evelyn King was a highly respected old-time Staten Island *doyenne*, an historian, a mentor, and a teacher for decades on Staten Island.

Evelyn King's body, the Black face taut, the skin shrunken, was curled into a ball on a hallway bed. I quietly said "Evelyn, this is Cleve. This is Cleve Overton." I touched the bones under her skin, she briefly moved her eyelids. I asked the nurse in charge if she knew who this lady was. She didn't, and I found myself beginning to tell her and my voice attracted attention on the ward. When I began to tell her about her charge, Evelyn King, her eyes quivered. I didn't know if it was anger, rage, or disgust, at seeing this body, at what had become of one of the premier figures of past generations on Staten Island and her connection to the very last slaves on Staten Island. I spoke again. "Evelyn." There were only slight eye movements. I desperately wanted to ask her about her books and records and family files, if they were now put in a place for safe keeping, for the future and education. And at her usual seat at the NAACP annual at Wagner High School, Evelyn King would be missing.

I looked at my notebook and I found something that was sent to me. It was from Moctar Toumbo, a Muslim. He sent me a prayer, and his initial comments were about my seeming depression, but the prayer is this:

O Allah! It is with your help that I struggle, move, and walk.

O Allah! I beg of you in this journey virtue, piety, and deeds which are acceptable to you.

O Allah! Make our journey easy and shorten for us its distance.

O Allah! You are the companion in the journey and the guardian protector of the household.

O Allah! I seek refuge in you from the difficulties of this journey and from the disagreeable sights and from the unpleasant return to my wealth, health, household, and children.

    Brother Moctar Toumbou.

Chapter 6

SANDY GROUND

As a Staten Islander, I have devoted a number of years trying to document the history of Black Americans on Staten Island. A chronology of this would take several volumes, and because of its unique nature, it would probably not be complete in all details. At this writing I hope to bring those concerned up to speed on this transition, from its beginnings to the present. From mimeograph hand cranked machines to electronic copy machines we now have the ability today to gather large amounts of material research and data. The ability to have all this comes with the assumptions that it is factual and correct, transparent and correct, it allows us to filter out emotionalism and ideology, like telling the future. My years of writing this book have been to get a decade long list of data to get my personal grip on the island where I was born. I admit I have entered on this with a skeptical, frame of mind, however reading the documents that make up this work I can say that I have remained close to the truths and confessions of being human to speak.

The idea was first spelled out by Mrs. Drusilla Poole and her husband Archibald Poole, who were then said to be the most knowledgeable people about the history of Black Staten Island - this was in the latter part of 1994 – she died soon afterwards. The ideal of a study did not die, and researchers at the Staten Island Institute of Arts and Sciences (SIIAS) formed a committee to seek funding. On March 16, 1970, Gail Schneider and I (aka Cleve), co-owner of the Potter's Wheel studio, along with members of the SIIAS, invited members of the community to view a 35MM color slide presentation in the Museum's auditorium. The list of Staten Islanders who joined in this effort was large – a broad spectrum of people came together. In the spring of 1970, the NYC Urban Corps approved the "Black Man on Staten Island" Project. Eight students were assigned from the College of Staten Island for summer work on the project.

Dr. Sonia Ragir learned of the project and developed a Free Black Historical dig in Sandy Ground. Gail Schneider, then archivist at the Institute, along with Cleve Overton, made a grant proposal in 1971 to the National Endowment for the Humanities. It was approved in late 1971 for $35,000. Gail Schneider wrote to George Pratt, pledging cooperation from the College of Staten Island and the Afro-American Institute. The following summer, Dr. George Cox worked with six interns on extensive interviews of local Blacks.

The Staten Island Advance ran an editorial that inspired Dr. Mary Meade, a member of the board of education, to propose that the project be adapted for Port Richmond High School. A joint participation between the board of the SIIAS and the College of Staten Island was made in January, 1972. Dr. Cox, Cleve Overton, and David Smith began the program at Port Richmond High School.

In April, 1972, the National Endowment suggested that the Institute supply equity funds to match those accrued by the Board of Education. The SIIAS approved an allotment of $4,550 to be sent to Washington, DC. The amount reflected the expenditures by the Institute for the project.

During the academic year of 1973/1974, I worked with five Urban Corps workers assigned to the project, along with Jane Ryder, Eugene Arnold, and Bill Givens, Natalie Surving, Richard Surving, Tim O, Martin and many others as advisors. The funding was minimal, and the concentration was on oral history. A videotape workshop was held at the Port Richmond library, its director assisted to a great degree in facilitating the event.

SIIAS contacted EXXON Corporation for additional funding. The funding director in Manhattan, Mr. Kingsley, visited the island and met with George Maginley, Bill Givens, Gail Schneider, and Cleve Overton.

The project was delayed because no students were assigned the following year. This was a serious blow, but materials were purchased through the Endowment Grant funds to continue the oral history interviews. Since the tapes are transcribed (although saved for future study), the transcriptions were first made in writing and then typed, a labor and time intensive effort at a time when there were no computers.

Dr. Touster, then acting president of College of Staten Island, suggested bringing the project into the open as an independent study for a continued source of students. Proposals were submitted to the Bicentennial Corporation and the Staten Island Council on the Arts. Drs. Ragir and Swiderski made substantial finds in the Sandy Ground area. It was Dr, Richard Swiderski a Richmond College Professor who I remember speaking only when necessary who said, "There is more history right here under your feet '. It took a many visits to Sandy Ground before excavations began when I understood his words.

At this writing I have difficulty struggling with the context of weaving through the decades of data, to find the significant correlations for this effort to tell the story, or stories.

Giving birth is difficult and the project "The Black Man On Staten Island" was an act of giving birth and a voice to many Staten Islanders ..... too many to mention here without disrespecting their involvement. The focus, however, was on Sandy Ground and its living descendants and those that had passed away, and those still living there.

It's 1970, Gail Schneider and I armed with recorders are in Sandy Ground, there was never a signpost that read Sandy Ground or even Bogardus Corners, or Little

Africa, Dogpatch or Harrisville, or Rossville. What everyone simply seemed to know was that this was the place where the colored people lived. On this first visit we conducted the first interviews for the Black Man on Staten Island Project. We audio taped them and took photographs, which I hope at this writing survive among the archived resources of the Sandy Ground Historical Society. The first interview was of Miss Flossie Henry, a black woman in her late eighties living in Sandy Ground. Miss Henry was a small slight woman, her delicate features suggested some Native American extraction, her mind and focused and sharp. She told of her parents, James and Elizabeth Landin, who were originally from Snow Hill Maryland and both of whom had Native American Blood. Flossie Henry was a living example of a vibrant oral history of Sandy Ground and Staten Island. I listened, and recorded her voice, while Gail took notes and asked questions. Miss Henry told of the difficulty of growing crops in the sandy soil. She said that the reason that they didn't starve was because pigs, goats and chickens bred in abundance, and strawberries grew easily in the sandy soil. She did not sound bitter or ashamed to recount the difficulties or the pleasures. Flossie recalled that Sandy Ground was not a utopia. Her mother kept her from attending school until she was seven years old for fear of her delicate, small framed child could not outrun the Whites who threw stones at the Black kids from Sandy Ground at the nearby school in Kreisherville.

Her brother, Everett Henry, eventually became the first Black school teacher on Staten Island. She said she learned the value of education when the oyster men were unable to find work after the pollution of Raritan Bay and the nearby harbor closed down the oyster beds. Some would ask for work at the nearby clay beds, no colored ever worked there. Flossie Henry was five years old in 1897 when the new church, now on Bloomingdale Road was completed . She told of carrying bibles and books from the old church to the new church, built on property purchased for $650 dollars. She remembers fractures in the close knit community, and the churches were the net that held together the fabric of the Black families. The community survived the splits and came together under the spiritual guidance of churchmen and elders. Elders she remembers were Bishop, Henman, Cooley, Purnell, Landin. The Rossville African Methodist Episcopal Zion Church (AME) the church remains today on Bloomingdale Road.

The next interview was of "Pop" Pedro, born in Sandy Ground in 1881. Pop was always ready to set-a-spell and recall the old days of Sandy Ground. Tapping his leg and foot he would sing "Swing them gals, round and round boys!!" and other square dance songs from the oystering days". They reconstructed their childhoods from memory. Pop Pedro recalled the annual bar-b-ques that drew whites and blacks from every corner of Staten Island. Pop Pedro had eight children, and his home was directly across the street from the AME Zion Church

Pop Pedro was remembered and called the unofficial historian of Sandy Ground, and he lived to be 107 years old.

Next to be interviewed was Joseph Bishop, an easy going soft spoken man with a ready smile. He always seemed to be wearing the same tattered baseball cap. His grandfather had migrated to Sandy Ground from Snow Hill, Maryland as did many of the original settlers here. He was still operating the family owned blacksmith shop founded by his father William Bishop in 1888 as stated by the sign over the front door. Joe

236

Bishop did not have the bulging muscles on expects on a blacksmith. He was slight but wiry, his carriage erect. Joe was one of five children and lived in the rear of the shop and simply did his thing. His works in wrought iron gates fences and window grills are unique, but I don't think he was ever awarded any artistic grants. Joseph Bishop was a delightful man – his blacksmith's shop the center of the community after the AME Zion Church. His workshop was on Bloomingdale Road, and his iron work was still standing at that time. Black/White relationships took many forms. Joe Bishop told us about the credit arrangements between the Black residents and the White store owners, the Bogardus family, some of whom lived on Bloomingdale Road They called it the "tick" system. For families unable to pay cash at the time of a store purchase, the merchant wrote up the charges on his Léger. The system had its advantages and it's disadvantages. For example, the customer did not receive a bill at the time for each item at purchase, so when the total bill summarizing the "ticks' was presented to the Sandy Grounder at the end of the month, the customer had nothing to compare to the statements for accuracy. Joe said that people in the community felt they were overcharged more often than not. Many recognized that education was the most important tool with which to deal with these problems, especially in the waning days of the oyster industry. Trades and hand skills were becoming less valued, and soon it became evident that higher education was necessary. Black men were never hired at the brick making clay pits, Balthazar Kreischer hired men that emigrated from Europe, he built homes for his workers who had to have wives and set aside a portion of their salary which was to support the church and pay for pew seats that he expected to be filled each weekend. I realized that when one culture dominates another it brings it's own literature, it's own language, it's own religion, and it's own architecture. Blacks "knew their place" and never asked, Black men had to leave their families and cross the river to New Jersey in search of work. What stress did to the families, we will never know.

The body makes no distinction between the immediate in-your-face stress and the chronic in your mind stress. I knew in my own prescient way that Black people living on this ground lived a very difficult, stressful, and traumatic life.

I would find that my own up and down erratic movements, the body's reaction to stress can become chronic, pernicious if it continues for a long time. My visits to Sandy Ground gave me the opportunity to look across the river and feel the place and the language, I knew nothing of the oyster raking and planting, or eating them, as a matter of fact I don't even like them.

Tempers flared from time to time and it was the church elders that held the community together when Whites living in the community rented homes to Blacks at rates that were living side by side. The Bogardus store at Bloomingdale Road that was the center of activity, they were White and had lived in Sandy Ground for decades. The second fire devastated the new store, and it was under suspicion as to it's origin. Whites and Blacks traded items at Bogardus, and purchased goods from the store, it was a needed resource to barter and to buy. The fracture in race relations began to show after the fire, was it an accident, or purposely set, both communities quietly set about to close ranks, each blaming the other. Tottenville was now the closest place to buy provisions for the community.

Joe Bishop was so knowledgeable, casual and social and his comments rolled into the stream of his life, he worked among Whites on the south shore for many years and his iron work and his personality still admired by those who remember him and had the pleasure of setting a spell to listen to him.

Listening to Joe Bishop was the first place we took occasional tourists or researchers who asked at the Staten Island Institute about Sandy Ground. He was the unofficial spokesperson in Sandy Ground until his shop was mysteriously burned to the ground in 1982.

That was a tragic loss, and end to a landmark, an era, and the Sandy Ground community, from which it never recovered. Joseph Bishop died four years later at 81 years of age.

He had donated his land and meager savings to the Sandy Ground Historical Society and the Rossville AME Zion Church. The SGHS promised to make an effort to rebuild the blacksmith shop.

An architect Anthony Tung made a stop at the site and said he would do preliminary work pro bono. The idea was to make a new blacksmith shop the home office of the SGHS, I had hopes that this rebuilding project would happen. It never did. I never knew if any other Black forbearers gave their property to the SGHS or to the church after their deaths, to be preserved for future generations, there is no transparency, and asking would be fruitless to find the answer what property still exists undeveloped.

On January 2, 1987 after a long illness, Gail Schneider died at her home in Kerhonkson, N.Y. Her letters to me during that time are intact in my files, the edges tinted brown, but her words will forever be with me. She was a mentor and dear friend who taught me to listen and to see. Her name is listed in the annual **Who's Who Among American Women** for her work as an archivist. Her list of accomplishments covers many pages. Gail Schneider's passing was another major reason for me to leave Staten Island, and go to Pennsylvania.

The hopes and promises to preserve the history and legacy, are long gone to development, awaiting the exit of those few left who tuck messy emotions away, never " putting our business in the street." And off the record those who speak will not do so on the record !! We no longer believe in ourselves. The young the best, the brightest, are all gone elsewhere. At this writing I ask, why did we give it all up? I look about and see a new economically integrated community, of half million dollar Mc Mansion homes, belonging to Whites and surrounded by a handful of Black "hangers on." The Blacks have moved elsewhere, except for a few isolated mavericks who persist in spite of it all, but who are not unified in purpose. The principals and practices that held the Black community together around the church has failed. There is no survival or success here.

I received a call from the president of the SGHS asking me to go to the site and remove anything of value, and to cover the old forge with a canvas to preserve it until a decision was made to rebuild. I moved many items to the home of the legal representative Carol Per Lee Plumb, whose great grandfather also had a farm in Sandy Ground, I stored items at my home in Mariners Harbor, and some items at the Museum.

The NYC Urban Corps workers under the direction of Dr, Sonia Ragir had chosen sites to dig. I knew nothing of how to approach or choose an archeological site, very often we did not know who owned the property selected. I did know and remember that Dr Richard Swiderski said there was more history beneath our feet . there was no money for tools or materials, where it came from I do not remember, my guess would be the College of S.I.

Most students came from the College and all were White students. Enthusiastic, budding archaeologists eager to find about what would be found in Sandy Ground. It was important to find the footprints of foundations and outhouses. Depressions and mounds, I simply followed directions. We found sites that had not been pilfered, or plowed or developed. Finding many arrow heads was an indication native Americans, had lived here, ceramic shards, and "jacks." We knew then that many people played the ancient game, a hook for buttons, a thimble, lots of broken pottery and bones made up the largest part of the finds after colorful glass bottles. Still the students dug and scraped, sifted and I guess we found salvation by digging and shoveling plain old dirt. I have filed away letters asking to dig, never receiving an answer. I knew I would never convince the church or the SGHS to give us permission to dig. The small sections were about 4x4 square to dig and hand sift sections and go down at least two feet because we had to cover it back up after a days work. Looking up the word "petro glyph " was our place holder or finder and we could then tell if someone else were here looking or digging, it would also give an incomplete site later if needed. I guessed that an academic would take a more utilitarian approach to excavating. Fingernails were damaged, scraped knees, unprincipled hunters of history. When one site was completed we went on to another. We had no precise dates or maps, the Sadie Collins property would not be cleaned or cleared for decades later, it was private property but left to the seasons to decay. It was a simple reason to avoid the site, some Blacks living nearby didn't bother us, we did not know if we were on city or private property, we had no hassle at all. Poison ivy and mosquitoes were the only pests we encountered. At this time it was clear that nature had triumphed.

The problems were for me to drive out to Sandy Ground and wait until the digs were complete for the day and load the excavated findings and tools and drive back home with my truck. At one time we decided to hide the tools so that I did not have to carry them to Mariners Harbor, after a bit of bad weather, and more than a week later, we found the entire lot of tools and sifters and grates had disappeared from the hiding place. The work continued by others at the Museum Archives, students worked at the museum archives three days a week studying maps New York State and Federal Census records, drawings, church records and personal letters and photos, health and birth and death records from the files in the Surrogates office.

On or about 1976, members from the AME Zion Church decided to form their own organization, and in 1979, it came into being as the Sandy Ground Historical Society (SGHS). The officers were Yvonne Taylor, Sylvia Harris, Lucille Herring, Wanda Butler, Elmore Taylor, and Ralph Cooper, who along with Gail Schneider, resigned. The Board of Trustees included Richard Dickenson, Reverend Ellis Freeman, Deldridge Hunter, Marie Spicer, Denise Pedro and Carol Per Lee Plumb. At that time I gave my paintings and pottery of Staten Island clay to the organization, I had naively envisioned a grand opening of a grand office building to house it; that was a long time ago.

In 1982 Yvonne Taylor was elected President of the Sandy Ground Historical Society. The next year 1983 Sylvia Harris became president and she has held the chair ever since. Letterheads came to me in 1988 announcing her daughter Julie Ojelade as president. I was never noticed of elections or changes in the directors. When I wrote asking for information I was told that my membership had been cancelled. I wanted in.

I voted for Sylvia Harris to become president of the Sandy Ground Historical Society in 1983 in the basement of the Rossville AME Zion Church. I felt the organization needed a much more vocal president. Her outspoken call for action to halt the destruction of Sandy Ground, first by the 1963 fire that destroyed many homes, and the grasp of land speculators and developers that were buying any and all vacant land in Sandy Ground and the surrounding community. Her call for a Land Acquisition and Restoration Fund I saw as a bold voice, and the need for Staten Islanders and Sandy Grounders to join in the call for concerted action on an island wide basis for help. I felt good about being there, seeing the development of a dream, working with Black and White people.

I was giddy and very happy to be chosen to be master of ceremonies at the 5th Annual Sandy Ground Proclamation Day dinner in 1983 honoring Joseph Bishop at the Pavilion on the Terrace in New Brighton. The year before, I had been given a special award by my dear friend Gail Schneider. I was walking on water after that surprise award, and the guest speaker was the New York Television reporter personality Bob Teague.

Milestones were being reached, Sandy Ground would be listed in the National Register of Historic Places, Sandy Ground was one of the oldest consistently inhabited places by Black Americans in the United States, for more than 175 years. The president at that time Yvonne Taylor realized that commitment to the cause was the key to success, she said that weather physical or historical this commitment would enable Staten Islanders to feel pride and jubilation in all the accomplishments. During the past year the SGHS received grants that would enable the organization to conduct historical research, not only about Sandy Ground, but also the entire Black community on Staten Island. The materials gathered and recorded as a result of the research would aid future generations in gaining a deeper insight into their heritage.

One of the priorities would be to gain a home repository in the Sandy Ground community for all the materials collected thus far. Ms Taylor said "our associations with other historical, educational and cultural groups on Staten Island has broadened, and we have reached out into the Staten Island community to disseminate information via video tape, and slide presentations and lectures. Her message went on to say that it was extremely important to create an awareness of the contributions of Blacks to the development of the country.

The goal of the Black Man on Staten Island Project was much broader, organized under an open transparent organization the goal was to open the entire island to its black citizens with assistance from whites who would join the historic lexicon to focus on slavery, the abolitionist movement, the civil rights movement, music sports, and entertainment. My own life became unraveled and I would begin to run, to Africa.

The postal service in 1990 Senegal was never swift, to mail a letter and to receive a letter was aggravating. But I did receive a letter with a front page of the Staten Island Advance, the local newspaper from a friend who knew of my interest in Sandy Ground. In October 1992 the Advance headlines read "Sandy Ground Society celebrates acquisition". The front page had a large photo of the society members Carol

Per Lee Plumb, Lucille Herring, Yvonne Taylor and Elmore Taylor. It stated that the society had received grants from the city and state as well as $15,000 from the estate of Joseph Bishop. Donations came from Brian Reardon, State Senator John Marchi, and Bear Stern. Mobil Oil which has a large depot and tank farm on Staten Islands south shore, contributed materials to the group, and the NYC Department of Cultural Affairs promised to help with the society's educational programs. With the help from the benefactors the article went on, the SGHS acquired its new headquarters from the Stapleton Realtors, Bartels and Eleford.

I was really happy to read that, and I was planning to return to the states in about a month, and that would be my first stop. When I saw the house at 1538 Woodrow Road and looked around the community I was shocked, I thought it looked like a firetrap that would go up mysteriously some night, torched by the night riders who I had always suspected torched the blacksmith shop a few hundred yards away. Construction was booming, builders were digging foundations, huge trucks were hauling dirt, they were quietly renaming the town "Rossville", the historical name for the area where Sandy Ground is located is "Woodrow". Looking at the building I was not sure it was a two story wooden house or a one and a half story building. It was built in the late 1800's and it was clear that adititions had been added several times.

I thought with dismay that it would need extensive repairs and remodeling. (This is the new headquarters of the Sandy Ground Historical Society?). The house was not fenced, there was no sidewalk. Little did I know that a survey would be locating the house in a tight space only inches from a new road to be built soon afterward. Rossville, or Woodrow, was now becoming the home ground of choice for people from other boroughs looking for space. Construction companies eagerly began to buy land in Sandy Ground that had tripled in value. I went to the site of the old blacksmith shop a few hundred yards away on Woodrow Road. A white homeowner had bought a large home next to the burnt out remains of the old blacksmith shop, which had become overgrown with tall weeds and cluttered with dumped debris. The canvas had rotted away and the roofless home in the rear was an eyesore. Tangled and twisted strips of metal lay rusted where they had fallen after the fire. The open water well was an accident waiting to happen for some hapless child wandering through these woods to fall into and die. The white homeowner saw me and asked me if I knew what was going to happen with this eyesore. I pointed out the SGHS office a few hundred yards away, I left a message at the SGHS office about the condition. In February, 1998, after more than 30 years, the city of New York cleared the final remains of the Bishop blacksmith shop. The property is again a weed-strewn lot, unfenced and still an eyesore, directly across the street from the new Public School 56.

An Oral History: The Story of Hettie

My personal trips to Sandy Ground included walking about the graveyard and meeting several times with the lady named Hettie. According to my notes, we met by accident or, as I would like to think, fate, in early 1967 in the Sandy Ground graveyard on Crabtree Avenue.

She was old; I never did have the nerve to ask her age. It would have been rude, so I didn't. At one time, she would say she was 87. It was difficult to understand some of her words because she did not have a full set of teeth. I learned much later that she did have a set of false teeth but they hurt, and did not fit. She may have been five foot, five inches and probably weighed about 130 pounds. She walked with her back straight and shoulders back, and wore a dress and a shawl that came to her ankles, soft brown leather shoes and a sky blue felt hat covering her gray/white hair; her glasses were large, with tortoise shell frames that covered most of her small, age-lined face. I wanted to know who she was and I wanted to see her full face and hair, was she a black person or a white person. I finally realized that she was both, mixed race. How to ask? I didn't, for fear of scaring her off.

She was alone, her black coat covered what seemed to be several print dresses, and she was wearing well-used brown gloves to dig shallow holes and plant small squares of geraniums at tombstones in the small black community cemetery. When I said I had been here in this cemetery many times before, she braced and looked at me. "This is a GRAVEYARD. You young folks change what you don't understand, and call it something else, this is a graveyard!" I erased the word in my note book. I watched quietly for a long time, there was a single unpaved road into the graveyard, and a car which I took to belong to this lady. She pulled the wooden tray of flowers to each stone with a string as she dug with a claw-like tool to carefully place each one. I didn't want to frighten her and said, "These are colorful plants, but will they live here in April?" In fact, this part of the world is known for its pharmacological cornucopia. Every shrub or weed is a botanical miracle: some weeds were for melancholy, some bushes were chills or bone pain, green flat leaves for intestinal gas, some for diarrhea.

"Only things the squirrels and rabbits won't eat or dig up," without looking up at me, "Water 'em good for a few days and they do the rest." I knew nothing about horticulture and was trying to think of something clever to say, something like dust to dust, make good soil. "Do you know people buried here?" I asked. "Yep. Mangins, Bishops, and Hunters, Roaches and Landins, Henrys, Purnells and Cooleys, Herrings and Pedro. Would you go and fetch that pail of water in my car?"

It was an old car, a well-kept four-door Chevy with imitation wood siding. Inside were three five-gallon cans of water. They were heavy; I could only get them out one at a time and I wondered how the old lady had managed to fill them and load them in there. I started to tilt a can over to pour water on the planted flowers, she said "Stop," looking at me for the first time. She then used a small saucepan to carefully water each plant. I had established what I thought was a reasonable amount of time to continue to speak to her and asked her name. "Name's Hettie, and who are you? You have kin buried here?" she asked, pushing her glasses to her nose.

"Probably," I said, "Can't be sure though. I come here to the cemetery to find out if I could find folks to speak to for an oral history project."

"I don't know much about any rural speakers here, "This is a graveyard." I did not correct her.

"There's a lot of history here, folks don't take care of this place, no longer care for the dead."

At the time I had nothing more than words, no papers, no photos, to show or to give her, I was entirely in another place. The Black Man Project at that time was only a dream. Blacks and whites on the north shore talked about it; teachers, workers, artists, librarians, Wall Street people, Unitarians, Catholics, and Jews, but there was no organization, no office, no phone number, nor any money to go beyond the tentative brainstorming thoughts from the museum and a mixed use art studio. The initial glimpses of the project did not seem like preliminary forays into a deep exploration of the black island community. The group would eventually grow and evolve, but there was no notion at the outset that we would discover a world within this place and Staten Island. I realized that the older generation could only engage in sporadic and scattershot efforts of memories, their private repositories remain intact sometime freed only by old age. Often the stories are amusing fables, or hard fights for survival.

She walked ahead, talking softly to the headstones. "I have no memories of all my ancestors, and my grandma died six or seven years before I was born, but I heard many times that she was a fierce, hard-headed woman who did what she wanted, starting with when she married my grandfather. There isn't much to see here now, most of em passed on. They all sleeps below us, right now."

I did not interrupt to ask questions about her parents, as long as she spoke to me and those who could no longer hear her speak. Little did I know that I had entered into my first oral history interview.

It was noon and she was going to have lunch with a friend Mrs. Munro, she lives over on Woodrow, and said I could ride along with her over to Bloomingdale road. She drove slowly, carefully, never going beyond second gear, while talking to me and her memory's eye. "We did a lot of gardens here, there was no lines, we just cleared enough space. We had everything; we growed fig trees, grape arbors, peach trees, crape myrtle bushes ten foot tall. Mrs. Collins said it wouldn't grow up, I told her I didn't think so. She's dead now."

"Red and pink roses grow very well here, growing wild, all tangled up. That mulberry tree should have been cut back, never been trimmed after Abraham died." Standing in her once beautiful yard and gardens, she said, "We had all this fenced in, but nothing growing here now. The flowers withered and so we withered," she said without a trace of resentment. I didn't want to comment, standing straight in this unkempt place, she saw the show place garden that it once was. "When you can't keep things up, you gotta let 'em go!"

She was a philosopher without portfolio, though I suspected she would have argued the point if I had wanted to explain or attach it to her. She would share her knowledge and insight gently and at times bluntly.

"If you live long enough, it's gonna get ya. Abraham worked all his life and we built this place when they wouldn't let us move in anyplace else. He lost some fingers and I wanted to die. He just drove a team like nobody's business up there. When he lost his job we couldn't pay them Cooley's the rent on our little place down Tottenville and we up and moved here. The Cooley's was colored and white you know."

"Abraham hired a man with two horses and a big wagon; everything we owned was piled up on that wagon, furniture, clothes, his tools, everything. He put the cast iron stove on top. Them roads was so bumpity it fell off and broke one leg; he got it fixed when we got here. That wagon groaned over them ruts and mud holes, them springs just groaning. They had to stop to tie that heavy stove up there. When we got here, first thing we did was put some clay bricks under it so we could fire it up; had corn bread and rice, black eye beans and some poke salad greens right here."

"We slept here and Abraham bargained for a plot. The first night we heard katydids all night. Folks here didn't take to me right away, called me Calico. Sticks and stones, I didn't pay it no mind. Cooley's had some white blood, didn't make no difference to me 'cause I was Abraham's wife. Some called him Uncle Abe."

"He was a good man. He would fight them if he heard insults; some whites here would look the other way, when you go by, sometime a wariness you can't shake. He never did want me to go to work down in Princess Bay for them people, he had pride, we had a Singer and I did sewing, made just about everything. I did take in some washing one time though."

"The first spring came and we planted squash and potatoes, peppers and tomatoes, and we had lettuces and beans and corn. Flora liked to sow the seeds barefoot, she would straddle the row using her bare feet, sweep the dirt back over the seeds. We could just about get the garden planted in one or two days. Early July we would have snap green beans, we would sit in wickers and trim away the ends and strings. We had some chickens and some guinea hens."

"Abraham didn't go to that church: he worked on the steeple and he made them new doors right there in the basement. They didn't much like my skin color no way, when he heard it he was going to fight. Abraham was contrary, but we had a place in nine months. And he worked down at the smelting place, be more than five years now. He got sick, and we had a hospital bed put right in the living room. I waited on that man night and day. He was terrible and in pain, he would drink water to cool that pain inside. He was sick right there for two long years."

"He was a good man. I cooked and scrubbed and baked, leg of lamb, pot roast," she said, laughing, "And he was a grouch, a nasty grouch, a cheap penny-pinching grouch, he was a cranky old sick man! You had to love him to be married all those years. But he was a good man."

"He laughed, he always laughed when I told him I wanted to be a teacher. I had a good teacher, a real good teacher."

"Who was that?" I asked. "You said you never went to school."

"No, I never went to school but I had a good teacher. Mr. Everett Henry was my teacher and I can read real good."

"And this marriage business ain't all it's cracked up to be, let me tell you. Your kids grow up and move out someplace, they ain't going to be what you wanted them to be. Your father and mother die. But I'm a member of the Eastern Star, and I'm on the missionary committee. I ain't much for singing in the choir. No, this marriage wasn't all that good. I was going to leave, but my child Flora got sick and we had no medical insurance in them days. Abraham took them bills and I never saw them again."

"He was a good man, but he was a jealous man, you hadta think every time you made a move. He say, "Woman you gonna have it your way huh?" I do miss him and I go to his grave all the time to tell him that this is the best time of my life. I don't say it like that because he would just jump up from that grave and pitch such a fit! I do tell him, "Honey you're there and I'm here, an' I'm doing all right. I'm comfortable and I did all I could for you. You out of your suffering," I tell him silly stuff like that. Ol' tall, dark, and handsome Abraham. He was a jealous man, didn't want me going over to New York City, terrible folks he said, baaad human beings, over there cross the water, I guess he was scared that I would run off or something, And I ain't never been there yet. He ain't buried over there, on Clay Pit Road either. Nope, he is buried over in Carteret New Jersey."

"You miss a lot of things. I got to say if I can't have them, I can't have them so why worry about them. A lot of old people can't do stuff. You get losses - energy, sight, hearing, memory, and friends, but I'm determined and I'm not going to be like that."

"Hettie will just move on. I still get up and read the Bible and make some breakfast. When I was sick I had a woman from Medicaid come to help me. By the time she got here, I was already dressed, got the dishes done, I just do everything a bit slower."

"I don't want to drive crazy and get speeding tickets, 'cause I never had none, no accidents either. When old folks lose their license they close the book. I know it's coming but I'll adjust, gonna fight like the devil to hang on. Let them youngsters pass me, that's why they have three lanes. I don't get upset. They are so rude, but they are young and have a lot of things to do. If I lose my license, I will just get a bus schedule."

"I been visiting Mrs. Collins before she got worse. Miss, Sadie was younger than me. She had a stroke and was bound in that wheel chair. Took her one half hour to answer the doorbell!"

"I had known her for a long time, what, like fifty years? We'd get in the car and she'd give me gasoline money, can you beat that? I try to get here once a week. She had to go to a nursing home. She's losing weight, 'cause she doesn't like the food there, says it makes her sick; there is no seasoning, and they don't serve pork, or bacon, or sausage, no this and no that. Don't laugh, if you were here you couldn't stand the food either."

"She tried to walk and fell going to the bathroom when her roommate died. She doesn't want a new roommate. She says she was always an independent person. She says, if they put garbage in front of you would you eat it?"

"Sometime when I'm there, she falls asleep, and they say death is like that; you just fall away, lay down and go to sleep just like a dream. She was the only one to stand up for me when Bogardus burned down. They said it was Calico. People got kerosene at Bogardus store, in bottles and cans, He had a big tank a ways back of the store and people filled their own cans and things, let it drip all the way to the store. It was bad and they had to leave them messy cans on the front steps where people smoked corn cobs and banged out the pipes on the stairs. That's where it started."

"Fire ran down the stairs and back to that big tank, fired it up and the whole store, the ground was so soaked it went right back to Bogardus, burnt up everything. Blacksmith Bishop knew this, he was there, trying to haul water; we had no fire brigade at that time anywhere close. People sat at Bogardus all the time talking, waiting, just setting there, smoking tobacco, ashes still lit on the ground. The smell of that fire and smoke was around here a long time. Last time I heard my name, Calico. "That Calico done that!" I did not do that. Why didn't they like me? I was attractive, I knew it. My shoes and my hat and my pocketbook all matched. I live in New Jersey now, Asbury Park."

I asked, "How can I reach you, Hettie?"

"If you just hush up and listen." "Hush up and just listen" was a phrase I had heard many times and from many people. It was one of those old folks' sayings, directions on life that came from many sources. I was "hard headed" so that many secret or overt codes came only after painful struggle.

I asked her last name, she paused and waited, "You can send mail to True Vine Baptist Church, 21 Dewitt Avenue, Asbury Park, New Jersey. Mrs. Hettie May Henman Cooley."

I later learned that Hettie had an accident, was forced off the road by some fool going nowhere fast, and then spent a year in a wheelchair. Often drifting through murky depths of her mind, she never complained one bit, never one word of complaint crossed her lips, her condition was hers, and she would bear it. "I'm smart enough to know how lucky I am. I remember them all and they will always be with me. When I have a friend I'm always with them. Of course, a lot of them have all passed away."

A pencil-written note book was not fast enough to keep abreast of the simple wisdom of her age. As I hastily scribbled to quote her, there was nothing platitudinous or flowery, or stogy, mean spirited, or cynical, no pompous aphorisms impatiently waiting to be carved into stone.

Hettie's wisdom was home grown, and all I had to do was hush up and listen to what would never be taught in schools. There was no woulda, coulda, shoulda; she led a worthwhile full life. "My life has been beautiful. To say that and believe that, we got up and did things when we were young. I never get depressed to tell the truth. If it's cloudy outside and you don't feel like cleaning the house, then go bake something. Keep busy, don't fuss with regrets, you see you have to not focus on the bad."

GENTRIFICATION

Race and class and gentrification mean many things to many people. My view of the issue in Staten Island, and Sandy Ground in particular, is that Blacks will move out and whites will move in. We saw all of this happen in a few short years. The first Blacks to sell their properties will do so because they want the money, and others will sell later because they will not be able to pay the higher real estate taxes brought about by the new development. Others will make no decision and lament gentrification.

Gentrification is here in all its glory. The standard script for gentrification is "White in, Black out." These few shotgun-type houses that are still Black-owned on Bloomingdale Road will stay that way for now, only because the residents have no resources to move and are too old to begin again elsewhere. The homes of the remaining Blacks are now unattractive eyesores in a place surrounded by new construction. They are eyesores only because they have not been well maintained. The homes could be a living statement and an historic site for us to see how this Black community lived in the past. It would require the will of the community as well as the resources of the Staten Island historical and cultural institutions. I doubt that it will happen.

There is a long-standing story that, "We Blacks buy what we want .... and beg for what we need." The State Attorney General's office of public information states that the SGHS has over $350,000 in assets. Yet, the Society has never been moved to clear the rubble and debris, or fence in their valuable property a few doors away. The Bishop property is on Woodrow Road, deeded to the Society by Joseph Bishop at his death in 1986. Sixteen years after the 1982 fire in February, 1998, the president of the SGHS, at the time Julie Ojelade, said she was not notified of the City's action to clear the site and that the Society was hoping the City would do an archeological dig there. The City cleared the property and sent the SGHS a bill for $5,865. The president stated, "We have no idea how we will get the money." The city responded that they will put a lien on the property and sell it at auction.

No one I asked has any information on this most valuable piece of land. But I am sure that developers are looking closely at it, and plotting how to acquire it. I also suspect that developers pressure city low and mid-level officials to make it difficult for the SGHS and the A.M.E. church to continue, so that, without strong will and legal clout, the property will go back to the City and be auctioned off. A similar fate awaits the last few Black-owned houses when their elderly owners die. I wait despondently, because it will mean another historical piece of the Black community has gone into a developer's hands without a whimper. The SGHS office has never had a sidewalk or wheelchair access ramp, while new construction to the left and right of the office has new sidewalks. Another newspaper story reads that the Rossville A.M.E. Zion Church has been presented a bill for $8,000 for a sidewalk they did not request. Blacks here lack the unity, will, and legal clout, and Whites, many transplanted from other boroughs, don't care.

The Rossville A.M.E. Zion Church and the SGHS and the two Bay men Cottages are the last visible parts left of the Black community. There seem to be no verbal or visual connections between them. The fragmented parts of a heritage desperately trying to survive in the 21st Century. The white community looks on in amusement.

This area, once rich in tradition, is fast disappearing. The failure of Blacks to secure a foothold in Sandy Ground was not "E Pluribus Unum." Out of many, one. But in this case, "Out of many, none." Sandy Ground's matriarchs and patriarchs must rest uneasily in the cemetery on Crabtree Avenue. It was their voices and direction that gave birth to the cohesiveness and brotherhood in the past, and all has been lost. If there is no history to protect, it gets plowed under. There is no museum on this island that will mention the African American contribution to Staten Island's economic and cultural development. Borough Hall in Saint George will consign a table display on Black History Month each year. Other articles and documents, voices and memorabilia, languish unseen by the public in the wood frame building which is the SGHS.

The historic event that had the most devastating effect on Sandy Ground and contributed to the continuing demise of the community was the devastating fire that destroyed many Black and White family homes in April 1963. It began as a small brush fire on the North Shore 6 miles away. The fire department hesitated to bring in reinforcements; they had seen this kind of fire before. The fire was blown south by ever-increasing winds from the north pushing the roaring fire in front of it with no resistance. By late afternoon, fire departments had a manpower force of more than 2,000 men. But it was too late. The conditions were perfect – a hot, dry season and low water pressure. Some reports were of no water at all on the South Shore. The Black community was now reduced to less that one dozen homes. Residents were depressed and pressured by others to sell their still smoldering ruins and move away. At that time, I felt the need to do more to memorialize the past for the future, and made efforts to become more involved in the day-to-day operations of Sandy Ground.

I received a call from the president of the SGHS asking me to go to the site and remove anything of value, and to cover the old forge with a canvas to preserve it until a decision was made to rebuild. I moved many items to the home of the legal representative Carol Per Lee Plumb, whose great grandfather also had a farm in Sandy Ground, I stored items at my home in Mariners Harbor, and some items at the Museum.

The Sandy Ground Historical Society had a Board of Trustees, Officers and Directors. President, Vice President' Recording Secretary, Financial Secretary, Treasurer, Parliamentarian. And a list of Members. The original White lady member would leave, The Annual Sandy Ground Dinner Commemorative Journals would stop. The presidents message would cease.

Many others sat in on the board of SGHS, Denise Pedro, Lucille Herring, Richard Dickenson, Elmore Taylor, Delridge Hunter, Dolores Morris, Marie Spicer, Julie Ojelade.

In 1982 Yvonne Taylor was elected President of the Sandy Ground Historical Society. The next year 1983 Sylvia Harris became president and she has held the chair ever since. Letterheads came to me in 1988 announcing her daughter Julie Ojelade as president. I was never noticed of elections or changes in the directors. When I wrote asking for information I was told that my membership had been cancelled. The paper formalities were always there, but one chief commanded.

The annual Sandy Ground Day Commemorative dinners would end after Sandy Ground family members were recognized, celebrated, and awarded a Proclamation from the Borough Presidents office. Only Sandy Grounders were feted at these events, no one outside the Sandy Ground community was recognized at an annual dinner at all. After the fifth Sandy Ground Proclamation Day Dinner and awards ceremonies in 1983 I left the United States to live in Niger Africa.

I remember some of the past Honorees who were, William "Pop" Pedro, James Sargent, Helen Henry, Joseph Bishop, and Vera Usry. Perhaps there were other people who did not live in Sandy Ground that were selected by the Sandy Ground Society for recognition, I do not know.

Sixteen years after the mysterious 1982 fire that burned down the blacksmith's shop and forge, in February,1998, the president of the SGHS, at the time Julie Ojelade, said she was not notified of the City's action to clear the site and that the Society was hoping the City would do an archeological dig there. The City cleared the property and sent the SGHS a bill for $5,865. Ms. Ojelade, the president, stated, "We have no idea how we will get the money." The city responded that they will put a lien on the property and sell it at auction.

No one I asked has any information on this most valuable piece of land. But I am sure that developers are looking closely at it, and plotting how to acquire it. I also suspect that developers pressure city low and mid-level officials to make it difficult for the SGHS and the A.M.E. church to continue, so that, without strong will and legal clout, the property will go back to the City and be auctioned off. A similar fate awaits the last few Black-owned houses when their elderly owners die. I wait despondently, because it will mean another historical piece of the Black community has gone into a developer's hands without a whimper. The SGHS office has never had a sidewalk or wheelchair access ramp, while new construction to the left and right of the office has new sidewalks. Another newspaper story reads that the Rossville A.M.E. Zion Church has been presented a bill for $8,000 for a sidewalk they did not request. Blacks here lack the unity, will, and legal clout, and Whites, many transplanted from other boroughs, don't care.

The Rossville A.M.E. Zion Church and the SGHS and the two Bay oystermen Cottages are the last visible parts left of the Black community. There seem to be no verbal or visual connections between them. The fragmented parts of a heritage desperately trying to survive in the 21st Century. The white community looks on in amusement.

This area, once rich in tradition, is fast disappearing. The failure of Blacks to secure a foothold in Sandy Ground was not "E Pluribus Unum." Out of many, one. But in this case, "Out of many, none." Sandy Ground's matriarchs and patriarchs must rest uneasily in the cemetery on Crabtree Avenue. It was their voices and direction that gave birth to the cohesiveness and brotherhood in the past, and all has been lost. If there is no history to protect, it gets plowed under. There is no museum on this island that will mention the African American contribution to Staten Island's economic and cultural development. Borough Hall in Saint George will consign a table display on Black History Month each year. Other articles and documents, voices and memorabilia, languish unseen by the public in the wood frame building which is the SGHS.

My return to Staten Island fifteen or more years later was primarily to write about it …. To find a closure to that chapter of my life and move on, as it were. The total deterioration of Staten Island was obvious, but my concentration on Sandy Ground is the reason for this dialogue. Sandy Ground was bleeding. The Black forebears who gave their property, always to be preserved for future generations, would bleed with the living. The hopes and promises to preserve the history and legacy, long gone to development, awaiting the exit of those few who tuck messy emotions away, never "putting our business in the street." And off the record, those who speak will not do so on the record! We no longer believe in ourselves … the young …the best and the brightest, all gone elsewhere. Why did we give it all up? I look about, and see a now economically integrated community, of hundreds of thousand dollar homes, belonging to Whites and surrounded by a handful of "hangers-on." The Black middle class has moved elsewhere, except for a few isolated mavericks who persist in spite of it all, but who are not united in purpose. The principles and practices that held the Black community together around the church has failed … no survival or success here. There were no church elders living to sound the alarm.

The hopes and promises to preserve the history and legacy, are long gone to development, awaiting the exit of those few left who tuck messy emotions away, never "putting our business in the street." And off the record those who speak will not do so on the record!! we no longer believe in ourselves. The young the best, the brightest, are all gone elsewhere. At this writing 2013 I ask, why did we give it all up? I look about and see a new economically integrated community, of half million dollar Mc Mansion homes, belonging to Whites and surrounded by a handful of Black "hangers on." The Blacks have moved elsewhere, except for a few isolated mavericks who persist in spite of it all, but who are not unified in purpose. The principals and practices that held the Black community together around the church has failed. There is no survival or success here.

A strong Black presence to head off the new influx is not possible in Sandy Ground. Most white homeowners do not use the term *Sandy Ground*, if they even know what it means. The hot housing market in NYC and the increasing lure of open space has led people to descend on this area and the entire South Shore of the island. The construction continues helter-skelter even now …. the city officials seem powerless (or disinterested) to control the construction and politicians get front page coverage on how to stop a renegade architect from making a three-home development into a plan that was originally for two homes.   New houses along Woodrow Road are example of a true McMansion mentality and architectural design, the fit into this landscape, a strange mix of Corsican Yurt huts, tall Greek columns and Monticello neo-Colonial renderings guarded by stone lions and tigers along with religious statues.

A plan was devised to keep Black home ownership in Sandy Ground, and some people approached the city and the U.S. Department of Urban Development. But the plan meant that Black homeowners, while still living there, would not realize the rising appreciation of their land value, and they rejected the idea. The issue was eventually dropped.

By 2000, giant digging machines were active day after day; water lines and sewers and foundations were dug, some illegally while the Building Department's inefficient and understaffed office looked on. One builder was stopped after putting in over 70 foundations without approval. The builder failed to get approval for removal of trees or to grade the land...or to subdivide the property. It left the SGHS building with a parcel that would be inches away from a sidewalk and a new street... SGHS never had a proper survey made, and it was too late to buy or negotiate with the builder for adequate space or land.

I would continue my research and photographs each year that I was in the U.S. so that the documentation and files would be an assist to the historical amnesia afterward.

The gentrification in Sandy Ground here of White families and businesses along the route 440 corridor are moving inland from the Raritan River. There is no racial mix here, although one might see a rare Black face waiting for a bus at times. The Black matriarchs of old Sandy Ground are buried in the old cemetery that has been recently fenced in to protect it from continued vandalism on Crabtree Road. It to will be lost in time. The ratio of Whites to Black homeowners here now is approximately 150 to 1 and rising. It is a familiar tale of gentrification which surprises no one, and this area will become one of the wealthiest on Staten Island with developments here called Platinum Ridge, Cobblestone Walk, and The Hamlet, with new homes now selling for $550,000 and more. The response from the Blacks is to get out into the suburbs, and that means move to New Jersey or upstate New York.

My view of Staten Island, this single island in the shadow of the Statue of Liberty, has been an excellent test case for me to see, witness and document. It is a microcosm, and my conclusions are by no means a simplistic answer to the United States social hierarchy that framed a continuing exclusion of others, or non-Europeans, to an oppressed status. The abstract words and proclamations ...the edicts and the political rhetoric, will never change my mind. The problem is that of skin color. We will never ever move forward until it is addressed, and people of color begin to walk through the doors of education. The starting line.

After more than 160 years no Black writers have written about this place. A gift from Gail Schneider was a book, "Up in the Old Hotel" written by a white man, Joseph Mitchell. It is a compilation of four books. In the book, Mitchell walked around Sandy Ground where he met Mr. George Hunter, the caretaker of a ramshackle cemetery, Hunter a black man lived in Sandy Ground, "The Bottom of the Harbor." This meeting resulted in the first printed recording about Sandy Ground, Staten Island in 1956. In an essay in the book titled, "The Bottom of the Harbor" Joseph Mitchell named the 20 page section, "Mr. Hunter's Grave." Another book of essays was written by a White lady Minna Wilkins. She began to write and speak to Blacks in Sandy Ground in 1940. This book is no longer available.

In 2003, a black woman, Lois A. H. Mosley, a 6th generation native Sandy Grounder, did write her book, "Sandy Ground Memories," family stories and voices of other Sandy Grounders, with essays by a white man, Barnett Shepherd. Her stories fill the generation gaps of one of the oldest black settlements on Staten Island, founded by freed slaves in 1850. The book of maps, photos, historical documents from her family, the Staten Island Museum, and Sandy Grounders that lived there, along with her extensive narrative, bring the lost history to life. Her final comment was "There is no more Sandy Ground, it's extinct as a Black community. It's 99 per cent White now.

Lois Mosley would send me an autographed copy of the book before she died at 81 years of age in June 2008. Her family traces its history back to 1850 in Sandy Ground founded by freed slaves. Lois Mosley played the organ in her church for 67 years; she would be buried in the old church cemetery on Crab Tree Avenue.

The existing oral history collections still consist largely of transcribed, audiocassette interviews, and access to them is limited and most are ill suited for easy transfer to today's media formats. Sandy Ground Historical Society now has the largest archival project that sits in a wooden house, the hand recorded interviews was methodic in it's attempt to capture the words and testimonies of black Staten Island Who am I to judge what seems to be a total takeover not only of property, but of the dreams and hopes of the living and the dead. Perhaps there is a reason that the records have left the SIIAS and are located in a flimsy wooden building waiting for fire or theft to come in the night, as it did to the Bishop forge shop. I asked Ms. Lewis if there was adequate security and fire insurance ... the answer covered in "Robert's Rules." I have tried many times to correspond with Ms. Lewis to offer my services and assistance. I have been questioned as to my motives, to become president of the society, or to take over any of the Staten Island organizations is the furthest thing from my desires or ambitions. The post-mortem landscape is as clear to me as to anyone who has taken the time to remember .... to remember when Sandy Ground had a Black florist who entered the floral contests at Madison Square Garden and had to wait outside to receive his prize ...

or the yearly homecoming, weekend barbecues, the many tuxedo-ed weddings from the church … the camaraderie of neighbors both Black and White. I had dreamed of a more poignant documentary of those moments, but now my mind grows dim, thoughts replaced with some lingering fears of inferiority. I suppose this is the price Black Americans pay for the privilege of entering the open door of mainstream America, and leaving behind our history and heritage for greener fields elsewhere.

OTHER PIECES OF THE PUZZLE

I was asked many times why it was important to me to do anything at all with respect to Sandy Ground, which is on the South Shore; I was on the North Shore. But being one of those that helped make up the Sandy Ground Historical Society, I wanted to bring together something that hadn't existed on Staten Island which was simply a place, a building, a group, that was in our own way trying to put together the puzzle which is, I guess, still going on.

I have in my files something that Franklin D. Roosevelt said, and when I read it over and over again, I think it's important to me to understand why I became involved: "To bring together the records of the past and to house them in buildings where they will be preserved for the use of men and women in the future, a Nation must believe in three things: It must believe in the past; It must believe in the future; It must, above all, believe in the capacity of its own people so to learn from the past that they can gain in judgment for the creation of the future." That was simple enough for me to put into my mental lumber yard.

I also believed in the statement that I assisted in convincing others of the importance of the Sandy Ground Historical Society, which was to preserve the history, the physical surroundings of the Sandy Ground community, to promote, to maintain this legacy where we could find it. It was, we all believed, a part of the real American history. In part, through the efforts of white and black, young and old, elementary and college level people, it happened. I believed that the years working with these people to promote the historical research of Sandy Ground would be the one item, the one issue, that I could leave behind.

I realize, even today, that our predicament, the black perspective at the present time, always throws up new questions. Sometimes we get trapped, many of us get trapped, in a previous moment of history, and you find it hard to carry on a conversation with anyone, because they are still out to defend something that you are not against. But you're not with it because it no longer maintains anything relevant. I essentially got caught up in making tremendous tirades against the initial Sandy Ground missionaries to this hope. I believed that was a formulation that was necessary at that particular point in time when we were still within the whole identity crisis. When we were still trying to evolve a kind of "peoplehood." I knew that we had to move beyond that to have a relationship with white, black, others on Staten Island. It was necessary to move beyond; to have, perhaps, a relationship with the rest of the world.

I have my own files which continued for decades. There was a haste on my part because I was acutely aware of the fragility of the historical records, and the first step was to rescue them wherever we would find them; orally, pictorially, physically, gather them whatever way we could from private repositories to get at important documents which were, as I viewed it, liable to be lost or destroyed by the indifference or neglect of those into whose hands they may have fallen. And without the aid of original records and documents and authentic narrations, history will be nothing more than a well-combined series of ingenious conjectures and amusing fables. I knew, but I didn't know. Historians made no mention of this island's black population. We were entirely absent from the Society's archives. The founders didn't seem particularly interested in blacks, Sandy Ground, perhaps finding it useless. Nevertheless, traces of black life did survive, did surface. Couched within a white context, as it were, Sandy Ground was located on the margins of white island history and presented from a white perspective. I believed it was left to members of my generation, so long ago, those born in the post-war 19th century, to begin the work of preserving, and committed to the point of collective memories of the black Staten Islanders.

My reason was that the Sandy Ground Historical Society had, in some way, removed The Black Man on Staten Island Project from the Staten Island Institute of Arts and Sciences in St. George. I received letters from whites on how it could have happened. I didn't know, I was out of the country. I had completely forgotten about my signature. In 1981, I signed the release of the papers and materials to the Staten Island Historical Society. I received this letter and I received a copy of the typewritten disposition of the material from the archives of the Staten Island Museum. Yes, I did approve the moving of the documents from the Museum to the Staten Island Historical Society. Yvonne Taylor sent a copy to me. At this late date, I guess it's a bit late to apologize, but my enthusiasm in the interim was, perhaps, something that should be a part of the puzzle and placed here in these letters.

Over the years I have tried, before the fateful letter of course, I tried to nudge the Sandy Ground Historical Society to fulfill its mandate of promoting and revering the history and the contributions of blacks on Staten Island. My approach and the approach of others range from polite suggestions, offers of assistance, and cajoling enquiries, to criticism intended to incite them to some kind of action, to perhaps catalyze a metamorphosis of the dormant, uninspired state of the Society and its Board of Directors. We did not know what direction it seemed to be. For the last 30+ years, Judy Moody Lewis and her mother, Sylvia Moody D'Alessandro have controlled the Sandy Ground Historical Society. Adrian Ross did preside in the Chair for a very short time in 1999, but the Executive Director was Judy Moody Lewis.

Most island blacks ignore or dismiss the Sandy Ground Historical Society, but blacks usually, mostly, always, decline to criticize their own. So it is with much shame that, when I did an oral history here on Staten Island, I talked to many and every black person and many whites on the island. Many have heard of it, many have not, and many just have not been able for some reason, to go there. There doesn't seem to be a Board of Directors, a Board of anything. Sylvia and her daughter have been more than 30 years at the helm; a clear-cut case that I've seen in my life in Africa, of mellowing benign leadership such as I witnessed in Equatorial Guinea; a dictator for more than 30 years, a benign dictatorial meritocracy. I would find most organizations on Staten Island to have leaders only because of their insistence upon maintaining their position of

Director or President of the organizations. One would have very easy access to the files of the organization. We have become our own worst enemy.

I will be leaving the pottery, the arrow heads, the Dutch pipes that we dug, so many years ago. They will be given to and delivered to the Sandy Ground Historical Society which is where it belongs. It's the common cultural heritage and the digging, the archeology below the ground still remains a way that we can tangibly do it. A way that we can touch that heritage ourselves. There should be volunteer programs. I know of none. Many people, I believe, looking for a career change, would be interested if the possibility were made to dig on our sites that have been left undisturbed. They may be simply curious about the work of archeology, about the work that historians and/or museum curators do; the lab work, the database management. It's so interesting; it brings to my mind the golden opportunity to find out more of who we are, of who we want to be. I don't know if there has ever been a program started, but I'm sure this could be a very valuable part of our history.

Housing development has taken a major portion of Sandy Ground. It is no longer possible to pick up Indian arrow-heads, pieces of the past that we were uninformed as to their meaning. The glass beads for trading with the Indians, they are here, pieces of pottery, brass buttons, a piece of a pistol. They have always been exciting for me and those of us that had the privilege at one time of freely picking a site to uncover the jigsaw puzzle with the many missing pieces. We don't know what we have here. I don't know. The work has yet to be done.

I have to be very careful of my work now in and around Sandy Ground. I carry with me a copy of the letter from the attorney who informed me many years ago, in 2000, that I might be subject to arrest. On one trip on the 4th July, 2003, I accidentally came out of the bushes and met, on Bloomingdale Road, Sylvia and her daughter. I carry with me a tape recorder for my own safety and after our meeting I had sent them a letter, return receipt requested, for my own safety. My letter to the Sandy Ground Historical Society, July 4, 2003, read:

Dear Julie: I was surprised to see you yesterday morning on Bloomingdale Road. You gave me such a fright when Sylvia beeped and came to a sudden stop. I had not seen you since September 17, 2000, at the Unitarian Church. At first, I imagined, someone may have telephoned you about my entering into the old Collins Property with my camera. The people in the bay man's house on the right saw me standing there and may have suspected I was up to something. For the record, I did not enter onto the lot because of those high weeds and I did not have my machete with me. You mentioned that it was private property. I had no idea that the Sandy Ground Historical Society owned it. I saw no sign; perhaps the tall weed growth had covered one. You asked me if I was at your last Fete. I had no way of knowing about it. Sorry about that. I leave my contact addresses with this letter.

I sealed it with name, address, e-mail, telephone number of Staten Island, and fax. I received no response. I follow this because I am continually afraid that my presence would somehow land me in jail, which I would be terribly upset about, and I do not enter into that area without another person as a witness. I have said in most of my correspondence with Julie Ojelade again and again, I was told that I was not welcome. I file the letters away, but I have made my position clear; that I did not want anything from the Sandy Ground Historical Society. I do not want to be on the Board or run for any office. There have been no nominations for members to become active in the organization. It is, as I have said, a meritocracy.

I do not want to destroy the organization. I represent to organization or persons attached to any organization. If at all, I would like to see the Sandy Ground Historical Society improved. I feel that the Sandy Ground Historical Society has alienated itself from much of the white and black Staten Island community that could assist and support it. I do not know if it is a function of the personalities involved, but an institution with as important a mission as Sandy Ground should not stand or fall because of personalities. The Sandy Ground Historical Society should be inclusive not exclusive in order to survive, but whether the Sandy Ground Historical Society improves or not is not my problem or my preoccupation.

What I have been lobbying, and picketing, and writing letters for, is to have all the original documentation, videotapes, photographs, and files relating to the work done for The Black Man on Staten Island Project returned to the Staten Island Institute of Arts and Sciences Museum. The primary reason, as I stated, was that they should find a place before they were authorized to move. Surely, little thought was given on my part that their fate, by directing them to the Sandy Ground Historical Society building, a comparatively unsafe, and unsecure location where they are subject to theft and fire. I have asked in writing to be provided with the insurance and methods taken to protect them. The loss of the blacksmith shop was terrible, but the loss of the irreplaceable documentation would be horrific. I have seen the results when greedy unscrupulous developers see property that impedes their continued construction of condos here, and I fear for the future of those files.

I realize that the body doesn't make any real distinction on how to survive the stresses. I believe that my life has been a series of stress episodes, but it's the long-lasting ones that kill. I have had to put together the pieces of the almost eternal struggle that black people deal with, but I am most familiar with the bits and pieces of the puzzle of my island. The puzzle has no medical title, determination, number, or code. We stumble, as I do, into forums of mental illnesses. I have avoided all my life that tendency to submit to the couch of a psychiatrist or psychologist, but sitting on the balcony listening to the medical mental doctors, people, I know from my life that their studies have not, would not, and cannot apply to the black situation.

Perhaps I should say that it is simply my own personal situation that I found while attaching the pieces of the puzzle to write this. The medical establishment would simply say these are adjustment disorders, the development of emotional or behavioral symptoms. Another would be the impulse control disorder. This category of disorders of impulse control is category number 61-5. It gets more interesting if you can read their findings. Trichotillomania, the pulling out of one's hair, increasing the sense of tension immediately before or after pulling out one's hair. Bulimia Nervosa, recurrent episodes of binge eating in a discrete period of time. It gets rather difficult for me to simply listen to try and identify some of these strange disorders, find out which one would fit me, my character, my body. I did realize that most people have some of them and the one that I found after many hours, days, and months, listening, sitting in the audience, to understand the somatoform disorders. What are somatoform disorders? A history of many physical complaints beginning before the age of 30 years that occuring over a period of several years, several decades, resulting in a treatment of yada, yada, yada and of importance to one's life malfunctioning.

I no longer expose myself to that as I said I would know when the medical society would find reasons that I have done what I needed to do to free myself of the addiction of Staten Island. A black man's addiction. Most white people, I believe, think that discrimination is on the decline, that racism is no longer a significant factor in the lives of people of color, and most white people are sincere that their black friends, neighbors, associates have some sort of a problem adjusting, but they know it exists and they comfort themselves in saying that well, equality will be shortly achieved.

As a black American, I perceive the situation quite differently. My findings over the global travels have come to the continued micro-aggressions; some are brief and some are commonplace daily. The micro-assaults, the micro-aggressions, the micro-insults, the micro-invalidations. I had to return to things that have happened so many long years ago. The micro-assaults placed gently on my skin, my head, my body, when I joined the US military. It wasn't done by white supremacists, it wasn't done by the Ku Klux Klan or the skinheads. The major micro-assault that has left me with the inability to find a place of life in the US. At over the age of 80 there are many black men who entered the military; patriotic, willing to kill, to fight, to stab, to learn the business of killing. Yes, my initial micro-assault was placed on me by the US Government.

I think very strongly that everyone, all of us make choices about where to place their efforts; where to bring about some understanding in this diverse worldview population. Where do you acquire the knowledge, the understanding of the cultural values and the differences? It was my naiveté, I suppose, in thinking that perhaps the Sandy Ground Historical Society would be a kind of think-tank, a kind of a place where there would be forums, discussions, that black writers would attend. We would give them that attention that's needed to sustain them. I can't believe how many books are being published by black writers. Simply getting the word out, at least here on Staten Island, to potential readers, black and white, it's not easy, trust me. We have no forum or place and the little private shelves that have any black or African American titles on their shelves receive very sparse coverage, especially in the mainstream media here on my island, and the little space that was allotted to any books other than the college books, that space has been dwindling. There is no place of interest of readers of African descent.

Yes, my naiveté, trying to bring an otherwise unheard-of black perspective about things that were happening. It hurts deeply to know that here in Sandy Ground the Society does not carry President Obama's *The Audacity of Hope*. A place like the Sandy Ground Historical Society would have been an opportunity to help another generation find a voice, but nothing here is sufficiently covered. One book dealer said that "We get so many books and our space is limited." I don't know where African American authors, especially here on my island, how do you do it? Word of mouth, church groups, books signings? I could not get one and the need for whites, I realized, was the only way. Hard to say, hard to swallow. The adage, the old adage, that sometimes we black folks are our own worst enemy.

The frustration remains and black authors don't succeed because of the system. This indicates to me that there is at least a perception of black people as active and engaged readers who are willing to read books, which is opposite to the way the book industry seems to think of them. I know, I believe, that an exposure would generate the needed excitement. Again, the reason I believe.

We were especially interested in finding the Esther Purnell place in Snow Hill. Esther Purnell was a free black woman who migrated in the early 1800s from Snow Hill to Staten Island. She was interesting to me because she was a driving force, a foundation for a school that she established on Sandy Ground. We took the walking tour and we found a Julia Purnell Museum. Well, we made inquiries, we asked questions, and we made notes. This Julia Purnell Museum was not a museum that was placed in Snow Hill, it was a white Julia Purnell, they said there was no black connection to an Esther Purnell, but it was quite obvious that the Julia A. Purnell Museum on Market Street in Snow Hill did recognize their place in the history of black slavery.

The Museum was small, but tastefully appointed with many articles about Snow Hill. The building was a former tiny Catholic church. The Gothic architecture was quite interesting. I thought before entering that it did have some significance to a religion. After questioning, asking the people inside, it sure was. But they carried a wide assortment of things; an assemblage of early American tools of different trades, different kinds, for agriculture, tobacco processing. Many artifacts, including slave chains, slave bracelets, the whips, and the tools that belonged to that era, to that time. Jude and I took the tour which was quite interesting.

It was the typical Market Street where we had lunch, and as an interracial couple, I found that we did not notice any awareness of our being white and black. As we strolled the streets from Market to Church Street, we would walk down Federal Street to see the grand 14-roomed homes with 9 fireplaces, constructed in the 18th century, the original carved woodwork. On East Market Street we entered the old cottage, known as the Little House; an interesting colonial-style dwelling, clapboard siding, wood shingle roof. Building after building. Grand 10 and 15 storey buildings. There was never any mention of how these huge homes were built, who built them, why they were here.

We looked for names that would be associated with any black person who came north. We found none. The churches; Presbyterian, Methodist, and the one church that belonged to the blacks, many of whom still attend services on Sunday. There were no black-run businesses that we noticed in Snow Hill. I thought that was interesting, but I was always reminded of the statement "When one culture dominates another, it brings its literature, its language, its religion, and its architecture." Worcester County was, to me, a place that the Staten Island black people would ultimately find a wisp, a wind, and a puff of smoke, leaving behind a white-sided clapboard church, locked securely, with dozens of grave markers at its side. It was an interesting and a fruitful day, but with it I saw and realized the bits and pieces of the puzzle in 2012 of what is happening at Sandy Ground. Their history had vanished.

I look at the Fifth Annual Sandy Ground Day Commemorative Journal of December 10, 1983. It was a very uplifting, I suppose, happy time for me. There were officers, Sylvia Harris became President, Sylvia Harris is now Sylvia D'Alessandro, still the President.

Yvonne Taylor was Vice President, Dolores Morris was Recording Secretary, Julie O'Gelliday was Corresponding Secretary, Julie is Sylvia D'Alessandro's daughter. Denise Pedro was the Financial Secretary. A very dear friend at that time, still is, Lucille Herring was Treasurer. Marie Spicer was the Parliamentarian. Members were Carol Per Lee Plumb, Delridge Hunter, Elmore Taylor, Eddie Martinez, and me. I also, at this time, was the Master of Ceremonies. There were men who were on the program, there are very few men in the Sandy Ground Historical Society, but I mention all of these positions because I do not believe that there are any elections. I don't have any lists, nor could I get any list provided to me, that name who the Vice President, Recording Secretary, Corresponding Secretary, Financial Secretary, Treasurer, Parliamentarian would be today in 2012. Sylvia D'Alessandro has been in this position for over 30 years.

Funny how my historical bits and pieces come together and as my mother would say "God puts you where you should be." I spent many years in Africa, many different countries on the continent of Africa, and on my return at one time I received a certificate of Merit from the New York State Assembly. The Assembly of the State of New York, in Recognition of the Achievements of Cleve Overton, Recipient of the Staten Island African American Political Association's Griot Award. June 24, 2006. And being older and a bit wiser, I find that I can fill the role of a griot. Having watched, having been a part of my Staten Island for so many long decades, seeing and working with blacks and whites, I think I can wear the cape, the uniform, of the griot, which is also why this style-type book is something that I have been destined to believe, to do. I do believe this is where God wants me to be.

For many years the people of Staten Island have been looking for an alternative and they have found it here in Sandy Ground. There is no other option, this place, this Sandy Ground, is a new version of the American Dream. There are still no landmark signs; the Landmarks Preservation Foundation says that they are not responsible to put up signs for passers-by. The two gigantic propane tanks stand boldly blocking any view from this historic district to the Kill Van Kull River below. There is so much that could have been accomplished, but the speedboats are too many, and race has been factored into all of this. The church has no foundation or no tools with which to place their faith. If and when they do find those, the machinery with which to fall in line will be white.

We on Staten Island have lived with white people all our lives. It will continue and if we, the black community, continue to work against one another rather than as a single voice, we will suffer the fate of Snow Hill. I will end my hope for Sandy Ground; I will retire any suggestions about the promotion, education, and the better business opportunities, the fundraising, all the things that I thought would find open and welcoming ears.

I have discontinued my campaign, I have discontinued the letters. The one man, Reverend Julius Ingram, is no longer with us. I will still receive, I guess, the deep throat midnight phone calls from people who always speak on the condition of anonymity. There are missing links in the puzzle. I'm not able to carry the banner. Any strong black presence, a leader in Sandy Ground, it's not possible. Most white homeowners here do not even use the term Sandy Ground, even if they know what it means. The hot market in New York and the increasing lure of open space has descended on this area and the entire South Shore of the island. The construction continues helter-skelter, and the city officials seem powerless or perhaps disinterested to control the construction.

I will carefully fold the records, perhaps to send them to their grave. But this, of course, ends my active participation. I'm finding a way to have some peace in my knowing that I have accomplished a little.

TROPHY SEEKERS

The Trophy Seekers notes began in January 2005. At that time I was speaking with a Black friend in the lobby of the Li Greci's Staaten Restaurant, while watching folks enter the dining room for the NAACP Annual Awards presentations. After a while, we simply ran out of small talk and I mentioned to him that I was thinking of writing an essay on Black Trophy Seekers. His response was, "You better watch yourself. I'd keep it to myself if I was you."

The conversation was brief, and I could tell that it didn't register as I'd meant it, simply a description of what was happening. Rerunning the conversation, I suppose it seemed to him to be a threat. Perhaps it was. Someplace I heard the expression "A Conspiracy of Silence," and I thought, yes, a conspiracy of silence right here on Staten Island.

It made me so pissed that soon after that encounter, I sat down at my desk, wading through my files to find the basis for my anger, why I was there in the first place, and why Black folks continue, year after year, to compulsively line up to spend their hard-earned money to receive awards and plaques. Most people could care less about or remember the names of the awardees, and the parallel worlds of the economics attached to all this a week later.

Anger and rage have been my constant companions, and I find it easy to tell you that because I'm Black. Hundreds of awards, accolades, grants, medals, proclamations, garlands, plaques, extravaganzas, and prizes, with the prerequisite gibberish attached, are presented to and by Blacks and a few Whites every year, decade after decade. Dinners, lunches, brunches, and prayer breakfasts, honors, awards, and proclamations continue.

I continued searching and I find that I do have lists; man is a list-making animal, and my first list from 2005 might very well fall short of a universal Staten Island appeal. The fact of the matter is basic: we need these lists. The years without them would make no sense. I think that, basically, is it is good to know someone is watching you, someone is paying attention, and that you need to realize the list in exactly the way that a drowning man needs a life-preserver.

So seeing or reading the list will tell you that the people who make these annual award lists have crossed the great divide of packaged amusement and entertainment. The sympathy, the pity, and the tenderness provide a distraction for everyone buying into it. Black folks will emerge with their trophies warmly held to their breasts to join others on the mantle of Hope. The inscriptions include their names, their rank, and are inscribed "You are the Best!" We all admire their grit and pluck and applaud after their acceptance speech to thank God and mom for their guidance. Of course, like all things that pretend to perfect transparency, it is a result of juggling and finesse. The list makes itself.

Now at the turn of the century, new presentations are here. The Unsung Heroes Awards are now into the 21st Century on Staten Island, while the myriad discrimination and racial problems have not changed one whit, here in the shadow of the Statue of Liberty. We were very nice colored folks and Negroes; now we are very nice African-Americans and Black people. We've never had to sit in the back of the bus, or go to the rear door for service at the lunch counter. We've never been denied the right to vote. There was never a Black riot or any unruly demonstrations here. We are all excellent citizens, home owners, taxpayers, workers, military personnel, and voters.

Yet year after year I see and hear the bell tolling for the Blacks that still live here. No speaker will address it from the podiums, though all will admit readily in private that Blacks have fumbled the ball. I will not find my Gold Ring here. Yet each year the processions to the podiums persist, the cast only changing slightly in a game of musical chairs of persons and organizations.

Behind my chair there hangs a plaque. I'm very proud of my trophy. It was given to me in 1982 by the newly-formed Sandy Ground Historical Society for my assistance in preserving Black History on Staten Island. It was not necessary for me to accept this gift because the gift came from a very dear friend before leaving the Society; that was Gail Schneider, one of the Whites who helped to preserve Black history on Staten Island.

I returned to the Island in October 2003, I was standing in the hallway outside the annual Urban League Awards luncheon. This annual event has become an odd and confusing phenomenon. Why do so many intelligent, honorable, and respectable Black folks distort reality and subject themselves to this painful theater of the absurd? I was asked if I was going inside and my response was "I cannot afford this," which was true. However, the larger issue is that I had no intention of supporting this charade, but I did accept a free ticket to go in to get closer to the attendees. I accepted in order to photograph the event. Besides, I also had not eaten and the food odors were tempting! This is an Italian-owned hall; there are no Black waiters, no Black servers, though some are perhaps Mexican.

I began to make notes of the occasion. I made notes of the seating—10 people to a table and there are 17 tables. I made some quick calculations: 10 X 17 is 170 people attending. The ticket price was $55 per person, for a total of $9,350. I would add another $2,000 for raffle tickets, clothes, haircuts, beauty parlors, dry cleaners, fingernails, jewelry, cosmetics, baby sitters, auto use, gas, and tips for the young White men who park the cars.

There were no Black boys for valet parking. We all tip very well; no one likes to leave knowing that Blacks have been frequently noted as being cheap tippers. We would tip above the $5 valet tip. Later I am hustled at my table while shoving food into my mouth by a lady who asked me to give her $5 for an "admit on" raffle ticket with a number. I will never know who won, or indeed if anyone did win this alleged raffle. I was cowed into giving her the $5 because I was embarrassed not to. When she ripped the stub from a huge roll under her arm and shoved it at me, it was a real tacky bit, but under other circumstances, I would have quietly said to her that I would rather not gamble.

As the award recipients at the podium thanked their friends and family and God, I left the hall.

Another time, I was at the same Li Greci's Staaten Restaurant for the annual NAACP "Freedom Fund" event luncheon. For this event there were more than 200 people in attendance. I made my fast calculations: $13,000. These two NAACP and Urban League Black annuals awards totaled $24,350 dollars. The NAACP and the Urban League also paid for events at other places during the year, but these events at the Staaten are the annual "biggies." The events have no creative spontaneity; it's simply déjà vu all over again.

Other Black Fraternal organizations, women's groups, civic groups, etc. which normally party at the Staaten can now party at the new Hilton Gardens on the West Shore, and other White restaurants, because there are no Black-owned businesses to cater to any convention or event on Staten Island. In March of 2004, the huge 15,000 square foot Whitney M. Young building on West Street in West Brighton, owned by the Urban League, was sold to the United Talmudical Academy. The Urban League chairman said the money was going to be invested in other programs on Staten Island. I will not hold my breath, but simply placed this notice into my Black Staten Island file.

Those of us who cheered for the creation of, and those who prayed for the arrival of, the Whitney M. Young Day Care Center, also fell silent when the Black director was convicted of larceny and the Center closed due to financial mismanagement. No matter; a new Day Care Center was built on Alaska Street and Castleton Avenue by a White guy from Brooklyn. It's déjà vu all over again.

In the 21st century, this legacy of single-minded traditions continues, and is actually presiding over the deathbed of the failed resuscitation efforts of the Black community. Most Blacks walk and talk the party line, not allowed to put "our business" in the street. I watched the glad-handing and back-slapping, the Colgate smiles of both Black and Whites. I knew none of the little face-to-face smiling conversations were about the perennial conundrum that another "annual" brunch would bring the races any closer to the truth. Blacks on this Staten Island cannot escape the appalling situation unless they reach out to Whites and *vice versa*, which is, historically, an American story. Black Americans have lived among Whites on Staten Island their entire lives, working together, living together on this island; in every way Blacks and Whites have interacted. Perhaps not socially or religiously, but Blacks have never gone one day of their lives into the streets and not met a White person. Blacks and Whites have been part of this island since the ships from Africa docked in the harbor in 1691.

However, my view from the balcony is higher than ever. I watch the White politicians, the CEOs, entering the Staaten when called, State Senator John Marchi, *Staten Island Advance* Editor Brian Leline, city councilman Michael McMahon, Snug Harbor Cultural Center CEO Paul Goldberg, Assemblyman John Lavelle.

A mental Theatre of the Absurd came to mind. I see the scene—the White movers and shakers at this annual "economical" huddle event, with Black men and women, ministers and businesspeople, 100 Blacks in Law Enforcement, Sisters With a Purpose, Brothers With a Purpose, the Sandy Ground Historical Society, the Urban League, Black Women of Achievement, The Borough President Distinguished Service Awards, Rotary Club honorees, honorees of past decades, all working to find a common ground to enable Blacks to acquire and operate a BSISR, a Black Staten Island Staaten Restaurant catering hall!!!

My dream ended when I awoke in a cold sweat on October 19, 2004. The Richmond County Savings Foundation presented a grant to the NAACP and the President, Ed Josey, immediately announced that the money would be used for a William A. Morris Awards dinner.

My living history does not allow me to fabricate these events, to obfuscate the facts, or to exaggerate. It simply allows me to be free of the chains that bound me for so long, no pun intended. I could demonstrate, yell, talk, and scream, pontificate and/or analyze all I wanted, but the bottom line remains that we have failed to move forward collectively to right the wrongs inflicted on the Blacks of the Island and continue to do so in a time of such tremendous possibilities, right here in the Shadow of the Statue of Liberty.

After a more than 40-year period, my math has tallied the rental of the Staaten Restaurant and other sites that the Black community has used for their affairs—my files track 10 major Black organizations—and the dollar amount paid is a staggering $2.5 million. And yes, we Blacks will continue to support them because we do not read or understand, and we will continue to buy anything that we want thinking that we are helping our communities, and paying dues to organizations and companies which do little aside from hold lavish events in White restaurants and hotels. And, by the way, concentration can make the difference, but it means concentration.

There is a kind of tribal subculture of Blacks on Staten Island. It's a weird and often wonderful, occasionally confounding, portrait of 21st century Staten Island. It has garnished itself with critical reviews in the *Advance* hometown newspaper, notices and photos; and the awards that are given are just as likely to leave some attendees and viewers befuddled and bemused. The charismatic leaders have been performing the same rituals and rites as leaders of a nascent religious cult, which takes place each year at the Staaten. Most will find ways to attend and enjoy, and perhaps dance and interact about the rituals that have lost their base and are now not worth pursuing or understanding. We are just curious about it.

I have made efforts not to seem nasty at being present. I found attending to be both intimate and quite claustrophobic. Everyone here wants CHANGE, but they don't want change. I found myself waiting at the doors to sell copies of my books, only to be involved in a conversation that never moved itself into the reason for being here. The coiffured men and women will enter and take their seats in the Imperial Room at Li Greci's Staaten. I look very closely at the richness of the challenge. It's seen in the faces of the youth, the energy and hope, the expectations. The youth arrive and accept awards here every year, most of it only to be lost in the fog of non....

My notes would make very little sense to others. Many years ago in 1998 I attended at event, one of the first events long, long ago, at the Columbia Lyceum in West Brighton, and I watched and I made notes of three young Black men who would receive the Charles K. Smith Memorial Scholarship Awards. This was a memorable occasion for me because I had known Charles K. Smith; I had worked in the shipyards as a welder and began to know more about him.

I wonder now, in 2014, where are these young men? What has happened to them? Their names, written in my notebook, are Kevin Serrette, Osmani Ofarri Eboa, and Nicholas Payne. I remember these young men accepting their awards and I wonder to this day, have they returned to Staten Island to take up the mantle of responsibility? It breaks my heart that so many Black Staten Islanders have no clue who paved the way for them. There is almost a willful ignorance on their part. For many years I have followed as best I could the young vigorous wide-eyed honorees. How many have returned to Staten Island to man the chairs and the positions as future Black leaders in this community? The torch, it seems, has not been passed. Will there be a booklet or a video to remember these events? Where do we find our accomplishments? The program books, the letters, the speeches, commemoration booklets? Where are the artifacts and the ordinary markers of this generation?

Will I ever find out whatever happened to the three young men that I met so many years ago? It is my hope that they have succeeded in rising above this Island. Have we taken our eyes off the prize? The Civil Rights Movement continues, but the struggle today is not so much in the streets as in the home and with our children. If systemic racism remains a reality, there is also a far more sinister obstacle facing African American young people today. A culture, steeped in bitterness and nihilism, a culture that is a virtual blueprint for failure.

Blacks born on Staten Island live in a dual world of cultural idioms, codes, styles, body language, and real life survival instincts. My living environment on Staten Island had always been between Black and White, and I realize that I had not yet dreamed a full text of in-house customs, mannerisms, of either Black or White. I knew I was a byproduct of this cumbersome way of life.

The Staten Island Chapter of the NAACP and the Urban League are at the top of the list of Black groups that support the funding and the enlargement and rehabilitation of White-owned Staten Island restaurants and catering halls. As I watched the proceedings from the sidelines I would never see a Black waiter inside.
I would buy no tickets. I watched and I listened at the doorway for a mention of who Mr. William A. Morris was. Does anyone know this honor in his name had even existed? No one mentioned that.

What is repellent about the celebrity awards is that it often represents fame unconnected to achievement. People want to be famous. They do not necessarily have to be famous **for** something. It's disconnected, it's unconnected, although it is always to be preferred anyhow, but no matter what, they want to be famous. Fame and these trophies provide meaning, supposedly, to meaningless lives. Fame is a rocket fuel. ZAP and you're up and over the mundane of the Island and because this is America it will perhaps make you rich and therefore happy.

I call this celebrity a disease, celebritis perhaps, because it makes us think that certain people are more important and more powerful than the rest of us, and of course that's a lie.

I don't intend or pretend to be perfect or to have my life completely together. I have my strengths, I have my weaknesses. I think it is time for us to stop lying to ourselves about the country and about this Island. There were certain days, I suppose, when I'm feeling so judgmental that even if I say the right words, my tongue is going to convey criticism. If I were committed only to being right, I would go out and talk anyway, but I'd like to think that because I'm committed to making a difference I wait until I'm ready.

There are times when I realize my feelings and writing are so fierce in their communication that it unsettles people. It is important that I know whether my fierceness is coming from my center, good judgment; sometimes it is better for me to simply shut my mouth. Perhaps it is a part of a spiritual practice that I know nothing about, about being open to receiving lessons from whatever source I might receive them.

I am a human being, I have a lot of faults, I get angry and frustrated and overwhelmed and cynical, just like anybody else. I've learned that I can find support and help from the most unlikely places, but I often don't do so well. Struggling with this, the micro-assaults, the micro-abrasions, can lead to depression, and I think of myself as a sensitive person.

Right now, when I think about all of this I might want to cry. I don't seem to have an in-between zone. I feel everything deeply. I didn't know so much because I didn't know how to be in this world. Even now there are occasions when I go into despair and numb my nerves, my head, with a drink too many. Frightened of being an addict of anything, I stop, throw up my hands, and say "Cleve, what the hell are you doing?'
I don't mind sharing any of this because I believe we have to be honest about our humanity, and I don't want other Staten Islanders or people to see me as some sort of hero, a gigantic hero, a little hero, a hero of whatever size without a cape. I am a human being who struggles with the same problems that we all struggle with. But I know that in order for me to heal, to feel when I know something is out of balance, when I know that something has gone wrong, I will not ignore the problem. I would consult my friends; I do have some very good friends with whom I can lay out my fears and struggles. I'm lucky.

And with the murals or the trophies, only the shallow-minded are excited over the publicity. Publicity is evanescent; it is here today and gone tomorrow. Whoever falls in love with this publicity, they are not fit to have it and will perhaps end up in misery.
The books of John Hope Franklin, the Black historian and thinker, have always had a place in my library. During an interview by *the New York Times,* the reporter said "And of course, you are a teacher yourself. In fact, you are said to be the most decorated professor in this country. I hear you have so far earned 130 honorary degrees. "
Mr. Franklin's response was "I think it's up to 137. But that's not the way you measure anything. Some of it is conscience pay. I don't want to belabor the point, but giving out awards makes the givers feel good. It is easier to give me an honorary degree than to make certain that all blacks have a decent place to live."

Today racism is no longer embedded in the law, and while it has by no means been banished from the hearts of men, its grip is far weaker than it once was, and if Dr. King could see America now, and look upon our Staten Island, I think Dr. King would be very disappointed and feel that his work is nowhere hear done.

I no longer wish to visit the Staaten or any other event on Staten Island. We talk, always, about our young. It is easy for me to see why the words and the ideas of the community have been massaged into gauzy slogans, meaning very little.
And money is not our problem: I think the problem is a loss of faith in ourselves. We Blacks need to restore confidence to accomplish something without White leadership, and understand that the fact of White is not important, or is it important? We live every day associating and interacting with Whites. Where do we stand with Reach a Sister Teach a Sister? Reach only Black sisters? Teach only Black sisters? Race sits like a

cancer on this Island, and I suppose others would say in America, but I know my Island very well. I know my Staten Island, New York, very well. All this is happening here and no one is writing about it. We have very little or no association with any of the awards committees personnel organizations. We work alone, we think alone. That's sort of weird, isn't it?

****

It was Saturday February 23, 2013, when I left home in D.C.at 6:30. I left the I-95 New Jersey Turnpike at exit 10 and crossed over the Outerbridge Crossing Bridge at the southern tip of Staten Island to stop at Sandy Ground. Earlier in the week I received a message that there would be a funeral at the Rossville AME Zion Church that day for Elmore Taylor, who died earlier in the week. I had not seen or spoken to Elmore Taylor for more than 5 years, but we used to bump into each other at Charlie's barber shop on Castleton Avenue or at the Cassidy Coles senior center in West Brighton. Being my own full time archivist, our paths had crossed because he was a member of the Sandy Ground community for more than 25 years, had been a board member and active in the SGHS and in the AME Zion church, and had been a commander in the Black 369th Infantry Regiment. Recently Elmore had been active in the AME Zion Church Building Committee to construct a 14 million dollar housing development for seniors on church property.

Elmore Taylor was on the committee of the Staten Island African American Political Associations Griot Award in June 2006 that selected me to be this island Griot, and being a card carrying Griot required me to ask questions. I would have asked Elmore Taylor, who had married Yvonne Usry, whose ancestors, freed slaves, were some of the first Black inhabitants of Sandy Ground, why he did not wish to be buried in the Sandy Ground Community graveyard on Crabtree Avenue just around the corner. I would make notes.

Sitting in a car beside the church were two women. I waved to them. "Do you need any help?" I asked.

"No we're fine."

"I simply wanted conversation," one said.

"Are you here for the funeral?" I asked.

"Yes."

After an awkward moment of the ladies and me looking at each other, I smiled and said "Have a nice day."

I looked up at the church door, and noticed that there was no ramp. There are about 40 older church members, white-haired seniors who are the core of the members, and I wondered how the old folks get up the stairs. How do they climb those stairs each weekend to attend the service?

Across the street from the church there were two White men on the stairs of Mr. Hunter's house. I quick glance told me all I needed to know. I had watched this house on Bloomingdale Road for a decade. At first it was empty, and still owned by one of Mr. George Hunter's kin. It was the best house still owned by Black Sandy Grounders; it had indoor plumbing and electricity. I watched this house for many years thinking it was still owned by a Black man, Deldridge Hunter, who was on the original board of the Sandy Ground Historical Society when I was on the board. I didn't ask questions when I saw a White guy working on the house. I took some photos year after year, and then one day I happened to ask a neighbor if the house had been sold. "Yes," he said. "What can we do?" I was under the impression that Blacks were not selling their property, and this was a particularly historic house; a long essay about it was in Joseph Mitchell's book *Bottom of the Harbor*, it had attractive spindle turned porch posts and other decorative features.

"What can we do?" That was what everyone else was thinking. No one would face the truth or ask the question as to who owned 575 Bloomingdale Road, the Hunter House, because the answers are fragile and uncertain and difficult. Bit by bit I began to see the pattern of the failed honest effort to toe the line and not to sell out. A White man eventually bought the house and made many changes and alterations to the house and the grounds. He sold it in 2011; I am sure at a handsome profit. The failure of avoidance and denial.

Mine was a personal initiative. As always I would take notes and promise to contemplate quietly when I am at home to add this to my continuing effort to free myself from Sandy Ground.

Primarily my voyage here was to attend the history roundtable discussion at the College of Staten Island. Usually, I have a list of things to do here, most of which I can never cover, but on this list I had a notation from an e-mail, and having some time before the event, I drove up the Howard Avenue hill to see the sprawling four story mansion that was purchased by a White Italian business woman, Gina Biancardi-Rammairone, four years ago for 3 million dollars. The story read that this was a way for the Italian Cultural Foundation to "give back" to the community. The mansion would be called Casa Belvedere, and was hailed as a welcome addition to the Italian presence in Staten Island. It is an amazingly beautiful white stucco building on 4 acres of land. She has secured tax exempt status as a non- profit and is seeking funds to make the 19-room mansion handicap accessible. (I thought *AME ZION Church - what a grand idea!*) I took some photos before driving away. We Blacks have been living on this island since the 1600's, working here in slavery and freedom, and have not been able to do more than pray for such a place. If prayer could only break these chains! I checked my mental temperature, took more photos, and simply drove away.

Earlier last month I opened my files titled "Trophy Seekers." This is a decades long running account of buildings built and lost, and money spent in search of the exact same purpose by Black Staten Islanders. The huge two-storey Whitney M. Young Building in West Brighton, the Martin Luther King Heritage House building on Castleton Avenue, the painful time and money effort to buy the first Staten Island City Hall Building, an historic building on Franklin Avenue. The voices were the same, "We want to give back to the Black community." We want a place to exhibit our art, our culture, and our history. The pieces of this dream came and faded in the fog of desire, again and again; the puzzles of the past.

2002 PUZZLE PIECE

At the guard kiosk at the College of Staten Island on Victory Blvd I ask which building is the Center for the Arts and get directions. I proceed to park, forgetting to notice which lot I was in, and dash to the building in the now heavy drizzle. It was the wrong building. I had not been here for a number of years and the campus is large with few signs, but I ask a student where the Center for the Arts building was and she pointed it out for me. Inside the huge building there are a number of people having coffee and talking in groups. I look about and see a friend from the Staten Island Museum, a good friend who has assisted me many times to have a book reading or an art piece hung at the museum. They also sell my books and have been quite helpful over the years when I could not find a Black organization or group to give me a book signing. She gave me a packet of information and I sat at a small table to read it. The panelists' bios indicated they were all PhD holders and one emerging scholar.

The topic was whether Staten Island really was a stop on route to freedom for Blacks escaping slavery. An article in the June 2002 edition of the *Staten Island Advance* stated that Sandy Ground was being proposed for inclusion in the Underground Railroad Network to Freedom by U.S. Congressman Representative Vito Fossella and the National Park Service. The article seemed to be a stamp of approval. A stamp of approval by a White man was proof enough for anything to be true and the Sandy Ground Historical Society (SGHS) had, apparently, done no further research or published any reports. The article stated that members of the Staten Island Branch of the NAACP and the New York Urban League toured the Sandy Ground site with Sylvia D'Alessandro, the SGHS Director. Ms. D'Alessandro was quoted as saying that John Jackson was the first Black man to buy property in Sandy Ground and that he owned a ferry that ran between Staten Island and New Jersey. The presumption was that he may have transported slaves across the Arthur Kill River, and SGHS would conduct research to provide evidence for that theory.

I looked around the group at the table, trying to find anyone I knew from Sandy Ground; I saw no one. One lady asked who I was, and she told me her name was Angela. She said she was a Staten Islander and a school teacher, and that she lived in New Brighton, a section on the North Shore of the Island. She said that there were a number of homes that had basements and cellars that were used as safe places for slaves to hide.

What I realize now is that many places that simply had root cellars for winter foodstuffs were now being touted as places that slaves hid during the march north along the Underground Railroad. I asked the lady if she knew about any Quakers that lived on the North Shore or in her community; she said no. We were soon joined by others at the small table. It was a friendly give and take, but I was not ready to tell them of my real reason for driving here to this event from Washington D.C. Most were enthusiastic to hear about the forum; they were all White and seemed to be very interested to learn if Staten Island was actually a stop on the Underground Railroad.

Conversations stopped and every head turned as a clarion voice rang out from the auditorium door. Her arms stretched out, Christine Dixon, a female singer in costume, sang the "Gathering Call" in an amazing, clear, powerful voice, welcoming patrons to the auditorium and stage, and then, in a graceful pantomime, performed "Follow The Drinking Gourd" to set the stage for the event.

I expected that there would be officials from Sandy Ground at the roundtable discussion, but was disappointed. I looked around at in the audience; about five Blacks were scattered in the audience of about 150 people. The panel members were professors, well-prepared and scholastically credentialed. I understood the historical context and content intimately, all too well. The numbers and dates of slave deaths, dates of Dutch colonialism, Black deaths at the stake, 1712 and 1741, the Five Points of New York, Irish/Black coexistence in solidarity in New York, the 1860's draft riots, race and class in the 1800's, Frederick Law Olmstead, Kreisherville Clay Company, and the contributions the Germans made to Staten Island.

One panel member, MA candidate Debbie Paige, went away from her written talk to say that she was not trying to make the case for or against the theory that there was an Underground Railroad stop on the Island, and that everyone should make up his or her own mind on the subject. At the break, I expressed interest in her thesis *A Slow Burn*, and requested a copy.

With playful cynicism, I mentally ran through what I knew all too well; that there would be no discussion time left on the program for a "community response." I would leave quite unobtrusively, not wanting to be the adroit cad who comes to the culture table, makes an ass of himself or preaches to the unconverted and then leaves! There was an elephant in the room but there would be no discussion of the contemporary racism on Staten Island. I did find it unusual that no one spoke from the Staten Island Historical Society or the SGHS.

My own research had revealed no evidence that there was an Underground Railroad stop on the island. While an intriguing theory, the practicality of escaping slaves from the South detouring to an island accessible only by boat, where another crossing would be required to continue their journey to the North and Canada, has always defied my logistical sensibilities. But I remain open to the possibility and await the evidence.

During the break I left to drive home. Stepping outside the building, I realized that I had absolutely no idea where I had put my car! It began to rain, and after an hour of walking through all the visible parking lots and trudging through the mud and Canada Goose poop, I hailed a security car and recited my tale of woe to the driver. She told me to get in and take a moment to remember while she returned to the gated campus entrance. She said this happens quite often and not to worry, and then pointed out the Toyota with the D.C. plates straightaway. I hesitated to get out of the warm car and asked her name. She said it was Devine.

"Did you say your name was Devine?"

"Yes, it is."

"Officer Devine, I want to thank you very much," I said, and thought about how cold and soaked I was, and that it was a divine stay none the less.

****

Alone on the drive back to Washington I reflect that I am embarked on my own personal journey to find the freedom of my life, as it were, to question the apparatus that sent me here, to become free and independent. I need to be free of the self-imposed limits and the limitations on my life to open the way to inner peace. And I believe that with Jude I have achieved a greater degree of success and an expanded consciousness; that a personal change has taken place in the 80th year of my life. It will all come together, materialized after several iterations written in various essays and ramblings, but not without support from some very special people that said "do it or shut up already."

Every nationality on the island has written a book on their triumphs. Until we embrace all of our past, the good and the bad, we can't move forward politically, socially, or as a community or a people. We are forced to deal with Black leaders in a different way. Racism isn't going to end just because we have a Black president; real change and equality will come when Black people can mess up just like White people and still succeed, and when a flaw in a Black leader is not looked upon as a flaw in all Black people. In the midst of the e-transformation of time and events around the globe, my task is just to work on my "island" community, and show the complexity here. The benefits and burdens of hindsight.

****

I have tried to follow the money, and why we Black Staten Islanders do not have it; it does seem that we Black folks buy what we want, and to me that becomes a painful legacy.

It's October 2003 and I am in the lobby of the Li Greci's Staaten Catering Hall on Forest Avenue speaking to a friend while trying to sell my book. The event is the Urban League Awards, an "annual" luncheon that is one of many "annuals" held here every year by Black organizations. It has become an odd and confusing phenomenon for me: why so many intelligent, honorable, and respectable Black folks distort reality and subject themselves to this painful theater of the absurd. My friend asks me if I am going inside, my response, was "no, I can't afford to do this," which was true. The reasons were two fold; firstly I **would** not support this charade economically and secondly I **could** not do it emotionally. The conversation was brief and I could tell it wouldn't register. Looking beyond him into the room I said "I think I'll write an essay about this."

He looked at me and said "You better watch yourself, Cleve. I would keep it to myself, whatever your thinking!" I just want to give people the background to make them aware of what's happening. Someplace I was hearing the words "a conspiracy of silence" and I thought *Yep, a conspiracy of silence right here on Staten Island.*

I knew immediately That I was in danger of destroying a long relationship; we had worked together, watching each other's backs, for the Mobil Oil company, and we shared a lot of interests in the island Black community. I needed to be a better friend but

269

I was so good at making up excuses not to bring up problems - to see the other side. I thought I would need professional help. I also knew that I had some very serious deep-seated resistance to asking for help or counseling. Maybe I could get a self- help book!

The words were already forming. I would return home and open the files already marked TROPHY SEEKERS, saved year after year, decade after decade.

At this "event" I did accept a ticket from a woman I met at St Phillips Baptist Church to get closer to the attendees so that I could photograph the event. Also, I had not eaten and the food odors were tempting! This is an Italian-owned hall, there are no Black waiters, a few servers are perhaps Mexican. I note that the tables seat 10 people and there are 17 tables. I make some quick calculations, 10 X 17 is 170 people attending. The ticket price is $55 per person, a total of $ 9,350. I would add another $8,000 for raffle tickets, clothes, hair cuts, beauty parlors, dry cleaners, fingernails, jewelry, cosmetics, baby sitters, auto use, gas, and tips for the men to park their cars, a total expenditure of $17,350!!!! Later, I am hustled at my table while shoving food into my mouth by a lady who asked me to give her $5 for a raffle ticket. I will never know who won this raffle, or if anyone did win the gift. I was cowed into giving her the $5 because I was embarrassed not to; when she ripped the stub from a huge roll under her arm and shoved it at me, it felt real tacky. Under other circumstances, I would have quietly said to her that I would rather not gamble. As the award recipients at the podium thanked their friends and family, mothers and fathers and God, I left the hall.

In lockstep, I watch the NAACP "Freedom Fund" luncheon at the same Staaten Restaurant. For this annual event luncheon there were more than 200 people in attendance. My calculations came to more than $17,000!!! These twin Black "annuals" totaled a participant outlay of $31,350 dollars, and since these two have taken place for over 20 years that I can recall, that would amount to a cost approaching half a million dollars. The NAACP and the Urban League also paid for events at other places during the year, but these were the annual biggies. The events have no creative spontaneity; simply déjà-vu all over again. My math may be incomplete, but I reckon a total of 2.6 million dollars have been spent at this one place by Black Staten Islanders over 41 years—and growing.

Other Black fraternal organizations, women's groups, civic groups, etc. which normally celebrate at the Staaten can now party at the new Hilton Gardens and other White restaurants, but there are no Black-owned businesses to cater to any event on the island. In March of 2004, the huge 15,000 square foot two story Whitney M. Young building, owned by the Urban League on West Street, was sold to the United Talmudic Academy. The Urban League chairman said the money was going to be invested in other programs on Staten Island. I will not hold my breath, but simply place this notice into my Black Staten Island file. Those of us who cheered, and those who prayed for the arrival of the Whitney M. Young Day Care Center, also fell silent when the Black director was convicted and the center closed due to financial mis-management. No matter, a new Day Care Center was built on Alaska Street and Castleton Avenue by a White guy from Brooklyn. Area Minorities make up 100% enrollment.

In the twenty first century, this legacy of single-minded traditions continues and presides over the death-bed of failed resuscitation efforts of the Black community. Most

Blacks walk and talk the party line, not allowed to put "our business" in the street. I watched the glad-handing and back-slapping, the Colgate smiles of both Black and Whites. I knew none of the little face-to-face smiling conversations were about the perennial conundrum that another "annual" brunch would fail to bring the races any closer to the truth. Blacks on this isolated island cannot escape the appalling situation unless they reach out to Whites and visa-versa, which is the case historically in America. I don't know about you, but I don't accept as valid the implied claim that most markings of racism are made in bad faith or that they are false, especially since those who habitually make this claim rarely attempt to validate it at all.

Attonement is one of my conditions of anti-racist work, and one of its substantive tasks, at least for White people, is public opposition to White expressions of racial bigotry and prejudice, which are ultimately signs and enactments of White privilege. Recognizing those signs and enactments without going on to oppose them is nothing more than an empty, private gesture.

I watched the White politicians, CEOs, etc., entering the La Greci's Staaten, State Senator John Marchi, Brian Laline, the *Advance* reporter, City Councilman Michael McMahon, Paul Goldberg, CEO of the Snug Harbor Cultural Center, Assemblyman John Lavelle, etc. A mental theater of the absurd came to mind, the scene....I see these White movers and shakers in an "Annual" economical huddle event with the Black men and women, ministers and business people, 100 Blacks in Law Enforcement, BWAP, SWAP, SGHS, Urban League, Black Women of Achievement, Borough President Distinguished Service Awards. Rotary Club honorees, honorees of the past decades, all finding a common ground to enable Blacks to acquire and operate a BSISR, a "Black Staten Island Staaten Restaurant" catering hall!

The Richmond County Savings Foundation presented a grant to the NAACP and the President, Ed Josey, immediately announced that the money would be used for a William A. Morris Awards Dinner. My living history does not allow me to fabricate these events or to obfuscate the facts, or to exaggerate. It simply allows me to be free of the chains that blinded me for so long, no pun intended. I could demonstrate, yell, talk and scream, pontificate and/or analyze all you want, but the bottom line remains that we have failed to move forward collectively to right the wrongs inflicted on the Blacks of the island and continue to do so in a time of such tremendous possibilities, here in the Shadow of the Statue of Liberty.

It is now 2013 and more themed awards continue at Li Greci's. I have not seen any creative changes in 45 years of monitoring the annual events and ceremonies. None of the honorees have returned to Staten Island to man the chairs as future Black leaders. The torch will not be passed. There will be no booklet or video to record and remember these events, where do we find our accomplishments? The program books, the letters and speeches, the commemoration booklets, where are the artifacts and the ordinary markers of this generation?

The richness of the challenge is seen in the faces of the youth, the energy; the hope, and the expectations arrive here each year to accept awards, they will leave with a fistful of fog, while the event planners rush to prepare for the same event next year. In 1998 I attended an event at the old Columbian Lyceum in West Brighton and I watched as three young Black men received the Charles K. Smith scholarship awards. I knew Charles Smith, a brother Mason, and I worked with him as a welder in the shipyards getting to know his voice about education for Black people. At this writing I wondered where were these three young Black men: Kevin Serrette, Ousmani Ofari-Yeboah, and Nicholas Payne.

It is a weird, often wonderful, occasionally confounding portrait of 21st century Black Staten Island that has garnished itself with rave reviews in the lone Staten Island newspaper, the *Advance*, with notices and photos of these events which are just as likely to leave the attendees and viewers befuddled and bemused.

The charismatic leaders have been performing the same ritual rites as leaders of a nascent religious cult, which takes place each year at the Li Greci's Staaten restaurant. I have made efforts not to seem nasty; being present I found attending both intimate and claustrophobic. Everyone here wants change, but they don't want **to** change.

Man is a list-making animal and my list may very well fall short of a universal Staten Island appeal. The fact of the matter is basic: we need these lists. The years without them would make no sense. Basically, it is good to know that someone has been watching and paying attention. You need to grasp the list in exactly the same way a drowning man grasps a life preserver. To read the list will tell you that the people that make these annual awards lists have crossed the great sea of packaged amusement and entertainment; the sympathy, the pity, and the tenderness provide a distraction for everyone buying into it, to emerge with their trophies held warmly to their breasts to join others on the mantle of hope. The inscriptions read, "You are The Best!" I try to imagine the fatigue the recipients must have suffered, waiting again and again while suffering through this daylong event. Of course, like all things that pretend to perfect transparency, it is a result of juggling and finesse.

A few organizations from my files

- SIWBA - Staten Island Women's Bar Association
- Leroy Dungey Scholarship Fund
- 369th Veterans Association
- Reverend Arthur D Phillips Scholarship Fund
- NCNW - National Council Of Negro Women'
- Gerald L Carter Awards Person Of The Year
- Business And Professional Women's Club Of Staten Island
- Reverend Hattie Daniels-Smith Davis Award
- Faith United Church Black American Achievement Awards
- Dr. Mary McLeod Bethune Achievement Awards
- Martin Luther King Awards
- Black Achievement Award
- Women Of Achievement Awards
- Henry Lee Collom Scholarship Award
- Urban League Staten Island Branch Annual Awards
- NAACP Freedom Fund Award
- Distinguished Gentleman Mother's Day Awards

Above: Sandy
Ground Historical
Society
Headquarters.

Right: Students'
early archeological
finds from Sandy
Ground area.

Above Left: Hunter home, newly purchased, renovated and returned to Black ownership.

Above Right: Twin cottages, formerly owned by oystermen, still occupied and never abandoned.

FRIDAY, APRIL 28, 2006

City plows down historic Island ruin . . . and then charges 6Gs

Five years after the city stepped in and demolished the remains of an old blacksmith shop, it wants Sandy Ground Historical Society to pay for the job

By TRACEY PORPORA
ADVANCE SOUTH SHORE BUREAU

More than five years after the city demolished the charred remains of one of the oldest blacksmiths shops on Staten Island — and possibly the state — the city has sent the financially strapped Sandy Ground Historical Society a bill for $5,865 to cover the cost.

Society members say they never OK'd the demolition work and tried to salvage a few artifacts from the former shop, but those historic remnants likely wound up in the Fresh Kills landfill.

On Woodrow Road — located directly across the street from the new PS 56 in Rossville — stood the Bishop Forge blacksmith shop, which was housed in a wooden barn for more than 125 years. It was razed by fire in October 1982.

The property was donated to the society by its owner, Joseph W. Bishop, a lifelong resident of Sandy Ground, who died at the age of 81 in 1986, said Julie Moody-Lewis,

ADVANCE PHOTO ■ MIKE FALCO

Julie Moody-Lewis, president of the Sandy Ground Historical Society, stands at the site where one of the oldest blacksmith's shops on Staten Island stood.

"WE DIDN'T KNOW, NOBODY TOLD US"

President & CEO

"WE DIDN'T KNOW THEY WERE GOING TO DO THAT"

Vice President

"WE THOUGHT THEY WERE GOING TO DO AN ARCHEOLOGICAL DIG"

Chief Operations Officer

"WE DON'T HAVE ANY MONEY"

Financial CEO

FACT: "The Joseph Bishop blacksmith shop property was donated to the AME Zion Church and the Sandy Ground Historical Society. Neither fenced nor secured for 16 years after the fire. Community complaints were ignored."

FICTION: "We didn't know anything." "The Sandy Ground Historical Society cares about the property."

SANDY GROUND GUIDE:
"WE HAVE MORE THAN A MILLION VISITORS A YEAR!!"

Staten Island Advance

SINCE 1886

FRIDAY, APRIL 28, 2006

50 CENTS

ROSSVILLE AME ZION CHURCH ANNOUNCES $40 MILLION HOUSING CONSTRUCTION FOR SENIORS AND MODERATE INCOME FAMILIES

- NAACP Annual William A. Morris Humanitarian Awards
- BWAP - Brothers With A Purpose Black American Achievement Awards
- SWAP - Sisters With A Purpose Awards
- The Brown Bombers
- Sisters with a Vision

How many of these annuals are worth recording, worth keeping a detailed record of? Why have we Black Staten Islanders failed to see this as a living archive for the future? Many have hoped for a repository in the Sandy Ground project many years ago, what remains of that? The words and ideas have been massaged into gauzy slogans and the failure of avoidance and denial. The changes in the lives of Black Staten Islanders have been superficial. We are still a segregated community, and I will leave it there, no longer needing to be caught up in abstract arguments or decisions.

On leaving Africa a man said to me "*Aucune condition n'est permenante en America.*" (No condition is permanent in America) I thought he was a lowly baggage handler, how did he know that.

CENTER FOR MIGRATION STUDIES AND DICK DICKENSON

There is no medical doctor or physician of any kind that can diagnose the/my problem. I am luckier than most to have had to opportunity of a forty year relationship. My lifelong friend has given me the tools to find my own way home. The former Staten Island Historian Richard Dickenson is also a Black man. 'Dick' Dickenson and I had a long relationship because of his work as a historian and as a person whose within Borough Hall to speak with in confidence. Many years ago I had made a promise not to speak ill of any Black man, the words above my computer screen hold me to that ideal, with these words.

THE IDEA IS TO EVOKE, AND NOT TO PROVOKE.

We served on committees and gave each other our sincere reasons for agreement or disagreement on any subject. I respected Dick and very often I wish that I had his friendly, open, island wide respect, and that I would like to have been more like him.

We did have disagreements. One strong disagreement was my objection to the murals at Borough Hall. The other was a book, **Holden's Staten Island**.

For many years it was well known that I objected to the murals as historically incorrect and racially offensive. After many months of demonstrating at Borough Hall the Borough President James Molinaro asked, instructed that Dick Dickenson write a long column to the Staten Island Advance Newspaper, in opposition to my demonstrating. Dick felt that my disagreement with the murals should have been a personal matter, meaning, not aired to the public, but I disagreed.

Most people knew Dick Dickenson, and Dick's Op-Ed letter would bring a certain amount of authenticity to the White B.P. it would validate his position, it was as if Black man Dick Dickenson represented all Black people. Many Black people have been reluctantly designated as the organizations "Black representative" who could speak for all Black people. There were dozens of others White people working at the Borough Hall building who could have been "consulted" asked or told by the B.P. on how to respond to my demonstrating. Getting White Americans to become aware of their "unintentional" racist views is a major challenge to society.

The "Mural" essay appears in another section of this book.

A photo of Dick Dickenson was on the front page of the July 15th 2003 edition of the S.I. Advance newspaper with his infectious smile. The caption in large print was ISLAND'S TALE BROUGHT TO LIFE AGAIN.

It was a story about Staten Island history, and a group of S.I. educators, history buffs and politico's gathered at Wagner College to celebrate the reprinting of a book written by an elementary teacher, Edna Holden, who was at the time diseased. The 260 page book was titled, "Staten Island - A Resource Manual for School and Community." The original work starts with the original inhabitants, the Indians of the Leni-Lenape Nation, describing each facet of their lives, such as how they dresses and how they ate. From there she would move through different time periods – from colonial times to the years of the Civil War, and finally the to the "cosmopolitan" period, covering such aspects as churches, business, family life and town infrastructure. Ms Holden ends with her predictions for the boroughs future after the construction of the Verrazano Narrows Bridge. "With this astonishing engineering feat, the Borough of Richmond really will become and integral part of the great metropolis, the City of New York. Ms Holden prophesied, "Many advantages will be enjoyed by its citizens who will find a richer, more fuller life emerging from continued and rapid growth of Staten Island."

Why I had never heard of this book before was a mystery. Reading this front page story, I knew it was fantasy. Ms. Holden would describe the original island inhabitants' lifestyle. There was no mention of the lives, condition, slavery, or the entire contribution of the Black people during that time frame.

Dick Dickenson had taken the original manuscript and doubled its original size. He entered lists of African American Churches and cemeteries. People should know their roots. This is another link to make that happen. There were crucial pieces of history missing Dick said he had updated and edited the book and added a text from the writing of the Black Staten Islander, Evelyn King. Ms. King was a retired teacher who had been the president of the S.I. Branch of the N.A.A.C.P. and he incorporated her work done in the 50's and 60's during the Black Man on Staten Island Project and papers done for her students. Dickenson concluded that the project started in 1991, the year he was appointed the borough's public historian. A dean at Wagner College praised the new book as a wonderful teaching tool. Dickenson must be praised, said Dr. Eleanor Meyer Rogg professor emeritus of sociology at Wagner College, who said that Edna Holden had finally received appropriate recognition. The Director of Education for Historic Richmondtown praised Dickenson for reviving the Edna Holden book, and for addressing local issues of historic preservation. New York State Senator John J, Marchi attended the book signing at Wagner College and said he had great admiration for Dick Dickenson for Staten islanders to get to know each other a little better by reason of your presence and your commitment. He said he could, "Relate to page after page, personally to people I know and love." I checked my file for the year 2004 and Senator Marchi had issued from his discretionary budget a grant known as "member items" a total of $10,000 dollars to the Center for Migration Studies for the support of the book.

Reading all this and looking at the photographs of these new efforts to bring more education about the history of S.I., I wondered where the Center for Migration Studies was located as I had never heard of it.

I wanted to have a copy of the book and I immediately e-mailed Wagner College and asked about the availability and the price of the book. I was told that they did not have any, but I could get a copy at the Center for Migration Studies. I was born on Staten Island but I had never heard of this Center for Migration Studies. I had been very active on S.I. and thought I would know about the Center for Migration Studies.

It was clear that there had never been any in depth study of Island history. I wanted to know about the Black migration and movements on Staten Island I wanted there to be something more than the half century memory records that have been used in school books. I would drive or take a bus to Staten Island for any event that would fill my need to have more information about Staten Island Blacks, slavery and history.

I had to search for the Center for Migration Studies, which was located on a hill overlooking the Atlantic Ocean, the Verrazano Bridge and Brooklyn New York across the bay. I have friends living on the "hill" at Flagg Place overlooking the Narrows. The beautiful historic mansion that the architect earnest Flagg built. There are no sidewalks on Flagg Place, indicating, that only wealthy people live up here. I did walk a friend's dog here a number of times never meeting a Black person.

It was important for me to go there and see the Center for Migration Studies. I drove up and down the narrow Flagg Place twice before I saw a sign that said, ST. CHARLES MISSION CENTER. CENTER FOR MIGRATION STUDIES, "STONECOURT."

I carefully and slowly drove into the gateway between the stone archways. On my right it looked as if it was a guardhouse, and a White woman was setting a potted plant on the doorway step. I stopped, daring not to proceed because I was a black person and blacks do not live in this area, so I stopped, and got out of my seat and looked at her over the car hood and smiled nicely, waving the paper directions. "Hi, I'm looking for The Center for Migration Studies?" She motioned and said, "That way," pointing up the gentle well care for drive past huge trees and a sign that said no dogs or visitors. That was cool I thought, I did not want her to summon the police, hoping my face was enough to place me out of suspicion. Call it my personal Black paranoia, but I was on a mission, and I knew how to act, smiled broadly and used my method acting to stay alive.

I drove past white statues of the Virgin Mary and followed the signs to the parking area. There was only one other car in the area and I got out and took a photo of the wide stairway and the glass front doors that leaded to the entrance. There was no sign. I walked up the stairs and opened the doors to another set of doors and pushed the buzzer. It was some time before a lady came into view on the opposite side of the wide glass door motioning what it was that I wanted. I said I wanted to buy the Holden book. I held up the notice of the Wagner College book fete. She opened the door and asked me to wait, I looked around and on a table was a small booklet of an awards celebration, and I opened after seeing some familiar names on the cover. When the lady returned she gave me a copy of the book and I paid her. I asked if I could take the book from the table and she said I could. I asked if there would be another book reading there and she said yes that Mr. Dickenson would be there to sign more copies of the book. She wrote a number for me to call before I came again to make sure of the date, which was September 17th which was my birth date. I also asked if there was going to be another award ceremony she said yes there would be another in the spring of 2005. She was cool, she offered more conversation other than what I had asked, and I thanked her and drove away carefully stopping to take more photos of the grounds.

At home I would read them through carefully, I was amazed at what I saw, The smaller 75 page booklet was the chronicle of the events of the November 16th 2003 Celebration of Arts an American Legacy, the 12th Annual Awards Brunch and Auction that was held at the Richmond County Country Club a few hundred yards away. I knew two of the awardees, both Black women the recipients, Silvia D'Alessandro, President of the Sandy Ground Historical Society. The other Black lady was Sadja Musawwir Ladner, the Executive and Artistic Director of the Universal Temple of the Arts.

I needed to know more, who were these people. The Center for Migration Studies founded in 1964, I never heard of them? Why were they giving awards to the two Black people. And how does this relate to the benefit to Black people on Staten Island, as a whole.

The Journal booklet describes the Center for Migration Studies of New York Inc, as an educational non profit institute founded in New York in 1964 to encourage the study of sociological, demographic, economic, historical, political, legislative and pastoral aspects of human migration, refugee movements and ethnic group relations worldwide. It continued, Center for Migration Studies brings an independent perspective to the interdisciplinary study of international migration without the institutional restraints of government analysts and special interest groups. (I noted again that my work was primarily confined to the Blacks of Staten Island, which would put me in the 'special interest groups') As the only institute in the United States the CMS is devoted exclusively to understanding and educating the public on the causes and consequences of human mobility at both origin and destination countries. This function is accomplished through the publication of the "International Migration Review," of which I was unable to procure a copy. The CMS is a nongovernmental organization NGO and it has Special Consultancy with the Economic and Social Council of the United Nations with a special representative there.

The Documentation Center links, extensive, performance sponsors, adequacy and quality of U.S. immigration data, housing needs for immigration, social and labor market incorporation, U.S. international refugee policy, non immigrant visa strategies, the historical role of churches on migration, undocumented aliens in New York. There were 16 other paper backs

Books CMS has promoted and funded along with the book that opened my eyes to CMS Holden's Staten Island.

There are five Archival collections at the Saint Charles Seminary at 209 Flagg Place on Staten Island.

Records of Saint Charles Seminary

Papers of father Pio Parolin

Records of the Saint Charles Province of St Charles –Salabrinians

Bouno Family Papers

The papers of Pamela Melcher

I continued to search for an island connection in the papers about CMS and Black people. There are no studies of and about Staten Island in the archives.

CMS founded in 1964 has done amazing work to establish a footprint on the island. I sit and wonder why Black Staten islanders have floundered in accomplishing work such as this. Blacks were on this island in 1639.

My work years ago in 1980 to bring about a similar study were The Black Man on Staten Island study.

As a black American interested in history, I find it hard to understand why so much of the cities African American history and its past are still unknown to students and the general public as well. People know little about the slave revolts, and the people burned at the stake, and the stories and history of people that advanced against impossible odds. Why have we failed?

Great I thought, my internal antenna however was buzzing for attention, and I thought, how I stop the underlying feeling that CMS as an academic work about migration it is BS. On checking my files I did discover that in 2004 I had opened a website into the center for Migration Studies. Re reading it I made a note on the margin, that the CMS was primarily interested in documenting the Italian American experience only to carry out its mission the CMS publishes a quarterly, **International Quarterly Review**. It appeared to have no relevance to in Black people and I filed it away.

I was curious and I knew that this was something odd, a strange voice filtering. I wanted to find out if there were other Black people on the island that knew of this organization, my internal antenna was working overtime as I looked at the books the, journal and the history, of CMS.

The Center for Migration Studies brochure was eye-opening. The pages were confusing because I wanted to know why this twelfth annual celebration was awarded to the two Black women. The former year's celebration numbers over 18 people all were Italian. Most were political Italian, Doctors, lawyers, newspaper editor, and restaurant owners, married couples accepting awards as husband and wife, there was one Dr, Chinese, person. There was no Black on the Honorary Committee. There were no

Blacks on the Program Committee; there were no Blacks on the Journal Committee, or the Auction Committee.

Previous Achievement Award Recipients were:

1991　Italian Americans

1992　Philippine Americans

1993　Korean and Pakistani Americans

1994　Indian and Sri Lankan Americans

1995　Irish Americans

1996　Greek Americans

1997　Immigrant Entrepreneurs

1998　Chinese American Community

1999　Jewish American Community

2000　Global Award Recipients (included 1 Black man)

2001　 'cancelled year'

2002　New Generation Awards Recipients

It was now November 16th, 2003 and the Center for Migration Studies Celebrates the Arts; An American Legacy Brunch and Auction was not exclusively for Black Staten Islanders as in the former years from 1991 to 2002, which recognized one ethnic group each year. The 2003 award ceremony included White people. Awards were extended to Black Americans, Silvia D'Alessandro and Sadja Musawwir Ladner.

It should be noted that the other awardees are White Staten Islanders. Solange Bila, Michel Fressola, Robert and Eva Gabriel, Frances X, Paulo Huber, and Gabriella Lamb.

I had instincts, I had enthusiasm, but I didn't know why this CMS business bothered me. Was I creating something that did not exist? What I did know was the all the words merely infect and ignore and blur, they darken everything it aggravated me so much that I had to find the reason.

I tried to ignore the feeling of my cultural uneasiness while going over again and again to find the bull-shit in the words of the CMS and the recipients.

So, I began with the journal words.

Sylvia Moody D'Alessandro, a descendant of the original settlers from Sandy Ground. Retired from the health care industry after 40 years of service. Sylvia was Client Services Manager at Empire Blue Cross- Blue Shield for 25 years, and subsequently worked as director of Network Development and Provider Relations at Health Plus. She was responsible for the contracting, educating and servicing of the physicians, hospital administrators and other health care professionals that were part of the Health Care provider network. Sylvia is a native Staten Islander, a descendant of the African Americans that first settled the community of Sandy Ground. She has always been interested in the history and role of the African Americans in our community. Her interest in history and art led her to develop a series of greeting cards and an activity book for children that are used to present the history of Sandy Ground in the public and private schools on Staten Island. In addition to being an artist, she is an accomplished quilter. Working with the Sandy Ground Historical Society, she formed the Sandy Ground Quilters Guild.

The Quilters Guild is developing a traveling quilt exhibit that tells the story of Sandy Ground. The designs for the quilts are based on the 21 paintings that depict the history of this re-Civil War African American community. The quilters interrupted their project to create a commemorative quilt honoring the 12 African American firefighters who died at the World Trade Center on September 11, 2001

Sylvia is a founding member of the Sandy Ground Historical Society and is currently serving as its president. The Society has established a library and museum in the Sandy Ground Community, the focus of which is to preserve the African American history on Staten Island. She was one of the founding members of the Harlem YMCA Mentor Program and is a recipient of the Harlem YMCA Black Achiever in History Award in 1984. In 1991 she was presented with the first with the first 'Excellence in Service Award from the New York State Congressional Delegation for her work with Medicare beneficiaries while at Empire State Blue Cross-Blue Shield. In 1998 she was recognized as a" Staten Island Woman of Achievement" by the Staten Island Advance. She has received awards for her community service and her work in health care from the Caribbean American Association, Project Teen Sid and the Aleh Foundation.

She has also served as Principal for a Day through the PENCIL program, and provided ongoing assistance to the school in her home borough. Sylvia is a lifelong member of the Rossville AME Zion church, where she serves as a trustee. Sylvia is the wife of Robert D'Alessandro, mother to Julie Lewis and grandmother to four, Idris Ojelade, Shamel Lewis and twins Camillah and Jamila Lewis.

The only thing motivating me is my curiosity, the "cultural uneasiness" about the relationship of the White Catholic CMS and the Black Sandy Ground.

Will there be a quid-pro-quo exchange of directors. Will Reverend Joseph Fugolo c.s. the CMS Executive Director speak at the Sandy Ground Church or the museum..?. Will any of the 20 member staff visit Sandy Ground?

Sadja Musawwir Ladner, Awardee

In 1967 when the civil rights and Black empowerment was a very strong social issue, Sadja and a few other artists incorporated their talents and skills to achieve a common goal of owning a business. Sadja Fine Art Fashion (SFAF).

A boutique which featured hand crafted jewelry, clothing and home accessories was formed. It was the first African American owned boutique on Staten Island and addressed the important social issue of African Americans needing a heightened level of self awareness and pride. SFAF sold merchandise that was representative of African American history, culture and future. This boutique was a catalyst and inspiration for many budding artists who were featured in the fashion shows which were presented in a theatrical manner.

In 1970, Sadja had a beautiful boutique called "Saadia" at 1090 Castelton Avenue which sold incense and burners, African beads, paintings, sculptures, dresses, hand-crocheted shawls, patchwork jumpsuits and liberation buttons, sun-streaked tye dye fabric, Aztec wall hangings, antique furniture, Spanish lace mini-dresses.

Sadja Musawwir Ladner is the executive and artistic director at the Universal Temple of the Arts (UTA) a nonprofit, community based organization founded by Maurice Phillips, along with a number of other artists, including Ms. Ladner. UTA offers a variety of programs and services for youth ages 6-12, ranging from dance, arts and crafts, sewing and computer literacy. The programs are designed to foster discipline, patience, confidence, self esteem and decision making skills. Their goal is for participants to become well rounded individuals, capable of better performance in both social and classroom settings. With Sadja at the helm as instructor, Universal Temple of the Arts was the first organization on Staten Island to provide multicultural education. In 1992, Sadja became a certified Cultural Diversity Awareness Trainer. Sadja was a member of "Increase the Peace Corps," a program offered by the administration of former New York City Mayor David Dinkins. Since then, she has been heavily involved in speaking on the beauty and worth of cultural diversity in schools and business throughout the New York City area.

Also trying to keep abreast and meet the ever changing needs of Staten Islands communities, Sadja has expanded the focus of UTA to include programs geared to offsetting the increased level of violence within these communities through the incorporation of Conflict Resolution and Peer Meditation through the Arts. In a nurturing environment, this program provides children with a positive outlet to express themselves by channeling their frustrations into creative energy to produce artwork capable of making social statements. These classes, in some ways, are therapeutic for the students. It is said that, "One who fails to plan, plans to fail." This is a phenomenon that disables many minorities from living up to their fullest potential. There was a deficiency of programs available to the youth of these communities to assist them in preparing for their futures as professionals in the workforce. Sadja introduced Entrepreneurial and Computer Training programs, as well as an introductory Spanish course, as being bilingual creates more work opportunities for people . The Spanish language class is also a part of Sadja's continued efforts to bridge the cultural gaps that exist on Staten Island. In addition to Universal temple of the Arts, Sadja is involved in a myriad of educational and social organizations. Sadja teaches a weekly Thursday evening sewing class to the parents and children housed in Project Hospitality, one of Staten Islands transitional housing facilities. She has given this class since its opening. Sadja Musawwir Ladner is also a substitute Paraprofessional in the Special Education department of the New York City Department of Education. She serves on the boards of Northfield Development Corp. Children's Montessori Schools and maintains her association with Big Brothers and Big Sisters. She recently joined the staff of the Girls Choir of Harlem as its wardrobe Mistress. She has received numerous awards from

Lambda Kappa Mu-Sorority, The New York City Housing Authority, and the Coro Foundation, among others.

There were African Americans on the island for centuries, and now the Liberian Community play a role, real Africans and real Americans. Black Americans are real non hyphenated Americans. Been here since Columbus, served in the wars slaved in the kitchens, totally American, perhaps more American than those who host these "Awards Celebrations" to salvage their old celebrations of other ethnic groups from 1991 to the present.

Why did this CMS need to recognize Black Americans ..? Perhaps they needed to fill their guilty consciences, and repent of being lacking in using a few Black American among the 5 other White Awardees . This 2003 fete is their final Awards celebration. I called to ask for information about a 2004 Awards celebration and was told there would be one in 2005.

Finally, there has never been a total Black American celebration as the other ethnic groups from Italian, Philippines, Korean, Pakistani, Indian, Sri Lankan, Irish, Greek, Jewish, and Chinese.

And finally, when will Black Staten Islanders look beyond their collections of "award" trophies and refuse to be added to fill a "Black person needed" slot for "Multicultural" PR publicity announcements for White Awards ceremonies.

The Center for Migration Studies' attempt to fete Black Islanders reflects the invisible world view of White supremacy in otherwise well intentioned individuals; they are manifested in individuals, institutions and the Staten Island culture at large and it promotes enormous psychological stress in all people of color.

ON THE VERGE OF EXTINCTION – PROPOSED DEVELOPMENT

My meeting with the new pastor at the AME Zion Church came quite by accident while touring Sandy Ground with a writer friend who volunteered to work with me, As we walked about the area there was one car in the church driveway, I imagined there was someone inside I opened the door and hollered "hello." A voice answered, "Yes." We walked inside and I followed the voice that came from up a narrow, winding, wooden staircase. At the top was a woman that I had assumed quite correctly was the new minister reverend Janet Jones. It was a very hot July day, at the top I found a place to stand next to her while my friend waited on the top step. The "office" was a cluttered closet, and I introduced myself and my friend who was still on the steps smiling as we shook hands. There was no air conditioner or window fan, and the remnants of discarded parts of mimeograph machines and fax machines lay amid books and other papers on what may have been a desk on the floor, there were no chairs. A thin layer of dust covered everything. She dejectedly at the refuse and said she must get this straightened out. Reverend Jones was a full figured woman with close cropped hair on her round warm face she wore glasses and a nice smile, I tried to study her mood hoping that we did not interrupt something. I told her of my mission to eventually write a book about Sandy Ground and the church would figure prominently in it. She said she was from New Jersey and she liked the area and would help me any way she could. I had known the previous minister, Reverend Julius Ingram, quite well, he lived in Port Richmond and we had a very good relationship, it was a conversation he declined to go into, his removal as minster of the Rossville AME Zion church, I saw no need to open any further conversation because the heat was now stifling in the cramped office-cum-closet space. I congratulated her on her on her appointment as minister, left my card and negotiated down the steep stairway and outside where my friend waited fanning himself in the cool shade of the building It would be the last time I would speak to her face to face, we would however correspond via e-mail and letters afterward.

A few weeks later my e-mail and post box would be filled with Staten Island Advance newspaper clippings, friends who new of my interest sent the incredible news of the Sandy Ground AME Zion Church considering a proposal to construct houses on the church property costing between $ 11 million to $14 million dollars. Some members of the church were very concerned about the wisdom of accepting such a proposal, as well as the lack of transparency in the proceedings. There was no mention of a relationship between the AME Zion church or the Sandy Ground Historical Society, about this construction proposal. Did Sylvia Harris know of this? Did the SGHS have a seat at the table?

I knew from Surrogate's office files and research of the land deeds that there was a mutual land use agreement by former black community members that left property in their wills to Sandy Ground and the AME Zion church. They died, thinking there would be a working relationship with the church and the historical society when land use would be an issue.

I had no idea what I should or would do with the land construction issue, I was now living in Washington D.C. and did not have immediate access to much of the information that came across my desk. I was not an architect or a lawyer, a builder or a banker, my activities and presence would be seen simply as a "disruptive influence," one who lacked subtlety, and I was loathe to open another Pandora's box, after my failed campaign to bring vitality and transparency to the Sandy Ground Historical Society. The newspaper articles continued: **CHURCH PLAN STIRS DEBATE ON THE SOUTH SHORE....SENIOR HOUSING PLAN BLASTED.....SANDY GROUND HOUSING HITS A SPEED BUMP.....SENIOR HOUSING PROPOSAL FOR ROSSVILLE SHOUTED DOWN.....RIGHT "AS OF RIGHT"...**

Before the Verrazano Bridge opened in 1964 thousands of working class people from crowded Brooklyn neighborhoods like Bay Ridge, Bensonhurst, Flatbush. The New Jersey Shore and Outer Long Island, much too expensive, Staten Island was the first choice to have a home of your own a yard and a pool, if you had more children you could add on to your home. The first wave was from the Italians, then the Russians, Contractors became builders, architects, and Real Estate dealers. A building frenzy through the 1960's thru the 1980's the Building Departments were overwhelmed, unprepared, and overworked to keep up with the codes and speed of construction. Farmland, swamps, and wetlands became prime property, on which to build a home. The elected leaders sat back hoping for a piece of the action. They were mostly young city workers that would become generally conservative politically, anti-government residents. Many police and firemen from this area would die in the World Trade Center attacks. Together they are a volatile force, that could bring Union, Police, Construction Trades, and politicians to issues they disliked to their knees.

****

The Sandy Ground area was now a community of million dollar homes owned by whites from Brooklyn, that wanted to leave the congestion and minorities that moved to Brooklyn after being evicted from Manhattan because of the high rents. Sandy Ground was now a community of New York City workers, mainly firemen, police, Wall Street brokers, traffic and sanitation workers, private business people most were Catholic and Italian. A volatile mix that would stand it's ground and meet at the Stolzenthaler, Knights of Columbus Hall in Charleston a mile away.

Their anger was not to have two four story buildings including a 1,900 community center on the 1½ acre property owned by the Rossville AME Zion church. Racism surfaced immediately, "these are projects," "What kind of people will live there?" … at the public meeting of 350 people at P.S. 56 across the street from the SGHS office, that remained silent, making no press statements. Some blacks were against the construction proposal, sisters Lucille and Theresa Herring church members, were vocal in their "as of right" designation used by the Church to continue, with limited input from city regulators, so the church is within their rights.

"Within rights does not mean it's right!!." Lucille herring a member of the Rossville AME Zion church maintains that the taller apartment buildings were too dense in context with the surrounding community. "The church ground should be revered, not desecrated, please consider the importance of preserving our history, the church grounds were always considered the center of this community, save this historic church grounds, do the right thing, Do not approve this housing development." She is right, four story apartment houses are too much in low rise one and two family homes.

The ugly comments would continue, about the lower classes status insisting that such people do not belong in "their community." Reverend Jones said she worried about racism, now she believes it may be ageism. "I'm sure that the church will call a meeting and inform the community of what's transpired," said Elmore Taylor a member of the AME Zion church.

I had begun to file everything with regards to the Sandy Ground building complex, what I did not get was anything of input from the SGHS.

The church had no telephone, e-mail or web-site, although Reverend Jones did have a personal e-mail address. I decided to drive to Staten Island with a friend and speak to anyone who would speak to me, Black or White, beside the church was described as an archaeological dig. What I photographed was a huge diesel front end loader backhoe that had gouged a long path between the huge trees to the center of the lots and dug some holes.

This was the archeological survey dig required by the City Planning Commission because the building project would require some public funding because the site was now designated on the National register of Historic Places. Reverend Jones said her congregation hired a contractor to conduct a dig, they discovered only a foundation and some utensils and the information had been sent to the state for review. The state identified a dozen problems with the excavation procedure, saying the excavated area appeared not to have been done in a controlled manner and had demonstrated, "sloppiness."

I remembered my work with students from Richmond College and people from the S.I. Museum so many years ago, we did not work close to the church building because we could not get permission to dig near the church in a controlled manner. Still many people expressed their concern about just what would be uncovered at this site if done properly. Our visit would give us a silent message in the windows of the white home owners across the street from the church, we photographed the disapproval in huge print in almost every window, I asked my friend who was White if she would ring some bells, while I got out of sight, and ask a person about the signs, when he did she was asked who she was and whom she represented, without fail,she got no long winded response from any homeowner except to say "we do not want to be involved" or "we do not want big developments over there", What became clear to me was that the White people were not against development, what they did want was a smaller footprint, and they wanted o be involved. Driving around the community to was fair to say that Whites had come to stay and they would fight decrease and racial tones, but they were also ready to" stand their ground" To anything that threatened "their" way of life in Sandy Ground Staten Island.

Reverend Jones and I would e-mail letters from time to time and respond to my letters, I felt that she would be under a great deal of stress being the voice of the black community.

CORRESPONDENCE WITH PASTOR JONES

March 12, 2004

Pastor Janet H. Jones
Rossville A.M.E. Zion Church
584 Bloomingdale Road
Staten Island, NY 10309

I would like to congratulate you on your appointment as Pastor to the Rossville African American Church. I offer my regards to you and your family and wish you a long and fruitful tender in the leadership of the Church which has a long history in the lives of generations of Black Americans on Staten Island. No historic account of our history is without mention of this.

I would also like to commend you on your initiative with the Church Trustee Ministry to improve the church land by considering a land development proposal. The area of Rossville, as you know, has been a centerpiece of development and discussion on Staten Island for the last two decades. I am curious as to why you and members of the Trustee Ministry did not respond to several designs and suggestions relating to the same area which I submitted to you. I mention this because there are members of the community who have asked me to comment on their behalf. Nevertheless, I applaud the committee's efforts to take direct action now to protect the cultural resources while trying to promote the economic revitalization of the area.

However, my understanding of the proposal by the Regan Corporation and the Danois Architects raises a number of concerns and questions. Foremost among them is the apparent lack of input by an attorney for the church. It is unfathomable that negotiations regarding the use of valuable church property in a commercial venture would begin or continue without the intervention of a commercial and real estate attorney. While I have not reason to impugn the integrity of the commercial entities who have made the proposal for a senior citizen residence, it is routine to involve an attorney early in the process, not after architects and city planners have already given their blessings. It is unclear that research into their past performance has been gathered, and whether the proposal is equitable and secure for the church in light of current business practices. We have certainly seen the disastrous results of other ventures involving seemingly forthright and competent development corporations.

There seems to be a general reluctance to ask, formally or informally, the hard questions that will have to be resolved before there is a "buy-in" from the church congregation. Given the historic legacy of the church, I would dare to suggest that this buy-in be extended to the entire Black Community. It would seem, at a minimum, that the Ministry Land Development Committee would be in contact with the Sandy Ground Historical Society to join this effort to use its historic resources and long-held vacant Black lands provided them by Black ancestors in thief wills, for just such a purpose. With all respect to the parties involved, a construction project of this magnitude, a whopping $11 to $13 million project, to which must be added the inevitable "cost overruns," begs the intervention and advice of more experienced legal and commercial parties before buy-in from the congregation can be sought. If the decision is to ignore the historic significance of the church by developing the land commercially, there are still many troubling features of the proposal.

Questions jump out to me, an admitted layman in such negotiations. For example, the church is to receive 20% of the revenue from the senior facility. Does the church have any rights as to how the facility is managed? Is the Regan Corporation the management entity, and if so, have they managed other senior facilities? If the facility goes bankrupt, either from mismanagement or other reasons, what is the church left with? If the church was unable to pay the taxes for such buildings, would the city take the buildings along with the church property? And what is a "development fee" and how will it be used? Putting aside such considerations as how the senior apartments will be filled and by whom, whether there will be a racial mixture, how much "affordable" housing costs, and where the services to attract seniors will come from, such as transportation, shopping, medical care, and entertainment, what evidence is there that 80 to 90 apartments could be readily filled in that location? Has anyone looked into the financial problems such facilities are already having in Staten Island and nearby New Jersey?

The proposal is to lease the land to the "entity" running the facility for 60 years. Yet, the church will receive 20% of the cash flow for only 30 years, at which point the entity, which has received 80% of the income during that 30 years, will receive 30% of the value of the building, presumably from the church. Assuming, and this is a stretch, that the percentages involve are equitable, and that the facility is still a profitable venture 30 years down the road, is the church then responsible for its management? Is the historic legacy of Staten Island's Black community being sacrificed for commercial gain?

In recognition of the church's financial difficulties, has any attempt been made to seek collaboration or advice from the city's premier Black history institution, the Schomburg Center in Manhattan? Little by little, we have seen land, cemeteries and resources owned by the Black community eroded away. This is certainly the last chance to retain the remaining historic property in Rossville.

In the mid-1970's I was one of those who worked and heralded the construction of the Whitney M. Young, Jr. Day Care Center on West Street in West Brighton. High hopes and celebration ended last week when the huge building was sold at auction to a Jewish group for a school in the very same building. The expectations for the Martin Luther King Heritage House on Castleton Avenue died and the building is being sold at auction by the city. The community center planned and promised decades ago for the property at Castleton and Henderson has been forgotten, and now private housing is to go there. These are just a few of the many development opportunities planned for the Black community that have failed, which should provoke healthy skepticism and caution in the plans for the Rossville project.

Is the goal of the project simply to provide the church enough income to maintain its building and pay for utilities? Or is the revenue estimated to be enough to protect the historic legacy of the area, and if so, how? Is the expected revenue from 30 years of hoped-for income, contingent upon the good management of the senior facility and a stream of paying customers, an amount more that the revenue the church would have from simple selling the property and living from the interest on the principal? Have other options for development of the land been sought or considered? Have the Regan Development Corporation and the Danois Architects been subjected to an in-depth examination of past performances and history, not just their portfolio and presentation? Certainly, an Internet search reveals that Danois Architects received an award for "Green Building" design in 2003, a commendable achievement. However, even if the architecture of the structure is impeccable, the building and managing of it will determine its long-term success. As for the Regan Development Corporation, they seem to have been embroiled in some controversy in Paterson, New Jersey. Even if they are determined to be competent developers, do they have a track record for senior residences, which require special consideration? Is such a residence intended to attract active people 55 and over rather than only the very frail and elderly? Many facilities built for the over 55 crowd are finding their residents in need of more assistance for which the facilities have not budgeted. The Patterson, New Jersey community was not against Regan's development of their historic site per se, but wanted something more in keeping with the district's tradition. Is it not up to the Black community and the Church Trustee Ministry to consider the historic relevance of the land to be developed and the risks of building and managing a senior residence on that land?

I send to you and the members of the community my heartfelt best wishes for success, and if I can assist in any way please let me know. I hope our myriad questions and concerns stimulate additional discussion. I represent no formal group or organization, but I can assure you that these questions are not mine alone.

Sincerely,
Cleve Overton
3301 9th St. NE
Washington, DC 20017
FAX: 1-202-526-5109 E-mail: cleveo@aol.com

cc: Ms. Yvonne Taylor

****

3 -18 - 2004
Reverend Janet H. Jones, Pastor
Rossville A.M.E. Zion Church
584 Bloomingdale Road
Staten Island, NY   10309

Dear Reverend Jones,

Your slogan, "Together Everyone Achieves Success" is true. However, there seem to be aspects of the land proposal that need to encompass the "everyone," now more than ever.

I will not waste your valuable time by simply suggesting what the problem is. I will try to encapsulate it here in a letter as carefully-worded as possible, because I have written you and Mrs. Yvonne Taylor several letters without receiving a reply. From the beginning of your very recent appointment, I have been concerned about the church and the future of the Sandy Ground community. As you have pointed out to Mr. Larry Regan, "There is a new climate in the church." I had hoped this did not reflect negatively on the departure of Reverend Julius Ingram. While change is often a good thing, impulsive and rash decisions can bring devastating and irrevocable results. I want to confirm to you that Reverend Ingram is also very much concerned.

I doubt your short tenure at the church has given you the physical or mental time to reflect on the entire package of facts and proposals presented to you, nor given you the opportunity to consult with diverse and interested parties on such a momentous decision as the future of the church property. By physical, I mean your accepting so great a responsibility without assistance and without means of communication such as a private office with fax and/or e-mail contact. A phone that is not answered leaves me and others, including Mr. Regan, to comment on how difficult it is for others to contact you. You have no listed cell-phone, and the standard land line is often not answered. I have no doubt that the Lord will show you the mental ways to accomplish your goals, and I hope you take the time needed.

The unanswered questions and sheer abstract nature of consideration of many important subjects regarding the construction is simply amazing. The drawing of the church and surrounding properties has no actual survey lines or notations as to scale, with the only measurement being the total size of the buildings' "footprints." I would be surprised if any member of the Land Development Proposal Committee had taken the time to go to Borough Hall to gather the actual surveys of each of the three properties in question. Block and Lot numbers mean absolutely nothing. The use of such a back-of-the-envelope drawing in formulating a proposal and making such a weighty decision is unprofessional, and frankly, appalling.

Your suggestion of "moving people across the street" is odd, and implies the church would be buying additional property, presumably the Taylor property. If the Taylors consent to sell their land, how will the selling price be determined? Who are the members of the Land Development Proposal or Committee...?..

The questions are myriad. What will attract seniors to this area? Answer: "The ministry will address their needs." What does that mean? Must all residents be practicing Christians? A major question for us is how the Regan Corporation will manage to obtain a mortgage from the New York State Housing Finance Agency. And why the corporation gets 80% of the cash flow. Why not 70% or 75% or 65%? What data are the figures based on? Fair market rents at $600 to $800 per month calculates out to about $54,000 to $72,000 per month provided 89 units (according to diagram) are all filled. What data were provided to decide that 80 - 90 units is the ideal size? Who will be responsible for maintaining heating and air-conditioning systems, indoor cleaning/housekeeping and landscape maintenance, for example, is not clear. Will this be contracted out to a private company? The suggestion to rent a bus to visit a construction site does not seem useful. Would it not be better to visit a fully completed and operating development rather than one under construction? Where are the completed sites that have been done by the Regan Corporation? Are the apartments only for fully independent seniors or will there by assisted living type services for those who need them? These services, such as food service, laundry and nursing assistance, become very expensive. The Regan Corporation suggests you form a for-profit corporation. What does your attorney suggest?

Have there been any alternative proposals submitted for the land in question? As for the sewer to be installed by the Perna Corporation, it is unclear why there is a demand to commit now when the project is in its infancy as to how many hook-ups will actually be needed? Has any inquiry be made into whether a package of this type might be presented to the N.Y. State Financing Agency to simply hire a building contractor for a smaller project now before going full bore into a $14 million project?

Why have the trustees or members of the Board or Committee who have assisted you with this packet of information not been able to sign on to it for identification, in any of the documents you have distributed? Should there not be a Corrash & Hollander legal representative or a neutral advocate at these discussions and meetings to take minutes for

287

future documentation and provide guidance? However well-intentioned the TEAM may be, do the members of the team have the necessary skills and knowledge to make this decision? Who are they? Do they have the interest of the Sandy Ground historical site in mind or only an income to keep the church going?

The full scope on the Regan Corporation involvement must he negotiated to the satisfaction of the full board and membership, and at this time there is a murky, if not sinister, atmosphere surrounding the entire project.

N.Y. State and Federal Government regulations pertaining to Senior and Assisted Living housing are stringent for all new construction. The Bush administration housing codes set to receive "Faith Based" moneys apply to the existing rules and can be costly to amend in older or new construction that do not have them. It is a warning best understood before signing contractors to begin. After all, "THE BUSINESS OF AMERICA IS BUSINESS." Please respond, as I am writing out of serious concern and confusion, as an older Black citizen born and raised on S.I. who has seen much sadness and deception in my long life. We would all be immensely saddened to see more S.I. Black-owned property go the way of so much similar property has before - to the city, and then to the auction block. Thank you for your kind attention.

Sincerely,

Cleve Overton
3301 9th St., NE
Washington, DC 20017   Fax: 202 526 5109 E-mail: cleveo@aol.com

****

Reverend Janet H. Jones, Pastor   3-24-2004
Rossville A.M.E. Zion Church
584 Bloomingdale Road
Staten Island, New York   10309

Dear Reverend Jones,

At vespers last evening, after receiving no responses, I quietly decided to conclude my mailings to you and others in the church. However, this missive is prompted by your not reading last Sunday any of the letter or quotes or bringing any of the points I made to the congregation for discussion.

You wonder if I am a member. Yes, I am a member in the personal club of our color; this is our fraternity. My not being with you in person is simply due to distance and not any lack of heart. Today's technology brings us together and closer via cyberspace. We have been together on Gorée and Elima ...... and countless other castles and hostels, before we arrived here in the United States.

Would you rather I did not speak? Would you rather I asked you not to look into the Sandy Ground Historical Society workings? Would you rather I did not suggest that your office should be in one of the church-owned buildings across the street from the church ... would you rather I keep my own counsel and not question how you became sole spokesperson and representative for such a large undertaking? I dare say that at the cornerstone laying, those who are now in the shadows will come forward for the photo shoot. When the brass plaque is attached to the building, there will be others dressed and smiling, witnessing the event with their names displayed.

I want to reiterate my position. I seek no employment, status or moneys. I am not representing any organization or group. I am accessible always by multiple means of contact. My C/V and my history and experience on S.I. are public record, available to you. And I am sure if you inquire, others will voice opinions about me. There has never been any reason not to have my name attached to any correspondence. I have nothing to hide and my intentions should be clear. Believe me, I don't want anyone to be confused at what I have said or the questions I have raised. We are geniuses at noticing racism and discrimination. But there will be no White person, however concerned or interested, who will dare raise such questions or who, witnessing the proceedings from some balcony, will comment as to the wisdom of the decisions we make for our community. If we ourselves don't speak up or voice our opinions, we are doomed to perpetuate the division among and between ourselves. Our "crabs-in-a-barrel" pathological attitude and fondness for secrecy will fail in the face of positive leadership. And you have the staff of leadership. The Lord has good plans for us even when things seem overwhelming, and I wish you wisdom and a large measure of luck.

                                        Most Sincerely,

                                        Cleve

3301 9th St., NE, Washington, DC 20017   Tel" 202 526 7072 Fax: 202 526 5109
cleveo@aol.com
****

289

Dear Pastor Jones, I would love to talk to you on the phone. Every time I try it is busy or there is no answer. Anyway, this is a good solution for now. Things really look positive! Our professionals believe we can build about 80-85 units of senior housing on the properties and keep the Church just where it is The best part is that they met with the NYC building dept. in Staten Island and they said we could do this without variances because the property is in the special district. The next step is for you to get me your surveys on the properties and the agreement you signed with the developer that gave you rights to hook into his sewer. I need to see that so we can determine sewer capacity. This is the most important point in the deal. We can't build 80-85 units of seniors housing without sewer. Please call me to arrange a meeting as soon as possible with our architect. With what I learned if we have sewer all we need to do is verify all items with the planning commission, let them agree and file for building permits. As we go through that procedure, I will start processing the deal with the State for funding and permanent mortgage. We do need to put an agreement together between our company and the Church. Call me in the office to discuss. First try the office then the cellular phone. We will get in touch. Thanks. Larry

****

Mr. Larry Regan
Regan Development Corporation
1055 Saw Mill River Road, Suite 204
Ardsley, New York 10502

Re: Property Development

Dear Mr. Regan:

It was a pleasure to speak with you this morning. I saw a number without any notation and decided to call it and was pleased to finally get connected to you. I am the new pastor of the Rossville A.M.E. Zion Church, Staten Island, New York. I am writing to reconnect with you and the Regan Development Corporation regarding developing church-owned vacant land in the South Shore section of Staten Island

About three years ago, you met with Rev. Ingram, Church Trustees, then Presiding Elder Louis Richardson, and Rev. Douglas Maven of First A.M.E. Zion church, Paterson, New Jersey, to explore options for developing this property.

Mrs. Yvonne Taylor, Chair of the Trustee Ministry at the church informed me that she and all parties present were impressed with your portfolio and presentation, and were anxious to proceed with a development plan, but nothing happened.

There is a new climate in the church now and we are ready to move forward in the process to develop our property. Barriers that may have hindered progress in the past are no longer obstacles to proceeding. We would like to meet with you to talk about creative ways to utilize our land to benefit the church and the community. The current consensus of the congregation is to build Senior Housing and a Multi-purpose Center.

I look forward to hearing from you in the very near future.
Sincerely,
Janet H. Jones, Pastor, Rossville A.M.E. Zion Church
****

Draft Building Proposal for Vacant Sandy Ground Land

This letter is by no means a definitive statement or an end all solution to the future of the Sandy Ground Historical Society and a new life for the AME Zion Church. It is intended to be a catalyst by providing an example of the kind of building that could serve as a real center for the historical archives and research of our history and legacy.

Recent phone conversations and talks have moved me to explore on paper the alternatives to this major move and task as I see it. There can be no doubt that extensive meetings and group actions will be needed to start this process, and I state it plainly here so there will be no misunderstanding of the difficulties.

The current members of the Sandy Ground Historical Society will have to be either included or replaced if this idea is to go forward.

Valuable property now sits idle in the hands of the SGHS. The Collins and the Bishop properties are vacant and valuable land, and for that matter, there may be more.

A new building is needed, and it should inspire pride and reflection. When the new building has been completed, the artifacts now in the SGHS can be moved to the new site, a solid and secure building, and the old site sold.

There will be many more questions, and I am unable to answer so this draft will also be short and to the point.

Do we reach for a higher plane, or continue to sit while the homestead of our forebears is lost?

Sample drawings and sketch attached.

Cleve Overton
3301 9th Street NE
Washington, DC 20017

Special South Richmond Development District (Staten Island)

The special South Richmond Development District was established to guide development of predominantly vacant land in the southern half of Staten Island. The special district maintains the densities established by the underlying zones and ensures that new development is compatible with existing communities.

To maintain the existing community character, the district mandates tree preservation, planting requirements, controls on changes to the topography, height limits, and setback and curb cut restrictions along railroads and certain roads. It restricts construction within designated open space (a defined network of open space set aside for preservation in its natural state). To preserve designated open space without penalizing the owners of such space, owners are permitted to transfer development rights from the designated open space to the balance of their property. A topographic survey and a report on the availability of public services must be submitted by the developer as a prerequisite to any application for development. A performance bond must also be provided to assure continued maintenance and improvement of public open space.

Pastor Jones attempted to contact The Regan Corporation via letter re. Development of vacant land owned by the Church.

Pastor Janet Jones finally contacted Larry Regan by phone and followed up with a letter expressing an interest in renewing conversations regarding property development. Attachment.

Sis. Yvonne Taylor, Chair of the Trustee Ministry, and Pastor Jones met with Larry Regan to discuss our options for development. Attachment.

Excerpt from Pastor's Report at the January Trustee Ministry Meeting.

Contacted L. Regan via email to get an update on his investigation as to the viability of developing affordable senior housing on the church's property. Attachment.

Sis. Taylor, Bro. Taylor, and Pastor Jones met with Larry and Ken Regan of the Regan Development Corp. and Mr. David Danois of Danois Architects, to review their findings, to get an idea of the scope of the project, and to get commitment from the Taylors of their willingness to sell their property.

Pastor Jones presented the project proposal to the Rossville AME Zion Trustee Ministry. Each Trustee (Taylors recused themselves) individually said yes to moving ahead to present the proposal to the congregation.

Present: Larry and Ken Regan, David Danois (Architect), Yvonne Taylor, Elmore Taylor, Rev. J. Jones

Project: To develop property owned by the Rossville AME Zion Church
Scope of Project: To build three affordable senior housing buildings with a total of 85-90 units for persons 55 and older and a Community Center on the ground floor of one building.

The property is located in the Special South Richmond Development Section that has many limitations on development.
Funding: NY State Housing Finance Agency
Long-term bond financing
Tax Exempt Long-term debt
Empire Loan Fund
100% Affordable Senior Housing

Sewer: Mr. Perna will extend sewer connection agreement beyond the April expiration date in his agreement with the church and will sell as many other connections needed at $5000 each. Cost savings of $200,000.

Estimated Project Costs: $11-13 million

Meeting Summary December 18, 2003

The meeting was opened by Rev. Janet Jones with the reading of Psalm 127 vs 1&2 followed by prayer.

Purpose of the meeting – To discuss the proposal for development of vacant land. At this meeting we will review the proposal. Another meeting will then be held to vote on the proposal. If the vote is affirmative a site plan will be developed by architect, David Danois.

Review of discussion
1. The corp. with which we have discussed this proposal is Regan Corp. They have done projects of this type, and did a development for Rev. Maven's church in Paterson, NJ.
2. We are interested in Senior Housing. A minimum of 85-90 units is required to make this a viable development.
3. The Regan Corp will derive 80% of the cash flow.
4. A partnership will be formed between the church and the Regan Corp.
5. The Taylors have been approached to see if they would sell their property (adjacent to the church owned property) to meet the area requirements for the number of units proposed.
6. Other contacts have been made for information from City agencies. The architect will meet with the Dept. of City Planning and representative of the church if the plan is approved.
7. The proposal was presented to the Trustees on Mar 4th who discussed it and each trustee expressed their approval. (The Taylors recused themselves)
8. (Refer to packet of information for other details of the project)

Sewer Connection Agreement
    The sewer connection agreement between the church and Perna is due to expire in Apr. 2004. Larry Regan contacted Perna who agreed to extend the deadline, and also allow us to buy additional tie-ins. An agreement will be drawn up to put this verbal agreement in writing.

For-Profit Corp.
    The Regan Corp. suggests that we form a for-profit corp. Ques. Raised – What is advantage of a for-profit corp. vs. a not-for-profit corp? We will seek an answer. During course of the project all land will be owned by the church and the Regan Corp. Land will revert to the church at the end of the agreement.

    The Taylors will determine an amount for their land, and after review the method of payment will be determined.

Some projected financial gains. At the end of the project the money derived from the Developers Fee for the church will be $200,000. The church subsequently will receive 20% annually of the net.

The apartments will rent at fair market value – approximately $600-$800 per unit (1 or 2 bedrooms)

Senior housing is needed in S.I. and this development is a way of doing ministry.

Ballpark figure for the development is $12-14 million, which will be financed by the New York State Housing Financing Agency.

Comments, Questions and Concerns expressed by those attending this meeting

1. The number of units in this small area will be hard on the existing community.
2. Maintenance – Who will maintain the property? Response – On-site management
3. No. of units – the no. of units proposed is no worse than building 40 attached housed as has been done in this area already.
4. Is parking provided? Ans. Yes. We will allow ample parking for the church and plan for expansion if and when needed.
5. We should consider concerns of those living in this community.
6. Footprint of development to the property on which the church building is situated allows for a community center and space for other uses such as office, meeting rooms, etc.
7. Will there be an environmental impact study? Ans. Yes, it's mandatory.
8. Are we doing this project independent of the Conference? Response – Yes, however the Bishop and Presiding Elder will be kept informed of the progress of the development for their approval if and when necessary.
9. Is the Regan Corp applying for a grant or loan? Ans. No, a mortgage.
10. Will this be 60 yr mortgage or will it be satisfied in less than this amount of time?

Who will represent the church? Ans. Law firm of Corrash and Hollonder. They will meet with us, review our project and do some research if and when project is approved. The attorney fee can be included in the initial funding package.

What will attract seniors to this area? Ans. As a ministry we will address their needs.

Why do we have to purchase additional property? Can we look at the church owned property across the street for development in lieu of developing entirely on the site identified? If we use this property and not buy additional property we could move people across the street. Response – It would create the same density in the area (Br. Spicer's response)

Will there be a hearing at the Community Board? Ans. There should not be a need because we are not requesting a varience. A hearing would only be required if there were some unforeseen developments.

The church will determine the design of the exterior of the buildings.

The Herrings will not allow their property to be landlocked. They suggest we talk it over with the architect. Response – It appears that their land is already landlocked because there is no access to the rear of their property.

Rev. Jones suggested that everyone review the material and pray about it and come back next Sun for further discussion and any questions.

Rev. Jones concluded the meeting with the slogan TOGETHER EVERYONE ACHIEVES MORE SUCCESS. We are a TEAM and need to work as such

Closing prayer by Rev. Jones

Respectfully submitted

Yvonne Taylor, church clerk

****

January 29, 2004

Reverend Janet H. Jones, Pastor
Rossville A.M.E. Zion Church
584 Bloomingdale Road
Staten Island, NY 10309

Dear Reverend Jones,

Your slogan, "Together Everyone Achieves Success" is true. However, there seem to be aspects of the land proposal that need to encompass the "everyone," now more than ever.

I will not waste your valuable time by simply suggesting what the problem is. I will try to encapsulate it here in a letter as carefully-worded as possible, because I have written you and Mrs. Yvonne Taylor several letters without receiving a reply. From the beginning of your very recent appointment, I have been concerned about the church and the future of the Sandy Ground community. As you have pointed out to Mr. Larry Regan, "There is a new climate in the church." I had hoped this did not reflect negatively on the departure of Reverend Julius Ingram. While change is often a good thing, impulsive and rash decisions can bring devastating and irrevocable results. I want to confirm to you that Reverend Ingram is also very much concerned.

I doubt your short tenure at the church has given you the physical or mental time to reflect on the entire package of facts and proposals presented to you, nor given you the opportunity to consult with diverse and interested parties on such a momentous decision as the future of the church property.

The full scope on the Regan Corporation involvement must be negotiated to the satisfaction of the full board and membership, and at this time there is a murky, if not sinister, atmosphere surrounding the entire project.

N.Y. State and Federal Government regulations pertaining to Senior and Assisted Living housing are stringent for all new construction. The Bush administration housing codes set to receive "Faith Based" monies apply to the existing rules and can be costly to amend in older or new construction that do not have them. It is a warning best understood before signing contractors to begin. After all, "THE BUSINESS OF AMERICA IS BUSINESS." Please respond, as I am writing out of serious concern and confusion, as an older Black citizen born and raised on S.I. who has seen much sadness and deception in my long life. We would all be immensely saddened to see more S.I. Black-owned property go the way of so much similar property has before – to the city, and then to the auction block. Thank you for your kind attention.

Sincerely,

Cleve Overton
3301 9th Street NE
Washington, DC 20017   Fax: 202-526-5109   E-mail: cleveo@aol.com

****

3-28-2004

Dear Reverend Jones,

I received your "E"mail note here and was very glad to get your response. I was a bit concerned that I was not being understood. I am sorry that some of my remarks were inaccurate, however the entire development proposal was presented to me in abstract fashion. Forgive me. And I am glad you realized that I intended no character insult or ill will with any letters or correspondence. I do feel there is reason for us to remember historically that land is at a premium in Sandy Ground and we must tend to it cautiously. Where I once walked freely about the area I am now told by signs that it is private property. My wish is that your crozier will be blessed with divine grace and wisdom.
Sincerely, Cleve

****

I found frustration simply trying to reach Reverend Jones, I sent articles to her only to have her respond that the Lord will pave the way. I would send a building proposal and drawings to her.

OTHER SGHS CORRESPONDENCE

109 Wayne Terrace
Staten Island, NY 10310
April 15, 1998

Ms. Moody-Lewis, President
Sandy Ground Historical Society
1538 Woodrow Road
Staten Island, NY 10309

Dear Ms. Moody-Lewis:

I would like to propose to you a group effort at fund raising to offset the cost of the city demolition that was recently cited in the Advance newspaper.

I spent a number of years in West and Central African countries, during which time I completed a series of collages and participated inn several art exhibitions, mostly in Senegal. My collages from that period were exhibited in a gallery in Virginia last year. I am proposing an exhibit with you at your headquarters if at all possible.

If you agree, I would like to hang the pieces at the SGHS headquarters for a one month stay. What I would like from you is to do the advertising only. I think this would be an exciting happening if we can work this out together. You can reach me at the above address, or at Phone # 718 981 5038. I receive fax messages at 1-202-526-0564, or Internet messages at cleveo@aol.com. If you need more details, please do not hesitate to contact me.
Sincerely,
Cleve Overton

3301 9th St., NE
Washington, DC 20017
May 7, 1998

Sandy Ground Historical Society
1538 Woodrow Road
Staten Island, NY 10309

Dear Julie,

Since the colorful season of Fall is here, I am inspired to propose a program of viewing a photographic study I did in Senegal called "Les Portes du Senegal" ("The Doors of Senegal"). It consists of an audiovisual slide presentation which I presented at the Sorano National Theater of Dakar. I would like to present it at Sandy Ground if your board of directors agree that it would be an interesting program. I would be happy to show the program and answer audience questions afterward, which would be a 90-minute program which I suggest showing twice a day for two days, preferably in November. The program comes fully-equipped with projector, screen, etc. All that is needed is an electrical outlet. The Sandy Ground Historical Society would supply the public relations/advertising and a fee of $125 for the 2-day program.

Please let me know if you and the board are interested in this proposal and would like a preview or more information. Attached is an English translation of the opening address to the program given by the representative of the Ministry of Culture in Dakar. I would appreciate hearing back from you, one way or the other, by the end of October. You can reach me by fax (202 526 0564) or e-mail: cleveo@aol.com

Thank you for your consideration.

Sincerely,

Cleve Overton

****

3301 9th St., NE
Washington, DC 20017
May 7, 1998

Sandy Ground Historical Society
1538 Woodrow Road
Staten Island, NY 10309

Dear Julie,

After a long drive home, I had time to review our meeting at the Sandy ground Headquarters on Monday. I have had four days now to go over the reasons for this letter, and to try to come to common ground about why I feel compelled to write this letter.

I will try to outline my reasoning for what I do and why, at our first meeting at the Unitarian Church, you said you wanted to nominate me for something. I had no idea what it was and did not have an opportunity after the meeting to discuss it with you. I feel that in my present life, I simply cannot afford to give any quality time to anything outside of my daily chores. I have never run for nor wanted to run for an office or position at Sandy Ground. My feelings then and now are simply to support the SGHS.

I simply wanted, as I wrote in the letter to the SGHS Board, to show that I had done a substantial amount of art work during my years on the African continent. I would like a place to show it to the public. I told you that I had approached the people at Snug Harbor, and that my feeling from that approach was negative.

I basically wanted to show this work to Black Americans because of the nature of the work and the themes. When you said you had a museum I thought, "Great." I called and made an appointment to come out to Roseville to see the museum. I thought there would be no better place to do it than SGHS. I was impressed by the location and the gallery.

However, during our talk I felt that we were talking at cross purposes. I showed you some photos of my last show at the La Taj Gallery in Alexandria, Virginia and my biography. You showed me some photos of the Frazier show. You told me that he made a lot of money at the showing. I said that I wanted to sell my work and make money also, but that this was not my sole purpose for doing it. If I can share these experiences with others, if others can understand what I am trying to say, and perhaps buy a piece, fine and dandy. I have been selling African Art for some time now and I am well aware of the market in African American art and African art. What your photos did not show at the opening of the "Frazier' show was the number of people attending. You said that he was from Texas and did shows all over the U.S. Julie, I am just a hometown boy, my work is in the collections of many Staten Islanders and I can submit the names of artists living on the Island for recommendation. I have done all of about 10 shows in my life, and have won a few awards here and there, but I have never supported myself with my art work.

You said that Frazier had submitted some of his work for your board to approve. Most galleries reject actual pieces from artists, and require the artist to submit 35mm slides for curators to examine and select to be shown. Most will not accept work shipped to them. You suggested that I bring a few pieces for the board to see.
This is logistically complicated. I cannot take my pieces out of storage and send/bring them to your board, who will meet and decide, after which I must cart them back to storage? And wait for word of acceptance? I have yet to receive a letter in response to mine to you of a month ago.... in which I asked you if the administration had approved of my showing. You had promptly replied, "Oh, yes."

All this is simply not cost effective. If submitted slides are not acceptable I will have to withdraw my offer.

Julie, what I feel is that you are wearing several hats there at the SGHS... when I used the term "Curator," I wanted to find out if there was another person who dealt with the museum portion of the SGHS. I realized that you did not, for whatever reason, answer my "E" mail. You said that I should put it on OYST20@aol.com and then download it and send you a copy...why..? You said your fax is not operating, why? I would have asked more questions, such as, can we compare mailing lists of people to invite to shows? A more important question is about insurance. You said "That is the way we do business here". I wanted a somewhat, in my perspective, more professional strategy. My work is a window of my thinking and life, and some of it is irreplaceable. I would like to help, not hurt, the cause. Please respond to my letter, and inform me of your ideas and intentions.

Thank you for your consideration,

Sincerely,
Cleve Overton

109 Wayne Terrace

Staten Island, NY 10310
September 26, 1999

Ms. Moody-Lewis, President
Sandy Ground Historical Society
1538 Woodrow Road
Staten Island, NY 10309

Dear Ms. Moody-Lewis:

I have applied for a grant from the Council on the Arts and Humanities for Staten Island (COASHI) to publicly present a photographic study called "The Doors of Senegal." I took the photographs in three cities of Senegal while I lived there in the early 1990s, and have added educational text and background material. It is an audiovisual slide presentation which I presented at the Sorano National Theater of Dakar in 1993. The photographs illustrate the creativity and ingenuity of the Senegalese people. In order to receive the grant, a nonprofit organization must agree to be the conduit for the funds. I am enclosing the application, and I would greatly appreciate your sponsorship. If you agree to be the conduit organization, please sign the attached application and provide me a copy of the following documents for submittal to the COASHI:

Proof of nonprofit status, in the fomr of any one of the following:
- Form 501(c) 3 of the US Treasury Department

- Charter from the Board of Regents under Section 216 of the Education Law

- NYS Charities Registration

- Certificate of Incorporation under Section 402 of the Not-for-Profit Law

If you agree to be the conduit organization, I will need an "agreement of responsibilities" letter stating the Sandy Ground Historical Society's willingness to fulfill the obligations and duties of serving as fiscal and administrative agent for the grant award. I have taken the liberty of drafting a sample letter for your signature (attached.)

Please contact me if you would like further information or a personal interview. You can reach me by telephone(981 5038), by fax (202-526-0564), or e-mail: cleveo@aol.com. Thank you for your consideration

.

Sincerely,

Cleve Overton

CORRESPONDENCE SENT TO THE SANDY GROUND HISTORICAL SOCIETY BY AN AD-HOC COMMITTEE OF CONCERNED CITIZENS

On April 28, 2000, Richard (Dick) Dickenson, Borough Historian for the Borough of Richmond (Staten Island, New York) faxed the following draft letter from the Borough President's Office of Staten Island to Cleve Overton in Washington, DC. He stated that he had had a death in his family and had not followed up on the letter, other than to provide it to Sheila Rohan, who made some edits and then sent it to Branch Addison. He suggested Cleve contact Sheila re the status of the letter. Cleve did so, and learned that the letter had been signed and mailed.

AD-HOC COMMITTEE OF CONCERNED CITIZENS

c/o Duane Felton, Esq.

805 Castleton Ave.

Staten Island, NY 10310

29 March 2000

Ms. Adrienne Ross, President

Sandy Ground Historical Society

1538 Woodrow Road

Staten Island, NY 10309

Re: Black Man on Staten Island and Sandy Ground Collections

Dear Ms. Ross,

A group of people of color met recently (March 23, 2000) to attempt to understand the complexities of issues that have been raised by Mr. Cleve Overton about the above collections, and – hopefully – try to resolve them in a manner acceptable to all sides. Those who participated were invited by Mr. Overton, but there was dismay noted by some of those in attendance at the absence of official representation by the Sandy Ground Historical Society (SGHS) by board members or staff. We were adequately informed that the invitation to participate was not accepted, however, we had hoped that the beginning of a dialogue could occur with SGHS. Nevertheless, it seemed incumbent to our concerns to proceed to establish an understanding, or a meeting of minds on this matter that may transcend Staten Island and may be of national interest.

We have carefully read your joint letter, with Ms. Julie Lewis, of March 11, 2000 and would like to further inquire into its content. First of all we welcome your invitation to visit your facilities and participate in your "continuous efforts to augment, preserve, and promote the rich history of African Americans on Staten Island." Secondly, it is in the context of yhour unique status as a majority African American, publicly funded, State chartered and tax exempt organization that we raise these issues.

Which brings us to a key issue, that of public access, and "making available to the public historical material as to the African American Community on Staten Island." Your letter states that SGHS has kept "the collection basically closed until further archival procedures and

300

assessments can be made." Would this mean that for some yet-to-be determined time members of the public are unable to have access to the collections? Some attendees at the Ad-Hoc Committee reported difficulties in obtaining timely access to the holdings, but have not found any visiting hours posted. Another aspect of the access issue is the alleged lack of return of some phone calls made to SGHS. We would welcome your perspective on the questions of access and availability, how these questions may relate to staffing and funding, and if we can be of any assistance in this matter.

We well understand the deep concern of the SGHS Board for the safely of the collection, but would like more details on the insurance policies you carry for fire, flood, theft, burglary and robbery. Would you be kind enough to tell us how much the collection is insured for and for what period of time? Much of what you care for is irreplaceable and we wonder what security measures you take to prevent the loss of any of the items in your care?

Since the physical aspect of Sandy Ground has irrevocably changed over the years, we believe that your mission is incomparable to any other in saving the history of the Americans of African Descent.

Yours truly,

Addison Branch, Jr.
Moderator

Issues for Discussion with SGHS

TRANSPARENCY – is SGHS modus operandi transparent? Are there by-laws and operating procedures? Are the books open to the public or secret? Are they affiliated with a church? If they are receiving public money, shouldn't the organization's functioning be transparent? Is there a financial secretary or accountant? Do they produce annual reports? Are there any salaried employees? Do they receive grants?

Do they have regular meetings, and if so, is the community invited/informed? Don't they want new members, fresh blood, or is it a secret society? When are they open? No hours are posted, and the gates are never open, calls are not returned, donations are not acknowledged. Why did they hold a meeting at the Unitarian Church in 1999 instead of in their own building?

What properties are owned by the Society? Weren't certain Black-owned properties deeded to the Society by people who wanted them preserved?

The blacksmith shop is burned to the ground. How long before the building, the photos and records are stored in it suffer the same fate? Is the building insured for fire and theft? Would it do any good if it were, given these files are irreplaceable?

There is an open well on the blacksmith's property – is there any liability insurance, or if someone sues the Society, does it go bankrupt and out of existence?

Director, or President, or what? Is it an elected post? If yes, who are the members who voted for her? What are the rights and responsibilities of the post? Shouldn't someone in this position be able to spell the word "throughout" which was "threw out" in her letter?

When she finally responded to my letter, she pretends not to know what files I'm referring to, although she knows very well they are videos, photos and records she took from the Staten Island Institute for Arts and Sciences (SIIAS).

We demand a full and detailed account of the items removed from the SIIAS, including WHO, WHY, and WHEN.

NEXT STEPS

The records insured a safe and fireproof storage.

The records accessible to supervised use by researchers.

Efforts made to publicize, publish, edit, reproduce, disseminate this proof of Black contribution to the economic development of Staten Island.

****

302

July 14, 2003

Mrs. Sylvia Moody D'Alessandro, President
Sandy Ground Historical Society
1538 Woodrow Road
Staten Island, NY 10309

Dear Mrs. D'Alessandro:

The recent events on Saturday, July 12th, prompted me to write directly to you as president of the SGHS. But first, I feel the need to recall the meeting with you and your daughter Julie during the previous week, when you stopped your car to speak to me on Bloomingdale Road. Julie shook hands and we spoke for a few moments, and she asked me if I had attended the recent affair at the SGHS grounds. She also said she wanted me to call her. I said I would and I did. The number I called, which I found in your recent "African American Quilting Workshop" bulletin, 718 - 317 - 5796, yielded only a recording saying the number was disconnected.

A week later, at ten minutes before noon, I came to the SGHS headquarters on Woodrow Road to introduce a person to the museum, the collection, and the recent exhibition. He is a Black professional writer who has been doing research into Black History. He was born and raised in Great Falls Montana, a recent arrival to the East Coast, now living in Washington D.C. He expressed an interest and came along with me.

He was shocked at the behavior of your daughter Julie at the gates and as she dressed me down, saying she was afraid for her safety, that I was dangerous, and that she would have to call her lawyer before I could enter the building. I had not told him that I disagree with the SGHS with regard to the files from the Staten Island Institute of Arts and Sciences. It was his first visit to New York and Staten Island, and I saw no reason to share that particular difference of opinion with him or lessen the enjoyment of his visit. I had told him about my work many years ago on the Black Man on Staten Island Project and I wanted him to form his own opinions about the SGHS. He then asked Julie if he alone could enter, and she answered sharply that it would be open at twelve. It was then five minutes to twelve. He was appalled that, whatever disagreement seemed to exist between Julie and me would lead her to behave in such a way to a stranger, an interested member of the public. He motioned for me to come away and we left. Fortunately, when he returned alone the next day, she had regained her professional demeanor and he had a pleasant visit.

I am at a loss to imagine how we can ameliorate our differences. I certainly do not believe she had any basis to call me "dangerous." While I have done picketing and leafletting, I have been a follower of Martin Luther King's nonviolent strategies all of my life, and have never been accused of physical violence. I will not call or write Julie again while she is the executive director of SGHS. I was shocked and embarrassed by her behavior.

Let me make my position clear. I do not want anything from the SGHS. I do not want to be on the board, or run for any office. I represent no organization or persons attached to any organization. I also do not want to destroy the organization. I would like to see it improved, because I feel the SGHS has alienated itself from much of the white and black Staten Island community that could assist and support it. I do not know if it is a function of the personalities involved, but an institution with as important a mission of SGHS should not stand or fall because of personalities. The SGHS should be inclusive, not exclusive, in order to survive. But whether the SGHS improves or not is not my problem or my preoccupation.

What I have been lobbying and picketing and writing letters for is to have all of the original documentation, video and audio tapes, photographs and files relating to the work done for The Black Man on Staten Island Project returned to the SIIAS. The primary reason is that they should never have been removed from there in the first place, and I have yet to see any documentation authorizing such a move. In fact, I doubt any exist!!! Surely, little thought was given to their fate by directing them to the SGHS building, a comparatively unsafe and unsecured location where they are subject to theft and fire. I have asked your daughter, in writing, to provide me with the insurance and the methods you have taken to protect them. The loss of the Bishop blacksmith shop was terrible, but the loss of the irreplaceable documentation would be horrific. I have seen the results when greedy, unscrupulous developers see property that impedes their continued construction of condos, and I fear for the future of those files.

There is no need for the files to be at the SIIAS in copy form and closed to the public. I have been told personally that these files at the SIIAS are closed to me. There is something illegal here, and I intend to continue asking questions and pursuing this until it has been addressed properly and professionally.

I await your response.

Yours truly,
Cleve Overton
Phone 202 526 7072
fax   202 526 5109
E-mail cleveo@aol.com

3301 9th Street, NE
Washington, DC 20017
****

304

June 10, 2003

Dear Marie,

     After the benediction of all the rain, I had to stop living inside and move out into the sun, to a large space outside to work on a project for the September show "Hidden Infrastructure," to take place here in D.C. I hope you can find the time to see it then... another part of my life...the part which keeps me sane.

     The phone call. I wanted you to hear what it was I have been doing for the last three or four years, with respect to Staten Island. And while talking to you, I realized that the subject has no quiet or peaceful place in my body. If I leave it dormant, and speak to no one about it, I am fine. However, when it is time for me to speak about it to another person, I tend to run on and all of my feelings and emotions become tangled, especially when I am actually on the island and need to do some research. It is a wonder we did not have an accident when I drove you around, and at one point you mentioned to Nic that my driving was a bit suicidal.

     I admire your ability to do what you do, write. Looking at your book, **Red Tails in Love**, I must say it is a remarkable work of patience that I find simply amazing. So please be a dear and have patience with me. As I grow older, I want not to waste time ...I do feel that to slow down a pace it will all fall to ruin in a sense. The result is this...hyper activity I suppose. I think that very often I come to understand the complete absurdity of the task of trying to do this memoir/book. I have this feeling of trying to go somewhere and not having any signposts to show me the way. Sandy Ground is but one piece of it, but a large and important piece. I have watched the political moves ...the Black people of the island ..the environment...the racism...sometime I have the feeling that I am going around in circles getting nowhere ..but then I continue. It's like trying to find water in the Sahara...the Black critics ask if I am going to put our business in the streets...my reply is ..."We have no business." While we were having lunch with Nic, I also realized that I could not take you to any place owned and operated by a Black person... there aren't any ... and I also felt uneasy being out at that end of the island ..it popped out while wheeling you about. My need to write about it makes me seem afflicted with something that will not leave me until I do find the voice, and it often seems as though I will suffocate on the bile of it all. It is difficult for me to put the mental thoughts into print ...and being articulate has never been one of my strong points.

     I sent Yvonne some of my notes about something that happened on my last visit, which I will add to this .... she returned the photos, which I will bring with me when I see you again. And she said she saw you at the homecoming day gig, which she now refers to as "Family Day." I hope you took photos. I recently took another late-night phone call about the church. The Reverend is being canned and a woman will be the replacement. The Bishop is mulling over the sale of the property next door to it. I could go on Marie, at times it seems so petty, but it makes my canvas say a great deal about our (read Black) presence on the island.

     Barnett Shepard will do the book with Lois Mosely, I think it will be "nice"...however, I don't think there will anything that will give the Sandy Ground people or readers a real view of what has happened and what is still happening. I will not allow the SGHS to use the works and words of others to feather their own narrow self interests. That project was a product of many of my friends, Black and White...And I will find a way to do it professionally and not personally if possible. I do not believe a White person will do anything but "nice," because there will be a charge of racism attached to anything negative. I will try to get my hands on a copy of the Mosley booklet.

     My files are huge. I can try to find anything you need and copy it for you, but it would be helpful if you could send me some specifics when you return from California. Also, please let me know more about what you are doing with the Hunter grave site. Actually, I feel that I have not been more sane in my life, while uncovering all this stuff. There must be a promised land out there.

There is a part of my book that may be important to you, namely my environmental concerns, and also Joseph Mitchell's awareness of the ecology of the island. Perhaps we could collaborate on this. I am sure you have noticed the effects of pollution on the environment. I would like to discuss that with you.

Cheers
Cleve

****

Thursday   July 31

Dear Yvonne,

Your letter with the copies of the 1981 SIIAS archive letters about the Black Man Project were eye openers, something I had forgotten about. But they were signed by me almost thirty years ago when I was not at all familiar with the workings of the Institute as a whole. I was interested mainly in the historical aspect of what we were doing and I trusted Gail Schneider to do what was best at the time. I also did not know what form the SGHS would take in terms of location and structure.

Rather than go into a long history dissertation on the subject, I want to clarify my position regarding SGHS. I honestly believe the original project material should remain with the SIIAS, because it would be available for historical students and researchers to work on/with them. Copies should be provided to the SGHS free and they should have access to them. Tampering with historical documents is not unheard of and I accuse no one of doing so. However, mistakes are made. For example, in the recent past, SGHS executive director Julie Moody Lewis said in the press that "Sandy Ground was a stop on the Underground Railroad. " My research at the Library of Congress and publications on the subject contradicts that. If true, the evidence should be made more public. If false, the statements should not be made.

Your question of contacting the SGHS for a dialogue is long past, and you must recall the meeting at Duane Felton's office, to which they were invited and failed to appear. I have copies of many letters in my files in which I attempted to engage them, all unanswered. I saw Silvia and Julie a few weeks ago while walking to the Collins property, (a copy of that sent to you), and at that time Julie asked me to get in touch. I wrote a letter to them in response to that request, and got no reply.

I went to the SHGS headquarters last week with an assistant who is working with me and Julie said she would not let me enter because she was afraid of me and she would have to consult with her attorney. McKinley Williams, shocked and embarrassed by her reaction, entered the next day and had what he termed "a pleasant visit."

My feeling now is that I want no further contact with Silvia or Julie, because I feel I am being set up for a fall that could lead me to prison, and I have no time for that now. I do believe *they* are dangerous. I hope the new Rossville community, private homeowners or developers will not find the SGHS headquarters' presence there offensive and will tolerate them. However I have little faith that the building is safe from fire or theft and fear that everything may be lost, as happen wipe out everything.

My book has now become larger than the Sandy Ground/SGHS issue, which is nevertheless a large and emotional one for me.
Sincerely,

Cleve Overton
****

307

Dear Yvonne,

At vespers I sit quietly and go over events, questions, responses, actions, feelings, a whole host of life theater stuff that must be clarified if I/one is to move forward, or stay put or safe....your questions about how I should have properly proceeded with the drawings and suggestions...frankly I did not know how. I did know that you were a long-time member of the church...in what position, I don't know. But after reflection, I do remember the last male minister saying to me, while I was in front of the church with the casket, that someone inside wanted me removed. I guessed it was you. You were right, I was brash and hold no bad feelings. I visited the new minister at the church with my assistant, McKinley Williams, in the tiny cluttered office up the staircase. it was a terrible hot August day and there were no fans or air conditioning. She said she wanted to have her computer repaired and could not contact anyone by e-mail ... how sad, I thought.. a dear soul ..a bit overwhelmed perhaps. It came over the Internet recently that Sandy Ground folks had a ML King day celebration ...and it quoted you, which leads me to believe you are still active there. I have been barred, and I was told by Julie Lewis Moody that she would need to call her attorney before letting me enter the premises. It is on tape, and after that Mr. Williams entered alone. I have to do this because I want not to go to jail.... to preserve my own personal safety. I may be brash, enthusiastic and committed to my beliefs, but I'm not violent, yet who would believe me versus a lady? What I'm wondering is, how involved are you with the mother-daughter team running the SGHS? Naturally, you need not answer any of my questions, but you should know that others are also asking questions. "Silent questions" .... like, how much salary Julie Moody Lewis makes as the director of SGHS, to be able to have a home built. I have asked the state Attorney General's Office Charities Bureau to send me a public information statement about the finances at SGHS. there is no other way for me to go, because my bottom-line concern is the safety of the archives. A point of information: I did not send SGHS the recent packet of the information I sent to you.

There is a mystery about the SGHS that permeates the entire Staten Island community, both Black and White. I sent more about this in a letter to you on July 31st 2003. I honestly believe it is your right to be/act as you have. I said many times to you that my impression of you is a very conservative, intelligent woman. I will always believe that. I also believe you have a "bully pulpit" that is dormant, and it is being questioned. Why has the SGHS office on Woodrow Road not seen it best to have a sidewalk placed in front of the office? If they have hundreds of thousands of dollars in the bank, will the funds be invested to enhance the accessibility and also the security of the building? Has the SGHS investigated the Bishop property for an archeological dig? And also fence it in and add a sidewalk? Has the White owner of the renewed "Hunter" house gone over his property lines and erected a deck over it? The State lawmakers budget has also left out the SGHS. See attached.

Just imagine a wonderful statement in the form of a new, first Black Staten island edifice, dual-purpose building on that site. Think of the potential and what it would mean....we, (read Blacks) have yet to build any structure such as this on the Island. Am I the only one that has a dream? And please ask the new reverend if she could use a very nice new office in such a building. I am and always will be open to you, and I have always provided my office address and phone, fax, etc. and always will. I wish the SGHS office could be as open and accessible.

In closing, let me reiterate what I believe are my good intentions and the reasons:
•The SGHS legacy and documentation are historic treasures that must be preserved. We need more people to recognize and support that.

308

•The SGHS is in a vulnerable building, often empty, surrounded by developments and people who would just as soon see it gone. Examples of such losses of Black archives around the country can be found in recent newspaper articles. A secure, fire-proof building is needed to house them.

•The SGHS leaders should be lobbying, advocating, planning, proposing and openly vetting their proposals in the press, in the Black and White communities.

•Our generation is in the Fall and Winter of our lives, and this is our last chance to influence the future and preservation of the Sandy Ground records. I have interviewed many Staten Islanders of all ages, and many who do care remain silent because of the secrecy and proprietorial atmosphere of the SGHS leaders. I am not afraid to say what I think, and I don't mind being the messenger who is attacked, but I can't do it alone.

Sincerely,
Cleve

3301 9th St, N.E., Washington   D.C. 20017

Phone; 1-202-526-7072, Fax; 1-202-526-5109 e-mail;   cleveo@aol.com

****

END GAME SANDY GROUND NOTES

http://www.citylandnyc.org/staten-island%E2%80%99s-sandy-ground-area-downzoned-2/

Staten Island's Sandy Ground Area Downzoned

02/15/2010

Rezoning proposed to prevent attached homes in area settled by freed slaves in 1827. On February 3, 2010, the City Council approved State Senator Andrew J. Lanza's rezoning proposal for the Sandy Ground neighborhood of Staten Island. Sandy Ground, also known as Rossville, is listed on the National Register of Historic Places and recognized as one of the country's oldest communities established by freed slaves. The rezoning impacts 35 blocks generally bounded by the West Shore Expressway to the north and west, Ramona Avenue to the south, and Lenevar and Alverson Avenues to the east.

The area is characterized predominantly by detached and semidetached homes, but over the past several years Sandy Ground has experienced an increase in the development of attached townhouses and multi-family buildings. The rezoning aims to prevent out-of-scale development by down-zoning the area from R3-2 to R3-1, a district that does not permit attached homes.

At the City Planning Commission's hearing, Nicholas Polly, president of the Civic Association of the Sandy Ground Area, which helped create the proposal, said the neighborhood's infrastructure was overburdened and the rezoning would stop out-of-character development. No one testified in opposition, and the Commission approved the plan.

At the Council's Zoning & Franchises Subcommittee, members and supporters of Sandy Ground's Rossville AME Zion Church testified in opposition. Reverend Janet H. Jones, the church's pastor, claimed the rezoning would prevent the church from building a planned senior citizen housing project. When asked why no one from the church spoke at any of the prior public hearings, Reverend Jones responded that it was difficult to speak in an environment where their concerns "were not being heard." Reverend Will Nichols, president of the Staten Island Council of Churches, citing a critical need for senior housing, asked the Council to reject the rezoning or delay it until the church completed its housing project. Council Member Vincent Ignizio, whose district includes Sandy Ground, expressed his support for the down-zoning and pledged to work with the church to help identify an alternative revenue stream for it or an "appropriate development" for its land.

The Subcommittee approved the rezoning, and the Land Use Committee and full Council followed suit, with only Council Member Charles Barron voting no.

ULURP Process
Lead Agency: CPC,Neg.Dec.
Comm.Bd.: SI 3,App'd, 35-0-0
Boro.Pres.: App'd
CPC: App'd, 8-0-0
Council: App'd, 48-1-2

Council: Sandy Ground Rezoning (C 090042 ZMR – rezoning) (Feb. 3, 2010).

Chapter 7

CEMETERIES

A friend on Staten Island, who keeps me informed of things that are in the

Staten Island Advance newspaper, sent me a story entitled "African American Burial Ground in Dire Straits." It was an article written by Karen O'Shea and Tevah Platt and it read:

> Broken bricks and a ruptured wrought-iron fence mark the entrance to Frederick Douglass Memorial Park Cemetery in Oakwood, a 17-acre cemetery named for the man who escaped slavery and went on to become a famous abolitionist, lecturer, writer, and trusted adviser to President Abraham Lincoln during the Civil War."

The cemetery, named after Frederick Douglass, was purchased on Staten Island in a white central area of Staten Island by a black funeral director from Harlem in Manhattan. The cemetery opened in 1935, solely for the purpose of African Americans at a time when segregation was very much a part of African American life – and death. This unique burial ground today is in danger of becoming an abandoned cemetery. Nearly three years after its Director was removed by court order a state-appointed receiver is trying to keep the cemetery afloat. The state attorney general said that money went missing from the cemetery's permanent maintenance fund under the direction of the former director.

Arthur Friedman, Superintendent and CEO of nearby United Hebrew Cemetery, was appointed the receiver of the cemetery. Arthur Friedman assumed the post without pay. Many years before, alarm bells began to sound about the management of this Frederick Douglass Cemetery in Oakwood. The cemetery's Performance Maintenance Fund was invaded, with much of the money used to pay the director's salary and benefits.

311

The receiver, Arthur Friedman, has been able to locate over $400,000 of the cemetery's money in bank accounts around the city. The money has been plowed back into a permanent maintenance fund. The trust fund can't be tapped but a portion of it is invested. The cemetery receives a small investment income -- about $20,000 to $25,000 a year -- to assist in the operational deficits.

Arthur Friedman and the nonprofit Friends of Abandoned Cemeteries have scheduled a Nov. 14 meeting at the Cromwell Center in Tompkinsville for the plot owners and the community. "We will help them get back on their feet if we can," said Lynn Rogers of the Friends of Abandoned Cemeteries, which is trying to avoid taking over the memorial park. "We already have 60 to 70 acres of cemetery property we maintain to the best of our ability," added Ms. Rogers. "We are the last resort."

Community Activist Janet Robinson, known as the Staten Islanders' as the "Kwanzaa Lady" for her community celebrations of the holiday, reached out to help Ms. Rogers after she went to the cemetery last summer to visit her grandmother's grave. "It took three people almost an hour to find my grandmother's grave," Ms. Robinson recalled of the overgrown trash-strewn plots.

A Brooklyn resident, Jennifer Stokes, also plans to attend the November meeting. Ms. Stokes, an urban planner, took up an interest several years ago in the life of Herbert Pope, an African-American studio photographer who documented the life of black families living in the city early in the last century. "It was interesting to me when I read a post that this cemetery was, perhaps, going to be abandoned," she said. "I responded to the post because I wanted to know more about it."

There have been some notable burials there in the 73 years since Rodney Dade, a prominent funeral director from Harlem, opened the cemetery as a place where blacks could be buried with dignity. Rodney Dade later was buried here at Frederick Douglas Memorial Park as were Lucky Roberts, a blues composer; Mamie Smith, sister of singer Bessie Smith; the father of author James Baldwin, and Rose Henderson, a popular blues singer of the 1920s and 30s who recorded for Victor Records; and many others.

And on September 25, 1971, 200 mourners gathered for the nighttime burial of three prisoners who were shot at Attica State Prison.

This was one of the first emotional responses from me when I heard about this burial of the prisoners that were killed in 1971 when Nelson Rockefeller refused to intercede in ameliorating a very hot, nasty, situation. I remember reading these words from my files because the four-day stand-off ended in a hasty government crack-down in which 29 prisoners and 10 prison employees died amid a storm of tear gas and bullets. The final death toll at Attica would reach 43. Some of the troopers firing into the mass described it as a "turkey shoot."

The iron fisted commander of Attica Correctional Facility in upstate New York would not concede to any conditions. It was an insurrection and he would put it down. I read from my files from the *New York Post* about the overcrowding. I look at the photos of the advancing state troopers and military, the helicopters. Overcrowding is one of the worst things that can happen in a prison because it scares everyone, both inside and outside those walls.

Several years of meetings to improve/repair S.I.'s Black cemetery have proven fruitless.

Fountain Cemetery, where man Blacks are buried, on Richmond Terrace at Alaska Street.

When the killings were complete, Arthur Lyman, the District Attorney and Chief Counsel of New York State said "It is now understood that all the prisons have re-examined their gates," and he wrote in his memoir "It is obvious that walls and gates, no matter how strong, cannot forever contain angry and desperate men."

The New York Times had a long article about the Frederick Douglass Memorial Park Cemetery. The article said that the cemetery is drowning in debt. Mr. Friedman said the unpaid workers' compensation judgment of $600,000 has not been paid, and there is a New York City water bill of $17,000, most of it interest and penalties.

In the cemetery's musty office, a one-story cottage on the north end of the grounds, a small dog-eared paperback biography of Frederick Douglass, sits chest-high on a wooden counter. Virginia Footman, now the cemetery's clerk, spends hours flipping through the old index cards like an old-time librarian, cross-referencing information with names in a handwritten ledger. "There's a lot of lost souls back there," she said, "because they don't have no gravestones," Ms. Footman was referring to the northwest corner of the cemetery, where there are fewer marked graves. "People come in and ask, 'Why is my father buried here?" she says, adopting a complaining voice. "At that time, it was a money issue for black people."

With the help of Lynn Rogers, executive director of Staten Island's Friends of Abandoned Cemeteries, Mr. Friedman held a town meeting for plot owners at the Cromwell Recreation Center, on November 14 in Tompkinsville. The hope was that family members would put up some money to keep the cemetery going. I wanted to know more about this Lynn Rogers, and I took a trip, one of the wild -ride trips, on the Chinatown bus from Washington DC to New York.

I would depart from Chinatown, Washington and arrive in Chinatown New York, hop on the subway several stops to the ferry terminal, board the ferry at South Ferry to Staten Island, taking a cab from the ferry terminal to the Cromwell Center. But first I wanted to know much more about the lady Lynn Rogers.

A native Staten Islander, Ms. Rogers grew up in Willowbrook, but attended St. Mary of Assumption School in Port Richmond because her grandmother cooked at the rectory for the monsignor. Ms. Lynn Rogers is now into her 13th year of involvement with the Friends of Abandoned Cemeteries on Staten Island (FACSI). During that time she has righted more than 500 headstones at Fountain Cemetery alone. She has dozens of old ledgers from cemeteries and churches and long-gone funeral homes stored at her home, and she has become an expert at deciphering the information that these ledgers contain.

But she's far more than a bookkeeper. On top of her paid position as an outreach coordinator with the City Parks Foundation, it's not unusual to find Ms. Rogers in one of 19 abandoned cemeteries in the borough of Staten Island, working with a tiny patchwork crew of volunteers and, before it closed, men from the Arthur Kill Correctional Facility. They would be righting headstones, clearing brush, directing front-end loaders and noting the locations of markers that need to be moved back to where they once belonged.

The work is under-funded; there are some grants to be had, but few officials pay it much mind. It's under-appreciated; families that seek help rarely donate any money or labor to assist with upkeep after Ms. Rogers has found their missing loved one's grave. And it's physically grueling.

Two years after Lynn Rogers started her genealogical research, she discovered that many of her forebears were buried in Fountain Cemetery and in tracking down what was left of their headstones, she ran across Woman of Achievement Marjorie Decker Johnson. Ms. Decker Johnson was quick to intuit that a person who could carry on her historical work was standing in front of her.

I checked my personal files because the name Fountain Cemetery rang a bell. I would find a fax cover sheet from Richard (Dick) Dickenson, who at that time was the Staten Island Borough Historian. I asked Dick some questions about some files from my family's history book and Bible. Dick Dickenson, who became a very dear friend, would say that "I have no documentation on black burials in Fountain Cemetery. It may exist elsewhere."

I looked in my files and I did find a receipt from the Fountain Cemetery Association, incorporated on Staten Island in 1974. The statement reads "Staten Island, December 15, 1882. Received from Mssrs Overton $11 for opening grave for Julius Cook. H.I. Fountain, Treasurer. Tier 4, Grave 3."

I was very happy at the time when I made a copy and sent it to Dick Dickenson who was one of the people, along with Pearse O'Callaghan, Marjorie Johnson, and Doris Lane, who were instrumental in bringing Friends of Abandoned Cemeteries at 140 Tysen Street, his home, to Staten Island in 2002.

I would find much more about Ms. Rogers and I was very impressed at her ability to gather together the men, women, and machinery to clear Lake Cemetery in Graniteville which was overrun by 10-foot high weeds, trees, rocks, stones, and debris from years of trampling. Not only Lake Cemetery, but Fountain Cemetery, and Ms. Rogers spends as much of her time in the dusty archives with her nose in these old ledgers as she does in the field.

As a black person I was peripherally interested, and I made a special trip to visit Ms. Lynn Rogers at her home and I found that the Second Asbury African Cemetery, which is now the shopping plaza in Port Richmond near the Boston Market on Forrest Avenue, was obliterated in 1980. I wondered when and where the records were of our black history. I would find that there would be none.

I did meet Ms. Rogers at her home on Myrtle Avenue and I promised that I would assist as much as I could, but I also knew that Patricia Salmon was the Staten Island Museum's Curator of History and I knew that Pat Salmon had written a book called *Realms of History: The Cemeteries of Staten Island*. This book was the culmination of 2 years research and preparation. Pat described growing up next to the Merrell Homestead Graveyard in Bull's Head as one of the best experiences of her life. "It was my playground," she said. "The cemetery confronted me with history and nature."

I made a note in my pad that, having relatives on Alaska Street, I too had played in a cemetery. I did not know at the time that cemetery that I used as a playground for hide-

and-seek with my friends was the very Fountain Cemetery where my relatives were buried.

Pat Salmon was a wealth of information and in my faxes and e-mails with her I would find out much more about the inner workings of a number of cemeteries on Staten Island and where to get more information. I received information from Pat that would make me very sad, but I also realized that there were few blacks on Staten Island who had access to much of the information about abandoned cemeteries.

I would see that the status of the old slave cemetery on Staten Island was unknown, its location undetermined. I would find that the old African Methodist Episcopal (AME) Zion Cemetery was also abandoned. It was never restarted. It was not a New York City or State landmark. No surviving records or verification exist and it denoted that it may have included a stop at the Underground Railroad for passengers.

The Rossville AME Zion Cemetery is active on Crabtree Avenue. It is maintained by the church and the note from my files says that it was vandalized in 1997 by the encroaching gentrification of the Sandy Ground area. At the time the church had to ask the community for funding to fence it in. I found notes of other cemeteries on Staten Island that have been abandoned, obliterated, or demolished.

A sad thing was happening and I decided that, against the wishes of my Jude, I would take the transportation and I would attend the Frederick Douglas Cemetery informational meeting on November 14, 2008. The introduction would be by Lynn A Rogers, Executive Director of the Friends of Abandoned Cemeteries, Arthur Friedman, the New York State appointed receiver, and Mark Russo, President of the Friends of Abandoned Cemeteries. There would be questions open to the public and responses from the four people.

I was not able to get into the building because it was so small. From the doorway I would snap photos and see and meet many of the prominent black Americans who attended this meeting. I stood, pushed to take photographs of this occasion, while outside I would listen to some comments from people who also could not get in. I would make notes and one of the notes struck me as rather interesting; a man who is a minister at one of the churches said to me "What are you doing here?" I said "I'm doing the same thing others folks are doing. I just want to find out." He said "I'm running for political office." I said "That's interesting. Does your position as the minister of your church allow you to become involved in the political arena on Staten Island?" He went into a long dialectic about God, man, and politics. I looked, turned off, and turned away. I would later find out he was running against the only black political person ever to come on board the political train to move into the position of political life.

There were a number of people; all black people were interested in saving this last very prominent cemetery from destruction or oblivion. I was not able to hear anything from the people behind the microphones, but I would find later that, of the hundreds of people, black people, who attended the informational meeting at the Cromwell Center, 22 would leave their e-mail addresses, and only one person would respond to Lynn Rogers and that person was Debi Rose.

It would also be interesting to note that, a few months after the meeting, the entire structure which was Cromwell Recreational Center would collapse and fall into the bay. But the life, I realized, of cemeteries is a strange thing. Cemeteries are unbeholding to the rhythms that govern the living. Cemeteries are a city of the dead. As it happens there are a lot of abandoned cemeteries on Staten Island. Some are being brought back to life. Some will disappear because of the need for land to construct houses.

The Friends of Abandoned Cemeteries of Staten Island have come a long way since 1985. The group has adopted many graveyards, restored paths, and reclaimed many stones from the poison ivy. The Executive Director, Lynn Rogers, is a person of extremely high energy. I hope she will continue.

I took a trip in the first part of July 2012; I took a photo of the sign on the brick column, the Frederick Douglass Memorial Park. The damaged wrought iron fence and brickwork remain as it was in 2008, but the grounds were well-trimmed, the gravestones cleaned, flags fluttered, and flowers were placed around flat headstones. The drive to the office building was now firm.

Before returning home I would notice in the graveyards things that I had never noticed before. One gravestone declared "CoD. 1 USCI." What was it? It was shorthand for Company D, the First US Colored Infantry. There were men buried here that served in the Union army during the Civil War.

And, my notes continued, cemeteries are spiritually significant landscapes and those grave markers tell many richly detailed stories about the people and the communities. They're loaded with important historical, genealogical, and biological information. Not to mention, if you tear down the walls of history built around them, you will read the dramas and the tragedies.

There are generations of local black American families interred. Some have been carefully tended; some have just passed on to dust. I can't help wondering who will care for this little known repository of this community and the family history that has gone.

The memory of some of these cemeteries simply tends to be forgotten. I wonder why can't we black Americans ever get it together anywhere. It may be that our ancestors inhibit our progress because we as a people have denied them. No other people have ever walked away from such a large number of their dead, and we continually pay the price for taking that walk. This is only a portion, just my island, of what must be done to sustain our progress to ensure a positive vision of the future and somehow to recognize our contributions in the developing world.

Lynn Rogers would send me an email in response to my questions on what has become of the interest generated at the November meeting. She's a very open, very well-intentioned lady. She said "Cleve you are so right about no one place on Staten Island to gather information. Wouldn't it be nice to transform the building at the Frederick Douglass Cemetery to a Staten Island Genealogy Center?"

Chapter 8

MURALS

This chapter includes essays about art, specifically public murals, and about the psychological effect they can have as one of many forms of subliminal visual messaging, in particular, the power of White supremacy as manifested overtly and also by omission in the WPA murals. It was inspired by a specific series of 13 WPA murals that adorn the walls of Borough Hall in Staten Island, New York. They depict the island's population participating in and enjoying the economic development of Staten Island. They were painted by Frederick C. Stahr from 1936 to 1938, although he proposed to paint then when Borough Hall opened in 1906. It took 30 years for the funds to support his paintings were found in the form of the Federal Art Project, the WPA. By omission, and in one case by deliberate depiction, the murals neglect and even negate any contribution by free Black citizens on the island. This chapter is also about history, and how the narrative a community chooses to accept as the truth about their past, about who did what, why and when, can be shaped and molded by those in power at any given time.

This chapter describes the murals and the decade-long efforts of the author to protest the continued showing of the murals in a public building without any explanatory text for the viewer. Further, the building in question is one where members of the public are obliged to enter if they wish to conduct certain government business or obtain information. There is no choice about many people's need to enter the building and view the murals. The chapter also cites recent psychological research on the effect of negative or derogatory subliminal messages, known as microaggressions, on individuals.

The chapter includes copies of letters published in newspapers on the Staten Island murals, and commentary by several individuals other than the author on the topic at hand. All in all, it provides food for thought and possibly, a call to action.

The Beginning

I have no beginning except to simply read from my notes and perhaps this could be called "Remembrances and Revelations."

Years ago, before my dear friend Gail Schneider, the librarian and archivist at the Staten Island Institute for Arts and Sciences, died in Kerhonkson, New York, I told her that I was ready to take a stand about the Borough Hall murals. After months of research about the WPA murals, I was ready to act. What I found, however, was that the dream of research would take me far away from the narrow corridors at Borough Hall.

It is difficult to add to the pages that I have already written on this issue. Like most Black men in America, I feel that we are always living in the shadow of an image; in a space that exists between fear, fascination, and wonder. More than 24 million Black men in the United States face a moment or a time in their lives when the decades of steady progress collide with disheartening setbacks. Like most people in other demographic segments, we are sorting out our futures as the country is changing in many dramatic ways. It is stressful to begin to speak about the years, the continued stalkings of Borough Hall, and how they led me to feel that now I am ready to write about it.

Tomorrow, I will take the bus and return to Staten Island again to photograph the murals, to make certain that my feelings, responses, words, are correct as I would see them. My work to uncover what I have witnessed in the art of documenting the murals, WPA art, is problematic because Americans inherently do not like to have their historical pictures messed with or the accepted narrative of the country questioned, even if those murals, the ones that grace the halls of government buildings across the country, are of questionable accuracy.

I thought initially that my findings were figments of my imagination. They were not. The conditions under which many Black Americans have lived for so much of our history in this country is real. Our fate has been in the hands of people who thought of us as less than human, or who hated us outright, could punish us on a whim, and could attack us with little or no fear of retribution. My reckless and sometimes self-destructive behavior has diminished as the process of understanding White supremacy in art evolves and explains my angst and frustration.

Yes, life and times have changed a great deal. There are no Night Riders on Staten Island, there are no church bombers or rashes of rogue violence, but what I feel in my gut and what I learned in researching this book tell me that there is a serious problem for Blacks; a serious problem with depression. It is caused primarily because of the conditions in which we, as Black people, and in particular, Black men live. Dr. Alvin Poussaint, psychiatrist, says that depression is deeply embedded in the DNA. No one has bothered to perform any in-depth studies.

At Atlanta's Moorehouse College School of Medicine they have begun pioneer research on depression and its treatment. The mental health diagnosis of Post Traumatic Stress Disorder, originally attributed to battle scarred soldiers, has been expanded to include people who experience horrible events, and now to include those who experience less dramatic traumas, but experience them chronically over a long period of time.

Since having been designated as an activist by the *Staten Island Advance,* it occurs to me that other activists must be heard from. White privilege and White power have engendered a personal betrayal for me and many other Blacks. The power maintains the indignity and finds the rhetoric to do nothing. There are those that can't grasp the concept of White privilege. Many are constantly looking for easy-to-understand examples.

For me, the murals carry enormous intransigent and negative intellectual and emotional baggage. A careful look is needed. I'm a senior now and not totally overwhelmed. There are many days and nights when things have gone terribly wrong. Tying together the coherent thoughts about this, at one time, reckless and destructive behavior has led me to process many years in civil rights activities.

What does all that have to do, you ask, with murals, art, or white power? It is about the whites, the blacks, the self-deceivers. It's important that the young vibrant black and white youth, both within the institutions, the arts, and outside of them. For a time the culture celebrated the rebel and the outsider, but the outsiders ended up achieving very little. Only the insiders, those that were not self-deceivers, those that can see, look at those murals for decades as I have been forced to do, will ultimately be aware of the personal betrayal. The Borough Hall murals glorify the White, European contribution to the development of the "New World" while omitting the contribution of Blacks and in one case by depicting a Black man as a lazy, disinterested bystander. The weapons, fine clothing, shoes and hats on the Europeans, the power of the workmen and the machines, the triumph of the priest holding the cross, all contrast sharply with the hatless, shoeless, tired Negro bystander.

For me to return, year after year, to picket alone in front of Borough Hall, to look, to see, to feel the murals, raised many difficult and fundamental questions. Of the painter's artistic intent, his assumptions, his expectations, we know little. The murals still continue to give me that touch of magic; the private investigations and interactions with art, especially the mural art, has seriously altered my life. The clumsy, outrageous negotiation with myself because I did not have a fine arts degree. I didn't know that I **could** speak about what it was that I saw.

When living in New York, I joined fellow Blacks and whites to speak about art, theatre, music, and dance. The conversations ranged wide: painting, sculpture, ceramics, print making, jewelry, paper art glass, wood, leather, metal, and photography. It was necessary to become erudite in these subjects.   No one was able to say why. We were deeply entrenched in our own silly quadrants of life. Meaningless. One night, one day, one afternoon, whenever, we would discuss Andy Warhol, Roy Lichtenstein, Jasper Johns, Jackson Pollock, Koening, Coe, all the 'biggies;' these names had cachet and power. It was supposedly a mark of some sort of intelligence to be able to rattle off those names. To become one of the "in" group.

I often wondered what the relationship was between artists and the general public. I don't have the vaguest idea what the answer is. After many years, I do have a number of questions.

The North Shore of Staten Island is a parody of a blighted community, a place where most have given up being or attempting to be integrated into the larger society. The island now becomes more a communal community, but down in the depths of their souls it is the most fundamental basis of our own struggles, that the human pathos inherent in every situation lives at the North and South Shore. Driving about, the scenes speak for themselves.

They speak most eloquently every day in the one newspaper when they publish stories about the many instances of the warped and the twisted, the harsh. The grind of Staten Island is overwhelming terrible and beautiful in its immensity. The following is what I see and observe. So will you if you look closely and not compromise.

It has taken me many years to understand, to photograph, and to visit, similar murals around the east coast. It has given me reason why I have known without much critical or any other kind of research that when the Municipal Arts Society (MAS) tours Staten Island, the first place they tour will be the halls of Borough Hall.

One mural in particular strikes the psyche of the discerning viewer.

A young black man sits in the forefront of the mural, the only Black person - barefoot, sleepy, snotty-nosed, a fishing pole in his hands but too lazy to drop it into the water. What it is, it's so much like everyday notable signals without a title that make tourists from all over the world remember what they see. The signals, the signs, that he or she visiting will remember.

I have known for many years now that my depression could be specifically diagnosed as some sort of a mental disorder. Like most Black men, we are not prone to present ourselves for mental therapy, our condition collectively could be called inflexible, maladaptive, even psychotic behavior that impairs our performance. In 1945, in the military, there was a term "shell-shocked." Today it's called Post Traumatic Stress Disorder or PTSD. Recently, the military was exposed (NY Times, 2/25/12) as having pressured mental health professionals to diagnose soldiers with PTSD, a military service-induced condition that engenders benefits, as having a personality disorder, a pre-existing condition which would result in discharge without benefits.

Black men have been living with the violence, portrayed in art, media, and murals; its violence will take various expressions. The same as war, the same as a civil conflict, human rights violations, slavery, colonial domination, the same domination for political, religious, ethnic, or social reasons; it may take many forms. It's the direct physical form and indirect physical violence. But there is also psychic violence that is directed at a person's self-concept or self-esteem. Those who inflict this violence on others, it comes in various forms. It's quite intentional and rational, in the outcome that they seek to produce in the lives of their victims. The intent is to produce in those persons afflicted; it becomes the narrative of the lie. The symptoms are very subtle; these covert racist incidents form a social back-up which racially marginalizes people who must function day to day. The incidents, the micro-aggressions, are never far from one's consciousness and require expenditures of a great deal of cognitive energy, and hyper-vigilance in coping. One incident alone may be traumatizing, but multiple micro-aggressions can build and create an intense traumatic effect or a traumatic impact.

Beyond being forced to stand in front of those murals so many years ago the most powerful, the micro-aggressions, that I was able to see, feel, in the white power structure maintains the right, the power, to house for decades the very symbols of racism, produce the laws, protect them from accidents. I began to see through my narrow lens a responsibility of action against this institutionalized racism.

Micro-aggressions, the insidious micro-assaults; those assaults daily cannot be treated by the current medical profession. These racial micro-aggressions are brief and commonplace. Sometimes daily, they are verbal, nonverbal, subtle, and environmental indignities, whether intentional or unintentional. They communicate hostile, derogatory, or even negative racial slights and insults to the target person or group. Black, pure, not even expressed them those micro-assaults come in three forms: the micro assaults, the micro-insults, and the micro-invalidations.

It has been many years since I knowingly have avoided any mental assistance because there simply is none. As Black men, permitting of their forcibly or personally to commit themselves for treatment is very difficult. I only skim the surface, and unfortunately it is very difficult to continue. The lesson is stark, the lesson is clear; in the community and perhaps in the world where there are serious impediments to freedom of expression we are far, very far, from having reached the stage of a genuine democratic culture in which thought and expression are truly free.

I suggested a panel from the art departments of the college and university on Staten Island. It went nowhere. I was naïve thinking that perhaps it would. My apocalyptic mural stands, perhaps it will forever be there.

I realized that there are few people that see the murals who really make an attempt to ask any questions. They probably ask themselves in a vague observation "Yes, I saw them," but there is no doubt in my mind that images, like the black young man front and center in the mural will remain in the minds of hundreds and thousands of people their entire life. I walk around the city, a city with hundreds of thousands of tourists, and know that those who trek up the hill to Borough Hall to see the murals will remember that image. Perhaps they will not speak about it; there will be no comprehensive discussion; the images like those that are part of our lives will remain in their heads, and because of the environment on Staten Island, that's as far as they will travel.

Writers increasingly use art to discuss art, to make a statement. Most art is political; there are no parameters. These historic themed murals are the patriotism that we all must have. There is no question. There is modernism, Dadaism, pop art, all the other conceptualisms. Artists are left with the question: What is it about? Do you like it or not? And no one knows why, really, no one cares as long as the artists get their 15 minutes of fame. And given that there doesn't seem to be any single definition of art, a vacuum has been created and nature fills vacuums. And these historic murals fill that void, the propaganda, the political correctness, funding to back the cleaning, to back their stability, ingratiate the politics, the building, and the politicians.

At the centennial it was simply an outrageous spectacle, a chance to party. In a video of my participation in the 350th anniversary at Borough Hall, I took every opportunity to be there before, during, and after what... I'm sure that most know of my feelings.

The creation and the discussions of art on the walls lead me to believe that art schools have virtually stopped teaching art. The best art schools are simply elementary crayon painters.

The first letter to me from Borough President Molinari said the $75 million to clean up and restore the murals in the Borough Hall lobby were private funds and that he was powerless to influence their allocation. He would however, he said, arrange to have an explanatory plaque to put the offensive mural in context. Companies, people, are increasingly relied on for funding and it's a wonderful marketing device to portray the history of our becoming who we think we are. The trashing and reconstructing of history can be perpetrated through visual art. The U.S. is a powerful nation and New York City is the seat of power and influence of the U.S. and that power is in the hands of the White bureaucracy.

Discussion about the murals does not occur and anyone attempting to discuss their merits, positive and negative, are declared elitist and their words less likely to appear in the *Staten island Advance* except perhaps to critique, criticize, unless perhaps a movie star or celebrity were to be quoted.

Finishing, I wonder what kind of legacy if any at all that we are leaving behind in regard to art of this generation. Could it be considered important art, which means that perhaps we will influence future generations? Not much, probably. There is a clear need for standards in art in public buildings. There are too many arguments about the good and the bad, that there needs to be some kind of new way of evaluating art. I think it's important to know how to proceed. The influences of the work, what is the work trying to say, contribute. Trashing history has always been continued. Does a people become extinct when it is no longer educated to have a creative capacity? Capacity to change the world or their environment?

Even the newer murals being prepared for an opening in the Courthouse on Richmond Terrace, which were painted by Black artists, perpetuate the Eurocentric vision of White power and supremacy. They avoid any controversial scenes and do nothing to promote the image of Blacks as contributing to the development of society. Blacks have been on Staten Island since the 1600s, but have still not attained historical relevance.

The current (through January 2013) show at the Museum of the City of New York, "From Farm to City," documents 350 years of Staten Island history. It features one poster of a photograph by Alice Austin of Black oyster shuckers and a White boss. The obvious conclusion for the viewer of this exhibit is that the only contribution Blacks made to Staten Island's economic development is the shucking of oysters. The truth is that Blacks on Staten Island were entrepreneurs and laborers and soldiers who had thriving business communities.

I bear partial responsibility (or credit, as the case may be) for this photograph being unearthed from the Austen collection and highlighted and brought to the public's attention through the Staten Island Black History Project. A member of the Unitarian Church alerted me to the existence of the photo in the collection at Richmondtown. We went there and located the photo, and several others, copied them and returned them to Richmondtown. When the Project published the oystermen photograph in its newsletter, I was threatened with arrest and chose to leave for South America until things cooled off.

What Is Art And Who Owns History?

This query is intended in a double sense: first, how might the history of the WPA be looked at or described differently than it was understood at the time of its existence? And second, since the images produced under its patronage may confront us as present-day viewers with representations that are problematic in a number of ways (among them, perhaps discriminatory in diverse, perhaps subtle ways), what should we do about this if so? Do we have a responsibility to signal our awareness of it, and how should that best be accomplished? Can these problematic viewpoints be affected retroactively at present by doing this now?

The touristic brochure-provided the fact that although that organization provided funding for their execution in 1936 and they were installed in 1940, it had been in 1904 when the Hall was constructed that the artist had independently conceived and proposed them as decorations for it, but they could then not yet be financed.

Stahr's Staten Island murals (although they are actually painted on canvas affixed to rather than painted directly on the plaster walls or *al fresco*) may be Modern examples of the long tradition of wall painting and its representation of political as well as social power.

Without "defending" the WPA and its intentions with respect to the topic of discrimination, there is no question that the WPA sponsored, in "real life," artwork by and the artistic careers of Black Americans as well as other non-Caucasian ethnic groups. The New Deal public works programs had as one of its primary goals making art and artists relevant to the general public.

This meant, in principle, "everybody" in American society: some of whom may have never before had exposure to a working visual artist (creating murals in buildings that were part of their everyday lives), or even to any work of art. And a similarly salient fact is that the WPA, or many of its participant members (as can be readily grasped from the existence of their Artists' Union, the contents of their publication *Art Front*, and the American Artists' Congress), were members of the Socialist party or at least of Socialist political orientation. That is, Public Works of Art Project participants were frequently the "politically correct" of their own time.

The author of one of the most important books on the WPA Federal Art Project (whose basis was the one its director Holger Cahill never managed to bring to publication), Francis V. O'Connor, pointed out in 1975 that the government endeavor was in part motivated by the "quest for a useable past... during a time of economic uncertainty... an art for the people," to reassure them.

Yet he too realized there were flaws in this effort, both inherent ones and others that stemmed from prejudices within American society at that time, even himself unintentionally participating in the latter while trying to be as "broad-minded" as possible. O'Connor relevantly stressed: "Our muralists, in particular, conscious of their 'people's audience' and inspired by the example of the Mexicans, sought to trace a national lineage which inevitably went back to our European origins." Yet he at the same time sees: "How tragic... that our mural artists ignored the rich, ancient, archetypal lore and icons of our continent's Indian tribes," and even why.

"The culture of the American Indian was not then—and is not today—a part of our usable past, and its absence from popular consciousness… is symptomatic of our continuing humanistic myopia." But it is when he speaks of "culturally undeveloped citizens" that we find the basis of our inquiry: "Of these, blacks were probably the worst off. The testimony… provides insight into the Project's effort to spread cultural democracy to even the least regarded citizens, to give them the training and encouragement they needed, and provide equality with whites insofar as the social conventions of the 1930s permitted." Could it be that that effort was in itself discriminatory?

The U.S. Narrative

Like every other country, the U.S. has a narrative that is presented in history books and which neglects to mention the more violent and sordid episodes of our past. Illustrations in many history books show fully clothed Europeans with hats and shoes trading goods with nearly naked American Indians. The artists did not try to portray reality, they wanted to portray primitive versus civilized.

Let's start with a premise not everyone is an artist and not everything is art. Its time to re-examine what is art, and particularly, why some art is still deemed to be "important" while other art is simply decorative or ephemeral. Why do certain dead artists still retain their power over us? And are there a set of artistic values that can be shared between artists that transcend style, medium, or even arguments over good versus bad art?

Questions, questions, and more questions. This essay seeks to provoke a lively discussion; a discussion initiated by the Stahr murals. Discussions I have had with the staff of other Universities in Staten Island and New York City did not result in increased interest in the subject or a wish on the part of the other party to pursue the topic. Nevertheless, the issue is real and however subtle, continues to perpetrate negative impressions or omissions of Black contributions to Staten Island's development.

How do we differentiate the innate desire to express ourselves from something called art – and is it important? What is the point someone's ketch/drawing/painting/expression become art? This essay was not intended to talk about good art vs bad art, or beautiful vs ugly, or any other contrary opinions about art. This discussion is to ask, What is art? Because if it is all straw and papers, or if parameters are just an exercise, then art is nothing. Why have museums? Why go to art school? Why study art? And, lastly, why make art work?

Because let's be frank: we are in danger of losing art altogether, at least the sense of collective recognition and appreciation of something; anything defined as "art." In other words, we can be losing the cultural literacy and the common touchstones that serve as markers and communication of a community, of a shared history. And there are very real consequences to this state of affairs, including, but not limited to, all contemporary art at least gets devalued

Art is subjective. Perhaps the relationship between the work of art and the viewer defines these boundaries.

And it is very hard - almost impossible - to make a living as an artist. How can a monetary value (the economic currency which places a unit value on something) be established when artists themselves resist the notion of artistic values? In other words, the intrinsic value of art and artists values, the beliefs and practices that define, that you can point to that are then recognized and monetized by others. For example, a Rembrandt is valued because of the skill, time, and vision that it took to paint the picture. Can the same be said today of a hack video producer today that just churns stuff out hoping it sticks to the wall? And contrary to the depiction of galleries as ogres with their 30 to 50 percent commission structures, I would add that most galleries as well are struggling mightily to exist. I would not want to be in that business.

Many superstar artists today have become producers and do not actually touch the work themselves. They direct or design. Or more importantly, beyond the actual "production" of something, they market themselves. They brand themselves. The artists have become their own art. And then they get old.

In short, art has become an excuse and platform – as therapy, to get laid, perhaps, to party, to become famous. And art itself, what is produced, has become a hook to market around. Again, I wonder what kind of legacy we are leaving in regard to art of this generation. What can be considered "important" art - which, to me, means what will influence future generations? As I see it, not much, I'm afraid.

I would argue that there is a clear need for standards in art - not in regards to medium (not this whole rip off that "painting is dead," or style, or substance/content. There have been too many arguments about the bad versus the good, the street versus the studio. But there needs to be a new/old way of evaluating art, and I offer some suggested standards:

- **Craftsmanship** - How well is the piece made? Is it archival? Does the artist show mastery of their chosen medium. Realizing that craftsmanship definitions are flexible and vary over time (the impressionists were described as sloppy painters and were later accepted as prized artists) does the work exhibit a firmness and surety of hand?

- **Aesthetics/ Beauty** - Does this artist deal with the question of beauty in the work - even if the piece is intended to be off-center, challenging or even ugly? This is particularly important in regard to painting. Spirituality - Here is what Kandinsky referred to as spirituality in art. Does the artist put something of themselves in the work? Does the work have essence?

- **Influences/ History** – The biggie. It is important to know what preceded you and the work of art. What or who influenced the work? What is the work trying to contribute/reference?

But I repeat the refrain, not everyone is an artist and not everything is art. Of my own work in using art to discuss art, my work is merely to make a statement. How did we get to a place that art, especially "fine art," has no parameters? There is a general perception that everything is art and everybody is an artist, resting on the notion that art singularly resists definition and so must be taken on its own terms. The conceit is conceptual.

Turned on its head, logically speaking, we are therefore essentially now saying: Nothing is art and nobody is an artist. Everything and everybody equal a big nothing. That is where we have been led, down the road from modernism, to dada, to pop art, to conceptualism, with all the thinking and ideas left far behind, to today's artists, who eschew paint for perfume and polemics. And nobody knows why – or really cares as long as they get their 15 minutes.

Given that there does not seem to be any definition to art, a vacuum has been created, and nature fills vacuums. So, non-art values have been filling that void: celebrity, propaganda, political correctness, marketing, corporate affiliations, art as commodity, shock, outrageousness, spectacle, and perhaps a chance to party, to name a few.

It is time to re-examine what is art, and particularly, why some art is still deemed to be "important" while other art is simply, as before stated, decorative. Who are the deciders of the public art and the public purchases?

Public support for spending on art is scarce due to public boredom and disgust at what is being purveyed as art, so companies are increasingly relied on for funding and buying art for their purposes and branding campaigns. Putting aside the excesses, the market is a wonderful thing in its organization, power to bring parties together, and to define. But it is self-interested. Artists need to stand up for their own collective interests to counteract that weight, and then perhaps for the public to care.

Here on the Island, and, I would say, in Manhattan, the art schools have virtually stopped teaching art. At best art schools are hand-holders, at worst they are hybrid amalgamations of other disciplines. The art school emphasis on marketing, concept, presentation, and commercial skills seems to be saying: Go to business school with a paint brush in hand if you really want to excel in the art world. And the true "patrons," the mentors and long-term supporters of artists, are an increasingly rare breed. They are now simply buyers of art.

Criticism - especially strong criticism - does not occur. As with the murals, when criticism appears it is declared elitist and less likely to be repeated. Most art critics today are second-tier journalists competing with the breathless reporting of celebrity antics on the style page. What has happened to art criticism? From the files you will find this:

Art criticism can content itself with description, but it then loses the run of itself, becomes something else, dissolves into the ocean of undifferentiated nonfiction writing on culture. Art criticism can be a parade of pronouncements or 'discriminations,' as the editorial in the New Criterion has it, but then it becomes conservative, or begins to smell of dogmatism. I find myself engaged by critics who are serious about judgment, by which I mean that they offer judgments, and – this is what matters most – they then pause to assess those judgments.

James Elkins *What Happened to Art Criticism*

"Meanings are made in people's minds. And what about those didactic panels once suggested? I'm not saying that artists should have to explain their work or that writers exist to explain it for them, but there could and should be a comprehensible public discussion about what art does for us. What is being learned from it? What might it enable us to do, or think, or feel that we couldn't before? Most of the public criticism of the arts is really an attempt to ask exactly such questions, and instead of just priding ourselves on creating controversy by raising them, trying to answer a few might not be such a bad idea.

And of the art schools? As I have noted they have virtually stopped teaching art. It is important to know what preceded you. What and who influenced the work? Who and what have any influence on the work of Frederick Stahr? What is the work trying to contribute? Traditionally when we had guilds, societies, a long apprenticeship was required of an artist before the individual would be allowed to put that one touch or one flourish that was his signature mark. Today's art seems to be very post-modern in orientation. Trashing history to always be creating the new "new." This is a race to the bottom and I do not wish to participate in that.

And I would add that the all-important ingredients of artistic success are there still: hard work, discipline, talent, striving for excellence, and, perhaps, luck. Predictably artists are going to resist standards and any values discussion, seeing it as repressive and paternalistic. One artist went so far as to react by stating: "I wish someone would explain to me why people feel that art needs to be defined, ruled, or standardized. Doing so is the antithesis of art. Does requiring artistic standards allow people to feel secure? By setting up a narrow path to creating art are they defining their own way of creating and trying to impose it on others?"

My response "no, no, that is not my desire. I, too, am digging, digging deeply, for fire, fire, fire …"

Background

Protesting the Murals

Staten Island's Borough Hall is bordered on one side by Richmond Terrace and on the other side by Stuyvesant Place, a few hundred yards from the Staten Island ferry. Beyond the building is the lower New York Bay, where the ferry passes the Statue of Liberty daily, bringing f thousands of tourists from around the world to view S.I.'s attractions, including the murals in Borough Hall. Borough Hall displays 13 Works Progress Administration (WPA) murals. During the presidency of Franklin D. Roosevelt and the Great Depression of the Thirties, the U.S. federal government sponsored visual and performing artists to an extent never achieved before or since. The WPA project saved thousands of artists from poverty and exposed many Americans to original art for the first time. Some 25,000 murals were funded, along with thousands of sculptures, paintings and prints. Many of the artists were politically active or socially conscious, others were racially biased. Their attitudes were reflected in their art, some of which became controversial as society changed. Artists like Ben Shahn and Harry Gottlieb painted the disparities between rich and poor and the plight of landless farmers and factory workers on picket lines. Some WPA murals were destroyed or painted over as too inflammatory. A 54-foot long homage to Jane Adams, Clara Barton, Harriet Tubman, Lucy Flowers and other women social reformers was deemed too controversial for its allusions to child labor, the abolition of slavery, women's suffrage and pacifism. Just a year after it was completed in 1940, it was ordered painted over by an all-male school board that considered it subversive. It was restored in 1995 by a project involved in restoring over 400 heavily-damaged and hidden WPA murals. According to Bryan Le Beau of the Smithsonian magazine, "The artists who did the murals and prints documented not only America's enthusiasms and fantasies, but also the nation's biases, ambitions and fears." Some artists, like William Sidney Mount (1807 - 1868), painted Blacks as individuals with character. He painted a series of Black musicians designed expressly for European buyers who coveted images of what they considered "American exotica."

Petitions and Protests

In 2000, I began a personal letter-writing campaign to Borough President Guy Molinari and all the elected political figures, asking for their support in the removal or covering of the most offensive mural. In July, 2000, I received a response from Borough President Molinari. He wrote that he had no jurisdiction over the mural in question, and that the property is in the hands of the Department of Citywide Administration Services in Manhattan. He noted that he had consulted the Borough Historian, Richard Dickenson, a Black man, for his input about informational placards to be placed next to the mural. I received courteously-written replies from all of them, but

329

there was no follow-up. I sat for many days deciding how to bring the issue to other Blacks and Black organizations. I naively convinced myself that large mailing lists existed and if I were to ask for them and explain my reason, I would obtain them from Black organizations on Staten Island. There seems to be no such list available. I decided to ask for one dollar per person to defray printing and postal expenses. With my first mailing of over 300 letters, I received a total of one dollar from a supporter. But I was cool; it dawned on me that asking for money was a mistake, since the Memory Lanes of Staten Island are washed thin with tales of people who have asked for money only to misspend or abscond with it.

I never advocated destroying the murals. I would prefer they be moved out of the public building or covered, but if that is not possible, the bare minimum concession to the sensibilities of Black viewers would seem be explanatory plaques. Such plaques have been used in similar situations, for example, the Environmental Protection Agency in Washington, DC, resolved the controversy over two WPA murals in its building which depicted Native Americans raping, scalping and pillaging. Although the murals were not covered, they are shielded by screens that prevent direct viewing by employees and visitors. Another WPA mural titled "Peoples of the World" was removed from Oak Park, Illinois, because Blacks felt their depiction carrying spears and wearing loincloths was a negative stereotype. The difference between these protests and the S.I. Borough Hall protests is the S.I. issue remains unaddressed. No Black Staten Islander, most of whom are home owners and tax payers, has ever said a mumbling word in protest, according to newspapers and records. It did make me feel a bit weird to mention it again, but after a trip to Gail's grave in Kerhonkson, I knew what I had to do.

In April 2000, I sent copies of the same letters about the murals to the Sandy Ground Historical Society; Universal Temple on the Arts; Ms. Josephine Tucker, Director of the S.I. Branch of the Urban League; and Mr. Ed Josey, President of the S.I. Chapter of the N.A.A.C.P., inviting them to join me at the next Arts Commission meeting in Manhattan. The letter read as follows:

> **The paintings show life-size figures of explorers, soldiers, statesmen, defenders of liberty, and clergy, elegantly dressed white men and women and proud Native Americans in full regalia. The only Black Americans in the murals are barefoot, ragged and sleepy.**

> **The murals are offensive, a comfort to bigots who would like to believe that Black men and women did nothing to foster the growth of New York City, and Staten Island in particular. Nothing could be further from the truth. Black children and adults visiting or working in Borough Hall can only feel shame a t the slovenly aspect of their alleged ancestors.**

One of the 13 Borough Hall Murals. It depicts a young Black man in the foreground, shoeless, hatless, uninterested in his surroundings. The Whites and American Indians in all the paintings have head and foot coverings.

Another of the Borough Hall murals. With a cross and a pike, Verrazano brings God to Staten Island.

I would like to draw your attention to an outrageous proposal to spend over 50 thousand dollars of taxpayers money to have the murals in the Borough Hall lobby restored. I urge you to join with me to deny the payment of public funds to restore these murals. I do not suggest their destruction but removal! They must be removed from this government building, the "People's House."

I suggest a panel be formed to fund a grant available to artists who can submit drawings and proposals for new paintings for the "People's House" that will more accurately depict the diverse population that contributed to the development of Staten Island during that period.

I created my own mailing list of Black Staten Islanders from friends and strangers, newspapers and the Internet. Whenever I encountered a Black person, I would ask for a name and address. Over time, I built a mailing list of more than 400 Black Staten Islanders. My first letters would explain my mission and ask for their signature on a petition to address the murals.

Staten Island politicians responded:

1) Assemblywoman Elizabeth A. Connelly: "Candidly, I am so rarely in it (Borough Hall) that I can't really recall what is on the walls. I most certainly recommend you bring your views before the City Arts Commission."

2) Councilman Jerome X. O'Donovan: "I am in receipt of your correspondence. Our children's education is very important to me and I am horrified with the budget cuts. I will keep you informed of any new information. Be assured of my continued support."

3) Assemblyman Eric N. Vitaliano: "Frankly, I was unaware of the proposal and have only the vaguest of recollections about the murals themselves. The failure to include an accurate depiction of the contributions of Black Americans to Staten Island's history is offensive and should be remedied."

4) Borough President Guy V. Molinari: "I have received your most recent letter regarding the Frederick Stahr mural at Borough Hall, and I appreciate your comments. My office has no jurisdiction over the mural in question. I consulted both the New York City Arts Commission and the Borough Historian Richard Dickenson for their input. At their suggestion, informational placards will be placed next to the murals to explain the artwork in a modern context."

Letters asking for support were also sent to Congressman Vito Fossella, State Senator John J. Marchi, State Senator Vincent Gentile, Assemblyman Robert Straniere, Mayor Rudolf Giuliani, Deputy Borough President James Molinaro, Public Administrator Gary Gotlin, Councilman Jim Oddo, and Councilman Stephen Fiala, none of whom replied.

The Borough President repeated that he had no authority to remove the mural, which was under the jurisdiction of the New York City Arts Commission. We gathered over 350 signatures and wrote a detailed letter to the Arts Commission and requested speaking slots during their next public meeting, scheduled for July 10, 2000, at the chamber on the second floor of City Hall in Manhattan. None of those who had signed the petition showed up at the meeting, so it was just Jude and I.

At 10 A.M. we added our names to the log book in front of the aisle. The choreography started when the Arts Commission entered, smiling, taking their seats on the circular dais. The chairperson, a Ms. Jean Parker-Phifer, made a short statement and opened the meeting, reminding the audience to be quiet and courteous. No one had yet looked at the big book where we had signed our names. Architectural firms came to the front and set up maps and drawings, then presented the 12 commissioners with papers and were given a microphone to speak into for the panel. Other men came to speak with their company logos attached to their large drawings, which they set up for the commissioners to inspect. It went on for so long without any comments above a whisper that I knew the scene was one that had already been planned. None of the speakers had signed their names in the book. It may just as well have been a bowl of plastic cactus. Other men representing companies wanted acceptance for window bars or "distinctive sidewalks." They droned on and on. The chamber was now humming with impatient citizens, who, like me, realized the die had been cast. We were simply spectators here, most would tire and leave. The meeting had a long agenda, and after several hours of discussions on various topics, it became clear that public input was not expected or solicited. I submitted a written statement to a woman at a desk and deposited a handful of the signed petitions. There was never any response.

James Molinaro succeeded Guy Molinari to the post of Borough President, and has been similarly unresponsive to the mural issue. In 2002, it was again reported in the Staten Island Advance that hundreds of thousand of dollars were to be spent on renovating Borough Hall and restoring the murals. The Borough President's aide and chief counsel, Dan Master, Jr. asked me to work with them and find some common ground. I agreed, and sent him letters on April 3 and April 19, reiterating the suggestion to set up a bi-partisan, multiracial panel to decide on the fate of the murals, and on whether to mount explanatory plaques alongside them, with public input on the text. The letters included suggestions for members of the panel as well as draft text for a plaque as a thought-starter. No response was forthcoming.

2002 was the third year of protesting and passing out leaflets in front of Borough Hall. Letters to the Borough President went unanswered.

Newspaper Coverage

Staten Island has one principal newspaper, the Staten Island Advance, and a few smaller ones, including the Staten Island Register and the Star Reporter. In the Sixties, our first Congress of Racial Equality marches and demonstrations barely made it to the back pages of the Advance, whose management has never been taciturn about its conservative views. It was a "home-town" paper and they were prepared to keep it that way without giving coverage to these civil rights rabble-rousers in the streets.

I had never met either of the Advance's reporters, Michael J. Paquette or Michael Fressola, the Arts Editor. Michael Paquette called me at my office in Washington, D.C. and, despite my long-standing suspicions about the White-power bias of newspapers and their reporters, I agreed to speak with him and discuss my decades-old feelings about the murals. Paquette listened and edited most of what I said and added what he wanted. In all my actvities in print and on the street, I never said I was a "self-described activist." I have not been an active member of any organization since returning to the U.S. and I found the description, one of the twists used by the newspapers, insulting. Michael Fressola intimated that he had met me in his front-page story on June 21, 2000. I never said I wanted to "tear down" the murals. In fact, the so-called "Art Editor" did not even look at the mural we disagreed about. I also had not met Jim O'Grady, who wrote the New York Times article on July 9, 2000.

My many letters over the years to Black leaders of organizations like the NAACP, the Urban League, the Sandy Ground Historical Society, and the Universal Temple of the Arts had elicited no responses. However, when the White press called on them, these same Black organizations and individuals had their responses on the murals ready, which appeared the next day on the front pages of the Advance. Sandy Ground Historical Society Black Executive Director, Julie Moody Lewis said, "I don't think images of an earlier era should be torn down, just because they are now seen as politically incorrect." Staten Island Urban League Director, Josephine Tucker, was "Disturbed by the image and wants it to come down unless borough hall includes a better reflection of the lives of Blacks during that time." Ed Josey, President of the S.I Chapter of the NAACP, said, "I support the effort to banish the mural, we should be more aware of how things are portrayed to the public today." Sadja Musawir Ladner, Director of the Universal Temple of the Arts, said, "Image is everything, and a lot of people are not going to read the text. Borough Hall is not just a building, it represents everybody."

Many Blacks seem to believe that it is politically correct to see a gray area, devoid of color, devoid of any solid ground. Refusing to look directly at the murals has made it easy to tolerate injustice. Too easy to resist raising ones voice against the prevailing mentality of White superiority so pervasive in our culture. We are told to be understanding, less judgmental, and to tolerate the biases and omissions of artists of another generation.

The Staten Island Advance editorial in the "OUR OPINION" column followed the theme, attempting to re-direct my words by using the title, **Old Art, New Offense**. The article runs on for more than 1000 words. At vespers, I sat down to respond, and burned the night away. How was I going to confront this powerful newspaper, its voice reflecting the thinking on Staten Island for as long as I can remember? Who was I to confront them? I had no organization behind me, no money to hire professionals to assist me, no masters or doctorate in fine art. Was I an art historian, a sociologist? No, I was a Black man who had become a militant and would always be. What right did I have to confront the Borough or the City or State of New York about a 60-year old mural? How could I resist?

I felt hurt and angry when the Black borough historian, Richard "Dick" Dickenson, wrote a long article in response to my demonstrating against the mural. I had corresponded with Dickenson months before, and he advised me not to complain about the murals, that it should be a private matter. He would not respond to me directly but did respond to the White Staten Island Advance reporter who called. To go public, he advised, would only open the floodgates to controversy and censorship of public art. His comments about art were not relevant to art in a taxpayer-supported building. Our backgrounds were somewhat similar - Black men in our early seventies, but our views were opposite. He was an appointee, not a career employee. I imagined that the privilege of being an unpaid volunteer would give him some freedom to stand on principal and not attack me, a Black brother. Dick Dickinson's serrated-edged article in the Advance cut deep under the heading, **Cultural Tyranny** as follows:

> **With regard to the recent and simplistic "politically correct" issue on the Borough Hall murals, I wish to further expand on remarks which Mike Fressola and Mike Paquette accurately depicted my position on the matter.**
>
> **I waver between both an ironic and exasperated reaction. Without a doubt, my old acquaintance, Cleve Overton, and those whom he has persuaded into his camp, have every right - constitutional and moral - to highlight an issue which they consider to be wrong. However, something I learned - in Army basic training in the months just prior to the Korean War - was that there are privileged rights and with those rights go responsibilities.**
>
> **To paraphrase the eminent jurist and Union soldier, Justice Oliver Wendell Holmes, Jr., "Freedom of speech does not extend to falsely shouting 'fire' in a crowded theater." I think that in the context of a perceived need in our borough for preserving our cultural heritage, tearing down all that one does not agree with**

is both irresponsible and reeks of cultural tyranny. What possible similarity is there between the South Carolina Confederate flag and the Borough Hall murals, other than the objections by some people? Mr. Overton's is a weak case as thus far reported.

But perhaps Mr. Overton's approach is not draconian and radical enough. Should each of the murals be searched for its political correctness, not only with regard to black history, but also in terms of te stereotypes of women and class orientation on Staten Island? And do they not meet current standards, tear them all down? What about the design of Borough Hall; isn't Beaux-Arts an example of elitist classism that excluded blacks and others from any engagement with it? Was the quarrying of the marble and construction carried out under affirmative action and/or equal opportunity principles during the 1904-1906 period of construction? If not, tear down Borough Hall.

Staten Island was then and is now a part of New York City, let us extend this process to the whole city, and where necessary, tear it down. Should not the same review be given to all other public buildings, visual and performing arts of any period prior to our own year 2000? If they cannot meet the criteria, tear them down.

Within these buildings - schools, libraries, museums, hospitals - are writings of literature, poetry and history. After they are scrutinized, should not those with evidence of past bias towards any group be removed and perhaps burned? This would, of course, particularly apply to dictionaries and encyclopedias, which include words and episodes (e.g., slavery, discrimination and segregation) in American life that were and are painful. The authors and publishers of these insensitive tracts should be indexed to determine what other materials need withdrawal from the public domain.

In addition to buildings, we should also extend our purview to removing street names of known and lesser-known historic icons of slaveholding (e.g., Washington, Jefferson, Dongan, etc.) school names and park names. But what cultural czar (or committee of czars) will be given this responsibility, and by whom? Should there be a referendum to set this cultural juggernaut in place and who will write the enabling legislation? Should black collectors of demeaning materials be excepted from such scrutiny?

It is exasperating that someone waited 60 years after the installation of the murals to publicly object to them. They were funded by a public program, the Works Progress Administration (WPA), that also funded black art, literature and theater.

Why wasn't this irony pointed out sooner, if the murals were objectionable? Moreover, by what stretch of the imagination can this one apparent youngster - can he be more than 16? - be a caricature of and embody all black Staten Island history"? Isn't the issue an absence of black history, not as excrescence of local history?

Alternatively, should the Council on the Arts sponsor (with funding assistance from public and private sources) writing and art contests to promote black history in the schools, museums, libraries and colleges on Staten Island? The black history exhibits in Borough Hall during Black History Month may set some positive precedent. Out of this could come some permanent art exhibits in Borough Hall - and elsewhere - unless the building has been officially demolished due to the demeaning image it has apparently fostered over the past 60-plus years.

Richard Dickenson

This author's comments appeared alongside Dickinson's as follows:

It's Demeaning.

This letter is a rebuttal to your recent editorial entitled "Old art, new offense" on the Borough Hall murals.

I would like to clarify what may be misconceptions about my views and comment on a few of your points and your proposal for compromise. You state that now this "well-intentioned society" is expected to defer to people and organizations who are "remarkably eager to take offense" over symbolic issues. You further state that the fight over the Confederate flag is a legitimate one, but that the murals just show a black child "looking and behaving as any boy would have in that era."

Although the mural is not raised up a flagpole every morning, people (including black children) enter Borough Hall every day, and the image is there to greet them. Any boy could have looked that way? Perhaps, but the black youngster happens to be the only person in any of the 13 murals who is shoeless. The other boys, all white are well-dressed. You ask whether the inclusion of a prosperous black family would serve history well, and my answer is yes, there were prosperous black people on Staten Island from the late 1800s to the early 1900s. There were black-owned oyster fisheries, retail and service businesses, funeral parlors and other commercial entities. That these businesses have not sustained into the current era does not detract from their place in history.

Let me be clear: I do not advocate "changing history," nor do I want to retrofit past works of art to suit current societal attitudes. I am not for destroying art that offends me. But a public building where people must go to take care of certain business is not a gallery or a museum where they may choose to go or not. Times have changed.

You ask why, after 60 years, we are raising this issue. It is simple. If hundreds of thousands of dollars are to be spent now restoring Borough Hall and its art, and the art is being touted as reflective of Staten Island's history, then now is the time to object because the "history" being reflected is distorted, inaccurate and offensive. The murals have been gradually decaying and darkened into obscurity. But now it is proposed that thousands of taxpayer dollars be used to restore them, freshen their colors, make them more prominent and glorify the contributions of yes, only white people, to Staten Island's development. Is there a statute of limitations on when we can object to something? Are the Native Americans out of line for objecting to the use of the name "Redskins" for a football team only now after decades?

The editorial seems to imply that the contribution of black Staten Islanders consisted only of service in the military during the wars. That is a common misconception by those unaware of Staten Island's history.

You are intrigued by my interpretation of the artist's portrayal, suggesting he may have been exercising social conscience in showing how the black youngster was being excluded from the higher rungs of society. Perhaps if Stahr had not painted in any blacks, we could have concluded that he just didn't think about them at all. But he included two: one in the forefront of a mural, inspiring nothing but pity or shame, and the other a hatless head in the midst of white men in top hats.

Furthermore, I believe there is ample evidence that Stahr colored the murals with his own bias, and that there are other historical inaccuracies in the murals. For example, the men shown building the Bayonne Bridge in 1933 are good-looking, muscular, blond men, bare-chested and carrying steel I-beams. Can anyone seriously believe that the labor that built many of Staten Island's monuments to progress did not include blacks?

The Native Americans portrayed in the murals are proudly dressed (and shod with moccasins), but did the Lenape Indians sell Staten Island or were they forced off the Island after the Peach Wars? British military are shown leaving merrily here after losing the war - hogwash !!!. And the adventurer-discoverer in the murals is backed by the cross of his God.

To some, it may seem a small thing, but how many small things have chipped away at a black person's soul? Black people have business in Borough Hall, and in no other mural is any person demeaned. In far too many historical portrayals of U.S. history, the contribution of blacks is omitted, consciously or unconsciously. The steam engine in one mural would never show that two black men invented a device to oil machinery while it is running, thus greatly increasing the efficiency of early steam engines.

I am, as the Delaney sisters said in their book, "Just Having My Say." In 1970 I was working with Mrs. Gail Schneider in the Staten Island Institute of Arts and Sciences (SIIAS) on a project researching the history of the black man on Staten Island. When asked if I had seen the large murals in Borough Hall, I said I had. She asked if I liked them, and I answered, "Yes."

Ms Elsie Verkiel walked me back to the murals and made me stand in front of the two with poor blacks. I had looked, but I had not seen. I swallowed hard. I had been wounded, but there was no blood ..... In a sense I became that person in the mural, and I never forgot.

It is the contact with people on the street that drives me to continue my protest. When I distributed flyers in front of Borough Hall last week, the police put out Dayglo cones and said that the public sidewalk was now a "restricted" area. The Corrections Department staff told me the public sidewalk on Stuyvesant Street is "off limits" to me and that "We have informed the police of the 120 Precinct of your presence."

I commend the Staten Island Advance for its coverage of photographs of a shameful period in history during which black people were hanged with impunity. And I applaud the proposal to add works of art to Borough Hall reflecting not only the experiences of black Staten Islanders, but their contributions, which include much more than military service. I urge you to investigate the real history of Staten Island and to support the effort to replace the Stahr murals with art that is historically more accurate and inoffensive. Thank your for your consideration.

Cleve Overton

The only other citizen, Black or White, who wrote to the Advance on the issue was William "Bill" Arrindell, whose August 7, 2000 letter follows:

> As one of the "community members" protesting the display of what is considered to be a racist symbol, I am most eager to see how an explanatory plaque can explain the racist propaganda which emanates from it. Displayed in a public building, as it has been for the past 60 years, it is, and has been, an insult to the many black citizens who, in the pursuit of their civic duties and/or obligations, are forced to be unwitting spectators to the lie that blacks played no role in the development of Staten Island beyond that of a shoeless, ragged, disinterested black man who was too lazy to fish.
>
> This painting is symbolic of the black stereotyping found in the 1920 movie, "Birth of a Nation." Anyone familiar with the movie must also be aware that it, too, received governmental approval and resulted in the loss of lives and property of countless innocent blacks. Considering that Mr. Stahr's painting comes less than two decades after the infamous "Birth of a Nation," it is not difficult to conclude that a) the painting is racist by intent, and b) that it was commissioned to be so.
>
> Symbols are very powerful tools. They can strike terror in the hearts of some, or they can inflame the passions of hatred due to the use of terror, in the hearts of others. The anti-black sentiments depicted in this one painting are unmistakably apparent to all but those who choose not to see.
>
> I speak not alone when I say that I see evil in that painting. I further believe that there must have been evil in the hearts of those government officials who commissioned and then displayed that painting in its current location. It has been said, "All that evil needs to flourish is for good men and women to do nothing."
>
> For those unfamiliar with these paintings, I would suggest that you visit the Staten Island Borough Hall and view them for yourself. It is important that the entire collection be viewed in order to fully comprehend the hate message being conveyed. I would ask that you subject the one painting (Erastus Wiman, First Steam Railroad, 1860) to the following test:
>
> 1) Does it possess any redeeming value?
>
> 2) Does it in any way foster racial harmony?
>
> 3) Is it consistent with the city's declared efforts to promote "racial harmony?"

4) Is it truthful?

At a time when the federal government and many states, including our own New York state, are passing laws to combat the unexplainable escalation of hate crimes, New York's elected officials chose to spend taxpayer dollars to perpetuate that which it seeks to outlaw.

The options are but two:

1) Remove the painting in question and, in so doing, reaffirm the commitment to building a "better New York City" for all of its citizens, or

2) Maintain the status quo and confirm to many that nothing has changed in our city government in the past 60 years but the names and the faces.

William "Bill" Arrindell

My last leafleting demonstration at borough hall was in May 2004.

The murals have been radiantly restored, and there is no explanatory plaque for the offensive mural.

Microagressions and Microassaults

Psychologists have identified categories of racial microaggressions and microassaults and have defined them as demeaning and invalidating messages reflecting beliefs of White supremacy that were unintentionally conveyed by perpetrators to people of color. Articles on the subject are found by Sue, Nadal, Capodilupo, Lin, Torino and Rivera.

According to the authors, racial microaggressions are "brief daily verbal, behavioral and environmental indignities, intentional or unintentional, that communicate hostile, derogatory, or negative racial slights and insults to a person or group, and are expressed in three forms: microassaults, microinsults, and microinvalidations.

Examples are given of each:

Microassaults – intentional acts, such as calling someone a "nigger," displaying the hood of the KKK, or refusing to serve a Black person.

Microinsults – usually unintentional actions that are rude and demean a person's racial identity or heritage, such as telling a person, "You are a credit to your race," or "You are so articulate." The authors listed four microinsult themes they identified in previous studies on racial bias: 1) assigning low or high intelligence on the basis of race; 2) assumption of criminal status; 3) pathologizing cultural values or communication styles; and 4) second-class citizenship. Two additional themes surfaced due to the authors' current study: assumption of inferior status and assumed universality of the Black American experience.

Microinvalidations - usually unintentional actions which make a person feel alien in his own land (asking "Where are you from?"), color blindness, denial of personal racism, and the myth of meritocracy.

According to the authors, Black Americans frequently report feelings of racial rage, frustration, low self-esteem, depression and other strong emotional reactions when subjected to microaggressions. According to Franklin, Hinton and Sue, racial microaggressions may be more harmful to people of color than overt bigotry because the "hidden, unintentional nature of microaggression allows them to flourish outside the level of conscious awareness of the perpetrators, thereby infecting interracial interactions, institutional procedures and practices."

The authors state that most White Americans believe racial discrimination is declining and that they themselves are not biased. Black Americans disagree, and see racism as more subtle but ever present, and view many White people as responding to them with racial insensitivity and treating people of color with less respect.

Microaggressions result when White Americans unconsciously feel superior to Black Americans, resulting in injustices that have a major impact not only on the mental health of the recipients, but also in maintaining equality in health care, employment and education.

The authors concluded that, "Racial microaggressions lead to psychological distress in Black Americans and that race-related stress occurs not only in response to overt racism but also in response to more indirect and subtle forms of racism, and may have a harmful psychological impact that may last for weeks or even years." Research participants often became visibly distressed, tearful and shaky when retelling their stories, indicating the long-lasting effects of the stress and trauma experienced from being subjected to various microaggressions. Racial microaggressions often reflect the invisible worldview of White supremacy in otherwise well-intentioned individuals who are unaware that their attitudes or actions are negatively affecting people of color.

In Conclusion

The continuous display of these murals without explanatory text amounts to the public punishment of the Black man. Such justice tempered by the wisdom of Christian mercy in the state displays its power by the micro-assaults by ignoring its own laws reaffirmed in its own justice. These are the games of a common culture which would never be displayed in a Muslim culture, one that has withstood the calls for its banishment on this Island. The uncaveated, unexplained display of these murals in the connection with everyday life manifests itself in the very staging of a spectacle. The choices did not take place behind the closed doors of a prison; rather, in the halls of supposed justice. These punishments occurred in many public spaces. Spaces that in other times were used for the very activities that led to the necessity of the gallows. Such displays drawn to the site of the criminal. The very publicness of the punishment made the viewers and its understanding crucial to the event. It was, after all, for the edification of the populace. Its appearance is that of the curiosity of the people let the authorities down. Yet the fascination that drew people to the spectacle could also undercut its effectiveness. Whether restraint or submissive, there was no guarantee that the lesson would be learned as it was taught. The state, through a ritual designed to reaffirm the bonds of a public community, might even risk turning the criminal into a martyr or hero. Integrated into everyday life with the whipping post and the pillory, they could not reach the soul and the heart of the victims of the continued micro-oppressions.

On September 14, 2012, New York Times writer Sam Roberts published a piece entitled, "Remembering the Forgotten Borough." The article announced the opening of the exhibition, "From Farm to City: Staten Island 1661 – 2012" at the Museum of the City of New York. The exhibit supposedly tracts the island's 350-year evolution. Does it document the contributions of the island's dark-skinned citizens? No! Why are we not surprised that the photographs and texts omit any mention of the indigenous Black population.

Chapter 9

SKIN, HAIR, AND COLOR

T his series of essays represents the documentation of more than five years of

work developed around the island of my birth, Staten Island, New York, and bits and pieces of the puzzle of travels around the globe. In the course of what I call my research I have arrived at a myriad of conclusions that are mine and mine alone.

Every day hundred and thousands of intellectuals and scholars study human behavior, and every day, like those eminent scholars, I too have a diary, make notes every day, and I file away these notes and studies because I find them bizarrely interesting. I hope my stories can sometime, in someone's future conversation, spark some thinking about these issues.

I have on many occasions used voices that were important to the events and situations in which I found them. I have tried to remove real names when necessary. I also have tried to evoke rather than provoke whenever possible. There have been a number of starts and stops because my life away from Staten Island and living in other countries make a constant direct approach very difficult.

So the uneven events and stories have a disconnect for which I am sorry and I apologize to the reader. Originally, I suppose I wanted to write a story about my life as a black man growing up on Staten Island. I did accomplish a work in 1995, in a book *In the Shadow of the Statue of Liberty*. In my middle years it became another book entitled *A Life Without Illusion*. This writing, it has become a final screed. There's still a puzzle, viewed as the Staten Island puzzle, or perhaps simply the puzzle.

There is in this writing a combination of all of the above. After many attempts over the years to ameliorate and understand the interracial situation on the island, I have witnessed a total breakdown in the communications by white voices as well as black voices. It is my hope in the following pages, to bring to the surface the failure of the island's educational institutions, the political and social organizations, the religious and social groups, and a final hardening of attitudes and position on both sides. It has become increasingly apparent to me that black people have been denied the in-depth assessment of their roles in the history of Staten Island.

Huge volumes of Staten Island written history have simply made for confusion and error in interpretation and content. Serious academic study of Staten Island history does not exist. However, individual attempts have surfaced in recent years to publish tracts for racial groups other than black Staten Islanders. My research finds no study or historical publication oriented toward understanding the black Staten Islanders and I have not met people that have any knowledge of the actual value of black islanders in its history.

Problems in black history research without an assessment of historic depth and a willingness to regard the historical past of an entire people as the equivalent of its written history can clearly be seen to have made for added confusion and error in interpretation, and misguided judgment in evaluating practical ends, and I am convinced perspective on the values of black American life cannot be had unless the academic teaching history treats the larger problems of cultural change or by practical men seeking to lessen racial tensions. While it has been necessary to throw into the mix the files neglect by others such as museums, foundations, and historical societies in the community, background materials in favor of historical statistical analysis are available.

The urgent problems of this 21st generation and the newer immigration racial emergence that seem to be unrecognized must be faced by blacks and white alike. On the contrary, this writing has attempted to show that present-day situations are more complex in their underlying causes than has been grasped and that, whether in analyzing intellectual or practical problems, every consideration calls for insight into the influence of pre-American and Euro-centric patterns. Much may be said regarding the gathering and documentation of the materials I have collected over many years, is that those works that have the widest influence in the past, and those that are the most cited today have been given extended treatment, for these are the sources upon which academic opinion is based. The works of John J. Clute, Charles W. Leng, and William Davis are considered the holy grail of Staten Island written history.

Citations that I have quoted are those which had had the sharpest bearings on the problems as envisaged. Where antiquarian, quixotic, or spectacular comments have also been included, it is only because they have produced a literary lineage. It would have been possible for the polemics, the aim of this discussion, to trace a consistent genealogy for many of the ideas that with slight qualification, may have surfaced in recent more authoritative presentations. It would have been equally possible, the use of the materials from the field study conducted to dissect current views on, say, the black family in terms of attitudes and customs prevailing there that are directly comparable to those found in other parts of the United States.

I have been asked dozens of times how I come to write these essays and what triggered the issue for me to sit down and do them. Well, what I know is that everyone's mind is a capacious mass of stuff, most of it bullshit. *On Bullshit* Harry G. Frankfurt, Princeton University Press, 2005. In his small book, Frankfurt says "One of the most salient features of our culture is that there is so much bullshit. Everyone knows this. Each of us contributes his or her share. But we tend to take the situation for granted. Most people are rather confident of their ability to recognize bullshit and to avoid being taken in by it. So the phenomenon has not aroused much deliberate concern nor attracted much sustained enquiry." For me, this is no earth shaking moment. It simply gets tucked away in the "Wow, bullshit" column when I hear it.

I have a friend here on Staten Island, a divorced white lady who has a single male child of 22. Her waking moments since his birth have been to cover him from head to toe with love and affection. He lives in a tidy well-planned two-door home; gardens and grounds are a statement to her tastes. Everything is in its place. There are no animals to upset the décor of the constant display of flowers on the dining room table. Weekly maid-service straightens, dusts, and cleans, each room, except, perhaps, the room of her son, which she straightens up each day to feel her continuing motherhood connection.

The grinding motor noise I heard was her son, Bob. The name has been changed. The sound was her son pressing the button to raise the garage doors. I had known Bob since birth, but now, over twenty years later, I hardly recognized him. He was tall and well built. His white teeth were now brace-less, reminding me of the last time I saw him. His head was close-cut but still full of dark brown curls. He came into the kitchen, and bent to kiss his mother who was smiling from ear to ear. "You remember Cleve," she said, pointing to me. He was wearing blue jeans; slash ripped at the knees, open sneakers, and an open-necked blue shirt with the logo of the mall electronics store where he worked. He reached his right arm out to fist bump "Hi." He was now standing eye to eye with me, a full, husky, 6 foot tall, and his voice was now a low adult register.

"Yes," he said. "You moved to Washington, right? You staying over?" He asked.

"No, just going to the island here for business." My eyes were still focused on his right arm. From the wrist to the folded shirt sleeve at the elbow his arm was a mass of colorful tattoos. Conversation was crisscrossed about other events and friends. He began to eat and drink from the fridge. I wanted to ask him about the tattoos. We spoke a bit more in the kitchen; then his mother walked me out to my car at the curb, and said to me softly, "Yes, I know. Weren't we the same when we were younger?" She did not look at me, she looked back at the house saying she wanted to resist but could not. She did not use the word tattoos. Benefit and burdens of hindsight, I guess.

"Yes, but he could have them removed," I said.

"It's painful and costly. No, No," she insisted. "I decided to get one also last year." She pulled up her sleeve and showed me her chain tattoo around her upper arm. "Like It?" she said.

"Wow, that's cool," I said.

"One here too," she said, pointing to her hip. "Can't show it to you now," she giggled. "It was a present from a guy who would eventually give me a hard time and we split."

"Got his name on it?"

She smiled. "Where are yours," she asked me.

"I missed that stage," I said. "I don't think they would go with black skin. Besides I have a very poor tolerance for pain and torture." We hugged and I drove away. I had never known her to be indirect or even to avoid opening her feelings ready for inspection. There was pain, I know. She did not like her son and his tattoos. This was bullshit. She was hurt and in pain. I would make my notes later that evening.

The third evening I sat watching a basketball game on the TV, I began to notice the tall black athletes on the court and their tattoos. They were tattoos that were simply ugly blurs on a beautiful brown, black, yellow skin. Most players had tattoos and there were some that did not have any, or perhaps, yet. Somewhere I read that the reason for tattoos is for permanence in an ever-changing world. Everything changes; our minds, our bodies, and our lives, and tattoos would also change. My take is that we are living in a very disposable society. Museums are gathering converts to tattoo parlors by curating Maori art and modern primitivism. One gallery hosts Japanese mafia lord tattoos. The entire back, torso, and arms of their women are tattooed to express the mafia lord's indelible identity.

Tattoos, once confined to motorcycle gangs, penitentiary prisoners doing time, and sailors aboard ships, have gone mainstream in America. I remembered a female friend that had alopecia, the hair-loss disease. When she told me that she had her eyelashes permanently fixed by tattoo, I thought that exceptionally creative.

Some colleges, black colleges I know, do special branding over the kitchen range using razors and tweezers, you want to wince, you want to belong, you will be branded. Greek letters branded onto skin, I have not seen an actual performance, but I have it on good secure voice that asked not to be identified because they were not authorized to speak. They were black men who were not authorized to tell me their fraternity, but I could hear the sizzle, the smell of burning flesh, and the snap, crackle and pop. He said it was merely a fad.

To me this branding moved me to dredge up historical branding of slaves and ownership, scarification that carried symbolism across many cultures. I found it difficult to swallow the verbal bullshit of branding of slaves and of Nazi Germany's branding of Jews. I would watch sports; I would watch simply to make notes, the teams, the games, but simply a distracting feature for me, black players, tattoos, is they are all a blue mass of ink. Nothing can be seen on their great beautiful bodies because black skin is simply not a canvas for tattoos. I could forgive the antics, flagrant fouls, leaps, hard physical contacts, even the cursing. I cannot find a mind-place for the guns, the drugs, and the tattoos. That behavior collects fans and money. The sheer bulk and weight, this agility sitting on multi-million dollar salaries are becoming nothing more than body-decorated celebrity jerks with tattoos. It is my wish that these men save enough money to have their tattoos removed when the curtain falls.

Conversation with my white lady friend filled into my pages about skin and color. I was not a dermatologist or an anthropologist. What I did learn is that the skin is the biggest organ on the human body and it is the most valuable raincoat for protection of everything else inside. Skin comes in a wide range of colors and people don't appreciate it as important until they need a dermatologist because of cutting, scarring, burning, or tattooing. The various skin colors are not about race; it's about the sun and how close our ancestors lived to the equator. Black skin evolved to protect the body from the sun's rays. Lighter skin evolved as people moved away from the equator and lost pigment, and white people living and being born on the African continent will have darker skin color and more melanin in their skin after decades and generations.

Living in Africa on and off for perhaps a decade I became aware of my own skin and the beautiful skin of the people of Zaire, in what was the Belgian Congo. Little did I realize that people lifting my shirt was to check if I was using skin-color bleaching creams. I was in the village open-air street market, and I would find a full array of skin bleaching creams.

I have become friends of Africans that have small scars on their faces, and after enquiring, gaining their friendship, I asked and was told that these are birthright marks to identify them and their tribes where scarification marks are common. I admit to being attracted to them and wanted to imitate my African side. But I did not know to which African tribe I belonged. I decided that I was an American that had limited knowledge of my past, and limited education of my past.

Africa for me was a submersion and an immersion to see what color is black and what color is white. Africa is an immense continent, so large that it would take a lifetime to describe a mere portion of the continent. Being born and raised on Staten Island, I believed that I had missed the part of body-painting and beauty. I have three sisters and I lived through a number of female evolutionary changes at home. They were as modern as most Americans and liked to adorn the body. Ear piercings seemed natural; it was something that happened, there was no ceremony, they often made or purchased store-bought earrings. I never saw much to do about lipstick or powder at home. I never saw eyeliner used and I guessed cosmetics were used later for sexual attraction. Attracting a mate for a chance to reproduce, makeup helps. We cannot see our beating hearts, or our filtering livers, or our food digesting tract. We can see our skin.

It is the pain of skin color that prevents me from digging into the subject. All black Staten Islanders purchased *Ebony* and *Jet* and *Sepia* magazines; I believe they also purchased fade creams, Magnolia Bleaching Creams. Black Americans have always had a thing about their bodies. Black Americans have always managed to dress stylishly even when we could not afford to do so. It was important to do it at least on Sunday, whether or not you believed or even sang of participated. You went to Sunday service to be noticed. You had your stuff for weddings and funerals and Saturday was the day to visit the barbershop.

Barbershops are just starters for black life. Our emphasis for long essays. My first barbershop, my first memory of being seating in a barber chair was a barbershop in West New Brighton. The window sign said "Bubbles" and in lower case, "barbershop." The red and white striped barber pole was just inside the window. Bubbles, the black owner was just that. Actually two bubbles: his close-cropped head was round and his body was round; he was not fat, he was simply rounded. Later when I was a bit older, brazen smart-ass young men would say, not to his face of course, because even they did not think it prudent to repeat that Bubbles was "Mr. 5x5."

Bubbles deftly wielded a straight razor. Bubbles was our barber, he was black, we were black, and this was the place we traveled to from our home, except, of course, when my mother would cut my hair. Bubbles cut hair the old fashioned way. No conking, no dying, no shampoo, no blow drying, no jelly curl settings; parents came with their kids for a haircut. There were no choices or any outrageous street styles. We would sit quietly until it was my turn to climb up on the chair. I don't think Bubbles knew my name; I was simply "one of Joe's boys."

This impromptu social setting was part of the life of black men countrywide, and especially for me, a tradition on Staten Island, formed over many years. Most of the black men were Prince Hall Masonic Lodge members. These black men were home owners who had worked on the island at the same shipyards, factories, plants, manufacturing, for generations. They were strong blue-collar family men. They knew each other's wives, family members, and relatives. There was a camaraderie to play a few numbers, talk politics, sports, and dissecting the weekly Gazette newspapers.

Bubbles would always use a cup, have hot towels for men, while using a straight razor. He decorously wielded the razor over a leather strop to sharpen it. An electric shoulder and neck massager for men would signal her was finished. Bubbles was always low-key. Many of the men would patronize their barber longer than the same wife, and at this writing, at 83 years of age, I have never had my hair cut by a white barbershop on Staten Island. When Bubbles passed away, it was natural for the black men to find another barber; one of the Dozier brothers on Broadway.

Finally, after many years of death and destruction of the black culture on Staten Island, Broadway, a new black barber would emerge. It would be Charlie's Barbershop. When I come to visit Staten Island, I would see Charlie. He would know my name and remember our last conversation; this was part of the black barber haircutting tradition. Charlie holds a Doctorate of Divinity degree. While cutting your hair the debates would begin, discussing the issues of the day, issues that affect the black West New Brighton community, religion, etc. Charlie would now occupy his barbershop for over 40 years. On his wall there are awards and commendations from many organizations. There are pictures of customers on one wall, on the other a full bank of mirrors, a huge television, a radio, and cable for watching boxing returns, and there are women customers having their hair relaxed and curled.

The community has changed dramatically, drastically. There are now tall housing projects where once the black community lived in single or double-storey buildings. There was a mix of many nationalities and colors. There are other barbers on the strip. Unisex haircutters. Many older black men that have moved to other parts of Staten Island continue to come to Charlie's barbershop for their haircuts. He would know their styles, their names, and their families. And I knew after many years that barbershops would be my training ground for what is happening on Staten Island. I would sit and listen to conversations to find the soul of this community. First they would need my patience, and I needed their trust for them to speak with me.

Barbershops, hair, black skin, have been places where stories begin, the young are taken there for their first haircuts, and perhaps a place for the old to end their voyages. A young man sat next to me in a barbershop looking at my face. He was not there for a haircut; he was there to run errands, or wash your car. He looked up at me and smiled "Why do you have a beard? Why don't you take the hair from your face away?" He may have been all of nine or ten years old. I looked at him and I remembered the story of why I did have a full beard.

It had been a long time for me and I was a strange black man in Africa. I was living in Zaire, the former Belgian Congo, and I went to the little village where I wanted to have my hair cut short. It would be cooler in the hot steaming climate. In the village of Kikwit a man sat on a concrete step under a tree with a towel across his lap. On the wall across the walkway were paintings of hairstyles. On my approach, he jumped up smiling and beckoned for me to sit. My first mistake was not to ask his price.

When I was sitting, he began to chatter quickly in Lingala. It was nice to sit under the tree, the wide branches forming the delicate ceiling of this one-man outdoor barbershop. I did not know how to speak to others in his language, but he understood my few words in French and I said "Je m'appelle Cleve." My name is Cleve. At the same time a few men and children, boys and girls, came to stand and watch. Some stood at a distance, some came forward smiling, holding out their hands for a handshake. I motioned to the man that I wanted a full, short haircut. He nodded that he understood. I motioned again, in my sign language, how much? He, being polite, said that I could pay afterward, as much as I wanted, only if I was happy.

He had a few tools, a pair of scissors, some combs, and other implements that were in a snakeskin-covered pouch nearby. Like any barbershop that I have ever entered, this became not much different. It is a fact that in my travelling life, if I wandered far enough from home, sooner or later I would need a haircut while on the road. It's an experience and I had learned early on not to dismiss this routine. But now I was had placed my head into the hands of a man I have never known. He didn't look like Bubbles, he didn't look like Mr. Dozier, and he didn't look like Charlie.

But I would learn early on not to dismiss this as simply routine. I had developed an open mind and a flexible attitude toward fashion and country standards. An overseas haircut can be one of the most edifying and satisfying experiences the world has to offer. There were now maybe a dozen children smiling, pointing, touching, smiling, skittering about as little kittens, it was then that I began to look about me. The community was black, the country was black, the village was black, and what I began to notice were the faces, the eyes, the ears, the noses, the chins, the bodies. I began to notice that I could see the differences; they were not just black people. I began to notice they were individuals. "Je m'appelle..." They would tell me their names. It was an introduction for me to know them and for them to know me.

Adults in the background simply sat smiling. I realized that the barber's chair was where I would experience the most intimate contact that I was likely to have with the local culture in any city or country. Even the friendliest guides and cabbies, three-wheelers, rickshaw drivers, they don't touch you; they don't run their finders through your hair or fuss over your head or discuss the possibilities of what they were going to do for you. I would let him decide what I wanted and what I needed as best I could with me body language. I was laughing and talking as if we were old friends. I let my suspicions go. He worked fast; spoke to everyone that gathered around. I was a customer and I was his.

He finished cutting, reached into his pouch and took out a straight razor. He swished it across a stone. I looked and I asked him why. He motioned to me that he was going to shape my hairline around my ears, my neck, and brushing my face he would give me a good close shave. I held my hand up to explain in pantomime that I did not want him to use the razor. There was no way to explain to him that I did not want any sharp instrument to accidentally cut into my skin. I had read the travelers warnings before coming to Africa about cuts and bruises. I had experienced a few travelers in Mali and Senegal that had become infected with worms between their toes and on their ankles while simply walking barefoot. I would visit pharmacies and realize that any cut that brought blood to the surface was bad, to be avoided. I made motions that I liked the result and I paid. It was the beginning of my having a natural growth of beard.

It was over; I had been transformed in more ways than one. If nothing else, you look a bit more like the locals, because no matter what kind of haircut you ask for, what you get is the local variety. Forget the charms, forget the colorful national clothing; the local haircut is your best shot at partial assimilation. A chance to assume a part of the local culture onto your own body. The barber finished cutting, he gathered up with a broom, with short sweeping motions around where I had been sitting; he would sweep up every bit of hair from the dirt and would take them and pour them carefully down the hole in the latrine nearby. After explaining why he did this, he said that he didn't want any of the nearby witchdoctors using my hair to work bad juju on me. That was a service and education that was worth a very handsome tip!

I began to remember names because I looked at faces. I began to know that remembering a person's name was one of the best openings into the culture that I could possibly learn. My submersion and immersion. It's difficult for me, I found, to come to the top of a moment in my life, to speak about life. I had to read something and to study other black and white writers to find acceptance or a place to start. My basics were always there for me: black, male, American. James Baldwin's writing and theatre seemed to be a voice that comes from my life when he said "Life is tragic simply because the earth turns and the sun inexorably rises and sets, and one day, for each of us, the sun will go down for the last, last time. Perhaps the whole root of our trouble, the human trouble, is that we will sacrifice all of the beauty of our lives, will imprison ourselves in totems, taboos, crosses, blood sacrifices, steeples, mosques, races, armies, flags, nations, in order to deny the fact of death, which is the only fact we have. It seems to me that one ought to rejoice in the fact of death--ought to decide, indeed, to earn one's death by confronting with passion the conundrum of life. One is responsible to life: It is the small beacon in that terrifying darkness from which we come and to which we shall return. One must negotiate this passage as nobly as possible, for the sake of those who are coming after us." James Baldwin, *The Fire Next Time.*

I had to check my baggage, stop, and read a number of the old essays before deciding to enter them into my life again. I thought about this topic for a long time, many years in fact, that the subject would pile up in my notes and files for many years. Notes, books

Skin lightening creams sold in African countries and S.I.

More skin lightening creams and a sign outside the store where they are sold.

would travel with me through many countries: the Caribbean, Sri Lanka, Senegal, Holland, Saudi Arabia, to name a few. The subject is now at a safe distance after 83 years of observation and fact.

I would like to point out that I share these observations cautiously because there is heavy criticism coming my way in the subjects of race and color. Skin color is an interracial as well as intraracial problem. It dwells in the lives of all cultures underground. It isn't racism, it's colorism; an unconscious prejudice that isn't focused on any single group because our brains are made from our history and our culture. It's stamped into the brains of every colonist that ever set foot in the New World to create a caste system for the privileged who was white. Black skin was immediately identifiable as a "lesser," was separated, cast into the fields to labor alongside the beasts. The lighter skinned hue had subtle advantages, more acceptable for making judgments about a darker skinned brother or sister.

A class structure within a class structure, and perversely the limits. It limits our ability to discuss prejudice honestly. In 2003 I became a certified griot. Placed on my head by the newly elected New York City councilwoman, Debi Rose. When I realized that I now had to use these credentials it gave me an escape from being a hit-man, or a meddler, or a sour-brained eccentric. It was an honor I deserved because I had learned from the mentors of Africa during my life there. I knew about my island and I was prepared to speak to it as a prescient griot, walk the streets of my hometown asking for voices, voices for an oral history story about black life on the island. There were stories both old and new, and stories that no one speaks about, perhaps because of the shame and risk of opening family secrets.

Being a griot is not easy, so be good and hang in here for a moment while I explain. We griots are originally from the African continent. Don't ask me to show documents; I carry them daily. All griots I ever met are colored; black, brown, and mostly male. We are working on some females becoming griots. That will take time because no one has signed my petition, time for griots is irrelevant. I'm having a difficult time with skin colors; however, we can all agree that to be colored you must show it up front. White folks are also colored; when they are born, they are red and pink. They become sick, they become yellow or grey, and when they die they become really white. When we real colored folks are born, we are cream to chocolate, and we stay that way until we die.

But let me tell you something that has bothered me for years. When I lived in Africa, streets sold skin whitening creams and I bought a few out of curiosity. I was amazed and horrified that the beautiful ebony skin around me, women wanted them and many used them. Medically a disease condition, ochronosis, is a skin disfigurement that inhibits the skin from producing melanin, melanin which is essential in protecting us from the sun's ultra violet rays, and these African women are stripping away protective skin layers just to look lighter. Most of these chemical products were made in European countries. The boxes sit in my archives; I have never brought up the subject until now. Becoming easier because a copy of the New York Times opened up the Pandora's Box, so I'm safe talking about a dirty little secret, and I want not to be accused of putting our business in the street.

One Saturday morning I was walking down Castleton Avenue in West New Brighton on Staten Island. A sign on the sidewalk said Beauty Supply Store and listed several products, the last of which was "Skin Bleach Cream." I walked in and asked for skin lighteners. The clerk pointed to a shelf and I chose from dozens of skin whiteners, all produced in the United States. I chose an Artra $2.99, Original Formula by J Strickland in Olive Branch, MS. Another product was Skin Whitener by Dr. Fred Summit, $5.99, made in Harvey, IL, with instructions on the box in Spanish and French. Nadinola Fade Cream, $6.99. skin discoloration fade cream, also made in Olive Branch, MS. At this point I noticed the tab for what I had chosen was about $20, I paid the clerk who did not look at me and left the store.

What I realize is that what had been a quiet practice years ago was now an open acceptance over the counter. Beauty use. The chemical ingredients are mind-boggling, and I wondered if blacks understood the dangers in using them. There's no attempt at disguising the use of these products. A lot of colored people want to be white. Mexican women, Pakistani women, and Indian women have suffered mercury poisoning as a result of using skin whitening creams. It's not racism, it's colorism.

The skin color paranoia has gripped many white people. Google the internet for "Man-Tan" and have it delivered to you door in five days, most of the products are made in Australia. A MAN TAN Rapid Tan solution can be sprayed on the body in twenty minutes. It must not be left on for more than 2 hours for a flawless tan; for a darker result, leave on for more than 3 hours, not showering for 5 to 7 hours, giving the body the ultimate bronze color. Using the Natural Tan Body Moisturizer daily will prolong a revolution for the well groomed White Man. A bottle of VuTan is $95.00 plus $15.55 for postage. Other selections are "dark tan' or VuTan 2 hour Blue spray. (I did not understand the 2 hour "blue" spray, and later I was told it was a California thing.) Tanning beds are under federal safety regulations and scrutiny now because of men and women developing skin problems.

The brains of many people have been shaped by the culture in which they live, and it has created caste hierarchies that give privilege to those that are physically lighter and brighter and fairer and punish those that are darker. Michael Jackson was asked by Oprah Winfrey if he had used skin lightening creams. His response was "There is no such thing as skin bleaching. I have never seen it and I don't know what it is." He continued, "I have a skin disorder that destroys the pigmentation in my skin. It's something that I cannot help." I made my notes, filed them away, and I wondered if others wishing to enter the entertainment business see Michael Jackson's white skin as a passport to success.

News stories tell us "Creams Offering Lighter Skin May Bring Risks" and dermatologists are treating more and more side effects from lightening creams. They contain steroids at levels illegal without a prescription, mercury, and other toxic substances doled out over the counter,. Use of such products has been rising due to Internet sales. People associate light skin with higher socio-economic status, happiness, and success. For a long time I carried the fantasy of what it would be like to be white. It took a number of years to see that fantasy trip of becoming a racial transvestite as a physically and mentally slow death. I know some people that have passed. I think of them, a ticking time-bomb until they are exposed. I could not think of the contradictory effects of forced assimilation of passing. The struggle for acceptance and discovery against self-hate.

If you're black the struggle is hard enough, and if you're true black it can become your life if you let it. It can dictate a person's most fundamental life choices. I wondered many times, when white people would say to me that they wanted to be black, voiced displeasure at their skin whiteness, I thought there must be some pills or creams or ointments that would do that. My entrepreneurial dream market! I was asked by a friend why I should want to write about this. My response was "Another brick in the wall." No white person on the island would dare to write about this or bring this subject into the open, into the daily newspaper. He or she would be tagged as a racist, or the magazine showered with epithets or stones. However, I am now a card-carrying griot. I have signed documents to prove it. So I am just having my say. What happened to the 60s mantra "Say it loud, I am black and I am proud?"

On a recent trip to Sri Lanka which has the language printed in three languages and one English, I noticed the ads for marriage in the newspaper. The ads always included long descriptions of a potential mate's complexion: light skinned and fair skinned brides, some paying a half-day's wages for creams and lotions. Despite the expense, the creams might as well be liquid gold for some young men and women who believe that pale skin will lead to well-paid jobs and wealthier mates. Products seen by critics as reinforcing the long-held discrimination against darker skins, especially those from northern Sri Lanka. It is often linked to lower-caste professionals. There is still the colonial hang-up that white is better, white is wealth, white is someone rich enough to never toil in the sun. Here in this magnificent beautiful teardrop of an island, the market is unstoppable.

Before shifting the pattern of skin creams, the kaleidoscope of tattoos, my files continue to surface of notes that I made many years ago while visiting the Gambia in West Africa. I was told after having my skin subject to imported bleaching creams and anyone found in possession of these creams would be fined $2,000 to $3,000, be imprisoned for three years; that of course has not taken the bleaching skin creams off the market. Smugglers have simply gained a pace. Skin creams there, and I suppose across the continent have made some people very rich. There is a lot of money at stake there.

We can no longer blame colonialism for this barbaric practice. We black people cannot expect others to see beauty until we see it in ourselves. I am conflicted, very conflicted. After paying monies to a tattoo exposition I can see the artistic beauty in many of the tattoos on white skin, many tattoos in truly suggestive places on the bodies of the female exhibitors. I received the literature given out by the Japanese tattoo makers and I view the extremely exquisite Yakuza tattoos on women. We Americans have taken their art, as it were, from Tahiti, or maybe from Borneo to copy the ancient warrior facial marks. I remain conflicted, I probably always will.

When I see black hop-hop artists exposing their bodies with tattoos, our beautiful brown skins subjected to the machines, as part of the hip-hoppers call the "bling" but enjoy the music, never the bling. 'Lil Wayne, 50 Cent, young black men, front page arrests, tattooed, faces scarred forever, whatever message they're sending besides the illegal gun possession, drug possession, this message that having these tattoos will place them in the center of the music. The fads continue and are now moving from the skin to the dental work. The bling and the gold and diamond teeth. Dentists and dental hygienists warn that metal with mercury in it on teeth can be dangerous, whether permanent or removable.

Many people cover their tattoos because they are Christians, not allowed. Many cover their tattoos because they are school teachers. Major businesses, hotels, industry not verbally or in writing, declare tattoo aficionados are off-limits. I worry about the toxic nature of the pigments that are used. Some of the pigments are supposedly used in automotive paints, in industrial printing presses. The American Academy of Dermatology says "Many of the tattoo inks may contain industrial or organic pigments." Many of the names I am unable to pronounce. Some are aluminum, calcium, copper, iron, phosphorus, silica, sulfur, titanium dioxide, and barium. Where is the American FDA?

On Staten Island, my home town, the Staten Island Historical Society, a staid historical unit of Staten Island, has posted an exhibit: "Skin Tattoos." I never saw it; it's another clipping to add to my files. But I guess tattoos are a mark of an era, decorations, perhaps of love, of loss, or even triumph, or perhaps youthful exuberance, or perhaps youthful foolishness. The removal of these tattoos will come to them as a regret; confessions that those landmarks are in the past.

I believe that the body is a temple. Fighting back are the new super powered lasers which can exhibit and produce faster tattoos on the face, on the neck, on the chest. The PR is there for the tattoo on to Mike Tyson; with this new machinery there is no pain. Those looking back or looking forward are told that new lasers can burn off these tattoos. I guess the future what will hold the truth…

As a black person and a black male I remember the distinct odor of burning hair and perhaps burning scalp in the kitchen of my home. We had three girls and it was my mother's job to use the weapon that was heated on the stove while she greased and pulled at the hair. Madam C.J. Walker was, perhaps, the inventor, I don't know, but Madam C.J. Walker did market these 'weapons of mass destruction!' While many people may have construed her ethics as having fed into the black woman's desire to be like, or perhaps to approximate, white beauty standards, Madam Walker denied the accusations about wanting to have white hair locks.

My notes now come to the surface; my jotting diaries, my notations, are a bit unsettling. I have no idea when I began making notes about my surroundings. Now, after 80 years of watching, looking, smelling, trying to understand my brothers and sisters and the white population around me, I understand Madam Walker's success; but I continue to wonder: are these products purchased over the counter are utilized by black women who possess a desire for whiteness or is it simply a desire to look one's best? Why, I wonder, do black women continue despite the great expense and the inconvenience and discomfort to straighten, perm, and relax their hair? Is it to stay stylish, or to look white?

I have no charts or graphs with which to measure the psychological development or the psychological effects on black women and I understand that personal beauty is frequently considered above all the most important virtue that a woman can possess.

That, along with occupation and education and status. The power in our society is often, for me, illusionary. In light of the inequality in social power it is no wonder that a woman will do all she can to enhance her beauty.

I wrote a heading many years ago that I thought was rather insightful, and it was "Resisting the Tyranny of Advertising and Movies and Magazines to Find Pride in our Own Appearance." I spent the entire summer of 2006 on Staten Island finding the courage to approach black women. I found that I had to discard the formal books on how one should approach and record black history. I happened to make conversation with one lady in particular while she was working on her hair with a stiff comb with white lather. After easing into the conversation and with smiles and patience, I asked her if she realized that if she were using chemicals on her body, on her hair, and I said "I think that there are so many things that we do that are not good for us." She smiled and forthrightly looked at me and replied "Yes, I know that watching TV and reading the papers is probably killing my brain cells, but I still do it. There are things that are good for you in the hair products and there are things that are bad for you in the drinking water and you just can't worry about everything."

Later, when I made these notes I realized that the women using these products don't fall into the 'victim' labeling. Most simply do not want to know because, as I continued to look, ask questions, and make notes, in order to straighten the hair that we have been given at birth, the product has to break down hair, which is why it stings and it burns and it smells. This is why the young lady proceeded to do that on her porch out in the open. There is no way to make any of that comfortable.

The hair is kinky, curly, permed, baked, dyed, and locks are now twisted and weaved; it is a system, a method that black men know little about. The cost, the time: most black women, will spend four to six times more time working on their hair than white women. I looked, time and again, at these shifting puzzles, pieces of hair. A black woman can spend over $2,000 per year on hair and beauty products.

I am a griot and society's griot. I am a storyteller for black history, but Black History Month on my island will never, ever, need any black man to speak of this. Could I ever have a private moment with a black woman about simply going natural? It is a term most recently recorded in *Ebony* and *Jet* about African American women who decide to stop chemically processing and relaxing their hair. Would I ever be able to quietly become a panel member in our African History Month to explain the tired and expensive time-consuming salon visits that many naturals are searching for? I think not. Black women are not happy to be nappy.

The proliferation of hair styles and dreadlocks, has entered into the political and racial lexicon. I'm told that black State of New York prison guards were made to cut their dreadlocks to comply with grooming codes. A quiet union political fight ensued. There has been as I remember, a whole rash of black people being fired and getting thrown out of schools for wearing locks and braids, and at the same time I see that more black people are becoming comfortable with wearing their hair like that. It is still unfamiliar; it is still a power struggle with their white supervisor. Men have a bit less of a problem as I see it in my daily life. A bald head – sexy, the dreads look sexy.

I have not come to any firm final personal conclusion, but what I do know and remember by living on the continent, is that the dreads belong to Africa. They were worn by the Masai of Tanzania, by the Somali warriors, and were adopted by the Rastafarians in Jamaica and Haiti for symbolic, patriotic and religious, reasons. The Rastafarians of Staten Island were heavily influenced by the Mau Mau Uprising for freedom in Kenya in the early 1950s that marked the uprising and the beginning of the anti-colonial movement in Africa, and the Rastafarian Mau Mau locked hair became a symbol of stark resistance.

Many black women are now transitioning; they are cutting off or removing their chemically straightened hair and embracing their natural Afro Black texture. I am simply an objective observer. I just wanted to highlight, to make notes, to understand the growing movement. Many black women with whom I struck up conversations randomly on the street or in a restaurant, I have noted that a vast majority have gone natural to some extent.

A top note I made was Natural Hair Journeys. The transitioning movement is quiet, silent, with no banners or fanfare. This evolutionary movement of transitioning is not an angry movement. Black women are not saying that their motivation to transition is simply to combat the Eurocentric ideals of beauty. No, I believe that this quiet statement, this movement, could be categorized by a personal self-discovery. My method to approach and to dialogue, even briefly, with black women was to first complement them on their hairstyle, whether it be natural, transitioning, dreads, or pressed. My approach had to be low-key, soft, with a smile.

I have many questions and I ask them very carefully: how do black men that wear dreads down to their waist clean their scalp? In this dusty, dirty environment that we all live in, especially the North Shore of Staten Island, how do you clean your hair? How do you clean your scalp? How often to you clean your hair? How often do you clean your scalp? The contemporary black African has hair shorn close to the skull for cleanliness for quick hair care, but then again I cannot, I have not made any charts or graphs about much of this.

Hair is our most personal attire and people are judged based on it. We are in a crucial crossroads in human history. We are losing ancient traditions and the way people live on this fragile planet. I wait for the major campus papers to come forth, to understand the trauma, to assist me and many others to understand the puzzle, to find somewhere to place these continued micro-assaults, the micro-assassinations on the black soul and heart. The traumatic, the institutions, the counselors, the researchers, all undoubtedly will produce at length their diagnoses.

"The problem with psychiatric diagnoses is not that they are meaningless, but that they may be, and often are, swung as semantic blackjacks: cracking the subject's dignity and respectability destroys him just as effectively as cracking his skull. The difference is that the man who wields a blackjack is recognized by everyone as a thug, but one who wields a psychiatric diagnosis is not."

On the Diagnostic & Statistical Manual of Mental Disorders (DSM), **Thomas Szasz**

Chapter 10

BLACK SPECIAL AGENT

I met Johnny Jones while tracking down Black active or retired policemen and fireman on Staten Island. I wanted to know about their relationships, their feelings in arresting Black men and women, about racism in the police department, and how they were treated as Black men by White or Black police officers. I had a guide to conducting tape interviews, which I would find to be completely useless; shoving a microphone in the face of a Black man was a non-starter from the beginning. Uncovering their internal lives, loves, family, friends, hopes and dreams, this would require a great deal of time and patience, and I had only this one hot summer.

There were not many Black cops or firemen on Staten Island, and the retired led casual, quiet, family lives on the north shore in well-kept houses. They were reluctant to discuss their time on the job; they had put in their time, and that was that. They were not interested in community organizations, churches, or clubs. In both groups of men I detected a quiet reserve that I suspected was a result of their police or academy training. Did the way they looked, thought, or interacted with the public change after leaving the police department? I would ultimately find the mask of indifference and air of distance was a Black man's protection from the outer world; a shield against both Black and White society, it is a safety chill that often covers genuine warmth of heart.

Johnny Jones was called JJ by the five men in his SOG (Special Operations Group), a 6-man special detail unit, a fallout of the 9/11 attacks. JJ was a Black man, 6ft 4in, and 200 solid pounds. Laid back and quiet, he knew the ropes because of three brothers already in the NYPD. JJ had climbed the ladder fast: patrolman, plain clothes detective,

Lieutenant, college and ROTC, Military service as a U.S. Army second lieutenant. His dark skin was smooth and his face unlined, and it was hard for me to tell or even guess his age. He could have been 27 or 37, or even 47. His hair was cut short in a sort of semi-military cut.

I would get to know a great deal about Mr. Jones in the torrid summer months of 2006 on Staten Island, and a great deal more after the sudden death of a team member.

JJ's wife, Brenda, was a full figured brown "lady." Well dressed, given to bright print dresses, she had a slight formal accent that said she was perhaps from the Caribbean. I would always refer to her as Ms. Jones. Their daughter, a smiling kid of about 8, was also wearing a colorful print dress. She came close, held out her hand "Hi, I'm Jessica," she said, giving a slight curtsy. Kid's been trained, I thought. She had a book in her hand and I think she wanted me to see something, but Ms. Jones stepped aside, her arm pointing to the kitchen door. "He's out back," she said.

Ms. Jones rarely said much. I could have walked down the driveway and past his car to the small gate that lead to the back of the two-storey home, but instead I would press the front door buzzer and wait for his wife to answer. I would greet her politely, perhaps saying something about the bone white built-in shelving holding her collection of Waterford Crystal, Corning Glass, and figurines. Only once, when I hesitated while looking at them, was there any conversation; she spoke about them and explained the craftsmanship, holding one in front of me. I was impressed and responded, surprised, that I dare not reach out and touch or hold one. I hoped that I had passed the "trust this familiar fellow face" test!

JJ sat in one of the two chairs that overlooked a wide fenced-in and well-cared-for apron of grass. This was his baby: the lawn and small shrubs along the fence line. The two colorful painted wooden toys on wheels that were pushed around the yard when his kid was much younger now sat idle. It was after 9:00 am, the day was already hot, and he asked if I would like a glass of iced tea. He turned his head slightly and called "Brenda." The only furniture was the two huge wooden lawn chairs, a Staten Island staple sold on the street from a pick up truck by a man that claimed to be a Pennsylvania Dutch woodworker. His rear yard was an immaculate green space of fresh cut grass and when I came to visit I would find him sitting in the shade with a glass on one side and an open book on the other.

He smiled and showed me the cover of his book and asked me, holding it up, if I had read this. It was a new book, written by Juan Williams, a Washington TV personality, the book was titled *Enough*. "No," I said, "I don't know about it." We would talk about books and I found out that he was interested in English classics. We would discuss *Don Juan in Hell* and other classics and it made the conversation, and, I guess, our friendship, easier after I amused him with my soliloquys of *Cyrano de Bergerac*. He would tease me about my reading and he asked me about current events and had I seen such-and-such an article in the *New York Times*, which I would purchase every morning religiously. Thinking, perhaps, that if I was a writer I would know more than he did, he held up his book and said "He's from DC."

I said many times that I was not a writer, only a freelance Black man trying to find the answers to the puzzle of the place of Blacks here on this island. I found it difficult to understand where we were and how we managed as Black people to be here. So I was asking him questions for a book that I had intended to write, but I was not a writer as such.

He always reminded me that he did not want to be taped and if I was going to talk to him I left my recorders in the car, I tried to remember what he said, and I took notes that I would put into context later that evening. But over the months I began to understand why he was reluctant for me to tape his voice.

One-on-one conversations with most Black men were totally different than talking in groups on the streets or in the barber's shops. If the setting was quiet and casual and I was patient, the topics and issues produced amazingly different results. I asked JJ why he wanted to be a policeman. He said his family wanted him to have a secure lifetime job with benefits. I would find a true story from a Black man that had been there. I would forget about the oral history, and the folklore study, and the guidelines from the books about how to do the best fieldwork. I needed patience, a lot of patience, and new batteries for my hearing aids as I found I had to wear them all the time to hear JJ's low, quiet monotone. Over the following weeks, these visits became special for me, and, as it worked out, for JJ.

I asked if he thought about arresting Black men, or seeing their numbers in jails. "No," he said. He wanted men in prison who had committed crimes. "Criminals belong in prison, White or Black," he said. "I don't make that call; I was a street cop." He thought it best not to arrest numbers runners who had to be released after they swallowed the only evidence.

He said that he had been under cover and had tried to understand the lives that Blacks lived, and he knew the reasons why there was a proliferation of drugs and dealers and the culture. They were only reflecting society, he said, reflecting society in New York City. He wanted me to know that if he did his job properly he could sleep at night. Which, he said, after a long silence and drink from his beer can, it was very hard to do as a Black wearing blue. He said he got tired of being a Black cop arresting men and women for buying or selling a nickel or a dime bag of weed.

I wanted to follow up but it seemed that he wanted to change the subject; I thought that we could return to it at a later time.

I asked him about his "special" unit, he looked surprised and wanted to know how I knew about it. I said he was in a photo at the Irish Pub. I told him about meeting the bartender there; he laughed and said he had never been in the place.

It was still early and the *Advance* newspaper had not yet been delivered to him. I showed him a copy I picked up on my way to see him, the newspaper article of his partner that committed suicide. "You said you weren't a writer," he laughed; I said that it was simply a coincidence. I promised that I would bring my truck camper on my next visit to let him see my traveling office.

He said the special security units were made after the 9/11 attacks by Mayor Giuliani and police commissioner Raymond Kelly. Senator Charles Schumer made an initial pitch that made headlines which resulted in an overdue new system of national security funded by Congress and implemented by the Department of Justice that would be copied coast to coast.

It sounded interesting to him, and he had become disillusioned after a Black eight-year veteran in plain clothes, a cop from Staten Island, was shot five times by a White off-duty policeman in a subway. The White officer said he did not see any identification 'color of the day' which undercover cops use to identify themselves. The case was settled after New York paid the officer, who survived, three million dollars. After the incident JJ asked for a change from the uptown 30th precinct and he filled out a brief questionnaire that he signed and submitted to his commander. Three weeks later he was assigned to SOG 6, a 6-man tactical team.

He heard that the Federal Government and the states were joining together to prevent another 9/11 and there were going to be funds to specially train men and women. A week later, he would have his first unannounced meeting with two men at his locker at the precinct, who looked him over, asked him the same questions he answered in the questionnaire, shook his hand, gave him their cards and left. One card was simply Mr. John Walsh, the other read Special Agent Martin Hall.

There was something left unsaid, but they did add that there would be an initial separation for as long as five months; and that the units were being made of men and women from various precincts, chosen by their precinct commanders. During their training they would have to spend most of the time together: they would eat together, sleep together, and train together. JJ said they were together so much that they could smell each other's shit!

They got to know each other's family affairs and legal problems, children and wives. They did not discuss race, but everyone got their chops broken: if you didn't get hazed that meant that you were not liked and it had nothing to do with race. You can't work as a team isolated, everyone is part of the team. That was a sit down discussion in class. They found out later that they were chosen because they had unusual qualities noticed during their rookie years and infractions on record, but they would never know why or how they were chosen, or the reasons for their assignment to that particular unit.

They introduced themselves:

Joseph Milazzo, he was born in Manhattan on the lower east side. It was important, he said, that his family came from Italy and owned a meat, sausage, and cheese store in same place in Little Italy since 1921.

Angelo Vitale was from Bay Ridge. He was a fireman before taking the police test five years ago and wanted some "action." He was not sure what this new unit would be but he was bored with the fire department.

Lionel Oliver Reginald Stamp was a White guy with a slight English accent; he said to call him Stamp. He had a formal way of speaking and the others waited for him to finish a thought or a sentence; not New York City quick-speak, JJ thought, and he liked the guy.

JJ, of course, was from Staten Island. He had graduated from Curtis High School and New York City College, and with his ROTC training entered the Army as a second lieutenant.

Dov Levy was Jewish, had attended private school, was married, and wore a Yarmulke. Levy was intelligent; he seemed lost in the police department, simply going through the motions. When asked why he was in this, he simply shrugged his shoulders. His political discussions engaged everyone within earshot.

Fernando "Nando" Ortiz was Dominican, quiet, street wise. Ortiz said he worked uniform housing patrol in Red Hook, Brooklyn, leaving after five years and numerous arrests and having his car so often damaged that he could no longer get it insured, and the last straw, he laughed, was getting concussion when a woman dropped a huge potted plant on his head. It was not clear that he was married, but he said he lived with his friend Lucy, also from the Dominican Republic, a child care worker he met while working in the housing project. Together now for over five years, Lucy and Nando were expecting a baby.

Eddie "Lucky" Doyle was Irish, a 27 year old Irish good looking young guy. Doyle was cool and he knew it! He learned his "loop" watching Denzel Washington and Morgan Freeman. Doyle was on top of his daily wardrobe: he had no baggy pants, no oversized shirts; he wore nothing that was uncool. He pumped iron, but told no one. He was naturally physical in a cool way: handshakes and hand smacks. Oh, yes, Doyle knew he was cool! Doyle wanted action and women; he didn't care which came first. He disliked being a crossing guard, and the application looked like a way out. He said he avoided wearing his street uniform cap because it messed up his "do", and he frequently comb-checked his Elvis pompadour. He did not want to walk a beat or be transferred out of the lower east side or central park south where he could meet the best of Manhattan's foreign young chicks. He had a Community College degree and said he was preparing to go to a four year college soon. Doyle was smart, but it was hidden under a façade. He had a repertoire of body movements, wore bling-bling jewelry and stylish clothes, and used a street slang that identified him as a man of the Manhattan world. He immediately confided to JJ that he was cool with the "sisters." JJ felt Doyle was rushing through his life, but he liked his energy.

They would not have to do crowd control or execute tedious search warrants; they did not have to do any of the day to day grunt work. Their work became similar to university students: they attended classes, studied, and took tests. They learned to read maps and understand airport layouts. They visited factories that made electrical parts and factories that made chemicals. They were told to pick a language to study, Spanish, Hebrew, English. Other units that had Chinese or Asian speakers were expected to learn similarly other languages. His instructors asked if any were Muslims. They had already checked their religions, but they were asked time and time again, many times. There were sessions regarding the use and manufacture and types of weapons used in various crimes around the city and surrounding states.

Most of all they were to be chameleons: tell no one of your job except that you were a cop—period. You're not special, but we will make you special, they were told. "I'm not interested in how you feel individually, but as a group you can't afford to offend each other if you want to get home safely at night. If you're dissatisfied with the training, your instructors, or instructions, or for any reason, you can return to your precinct, no questions asked."

Walsh was an ex FBI agent. He was about 60 and carried a body weight of over 250 pounds. His hair was thin and combed from the top to the rear to make his huge round head sitting squarely on his shoulders seem completely bald. He wore wide bone-rimmed eyeglasses, and a blue work shirt that was never fully closed or buttoned. His pants were always dark steel gray. He always carried a grey briefcase but he rarely opened it. He spoke without the notes which he always placed on the desk, never leaving them out of his sight. He had no badge or lapel pin or identification.

His voice was a commanding low-key bass. While often humorous, he was a strict disciplinarian, who lectured on the importance of hard work, making sure each man paid attention to every detail. He was commissioned as a first lieutenant in the Marine Corps, although, realizing that while he liked the discipline of the military he would not make a good soldier, he left after three years. He also added that he was not a physical fitness fan. No one decided to chance the obvious and laugh.

Walsh had started as a patrolman before getting a law degree and working at the FBI office in downtown Manhattan, and he said he was from the South Shore of Staten Island. Looking directly at JJ he said "So are you Mr. Jones, huh?"

"Yes," JJ said, "I live on the North Shore."

"Mariners Harbor, right?" Walsh continued.

"Yup," Jones replied, "Mariners Harbor." Was he being tested, or was he being assured that he had been vetted. Was it because he was Black? He didn't ask.

These small newly created unabashed elite Federal programs were not to catch crooks or druggies or red light runners or fare jumpers. "You will be sent to assignments at airports and train terminals, port facilities, and office buildings. We want you to excel. We want you to use instinctive judgment." Walsh was a combination of Mickey Rooney and Captain Bly!

He said that he wasn't sure why there were so many Italians and Irish on the New York Police Department, but a strong hand was sometimes necessary to control crime on the mean streets and both groups have a liking for the badge and the uniform. He also felt that if recruitment had done a better job with applicants there would have been more African Americans on the job.

He would continue to soldier on, as though it were a passing mental thought that he had forgotten to mention. You are now a larger team, he would say, and you'll be field tested again and again. We hope to train men and women, give them tools that are not taught at most academies. Hazmats will be explained, taught, and used by everyone. By the way some of your trainers will use live ammo. You will use paintballs for returning fire. No one laughed. No one smiled.

The team would travel by special bus and plane to army training bases in New Jersey, Virginia, and Georgia, and the FBI Academy. They would receive psychological tests and memory tests, and exams in darkened rooms. There were weekly medical tests and vaccinations, dental care, blood tests, and urine tests at strange hours during the weeks.

Six weeks later they were dressed in white shirts and ties, landing at O'Hare airport in Chicago where they entered an FBI regional headquarters and listened to a speech by the United States Attorney General. There were no programs, there were no handouts other than that they were told during the flight there would be no uniforms at all. Walsh wore his favorite blue work shirt and grey trousers. He did not have his briefcase. Martin Hall, moustache and black eyebrows looking more like Albert Einstein, would be there in the same brown hunter's shirt and black trousers, smiling but saying little.

They would receive no certificates or awards. After raising their hands and being sworn in as Special Security Agents, they were inducted into the official government records. They were sworn in and dined with hundreds of other men and women from around the country who had undergone the same training. They were given rooms at a nearby hotel and told by Walsh that they would be leaving at noon the next day on a flight to New York. They had made the unit intact. Six in, six out. No one flunked out.

SOG 6 was breaking into one or two man assignments, though they all continued to study, work, and travel together intermittently. JJ spent his first month at Newark Airport, and was home after ten hour days, working different shifts, different times, and Sundays. The assignments were different for the others and they would exchange information and problems. If possible they didn't make arrests, moving the court appearances and arrests to uniform guys at the specific job.

There was the usual grab-bag of problems. Doyle didn't like being undercover without his well pressed cop uniform, he was told more than once to move on by the hotel security and doormen; he did not like to blend in. Ortiz was always thankful for any assignment; he never complained. He worked the subways and bridges, and was often asked for identification, and asked why he was taking so many photos. Dov liked working the office alone, working with hazmats and chemicals; he was a wiz at mathematics and electrical problems. He liked the fact that they were not required to carry firearms. Joe Milazzo was excited to be assigned to the garment district and trucking; he said that the Italian could do that better than anyone else. His brother worked on the ferry boats and they would meet together wearing tight fitting pants and tee shirts and cruise the decks crossing the harbor. It was a chance to exhibit his physique. Never picked up any chicks though; he was going steady.

Angelo Vitale was either from Bay Ridge or Atlantic Ave or Bensonhurst. He spread his time around, he was a baseball fan, now supporting the Mets after the Brooklyn Dodgers left town, never missing a game. He carried game statistics and teammates' numbers and scores statistics around like a weights and measures scorecard.

Vitale hated the Yankees and Steinbrenner was a crook that bought his team with cash. After this season the Yankees would be a dead team walking...The Mets would come in worst in batting in the National League, worst in home runs and worst in slugging average   Jeff D'Amico would be a star this coming season, his rotator cuff was healed and he had been shifted to second base. Angelo's assumptions turned out to be wrong, but there was no one to challenge him outright in the heat of baseball conversation. A week before a Mets starting pitcher gave up a 4-l lead, Angelo would parade up and down the aisles in the hometown rituals with Mr. Met the mascot, tossing popcorn on everyone, Mets fan or no. The Mets did rally to win against the Atlanta Braves, 5-4 in twelve innings.

JJ suggested that he have a barbeque at his place, with wives and kids and girlfriends and family friends. He rented chairs and tables and things, and added some music tapes, beer, soft drinks, cooler food, shrimp, and barbeque. Brenda tried to cover each food taste making spaghetti for the Italian guys and beans and rice for Spanish guys; she rushed around for two weeks trying to make this special.

Milazzo was going to bring food from the family store. "What do you want?" he asked. He suggested a number of delicacies and JJ told him to get what he thought would be best.

I met Walsh and invited him to the barbeque. He didn't respond at first but asked me for my address and phone number.

Stamp came with Essie, his demure shy girl from Flatbush.

The bartender at the Sports Club takes up the narrative

Lionel's full name was Lionel Oliver Reginald Stamp. His family was originally from England where his father, Sir Gordon Fraser Stamp, was a Brigadier General. After an internal political disagreement, Sir Gordon had moved with his family to Australia where Lionel grew up in Melbourne.

They had nobility and style plus cash, and the family were definitely old-style Brits. A good-looking only kid, Lionel was an intelligent bookworm, had learned several languages, and learned skills at a tough military school: rifle, pistol, archery, fencing, wrestling, you name it. He was quiet, not a ladies man at all.

Story is that Lionel took a young girlfriend to a movie and on the way he met a school chum who introduced himself, and Lionel in turn introduced his girlfriend. The guy was pushy and asked Lionel's girlfriend embarrassing questions as they tried to move on to the theater. She asked Lionel to walk between them. The fellow followed them into the movie theater and sat in the same row with them, continuing to talk loudly. Lionel said politely that he should be quiet, that he was behaving badly. The student objected loudly, causing others to look around. "Piss off," Lionel finally shouted.

Lionel asked his girlfriend to leave with him. She followed, visibly upset. Outside Lionel took the man aside to say he was being an ass and if he did not stop he would call the authorities. He shrugged his shoulders speaking directly to the young girl who now was simply looking at the ground. Lionel asked him why he was busting his chops and would he leave them alone. The evening was spoiled and his girlfriend, who was now angrier at Lionel, said "Get him out of my face." Lionel looked at the guy, and, saying nothing, grasped his right arm and twisted it up and around forcing the man to yell while falling onto the pavement. An audible crack came as Lionel released the arm and stood facing the fallen man as he writhed in pain holding a deformed right arm to his body "Be quiet! You're making an ass of yourself," Lionel said. "We've heard enough from you this evening." They walked away in silence and a group began to gather around the writhing figure on the pavement.

Lionel was accused of not calling an ambulance and of assault, and Lionel's girlfriend refused all calls from him and his attorney to give testimony on his behalf. Lionel was charged; his father intervened, and paid an enormous fine. Afterward Lionel would make plans to leave Australia and move to the United States after graduation.

JJ continues the story

"I thought Lionel was solid. I never asked him anything about his past. His CV was top shelf and I believed he would be a good team man. My first big hit with Lionel was a sort of a minor Mafia group, a dozen small fry. Lionel could have taken the credit for the big bust but he was laid back, never used his weapon after the initial contact. I think he would use pepper spray on an elephant if he could! That bust could have been chaotically messy if there was any need for firearms. We had been together for all of three weeks in the real world like we were supposed to be and he became used to being able to leave the official uniform work behind.

"Most everyone knows that Angelo hit on Essie, Lionel's woman. It was a hot day, but Angelo came in his tight shirt and camouflage greens; he seemed ready to bark, his usual blow. But no one gave him a hard time. All had worked with Angelo at times and you needed patience; you had to get out of his way or be pulled into a set-up. Angelo really just wanted to be a Mets first baseman and I could head him off when he got heated and toss in some scores from the *Daily News*, but Lionel, he didn't care for baseball. Lionel was just what he appeared to be, blue-eyed blond kid, hair combed down the middle, with a silly smile, friendly, kind.

I'm sure that he knew Angelo had a short fuse and I think Walsh knew it too, so why was he on the team? I don't know; I guess he was special. My wife said he was a loose cannon after the incident we had here. I admit I was skeptical at first why there were so many strange attitudes added to the units, but I know now that we were a test unit. Typically, 'paramilitary' units like the SOGs are self-policing, using internal controls to catch the 'shooters' and, although I hoped I was wrong, I was concerned that Angelo was a shooter. Takes all kinds I suppose.

The arrest and control is finesse, subtle. A lot of instructors are afraid to take risks, but Walsh and Hall had been in the business for a long time and they also study psychos in blue; their most avid students became good patrolman.

The bartender resumes

Somehow Angel got Essie's phone number and called her, and she asked Lionel if he had given her number to him. Lionel is given to complicated vocabulary when he's angry: "Bloody bastard! Bloody cur!" However, I could tell his agitation was only temporary. "I must be firm," he said. "Very firm." He stared at the TV screen, seeming to watch the game, although I knew he wasn't a baseball fan. I set a fresh beer in front of him and walked away. Lionel sat there for more than an hour, and then he got up and waved as he left.

Lionel came in a few times and he never again mentioned the call from Essie. I wasn't going to ask about it if the subject was off limits; I was his bartender friend, not his mother. I was sure he would talk to me when he wanted.

Lionel waited several days before calling Essie to say he had no idea how Angelo got her phone number. He was low key, remembering the trouble in Australia, and he said he would ask Angelo how he managed to get the number. Everyone mentioned that Lionel was really casual, more casual than they had seen him. It was as though he had figured a way to meet Angelo and get this straightened out. There must be some easy explanation.

He would meet Angelo at the briefing at the storefront downtown Saturday morning, after JJ and Fernando saw Walsh and Hall in the rear room. JJ had a hunch about the briefing. He knew when trouble was brewing between men, when each person had access to legal guns, when conversation was reduced to polite utterances and phony smiles; he had been a cop for so long he thought and he was only 45 years old…he knew the players and he knew the personalities all too well. JJ asked Ortiz to watch the front door when he went inside to listen to Angelo and Lionel. There had been a distance in communications since the barbeque and the dust up and he wanted nothing to end up badly. But he could not shake the sticky web of apprehension under his armpits.

Lionel waited across the street for Angelo to go inside. He would explain his resignation to Walsh and Hall. He would not give any reason other than he wanted to return to street patrol and regular hours.

Walsh looked surprised but added that if he wanted to change his mind and return he would be welcome. Walsh asked if there was a problem, "No," Lionel said.

Did he want another assignment, Walsh asked? "No,"

Hall began to ask questions and Lionel told him that he was not on drugs or ill, and he would turn in his reports. "Did you have a clash with anyone?" Hall continued. Lionel thought of Australia and his fight there. "I want you to trust me," Hall said. He had never talked so much or so long since Lionel could remember.

He opened a box on the wooden desk and opened it; it was a gold plated refillable ink pen and pencil set. The pencil was for any mistakes, he added, smiling as he placed them in Lionel's breast pocket and giving him a firm hug. Hall got up heavily and gave Lionel a handshake, saying he read his steady handwriting reports and he would not need an eraser. 'You have my card, no? Let me hear from you." It was all so casual, even more so than Lionel had hoped.

Angelo was waiting in the outer room; Lionel told him that he was leaving SOG. He asked Angelo to have a beer with him down the street. Angelo feigned surprise and said "You pick up the tab and we go"

JJ picks up the story

What Lionel did not know was that the pen Walsh had given him was a mike. I was going to be the point man when they walked away from the storefront and monitor the conversation. Ortiz would follow me and step in if he was needed. I also wanted to know how Angelo got the phone number.

Angelo was bold; he looked at Lionel, raised his glass, and said "I got it from JJ's kitchen table. She gave it to his wife and I snagged it and copied it in the toilet while you were tending the burgers. That's what we do right? Keep our eyes open."

Lionel did not respond, he thought "Is it possible that I'm afraid of this cur?"

"She's a spick and you're a White guy; you can't handle her. She won't answer the phone now; maybe I could just drop in tonight. What? How're you going to stop me? You gonna kill me?"

It was as if some force of will had possessed him, something stronger than any words he could formulate. His hands began to shake.

"Essie is a beauty, Stump. Arm candy," he said raising his voice. He continued. "How did you find her? Was she hooking?"

Lionel backed away and stood up. He looked into the mirror behind the bar between the bottles, and he saw his reflection. It was a strange face looking back. He did not recognize the still-young very pale face, the hair parted in the middle. He had never seen this man before.

He looked at Angelo and said, "Yes, Angelo, that's what we are taught right? I will find a way to repay you. No!! I'm not finished!" His heart beat furiously. "You had the floor, now let me speak! You've crossed the line, Angelo, and I must force you to return to your burrow, I will stomp you into your burrow! And it's Stamp! Stamp!! Seems you've mispronounced it. I intend to stamp you down." He turned around and pushed the door walking out into the cool of the coming evening.

The bartender carries on

Lionel went back to work with SOG. He seemed unusually happy and upbeat. He came in with his sweetie Essie; they were here for some time, eating corned beef and cabbage, laughing, happy, playing shuffleboard. She said she made the colorful flowered dress she was wearing with Brenda, JJ's wife.

Lionel was afraid to be alone with himself without Essie's voice at the end of a call. His dreams were of the dead, covered with stark white sheets, lying on his bed; dozens of them on his bed, and he wanted to uncover each one to see who they were. Was he one of them, with open staring eyes, and hollow cheeks, and limp hands that never stir? He looked back from his cold shower conceiving a fear of his bed. He took a towel and ran to the other room to dry, he wanted a cigarette, he had none: he didn't smoke. He wanted a strong drink, he had none.

He was cold. He began to pace. He turned on the TV, raising the volume to drown out his raging thoughts.

Am I afraid? His hands were shaking again.

September was mild but Lionel pulled his jacket collar closer to his neck, he would stop for coffee and something to put into his stomach, that's want he needed, he thought, he was not afraid.

He opened the crumpled letter again, a letter from his father that came two weeks ago. He wanted Lionel to come to Australia for a family portrait. It would be a great time, he thought, to use some of the vacation time he had stacked up. It would not be an excuse, he would even call Essie and invite her to join him.

He looked at the letter; Colonel A. Kerr, CH (ret.). He did not know these relatives at all, Dr Humphrey Milton, DDS, London; he did not recognize this name either. The Honorable William G. H. Hartzell, DD. Nobles, soldiers of the Queens Fusiliers, ministers. He resented his father's continuing determination to remind him of his origins, his duty, his family, his country. He laughed at how his name would be at his death with no noble title attached.

He was not afraid of that brute!

The bottle said to take one capsule once a day; the first one did shit! He took the prescription bottle from a mole he trusted. Ha! Now I trust a MOLE? He could feel his head tilting, he discovered he was thirsty and drank water, glass after glass, then resumed his pacing. He stared at the cell phone: ring dammit! Shit!

Was his father right? Was he just like them? He would not go home, he didn't trust his father; he thought Lionel was soft, too. He was now using profanity with ease. Shit! It was just that: shit! And every one used that. Shit!

Stuck up, erudite bastards, he would be asked to wear a white tie and pose, chin up, steady. There were photos and paintings of generations lining every wall and staircase. Shit!

That brute had a number of words that he found no place to use; he could not even now find a proper place for them. He never used "nigger" or "motherfucker" as easily as the others. He had bohemian genes and bourgeois tastes; he hated his father. He will tell him so. Was he not yet flamboyant enough in the eyes of his superiors? He didn't like violence, he hadn't used his weapon, he didn't bring a man down needlessly.

He needed more water.

Essie called; he let it ring several times. He was asleep, he said, sorry. She would not be going with him to Australia. It was a difficult time for her, she need to concentrate on her studies for graduation. He smiled into the phone. "No problem; I was also deciding whether to go," he replied. "Corned beef and cabbage tonight?"

She said lightly "Yes. Tonight at 8."

He looked at her photo on his night table; she was smiling insolently. Bitch! He felt a fierce anger. Australia, the movie theater, defending his honor. Was it not disgusting that a total stranger could cause him such grief so many years later?

He took another capsule, drank more water. He was not a coward! Shit!

He was not a motor mouth, he didn't add gloss shit to his hair, nor have his clothes tailored to fit. He steadied his hand and began to write. He decided he would kill Angelo Vitale and violate his signed DRR rule #2648 and (∞) DRR rule #60404, 102 (d). If you have any questions, please contact ethics assistant, Mr. Frank Donner. He had signed it with the others; he would never think of committing this infraction. He laughed aloud, really loud. It was so stupid; no one challenged it, it was just a formality, internal matters. Shit!

He drank more water; he was becoming exhausted.

It was simply marked memorandum and countersigned by the district inspector. Department for the Preservation of Order and Public Safety. Everyone signed them;

He looked at copies of the forms he filled out each week covering his assignments. His name, occupation, antecedents, Christian name and paternal name of the person or persons under surveillance, street, zip code, house and room number. Does he take meals at home or elsewhere? Does he have any servants? If so, what are their names? Who takes care of his room? Where and from whom does he receive letters? Does he visit the library, and which one? How much time does he spend in his room? What are his means of subsistence? Have you seem him at any time intoxicated? At what time does he leave the house and what time does he return? Where did the officer who is now watching him first see him? Under what circumstances? Does he know the officer by sight? This sheet is to be signed by the officer of surveillance.

He began to laugh harder and louder, crumbling more of the papers around his feet.

Another capsule, more water. That would steady his hands.

He was aware that the dossiers were being gathered; he did not believe they were going to hurt anyone. Querying bosses, ex-wives, educators, all were a fertile source and anyone could do this, his job was to fill in the spaces on forms.

He was not a coward.

He had carried his Charter Arms Cougar in his ankle holster; it was light, small, firm, sleek, feminine he thought, not a huge Glock bulge. He looked at the round small hole at the barrel end, continuing to gaze at it.

He felt a sudden rush of calm. He was not a coward, he was brave.

Removing it from his sight, feeling the steel on his earlobe, he squeezed.

The rushing red stain from his head covered the table and papers.

He had written one line:

Dear father, forgive me.

Johnny Jones got a call from Walsh at 5 in the morning asking him to go to this address. That's Lionel's, right? Whats up? That's what I want to know. You're on the island. Would you please get there a.s.a.p.?

Walsh never said please before giving any order. When J.J. got to the address, there was a single NYPD cruiser blocking the street, and a black SUV at the curb. Not good, he thought, senior cops, there was no yellow tape. He thought, how bad can this be. He walked up to a young cop, showed his shield and asked him, "What's up?" He looked at J.J. and said, "Young guy from the 7th precinct, looks like he got jammed up and couldn't find a door." "You mean suicide?" "Yep. Waiting for forensic now, medical examiner is inside."

The Staten Island Advance article read:

STATEN ISLAND COP FOUND SHOT TO DEATH; SUICIDE PROBED AS TO POSSIBLE CAUSE. THE OFFICER, WHOSE NAME WAS NOT RELEASED, WAS PRONOUNCED DEAD AT S.I. UNIVERSITY HOSPITAL. A POLICE SPOKESMAN SAID THAT THE SHOOTING OCCURED IN HIS APARTMENT.

Chapter 11

REFLECTIONS ON
BLACKS IN THE MILITARY

T here doesn't seem to be any one book, magazine, or historical document, either military or civilian, that chronicles the stories of Black military men. As a Black WWII veteran who served in one of the last all Black units, I have made an effort to collect newspaper and magazine articles, but to my knowledge there has been no central effort to preserve this part of history. My own modest files about American Blacks who fought and died, and who are still dying today, would fill a huge volume.

I was a soldier in the military in 1945, in the segregated army, and I witnessed racial discrimination firsthand, as I was transported and transferred to another country, Japan. I was a member of the 8th Army and most of us were soldier civilians at heart. We were intent on enjoying the pleasures of life in an occupied country, and our salaries financed our enjoyment of the many pleasures offered in Yokohama, Tokyo, Gifu, and other places in the islands of Japan. We were poorly trained, badly equipped, and very short on experience in the field. I don't know if this baggage was carried by the white units in Japan at the time, but I do know that the problems of trust and the lack of confidence in the system that segregation imposed was disastrous, and in the minds of many Black men who knew that their white officers were racially prejudiced, there existed a deep mistrust and a resentment that built up. It ate at the minds and the bodies and into the bonds that must hold any military unit together.

West Point

Established in 1682, West Point Military Academy saw the admission of the first African-American cadet, James Webster Smith of South Carolina, in 1870. Smith endured harsh treatment and was eventually dismissed for academic deficiency in a controversial Natural and Experimental Philosophy examination in 1874. Almost 100 years later, in 1987, a posthumous commissioning ceremony was held for Smith in South Carolina State University in Orangeburg. During his years at West Point he suffered racist slurs and taunts; he had slop poured over him in the night, he had to eat his meals served cold, and experienced ostracism and silence from the entire Cadet Corps. Frederick Dent Grant, son of President Ulysses S. Grant, was reported as saying that no damned Black—he used another derogatory term—"will ever graduate from West Point."

As a result of Smith's dismissal, Henry O. Flipper of Georgia became the first African-American graduate in 1877, graduating 50th in a class of 76. Second Lieutenant Henry O. Flipper was assigned to the Tenth U.S. Cavalry in 1877, one of the two Black cavalry regiments organized after the Civil War. Flipper's military career was cut short when he was court martialed at Fort Davis for embezzlement of Commissary funds. The trial, weighed down with prejudice against the Black Lieutenant Flipper, resulted in his being relieved of his commission. Henry Flipper died in 1940 at the age of 84, never knowing that his rank would be restored in 1976, when the United States Army reviewed his case and posthumously awarded Henry O. Flipper an honorable discharge dated June 1882. This event came 59 years after his death and 117 years after the young lieutenant had been found guilty of conduct unbecoming an officer and a gentleman.

In 1887 John Hanks Alexander became the second Black West Point graduate. During his four years at West Point, Alexander was popular with the corps and escaped some of the mistreatment experienced by previous Black cadets. Second Lieutenant Alexander became the sole Black officer in a command position with the Ninth Cavalry, the famous Buffalo Soldiers. The Department of War, citing Alexander as a "a man of ability, attainments, and energy," honored him by naming Camp Alexander at Newport News, Virginia in 1918.

Charles Young was the third African-American graduate of West Point where he had shared a room with John Alexander for three years. He was to become the first Black U.S. national park superintendent, first Black military attaché, first Black to achieve the rank of colonel, and highest-ranking Black officer in the United States Army until his death in 1922. He served in Cuba during the Spanish-American War and also served in the American west. Colonel Young was later sent to Liberia as a military envoy where he died of a tropical illness.

The first Black to graduate from West Point in the 19th century was Benjamin O. Davis Jr., who rose to the rank of three-star general. But when he entered the academy in 1932, he was given the silent treatment by his fellow cadets. For four full years, nobody was assigned to room with him; nobody invited him to eat at his table. When Davis graduated from West Point in 1936, he was the first Black to graduate in forty-nine years.

As recently as the early 1970's, Black graduates numbered no more than nine each year.

Blacks in the Civil War

News from Fort Sumter in 1861 had set off a rush by free Black men to enlist in U.S. military units. They were turned away, however, because a Federal law dating from 1792 barred Negroes from bearing arms for the U.S. army (although they had served in the American Revolution and in the War of 1812). The Lincoln administration wrestled with the idea of authorizing the recruitment of Black troops, concerned that such a move would prompt the Border States to secede, and when Gen. John C. Frémont in Missouri and Gen. David Hunter in South Carolina issued proclamations that emancipated slaves in their military regions and permitted them to enlist, their superiors sternly revoked their orders. By mid-1862, however, the escalating number of former slaves, the declining number of white volunteers, and the increasingly pressing personnel needs of the Union Army pushed the Government into reconsidering the ban.

As a result, on July 17, 1862, Congress passed the Second Confiscation and Militia Act, freeing slaves who had masters in the Confederate Army. Two days later, slavery was abolished in the territories of the United States, and on July 22 President Lincoln presented the preliminary draft of the Emancipation Proclamation to his Cabinet. After the Union Army turned back Lee's first invasion of the North at Antietam, MD, and the Emancipation Proclamation was subsequently announced, Black recruitment was pursued in earnest, and many Blacks, both slaves and freedmen, hastened to volunteer in the Union Army, and in May 1863 the Government established the Bureau of Colored Troops to manage the burgeoning numbers of Black soldiers.

By the end of the Civil War, roughly 179,000 Black men (10% of the Union Army) served as soldiers in the U.S. Army and another 19,000 served in the Navy. Nearly 40,000 Black soldiers died over the course of the war—30,000 of infection or disease. Black soldiers served in artillery and infantry and performed all noncombat support functions that sustain an army, as well. Black carpenters, chaplains, cooks, guards, laborers, nurses, scouts, spies, steamboat pilots, surgeons, and teamsters also contributed to the war cause. There were nearly 80 Black commissioned officers.

In addition to the perils of war faced by all Civil War soldiers, Black soldiers faced additional problems stemming from racial prejudice. Racial discrimination was prevalent even in the North, and discriminatory practices permeated the U.S. military. Segregated units were formed with Black enlisted men and typically commanded by white officers and Black noncommissioned officers. Black soldiers were initially paid $10 per month from which $3 was automatically deducted for clothing, resulting in a net pay of $7. In contrast, white soldiers received $13 per month from which no clothing allowance was drawn. In June 1864 Congress granted equal pay to the U.S. Colored Troops and made the action retroactive. Black soldiers received the same rations and supplies. In addition, they received comparable medical care.

Because of prejudice against them, Black units were not used in combat as extensively as they might have been. Nevertheless, the soldiers served with distinction in a number of battles. The July 1863 assault on Fort Wagner, SC, in which the 54th Regiment of Massachusetts Volunteers lost two-thirds of their officers and half of their troops, was memorably dramatized in the film *Glory*. By war's end, 16 Black soldiers had been awarded the Medal of Honor for their valor.

On July 16, 1861, William Tillman, a free Black man who was a cook on a merchant ship, became one of the Civil War's first heroes after his vessel was captured 150 miles off New Jersey by a former slave ship turned privateer, the *Jefferson Davis*. After the *Jefferson Davis* captured Tillman's vessel, five Confederate crewmen were left onboard to sail it to a Southern port. The Confederates also told Tillman, then 29, that they would sell him into slavery. However, they underestimated Tillman, who, after killing three of the rebels with a hatchet, gave the others the choice of helping to sail the ship north or dying. They complied with his demand, and the *Jefferson Davis* sailed into New York Harbor five days later. Tillman received adulation as a war hero and a $6,000 reward.

Dr. John van Salee DeGrasse, only the second African-American to be formally educated as a doctor in the United States, was a very active abolitionist and helped organize vigilante groups to intercept slave hunters in Boston immediately after passage of the 1850 Fugitive Slave Law. In May 1863 DeGrasse volunteered for the Union Army and in September he received a commission as Assistant Surgeon with the Thirty Fifth United States Colored Infantry, one of only three African American physicians to do so. He was the only Black surgeon to serve in the field with his regiment in South Carolina and one of only eight to serve in the Union Medical Corps.

Robert Smalls was a slave on the Confederate gunboat *Planter* in Charleston Harbor. Very early one morning, Smalls, along with his fellow slave crewmen and their families, sailed the *Planter*, flying the Confederate flag, slowly out of port and into the harbor, saluting the harbor forts with the customary blasts on the whistle and passing under the forts' heavy guns manned by Confederate guards. When the vessel was safely past the Confederate outposts, Smalls and his tense but jubilant crew brought down the Confederate flag and replaced it with a white flag. They not only delivered the vessel to the Union forces, but also brought invaluable knowledge of Confederate defenses and local waterways. The northern press hailed Smalls and his crewmen as heroes, and Congress ruled that they should receive half the value of the prize they presented to the U.S. cause. Smalls joined the fight against slavery, enlisting in the U.S. Navy. He was commissioned as Second Lieutenant with the Thirty Third Regiment, United States Colored Troops, and was assigned as the pilot on the *Planter*. When, in 1863, the *Planter* engaged in fierce combat with Confederate forces, and the ship's captain contemplated surrender, Smalls fearlessly rallied the crew and urged the gunners to continue firing, saving the ship and the crew from being captured. When word of his actions reached the military hierarchy, navy officials dismissed the captain and promoted Smalls to his position. In later life he served as a Congressman from South Carolina.

Andre Cailloux was born a slave on a plantation in Louisiana. By the age of 21 he had been emancipated and was living in New Orleans where he was well-known and well-liked. It was traditional for free people of color to offer their military service to the government in power. Since they had done so since colonial times, it was expected of them and it would have aroused suspicion had they declined. So Cailloux enlisted 100 men into the Louisiana Native Guards, including working slaves, runaway slaves, and free Black men. He was made their captain. When New Orleans fell to the Union forces, the Native Guards offered their services to Union Gen. Benjamin Butler. Cailloux's company became the colored company, carrying the banner for the 1st Regiment. On May 27, 1863, General Nathaniel P. Banks launched a poorly coordinated attack on the well-defended, well-fortified Confederate positions at Port Hudson. As part of the attack, Cailloux was ordered to lead his company of 100 men in an almost suicidal assault against sharpshooting Confederate troops. Cailloux's company suffered heavy casualties, but Cailloux, shouting encouragement to his men in French and English, led several increasingly futile charges. On his last charge, a ball tore through his arm, which was left dangling uselessly by his side. Severely wounded, Cailloux continued to lead the charge until a Confederate artillery shell killed him.

From the field and slave cabin to the Confederate White House, Black women also took an active role in assisting the Union military in winning the Civil War.

Susan King Taylor, Civil War nurse, cook, and laundress, was raised a slave on an island off the coast of Georgia. In April of 1861, Major General Hunter assaulted Fort Pulaski and freed all the slaves in the area, including Mrs. King. When Union officers raised the First South Carolina Volunteers (an all-Black unit), Mrs. King signed on as laundress and nurse. Able to read and write, she also set up a school for Black children and soldiers. She was the only African American woman to publish a memoir of her wartime experiences. She was also the first African American to teach openly in a school for former slaves in Georgia.

The activities of Harriet Tubman are now legendary. Tubman returned to the South early in the war to assist liberated slaves in Port Royal, South Carolina. By 1863, serving as a scout for the Union, she would don disguises and lead local Blacks in dangerous missions behind enemy lines to gather information on rebel troop location, movements and strength. She even accompanied, and by some accounts led, troops under Colonel James Montgomery in daring raids into enemy territory which destroyed thousands of dollars' worth of Southern property and liberated hundreds of Blacks from plantations.

The story of Mary Elizabeth Bowser, less well-documented than Tubman's but no less intriguing, is a fascinating tale of a brilliant woman who worked with an urban spy ring in the Confederate capital said to be "the most productive espionage operation" in the Civil War. Bowser is said to have had a photographic memory. When she assumed the identity of an illiterate slave woman and found a place as a house servant in the Confederate White House, she was able to gain access to lists of troop movements, reports on the location of Union prisoners, military strategies, and treasury reports. She passed the information along to Union forces until she was discovered and had to flee Richmond near the end of the war.

Mary Touvestre, a free Black woman working for a Confederate engineer in Norfolk, VA, overheard plans for building the *C.S.S. Virginia*. After obtaining a copy of the plans, she daringly crossed enemy lines to take this information to Secretary of the Navy, Gideon Welles, which caused the Union to crank up construction of its own ironclad warship, the *U.S.S. Monitor*.

The list of Black soldiers goes on and on throughout history, much of it lost, never historically placed in any context.

The Tale of Fort Pillow

Fort Pillow was a Confederate-built earthen fortification with a Union-built inner redoubt, overlooking the Mississippi River about forty river miles above Memphis, and the Union garrison comprised 295 white Tennessee troops and 262 U.S. Colored Troops, all under the command of Maj. Lionel F. Booth.

Confederate Maj. Gen. Nathan Bedford Forrest (who was to become an important figure in developing the Ku Klux Klan in the south) attacked the fort on April 12th with a cavalry division of approximately 2,500 men and quickly overran the fort, suffering only moderate casualties. Though most of the Union garrison surrendered, and thus should have been taken as prisoners of war, some 300 soldiers were killed, the majority of them Black. Union survivors' accounts, later supported by a federal investigation, concluded that African-American troops were massacred by Forrest's men after surrendering. Of the Black members of the garrison, only 58 (around 20%) were marched away as prisoners; 168 (almost 60%) white soldiers were taken prisoner.

The Confederate refusal to treat these soldiers as traditional POWs infuriated the North, and led to the Union's refusal to participate in prisoner exchanges.

On April 17, 1864, in the aftermath of Fort Pillow, Grant ordered General Benjamin F. Butler, who was negotiating prisoner exchanges with the Confederacy, to demand that in the exchange and treatment of prisoners, Black prisoners had to be treated identically to whites. A failure to do so would "be regarded as a refusal on their part to agree to the further exchange of prisoners, and [would] be so treated by us." This demand was refused and in June 1864 Confederate Secretary of War James Alexander Seddon stated the confederate position:

I doubt, however, whether the exchange of Negroes at all for our soldiers would be tolerated. As to the white officers serving with Negro troops, we ought never to be inconvenienced with such prisoners.

The Union already had a policy about killing prisoners of war. On July 30, 1863, prior to the massacre, President Abraham Lincoln wrote his Order of Retaliation:

It is therefore ordered that for every soldier of the United States killed in violation of the laws of war, a rebel soldier shall be executed; and for every one enslaved by the enemy or sold into slavery a rebel soldier shall be placed at hard labor on the public works, and continued at such labor until the other shall be released and receive the treatment due to a prisoner of war.

Frederick Douglass was reported to have said that he pressed the point on Mr. Lincoln and the President's reply was that, as to the exchange and general treatment of colored soldiers when taken prisoners of war, he should insist on their being entitled to all privileges of such prisoners.

But on the question of retaliation, Frederick Douglass differed entirely from Lincoln. Douglass stated "I shall never forget the benignant expression of his face, the tearful look of his eye, and the quiver in his voice when he deprecated a resort to retaliatory measures. "Once begun," Lincoln said, "I do not know where such a measure would stop." He said he could not take men out and kill them in cold blood for what was done by others. If he could get hold of the persons who were guilty of killing the colored prisoners in cold blood, the case would be different, but he could not kill the innocent for the guilty."

On May 3, President Lincoln sent a memo to his Cabinet: "It is now quite certain that a large number of our colored soldiers; with their officers, were, by the rebel force, massacred after they had surrendered, at the recent capture of Fort-Pillow. So much is known, though the evidence is not yet quite ready to be laid before me. Meanwhile, I will thank you to prepare, and give me in writing your opinion as to what course the government should take in the case." President Lincoln received very different replies. Four of his Cabinet argued that Confederate troops equal in number to the Union troops massacred should be held as hostages. Three advocated no retaliation against innocent hostages, but argued for orders to commanders in the field to execute the actual offenders. President Lincoln drafted instructions for Secretary of War Edwin M. Stanton but never completed them. It apparently proved easier to threaten the Confederate government than to put a policy into writing.

Buffalo Soldiers

The Buffalo Soldiers originally were members of the Tenth Cavalry Regiment of the U.S. Army, formed on September 21, 1866 at Fort Leavenworth, Kansas. The nickname was given to the "Negro Cavalry" by the Native American tribes they fought, and the term eventually became synonymous with all of the African-American regiments formed in 1866: the Ninth and Tenth Cavalry Regiments and the 24th and 25th Infantry Regiments.

The Buffalo Soldiers, Black men, fought Indians and outlaws on the Texas frontier. Black men would be trained and equipped to fight and kill Indians, who were fighting for their lives to remain in their own place of birth. Black men covered themselves with glory on San Juan Hill in Cuba. Black men served in the Spanish American War, and in two World Wars, and one of the first questions that I asked myself upon returning to the United States after my enlistment in the Pacific was, "Why did all-Black units like mine still exist in 1951?" The Executive Order issued by President Truman regarding integration of the troops meant nothing to commanders on the ground. The commanding officers in the 8th Army in the Pacific theater read statements such as, "As long as I am commander here, there will be no changes. There will be an Officers' Club # 1, White, and an Officers' Club # 2, Black. There will be NCO Clubs # 1 for whites and NCO Clubs # 2 for Blacks, including swimming pool, entertainment facilities, etc." Hearing that while sitting in the audience, I wondered what the other Blacks thought. I guess we all were too embarrassed and resigned to our roles in the Army to find a way to talk about the reality.

Although several African-American regiments were raised during the Civil War as part of the Union Army (including the 54th Massachusetts Volunteer Infantry and the many United States Colored Troops Regiments), the Buffalo Soldiers were established by Congress as the first peacetime all-Black regiments in the regular U.S. Army.

From 1866 to the early 1890s, these regiments fought with great distinction throughout the western United States in numerous campaigns against marauding American Indians, Mexicans, and lawless settlers. They were often the only source of security on the frontier and were frequently at odds with those who would profit from banditry. They participated in most of the military campaigns in these areas and earned a distinguished record. In addition to the military campaigns, the Buffalo Soldiers served a variety of roles along the frontier from building roads to escorting the U.S. mail.

After most of the Indian Wars ended in the 1890s, the regiments continued to serve and participated in the 1898 Spanish-American War, although the men of the Buffalo Soldiers were only some of the 5,000 Black men who served in the Spanish-American war.

The Buffalo Soldiers were often confronted with racial prejudice from other members of the U.S. Army, and civilians in the areas where the soldiers were stationed occasionally reacted to them with violence.

World War I

For most African Americans, the United States' entry into World War I in the spring of 1917 held the promise that patriotic service could improve their opportunities and treatment in postwar America. W.E.B. Dubois, an African American leader, stated that war seemed to be the venue for Blacks to gain their own rights though their involvement as soldiers, and said that fellow Blacks should close ranks, shoulder to shoulder with their white fellow citizens. "Unstinting patriotism," he wrote, "would result in the right to vote and the right to work and the right to live without insult."

But politicians in the southern part of the United States continued, year after year, condemning any mobilization plan of African Americans in the military. Sen. James K. Vardaman (D-Mississippi) condemned any mobilization plan that would result in "arrogant, strutting representatives of Black soldiery in every community." Black leaders had to overcome considerable resistance, especially from southern Democrats, to their insistence that African Americans be included in any wartime draft. Ultimately, their efforts were successful, and 367,710 African Americans were drafted during the war.

By this time, however, Blacks in the American military had come to expect little in the way of recognition for their service in any branch of the armed forces. Few African Americans served in the U.S. Navy and none in the Marine Corps. The army was strictly segregated, maintaining four Black units, the 24th and 25th Infantry and the Ninth and Tenth Cavalry Regiments—all under the command of white officers.

But WWI did have a transforming effect on African Americans. Despite the white reluctance and hostility, the Black community took pride in its contributions to the war effort at home and overseas. Many southern Blacks moved to the North to take industrial jobs created by the wartime economy. Their numbers added to what would later be known as the Great Migration, a population movement that created or greatly augmented Black communities in many northern cities.

In addition, 200,000 Black soldiers were deployed to Europe, some serving with the American Expeditionary Force and others detailed to the French Army. But the vast majority of these troops were relegated to Services of Supplies (SOS) units and labor battalions. The War Department did not order its four Black regiments to Europe. Rather than taking part in World War I, the army's most experienced Black soldiers remained at their posts along the Mexican border.

During the war, no Black soldier received the Congressional Medal of Honor, America's highest award for military heroism. In 1991, however, President George Bush presented relatives of Cpl. Freddie Stowers with what he termed a "long overdue" Medal of Honor in recognition of Stowers's heroism on September 28, 1918, while serving in France with the 371st Infantry Regiment, 93rd Infantry Division. Stowers rallied his company after it encountered withering machine-gun and mortar fire that exacted 50 percent casualties and killed or wounded all of the company's more senior officers. After capturing a German machine-gun position in the first trench, Stowers was leading his men against a second trench line when he was mortally wounded by machine-gun fire. Even after being hit, he continued to crawl forward, and when he could crawl no farther, he continued to shout encouragement to his men. Inspired by Stowers's heroism, the company overran the remaining German positions.

World War II

Despite a high enlistment rate in the U.S. Army, African Americans were not treated equally. Racial tensions existed. At parades, church services, in transportation and canteens the races were kept separate. In Europe and across the war theatre, the Red Cross segregated the blood in its banks as if there were any real differences between white blood and Black blood.

Many soldiers of color served their country with distinction during World War II. There were 125,000 African Americans who were overseas in World War II. Famous segregated units, such as the Tuskegee Airmen and 761st Tank Battalion and the lesser-known but equally distinguished 452nd Anti-Aircraft Artillery Battalion proved their value in combat, and there are many examples of individual bravery.

And I will never forget during my childhood when Joe Lewis, the "Brown Bomber," who held the heavyweight boxing championship, gave that up to join the U.S. Army as a private in a segregated cavalry unit. Realizing Louis's potential for elevating esprit de corps among the troops, the Army placed him in its Special Services Division rather than deploying him into combat, and during his three and a half year enlistment, he traveled more than 21,000 miles and staged 96 boxing exhibitions before two million soldiers.

Carl Clark

In January 2012, at 95 years of age, Carl Clark received what probably will be the last combat medal awarded to a living veteran of WWII, when he was awarded the Navy and Marine Corps Commendation Medal with the Combat Distinguished Device, an honor he had been denied because of his race and which he received some 66 years after the event.

During the battle aboard the *USS Aaron Ward*, when Japanese kamikaze pilots attacked the destroyer near Okinawa in 1945, 29 year old Clark, despite a broken collar bone, pulled several men to safety and put out the fire in an ammunition locker that, it was said, could have potentially cracked the destroyer in half if it had exploded. He was the only survivor of the 8-man damage control team. Even though the destroyer's captain acknowledged that he had saved the ship, it took 66 years to be recognized for his actions, according to Clark, because of "bigotry." "It wouldn't look good to say one black man saved the ship," he said. The honor was further stalled due to the lack of documentation and living witnesses. Representative Anna Eschoo (D-CA) said "Carl Clark served our Nation during a time when the Navy was deeply segregated, and a culture of racism was prevalent. His courage stands as a symbol of the greatness of our nation, and this award makes Mr. Clark a true American hero." Clark remained in the U.S. Navy for 22 years, rising to the rank of Chief Petty Officer.

Vernon Baker

In the early 1990s, responding to requests from Black veterans and a white former captain who had commanded Black troops in combat, the Army asked Shaw University, a historically Black college in Raleigh, N.C., to investigate why no Blacks had received the Medal of Honor during World War II. The inquiry found no documents proving that Blacks had been discriminated against in decisions to award the medal, but concluded that a climate of racism had prevented recognition of heroic deeds.

Military historians gave the Army the names of ten Black servicemen who they believed should have been considered for the Medal of Honor. Then an Army board, looking at their files with all references to race deleted, decided that seven of these men deserved to be cited for bravery "above and beyond the call of duty."

Four of the men had been killed in action and two others had died in the decades after the war; those six received the medal posthumously. Vernon Baker, the lone survivor among the seven, was greeted with a standing ovation as he entered the East Room of the White House on January 13, 1997 to the strains of "God Bless America" played by the Marine Corps Band.

The Medal of Honor recipient died at the age of 90. "You don't have to remember me as a hero," the retired Army Lieutenant told me in Washington, DC. "Just don't forget the sacrifices made by African Americans during WWII." In his memoir, *Lasting Valor*, he wrote about the fierce battle in Italy, when his all-Black platoon of the 92nd Infantry Division was fighting the Germans. "*Our assignment was an ass-chewing assignment to scout for the white soldiers. It was a way of life for my men that made me furious. It was to break our spirit. We had made an ass out of everyone who said that we couldn't do this. We held it so that the white troops could go all the way through those lines without firing a shot. I still wanted respect, and the acknowledgement that we were good."*

"It was justice delayed," Baker said. "It was justice denied."

Cameron Wade

Cameron Wade was the first Black American soldier to be integrated into Army combat units. He died recently at the age of 87. Mr. Wade became a truck driver on the front lines as part of a little-known cadre of 2,221 Black soldiers who fought alongside their white counterparts. Afterwards, he and many Black soldiers discovered that their wartime service had gone unrecognized by Army authorities. Cameron Wade formed the Association of the 2221 Negro Volunteers, World War II, and launched a lobbying effort to have their benefits, ranks, and medals that had been denied restored to them.

He was a teenager when he was drafted into the Army in 1943. In basic training, he won awards for marksmanship, yet he was assigned a job as a truck driver. A similar fate awaited many other Black troops, who were often relegated to supporting roles in supply, transportation, or food-service units.

Mr. Wade became a sergeant in the "Red Ball Express," a renowned and heavily African American unit in the Army Transportation Corps that supplied Gen. George S. Patton's troops in Europe.

But after U.S. infantry forces were depleted by heavy casualties during the Battle of the Bulge in late 1944, Gen. Dwight D. Eisenhower, the supreme allied commander, signed an order allowing volunteers from Black service units to join white soldiers on the front lines.

The volunteers served in all-Black platoons, with many of them, including Mr. Wade, accepting demotions so as not to outrank white soldiers. Otherwise, they fought as equals.

"I was a member of the first platoon to integrate the infantry, which had been a sacred cow for whites only," Mr. Wade told the *Cleveland Plain Dealer* in 1995. "The results were amazing. We ate together, slept together, and fought together. There were no incidents. The Army couldn't believe it."

The Black infantrymen were rated extremely highly in battle. "These guys," David P. Colley, author of *Blood for Dignity: The Story of the First Integrated Combat Unit in the U.S. Army* stated "were essentially the first Black soldiers to be integrated into units in the Army since the American Revolution."

During that time, Mr. Wade, a member of the 99th Infantry Division, was among the first U.S. troops to cross the Rhine River at Remagen, Germany in 1945. He was leading a squad of 12 soldiers when they were hit by a shell from a German tank. Six men under his command were killed. Mr. Wade was evacuated to a hospital in England with shrapnel in his lungs, shoulder, arm, and eyelid. When an army officer strode through the hospital awarding Purple Hearts to the wounded troops, "He went to each bed." Mr. Cameron said, "He shook each solder's hand, he made a short speech and presented each man with a medal. When he reached my bed he took a medal from a cart and threw it on my bed without saying a word to me." The Black troops were afterward sent back to the United States without having their previous higher ranks restored. In most cases their combat experience was omitted from Army records.

In 1948, President Harry S. Truman signed an executive order prohibiting segregation in the armed forces. But the story of the 2,221 African American volunteers of World War II was all but lost until Mr. Wade made it his mission to keep it alive.

He took his concerns to the Army Board for Correction of Military Records and gained the support of Gen. Colin Powell, then the Chairman of the Joint Chiefs of Staff, and influential members of Congress. President Bill Clinton presided over a ceremony honoring many of the volunteers and other Black veterans in 1994, but Mr. Wade still wasn't finished.

Eventually, at a Pentagon ceremony in 1998, Mr. Wade and hundreds of other members of the 2,221 volunteers received Bronze Star Medals and had their old ranks restored.

Mr. Wade was present at the White House on Jan. 13, 1997, when President Clinton conferred the Medal of Honor on Vernon Baker and the other six posthumous African American soldiers whose wartime valor had been overlooked for more than 50 years.

"They were prepared to sacrifice everything for freedom," Clinton said, "even though freedom's fullness was denied to them."

Doris "Dorie" Miller

On the morning of December 7, 1941, Mess Attendant Second Class Dorie Miller was awake at 6:00 AM on the *USS West Virginia* in Pearl Harbor. He had volunteered as a room steward and made an extra five dollars each month providing wake-up services to duty officers, as well as doing their laundry, shining their shoes, and making their beds. When the alarm for general quarters was sounded, he headed for his battle station, the anti-aircraft battery magazine amid ship. However, the ship was under attack by more than 200 Japanese torpedo planes, bombers and fighters, and a torpedo had destroyed his battle station. Because of his size and strength he was ordered to run across the deck to retrieve injured shipmates and carry them to the quarterdeck where they were somewhat protected from the attack.

Miller was next ordered to help Ensign Victor Delano and Lieutenant Frederic H. White load two anti-aircraft machine guns. Lt. White loaded both guns and, despite his lack of training, Miller manned one of the guns and began firing into the air at dive-bombing Japanese planes. Miller later recounted: "It wasn't hard. I just pulled the trigger and she worked fine." Miller fired the gun until he ran out of ammunition. Japanese aircraft eventually dropped two armor-piercing bombs through the deck of the battleship and launched five aircraft torpedoes into her port side. When the attack finally lessened, Lt. White ordered Miller to help move injured sailors through oil and water to the quarterdeck, thereby "unquestionably saving the lives of a number of people who might otherwise have been lost."

With the ship heavily damaged by the bombs, torpedoes and following explosions, the crew prevented her from capsizing by counter-flooding a number of compartments, and the *USS West Virginia* sank to the harbor bottom as her crew—including Miller—abandoned ship.

Dorie Miller was a Black Mess Attendant, and like virtually every other African American in the U.S. Navy, he had been ineligible for military training. On January 1, 1942, the Navy released a list of commendations for actions on December 7. Among them was a single commendation for an "unnamed" Negro. On March 12, 1942, Dr. Lawrence D. Reddick announced, after corresponding with the Navy, that the name of the unknown Negro sailor was Doris Miller. On May 27, 1942 Miller was personally recognized by Admiral Chester W. Nimitz when he presented Miller with the Navy Cross, the third highest award for gallantry during combat that the Navy awarded at the time.

Dorie Miller was then assigned to the aircraft carrier *USS Liscome Bay*, but a year later, back at sea, when a Japanese submarine sank his ship, the Black Hero of Pearl Harbor, Navy Cross awardee Dorie Miller, died as a Ship's Cook Third Class.

The Tuskegee Airmen

Colonel Kenneth O. Wolford, a Tuskegee Airman, passed away in 2012 at the age of 88. Perhaps only a dozen of the initial airmen are now living. Colonel Wolford spent his entire 32-year career in the military, was with the famed 99th Fighter Squadron in WWII, America's first and only African American Fighter Squadron in Europe. Germans called the Tuskegee Airmen "Die Schwartz Vogelmenschen" – the Black birdmen. The Tuskegee Airmen really fought two wars: one against Nazi Germany, and the other against segregation at home.

Like many Black men, they were in fact initially thought of as incapable of being pilots. In 1925 the War College stated that Blacks did not have the courage or intelligence to be pilots. One General Officer said "The Negro type has not the proper reflexes to make a first-rate fighter pilot."

The War Department was reluctant to allow the unit to exist and in an effort to eliminate them before they could begin, they set up a system to accept only those with a level of flight experience or education that they thought would be difficult to fill. However, the Air Corps received an abundance of applications from men who were qualified even under those restrictions.

The Tuskegee Black airman program was an experiment. It was set up to prove that the American Negroes would fail, that they did not have the capability to fly, and that they would be cowards in combat.

That plan backfired.

In June 1941, the Tuskegee program officially began with formation of the 99th Fighter Squadron at the Tuskegee Institute. Four hundred and fifty of the pilots who were trained at the Tuskegee Army Air Field served overseas in either the 99th Pursuit Squadron (later the 99th Fighter Squadron) or the 332nd Fighter Group. Despite segregation and other adversities, the Tuskegee Airmen flew with distinction in 15,000 missions on record. Their success was initially due to the leadership of Benjamin O. Davis, Jr., the first Black General in the United States Air Force. During World War II, Davis was commander of the 99th and the 332nd Fighter Group, which escorted bombers on air combat missions over Europe. In breaking racial barriers, Davis followed in the footsteps of his father: Benjamin O. Davis, Sr., the first African-American general in the United States Army.

Even at that time, a half century before racial injustice against Black soldiers was still emerging, there were many questionable discharges of Black veterans, who received a so-called blue discharge which would deny them the education and job-training benefits of the GI Bill. The GI Bill was highly regarded as a gateway to the middle class. Black soldiers received more than 22% of the blue discharges. Blacks had been victimized once again by institutional racism, with economic consequences that continue to persist to this day.

The famed Red Ball Express in Europe was the overwhelmingly Black unit that drove supplies to the front following D-Day. My brother Eugene was a member of the Red Ball Express during 1943 and 1944, and he saw service at the Battle of the Bulge in late 1944. The Red Ball Express drivers were not combat troops, but their jobs involved great danger, transporting the munitions and high octane gasoline and explosives. In December of 1944, during the worst of the Battle of the Bulge, the US Army issued directives requesting African American volunteers for racially integrated combat units. That request marked the final beginning of the end of Jim Crow in the Army. The Army found many of those volunteers among the Black cooks, engineers, quartermaster personnel, and truckers. Some men recalled that those Blacks who did volunteer did a credible job, which shows that all they ever needed was an honest to goodness chance. In 1948, President Truman signed an Executive Order, 9981, ordering the integration of American forces and establishing the President's Committee on Equal Treatment and Opportunity in the Armed Forces.

Korea

The Korean War started in 1950 and ended in 1953. This was the last American conflict involving segregated units of the armed forces. I was with the 933rd Antiaircraft Artillery Automatic Weapons Battalion, combined later at Gifu with the 76th Field Artillery Gun Battalion. I had a very privileged job in the Headquarters Message Center, the mail room, and because of my job I was required to carry a 45 caliber pistol. I never had training to use it; I don't think I would even remember how to load the weapon with ammunition. That was the extent of my training before our units were sent into Korea as combat troops.

These two outfits, the 933rd and the 76th, went to Korea and lost many men trying to cross the Han River near Seoul, where they were told to use their weapons in a lower

Above: Black soldiers off to war with Colonel Robert Shaw, who commanded the all-Black 54th Massachusetts Infantry Regiment in 1863. Displayed at the National Gallery of Art in Washington, DC.

position to fire across the river at the North Korean or Chinese Army. When I have attended reunions with survivors of the battle, they recount that more than half of the men were killed or wounded. The officers were white, the only Black officers being the chaplains, and the men that fought in these battles had very little field practice with their weapons. Most of the men from the 8th Army that went to Korea were unprepared for the major battles in which they would ultimately fight and die.

I'm sure that historians will present their conclusions of why many of the Black military units failed in Korea, but the significant attack that was conducted by the 8th Army at the Han River will forever stay in my mind.

It was a very sad time for me to know and to remember. The officers in command were white, and they failed to enforce high standards because they refused to admit that there was racial prejudice in recruiting, training, and preparing these Black men for all-out war. To me, they were simply poor leaders, and the bonds of mutual respect between the soldiers and their officers and commanders were weak. I guess on the surface all seemed to run well within the units at our base in Japan. Underneath, however, hostility and frustration were there, and it would break forth when the units were facing combat, and these soldiers, these Black men, would realize that their lives depended on officers that they did not and could not trust.

The mistrust that resulted on both sides was largely hidden behind a screen of military conventions and good manners, but it was still there. Black officers were frustrated and resentful. They saw that most promotions and career-enhancing assignments went to white officers, some of whom were clearly inferior to them in education and military competence. Aware, as well, that few if any of them would ever rise to a rank above captain, they could only conclude that the Army considered them second class.

There were many misadventures during the Korean War, probably for many reasons. An aggressive enemy, inadequate equipment, inexperience at many levels, high rates of leadership failures, casualties among key personnel, and the lack of bonding and cohesion, all of these played their part.

I remember, on my daily rounds in Yokohama, that it was just as important for me to prepare the new movie and the new music for the servicemen's club as it was to get the messages hand delivered between the two or three regiments or headquarters.

A Scout with the Buffalo Soldiers - An Essay by Frederick Remington

Slightly abridged from *The Century; a popular quarterly*. Volume 37, Issue 6, April 1889.

I sat smoking in the quarters of an army friend at Fort Grant, and through a green lattice-work was watching the dusty parade and congratulating myself on the possession of this spot of comfort in such a disagreeably hot climate as Arizona Territory offers in the summer, when in strode my friend the lieutenant, who threw his cap on the table and began to roll a cigarette.

Marching in the Desert with the Buffalo Soldiers

"Well," he said, "the K.O. has ordered me out for a two-week's scouting up the San Carlos way, and I'm off in the morning. Would you like to go with me?" He lighted the cigarette and paused for my reply.

I was very comfortable at that moment, and knew from some past experiences that marching under the summer sun of Arizona was real suffering and not to be considered by one on pleasure bent; and I was also aware that my friend the lieutenant had a reputation as a hard rider, and would in this case select a few picked and seasoned cavalrymen and rush over the worst possible country in the least possible time. I had no reputation as a hard rider to sustain, and, moreover, had not backed a horse for the year past. I knew too that Uncle Sam's beans, black coffee, and the bacon which every old soldier will tell you about would fall to the lot of any one who scouted with the 10th Dragoons. Still, I very much desired to travel through the country to the north, and in a rash moment said, "I'll go."

"You understand that you are amenable to discipline," continued the lieutenant with mock seriousness, as he regarded me with that soldier's contempt for a citizen which is not openly expressed but is tacitly felt.

"I do," I answered meekly.

"Put you afoot, citizen; put you afoot, sir, at the slightest provocation, understand," pursued the officer in his sharp manner of giving commands.

I suggested that after I had chafed a Government saddle for a day or two I should undoubtedly beg to be put afoot, and, far from being a punishment, it might be a real mercy.

386

"That being settled, will you go down to stable-call and pick out a mount? You are one of the heavies, but I think we can outfit you," he said; and together we strolled down to where the bugle was blaring.

At the adobe corral the faded coats of the horses were being groomed by black troopers in white frocks; for the 10th United States Cavalry is composed of colored men. The fine alkaline dust of that country is continually sifting over all exposed objects, so that grooming becomes almost as hopeless a task as sweeping back the sea with a housebroom. A fine old veteran cavalry-horse detailed for a sergeant of the troop, was selected to bear me on the trip. He was a large horse of a pony build, both strong and sound except that he bore a healed-up saddle-gore, gotten, probably, during some old march upon an endless Apache trail. Well satisfied with my mount, I departed.

On the following morning I was awakened and got up to array myself in my field costume. My old troop-horse was at the door, and he eyed his citizen rider with malevolent gaze. Even the dumb beasts of the army share that quiet contempt for the citizen which is one manifestation of the military spirit, born of strength, and as old as when the first man went forth with purpose to conquer his neighbor man.

Down in front of the post-trader's was gathered the scouting party. A tall sergeant, grown old in the service, scarred on battlefield, hardened by long marches, -- in short, a product of the camp -- stood by his horse's head. Four enlisted men, picturesquely clad in the cavalry soldier's field costume, and two packers, mounted on diminutive bronco mules, were in charge of four pack-mules loaded with *apperajos* [rigs] and packs. This was our party. Presently the lieutenant issued from the headquarters' office and joined us. An orderly led up his horse. "Mount," said the lieutenant; and swinging himself into his saddle he started off up the road. Out past the groups of adobe houses which constitute a frontier military village or post we rode, stopping to water our horses at the little creek, now nearly dry -- the last water for many miles on our trail, -- and presently emerged upon the great desert. Together at the head of the little cavalcade rode the lieutenant and I, while behind, in single file, came the five troopers, sitting loosely in their saddles with the long stirrup of the United States cavalry seat, forage-hats set well over the eyes, and carbines, slickers, canteens, saddle-pockets, and lariats rattling at their sides. Strung out behind were the four pack mules, now trotting demurely along, now stopping to feed, and occasionally making a solemn and evidently well-considered attempt to get out of line and regain the post which we were leaving behind. The packers brought up the rear, swinging their "blinds" and shouting at the lagging mules in a manner which evinced a close acquaintance with the character and peculiarities of each beast.

The sun was getting higher in the heavens and began to assert its full strength. The yellow dust rose about our horses' hoofs and settled again over the dry grass and mesquite bush. Stretching away on our right was the purple line of the Sierra Bonitas, growing bluer and bluer until lost in the hot scintillating atmosphere of the desert horizon. Overhead stretched the deep blue of the cloudless sky.

A Halt to Tighten the Packs

Presently we halted and dismounted to tighten the packs, which work loose after the first hour. One by one the packers caught the little mules, threw a blind over their eyes, and "Now, Whitey! Ready! eve-e-e-e -- gimme that loop," came from the men as they heaved and tossed the circling ropes in the mystic movements of the diamond hitch. "All fast, Lieutenant," cries a packer, and mounting we move on up the long slope of the mesa towards the Sierras. We enter a break in the foothills, and the grade becomes steeper and steeper, until at last it rises at an astonishing angle. The slopes of the Sierra Bonitas are very steep, and as the air became more rarified as we toiled upward I found that I was panting for breath. My horse -- a veteran mountaineer -- grunted in his efforts and drew his breath in long and labored blowing; consequently I felt as though I was not doing anything unusual in puffing and blowing myself.

On the trail ahead I saw the lieutenant throw himself on the ground. I followed his example, for I was nearly "done for." I never had felt a rock as soft as the one I sat on. It was literally downy. The old troop-horse heaved a great sigh, and dropping his head went fast asleep, as every good soldier should do when he finds the opportunity. The Negro troopers sat about, their black skins shining with perspiration, and took no interest in the matter in hand. They occupied such time in joking and merriment as seemed fitted for growling. They may be tired and they may be hungry, but they do not see fit to augment their misery by finding fault with everybody and everything. In this particular they are charming men with whom to serve.

After a most frugal lunch we resumed our journey towards the clouds. Climbing many weary hours, we at last stood on the sharp ridge of the Sierra. Behind us we could see the great yellow plain of the Sulphur Spring Valley, and in front, stretching away, was that of the Gila, looking like a bed of a sea with the water gone.

Here we had a needed rest, and then began the descent on the other side. This was a new experience. The prospect of being suddenly overwhelmed by an avalanche of horseflesh as the result of some unlucky stumble makes the recruit constantly apprehensive. But the trained horses are sure of foot, understand the business, and seldom stumble except when the treacherous ground gives way. On the crest the prospect was very pleasant, as the pines there obscured the hot sun; but we suddenly left them for the scrub mesquite which bars your passage and reaches forth for you with its thorns when you attempt to go around.

We wound downward among the masses of rock for some time, when we suddenly found ourselves on a shelf of rock. We sought to avoid it by going up and around, but after a tiresome march we were still confronted by a drop of about a hundred feet. I gave up in despair; but the lieutenant after gazing at the unknown depths which were masked at the bottom by a thick growth of brush, said, "This is a good place to go down." I agreed that it was if you once got started; but personally I did not care to take the tumble.

Taking his horse by the bits, the young officer began the descent. The slope was at an angle of at least sixty degrees, and was covered with loose dirt and boulders, with the mask of brush at the bottom concealing the awful possibilities of what might be beneath. The horse hesitated a moment, then cautiously put his head down and his leg forward and started. The loose earth crumbled, a great stone was precipitated to the bottom with a crash, the horse slid and floundered along. Had the situation not been so serious it would have been funny, because the angle of the incline was so great that the horse actually sat on his haunches like a dog. "Come on!" shouted the redoubtable man of war and I started. My old horse took it unconcernedly, and we came down all right, bringing our share of dirt and stones and plunging through the wall of brush at the bottom to find our  friend safe on the lower side. The men came along without so much as a look of interest in the proceeding. Down came the mules, without turning an ear, and then followed the packers, who, to my astonishment, rode down.

Our camp was pitched by a little mountain stream near a grassy hillside. The saddles, packs, and *apperajos* were laid on the ground and the horses and mules herded on the side of the hill by a trooper, who sat perched on a rock above them, carbine in hand. I was thoroughly tired and hungry, and did my share in creating the famine which it was clearly seen would reign in that camp ere long. We sat about the fire and talked. The genial glow seems to possess an occult quality: it warms the self-confidence of a man; it lulls his moral nature; and the stories which circulate about a campfire are always more interesting than authentic. Soldiers have no tents in that country, and we rolled ourselves in our blankets and, gazing up, saw the weird figure of the sentinel against the last red gleam of the sunset, and beyond that the great dome of the sky. Then we fell asleep.

A Campfire Sketch

When I awoke the next morning the hill across the canyon wall was flooded with a golden light, while the gray tints of our camp were steadily warming up. The soldiers had the two black camp-pails over the fire and were grooming the horses. Everyone was good-natured, as befits the beginning of the day. The tall sergeant was meditatively combing his hair with a currycomb; such delightful little unconventionalities are constantly observed about the camp. The coffee steamed up in our nostrils, and after a rub in the brook I pulled myself together and declared to my comrade that I felt as good as new. This was a palpable falsehood, as my labored movements revealed to the hard-sided cavalryman the sad effeminacy of the studio. But our respite was brief, for almost before I knew it I was again on my horse, following down the canyon after the black charger bestrided by the junior lieutenant of K troop. Over piles of rocks fit only for the touch and go of a goat, through the thick mesquite which threatened to wipe our hats off or to swish us from the saddle, with the air warming up and growing denser, we rode along. A great stretch of sandy desert could be seen, and I foresaw hot work.

In about an hour we were clear of the descent and could ride along together, so that conversation made the way more interesting. We dismounted to go down a steep drop from the high mesa into the valley of the Gila, and then began a day warmer even than imagination had anticipated. The awful glare of the sun on the desert, the clouds of white alkaline dust which drifted up until lost above, seemingly too fine to settle again, and the great heat cooking the ambition out of us, made the conversation lag and finally drop altogether. The water in my canteen was hot and tasteless, and the barrel of my carbine, which I touched with my ungloved hand, was so heated that I quickly withdrew it. Across the hot-air waves which made the horizon rise and fall like the bosom of the ocean we could see a whirlwind or sand-storm winding up in a tall spiral until it was lost in the deep blue of the sky above. [These "dust-devils" are still common in southern Arizona.]

Lizards started here and there; a snake hissed a moment beside the trail, then sought the cover of a dry bush; the horses moved along with downcast heads and drooping ears. The men wore a solemn look as they rode along, and now and then one would nod as though giving over to sleep. The pack-mules no longer sought fresh feed along the way, but attended strictly to business. A short halt was made, and I alighted. Upon remounting I threw myself violently from the saddle, and upon examination found that I had brushed up against a cactus and gotten my corduroys filled with thorns. The soldiers were overcome with glee at this episode, but they volunteered to help me pick them from my clothes. Thus we marched all day, and with canteens empty we "pulled into" Fort Thomas that afternoon. [Fort Thomas was north of Fort Grant and less than a mile south of the Gila River.]

At the fort we enjoyed that hospitality which is a kind of freemasonry among army officers. But for all that Fort Thomas is an awful spot, hotter than any other place on the crust of the earth. The siroccos continually chase each other over the desert, the convalescent wait upon the sick, and the thermometer persistently reposes at the figures 125 degrees Fahrenheit. Soldiers are kept in the Gila Valley posts for only six months at a time before they are relieved, and they count the days.

TROOPER IN TOW.

On the following morning at an early hour we waved adieus to our kind friends and took our way down the valley. If the impression is abroad that a cavalry soldier's life in the Southwest has any of the lawn-party element in it, I think the impression could be effaced by doing a march like that. The great clouds of dust choke you and settle over horse, soldier, and accouterments until all local color is lost and black man and white man wear a common hue. The "chug, chug, chug" of your tired horse as he marches along becomes infinitely tiresome, and cavalry soldiers never ease themselves in the saddle. No pains are spared to prolong the usefulness of an army horse, and every old soldier knows that his good care will tell when the long forced march comes some day, and when to be put afoot by a poor mount means great danger in Indian warfare. The soldier will steal for his horse, will share his camp bread, and will moisten the horse's nostrils and lips with the precious water in the canteen.

Through a little opening in the trees we see a camp and stop in front of it. A few mesquite trees, two tents, and some sheds made of boughs beside an *acequia* make up the background. By the cooking-fire lounge two or three rough frontiersmen, veritable pirates in appearance, with rough flannel shirts, slouch hats, brown canvas overalls, and an unkempt air; but suddenly, to my intense astonishment, they rise, stand in their tracks as immovable as graven images, and salute the lieutenant; then these men were soldiers! It was a camp of instruction for Indians and a post of observation. They were nice fellows and did everything in their power to entertain the cavalry. We were given a tent, and one man cooked the army rations in such strange shapes and mysterious ways that we marveled as we ate. After dinner we lay on our blankets watched the groups of San Carlos Apaches who came to look at us. Some of them knew the lieutenant, with whom they had served and whom they now addressed as "Young Chief." They would point him out to others with great zest. Great excitement prevailed when it was discovered that I was using a sketch-book, and I was forced to disclose the half-finished visage of one villainous face to their gaze. It was straightway torn up, and I was requested with many scowls and grunts, to discontinue that pastime, for Apaches more than any other Indians dislike to have their portraits made.

All along the Gila Valley can be seen the courses of stone which were the foundations of the houses of a dense population long since passed away. The lines of old irrigating ditches were easily traced, and one is forced to wonder at the changes in Nature, for at the present time there is not water sufficient to irrigate land necessary for the support of as large a population as probably existed at some remote period. We "raised" some foothills, and could see in the far distance the great flat plain, the buildings of the San Carlos agency, and the white canvas of the cantonment. Nearer and nearer shone the white lines of tents until we drew rein in the square where officers crowded around to greet us. The jolly post-commander, the senior captain of the 10th, insisted upon my accepting the hospitalities of his "large hotel," as he called his field tent, on the ground that I too was a New Yorker. Right glad have I been ever since that I accepted his courtesy, for he entertained me in the true frontier style.

Being now out of the range of country known to our command, a lieutenant in the same regiment was detailed to accompany us beyond. This gentleman was a character. The best part of his life had been spent in this rough country, and he had so long associated with Apache scouts that his habits while on a trail were exactly those of an Indian. I jocosely insisted that Lieutenant Jim only needed a breech-clout and long hair in order to draw rations at the agency. In the morning, as we started under his guidance, he was a spectacle. He wore shoes and a white shirt, and carried absolutely nothing in the shape of canteens and other "plunder" which usually constitute a cavalryman's kit. He was mounted on a little runt of a pony so thin and woebegone as to be remarkable among his kind. It was insufferably hot as we followed our queer guide up a dry canyon, which cut off the breeze from all sides and was a veritable human frying-pan. I marched next to our leader, and all day long the patter, patter of that Indian pony, bearing his tireless rider, made an aggravating display of insensibility to fatigue, heat, dust, and climbing. On we marched over the rolling hills, dry, parched, desolate, covered with cactus and loose stones. When we reached water and camp that night our ascetic leader had his first drink. It was a long one and a strong one, but at last he arose from the pool and with a smile remarked his "canteens were full." Officers in the regiment say that no one will give Lieutenant Jim a drink from his canteen, but this does not change his habit of not carrying one; nevertheless, by the exercise of self-denial, which is at times heroic, he manages to pull through. They say that he sometimes fills an old meat-tin with water in anticipation of a long march, and stories which try credulity are told of the amount of water he has drunk at times.

Yuma Apaches come into camp, shake hands gravely with everyone, and then in their Indian way begin the inevitable inquiries as to how the coffee and flour are holding out. The campfire darts and crackles, the soldiers gather round it, eat, joke, and bring out the greasy pack of cards. The officers' gossip of army affairs, while I lie on my blankets, smoking and trying to establish relations with a very small and very dirty little Yuma Apache, who sits near me and gazes with sparkling eyes at the strange object which I undoubtedly seem to him.

It seems but an instant before a glare of sun strikes my eyes and I am awake for another day. I am mentally quarreling with that insane desire to march which I know possesses Lieutenant Jim; but it is useless to expostulate, and before many hours the little pony constantly moving along ahead of me becomes a part of my life. There he goes. I can see him now -- always moving briskly along, pattering over the level, trotting up the dry bed of a stream, disappearing into the dense chapparal thicket that covers a steep hillside, jumping rocks, and doing everything but "halt."

We are now in the high hills, and the air is cooler. The chapparal is thicker, the ground is broken into a succession of ridges, and the volcanic boulders pile up in formidable shapes. My girth loosens and I dismount to fix it. The command moves on and is lost to sight in a deep ravine. Presently I resume my journey, and in the meshwork of ravines I find that I no longer see the trail of the column. I retrace and climb and slide down hill, forcing my way through chapparal, and after a long time I see the pack-mules go out of sight far away on a mountain slope. The blue peaks of the Pinals tower away on my left, and I begin to indulge in mean thoughts concerning the indomitable spirit of Lieutenant Jim, for I know he will take us clear over the top of that pale blue line of far-distant mountains.

In course of time I came up with the command, which had stopped at a ledge so steep that it had daunted even these mountaineers. It was only a hundred foot drop, and they presently found a place to go down, where, as one soldier suggested, "there isn't footing for a lizard." On we go, when suddenly with a great crash some sandy ground gives way, and a collection of hoofs, troop-boots, ropes, canteens, and flying stirrups goes rolling over in a cloud of dust and finds lodgment in the bottom of a dry watercourse. The dust settles and discloses a soldier and his horse. They rise to their feet and appear astonished, but as the soldier mounts and follows on we know he is unhurt. Now a coyote, surprised by our cavalcade and unable to get up the ledge, runs along the opposite side of the canyon wall. "Pop, pop, pop, pop" go the six-shooters, and then follow explanations by each marksman of the particular thing which made him miss.

That night we were forced to make a "dry camp"; that is, one where no water is to be found. There is such an amount of misery locked up in the thought of a dry camp that I refuse to dwell upon it.

We were glad enough to get upon the trail in the morning, and in time found a nice running mountain-brook. The command wallowed in it. We drank as much as we could hold and then sat down. We arose and drank some more, and yet we drank again, and still once more, until we were literally water-logged. Lieutenant Jim became uneasy, so we took up our march. We were always resuming the march when all nature called aloud for rest. We climbed straight up impossible places. The air grew chill, and in a gorge a cold wind blew briskly down to supply the hot air rising from sands of the mesa far below. That night we made a camp, and the only place where I could make my bed was on a great flat rock. We were now among the pines, which towered above us. The horses were constantly losing one another in the timber in their search for grass, in consequence of which they whinnied, while the mules brayed, and made the mountain hideous with sound.

By another long climb we reached the extreme peaks of the Pinal range, and there before us was spread a view which was grand enough to compensate us for the labor. Beginning in "gray reds," range after range of mountains, overlapping each other, grow purple and finally lose themselves in pale blues. We sat on a ledge and gazed. The soldiers were interested, though their remarks about the scenery somehow did not seem to express an appreciation of the grandeur of the view which impressed itself strongly upon us. Finally one fellow, less aesthetic than his mates, broke the spell by a request for chewing-tobacco, so we left off dreaming and started on.

That day Lieutenant Jim lost his bearings, and called upon that instinct which he had acquired in his life among the Indians. He "cut the signs" of old Indian trails and felt the course to be in a certain direction -- which was undoubtedly correct, but it took us over the highest points of the Mescal range. My shoes were beginning to give out, and the troop-boots of several soldiers threatened to disintegrate. One soldier, more ingenious than the rest, took out some horse-shoe nails and cleverly mended his boot-gear. At times we wound around great slopes where a loose stone or the giving way of bad ground would have precipitated horse and rider a thousand feet below. Only the courage of the horses brings one safely through. The mules suffered badly.

At last we reached the Gila, and nearly drowned a pack-mule and two troopers in the quicksand. We began to pass Indian huts, and saw them gathering wheat in the river bottoms, while they paused to gaze at us and doubtless wondered for what purpose the buffalo-soldiers were abroad in the land. The cantonment appeared, and I was duly gratified when we reached it. I hobbled up to the "Grand Hotel" of my host the captain, who laughed heartily at my floundering movements and observed my nose and cheeks, from which the sun had peeled the skin, with evident relish at the thought of how I had been used by his lieutenant. At his suggestion I was made an honorary member of the cavalry, and duly admonished "not to trifle again with the 10th Nubian Horse if I expected any mercy."

In due time the march continued without particular incident, and at last the scout "pulled in" to the home post, and I again sat in my easy-chair behind the lattice-work, firm in the conviction that soldiers, like other men, find more hard work than glory in their calling.

Frederic Remington was born in St. Lawrence County New York, in 1861. He studied drawing for a year in the Yale School of Fine Arts at New Haven, and went West in 1880. With the exception of this single year of instruction, he derived all his knowledge from constant observation and study. He wrote entertainingly and accurately of life in the West, as well as illustrating it in his drawings and pictures.

###

The following is the text of a communication between French Army commanders during World War I which cites shows how Black American soldiers assigned to Europe were to be treated.

Headquarters of the Army

August 14, 1918

The General of the Boissiudy Division

Commander of the 7th Army

The Chief of Vosges

The Chief of the Leurthe-et-Loselle

"The American 92nd Division, a division composed entirely of colored soldiers, is at the disposal of the 7th Army as of the 12th of the current month, the date of its arrival at the Arches camp.

This Infantry Division, which will later fight in the Saint-Dié sector, will be stationed on the territory of the Vosges province and near the Meurthe-et-Moselle to the north of the area (Raon-l'Etape – Thiaville). "The negro question" is considered by our allies to be a particularly delicate matter, which point of view should not be discussed but should be accepted.

The French Mission to the American Army has explained to the General commanding the Army the attitude that we should adopt regarding colored troops, which is the attitude of white Americans, in military matters as well as in contacts between negroes and our local populations.

The Commander-in-Chief of the Army has the pleasure of communicating these observations to the Commanders concerned in order that these officials let it be known that local authorities should act in a reserved manner in dealing with colored men.

Try and make local people understand that they should not spoil the negros. The Americans are indignant at any <u>public intimacy</u> between white women and blacks. They have recently raised vehement protests against an engraving of the <u>Vie Parisienne</u> entitled: "The Child of the Dessert" representing a woman in her room with a negro.

Furthermore, American negro troops in France have by themselves raised as many complaints of attempted rape as all the rest of the Army although we were sent only the physical and moral elite."

Chapter 12

NASCAR MOCKUMENTARY
A STRUGGLE ISLAND
VIDEO PRODUCTION

T his Borough of Staten Island, one of the five that make up the City of New York,

is, like others, seemingly filled with unending contradictions and monumental problems. Young people must be encouraged to believe that there is a possibility for change. My view is that many people here are frozen into a state of limbo. They are unable to act or think rationally because of the sheer magnitude or complexity of life's problems. Some people here are so frightened by the future and so discouraged by society's ills that they simply drop out. There are others who foolishly believe that if someone simply recognizes a problem and states it, it will somehow automatically be solved.

Me, I am in limbo. It would be generally, I feel, recognized that Staten Island has changed. Staten islanders believe that it has changed because of The Bridge. The bridge is the Verrazano. The feelings about the bridge run deep. There are three other bridges, but they do not lead to New York. One bridge is the Goethals Bridge which leads to Elizabeth, NJ. The Bayonne Bridge leads to Bayonne, NJ, and the Outer Bridge Crossing leads also to New Jersey.

Many who crossed the Verrazano Bridge in the mid-60s felt that they were moving to a Shangri-La. Perhaps today in 2012 many of those feelings have changed. It is no longer a sleepy, warm, home Borough. The Borough's population is almost 500,000. The triangular shaped Borough is seven miles wide and thirteen miles long. At one time, Staten Island was a place of 61 individual neighborhoods. Today, Staten Islanders have been divvied up into a Borough of four wider designations. There is the North Shore, the South Shore, the West Shore, and the Mid Island Section. The Island's history is hidden within the names of communities that no one knows. Ask a pedestrian where would I find Bay Terrace, Arrochar, Chelsea, Huguenot, Shore Acres, or Ocean Breeze? Very few could point out those destinations, and I'm sure that there are very few people who would know where to find Bloomfield.

From my files I find that the International Speedway Corporation, the ISC, NASCAR, the country's largest motor sports raceway, announced that it had signed a deal to buy 600 acres in Bloomfield to build the New York Metropolitan Area's first NASCAR race track. The representatives from NASCAR had said they would build an 80,000 seat raceway stadium in the shadow of the Goethals Bridge. Reading this, I simply tore it out and filed it away.

I knew where Bloomfield was located, but Staten Island is no longer the unhurried, uncongested, and unpolluted place it was before the mammoth span Verrazano linked Staten Island to its other gritty urban siblings, the other Boroughs New York and Brooklyn. And much of the blame belongs to the unplanned and unbridled development that has caused the population of the Island to skyrocket. Looking back at five or six decades in hindsight, it appears that the Staten Islanders were sold up the proverbial river with promises and more promises. After the bridge, they were promised a superhighway system that would traverse the Island from east to west and west to east. A never-completed highway now carries trucks, cars, vans, vehicles, across the Island, speeding between Brooklyn and New Jersey. Compounding the traffic is the Howland Hook Shipping Container Port which is also in the shadow of the Goethals Bridge. I wonder if many Staten Islanders still enjoy their geography, the closeness to Manhattan as being the center of the universe. No, this is not country laid-back living.

I would find again and again articles about NASCAR, usually front page articles of the only newspaper on Staten Island, the *Staten Island Advance*. I'm familiar with the Bloomfield land. I remember in 1973 there was an explosion inside a liquefied natural gas tank that was operated by the Texas Eastern Transmission Company. It killed 40 men who were working inside the tank. One of the men happened to have been a friend of mine.

The articles continued almost weekly. The NASCAR affiliate, based in Daytona Beach, FL, announced that they would transform these 450 acres of unused industrial land on the northwest tip of Staten Island for the country's most popular sport. Questions at their news conference at the *Advance*: What about the traffic? How can you relieve the inevitable traffic? Their answer came from their heavy-hitters; they proposed a complex network of ferries, charter buses, and park-and-ride lots that would allow the fans to reach the site during their three race weekends per year. That's right, three scheduled races in one year. They also promised more than $350 million in construction wages during the two years it would take to build the track, and this track would contribute over $200 million to the Staten Island economy every year, including ticket sales, food &

beverage sales, hotel bookings, and they would help Staten Island navigate the shoals of city politics.

The rotten smell began for me when I would read that the former Borough President, Guy Molinari, was hired as a lobbyist. Phone calls to Mr. Molinari at his office seeking comment would not be confirmed. The newspaper would not rest. Learning that the Molinari Group would consist of Guy Molinari, a former United States Representative and former member of the New York State Assembly, and Staten Island attorney John D'Amato.

When Guy Molinari appeared at his office front, facing a group of citizens asking questions, Molinari said that he planned to shop the proposal for the stadium with Mayor Michael Bloomberg, before the City Comptroller William C Thompson, and he would shop this before Governor George Pataki in the near future. There were major sticking points and Molinari refused answers, waving his hand, returning to his office in West Brighton. "Wait, wait," one person called. "Who is going to to use the stadium if they are only going to use it for three big races a year? Who is going to use it over the course of the year?" "I just don't understand the sport of racing," he mentioned. "We will cover this eventually." His reply to the reporter standing beside him was "Well, beside the races the track would be available for events like car and boat shows, or even charity functions."

The political smell gathering around the voices of NASCAR grew more pungent; it is perhaps no laughing matter that most Americans, like Staten islanders, have given up hope about the possibility of honesty in politics. What is happening today is hardly new. It just feels that way.

The Staten Island Advance would continue probing for answers, touching on the past history of the former Borough President, who was a real estate lawyers before he entered politics in 1974. He told the *Advance* that he purchased a number of properties in early years, but he also declined to say how many parcels he still owned. "I stopped investing in real estate when I went into office," Molinari said. "In my twelve years as Borough President I never met with a builder or developer to buy or to sell property. People don't believe that, but I don't care. Did I make any profit in real estate? That's none of your business. It's a nice term," he said. "If you have a piece of property that you've owned and you sell it, is that profit?"

Some observers in the real estate industry maintain that, unlike his associates, Molinari was never interested in buying property and selling it for profit. One friend of Molinari's, Robert Fitzsimmons, said "Why I've known Guy for about 35 or 40 years and money was never important to him." Molinari said that he should have the same rights as any land owner and he would tout his record on re-zoning and his Borough-wide efforts to seek less dense housing on Staten Island. "I've invested much time in the program of rezoning Staten Island. We've cut in half the number of homes that could be built here. It's all BS, that's what it is." And he said that he was not bothered that the land that he and his partners would be selling might eventually be covered in town houses. "Well, you can't control what buyers are going to do with the land you sell them." Molinari, indignant, stormed back inside his office again.

The problems would not subside. James Oddo, the Mid-Island councilman called one of Guy Molinari's real estate friends "The Man in the Black Hat." Oddo said "He's the guy to go to if you want to exploit a piece of property." Who is this? Who is this?" someone shouted. "Stanley Krebushevski," Oddo said. "He's the guy in the black hat." Molinari would not comment. He said, "I'm in support of a mid-Island blue belt and it would limit development in the wetlands. That's all it is."

The current Borough President, James Molinaro, when asked about the real estate controversy said "If I knew Guy Molinari owned that land, I would not have made the same statement." He added that any property owner who sells land should get a fair market value for it. Jimmy Oddo agreed, but if this property is deemed by the DEC or the DEP, it's vital to the greenbelt then, regardless of who owns it. I will still move forward to stop any building from taking place." Molinari in response acknowledged that he and his co-owners are under contract to sell the property. The newspapers had obtained a copy of the signed contract of sale that notes a $750,000 purchase price and lists Molinari as one of the owners. Molinari said that he fully supports the blue-belt concept but he had said that, "The city has an option to move swiftly and come up with a plan and adequately compensate affected property owners. That's my position."

The newspaper articles would continue to command the front pages of the *Advance*. One article referred to the developer, NASCAR, having to put down more than 1 million cubic yards of clean fill as part of the State mandated cleanup of Bloomfield. He said Michael Printup would appear at the *Advance*. He said "We have obtained a developer that would spread out and compact fill as it comes onto the property." "This is in response from the State after decades of petroleum contamination at the site."

"Of course, the company doesn't break down item by item how it will spend the money on Staten Island, but this will likely come from the site improvement work." Michael Printup, the ISC Staten Island Manager for NASCAR said.

"Yes, we understand that the track land once housed an above-ground oil tank farm, and they have been demolished, and we will remove any contaminated soil." The statement, a few days later, would appear in *The New York Times* that Mr. William Kilgannon, an employee of the ISC NASCAR, employed in the planning and design of the proposed NASCAR track on Staten Island. Mr. Kilgannon would plead guilty in an indictment that was handed down by the US Attorney. Another man, Mr. Todd Polakoff, a construction manager at the site of the ISC subsidiary would also be indicted. Both worked for the North American Testing Company.

Following the smell, the odor not of Bloomfield, but of the machinations in the papers, headline "Officials demand answers on tainted soil at the proposed NASCAR site." The article on the front page mentioned that the ISC, the company hoping to build a NASCAR track on Staten Island, voluntarily relinquished its license to cart soil onto its property, and local officials are demanding to know what was wrong with the fill. One Assemblyman said "We are here to ask the ISC to be good neighbors. We need an answer."

At a news conference hurriedly convened outside the acreage, Michael Printup would say "It's troubling to see these reports about contaminated soil, and we're not sure what that means." The State and City agencies investigating the soil have refused to say what triggered the termination of the permits, and any subsequent investigations. The agencies have been vague when explaining the problems with the fill, and the ISC NASCAR has been equally reticent to discuss the issue.

John E. Graham, the first Vice President of ISC, issued a strongly worded document "We are continuing to work with the State Department of Environmental Conservation and the City Department of Sanitation toward a completely satisfactory fill material operation at our project site. The condition of the site is vastly superior to its condition when we purchased it in 1904. The remediation has been undertaken ever since then." John E. Graham did not answer further questions.

Later the ISC lost a separate permit also issued by the Sanitation Department to cart fill to the site. The Department of Sanitation would also not disclose any information. A spokesman from the State agency would divulge only that the soil samples provided by the development contained just a slight level elevation of a semi-volatile organic compound, and they would not say which compound was discovered, or its potential impact on any other soil tested at the site. The US EPA defines a semivolatile organic compound as having a "boiling point higher than water, and it may vaporize when exposed to temperatures above room temperature. Semivolatile organic compounds include phenols and polynuclear aromatic hydrocarbons." Councilman James Oddo said "That's nothing that we don't know. We think it's incumbent on the ISC and NASCAR to step up and explain what the scope of this issue is."

Michael Printup was the ISC NASCAR New York Project Manager. He had met several times with the Staten Island Chamber of Commerce President, Linda Baran, who called the ISC's project "A benefit to the community." And she would enter with the sports motor giant into a Community Benefit Agreement, or a CBA. Linda Baran also pointed out that the Economic Development Corporation, headed by Cesar Claro, would also seek to back the NASCAR project. Speaking at the Chamber office, Linda Baran said that the Chamber would seek guarantees on jobs for residents, promises for residents, and assurances that local contractors and vendors would be used. She also promised that the CBA with NASCAR would give preferential treatment to Islanders and Staten Island based businesses.

The word "promises" continued to raise my ears. The Chamber of Commerce would appear several times in the *Staten Island Advance* presenting multimedia presentations from the ISC. Linda Baran said "This is a guarantee before settling on the idea of any binding agreement." Linda Baran said that the binding agreement would focus solely on guarantees for Staten Island business residents, and she stated that the transportation infrastructure is a separate issue. She noted that the ISC recognizes that, but the ISC would become an ally of Staten Island when pushing government agencies to make transportation improvements like passenger rail lines along the North and West Shores, "While the Chamber acknowledges that traffic is an issue," she said, "we feel it is unfair to expect or demand that NASCAR alone should cure the problems for both you and I after decades of poor planning."

Again there were promises. Somehow, reading the bits of information began to worry me. Like many other businesses that came to Struggle Island they would promise jobs and hope to the people of the Island, and I wondered if this 600 acreage would really make history for Staten Island. The articles would pile up on my desk, my little notebooks grew, as the statements would appear in the papers.

I realized that the contemporary people on Staten Island knew very little about the Bloomfield property or what the Chamber of Commerce and the Staten Island Economic Development Corporation were doing. There was very little about the background published. Again and again the Project Manager from NASCAR, Michael Printup, would make front page statements, such as "We are not seeking public funding on Staten Island, but Staten Island will see millions of dollars a year in tax breaks for the next 15 to 25 years. We have an as-of-right city incentive program."

I didn't understand "as-of-right city incentive program." It didn't smell right, and when I asked those at these impromptu meetings what it meant, very few knew any more than I did about the "as-of-right incentive program." Who was behind it? Who was proposing the tax break? And who was proposing to give away to a builder such vague references as "right of effort, as of right." Never could understand it, but I would copy articles, vague details, about how they would fill the 80,000 seat stadium, how they would operate ferries from Brooklyn, Manhattan, and various points in New Jersey.

The lobbyists and consultants would submit beautifully rendered pictorial pages in the newspaper, all of which left me baffled. I was also constantly baffled by the lack of response from the councilmen. When asked by reporters, one councilman responded "Why, I'm not looking to bash them. I just say there are large pieces of this puzzle missing and this piece of that puzzle shows what benefits Staten Islanders will have out of this NASCAR stadium. Why would they build a stadium that would only be used for three days a year?" That councilman was Michael McMahon. Another councilman, Jim Oddo, said "This notion that there's additional capacity for 8,400 cars I think is a false premise, and I think there remains a fundamental flaw in their traffic plan."

But there were heavy hitters working in the background for NASCAR. Besides the Molinari Group of lobbyists from Staten Island, there was Ostroff, Hiffa & Associates, a New York lobbying firm. There was the Yoswein New York public affairs firm based in Manhattan, and Eng-Wong, Taub & Associates, based in New York and New Jersey, a consulting firm specializing in traffic engineering and transportation planning. There was Wachtel Masyr & Missry, a land use law firm based in Manhattan and Albany, and Dmjm Harris, a traffic planner and engineer specializing in marine transportation and port infrastructure. There was also Game Day Management Consultants that would provide traffic management plans for major spectator events, home base in Florida. These heavy hitters were constantly working behind the scenes, their powers would be felt whenever their voice was needed.

Anthony Lanza would continue to ask "Before you start to figure out how you _can_ make it work, you've got to tell us why we should make it work. I don't have people beating down my door on Staten Island demanding that we bring Staten Island and NASCAR together." Bit by bit the sides were beginning to take shape.

I was born on Staten Island and know very well that the Borough has faced many years of frustration in getting an additional piece of property sited for a fast ferry to Manhattan, or any improvements for the commuters. Where would those fast ferries go on the non-race days? NASCAR promised 83 ferries. What would happen to the 83 ferries on the

A 25

THURSDAY
MAY 4, 2006

GOSSIP   A 26
MOVIES   A 27
YOUNG ADVANCE   A 28
TV   A 29
ADVICE   A 30

FEEDBACK

NASCAR mayhem: Prelude to a war of words

PRO-NASCAR TRACK GOONS HIJACKED THE HEARING

I was in attendance [Thursday] night at the ISC/NASCAR hearings at the Petrides Complex. If I were not already against the track, that would have made my decision for me. Those against the track were well-behaved until the riff-raff that NASCAR so obviously loaded the meeting with started getting way out of hand. It was almost frightening and should stand 'as a small example of what we can expect from this gang of goons when they get a tank full of high-octane booze in them on a race day I was proud of the way Councilmen Andrew Lanza and James Oddo conducted themselves and handled the situation.

Also, the NYPD and its commanders present should be lauded for the patience and prudence they displayed in exercising great restraint and calling an immediate halt to the whole fiasco before it got further out of hand. I am convinced that a very major incident had been averted.

DOROTHY SARANTOPOULOS
GRANT CITY

BLAME UNION 'YELLOW CAPS' FOR DISRUPTING HEARING

My husband and I attended, if only briefly, the NASCAR meeting at the Petrides Complex. While we waited on line to sign in, we noted a large contingent of yellow caps in the front of the line.

Once in the auditorium, we

"I admired Mr. Lanza's courage in facing this crowd."
— GLADYS DIXON, RICHMOND

"Lanza succeeded in baiting an individual and a lesser person may have been charged with inciting a riot."
— ROBERT PRINDLE, GREAT KILLS

LANZA COULD HAVE BEEN CHARGED WITH INCITING RIOT

Arriving at Petrides on a nice Thursday night, I was pleasantly surprised by what appeared to be an overwhelming majority of NASCAR supporters. There were in my estimation, another 200 protrack people outside who could not gain admittance.

As a vocal supporter of NASCAR, I was happy that the day finally arrived where International Speedway Corp. would make their presentation and shoot down the lies and half-truths that anti-track doomsayers put out there.

All three of Staten Island's councilmen were present – all three who had no problems or concerns for the people of The Bronx voting for a new Yankee Stadium with its 80-plus days of 25,000 cars.

Councilman Lanza succeeded in baiting an individual and a lesser person may have been charged with inciting a riot.

It's well documented by now what happened, but only an ignorant person would say that union personnel, looking out for their own interests, are the face of NASCAR. Unfortunately for the people of Staten Island, they are represented by two councilmen who fit that description and I'm not so sure about the third.

ROBERT PRINDLE
GREAT KILLS

LANZA BLEW UP MEETING DELIBERATELY

Let's tell the truth about what really happened to cause

Staten Island Advance

50 CENTS

FRIDAY, APRIL 28, 2006

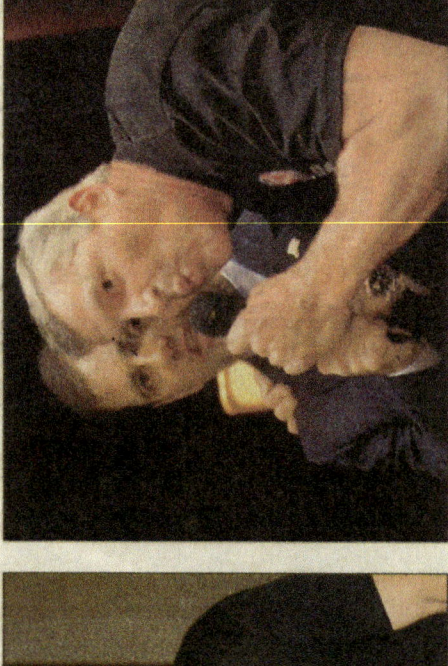

THE CONFRONTATION: Wallace takes over the microphone and denounces the councilman's comments.

STATEN ISLAND ADVANCE/NICHOLAS FEVELO

THE STAREDOWN: Wallace was upset by Lanza's assertion that the labor activists were not Staten Island residents.

STATEN ISLAND ADVANCE/JIN LEE

THE ANGER: Labor activist Christopher Wallace of Westerleigh tries to shout down Councilman Andrew Lanza.

STATEN ISLAND ADVANCE/JIN LEE

NEAR RIOT SHUTS NASCAR HEARING

Jammed forum turns to mayhem when official goads labor activists

By JOHN ANNESE
STATEN ISLAND ADVANCE

The first public hearing on the proposed NASCAR race-track here turned so rowdy last night that police shut it down in less than an hour.

The crowd — which numbered close to 1,000 people — jammed into the Petrides Educational Complex auditorium in Sunnyside and was unruly from the beginning, shouting down track developers and elected officials alike.

Emotions ran so strong that one Staten Island track supporter nearly put a borough councilman in a headlock.

"He doesn't have a right to that mike!" screamed Westerleigh resident and union official Christopher Wallace, as he wrapped his arm around Councilman Andrew Lanza's shoulders and tried to yank a microphone out of his hand.

Lanza had triggered that reaction by suggesting that track developer International Speedway Corp. (ISC) shipped construction union members from off-Island to support the Bloomfield project, which would provide jobs.

STATEN ISLAND ADVANCE PHOTOS/JIN LEE

Police officials shut down the hearing and ordered an estimated crowd of 1,000 to leave less than an hour after it started.

The author (circled in red) amid the chaos at the NASCAR hearing.

Above: NASCAR representatives seek S.I. support for the stadium.

Right: Councilman Andrew Lanza at the NASCAR confrontation with Christopher Wallace.

non-race days? How would they justify the capital investment that they were speaking of? Again, there were promises.

Staten Island people were working behind the scenes: former Borough President Guy Molinari, and his political ally attorney John D'Amato made up the Molinari Group. They spoke of jobs, community events; I wondered what community event on Staten Island would require an 80,000 seat facility. There was a brand new baseball stadium in St. George with immediate access to ferry and train transportation, and the attendance numbers were always less than hoped for.

The Goethals Bridge, that would lead almost directly to the NASCAR stadium, would serve as an entry point for the prospective race fans from New Jersey. This 80-year-old relic was incapable of accommodating the endless stream of busses it would take to bring tens of thousands of people from remote parking spaces elsewhere to the track on race days. The daily traffic of containers from the Howland Hook Container Port is a constant flow holding up traffic on the Goethals Bridge that seems to be always under constant repair.

I began to see the larger picture of a hopelessly impossible dream. It was finally revealed that the former Borough President, Guy Molinari, at one time the Republican Party Chairman, who had formed the Molinari Group lobbying firm was in trouble. There were reports of Guy Molinari seeking concessions quietly from his old friends. There would be reports of him privately escorting councilmen to off-Island NASCAR events. There was also a continued newspaper articles of NASCAR paying the Molinari Group $1.5 million for their lobbying efforts. The Molinari Group, it was said, pulled in $15,000 a month from the ISC. This was according to lobbying records filed with the state. However, sources from the *New York Post* newspaper found that Molinari's company was paid an additional $35,000 a month to rev up community support for the 80,000 seat racetrack. The latter figure, it was found, included in a separate contract, previously unknown to the public.

When asked about the $35,000 state lobbying records uncovered Guy V. Molinari would not comment on the compensation issue, citing a confidentiality agreement with ISC. Michael Printup would interrupt saying that the dollar amounts paid to the Molinari Group was "a great idea for the job that Guy is doing for us and we are moving on."

I know this Staten Island a bit. I know a bit about its people. I've been a Staten Islander for over eight decades, and I listen and I see a parallel universe, and I'm acutely aware that…

I would note that the well-dressed white men wearing suits and ties, white shirts and polished wing-tipped shoes were somehow different. How, you may ask. Just a feeling. NASCAR would use the "carrot and the stick" approach. An article on the front page of the *Staten Island Advance* read "NASCAR Raises Money for Island Causes." Drivers from the NASCAR Company would tour the Staten Island University Hospital; they would sign autographs, and meet the public. The well-publicized arrival of these drivers would ultimately raise $151,000. One NASCAR driver, Carl Edwards, who wouldn't know Staten Island from Rikers Island, came in by helicopter. "Is that Staten Island," he asked, pointing?" "Gosh! And I saw the Statue of Liberty for the first time." He announced. "I felt like a kid again!"

The other drivers, Jimmie Johnson, Kurt Busch, and Brian Vickers, would hold a silent auction at the Vanderbilt Restaurant in South Beach. When asked why they had come to Staten Island to raise money for a burn unit at the Staten Island University Hospital, one of the drivers said "There are times when a car accident happens. The vehicle catches fire, and many times when that happens the driver is burned, so we will need to know that there are hospitals available to treat burn victims." The carrot and stick approach was working perfectly.

I had to step back just to find out what I knew about automobile racing, which was very little. I knew virtually nothing about NASCAR, the ISC, and NASCAR racing. There was a time when Staten Island had its own demolition derby which was held at the Weissglass Stadium on Richmond Terrace in Port Richmond. Gabe Rispoli was top man, top dog, at smashing them up every weekend. When I did find myself able to afford a stadium seat, I realized that Staten Island demolition derby was a joy to watch. The huge vehicles, 700-800 horsepower, 2-3 ton Oldsmobiles, Buicks, the souped-up Caddys and Fords with the straight-pipe muffler which was to give it a more fearsome sound. They were, as many of my friends would say, "bad mothers."

It was a joy, even if I could not understand this ungodly racket, and why the bashing was necessary. It was the noisiest place on Staten Island. You could hear the sound of the engines a mile away. 30 to 40 jalopies smashing into one another at 50, 60, and 70 miles per hour, propelled by these souped-up horsepower engines. They would sound like dive bombers, or angry bees coming out of their nests. In order to communicate with anyone next to you, you had to shake them and scream in their ear. I also realized that there were many accidents after leaving the stadium when men, drinking, would attempt to race other testosterone-loaded, boozed up friends down Richmond Terrace.

This was a NASCAR that I knew. But the NASCAR that was asking for a place on Staten Island is quite different. Cesar Claro, the Staten Island Economic Development Company CEO would continue to say that the track and the adjoining retail center would spark millions of dollars in activity directly on Staten Island. This would generate tens of millions of dollars in annual tax revenue and create jobs for the Borough's unemployed. I didn't know what to believe, I didn't know what questions to ask.

The pro and con factions on Staten Island were beginning to take shape. The ex-Borough President Guy Molinari usually issued statements to the *Advance* more often now; he would be hunkered down in his office, appearing from time to time to answer questions from the public that would gather in front of his office. He would emerge from time to time to confront a new group from Staten Island called SCAT (Staten Island Citizens Against the Track). SCAT was a group hurriedly formed to fight the proposal to bring NASCAR to Staten Island. The signs were hurriedly made, some reading "Would you want motor homes parked in your driveway?" Attorney John D'Amato, a partner in Molinari's lobbying firm would stand out front and argue that the track would be more benign than the usual industrial warehouses or other options for this property. "How do you think you'd feel if you woke up one day to find a couple of RVs parked on your block, and the people who came along with them were breaking out the grills and lawn chairs?" the woman screamed over and over again.

John E. Graham would e-mail Molinari and D'Amato constantly. "Take them down to the Tennessee track. Take them down for free. Let them see, let them hear."

The SCAT people would not be deterred. "This is not going to happen. There is no opportunity," the SCAT citizens would respond. D'Amato was forced to retreat inside the Molinari Group offices while a policeman would be stationed on the sidewalk outside the doors.

The timeline would continue in the *Advance*. The NASCAR events would sign a $4 billion eight-year television deal. **The** ISC would secure endorsements from the Staten Island Economic Development Corporation and union officials. The City Council speaker Christine Quinn would counsel a sit-down meeting with ISC NASCAR officials and the three Staten Island councilmen. One councilman said he would not attend, not after the mob-tied conviction of the site people, unless there was more information. The Department of Sanitation would issue nothing more than had been published.

The followers would meet the fans, the standoffs would continue in the streets, in the newspapers, in paper handouts at the ferry terminal and in the streets. I would listen to both sides of the issue. What I did realize was that there were powerful forces in the wings NASCAR was a fast-growing sport; it came out of the makeshift dirt tracks in the south. One of the promoters of NASCAR, Bill France, (France Sr. was the co-founder of NASCAR, Jr. was the CEO) gave a long talk on how and why the NASCAR business was founded. Many of the NASCAR folk heroes came out of the south, and France spoke of the biggest races for NASCAR at Daytona 500, when they were driving without sponsors, when their beat-up automobiles would trounce the Detroit automakers, but he would also concede that the moonshining connection helped NASCAR a lot more than hurt it. It was no longer a P.T. Barnum event.

"Yes," he continued, "many of the original drivers grew up hauling moonshine when all the roads were dirt. We didn't have no paved roads out in the country, so we learned to drive dirt. It was very good because that's where we would go to get away from the law was how we did it. We was moonshine runners."

Moonshining was a cat and mouse game that had been going on in the Appalachian Mountains for more than 200 years. The federal government had imposed a tax on whiskey that sparked an armed uprising in the hills. Many people forgot the Whiskey Rebellion. When the revenuers came it was a high speed road race and guys who could outrun the Revenuers became local heroes. They had their own mechanics skilled at goosing up cars to get their maximum speed. Yes, racing reeked of red necked stereotypes: hillbillies, bootleggers, the whole dog patch tobacco road aura that middle class southerners were struggling to overcome. And with it was the corn liquor and hillbilly music.

Many of the men who are racecar drivers originally came back after serving in WWII. What a world war taught the rural southern boys was that there was more to life than working on farms or in furniture mills. They wanted the adventure so racing attracted them.

Research was necessary for me to find out what should be said about things like NASCAR. I had a feeling, and the feeling was correct, about the $146 million NASCAR

Hall of Fame that was taking shape in Charlotte, NC. The racing fans were then arguing over the nominees for the first five inductees to be honored there. There was a debate over a name missing from the 25 contenders. The missing name would be a NASCAR pioneering Black driver, Wendell O. Scott.

Wendell Scott was a hero NASCAR didn't want. The omission of the Black driver would stir up broader discussion of NASCAR's past discrimination and what the critics say is a continued record as the nation's least diverse major sport. Wendell Scott broke the racial barrier more than a half century ago, and now, despite a nine year diversity program, all but one of the 130 regular drivers in NASCAR's three national racing series are white males. The sole ethnic minority is Juan Pablo Montoya who is Hispanic.

The history of Scott's roadblocks remains largely ignored by NASCAR. Wendell Scott never received corporate sponsors which could have afforded him a first-rate vehicle and a professional crew. Wendell Scott served as his own mechanic, made do with inferior cars and amateur crews, and sometimes ran a race on recapped tires. "They wasn't going to help a Black man. That's all there was to it." And until sponsorship is attached to diversity drivers no one is going to make it. Wendell Scott died in Virginia in 1990 at the age of 69.

Wendell Scott also honed his skills by outracing law enforcement men to haul moonshine. In the racing business Wendell Scott is called the Jackie Robinson of racing. The most egregious humiliation came in a minor 1963 race in Jacksonville, FL. Wendell Scott won the race by two laps, even beating Richard Petty, but the officials at the race apparently blanched at the prospect of the winner's customary kiss for the local white beauty queen, so the scoreboard went blank, the chequered flag was withheld, and the runner up was crowned the victor. Everyone in the place knew that Wendell Scott won the race. Officials later conceded that it was a "scoring error" and privately gave Wendell O. Scott a crude wooden trophy with no inscription.

In October of 2010, after a 47 year odyssey, Scott's family was finally presented with a replica of the trophy he should have been awarded. As a possible nominee for the 2013 inductees into the NASCAR Hall of Fame Wendell Scott did not receive sufficient votes to be inducted.

On Staten Island I would continue to try to monitor the papers, and the pro and con conversations. The wheelings and dealings, the lobbying, was in-your-face. This was Staten Island and Guy Molinari would use whatever was necessary to convince the politicians to use their votes to allow NASCAR to bring its racing to Staten Island. There were dinners and late night meetings at the La Fontana restaurant in Oakwood. Guy Molinari would discuss the project with Jimmy Oddo; another dinner with Andrew Lanza. Around the dinner table there were smiles and toasts. Molinari was easily excitable and he was overheard loudly saying "My God. Don't you see it? This is a benefit." Afterward, Molinari in his anger would leave, saying to everyone within earshot "I'm not going out of here to support Oddo or Lanza."

As a highly paid lobbyist, ex-Borough President Guy Molinari was frustrated, and the public sides were gearing up. Audiences were demonstrating at Borough Hall, and different groups were being interviewed. Margie Bald Eagle, whose roots go back to the Lenape Indian Tribes, believed that the site at Bloomfield may be the graveyard for artifacts that her relatives used to hunt, build shelters, and cook in this area. "We know that the Tribes were here on Staten Island," she continued. "Because of the location of the creek, the wetlands would have been an ideal place for the Lenapes, an occupational site."

Mr. and Mrs. Gene Cosgriffe, the Staten Islanders from Rossville who waged a successful fight against the liquefied natural gas tanks in Rossville, came out several times against the building on this site without a memorial to the men who died there.

I would note from articles time and time again that there was no Black voice and no Black organizations to take a stand, pro, or con.

Staten Island is unusual among the Five Boroughs. A quarter of a mile away in Bloomfield is the only trailer park in New York City. People have lived in trailers on Staten Island for over 30 years, and it is just over the road at 278 Forest Avenue, 200 yards from the Goethals Bridge. The people in the trailer park were silent, never asked for their opinions. My visit there was strange. There were very few people with whom I could speak. One man asked "What's in that stadium for Staten Islanders?" I responded that the developers said they would have more jobs, national recognition, tax revenues, and a "fuel-boost" of cash into the island's economy. The response was, as usual, a shrug.

Again and again, NASCAR would host families and groups from Staten Island to a race track in Kansas City, KS; it would be the first of several trips the developers used to woo the local dignitaries and families.

A point man, Michael Printup, was actively involved in the PR to downplay the actions of SCAT, while playing up the $4.8 billion television deal. There were constant references with the Staten Island Economic Development Corporation and the city's union officials. The EDC released a 40-page accumulation of the traffic feasibility assessments. I realized that the inner circle was moving rapidly.

The dinners and the late night meetings at La Fontana restaurant would continue. A special emissary from ISC NASCAR was sent to Republican John Markey's office in Albany, but it was reported that Senator Markey was ill; he had been hospitalized, and he was pending retirement. But the push would never cease and the staggering price of NASCAR's dream would continue to rise. Six members of ISC would fly in for a personal meeting at the Staten Island headquarters, among them H. Lee Combs, SVP, John E. Graham, Jr., VP, and Robert Orsini, VP. They would lay out their plans and present documents. They would ask for a public review, they asked for questions, and they would respond with more documents.

The senior officials of NASCAR would leave with a firm commitment that they would have a public hearing on Staten Island to present their case about the proposal to the public. In May 2006 an article in the *Staten Island Advance* announced that there would be an open public meeting at the Petrides School complex. I had been on Staten Island during that spring, and I would make it my business to attend the NASCAR meeting at the Michael J. Petrides School just off the expressway.

I knew the school, I knew the environment; I would drive there and make it my business to attend this forum. I arrived at the Petrides School about three hours before the City

Planning Commission where the public hearing was to take place. The various factions from island organizations, the pros and the cons, had staked out their spaces in the outside quadrangle. The cons were easily visible with their signs: "Save our Wetlands" and "Raceway No Way." The NASCAR yellow caps and the red t-shirts were handed out from boxes freely to anyone who asked for them. There were plastic bags along with paper signs promoting NASCAR's position.

Several men standing nearby in suits and ties quietly observed the NASCAR group. They were huddled together at one side of the building, occasionally walking to one group or the other, shaking hands, and saying "Glad you could be here." There were a few western hats and boots, blue jeans, bikers, motorcycles, and souped-up cars. I thought I was parked safely at a distance from the gathering because the union buses had dislodged members with shirts indicating that they were from different trades unions: steamfitters, firemen, roofers, water proofers, and carpenters; they also laid out their coolers of beer and relaxed.

It was obvious to me, looking at the people in the quadrangle, that they were clearly upset.

I knew from having been here many years before where the auditorium was located and I knew what doors would open. I was the second person to enter the lobby and I approached one of the tables set up there. A lady behind the table asked me to read the Department of City Planning Scoping papers. She gave me two papers that were headed Environmental Assessment and Review Division, Amanda M. Burden, Director, Department of City Planning. The papers were titled Protocol for Public Scoping Meetings, NYC Department of City Planning, Environmental Assessment and Review Division. I glanced at the two pages, telling the lady that I would read them. She seemed a little uneasy at the people behind me pushing and shoving to get at the tables.

She presented me with some 4" x 3" papers that were titled City Planning Commission, Appearance Card. It had printed "I intend to appear and speak on C.P. [blank] Cal. No. [blank]. Two small checkboxes indicated either "in favor" or "in opposition." I was told to fill in the date, my name, my address, as well as whom I represented and their address. She said that I should complete this card, return the original, retain the duplicate, and present it to the clerk at the speakers table when I came forward to address the commission. It was all so weird to me. I said I would read the Scoping Meeting Protocol and follow her directions. She continued to speak, telling me about the rules, about the etiquette of the Planning Commission, that when I introduced myself I should speak clearly, and that I should not eat, drink, or use foul language. I thanked her, accepted the papers, and moved away.

The crowd started to push toward the doors to get into the auditorium space. I looked at the Appearance Card and the two checkboxes indicating that I was appearing either "in favor" or "in opposition." There was no box marked "other," or "undecided." I was neither for nor against, so I left them blank, signed the card, and took it to the clerk at the speakers table when it was time for me to speak. I had no intention of actually speaking, but I followed the kind lady's protocol.

For some reason, I realized from my usual inner paranoia, which was always on target, that the game was fixed. I moved to a seat on the aisle in the third row. I realized that the seat on the aisle was something that would give me an escape route.

My paranoia would prove to be right. I looked around the room and on each wall there were dozens of video cameras. As the crowd became louder, the voices began to shout, and Borough President Molinari took the microphone from the speaker's platform and began to tell the audience that they should look around the room and behave because the entire country was watching. Before leaving the podium he said "Let the games begin."

And begin they did. In the first row on my left on the audience floor was the former Borough President Guy Molinari, James Oddo, Michael McMahon, and the other council man, Anthony Lanza. James Oddo stood up, took the microphone, and began to address the crowd. He began by telling the audience to calm down, to be cool, and to let the voices be heard. There was a big guy behind me. I had noticed him earlier because he was shouting directly in my ears. The big guy seemed about 10 feet tall and 300 pounds, and I would learn later that he was named Christopher Wallace. He was a union man, dressed in a blue t-shirt with a paper stuck on his shirt reading "I support the speedway."

He stood up, walked the few feet to the front of the auditorium, reached out, and put his right arm around the neck of councilman Lanza. With his muscular left arm, he reached out, seizing the microphone from the councilman's hand who looked up and at him, stunned. The big guy was a foot taller and perhaps 150 pounds heavier than councilman Lanza. As he began to speak, a man within an arm's length of me, also in the row behind, stood up and began to scream. I didn't understand what he was saying, but......

As I watched it all, I debated whether I should get out or go to councilman Lanza's defense. I realized that would be irrational and that I should not interfere in any way. I knew the consequences; I would have been photographed as an aggressive person, arrested, and hauled off to jail. It was not a sudden realization that I was a Black guy; I had been there before, and done that.

I looked around, raised my camera, and began to take photos. There was a little fat guy behind me with a huge head and a bigger lung capacity. I looked at him and realized that he was depriving some village somewhere of an idiot! I looked at the huge man with his arm around the councilman's neck. I believed that this guy could be in a boxing ring and would be designated the next "Great White Hope." This was Christopher J. Wallace, and I appreciated that the other men in these t-shirts would follow him anywhere, but only out of morbid curiosity. The little fat guy never closed his mouth. He yelled, he hollered, and I never understood a word he was saying. He was merely shouting to be heard, not to be understood.

The audience began to shout. I noticed Jimmy Oddo. I always liked Jimmy Oddo because he reminded me of a little fellow called Willie Pep, who was a world champion featherweight boxer. I followed Oddo's career and I knew that Jimmy Oddo would become the next Borough President. I wondered why he didn't step up. But I thought of

409

Willie Pep, whose nickname was Will o' the Wisp. He won 230 fights with 65 knockouts, losing only 11 bouts in his 26-year career with only one draw.

Willie Pep lost one title bout against a heavier fighter, a Middleweight named Sammy Angott. This would have been the Chris Wallace knockout – "stand up, get up, Jimmy Oddo." Like Willie Pep, I imagined Oddo as the master of finesse, a one-two punch, and a ten round decision, Wallace would have went down. It would have been 135 straight wins for Jimmy Oddo like Willie Pep. Jimmy Oddo was skinny but he wasn't scared of nobody. He was a superior defensive boxer. I loved Willie Pep. He only lost to Sandy Saddler, A tall slender fighter from Harlem. It was the first time that Willie Pep had been knocked out, some people though he took a dive. He went down for the count, never got up. The city newspapers said he took a dive and he sued them for $75 million. He lost the case.

But Jimmy Oddo never stood up, he got lost in the crush of bodies. Jimmy Oddo – he would get the fast ferry moving.

Jimmy Oddo – he would get the Department of Consumer Affairs to revoke business licenses if they didn't operate properly.

Jimmy Oddo – who found industrial waste and hazardous materials and informed the Department of Environmental Protection.

Jimmy Oddo – a representative of all the City agencies examined by the facility in May that held up all of the NASCAR investigations.

He stood up to Curtis Sliwa with the red hat and had Sliwa accept the soap in his motor mouth, the radio host who made a crack about the mafia on Staten Island. He took his mouthful of soap because Jimmy Oddo was standing behind him. Jimmy Oddo wants to become the next Borough President and he was securing a deal, he was getting the best consultancy to run for the office. I was upset that Jimmy didn't stand up to that fucking Wallace. One-two punch, Jimmy. One-two punch, Jimmy.

But I had to leave. By now the city police were coming down the Island to the Petrides School, and I decided it was time for me to leave, and I made my way, pushing up the aisle and out of the audience. I made my way to the lobby and out of the doorway where the people were still trying to enter. I listened to the police sirens coming; I knew that they were the regular city policy and I didn't know what would happen in the group. I didn't wait to find out.

But the police who were in the auditorium were simply security guards, there were men and women. They were not armed and I am sure they also were afraid of the hundreds of people shouting and waving signs. I made my way, walking very fast out across the road and up a few steps.

I hopped into the cab of my huge camper and backed my vehicle out of the parking lot onto the road. I did not stop at the gate; I simply slowed down and waved. There was no one there and I continued onto the main road.

It would be a few days later when all of that was happening in the auditorium came out. The papers would record what happened after I pushed by way out of the building and off the campus. The headlines were "Near Riots Shut Hearings. The jammed forum turns into mayhem when officials goad labor activists." No one asked me then and no one has ever asked me, but what I noticed on the front page of the *Staten Island Advance* in color in the midst of all of it, there I was with my hands raised and my camera snapping pictures.

I knew that I had taken the best position to leave. I saw the man reach up and put the councilman in a headlock. I thought he would be arrested; he never was. He was never charged with any assault and there were many other people who saw this. But as I made my way slowly back to Mariners Harbor, I would stop at Jonesy's Tavern on Holland Avenue to have a drink. I was a bit..., no I was very confused. I was not prepared for what happened, nor did I expect to be involved in what had happened, but then I should have known. I am a Staten Islander.

On Monday, May 15, there would be front page coverage of the incident between councilman Lanza and Christopher J. Wallace. Christopher Wallace was now dressed in a suit, white shirt, and tie, his hair was trimmed and combed. He had a benign expression on his face, much different from the expression that I saw and photographed, and that hundreds had seen. Many people, when asked about the incident, would say that Christopher J. Wallace, who supported the speedway, tried to pull the microphone from councilman Lanza's hand. He simply mentioned in the article that he was wrapping his arm around the councilman's shoulders.

No one asked me about what happened. My pictures show something quite different about the incident. Councilman Lanza would say "I was attacked. I wasn't trying to be a tough guy." All of the officials seated nearby did nothing, they said nothing, and they failed to demonstrate any political leadership when it was desperately needed.

Lanza's voice would appear in the newspapers almost daily. He said "If this idea of bringing 80,000 people to Staten Island happens, then I think all of this is irrelevant." "It's paid for by NASCAR." A television interview with councilman Lanza was interesting. There were no police to arrest this man Christopher Wallace. Councilman Lanza, looking into the lens of the camera, said he was "describing his views on the project when a guy put a bear hug on me, threatening me, while guys standing in front of him urged him on. " Punch him. Punch him. Hit him. Hit him." they screamed."

Mr. Lanza would identify the man as Christopher J. Wallace, president of Local 20 of the United Brotherhood of Carpenters and Joiners of America. Mr. Wallace, whose union has 630 members, said yesterday "Oh, that's silliness. Clearly not true. The speedway and the benefits to Staten Island are what we should be speaking about, not this silliness."

The ISC official, Michael Printup, said "Oh, we all saw Mr. Wallace place his arm around Mr. Lanza while trying to grab the microphone. It's a shame the elected officials couldn't speak and finish their thoughts," continued Mr. Printup.

There would be no statement from a police department official. The officers said they disbanded the meeting shortly afterward saying simply that the auditorium's capacity had been exceeded. They would make no arrest.

No new hearing date had been scheduled. The city officials each made statements declaring that they were against the speedway and the speedway could now be considered dead.

At Jonesy's Tavern I described what had happened at the Petrides School and how the NASCAR hearing had turned into a free-for-all. Audrey, the bartender, listened and said "I'm glad you didn't get involved, Cleve. Your ass would be sitting in the 120th precinct by now in a jail cell."

But day after day articles would appear in the paper, some paid for personally by individuals, many describing how unfortunate it was to see the testosterone poisoned Christopher Wallace and what his actions had done to Staten Island. Many people I met in the following days said that it should all be much calmer next time. But "There will be no next time for me," councilman Oddo said. The Department of City Planning did not set a new date.

And Christopher Wallace? He would deny that he assaulted the councilman. "I shouldn't have been gullible," he said. "Lanza said that I was simply inciting the union members present by saying they were "lured in" from off island."

Printup from NASCAR said "We had a couple of people who got a little riled. They just weren't following instructions."

Many articles would appear in the *Staten Island Advance,* many saying that it showed that we were uneducated, uncivil, narrow, and disrespectful. The real issue was the terrible disservice that the people have done to their Borough's image. Christopher Wallace continued "You ain't seen nothin' yet."

A week or so later, I would drive around the community that I knew so very well. I watched the loading and unloading of container ships at Howland Hook. The ships were being refueled by oil barges snuggled against the huge container ships, transferring bunker fuel during the loading and unloading processes. And this activity will be carried on within half a mile of the proposed NASCAR track, which, if had been completed, would draw 80,000 people for an event.

Across the Kill Van Kull in New Jersey there are huge oil refineries, and anything that would cause the Goethals Bridge to fall and the nearby trailer park to be incinerated reminded me of the USS Kohl incident, after the ship was struck in Yemen. Has anyone noticed the Texas Eastern jet fuel pumping station line that surfaces at the corner of Western Avenue and Goethals Road North? This line sends highly volatile jet fuel to the three major airports. Will the 2-truck Fire Engine Company 157 on Harbor Road or the Engine Company on Richmond Avenue have enough equipment or manpower?

The pathetic little blue and white signs that point to the Michael J. Petrides School as an evacuation reception center seem a bit puny. Have there been any current plans for Borough residents? I think of Katrina. I think of the EPA report that there is a toxic dump under the Goethals Bridge that has been designated for a Superfund cleanup. And this, also, a few hundred feet from the proposed NASCAR racetrack site.

And to the south of the track, at the former Fresh Kills dump, rest the remains and remnants of 9/11 that are all too familiar for Island residents. Reports are that this is now to become a bucolic retreat, but, of course, only on those days when the NASCAR is silent. Has anyone at all noticed this? Is Al-Qaeda watching? Is Homeland Security watching? Is anyone watching?

It would not take an elaborate terrorist plot to endanger many lives in Bloomfield. In the past few years we have seen too many accidents; home-grown incidents, and numerous warnings. It's time for public safety. If a terrorist were to target the chlorine gas facility in New Jersey, what would happen to the hundreds of thousands of people living downwind of this on Staten Island? I would submit this, but I think it is already too late.

Of course, Christopher Wallace will command a place at the table of the *Staten Island Advance*. Many more voices would be calm or silent, hoping for a peaceful settlement. They will be dismissed.

Chapter 13

MY STORY OF GOD

After looking through the notebooks for a title, I think the best title to give this

would be My Story of God.

In all probability, before I complete this I will be struck by lightning; however the past lingers in the present.

The past brings me to the poetry that, as a child, I had to recite each night before I climbed to the top bunk in my bedroom, and the memories are still vivid if I pause for a moment.

Now I lay me down to sleep,
I pray the Lord my soul to keep.
If I should die before I wake,
I pray the Lord my soul to take.

I no longer get down on my knees. Am I unable or perhaps conflicted about what I was to remember? These are the paths that many young men, Black and white, in my neighborhood had stamped on their foreheads. They are still there. These ideas are implanted at a very early age and we are immediately weaned from any suggestion that might bloom into self-worth or self-value. We were somehow bred to ignore our own presence on this earth.

As a little Black kid this was the lifestyle. The fictional characters also are important; they kept us from sin: the boogeyman that would kidnap us, ghosts who would come back from the dead to get us, the monsters, and the horrible creatures that would claw at my skin and gobble me up if I was bad! The tactics to train us to avoid the devil are not forgotten by this Black boy.

An Inuit asked a priest "If I did not know about God and sinned, would I go to hell?" The priest answered, "No, not if you did not know." The Inuit replied, "Then why did you tell me?"

The little Black boy could avoid hell if he listened to the teachings of God and of Jesus. From kindergarten on we were fed more and more of these details, but around them the holidays are firmly implanted in our brains. The Easter Bunny would bring colorful eggs in cute little baskets of green straw and all sorts of goodies that we could eat if we were good, if we did not sin. We never asked if the little bunnies laid eggs or not!

We looked and waited for these yearly festivities; the symbols and myths that surrounded the holidays were merely to reinforce the church and our behaviors, and I guess the predictability of all these holidays would make the child feel more secure.

An entry in my notebook says that in order to save the human race and the planet we inhabit, we have to encourage strange bedfellows and forgive many trespasses. Science and religion, capitalism and socialism, cast and character are all on the auction block now and the waters are rising while we are dreaming of *Dancing with the Stars*. We call ourselves social creatures when indeed we are simply pack animals. Many of us say we are middle class, but in reality we are lower class, salt of the earth, working class drones. We exist at the whim of the systems of these religions that distribute our life's blood as so much spare change.

These subjects can be addressed in fiction, in the theatre, even in poetry, but now and again, as I re-read this, the plain talk of nonfiction is preferred. Walk with me through this difficult period.

GENESIS

I would delight over and over again, reading the stories of the Bible.

In the Beginning...

And in the beginning God made Heaven and Earth, but God was lonely and he made mistakes. God, like a lot of men, lived alone but he was unhappy and he had no one to go out with or hang out with, there weren't any people around, and so God created Adam and Eve, and God made this beautiful garden where he had all kinds of fruit and vegetables. They ate a lot of fruit in those days, they were the original vegetarians.

So God let Adam and Eve hang out in his garden. "You can have anything to eat in this garden," he told them, "but you can't eat from this one tree; it's a forbidden tree." When God went out to do some shopping, he came back and found that Adam and Eve had eaten some of the forbidden fruit which made them very uptight about being naked. "Who told you being naked is bad?" He asked. They said "The serpent made us do it." God was really pissed off. "The serpent made you do it, huh? Well, I'm going to put a stop this this." And he yelled and he evicted them, got them out of the garden, and for extra punishment he made it so they would become parents.

Adam and Eve had two children, Cain and Abel. Abel was a shepherd boy, and Cain grew crops, but when they came to offering up the results of their labor to God, God didn't think too much of the seeds and fruits, and that pissed Cain off. So Cain murdered Abel. Cain went away, got married, and had many children, and his descendants inhabited the globe and murdered, killed, and created mayhem

Adam and Eve had a third son, called Seth, to replace Cain, and then many other sons and daughters during the 900 years of Adam's life. Seth lived 912 years, also working hard to populate the earth, and Noah was his descendant.

Noah

God got fed up with the wickedness of Man and decided to destroy him and every other living thing on the earth. Except for Noah and his family. God said to Noah "I'd like you to build an ark of cypress wood. You need to caulk it inside and out with pitch, and make it 300 cubits long, 50 cubits wide, and 30 cubits high."

Noah began to build the ark; after all, it was a commandment from God. And, when it was built, two animals of every sort; of fowls, of cattle, and of every creeping thing of the earth, two each came to Noah and went into the ark, male and female.

And so, when Noah was 600 years old, it began to rain. Noah and his wife, with his sons Shem, Ham, and Japheth, and their wives, went into the ark and closed the doors, and the rain fell on the earth for 40 days and 40 nights. And all flesh that moved upon the earth died. Everything perished; from humans to cattle to crawling things; they were wiped from the face of the earth. Water covered the face of the earth for 150 days. Then God remembered Noah and all the beasts, and the rain stopped and the waters ebbed, and the ark rested on the mountains of Ararat. Noah had sent out a dove; the dove returned with an olive leaf. A week later he sent the dove out again, and the dove did not return, so Adam released every beast, every crawling thing, and every fowl; everything that stirs on the earth went out of that ark.

Noah planted a vineyard, and one day he got drunk on his wine and he staggered about butt-naked in his tent and his son Ham saw him and spoke to his two brothers about Noah, their father, being drunk and naked. Noah got pissed off and cursed Ham's son, Canaan, saying that he would be the lowest of slaves to his brothers.

I wondered: would this be where the Black Africans were later designated as the 'descendants of Ham" by white Christians? This biblical passage really bothered me for many years.

Abraham

Abram was a descendant of Noah's son Shem. He married Sarai (who was his half-sister), and she was barren.

God told Abram to leave his country and his family and travel to a land that God would show him. God promised to make a nation from Abram. He would have enough children and grandchildren and further descendants to populate a nation. So Abram goes off into the wilderness to Canaan to start his nation, and he takes his wife and his nephew Lot with him.

There was a severe famine in the land of Canaan, so Abram and Lot and their households travelled south to Egypt. On the way, Abram told his wife Sarai to say that she was his sister, which she kind of was, so that the Egyptians would not kill him. When they entered Egypt, the princes of the Pharaoh praised Sarai's beauty to the Pharaoh, and she was taken into his palace, and Abram was given provisions: "oxen, and he-asses, and menservants, and maidservants, and she-asses, and camels." However, God was pissed off and afflicted Pharaoh and his household with great plagues, which he tried to find the reason for. Upon discovering that Sarai was a married woman, Abram's wife as well as his sister, Pharaoh demanded that they and their household leave immediately, along with all their goods.

So Abram went back to Canaan to start his nation, and his nephew Lot tagged along. Lot, however, had developed a severe case of city living while in Egypt and left Abram, moving to the twin cities of Sodom and Gomorrah.

After 10 years of living in back in Canaan, no child had been born to Abram and Sarai, their geriatric sex had produced nothing but dislocated hips and swollen ankles, but God had told Abraham that he would build a great nation out of them. So Sarai told Abram to sleep with her maid so at least they could have some back-up kids. Abram did as he was told and slept with Hagar, one of her slaves. Hagar gave birth to a son called Ishmael.

Then, when Abram was 99 years old, God came to him and said "Do I have a deal for you! I am going to make you the father of many nations. Your descendants shall be kings, and I will give you the land of Canaan to be yours for all time. All you have to do is cut off your foreskin and the foreskins of every male in your household, including your family, your servants, and your slaves. Oh, yes, and your name will now be Abraham and your wife's name will be Sarah."

Free circumcisions everybody?

But Sarah did get pregnant, when she was 105.

Is the book a real story or has it been made up and twisted, from the top down and the bottom up?

Sodom and Gomorrah

God really hated Sodom and Gomorrah. The people in Sodom and Gomorrah were really sex-crazed. They wanted to have sex with everything and everybody. But they took it too far. They wanted to have sex with God's angels, and angel-rape will get you on God's bad side.

It seems that Lot was hanging out at the city gates of Sodom when two strangers come by, and Lot invited them home. Lot prepared a feast for them, baked unleavened bread, and Boy, did they eat! They had not lain down yet when the men of Sodom, the young and the old, gathered at the house and they shouted to Lot, "Where are the men who came to you tonight? Bring them to us so that we may know them."

Lot went outside and he says "Please, brothers, do no harm. Look, I have two daughters who have known no man. Let me bring them out to you and you can do to them whatever you please. Only do nothing to the men that came under the shadow of my roof for protection."

Apparently, raping his daughters was an OK substitute for attacking the two strangers in his house.

"Get out of our way," they replied. They kept bringing pressure on Lot and moved forward to break down the door. Lot ran inside and slammed the door, and all the men outside the door, from the smallest to the biggest, were immediately struck with a blinding light and they could not find the door.

The men inside reveal themselves as angels who had come to the city, and they tell Lot "Lot, you gotta get out. God told us to destroy the city. Now, hurry! Take your wife and your two daughters who are here, or you will be swept away when the city is punished." Lot didn't linger. The men seized his hand, and his wife's hand, and the hands of his two daughters, and led them outside the city. "Flee for your lives, don't look back, don't stay anywhere in the plain. Flee to the high country or you will be consumed.

But Lot said to them, "I can't flee to the mountains; this disaster will overtake me, and I'll die. Look, there is a small town nearby that we can run to. Let me flee to it. Then my life will be spared."

The angel said, "Very well, I will grant this request; I will not overthrow the town you speak of. But flee there quickly, because I cannot do anything until you reach it." So Lot and his family fled to the nearby town of Zoar. The next day the Lord rained down fire and brimstone on Sodom and Gomorrah, but Lot and his family were safe in Zoar. But Lot's wife turns around for one last look at her home, and she is immediately turned into a pillar of salt. Are we ever told the name of Lot's poor wife?

Lot goes out of Zoar and resettles in a cave in the mountains with his two daughters who, it seems, were also not worth having their names mentioned. The two daughters were concerned that there were no men around to mate with, to carry on the family lineage. His daughters were, I suppose, well endowed, and the older daughter said to the younger "Our father is old, and there is no man on earth to come to bed with us like the way of all the world. Come let's give our father wine to drink, and let's lie with him so that we may keep alive the seed from him."

That night they gave their father all the wine that he could drink and the older daughter went in and had sex with her father, and Lot was not aware when he arose what had happened. Those alcoholic memory losses can be a bitch, but they're so convenient! The next day the elder daughter said to the younger one "Last night I lay with my father. Let's get him drunk again tonight, and you go in and lie with him so we can preserve our family line through our father." So they got their father to drink wine that night also, and the younger daughter went in and slept with him. And the Bible says "He knew not when he lay down or when she arose."

His two daughters did have children; each one of his daughters had a son.

Jacob

God woke up Abraham one time and said "Tie your son Isaac to the altar and kill him as a human sacrifice." This, of course, is the kind of thing God only does to people he likes. Abraham was upset but he had to do what he was told. He took Isaac to the top of the mountain and tied him to a stone at the altar and when he was ready to plunge his sacrificial knife into Isaac's chest, God stopped him. God looked at Abraham and smiled and said "Let him go, that was just a test of faith." It was really a vicious prank of course, depending on how you read it.

After his narrow escape from human sacrifice, Isaac grew up to be a man and had a couple of kids of his own, named Esau and Jacob. Jake was a bit of a sugar-foot, staying at home with mom, helping her cook and clean, and bake bean pies. Esau, on the other hand, was pretty much more butch. He was a hunter and outdoorsman.

Jacob messed up and God sent him out. As Jacob was going down the road, he met a farmer. He said "Farmer, I'm tired and I'm hungry, would you help me?" The farmer said "Fine, I'll help you but don't you be messing with my daughters." But Jacob fell in love with his daughter Rachel and offered to work on the farm for seven years if the farmer would allow him to marry her. After seven years of slavery and no money, the farmer tricked him into marrying the other daughter, Leah. Jacob said "I worked for seven years and I wanted to marry Rachel." The farmer said "That's cool; you can marry her too, but you gonna have to work for seven more years." Jacob spent 14 years working on the guy's farm.

Jacob had had enough. He put his children and his wives on camels and gathered all his livestock and everything he had gotten, everything he had acquired in 14 years, to go back home to his father Isaac in the land of Canaan.

He finally got to Shechem in Canaan and bought the land where he pitched his tent from the sons of Hamor, the ruler of Shechem. Dinah, the daughter Leah had borne to Jacob, went out to visit the women of the land. When Shechem, the son of Hamor, saw her, he took her and raped her.

Jacob heard that Shechem had raped his daughter Dinah, but his sons were out in the fields with the livestock so he didn't say anything until they got home. Hamor, Shechem's father, went to Jacob to work out marriage arrangements. Meanwhile Jacob's sons on their way back from the fields heard what had happened. They were outraged, explosive with anger. Shechem's rape of Jacob's daughter was intolerable in Israel and not to be put up with.

Hamor spoke with Jacob and his sons, "My son Shechem is head over heels in love with your daughter—give her to him as his wife. Intermarry with us. Give your daughters to us and we'll give our daughters to you. Live together with us as one family. Settle down among us and make yourselves at home. Prosper among us."

Shechem then spoke for himself, addressing Dinah's father and brothers: "Please, say yes. I'll pay anything. Set the bridal price as high as you will—the sky's the limit! Only give me this girl for my wife."

Jacob's sons answered Shechem and his father with cunning. Their sister, after all, had been raped. They said, "This is impossible. We could never give our sister to a man who was uncircumcised. Why, we'd be disgraced. The only condition on which we can talk business is if all your men become circumcised like us. Then we will freely exchange daughters in marriage and make ourselves at home among you and become one big, happy family. But if this is not an acceptable condition, we will take our sister and leave."

This seemed fair enough to Hamor and his son Shechem. So Hamor and Shechem went to the public square and spoke to the town council: "These men like us; they are our friends. Let them settle down here and make themselves at home; there's plenty of room in the country for them. And, just think, we can exchange our daughters in marriage. But these men will only accept our invitation to live with us and become one big family on one condition, that all our males become circumcised just as they themselves are. This is a very good deal for us—these people are very wealthy with great herds of livestock and we're going to get our hands on it. So let's do what they ask and have them settle down with us."

Everyone who was anyone in the city agreed with Hamor and his son, Shechem; every male was circumcised.

Three days after the circumcision, while all the men were still very sore, two of Jacob's sons, Simeon and Levi, Dinah's brothers, each with his sword in hand, walked into the city as if they owned the place and murdered every man there. They killed Hamor and his son Shechem, rescued Dinah from Shechem's house, and left. When the rest of Jacob's sons came on the scene of slaughter, they looted the entire city in retaliation for Dinah's rape. Flocks, herds, donkeys, belongings—everything, whether in the city or in the fields—they took. And then they took all the wives and children captive and ransacked their homes for anything valuable.

Then Jacob said to his sons, "You have stirred up a lot of trouble by making me odious to the Canaanites and Perizzites, the people living in this land. We are few in number, and if they unite against me and attack me, my household and I will be destroyed." But they replied, "Should he have treated our sister like a whore?"

Then God said to Jacob, "Go up to Bethel and settle there, and build an altar there to God, who appeared to you when you were fleeing from your brother Esau."

But God said to Jacob "You will be a big success. He was losing his sons and daughters left and right and when God left him he would have nothing. The parable is - just because God put you in the position to pull shit like that, it doesn't mean that he has to let you get away with it.

Judah

I guess I didn't realize it at the time, but I was becoming addicted. The sexual narratives that I absorbed were reaching deep. I searched out the erotic. I enjoyed trying to find sections that gave me a jolt. I could not understand why, when old Noah got drunk after the flood, staggered around the tent naked, and was seen by his son Ham, Noah cursed Ham's son Canaan. "He shall be the lowest of slaves to his brothers." Thus were Black Africans later designated as the descendants of Ham. I wondered whether this Biblical passage served as a righteous rationale for the enslavement of Black people. I would continue to find more pornography, racy stories, before I was introduced to sex. The stories in Genesis would not leave me.

Judah was a story I had to read several times before I thought I understood it, though after trying write about it, I doubt that I ever really did.

Judah was the fourth son of Jacob. He met the daughter of a Canaanite man named Shua. He called her his wife, took her to bed, and she bore a son. The son's name was Er. She conceived again and gave birth to a son and named him Onan. She gave birth to still another son and named him Shelah. When Er became a young man he was married off to Tamar, but Er was a real bastard. He was a sly and evil sucker and the Lord put him to death. He had a miscreant from the neighborhood cut his throat.

When Judah heard this he told his second son, Onan, to sleep with his brother's wife and fulfill his duty to her as a brother-in-law to raise up offspring for his brother. But Onan knew that any child would not be recognized his; so whenever he slept with his brother's wife, he spilled his semen on the ground to keep from providing offspring for his brother. And what he did was evil, and the Lord put him to death as well. How anyone knew that he was "wasting his seed" I had no one to ask. I had only to think about what happened and leave it at that.

Judah then told his daughter-in-law Tamar, to go live at her father's house to wait for the third son, Shelah, came of age.

After a long time Judah's wife died. When Judah had recovered from his grief, he went up to Timnah, to the men who were shearing his sheep.

Tamar, still a comely young thing, was told "Behold, your father-in-law is coming to Timnah to shear his sheep." She took off her widow's clothes, covered herself with a veil to disguise herself, and then sat down at the entrance to Enaim, on the road to Timnah. When Judah saw her, he was hooked. He thought she was a whore because she had covered up her face. Judah came up to her and said "Here, let me come to bed with you." He did not know that she was his daughter-in-law. He promised to send her a goat from his flock, but she asked for a pledge until it arrived. She wanted his seal and its cord, and his staff. So he gave them to her and slept with her, and she became pregnant.

Judah sent the young goat by his friend in order to get his pledge back from the woman, but he did not find her. His friend asked the men in the village, "Where's the hooker on the Enaim road?"

"There is no hooker on the Enaim road," they replied.

He returned to Judah and said "Well, I couldn't find her, and the men who lived there said that there hasn't been any prostitute there." About three months later Judah was told, "Your daughter-in-law Tamar is guilty of prostitution, and as a result she is now pregnant." Judah said, "Bring her out and have her burned to death!"

As she was being brought out, she sent a message to her father-in-law. "I am pregnant by the man who owns these," she said. And she added, "See if you recognize whose seal and cord and staff these are." Judah recognized them and said, "She is more righteous than I, since I wouldn't give her to my son Shelah." And he did not sleep with her again.

When the time came she gave birth to twin boys.

Joseph

God changed Jacob's name to Israel, which means "one who wrestles with God," which reminds me, I was told, before I was asked to leave the men's group, "Mr. Overton, your arms are too short to box with God." That's the closest anyone ever came to putting me in such a wonderful space.

Israel, the new Jacob, had twelve sons. One of them was named Joseph; the other sons mostly hated Joseph. It was hard to blame them because he was clearly a favorite' he was always getting nice presents from their father and he wasted no opportunity to remind his brothers of this fact. His brothers grew tired of his bragging so they threw Joseph into a pit and sold him as a slave. "That ought to take him down a peg," they said as they sold him to a slave caravan, disappearing over the hill in the distance.

But Joseph really was a good guy; he was a lot better than his brothers who wanted to kill him. Joseph was sold in Egypt to Potiphar, a captain of Pharaoh's guard, but the Lord blessed him and Joseph did very well; in a few years he was practically running the place.

Joseph's Egyptian master put him in charge of everything. He kept the numbers and the charts and everything while the Egyptian master left everything in Joseph's hands; he sat about listening to music, watching the naked dancers, eating, and sleeping, and Joseph was left to tend to Potiphar's wife. And it came to pass that his master's wife raised her eyes to Joseph and said "Lie with me." I didn't know what that meant. She asked Joseph again "Lie with me." I found later that she meant "Joseph - I want to go to bed with you. Come, lie next to me."

But he refused and said to his master's wife "With me in charge, my master does not concern himself with anything in the house; everything he owns he has entrusted to my care. No one is greater in this house than I am. My master has withheld nothing from me except you, because you are his wife. How then could I do such a wicked thing and sin against God?" And though she spoke to Joseph day after day, he refused to go to bed with her or even be alone with her.

One day he went into the house to attend to his duties, and none of the household servants was inside. She caught him by his cloak and said, "Come to bed with me!" But he left his cloak in her hand and ran out of the house.

When she saw that he had left his cloak in her hand, she called her household servants. "Look," she said to them, "this Hebrew has been brought to us to trifle with us! He came in here to sleep with me, but I screamed. When he heard me call out, he left his cloak beside me and ran out of the house."

She kept his cloak beside her until his master came home. Then she told him this story: "That Hebrew slave you brought us came to me to trifle with me. But as soon as I called for help, he left his cloak and ran out of the house."

When his master heard the story his wife told him, saying, "This is how your slave treated me," he became incensed. He took Joseph and put him in prison. Where he was left to rot. (The Bitch lied big time!)

But while Joseph was there in the prison, the Lord granted him favor in the eyes of the prison warden; the warden put Joseph in charge of all the prisoners, and made him responsible for all that was done there. He also became known as an expert in interpreting dreams.

A couple of years later, Pharaoh had some horrible dreams and his dreams would not let him sleep. He called all the soothsayers in Egypt and recounted his dreams to them. They looked about and pondered what could be done until someone said "The only one who can understand these dreams would be Joseph." They shaved him, cleaned him up, dressed him, and sent him before Pharaoh.

The Pharaoh said to Joseph "I dreamed a dream and none can solve it, but I heard that you can. You understand dreams, and you can solve this."

"Well, I can't," Joseph replied to Pharaoh, "but God will give Pharaoh the answer he desires."

Then Pharaoh told Joseph his dreams. Seven fat cows that came up out of the river, followed by seven scrawny and lean cows that devoured the seven fat cows. In a second dream seven heads of grain, healthy and good, were growing on a single stalk. After them, seven other heads of grain sprouted—thin and scorched by the wind—and the thin heads of grain swallowed up the seven healthy, full heads.

Then Joseph said to Pharaoh, "God has told Pharaoh in his dreams what he is about to do; it is one and the same dream. The seven good cows and the seven good heads of grain are seven years of abundance. The seven lean and ugly cows that came up afterward are seven years of famine, and so are the seven worthless heads of grain scorched by the east wind."

Pharaoh's sleep returned and things seemed good in Pharaoh's eyes. He was feeling better, he was sleeping better, and Pharaoh was so pleased he put Joseph in charge of the whole land of Egypt."

Then Pharaoh took his signet ring from his finger and put it on Joseph's finger. He dressed him in robes of fine linen and put a golden collar around his neck. He had him ride in a chariot as his second-in-command, and people shouted before him, "Make way!"

During the seven years of abundance the land produced plentifully, and Joseph collected all the food produced in those seven years of abundance in Egypt and stored it in the cities. Joseph stored up huge quantities of grain, like the sand of the sea; it was so much that he stopped keeping records because it was beyond measure.

Then the seven years of famine began, just as Joseph had said. There was famine in all the other lands, but in the land of Egypt there was food. When Egypt began to feel the famine, and the people cried to Pharaoh for food, Pharaoh told all the Egyptians, "Go to Joseph and do what he tells you." Joseph opened the storehouses and sold grain to the

Egyptians and all the world came to Egypt to buy grain from Joseph, because the famine was severe everywhere.

Back in Canaan, Jacob told his sons to go to Egypt and buy grain. Joseph saw his brothers and recognized them. And his brothers bowed down in front of him. That was humiliating for them but it was less embarrassing than starving to death. So the brothers all packed up and moved to Egypt and the descendants of the twelve brothers would go on to become the Twelve Tribes of Israel. And God made a nation out of Israel's 90-year-old body.

I just need a few friends I can count on, God said. "That's all I need."

That was my reading of Genesis.

****

I will attempt to avoid trying to establish a dialogue while talking in tongues. They sometimes make those who speak in tongues feel lighter, freer, and better. As the prayers continue to God they feel increasingly more involved. God is the therapist for reality. The God of our creation is beautiful, but it's not safe. Our reality in everyday situations is corrupt and broken but what should one do? Get to know God and learn to hang out with him? Those guiding our minds, our souls, our bodies, our lives, approach this problem, this age-old problem of theodicy. It's not really available to the mainstream. Difficult to gather together. I will continue on and try.

I continue to write, walk this structural high wire routine of daily life and its philosophical balancing acts day after day, night after night. I will sometimes distance myself from you, from the heartache that provides no cushion to protect us against its reality. This is the spice and flavor of my 85 years. Bizarre and funny moments of this human variety show, these memories. If you put nonsense in, you will get nonsense out. It doesn't stop as a child, if you live long enough education will be continuous. If you look and feel, it's an ongoing process, and yes, it doesn't stop at elementary, high school, college, or graduate school; it continues until you die.

I began to realize how much I didn't know many years ago, and I began to educate myself. It allowed me to view my existence from a totally new experience, other places, and other countries. Everything is rooted in the past, in knowledge. Memory is the common highway between all of this. Knowledge can be obtained at any time. My growing up on Staten Island gave me no creative presence. There were the masses of people, the quantity, but the people, the Blacks and the whites where I was born, become extinct where there is no creative capacity or the capacity to change our existence. I had to reconnect my brain to free the other memories on that structural high wire of life. And as I write, I realize that to gain the understanding of the human condition required that I bring all of these stories to fruition, each so beautiful and each steeped in so much pain.

I also realize that much of the inconsistency may leave the reader confused and frustrated, but also undeniably intrigued and provoked. The writing is on my wall. What alarms even me is that I must probe even further, even deeper. The handy Holy Bible given to me by my family, the exposure to Gideon's Bible in hotels and motels. I find clarity in my own ability to understand the Bible.

I tried to understand the Bible by becoming a member of the church group, many churches, many men's groups, many brothers; I found out after some years that the popular King James Version of the Bible just didn't provide the solutions to the problems that existed then and that continue to exist. Oh, those countless hours!

One thing that everyone had an opinion about was the white, blond, blue-eyed image of God and Jesus displayed in the church sanctuary. Some brothers were adamant, saying they will no longer worship no white man. They would not worship anybody that did not look like them. I understood because I had a problem with the Easter Bunny and the white eggs! I understood very clearly because, in the movies at Empire Theatre in Port Richmond and on our early black and white television screens, the Lone Ranger, Tonto, Moses, Cleopatra—everybody was white. The stamp on my forehead was that the heroes of my life were white. No, many brothers left the church because they could not attend while that image was on the walls. Most of the brothers were Black; all of the churches I attended and went to Bible study at were Black, and the eurocentrism always came to the surface.

There was always a frustration that began and ended in the men's Bible study groups when I, along with many others, would silently confess they didn't understand why a church service would last all morning and half the afternoon. We usually wanted to break up to have something to eat or something to drink. In some churches, the brothers explained, the services, the masses, were half an hour or 45 minutes.

The other problem was the criticism about the minister and about the church, that they were not addressing the problems of the North Shore, of jobs, of housing, of public services. The churches and the halls of worship were only open on Sunday, and all they did was holler, jump up and down, and clap. Many of the Black brothers said that there was too much contradiction between what was being said in church and what was being done in the community.

There were times when I would attend the church meetings with all the brothers simply to open my Bible and try to understand the Bible study class from the very beginning. There are readings in the Bible that were always deflected when the minister was present. I wanted to understand Sodom and Gomorrah. I wanted to understand, I wanted to speak about...God send Lot out into the midst of this destruction, and Lot would go up and out of Zoar and settle in the high country with his two daughters. He was afraid to dwell in Zoar and so he dwelt in a cave with his two daughters. There was no discussion. I wanted to know, I wanted to understand, and I wanted to discuss so much of what I read.

I wanted to understand, I wanted to know if my readings were incorrect. I wanted to know about the children of Israel who came to Egypt, Jacob and his sons. Jacob's firstborn, Reuben, and the sons of Reuben: Enoch, and Phallu, and Hezron, and Carmi. These were the words in the Bible. Who are the sons of Simeon. What are their names? Who were the sons of Levi, the sons of Perez, the sons of Issachar, the sons of

Zebulon, the sons of Gad? I never, ever, found a description of much of what happened in the Bible, in Genesis.

I would one day, I promised, go to Egypt, I would one day walk on the land of Egypt. There are many who came to the land of Egypt with Jacob. Genesis gave me many hours of my mental vision of what it would have been like in Egypt and the land of Goshen. I would see the museums, the Pyramids, the crypts, the chariot that was harnessed by Joseph when he went up to meet Israel, his father, in Goshen.

I would delight over and over again, reading the stories of the Bible. Some of the stories, many of the stories, leave me quite empty. The incest, the fornication, the rape, the robbery, this was the new world, the globe that we were to inherit.

Reading the Bible became a very private pastime for me. It was very funny and very sad in many places, but I realized I had to read the Bible and understand it in the context of the life that I was living, day in and day out.

AN IRRITABLE SONG

Of course, from time to time, daily life would interrupt my search to find the puzzle of belief. Why did people believe in God? What was the evidence that there was this invisible person? How can those delivering the messages from the pulpit be so bloody confident? But of course they were always abstract and intellectual. They are not preachers any longer. They are doctors who have these arcane physiological questions. The simpleton I was, I would enter quietly at 9:00 am with my little notebooks. I wanted to speak about what I was reading in Genesis; I wanted to understand—have someone respond to me about the sin of Onan. What he did was evil in the sight of the Lord and so the Lord killed him.

The arcane language always confused me, but then again, Bible studies were not Bible studies of what was, at the time for me, the most important book in history. It accounted for the major religions of the world, but not too many people, I found, would know what the Bible actually says, and they, like me when I began to take notes or write about this, probably only knew a little bit, a tiny morsel of the Bible that was spoon-fed to them in Sunday School. The rest of the Bible remains in most of our heads as a pot of phantasmagoria. We have little knowledge of the first clue of what is actually in this Bible.

I realized actually how little I knew of the Bible, even though I grew up in several Christian churches. I realized that my teachers and those leading the study groups didn't know either. They omitted or sanitized the texts, or simply got it wrong. They didn't know. But I wanted to learn. I became a sinner, for whatever reason, and I began to feel guilty. Whatever the case, no one ever really taught me what the Bible was, who God was, or even why I should love God or Jesus. There were 60 books in the Bible, and many of the stories, like Genesis, that continue to appear in every Bible, whatever version, are stories that we probably were never supposed to hear, stories that we were never supposed to discuss; stories of incest, prostitution, harlots.

The genealogy, the language, the repetition, is something that would keep most people from really reading the Bible. But what is the Bible? I had to look at myself, my files, and

426

wonder about the bits and pieces of my life. As Geoff Crozier, the magician friend from Australia would say, I'm a rag and bone man. I don't have an MD or a DM, but what I do have is something that gave me the reason to look at the Bible to try and understand it and from my notes of a decade ago I started and I dedicated it to this next essay.

SEARCHING FOR GOD IN THE CHURCHES OF STATEN ISLAND

Churches, God, my life, and my family here on Staten Island were never far apart. I belonged to many churches; I belonged to St. Michael's; I belonged to the Summerfield United Methodist Church; I could also say I belonged to the Holy Rollers church because they gave out the best gospel and the best choir music in the neighborhood. But we also belonged, as did most Blacks, to the Baptist church on a tiny side street in Port Richmond. They were the major Sunday churches.

I needed to reorient myself a great deal on my return to Staten Island. But while the geography had changed some, the churches remained the same. The only difference was that a few steps away on Richmond Terrace and Castleton Avenue there were storefront churches. They were special and they attracted me because their doors were always open.

I continued to make notes, to attend churches. It seems to me that the people currently in charge of this country's religions have spiritualized their hysteria. The ministers, the rabbis, the priests, the ethical consultants, they alone know or believe that they know, God's will for all of us. But no one can appropriate God, the Bible, or Jesus. The opposite of faith is not doubt, it is certainty. You know you've created God in your own image when it turns out that He or She hates all of the same people that you do.

In my work to discover the roots of the Blacks and whites on Staten Island I would uncover many religions, some rather comical. One of the most notable religions was perhaps the Shaker movement, founded by Mother Ann Lee. Mother Lee preached the evil of sexual lust and insisted that her followers practice celibacy. They were known as the Shakers because they would form lines three abreast, and parade around the room, singing and dancing, shaking and shouting. Perhaps they were shaking the sin from their bodies. My observation was that the Shaker movement did not really die out; it was transformed by the Blacks in many of the storefront churches that I witnessed in West Brighton, altered only by the inclusion of sexual participation. It's home-grown Shakerism.

I somehow became attracted to the store front ministers, these itinerant preachers who had, perhaps, little formal theological education, but were the most mesmerizing, the most theatrical, and with an unparalleled ability to summon their worshippers to repent their sins and reform their lives. It seemed to require a great deal of physical involvement. These New Shakers would have their emotional orgies, the men and women tearing at their hair, beating on their breasts, and rolling on the ground begging for God's forgiveness, publically confessing their sins and promising to devote themselves to improving their society.

Quintessentially, Black Americans are very much American. We try more and more to identify with our church, even while our churches, such as the Rossville AME Zion

427

Church, which was built in the 1800s by a white builder, are now reaching out for funds to maintain their building, and stay alive, relevant.

HOPE OR DESPAIR

On the North Shore, Blacks are beginning to erect a church, one of the first in over 90 years, and an amazing thing is happening. Back in 2005 a business building work permit was issued to the North Shore Church of Christ and for the last fifteen years, the North Shore Church of Christ has been trying to erect a church. The church is one block from an already established Black church. The community gossip is that the Blacks who worship now in a former clothing store on Port Richmond Avenue are dissatisfied with their minister and so they have literally been building a church, brick by brick, on Heberton Avenue. I have no idea when this, the first physical church to be built on Staten Island by Blacks, will be completed.

I wasn't seeking God that summer morning in 2006, I was simply waiting for my laundry to dry. A lady attendant asked me if "that," pointing through the glass windows at my camper parked outside, belonged to me, I put my newspaper aside and said that it was and that I would open it if she wanted to see the inside. She was a middle aged Black lady, full figured, and with the most amazing green eyes. I would use any excuse to enter into a conversation with people, but this time there was no need and she continued to ask me questions, I told her I had lived on the island at one time and I was back to see the changes; political, social and environmental. Before I could ask her my standard list of questions she asked if I was saved. I said that I was still seeking the pathway to heaven, and she reached into her apron and gave me a small pamphlet. She began to talk to me of the benefits of God and asked me to come to a Sunday service at her church. Then a white man came in and the subject quickly changed to asking me if I wanted to know about the benefits the Laundromat gave to regular customers, a two for one on detergent, free drying if I came on certain days, free folding, and certain money back if I had not had all the holes punched in my card.

I had no need to become attached to any offering beyond the month I would be on the island, so I put her pamphlet in my pocket and my laundry in the camper and drove away.

Little did I know at the time that this would become another chapter in my life of looking for God. The church she spoke about conducted Sunday Services on Port Richmond Avenue. The oldest shopping center on the north shore, it was rebounding after years of neglect and the movement of Jewish business establishments to the newly built shopping plazas and malls. The street was now being reclaimed by Mexican entrepreneurs doing a lively trade in everything: restaurants and night clubs, furniture and thrift stores, supermarkets, churches, banks and services to transfer money directly to Mexico, and employment and social services agencies that catered to a constant stream of men waiting for work.

In the middle of this new energy the older Black established homeowners remained, joined with the new and younger Hispanic community.

The North Shore Church of Christ, the subject of the brochure given to me by the Laundromat lady, was housed in a former clothing store on the busy Port Richmond Avenue. It was Sunday morning and the steel door front had been raised and two men were standing in front on the sidewalk, I parked my vehicle around the corner and walked to where they were talking. They were dressed in suits and ties, it was obvious that they were members of the church, I said "Hi," and asked if this was actually the North Shore Church of Christ.

"Yes," one man said, pointing, "And we are building a new church up the street on Heberton Avenue."

"Hey that's great," I said. "I will go and look, see you later." Sure enough there was a foundation dug and concrete walls completed, there were several stanchions with steel beams crossing the large opening waiting for the floors.

This would become a decade long construction watch for me. There was never a church constructed by Blacks on Staten Island. My research revealed Blacks were assisted by whites in building Saint Clements in the 1800's on Van Pelt Avenue in Mariners Harbor. For some reason, it floundered and became part of the Catholic Diocese and the parish on Harbor Road provided the priests. The founding of a church was one of the ways Blacks expressed their new freedom. And this seemed to be a crash program of self-help. It seemed to me that the island churches had lost their zeal for freedom after the civil rights activities of the 1960's. It seemed that period also softened their drive for equality. White churches showed their power, building and expanding, while the Black churches moved into vacant premises to listen to the innocuous homilies of the past, preaching of the dangers of drinking, drugs, and fornicating. This meant endurance now, liberty later.

But this seemed to be different, Black men and women were actually putting bricks and mortar in to their own church. I found no evidence of this ever happening before on Staten Island. I would monitor the building site whenever I returned to the island, outer stone walls began to go up and the concrete floor was finished.

After three years the construction stopped and an 8 foot fence was erected around the entire site, there was no notice or explanation except the names of the architect, the construction company, and the bank. After more than ten years the weeds grew higher, and I would asked anyone walking about if there was any reason for the work stop, but no one knew why. I refused to listen to the gossip that this church was being constructed because of dissatisfied members of another church minister in the area.

I was told that there was a group within the church that considered buying an already built church, Halls Temple Reformed Church a mile away, and I drove to see it. Halls Temple Reformed Church, a three story red brick building with stained glass still in some of the windows, had been empty for a long time. The wooden windows, some arched, some square and some oval-shaped looked like they had been open to the weather for many decades. The well-constructed timberwork bell tower gave it an imposing corner presence. There was no cornerstone and I did not want to go beyond the sidewalk, I think it was erected in the 1890-1910 era, I noticed the grass had been recently cut and on the huge red painted front doors was a paper sign that said it was founded by Reverend Arthur Hall and the pastor Emerita Lula Hall, now closed for renovations. No Loitering! No trespassing on property! We will prosecute all! PROTECTED BY SLOMINS SHIELD.

Men of the two congregations had conversations about merging the congregations and repairing the Halls Temple building. Fifteen years later, the fenced in North Shore Church of Christ remains fenced in and the Halls Temple Reformed Church continues to be a victim of time and weather.

I realized long ago that when one culture dominates another it brings with it its literature, its language, and its religion. The art of history is the art of arguments. Many textbooks, while they may mention religious organizations, rarely treat religious ideas in any period seriously, for any in-depth portrayal of any religion would be controversial. To mention atheism or to mention deism would be even worse. Treating religious ideas neutrally, non-religiously, simply as factors in our society won't do either, for that would likely offend some adherents. So the textbook solution is to leave out religious ideas because ideas have power.

Many people came to America to search for religious freedom. Their hope was to escape the religious persecution they were facing in their own countries. They wanted a chance to worship freely and have an opportunity to choose which religion they wanted to take part in. However, although the plan was to escape persecution, that wasn't exactly how it worked. In order to ensure that Puritanism dominated the colonies, nonconformists were fined, banished, whipped, and even imprisoned for not conforming to the way of the Puritans.

Many of the colonists that came here from Europe, even the Pilgrims, left Europe to make money, but their driving force was their religions. The European view of the inherent right to conquest and domination in the New World was captured in a declaration addressed to native populations known as "El Requerimiento" (The Requirement). This was a declaration by the Spanish monarchy of its divinely ordained right to take possession of the territories of the New World and to subjugate, exploit and, when necessary, to fight the native inhabitants. The Requirement was read, in Spanish, to Native Americans to inform them of Spain's rights to conquest. Those who subsequently resisted conquest were considered to harbor evil intentions. The Spaniards thus considered those who resisted as defying God's plan, and so used Catholic theology to justify their conquest.

"I implore you to recognize the Church as a lady and in the name of the Pope take the King as lord of this land and obey his mandates. If you do not do it, I tell you that with the help of God I will enter powerfully against you all. I will make war everywhere and every way that I can. I will subject you to the yoke and obedience to the church and to his majesty. I will take your women and children and make them slaves. The deaths and injuries you will receive from here on will be your own fault and not that of his majesty nor of the gentlemen that accompany me."

This was The Requirement.

As pictured in the murals in Borough Hall on Staten Island, behind the explorer was always the military with their weapons; the sword, the pike, and the cross of his God. The textbooks fail to mention this as a facilitator of exploration and domination. History will omit such crude factors as military power or religiously sanctioned greed—they are perceived as reflecting badly on us—but look at the murals and see who, exactly, are the Americans.

Who are these textbooks written for and by? Plainly descendants of the Europeans. When Columbus landed on the American shores, the murals show him dominating immediately, the cross of God behind him held aloft by his ministers. He would raise his hand and claim everything that he saw right off the boat as his kingdom.

Slaves transported to this New World brought with them a wide range of their local religious beliefs and practices. It is very difficult to numerically establish, but it is estimated that at least 30% of the enslaved people were practicing Muslims and came here from the west coast of Africa.

The American way says little about slavery as experienced by slaves, but slaves' narratives survive until the 21st century. I do believe that the influence of religion on African Americans has been extensive. On Staten Island, I remember Blacks hating the fact that Black Muslim Minister Louis Farrakhan would sell his newspaper on the streets. They would dismiss anything without reading or purchasing it. But in the copy of the *Final Call* that I have, Farrakhan made the front page statement that slavery in the United States was sanctioned by the church through divine providence as a means of bringing salvation to a soulless people.

Bringing the historical truth to religion is an endless process, but truth can never be validated by ignorance or denial.

> *Tear it out of the history books!*
> *Bury it in conspiracies of silence!*
> *Fight many wars to suppress it!*
> *But it is written in our faces*
> *Twenty times over!*
> *It sings in our blood,*
> *It cries from the housetops,*
> *It mourns with the wind in the forests,*
> *When dogs howl and will not be comforted,*
> *When newborn lambs bleat in the snowdrifts,*
> *And dead leaves rattle in the graveyards.*
> By Pauli Murray

BUY ONE GET ONE FREE, OR MISPLACED QUANDARIES

For many other religions the commercialization we see of Christian holy days would be considered irreligious. Many religious organizations strictly forbid the exploitation of their sacred rituals and their divine doctrines. How can we intellectually understand the commercialization of Thanksgiving and Christmas, the frenzied sale of merchandize, and the exhortations that the best way to celebrate the holy season is to buy a new car? And let's not forget the shopping phenomenon that can be witnessed in the days leading up to Easter. As I've noticed in New York, everyone participating in the Easter parade must make sure they are dressed to kill in their new dresses, new shoes, new suits, new hats, all to be worn to church for the Easter Sunday service.

I guess this makes me sound like some sort of a spoilsport. But it seems to me that as the religious significance of both Christmas and Easter is overshadowed by materialism and these same materialistic emotions are passed on to our children through the fabrication of such fictitious individuals as Santa Claus and the Easter Bunny, over and over again it just lays the foundation for another generation of pre-programmed consumers.

As a young kid, I remember hearing the angelic voices of the singers at St. Michael's Catholic Church on Harbor Road. I would sneak up and sit on the stairs to listen to the celestial voices of the female singers. The feeling that this was as close to heaven as I would ever get remains. It is a feeling that came very close to me while visiting the Middle East; Saudi Arabia and Jordan. That feeling overwhelmed me at Mecca, at the Mosque, at the Kaaba. We may reject the influence that comes from it into our very souls, but the ignorance of that denial and its effect are somewhere lingering.

I make no criticism because everyone has been afraid, ignorant, or lazy at some point in their lives. As for me, it came very slowly. I just had to get busy, to get to know myself and to move through my life without the fear, given to me by religion, which has bound and held me, binding back the source of my own creation.

As a child, I was given a copy of the Old Testament. It is and has been such an intense personal and emotional area for me that during my early days, my younger years of trying to develop an understanding of religion, I held fast to opinions of the great leaders in the churches. I remembered the words of one minister that this relationship should remain very personal and private, and I tried to stay away from discussing it. But so many people wanted to know about my conversion to Islam that I found that I had to address those concerns.

I believe that every person, every seeker after truth, must attempt to learn how and why the stories are there and why they were changed. Only then will the real truth be known, if there is a truth to be found.

When I was living in Senegal, I realized that there were few people who understood the history of Timbuktu, and how it was once a center of learning, the academic center for many African leaders on the continent. Even while the history of Timbuktu is still being uncovered, it has been dismissed by all of the major religions. There have been attempts by individuals to wipe out Timbuktu as an historic learning center. Yes, in 2013, attempts are still being made to burn, to defile, to discredit the learning center which still survives.

The new generation of religious historians will undoubtedly uncover historical ancient texts in Timbuktu and document stories of the Immaculate Conception, the virgin birth, and the world's first savior, who was proclaimed the son of God. And all of those narratives written in Timbuktu will have been written over 4,000 years ago, before the birth of a Christian God. The documentation can be found in the writings of the ancient Egyptians and Ethiopians and inscribed on the walls of their temples.

I believe the new undeniable historical realities will help to explain the existence of over 125 versions of the Holy Bible. Versions of the Holy Bible, versions of religion.

INVOCATION

What I hear is the prattle from ministers while the violence around them continues, and guns and death and hate are readily available from the North, East, West, and South Shores of my island.

I have often dreamed a street theater scene when I see dozens, hundreds, thousands, or maybe millions of black hooded men and women, silently moving in unison past the front of the White House. There would be no banners, no sound, except perhaps a subliminal moan, Bringing up the rear is a cortege of white-robed figures pulling the flag draped coffin of a young soldier. They move away, silent, orderly, peaceful, breaking no laws, speaking to no one. I have had this recurring dream so many times after attending the funeral at Arlington National Cemetery for Jude's great nephew Nils, who was shot dead in Iraq in 2005, the day after his 19th birthday.

When explaining this dream to friends, I prefer them to not think of me as an eccentric, but it's cool; I am not nearly as offbeat as some might expect. I've simply been trying to realize that I want to find my own religious center and that can in itself make me seem a bit odd. An African friend said that I have *barka*. When I asked him to elaborate, he said I am bits and pieces of recycled things, and that I have both *faida* and *kersa*. For further clarification or explanation, ask a West African what that means, preferably a Senegalese.

I read at one time, "Don't let your honest convictions be laughed down." You can no more exercise your reason if you live in constant fear and dread of ridicule than you can enjoy life while in constant fear of death. If you think it right to differ from the times and make a point, then do it! Not for insolence but seriously and gravely as a man who has carried a big soul on his bosom and did not wait until it was breathed upon him by the breath of fashion. My own conscience will be my approval.

But Christianity was like one of those things kids play with that you push down and it comes back up. I'd give it my best shot, but it would take me ten years just to investigate this.

You have to visit the dark places to find God. You must dig, you must travel, you must let your senses direct you, divesting yourself of all the fears and shit that you carry around in your life. You must admit that there is something you don't know; most adults are ashamed to admit that. Adjust to being an idiot if you must. There is no knowing where your monitors or guides will come from or where they will lead you. There are no signposts, no road markers. The dark places are under the surface, in the small print, in the jumble of text, in the manufacturing of words to fit the crimes.

One Sunday I went down to Richmond Terrace to listen to a minister in a store front church. I had no idea why, only finding myself listening intently to his preaching. I recognized the Genesis verse "and God created mankind in his own image, in the image of God he created them; male and female he created them."

433

I would go back to the storefront church on Richmond Terrace because of its intensity. Nothing was made clear; I simply exposed myself to the feeling, unafraid, of the unsophisticated multi-syllabic exchange of the live theater and this reality. Everyone in the audience was Black and the angst of life was released. I could close my eyes and hallucinate unashamed.

By the late 1960s, I had lost my faith. I had tried; I read the books, Catholicism, Mormonism, Buddhism, Judaism, Islam, the world's religions.

In my search for my connection, a very dear friend suggested I go with her to the Tivoli Catholic Worker Farm in New York. She introduced me to Dorothy Day at the soup kitchen in downtown Manhattan. Dorothy Day was peeling potatoes. I shook hands with her enthusiastically; she had arthritis and winced.

I planned a short stay, and I helped with chores and minor work in the company of priests, nuns, men, women, and family groups. There were no scripture lessons, no pastoral prayer, no choral response, no general offerings, offertories, or doxologies; all were done away with at Tivoli. Our participation was to assist in the kitchen, assist in the serving.

Guest speakers would be asked to explain their idea of God and the answers were quietly spoken to the group. The idea came to me from one speaker that God was a hopeless idea, that there is no such thing. "Churches," he said, "have given us great treasures of art and architecture." He went on and on about the paintings, the sculptures, the creations of the greatest artists to glorify God. His last remarks asked us if all of that we see can pay in kind for the harm that the churches have done.

I did not know where to put much of what I would hear at Tivoli. I realized that among other religions and with the Catholic workers, there were many who, like Mother Theresa, who would speak about their personal spiritual depressions, the loneliness and the doubt. Mother Theresa would say, before she passed away, that "God loves me and yet the reality of darkness and coldness and emptiness is so great that nothing touches my soul." She shocked many people with her constant cheerful and smiling manner; she would call it "The cloak by which I cover the emptiness and misery."

I would always save the little pamphlets given to each person when they entered the churches that we went to on the North Shore and place them in my God file. I would not find pamphlets at Tivoli, I would not find choirs. I would find strangeness.

I did not find God.

ON BLACK SUFFERING

The social gospel inspired many Christians for many decades to create this New Deal. We all understood what Roosevelt was saying and we believed in him. He was our messiah. But today we are still victims, white and Black, of the massive Ponzi schemes. I knew many years ago that I had to leave all of the church teachings and the question and answer periods. The pain continues.

For most of the men, these Black men, many I knew, many I've just met, a rebellion, especially here on this island, is very rare. We do not rebel; we dodge and evade. We kneel each Sunday in lowly submission and kick our duty under the bed while God is not looking. Sin mattered; sin matters greatly for those of us who are having a little nookie on the side. It's accepted; we're the male head of this household; don't be disappointed or offended, because we have not alienated God. It's in the most exotic book you'll ever read - it's called the Bible. It's there you will read of disrupted relationships, of love and justice in human affairs, and we rarely sin alone. Science supplies the means of killing around the globe, finances the methods of stealing. Through the murals and the newspapers I've learned how to bear false witness. Who bore false witness against me I've forgiven.

Many Blacks have moved here from the larger outer boroughs and they've adopted what they feel are protective practices. They have developed a tendency to be selective in the places they frequent, with the preference for those where other Blacks are likely to be found. The search for the good life on Staten Island continues for the Blacks, but it's continued with caution. While there may have been some, mostly Puerto Ricans, Mexican, Chinese who ventured into predominately white neighborhoods, many others opted for the familiarity and safety of these neighborhoods where other Blacks have already settled. The lifestyle of the new Black class continues to be constrained by racism. It's still active in this American island - my Staten Island - where the pain continues.

All of this is not a new development. Regardless of the economy the job prospects for African Americans have long been significantly worse than the country as a whole. The most obvious explanation for this entrenched disparity is racial discrimination, but in my research I've found another difficult culprit. That culprit is favoritism; getting the inside edge with help from family and friends, it's a powerful hidden force driving inequality on this island. And such favoritism has a strong racial component. Through such seemingly innocuous networking white Americans tend to help other whites on the island because social resources are concentrated among the whites. Look about you, brothers and sisters, African Americans are not part of the same networks. They will have a harder time finding decent jobs. Check your personal networks.

More than ever before, people want to talk to me about religion. Perhaps it's because we old people are closer to the departure zone or that we look and act as though we want to leave here for the Promised Land. I do not know that religion, age, and death go hand in hand. When I sat down to do this, I thought I would separate the primary issues—politics, religion, sex, and so forth—but I can tell you now that I was wrong. There are no single issues that make up our lives; everything is intertwined. Decisions—they all come from the sounds, the sights, the experiences that fall on us like autumn leaves and make up the entire person from day one.

Sunday mornings, especially when I was a kid, used to mean something special to me. Going to church not only meant clean clothes, but after church services, if I behaved, there might be a movie or a trip to Al Deppie's for a footlong hot dog, while my father would have a plate of oysters or clams. Now when I see churches, I face them with dread, a kind of bittersweet sorrow that pulls at my heart and soul, so much so that the tension makes me reach for an aspirin.

Every Sunday in my teens I attended Sunday school and then, with my family or a member of my family, participated in the church services upstairs. But I began wondering about the truth of the religious stories and teachings. I remember my mother warning me that if I didn't go to church, something bad would happen to me. And of course, I knew about people burning in hell. I knew that God was up there, watching me. I would ask my mother, what if there were no heaven or hell? My mother would give me that look of disbelief but her response never varied. "What do you mean, no heaven or hell? It has to be true because it says so, right there in the Bible." Of course, that would silence any further questioning. But quietly, inside, I began to realize that most people do not and cannot accept any statements that do not conform to what they presently believe, or questions that challenge those beliefs. How can they? How can Biblical statements have any false information that is inconsistent with reality?

Most people, I began to realize, refuse to accept a new belief, especially a new religious belief, because it would contradict their present belief system. Now, I was evaluating my own belief systems because I was given The Good Book. I had read The Good Book. There was only one book in our home and it was the Bible. When the authorized King James Version was replaced by the new Bible, I realized that many of the belief systems were influenced and determined by which particular version of the Bible we read.

Even today, I remember the gigantic murals behind the preacher in the church of the blue-eyed, blond Jesus in his white shawls holding a cute little white lamb. That was my Jesus. Most Black churches had the same figure on the wall behind the preacher who was preaching to his Black audience weekly. This man, this Jesus, was our likeness?

Saint Michael's Catholic Church was the biggest building in Mariners Harbor. It was a huge redbrick building with a steeple and bells. The wide stairway on Harbor Road was often filled with members of the community on special occasions, mostly weddings and funerals. I knew about Saint Michael's at a very early age; my mother worked there for years as a housekeeper and cook, and when I was born, everyone knew everyone in Mariners Harbor, Black, white, catholic, and protestant. There were three priests that lived in the parsonage in Harbor Road who served the two catholic churches in Mariners Harbor, St. Michael's and St. Adalbert's, and Father Molinelli was the head priest.

I remember when I was in my early teens, maybe 13 or 14, I would sit on the winding staircase leading up to the choir of St. Michael's listening to choir practice. I was there to listen to the music, the sound, and it was that sound, the voices, that interested me. Many other young guys in the neighborhood would sneak up the stairs to ogle the young girls, and make sounds to distract them, but I honestly believe, even today, that I was captivated by the voices and the music rather than by the women.

One time I was caught by Father Molinelli. I thought he was going to ask me to go to the store and get a Phillies Cigar for him; he was a cigar smoker and it was my duty to go to the store and get him his cigars. But on that occasion he gave me a small red imitation leather booklet of about 85 pages titled *The Safeguards of Chastity: A Frank Yet Reverent Instruction on the Intimate Matters of Personal Life for Young Men* by the Reverend Fulgence Meyer, OFM.

Father Molinelli didn't say anything at all, he merely placed the book in front of me, and I took it. It was unusual because I didn't ever remember him giving me anything before. I realized later that every young man in the neighborhood would have one of these, but for some reason, no one ever discussed its content. No one even mentioned that they had one. I didn't know what chastity was—I had to look up the word in the dictionary. But I found out, after reading the entry, that I was clean, decent, modest, and morally pure. I was pure in thought and in conduct. I had not experienced sexual intercourse and I was also celibate.

The first page in the book was a picture of a young teenage Jesus, the divine model of chastity. "Blessed are the clean of heart for they shall see God." Since, according to the dictionary, I had passed the test of chastity I didn't read much of it, and I would take it home and place it with my other notebooks and diaries, and I wouldn't read it again until more than 50 or 60 years later. It was in the basement of my Lockman Avenue home where I would find it after the death of my mother and the sale of the family homestead.

Looking at the book again, I remembered the incident and I thought about Father Molinelli. He had no children; what did this white priest know about young Black men, their intellect, and their feelings? But, on reflection, I realized that by giving this book to the young men of the neighborhood, Father Molinelli was casting about for possible recruits to the priesthood. I don't ever remember if there were any takers in the neighborhood.

I would find the time to read the little book more closely. Chapter after chapter was given to the very intimate matters of personal life of young men. The beginning text read "O how beautiful is the chaste generation with glory: for the memory thereof is immortal: because it is known both with God and with men. When it is present, they imitate it: and they desire it when it hath withdrawn itself, and it triumpheth crowned forever, winning the reward of undefiled conflicts." (Wisdom 4:1-2: Douay-Rheims Catholic Bible). The secrets of sex were in the first chapter: Living With the Temple of God. Know thyself, know male and female, the human body, the human passions.

This strange method of reading about the erotic drives of the young was strangely off-putting to me. I didn't receive any sexual knowledge at home; my mother and I guess my father each believed that I had gotten some instruction from the other. I guess my father was worried that I might get someone pregnant in high school. There was absolutely no intercourse or sexual activity at the time. I did not have any experience I was simply a victim of my own, as it says in the book, "self-pollution," or masturbation.

Were things different with girls than with boys? I didn't know. I didn't know how to ask. I didn't know who to ask. I wouldn't have known how to describe what it was that I wanted to know. A few people pointed out that it was the school's responsibility, but my public schools gave me no information; there was no public document that was given to me or that I could lay my hands on. Somehow sex came into my life like products in a supermarket. It was on display for me to pick and choose, it was a trial offer. It would be interesting to know what God knew about my fumbling and bumbling around the sex act with the women in my life. That could be a humorous tale; wild and chaotic.

I was very happy. I believed at an early age that I wasn't disobeying the rules of God. I wasn't preparing for the absolute catastrophe. I absorbed the lesson of Lot's wife, the woman who was transformed, after glancing back to the inferno of Sodom and Gomorrah, into a pillar of salt. I would obey the simple rules and I believed that I should always love Jesus. It wasn't evasiveness; I merely wanted to get on the right side of God.

I did love God and I loved the church, knew the church-speak, and I felt very comfortable shouting "Halleluiah" and "Amen" in the sanctuary. I guess there was a time when I literally danced in that religious spirit. I attended many, many services, yet, bitter in my young adulthood, I began to feel disconnected. The fact is that I am disconnected, not necessarily from the God for whom I'm searching; I'm disconnected from the church.

I guess it's probably the same thing that has happened to many other Black American men who often wonder why, despite the years of money put into envelopes, put into collection plates, much of it from the poor colored folks of the North Shore, they see very little that the church has done. We have no coffee shops, offices, museums, bowling alleys, anything that perhaps would entice the Black men who hang around, perhaps even outside the church waiting for his wife inside. I guess what I'm looking for is responsible stewardship.

I know that many Black men seek the solace that they need. I suppose they find it in a bottle of liquor or even drugs. But I guess that as long as our mothers, sisters, wives, and children attend, while our money still flows through the church doors, as long as there are still a few bodies to fill the seats, as long as the church can claim a semblance of relevance to the community, as long as some of us on the outside stand as potential critics of the heart and the stewardship of those Black men charged with leading our church, very few of them are ever going to come looking for us, asking us what we need.

I still miss the organ, the voices, and the misty spiritual sounds of song drifting and rising in the sanctuary. I've always loved the sound and the spirit of the choir. I miss the sight of the older women, the church mothers, in their Sunday dresses, their warm embraces, and their smiles. I guess some men will continue to file into baseball or football stadiums on Sundays instead of heading to church, while other Black men will lose themselves in the scent of gasoline while mowing the lawn, or washing and waxing the cars.

I could be wrong; I might be too harsh, but that's where the pain of searching for God in buildings lies. I very often think that many Black churches, even those well established in the community, are being dismissed as an irrelevant social club.

Inwardly, somewhere along the way, for me the church, the collective Black church, and the Christian faith, have lost their meaning, lost their relevance. I know that there are still many Black men who do go to church, but most Black pastors will readily admit there are far more Black men who don't. And the shadow of the church never falls on the souls of those Black guys who are most lost and drifting in a destructive sea of fatalism. There are no rescue workers who seek the Black men out.

****

Virtually everyone defers to persons of superior competence in their given fields. In the words of physicist Michael Ziman, FRS, priests, like scientists, *"favor the passive voice, the impersonal gender, and the Latinized circumlocution, because these would seem to permit, in the circumstances, a climate of opinion within which, as it were, one can express relatively positive assertions in a tentative tone to which one would not be utterly committed if it should happen that complete coincidence had not been achieved with objective reality. This sort of shyness is not just a trick for escaping when one turns out to be wrong; it is a device of 'inverted rhetoric', by which an apparently modest and disinterested tone enhances the acceptability of one's utterances...It's a cunningly contrived great piece of rhetoric. It has only one purpose; it must persuade the reader of the veracity of the observer, his disinterestedness, his logical infallibility, and the complete necessity of his conclusions."*

You continue to read, but this, my friend, is not the whole earth category or rather the Whole Earth Catalogue, which in the '60s and '70s was THE book. But in the end the Rev. Dr. Fulgence Meyer, OFM, has both the language and the design which seem to proceed, it's the same, it's a compartmentalized, standardized, technological environment, choking in fluff. In all of what I read continually is a confusion of tongues and that can have practical consequences. If you debauch a language you run a grave risk of debauching the minds of those who use it.

As Arthur Herzog, III said in *The B.S. Factor:*

"One of the main results of continual fakery is confusion—confusion about objectives, means, ends, and meanings. This confusion is not coincidental. It might be compared to a protective screen behind which Americans can hide their fears, their failures their true preoccupations. The obsolescence of some of their polar ideas, the selfishness of interest groups, the shortcomings of their society. The language seems to speak of false bravado, of a superiority complex of an increasingly regimented form of life, and most loudly of all, of self-delusion. It buries everything all together in the haze of splintered intellect."

The safeguards of chastity would be put aside, the sex that I knew came from the street, traded magazines, little "dirty" books. The stories all seemed kinky, but they also seemed nice. They were not a complete turn-on but they were also not a total turn-off. The most erotic stories came from the Bible and I was allowed to read that openly. Much of it abstract, yes, but I used my imagination.

At birth I had my tonsils removed, was circumcised and vaccinated, and some guys even had their appendix removed. It was the right of parents. These were body parts carefully discussed in the open and dismissed. This was for our own good. There were no questions. The Bible, again, was even more interesting. We would always read more about this circumcision business. God, the extremely patriarchal deity, assures Abraham that kings shall come forth from him, but part of the deal was that Abraham must be circumcised, together with all the members of his clan group, even his slaves, and any male not circumcised must be cut off from his people. So the cutting of the foreskin becomes an initiation rite, branding all the males as members of God's Chosen

People, as well as ensuring that the rights to the land God gave them would be handed down to the male descendants of the clan. I was a chosen one also.

THE THEATRE OF EXECUTION

The night Jesus was arrested they took him up to governor Pontius Pilate's house, and they made a charge against Jesus that he was trying to lead a revolt and make himself king. Pilate found Jesus to be more pathetic than threatening, and he didn't really want to deal with this whole mess, so he sent Jesus to King Herod and asked the king to figure out what was with this guy. Was Jesus actually trying to put himself on the throne?

Herod was really excited to have Jesus in his palace, thinking he could get him to put on some kind of a magic show after hearing of his exploits in the community. But he was disappointed. King Herod found Jesus to be boring and something of a mope, so, as a joke, Herod dressed Jesus up in a king's robe and sent him back to Pontius Pilate. Pilate, seeing the skinny sad man in a loincloth draped with a royal purple robe, busted out laughing; it was such a funny mean-spirited joke, that it instantly made Pilate and Herod the best of friends. They were still not convinced that Jesus was much of a threat, but in order to keep everyone happy, Pilate relented and had Jesus executed, crucifying him on the outskirts of town.

As he slowly bled to death it seemed like the whole world had gathered around to ridicule Jesus. As he hung there dying they threw stones at him, and mocked him for being so naïve as to waste time on such pathetic and misguided ideas like forgiveness.

Out of Nazareth

1

pilate the procurator, mean bastard that he was
thought three hours a mercifully quick death
for this, what's his name? jew. he, pilate
was satisfied that he's played the rabble well

the soldiers thought it a routine dispatch
for a slave or one not graced to be born roman

tired of holier-than-thou ascetics
in a town where prophets pitched gnosis
on every corner, the sadducee rabbis were smug
they dared him to miracle his broke ass
out of this one

his buddies lay low as he said they would
if the distant patriarch he called on
in the only prayer he ever taught noticed
his response was skimpy: black sky, small tremor
cracked rocks, a few crypt doors popped open

Hall's Temple Reformed Church on Caroline Street. Black-owned church remains unused and deteriorating for 35 years.

Above: Attempt by Blacks to build a house of God remains unfinished after more than two decades.

Below: Minister asks the congregation from the pulpit, "Where are all the Black men?"

The author's visit to Mecca

The author's visit to the Mosque at Medina, Mohammed's burial site.

Above: Sale of stamps honoring Muslims denied to the author by
S.I. postal worker.
Below: Dialogue between Eskimo and missionary priest.

Eskimo: "If I did not know about God and sin,
would I go to hell?"
Priest: "No, not if you did not know."
Eskimo: "Then why did you tell me?"

nothing major, nothing grand

2

manual for crucifixion: you prepare the apostate
by flogging. have him carry the crossbeam through the streets
to where the stake is securely planted. a crowd
always turns out for a lynching & they will taunt him
with insults & refuse. let them. it makes a good show
keeps the people happy & gives the prisoner the full benefit
of the experience by letting him die humiliated. attach his feet
one atop of the other to a little plant of olive wood
with a single spike & drive that into the stake. do not
nail the hands to the crossbeam - they will break free&
then you've got a mess. instead affix the forearms
to it. a board under the hips will hold the body up
& better excruciate the miscreant. he'll eventually die
of suffocation & if you do it right the demise
will take days. to check for the imminence of death
look for the bottomless thirst, then awful shudders
of course, you could be nice & break his legs
or ribs so that the shock releases him faster. always
stab him in the heart to make sure he's dead
so he doesn't get buried alive. no need to be cruel

3

the marys came for him loaded with perfumes
to defend against the awful reek
of deadtown. instead they walked into a light
in the gloaming, a speaking light in the room
of the dead. speaking light that threw no shadows
in a voice that made no sound. he is not here
the light said you won't find him in deadtown
the terrible voice in the glow said to the marys
in this putrescent place of the missing dead
words in the glow of the life of the dead
shook the marys to the quick. the men
thought them hysterical

4

paul, jew of tarsus, snitch for the pharisees
fresh from the lapidation of stephen
met jesus from the foot of his horse
in a coma, blind from the light, the word
of the way in his ear, paul fell into the faith
he would make from scratch & take
to the uncircumcised of flesh & uncircumcised
of heart & out of the uptight law of moses

now off to fight the bloody bull of mithras
sweet isis, daughter of earth & sky
cybele, great succulent mother of us all
writing letters to the faithful as he went

5

celsus, pagan & proud of it, thought he'd look
into this new galilian custom: the unanimity
was impressive, & you hadda give him the morality
which was hard to come by in rome. & man
could they blow. but face it, their audience
was children & silly women, especially widows
especially widows with money, & their eloquence
was the eloquence of frogs
but who could take seriously their dictum
that the cosmos with all of its back & forth
lived in each of us. rome had it right. better
to take the gods of all nations into battle
with them. especially the ones more manly than this

A.B. Spellman, Things I Must Have Known, Coffee House Press, Minneapolis 2008

MEN'S GROUPS

For many, many years I tried to understand the Bible, wondered what I was supposed to extract from the Good Book. The Bible Study groups in all of the churches that I went to, the men's groups, would usually meet on Sunday to study the Word of God. Some men would come all the time, every week, and others would only come occasionally. Most of the men there were older men, over 50, and married. Sometimes the group was led by the pastor and sometimes other men were appointed, and whoever was running the group would present extracts from the Bible for discussion that they thought would be helpful to the Black men.

It was an excellent time; it felt like the only time that I would see this number of Black men together. The camaraderie was amazing, and I would go to this group or that group. But I always wondered, what was it that we were really here for? What was the important question?

We never really got into the economics of our situation. Most of the men knew someone in their neighborhood or in their own household that was using or was addicted to drugs. This was Staten Island, my part of Staten Island, and in private conversations and in most of the conversations that took place when we were reading or studying the Bible, it was clear that drug abuse was a big problem.

It was simply a matter of understanding and reading the Bible.

I noticed that conversations about AIDS were anathema. I realized that there was a great deal of avoidance of talking about sexuality, classism, unemployment, and education, although I knew that most of the Black men in these groups were unemployed or underemployed. And questions in the group about sex, sexuality, or anything intimate between men and women were way too sensitive to open up for any kind of discussion; they were usually dismissed.

The men that were not employed would put their feelings on the table immediately. "Why would I go to church if I have nothing to put in the basket?" "What is the preacher doing to help us get a job?" Many of them said they simply could not understand what the preacher was saying. What was he getting at? I had my own reasons for being there and I knew that like other the Black men in this group, I had to be more forceful in order to find any answers here.

The Bible always fascinated me, especially Genesis, with its slavery, racism, and pornography. I wanted to talk about Noah. The Bible tells us that when he got drunk and naked in his tent, his son Ham saw him and told his brothers. Noah got pissed off at that and cursed Ham's son, saying "You will be the lowest of slaves to your brothers." And I wondered, would this be where the Black Africans were later designated as the descendants of Ham by white Christians? This biblical passage really bothered me for many years. I could never get that discussion on the table.

I wanted to discuss the destruction of Sodom and Gomorrah; that was a bizarre reading. There was Lot's wife, leaving her home in Sodom, looking back when she was told not to do so and being turned into a pillar of salt. And there were Lot's daughters who got him drunk and slept with him in order to have children. I could never understand why that discussion was tabled. Whenever I opened these pages I was told that it was not welcome here; another time, perhaps.

The deacon, Mr. Williams, had been appointed to lead the morning Bible study class. It was a hot morning in August and the deacon was dressed in his full suit, shirt, and tie. I remember this because he was always pissed at me for what I was doing, but at the time I was wearing shorts. The temperature in the basement was 99 degrees or maybe more. There was one window fan working. I had a bunch of papers that I was prepared to give to the other Black brothers about homosexuality in the church but I never got to it. I would never even get to first base with it.

But I realize now the dress code was just that. The women upstairs, the matrons, were always dressed in white and white gloves. The minister encouraged the men, the deacons and the trustees, to follow him wearing shirts and ties but no sports jacket. I couldn't handle it, I wasn't going upstairs, but I don't remember anyone suggesting that the dress code be somewhat relaxed during the hot summer months. Most of the men who wore a suit, were not comfortable in them, they wore a suit only for weddings and funerals and other formal affairs. The church was, as I remember it, only somewhat air conditioned upstairs. I know that the men could afford to wear fine clothes but they happened to have become so involved in the dress code, it was just that, it was a code, no one really pushed the issue.

That day, Deacon Williams wanted to talk about where all of the Black American men were. Where are the brothers? The previous Sunday I had taken dozens and dozens of photos of the hundreds, perhaps a couple of thousands, of Black men on shiny motorcycles in Tompkinsville, but I couldn't bring myself to tell him that most Black American men were not into being inside dressed like this. Neither were the sisters.

Besides, many of the ministers, pastors, preachers, would be browbeating the few men that were in the pews anyway. The people who needed to be there simply weren't there.

I thought for a long time why most Black men on Staten Island don't go to church long before I ever thought about writing about it. There were just notes of what I saw, but you can't be what you don't see. Many of the brothers, the Black men, grow up anti-church not wanting to be a part of the church, the tithing, the dressing up, but I saw very much in my travels around Staten Island that they just couldn't be a part of what was a loving community church, supporting the church with tithing. It just wasn't their thing. It was irrelevant.

****

"Cleve, perhaps you should go back to where you came from." I had heard that before, many times. Go back, with your Bible. Go back to where you were born. Go back and find there what it is that you really want to know.

In Genesis it says that the Hebrews are God's chosen people. They are divine beings. But nowhere in the Bible does it say that the God of the chosen people is the only God, which is where I, in my infinite wisdom, I thought perhaps Allah would be found.

What did that have to do with my being a Black person? It was very difficult for me to be carrying a Bible, reading it, and wondering why Abraham seemed to be pimping his wife to pharaoh in exchange for camels and slaves. That kind of morality is murky at best, and it didn't make any sense to me. Probably it was a distortion that was twisted to fit the legend. How much did I believe in the magic that was expressed so many times in the Bible; the spiritual powers, the dreams, the visions, the oracles, the spells, and the curses? I would continue to educate myself. The Bible always fascinated me, and I would read it again and again.

Most of the brothers in the Sunday morning meetings became as frustrated as I when our gatherings produced nothing. Once we were given a questionnaire that we were supposed to fill out. Again, I wanted to discuss the things in the Bible I had difficulty understanding. Again, I wanted to speak about things like going to hell and being saved. And it wasn't just me. The brothers wanted to talk about these things too. These were the FAQs.

Brother Bill said "I've got a problem with all this heaven stuff. The White man, he kick my butt every day on the job down there. Pay me just enough to live on while he enjoys a nice house up in Westerliegh someplace. I live in the projects across the street. I'm told the more I suffer the more I'm going to receive in heaven Well, I gotta tell ya, I've gotta problem with that. Yea, I gotta problem with that. I can sin all my life and like the brother who's hanging on a cross next to Jesus at the last minute the white brother goes to heaven, he can cop a plea, but I hope that every white person who's been involved in oppressing my ancestors, I hope they rottin' in hell right now. I don't want 'em to be saved; I want 'em to be rottin' in hell right now. Why do us Black Americans always have to suffer and wait? I want my 40 acres and a mule right now. I can't be talkin'

444

about heaven; I can't be talkin' about some place I can't see. I can't even talk about some God I can't see, but I know camel shit when I see it."

The Deacon running the group, he had other things on his mind. He wanted to bring all of these men together, young and old, like we were in some kind of a club, a Christian club. But how can you say that God loves these people when they spend their whole lives ignoring His commandments? How can someone who despises the laws of Moses ever become a real man?

He told them about the prodigal son. That's about some rich kid who went on a drunken spending spree with his father's money. The prodigal son bugged his father to get an advance on his inheritance. Once the kid got his hands on the money, he left his home, he left his father, and he left the farm and ran off to the city. Yup, just like your sons. They go over to Manhattan, buy expensive clothes, take their friends out for drinks, barbeque, and women.

But it wasn't long before the boy ran out of his papa's money. His party friends left him; he was forced to live on the streets and pawn his clothes, and one day he hit rock bottom. Having blown his inheritance he returned home hoping his father would hire him as a servant. The father saw him coming up the driveway and ran out and put a warm coat around his shoulders and a gold ring on his finger to celebrate his return. The older brother didn't understand why his brother should get a party with balloons and cake for throwing his life away and wasting everything he had been given. His papa looked at him and said, "Son, the fact that I love your brother doesn't mean I love you any less. You still get everything that's coming to you for leading a good life. But today you just gotta be happy that your brother is back with us."

I had become frustrated and impatient and I wondered how I ever became suckered into this Black American man's room, this house, this place, this church.

My last attempt at anything, humorous or serious, would come to an end when the deacon running the Group I was in gave us a lesson plan for the following week so that we could study certain passages in Proverbs. No one would really study Proverbs and wish to discuss them, I knew that. It was bluff; it was bullshitting bluff. It's sort of a "who's on top" calculation, but bluffing and bullshit always seemed to be part of what happened when we were studying the Bible. I wasn't happy but I would do it. I would do whatever I could to, perhaps, eventually, get back to Genesis, which I loved.

I next week I came prepared. I had my papers; I had my responses to the Proverbs. We were all speaking in sort of a Black American male one-upmanship game called playing the dozens. I don't recall how we got into this, but, to give you an idea, the deacon read from Proverbs "A fool spurns his father's admonition, but prudent is he who heeds reproof."

He looked at me and I said "A stitch in time saves nine." He didn't laugh.

He went on. He chose to read Proverbs 17. "A quick-tempered man makes a fool of himself, but the prudent man is at peace. Well, Mr. Overton?"

I looked up and said "Don't take any wooden nickels."

He didn't see any humor in that and he went on to Proverbs 16; "Better a little with the fear of the Lord than a great fortune with anxiety."

I answered, "Birds of a feather flock together."

He turned a page, looked at me, and said "Guilt lodges in the tents of the arrogant, but favor in the house of the just."

I love that one. I said "Father, Son & Holy Ghost, who eats the fastest, eats the most."

He looked at me. He was pissed off, I knew he was, and I said that I would not be there the following week. I was going back home; I wasn't feeling the spirit; as a matter of fact I was believing less and less in God. It's all a game. I bid them farewell and I left.

Arthur Schopenhauer said in his essay The Wisdom of Life:

> *The only way of putting an end to this universal folly is to see clearly that it is a folly; and this may be done by recognizing the fact that most of the opinions in men's heads are apt to be false, perverse, erroneous and absurd, and so in themselves unworthy of attention; further, that other people's opinions can have very little real and positive influence upon us in most of the circumstances and affairs of life. Again, this opinion is generally of such an unfavorable character that it would worry a man to death to hear everything that was said of him, or the tone in which he was spoken of. And finally, among other things, we should be clear about the fact that honor itself has no really direct, but only an indirect, value. If people were generally converted from this universal folly, the result would be such an addition to our piece of mind and cheerfulness as at present seems inconceivable; people would present a firmer and more confident front to the world, and generally behave with less embarrassment and restraint. It is observable that a retired mode of life has an exceedingly beneficial influence on our peace of mind, and this is mainly because we thus escape having to live constantly in the sight of others, and pay everlasting regard to their casual opinions; in a word, we are able to return upon ourselves. At the same time a good deal of positive misfortune might be avoided, which we are now drawn into by striving after shadows, or, to speak more correctly, by indulging a mischievous piece of folly; and we should consequently have more attention to give to solid realities and enjoy them with less interruption that at present. But what is worth doing is hard to do.*

I thought very hard, very deeply and I came away from that final meeting with the Black brothers in the church basement with the feeling that you do all you can diplomatically and hope that eventually you will make some kind of a breakthrough. After all, it couldn't hurt, could it? As T.S. Elliot said *"The only wisdom we can hope to acquire is the wisdom of humility: humility is endless."*

ISLAM & MY JOURNEY TO MECCA

Some years later when I returned to the United States from Africa, I would move to Washington D.C. I began to act upon a very private decision: I would begin to read about and make a conversion to Islam, and I would travel to Mecca. I would tell no one but the very close Muslim friend, who would accompany me. I had a lot of reading and a lot of homework to do!

My dear friend Omar Abdoulaye was an educated middle-class Mauritanian whose family had been in the military and suffered greatly during one of the many purges there. His present to me of the Quran was something that he merely presented as a gift.

The Quran, I found, is both magnificently simple and unspeakably complex. Of course my version was translated into English, which did not make it any easier, but trying to read the Quran was very difficult and complicated because of its contradictions and ambiguities.

As the Muslims that I joined at the mosque read and hear the text, they strive to suffuse themselves with the spiritual dimensions of its message. The Quran is beyond time, beyond history, beyond the millions who populate the earth. The Quran is inviting, guiding, counseling, and commanding. There is no intermediary. The simplicity makes one fall silent, lost in thought, reading the Surah. The Quran is revealing in sequences of varying length and the entire chapters of its Surahs are in neither chronological nor strict thematic order.

I believe it is impossible to obtain general information on this or that aspect of Islam. One must study and study to derive the principles. It is a demanding task which took me long into the weary hours of the night. The Quran requires study and also extreme caution. It is at times light linear reading, likely to disorient the reader and to give rise to incoherence and perhaps even contradiction.

I remember asking Omar Abdoulaye questions about the continuing bravery in his country and in many Islamic regions, at the ill-treatment of woman under Islam, at the dreary Jew-bashing. He did not flinch, merely gave me another book, much simpler for me to read and to digest. He presented me with the Sunnah. The Quran is the words of Allah sent down to Prophet Muhammad, while the Sunnah is the teaching of Prophet Muhammad.

There is no translation of the meaning of the Quran beyond what is revealed in the book. The Quran exists exactly as it was revealed in the original Arabic language some 1300 years ago, and it will remain exactly the same for all time as God's final message to all mankind. Unlike the Bible there is only one version of the Quran. Any other translation would be merely an attempt to convey the meaning of the Quran. The Quran is Arabic and must be studied in Arabic. I found it to be terribly difficult. There are many translations from Arabic to English, French, and other languages, but it is hoped by those that practice the Quran, that the meanings of Muhammad the Messenger remain the same.

I didn't know how much I would gain, if anything, from a pilgrimage to Mecca, but I did realize that, at the minimum, I was gaining insight through my continued reading. There are many parts of the Sunnah that makes one's fulfillment to one's duty very similar to the life that I realized I was already leading.

Before my journey to Mecca, I talked to many people who raised questions about my going. I found that many of my friends were against my travel to Mecca. They warned me how the women of Saudi Arabia are not allowed to travel alone, or to sit with a strange man and talk and laugh and drink coffee together like they were married. They had religious police and women are not allowed to drive. They have a monarchy. They are socially intolerant and conservative. They are extreme. Why would I go there?

At this point I didn't really know what I was getting into. I simply had convinced my brain that this was what I needed to do. I knew that I wanted to journey to Saudi Arabia; I knew that I wanted to make that hajj to the heart of Islam; I wanted to make the pilgrimage to the center of the Muslim faith. Hajj at Mecca; I had to do it.

The hajj is the fifth pillar of Islam, and every Muslim who can afford it is obliged to travel to Mecca for the hajj at least once in his life. Its origins being in the story of Abraham, the hajj is a set of strict rituals performed every year for five days and with this hajj the pilgrims must follow the route of Muhammad, who did the hajj before he died. The hajj begins in Mecca.

You don't have to go overseas to experience the birthplaces of the religions here, but I decided to take a voyage, to perhaps slow down, relax, and discover the truth, the truth of my own spiritual identity, my own deeper truth. I decided with my friend Jude to visit St. Peters in Rome. We spent four days with the throngs of people moving in, around, and about. Past the paintings on the walls and ceilings, past the hundreds of sculptures, trying to move slowly and breathe in the history and the culture of this place if possible.

We came face to face with Michael Angelo's famous sculpture, the Pieta. Of course one could not get close; there was a thick glass protective cover, and lots of people in front of me and behind me. But we did see it and I was struck to my very core. Looking at the Pieta one could feel the anguish and the pain of this mother at the death of her son. The face is alive with anguish, it's tortured by the finality she was facing. It's of breathtaking beauty.

The simple 4-day tour of Vatican museums, the Sistine Chapel and St. Peters Basilica; the crush of the tourists and the faithful; the art and the faith; this was a spiritual experience and the art and beauty would perhaps be more real to me than they were before from viewing them in a book or the National Geographic, but the trip did not touch my need.

You don't have to be a Catholic to go to the Vatican. You don't have to be Jewish to go to the Western Wall. You don't have to be a Buddhist to hear the Dalai Lama speak. But Mecca is a special case. It is written in the holy book that only Muslims can enter. My odyssey to Saudi Arabia would be nearly impossible for me to experience without conversion, and my conversion would be complete.

I had accepted the invitation to visit Mecca from my dear friend Omar Abdoulaye, and I said I would study as hard and as much as I could before our trip. First we would spend some weeks in Jordan, and then we would travel from Jordan to Saudi Arabia. And I liked the idea that if I respectfully completed my hajj I would become respectfully referred to as an El- hajji.

So, in 2008, armed with my passport stamped with the bold national emblem of Saudi Arabia, the palm tree and the crossed swords, I realized my long-held dream, to go to Saudi Arabia, and to visit Mecca. I first went to Amman, Jordan to visit with my friend Omar, his wife Maryam, and their four children. My visit to Amman was an eye-opener.

Omar was at the time employed by an NGO company in Jordan, and while he worked in the capital, I would see and experience much more about Islam and the people of Jordan. I visited the mosques with his family, and lived in their gorgeous home in the outskirts of Amman. It was a very, very welcome time for me to understand the people of the country. In Amman, I visited the archeological digs, the excavated roman amphitheater, and the museums. But I looked forward eagerly to the plane that would eventually take Omar Abdoulaye, his wife Maryam and me to Saudi Arabia.

We would land in Jeddah, Saudi Arabia, and then take a short flight to Mecca. We would stay in Mecca for two or three weeks, then we would take another plane trip to Medina in Western Saudi Arabia, stay there for two weeks, then fly back to Jeddah, and return to Amman, Jordan. Omar Abdoulaye, having been to Mecca twice before would be my guide and leader while in Saudi Arabia.

Welcome to Saudi Arabia

My plane from Amman landed in Saudi Arabia at the King Abdullaziz airport in Jeddah in the late afternoon of July 1, 2008. From the tarmac, we stepped aboard a new ground transport bus to the terminal, which is about 30 feet across the roadway to the main air conditioned arrival building. The heat was oppressive, heavy, and felt like 110 degrees Fahrenheit (at least 43 degrees Celsius.) Some passengers waited for the baggage at the carousel and I walked straight to the immigration and visa check booths to present my documents to the agent, who scanned and stamped my passport. I replied to him, "Shukran," thank you, with my few Arabic words.

Beyond the booth and a few feet away was a conveyer on which I placed my bags. I removed my belt, wrist watch, and metal for x-ray, then walked through the electronic body scanner next to the conveyer. I noticed that no one removed their shoes. The officer on the other side motioned me through to collect my bags. As I walked towards the exit door an officer in uniform behind a desk motioned me to leave and I again felt the humid, enveloping heat.

As I stood for a moment looking at the names printed on paper signs and looking across the street to the taxi area, four young men in their twenties, wearing white shirts and black ties and black trousers, came forward, saying "Passport, passport," with open palm gestures suggesting urgency. I looked around and hesitated, having just gone through the immigration and inspection process. "Passports, passports!!" The demands were repeated and the extended hand movements said, "Quickly." I looked around and other passengers were asking questions in Arabic and languages I did not understand while still others were handing the men their passports. They continued to take passports saying loudly, "Passports, passports" to those of us that did not respond.

The men had no uniforms, name tags, insignia or identification and I was still reluctant to hand over my passport to anyone. The officer inside the door behind me said nothing and looked away. I gave one of the men my passport. He then said to us all, "Come, come," and we walked behind him across the road to the taxi area and then to an old, low, white trailer that had no windows and only one door. One of the men motioned us to an area with chairs with a flick of his hand, as though he were whisking insects away,

449

indicating we should go and sit. Many were women in long robes and men who were going to Mecca dressed in their white two-piece cloths and sandals.

The area with the chairs was next to the wooden structure, amazingly different from the spotlessly clean area I observed as we left the bus and the airport terminal building. I didn't like the feel of what was happening. The men entered through the doorway of the white building with the passports and another man stood in the doorway barring anyone from entering. It was beginning to get dark, and I felt something weird was happening.

The seating area was under a metal roof with fans moving the humid air. The signs read, "Tas Heel." Dozens of filthy, white molded plastic chairs sat in pools of water and food debris, cigarette butts, and soda cans, and the place smelled of urine.

The young men who had collected the passports were now lounging about smoking and drinking coffee, laughing, seemingly waiting for another plane to arrive.

My senses were heightened and I jotted down what was happening in my notebook. My anxiety grew and I listened to people who are now shouting and gesturing. About an hour had gone by and now I joined the men with my gestures, "Why?" "Where are our passports?" "Who is in charge?" I had been looking forward to this voyage for a long time and I was prepared to relax and submit to airport authority. But this seemed to be unofficial. I am used to searches and being ordered around. I know that there are cameras, seen and unseen. But I was an American in the Middle East and I did not want to be the center of an international incident, so I remained silent. I had names and addresses and phone numbers of people in Jeddah but I had no way of reaching them; I had neither a cell phone nor coins for a public phone. It was now sundown, and after a half hour of shouting, I decided to open my bag and take pictures, remembering that the flash at an airport might attract some authorities to this section that now seemed to be getting out of control. I began to take pictures and still no one came to see what was happening here, and the shouting continued.

Make a scene, I thought. Make a scene and attract attention. But without that passport, that document, I was nobody, nothing. In making a scene or creating a disturbance, would I would be guilty of a heinous Saudi Arabian crime? Would I be given 80 lashes, buried up to my neck in sand, put to death by stoning, wrapped in a white sheet, placed in a shallow, unmarked grave, and buried somewhere in the Arabian Peninsula desert? I took out my camera, hoping that the flash would bring someone. There were no police officers or camouflaged soldiers holding AK 46 guns. But after my loud protestations, and many camera flashes, nothing changed.

Later, a small, thin man, about 5 feet tall with salt and pepper hair and glasses, dressed in a white robe and sandals, came to the group of men shouting at the doorway. He seemed frightened but calm, and was grasping a handful of papers in his hands. I asked him who he was and if he had a card. He pointed to some words in Arabic on his papers and pointed to the doorway of the trailer. After a few minutes, he turned and walked away. No one came after the camera flashes, and I could not leave the area without my passport in a foreign country, so I stood at the door. Finally, a man holding a handful of passports appeared at the doorway and I recognized the blue cover with the eagle and words United States of America and took it from his hand.

I had no idea what they did with my passport. I had no idea if the information in it would appear some time or somewhere later. I had no idea what had just happened. I was tired, hot, and angry. I would keep my notes and photos for later reference when my pilgrimage/voyage was over and decide what to do.

I decided not to linger in Jeddah and took a taxi to the connecting airport, changed my ticket and spent the night waiting for a flight out.

Later, I would write to people, agencies, groups, anyone that might give me the reason for this less-than-humane treatment of so many people here in Saudi Arabia. If this is how visitors are treated; this would be my last visit.

Mecca

Once in Mecca, Omar Abdoulaye and I would purchase two ihrams and two pairs of flip-flop sandals, without strings, buttons, or clasps. An ihram consists of two unstitched white sheets of cloth, resembling something like a shroud, which are worn during the hajj and the shoes are necessary to protect your feet from the hot tiles of the mosque.

We would carry around our necks a booklet that contained all the steps that were necessary to make a proper hajj. Omar showed me how to put on the ihram, and told me about the recommended prayers for different stages of the hajj.

On my first day we boarded a bus to the Kaaba. The Kaaba is an immense cube-shaped granite building and it is the holiest site in Islam. Before we boarded the bus I had to change into my ihram, which is traditionally all a pilgrim may wear, but because of my age I was allowed to wear a wide belt under the ihram that could hold medicines, and in it I placed my very small camera. I did not know at the time whether cameras would or would not be allowed inside the Kaaba or the mosque.

The buses were very crowded with women seated, the men standing. I did not have a pencil or pad, and everything that I saw I had to jot down in my memory. People were carrying the Quran, people were constantly praying saying, in Arabic, "I come Lord, and I am here. You have me, I am here. Grace and sovereignty belong to you."

From time to time I tried to flip the pages of the guidebook around my neck. On that first bus trip from the hotel to the shrine we were standing shoulder to shoulder, and, since I was unsure how to secure them, I found it very difficult to keep my flip-flops from being scooted away!

We came to the old quarter of Mecca. Although I couldn't ask anyone, it seemed to me as though giant machinery was tearing apart the large old concrete and stone houses, homes, and buildings. Development, development, development was going on. I wanted to photograph it, but at this part of my visit I did not want to reveal that I had a camera, although I would find out later that the camera was not illegal.

We came to an overpass at the Al-Masjid al-Ḥarām, or the Grand Mosque. The Grand Mosque houses the Kaaba, and it lies in the lowest point of the city. We left the bus and climbed the stairs. There was a moving staircase but it was so jammed that we decided to walk up. We came to the western side of Mecca sort of like coming out of a metro from the long tunnel. I looked up and there were the seven giant minarets and all I could do was marvel. I found myself almost speechless.

Beyond this white granite space I noticed that there were areas that were sectioned off with partitions that looked like Jersey barriers. In some there were only women, and in others there seemed to be people, who I guessed were Indonesians, huddled together praying. Many other groups followed their leader under an umbrella or flag. People were praying, moving quietly, most of the men in their two-piece white garments. Many now had the bare right shoulder preparing to enter the Mosque at Mecca.

I follow closely behind Omar and his wife. Before entering I remove my sandals and carry them in my hand. In the courtyard sat the Kaaba, a huge black cube. I am speechless, silenced by wonder. It is so prominent that around it men seem so infinitesimally small, so unnecessary. I notice that the men and the women are shoulder to shoulder, there is no sex separation or discrimination. There are Blacks, there are whites, there are old, and there are young. Men are constantly driving floor cleaning machines, expertly avoiding people. There are no trash baskets or receptacles, no litter. Men pray on their prayer rugs, thousands move about in groups before entering the Kaaba.

We enter one of the openings, a man stands at the entrance to check for proper attire, we can leave our sandals outside or carry them in our hands. On the outer rim inside there are hundreds of white marble columns and people sitting or sleeping resting in white. We move toward the center, and the huge black stone.

The white marble is so hot. There are so many bodies that walking normally is not possible. We begin to glide to our right toward the slow moving mass circling the center and the cube that seems to become larger.

I begin to feel my body float up. There is a constant M-M-M-M-M-M of voices reading the Koran, some calling out "God is Great." I have entered a theatre, an intruder who is lost in special effects, as my brain processes an increasing out of body experience. The heat and the feeling that I am about to lose consciousness cause me to move to the outer part of the circle, to the long lines of brass water fountains. I am exhausted. Nothing stops; the circling continues, the sound has gotten inside my body and I need even more water to pour on my feet and wash my face and find a place to sit down. There are no chairs, but there are many prayer rugs on the white, hot, marble.

I didn't realize at first, though I would on our third or fourth trip around, that we are moving counter-clockwise, and I pull Omar wanting to get closer and closer to the huge Kaaba in this open courtyard. I move through the people, the old, the young, the fat, the thin, some men with scars on their shoulders that I would learn are from a group that beat themselves with chains and scar their bodies in the name of Allah, but I say nothing to anyone.

The closer I get to the black cube I realize that I want to touch it, why I don't know. I motion to Omar Abdoulaye and hope that he will hear me over the prayers. "Don't lose me. I will be over there." I point to a section where I will be, a place that I can move to after. Pushing myself, humbly and quietly, through the men and women, I am able to move to the black covering. It is made of a very fine but stiff and strong material. Embroidered around it in gold are Quranic verses and the 100 names of Allah.

As I move around I am literally pushed into the black structure by the many people wanting to touch it, to feel it, to press their faces against it. About ten feet up from this granite structure there is a part that's left uncovered. On one corner there's a police officer, telling people who want to reach out and touch the smooth part to "Move On. Continue. Don't Stop." I find myself repeating the words as I pray for my mother, my father, my friends. I have prayers and names that were given to me that I left back at the hotel, but if I come again I will mention their names here at the Kaaba.

It is not a stampede; it is a very determined walk around the center. I can't help but look at some of the faces, the Black faces, the white faces, I look at the eyes. People press their faces and their lips to the stone. The policeman standing on the ledge says "Keep moving! This way! Go! Move!" Some people lose their balance, and are held up by others whether they are friends or just fellow pilgrims.

I reach the stone; I look up at the black fabric. My feet only hurt when I remember that I am barefoot. I feel as though someone is speaking to me inside. I am receiving what I think might perhaps be a blessing, from somewhere, somehow. It is quite upsetting, but also quite calming.

I reach the place that I had indicated to Omar Abdoulaye and I stand up as high as I can. I notice that men and women are drinking water, there are paper cups available, and the water is running constantly. Oh, how I need that! I reach into my waistband, step back, and I take a photo, hoping that I can bring back at least a photo of what is in front of me. There's no way that I can speak about this.

There is a sound of thousands of voices, all merging into one entering my ears, entering my mind, entering my brain, and I can readily understand why the Islamic faith is.

There are men and women pressed shoulder to shoulder walking seven times around the Kaaba. I step back, I look up, and I hold my camera up to take photos.

I would not remember much of what I was feeling until I was back in the US and I could have these photos developed for Jude to see. I knew that I would have to return, but for now I motioned to Omar Abdoulaye that I had to leave; that I would find my own way back to the hotel. The emotion of being here, being here in this outdoor mosque was overwhelming, but I found that I also needed to rush back to empty my brain into my notebooks and prepare myself, I guess, for another day. I was certainly filled with whatever I was receiving. I had to leave.

I was happy to be back in the air conditioned corridors of the hotel, to cool my feet, and to order orange juice. I would return the next day, refreshed, and look at the new city of high-rises and shopping malls which is directly across from the Grand Mosque. One can walk from the Kaaba to the city's new high-rise buildings and shopping malls and two storey escalators with people constantly moving up and down. I had never seen anything like this before but I noticed that many of the shops were selling the high-priced articles that one would find in Paris or London, or New York City. The most interesting thing was the stores advertising the prayer watches which sounded an alarm five times a day. I didn't think I could afford that, or the Italian shoes, high-priced articles.

On the third day I would hear the Muezzin call for the afternoon prayer; I sat respectfully, watching the devout carry out the ritual that is repeated five times a day. I often wondered while I was there, were there many Blacks who had become true followers of Islam that maintain the daily devotions? The strong voice of the Imam recites prayer from Koran.

On the street, there was a constant flow of huge dump trucks going up and down the road. When I asked a man next to me where they were going and what they were carrying, he said, simply by pointing, "There." I didn't speak the language to understand more, but I would soon find out that around the Grand Mosque of Mecca, mountains were being moved and leveled. Constantly, six days a week, from sunrise to sunset, the drilling, the dynamiting, and the giant earth movers continue.

Saudi Arabia has a great deal of oil revenue which was being used to move mountains and to bring 21st century modern technology to Mecca, and I realized that the classic Islamic architecture was disappearing rapidly. The history and the tradition of centuries were disappearing, being replaced by the sprawling imitation height of modern city architecture. Chicago, New York, or Los Angeles in the desert. It seemed like the old must go and the new will take its place, these gleaming glass, steel, brick, and concrete skyscrapers are changing the Wadi forever.

It was interesting to see the old side by side with the modern technology that will now take Mecca into another century. I wondered if all of this would continue to follow the strict religious doctrine of Islam after all of these old buildings are washed away.

I realize that there are many wealthy people that spend thousands of dollars to make this pilgrimage to Mecca, and I am sure that the rulers of this country know that a major source of revenue is from the people who come here for the hajj. They will no longer find the Wadi of Islam. Mecca will become a mecca, a mecca with luxury hotels, luxury prayer rooms, and helipads.

Every evening before night fell I would see dozens upon dozens of people spread cardboard or pieces of white cloth on the white marble where they would sleep. Many were guest workers, Africans and South Asians. I would seek out people who did not look to be Saudi Arabian. I would see many Black women, bags on their heads, coming out of the courtyards and into the alleyways walking to the main roadways. They would simply sit on the sidewalk and spread out their bags of fruits and vegetables and odd-looking packets of food, for sale. Many of the store-keepers would shoo them away from the sidewalk in front of their shops with gestures as I watched "You can't sit here! You can't sit here! Go away!"

The people who had the bright white clothes, the gaudy chequered headdresses, or the watches on their dainty hands were not the ones who were moving the mountains. They were not the ones that were driving those trucks; they were not the ones who were operating the cranes and the digging shovels. I am sure that many of the people sleeping in the courtyard, African, European, and South Asian workers would be mainstay of the brawn and the muscle needed to build these towers, these unusual, strange, 39 or 40 storey buildings of concrete, granite, and stone. What was I looking at in the building around the holy area? Was I looking at New Mecca or was this the new Disneyland of Saudi Arabia? I wondered if I would ever be able to describe this when I reached the United States again. The only memorabilia that I kept was the ihram that I wore on the pilgrimage.

On the plane trip to Medina I was able to look closer at the landscape. The Arabian Peninsula is a vast sea of sand that covers more than 250,000 square miles. It's bigger than France, Belgium, and Holland combined. It's also the hottest place on earth – believe me! The summer temperatures very often reach 140 degrees Fahrenheit, in the shade that is. It is, as I looked down, one of the most forbidding environments I have ever seen, or perhaps the most forbidding environment on the entire planet. I was lucky to be seated next to a Pakistani who pointed out the massive dunes and tried to explain how the ravine-shaped dunes were formed by strong winds that made these long ridges across the flats.

Some of the only modern trails visible are made by roads built by the Saudi oil companies' crude oil processing facilities, but most of the workers, servants, are flown in by plane. The only thing that would come by road, my neighbor told me, would be the heavy equipment. Many parts of the desert looked as though they had been smashed by meteorites from the sky and that asphalt lifeline, I suppose, could disappear at any time if Nature acted up.

This also, he mentioned, was the important crossroads for camels bearing frankincense from the Persian Gulf through Petra to the Mediterranean. As he said, it still is a very normal route from wadi to wadi, lifelines on the Frankincense Trail that the caravans still use. We still use frankincense in our religious ceremonies.

Medina is the second holiest city in Islam, known primarily for its importance in the early years of Muhammad's preaching as well as the site of the Mosque of the Prophet, which contains Muhammad's tomb. The mosque at Medina is quite different from the mosque at Mecca. The Medina mosque is quite large, has eight minarets, perhaps ten or fifteen stories high. It is a covered mosque; with a marble walking area around it, which is constantly cleaned by men driving machines.

The mosque is in the center of Medina. It is the reason for life, the reason for being, and the building is faced so that the prayers of the people would be facing the Kaaba in Mecca. The mosque is usually overflowing with worshippers so the people pray outside on the marble. It is said that the original mosque constructed by Muhammad was built in the year 623. The mosque at Medina is another powerful place of prayer, a place where one can reach out and touch his or her God.

The climate is very hot and humid and the roof of the mosque is raised so that there are hundreds of thousands of openings for the circulation of air. Ventilation towers are equipped with a kind of exquisitely made wooden opening that somehow captures air and circulates it so that there is a continual movement of air inside the building.

I stayed at Medina for three days. It is a very solemn, a very quiet place, this place where, according to tradition, the prophet Muhammad was buried. It's the place where Muhammad's camel stopped; the place that became his home, and his final resting place. I would try to carry with me something other than the photographs I had taken. Clean streets constantly cleaned by men with brooms and brushes. Women in black or white. Constant movement to the places just outside the mosque that carried the only English words that I saw—Toilets. The minarets and the lights are covered in severe white stones. We would come in the evenings, to look at the mosque and find that there were thousands of others who had decided to do the same thing. The lighted minarets gave off a golden hue, Here in Medina the bodies moved more slowly; the faithful spread their rugs and prayed.

I would close my books ready for the return to the United States, carrying very few mementos with me except the cloth that I had worn. It was a very unusual visit. I would like to have stayed longer to speak to the people. Though there were few that could speak English; there were some of those that were anxious to speak to me. I did ask one taxi driver why women were not allowed to drive in Saudi Arabia. His response was that they wore head veils and that could be dangerous. I would file it away in my little note books, try and sort out whatever would be interesting to others.

From the Margins of My Note Book

Many times in my life I would gather together the comedy, the errors of my life, and weeks after my conversion to Islam I would visit a friend on Staten Island who would invite me to go to a West Indian smorgasbord at the Brighton Heights Reform Church in Fellowship Hall. The invitation came very suddenly; I was tossed between what I needed to do on my trip to Mecca, but it was easy for me to refuse his offer and decline when I read the menu - suckling pig, roasted and stuffed! The menu I folded and put into my pocket. I phoned my friend and thanked him for the invitation but I would have to decline.

RELIGIOUS PREJUDICE

Since 9/11 the hatemongers and the white supremacists on Staten Island have been very active. The Sikhs, with their uncut hair, their turbans, and their beards, have been particular targets of discrimination on this island. The rationalization has been simply, "Oh, mistaken identity." One protester arrested by the police shouted "This is not your country. It belongs to white men."

Since 9/11 many Arab Americans, whether Muslim or not, are beginning to legally change their names to resemble names and titles that are more "American." One Arab said "It's unfortunate, but your name does define you. It incorrectly defines me." Many said they Americanized their names because they were being harassed or were having problems getting a job and thought a new name would help.

In 2006 I entered the large post office on Bay Street on Staten Island. I wanted to buy a sheet of the royal blue Christmas Greetings stamps that were written and printed in Arabic with the English word "Eid." Like many others, I found the stamp attractive. However, when I went to the window and asked the sales clerk if he had any of these for sale, he said "None of us will handle those after what happened over there." He nodded and pointed his thumb toward Manhattan.

I immediately understood what he meant. It was the 9/11 bombing. I said, "Oh, I know what you mean, babe. Yeah. You can't get any, huh?"

"Nope, not gonna sell 'em."

I said "OK, babe," turned around and walked away. I took out my notebook and I made a note. Later on that evening I sat thinking for a long time. Imagine if your perceived ethnicity determined what products you were able to buy. For many Americans, and certainly for me, a Black man, it's not hard to imagine.

If I had been a man with a beard and a cloth around my head, would he have said the same thing? Of course, it may have been an isolated episode that could be dismissed as the work of one bigoted or misguided employee. But then I thought, has the US Post Office allowed this, or is it just freelance xenophobia? Discrimination is one result of trying to enforce flawed and haphazard controls against countries and peoples. Was this retail clerk, an employee, empowered to interpret and implement a Federal policy that results in racial profiling?

These workers are supposed to dole out the Christmas, Hanukah, Kwanza, and Eid stamps, assisting in the celebration of a holiday whose secular folklore is based on what is ultimately a grand postal miracle: millions of people, one sleigh, one night, one red suited mailman.

After living abroad, I admit that our mail situation is a kind of liberation. It's very impressive; a system by which one of us billions of people can send an object to another for less than a dollar in less than a week. Quite frankly, I think these employees are geniuses. However, they are not lawyers or law enforcement officers.

It is illegal in the United States under the Civil Rights Act for a private company to discriminate against individuals based on race, color, religion, or national origin. This protection extends, of course, to all retail stores. Must there be printed, posted, sanctions that would punish ordinary clerks that undermine the democracy that we so love?

Beyond the wisdom of American foreign policy, the issue here is the unfair and perverse impact on some Americans who had no involvement in that policy, but quietly exist. The potential for abuse is great unless we speak out and enact policies to prevent discrimination like this, and American policy makers act to stop illegal enforcement activities.

The incidents continued on Staten Island. Hindu worshipers in Dongan Hills at the American Legion Hall were barricaded inside from the outside by large potted plants and heavy concrete. A group running about the building shouted "Go back to your own country. We are going to make sure you go back to your own country." One of the Hindu worshippers said that they are a pacifist community but they will not stand by and allow these incidents to happen without trying to nip it in the bud. Police escorted people away from the building.

When speaking to Muslims it is apparent that they have grown accustomed to the fact that hundreds of mosques have been infiltrated by undercover officers and that the police have compiled extensive dossiers on Muslims; where they work, where they eat, where they transfer money to relatives; and that even the Imams who work closely and courageously with the police have found themselves spied on and listed as suspects.

I became very uncomfortable with the openly anti-Arab, xenophobic, and racist rhetoric that I heard from many people while walking about the island. Supposedly friendly conversations would start and turn immediately into discussions of the enemies in our midst; the "rag heads," the enemies of the Jews who are always ready to attack us, who are always ready to downplay our patriotism.

In my memories of life on Staten Island in the '40s and '50s there were no mosques at all on the island. I was very unfamiliar with Islam until I was faced with the Black Muslims in the '50s and '60s. Malcolm X of the American Black Muslims was killed, shot dead in Harlem. I didn't really know what to believe or to understand about that.

Years later, when there were mosques, at least three that I know of, on Staten Island, conversations with friends and relatives revealed that most Staten Islanders largely thought unfavorably about Muslims in general. I'm sure that numbers have gotten higher, solidified, hardened, since the September 11, 2001 attack in Manhattan on the World Trade Center. The climate today makes it easy for people to lose sight of the fact that the majority of Muslims dislike terrorism and violence as much as they do.

In 2010 there was a plan for a disused Roman Catholic convent on Staten Island to be sold to a Muslim group for use as a mosque. But neighbors who opposed the mosque claimed it might become a front for terrorism. Many members of the parish would gather at the Borough Hall at St. George with placards and signs. The signs read "No Hate, Yes Faith" and "This is My Country." A reporter standing around watching the event would hear such statements as "We have our right to say no. There will be no mosque in Midland Beach." Another would say "Down with the mosque, up with 9/11." One protester commented "What I don't understand is why they want this place when they know they're not wanted. They don't even live in this area."

In the face of this community opposition the Archbishop sent a message to Father Keith Fennessy, the pastor of the St. Margaret Mary R.C. Church which owned the convent in the Midland Beach neighborhood, saying that said he had given the deal a second look and concluded that the contemplated sale would not serve the needs of the parish.

When, in 2011, the Muslim American Society of Staten Island and Brooklyn quietly purchased a former Hindu temple in Dongan Hills, neighbors voiced their concerns about the project, saying "Muslims need to adhere to our Christian ways and NOT those of Islam," and "The worst part about a new mosque in your neighborhood is Muslims will start moving into it. Your property value will plummet and you will sell at a loss to get the heck out," and "Did they kill or threaten all the Hindis so the temple came on the market?"

In 2010 Borough Hall hosted the first annual Staten Island Iftar meal. The Iftar meal is the evening meal during which Muslims break their daily fast during the month of Ramadan. Borough President James P. Molinaro and the Secretary of the Albanian Islamic Cultural Center met in Borough Hall with stiff forced smiles and the Borough President said that he felt no discomfort in hosting this event. However, he went on to say that the Islamic Cultural Center two blocks from Ground Zero was insensitive to the family members of 9/11 victims, and that he had written to its Imam saying that it should be removed.

In 2012 Islamic leaders reported to the police that organizers of the outdoor end-of-Ramadan ceremony found several strips of bacon strewn across the artificial turf where worshippers were to gather.

Although the religious community on Staten Island strives to build bridges, the incidents continue.

THE STORY OF THE POPES

Based on *The Bad Popes* by E.R. Chamberlain, 1969, the Dial Press; *Keeper of the Keys of Heaven: A History of the Papacy* by Roger Collins, 2009 Basic Books, a member of the Perseus Books Group; and *The Cadaver Synod: Strangest Trial in History* by Donald E. Wilkes, Jr., University of Georgia School of Law.

The dominant families of Rome feuded, using the papacy to advance their own ends. Popes were elected, deposed, manipulated, and murdered with astonishing frequency. A staggering 24 held the office between 872 and 965.

Pope John VIII (872-882) was the first pope to be assassinated. He was initially poisoned, but when the poison was too slow in acting, he was bludgeoned to death. Adrian III's short reign (884-885) was marked by increased internecine violence and grudge settling. He had George of Aventine, a civil official, blinded, and the wife of a murdered Nomenclator whipped naked in the street. In spite of this dubious behavior, he was eventually sainted.

Pope Formosus' tenure (891-896) was troubled by botched protocols and continued factionalism. In spite of this his pontificate was a stable if heavy-handed one. Formosus himself had a reputation for piety and asceticism. He died shortly after crowning Arnulf as Holy Roman Emperor, a controversial coronation owing to the questionable legitimacy of Arnulf's birth.

Stephen VI (896-897), his replacement, was haunted by his predecessor. He felt compelled to rectify his perceived missteps and took extreme measures in doing so in the legendary Cadaver Synod of 897.

Formosus' seven months dead, putrid corpse was exhumed from its resting place, dressed in papal robes, and placed on a throne, a mockery of Formosus's station in life. A young deacon was appointed as the dead pope's counsel and thus began history's strangest trial.

The charges were read with a madman's fervor as the witnesses looked on in horror. I-Perjury. II-Coveting the papacy. III-Violating the church canons when he was elected.

Stephen ranted, accused, and demanded that Formosus voice his defense.

Of course, there was no reply.

Stephen persisted, and Formosus' counsel wisely remained mum. Eventually finding Formosus guilty of all charges and unable to contain his rage any longer, Stephen had the former Pope's corpse stripped, the three fingers of benediction on the right hand hacked off, and the remains thrown to the mob outside, who dragged it through the streets and threw it into the Tiber. His corpse was recovered later and given a proper burial. Mere weeks after the trial, the Lateran Palace was destroyed by fire.

The Roman clergy, having been pushed to its limit, revolted. Stephen was imprisoned and strangled, and a further synod overturned his rulings and forbade future trials of the dead.

Sergius III was elected in 898 and promptly fled for his life as imperial forces again intervened. A successor, Leo V, was elected and shortly overthrown and imprisoned by Christopher (who was later declared anti-pope and removed from the list of papal succession).

This would have been a suitable end to the saga but the following years were filled with strife. Several popes ascended and died in the six years following the Cadaver Synod, but in 903 Sergius returned with military backing. He had both the long-imprisoned Leo and Christopher put to death.

Sergius reinstated the verdict of the Cadaver Synod. Formosus' much-abused corpse was exhumed once again. This time his body was decapitated in a posthumous execution.

However you deal with the problem of the basic questions of religion, you will undoubtedly appreciate the spiritual power locked up in every personality which can be released by faith. Do not play around with religion. Accept it or reject it. Most make it the center of their lives with a brief casual nod every Sunday. It is much better to have your own inner sense of faith in the possibility of man, or humanity, which you can use each day to maintain your equilibrium, but make no grand sermons or protestations that are never heard beyond the doors of the church.

But I first had to understand the Bible. I came to realize that I had to read the text very carefully and closely in order to record it as accurately as possible. Five books of Moses were initially compiled by the priests; the Torah is made up of Genesis, Exodus, Leviticus, Numbers, and Deuteronomy. They have survived for millennia, though many of the stories are buried and forgotten.

I began my reading and understanding that many of the passages in the Bible are made up of narrative dialogue in an attempt to streamline and modernize the old scriptures. There were various attempts to adhere to a format, a narrative format, that the Bible is the Word of God, or inspired by God. I do not believe the Bible is the word of God, I believe the Bible is the words of man. I was always intrigued by the chapters of Genesis, and I realize that through the years and successive Bibles much of the meanings and intentions have been lost. Things have been altered, they have been changed by increasingly entrenched priests, and the triumph of the patriarchy over an ancient and ever more dimly remembered matriarchy. A great deal has been lost in the mists of time, and many of the scholars will say that much of it is educated guesswork. They will pontificate and pour over the clues and try to fill in the missing fragments. The literal interpretation of the book of Genesis offends or outrages some readers, but then again some of that text is revered by many people. I had no intention of trying to ridicule the hypocrisy, I was irregularly educating myself.

REFLECTIONS

Many people on Staten Island, white and Black, feel and witness the frustration, the suffering, and the futility of Blacks. The Black leaders must have cohesion, discipline and organization in a society numerically too small to be effective. When I look at the North Shore and the East Shore it is a microcosm of the new ghetto. Blacks have been accustomed to the conditions here unlike the South Shore white communities. And the whites that do live here on the North Shore live in tight neighborhood patches and are reluctant to put their noses in places that will jeopardize their place in the system. The Black churches will continue to use the pulpit for hope; hope that the white community will wake up to the misery of this place that is also shared by many lower class working whites that find on the North Shore lower costs for housing and a place to do environmentally destructive business.

RETURNING HOME

In writing this I have done my utmost to come up with an intelligent, and intelligible, piece of work. It will not be perfect; some parts will be better than others. The editors will send things back to me for more clarification and in all probability the end result will have little to do with what I originally thought, but it will be fine. It may not be made so perfect or fashioned so well as to be understood by all; however, it will hit a mark somewhere for someone; and since I will be older, I will be wiser!

Finally, if God did create all this in seven days, he did a damn good job and is entitled to a bit of vanity. But as I read, again and again, there are a lot of mistakes, and he has returned to his tent for some revisions. So, is this a perfect universe? No. It will mess up a lot of folks; it will mess up their brains. The religious orders will have a job to clear up this moral confusion if there is to be a future in it for all of us. I will be satisfied listening to the gospel voices I love. I listen to them again and again, amazed and entranced by the pageantry of the ritual.

In reviewing my life work with finding God, it has been difficult, very difficult, and I realize that a lot of people have been where I was at. I was not a religious writer or student, I was a Black guy looking for my people in a book, and on one voyage to Saudi Arabia it came to me. Who the fuck are you to question the Bible? Who's going to listen to your voice? And why do you want them to know?

The Good Book was given to me by my family, and it seemed to be the right way to live. But on closer inspection, I didn't want to be the same as everyone else in my family. I was many times told that I was simply hard headed, and this, of course, would get me bitten by a serpent or struck dead by lightning, or perhaps I would wake up with a lot of warts or boils! Would I be opening the family door for a plague? I was silent for many, many years. I did know that, living and dying, I was a member of a very large family, but I also knew that I was not going to live for 900 years.

However, nothing in the world can take the place of nagging persistence. Talent will not, genius will not, education will not; the world is full of educated derelicts. Resistance and determination alone are omnipotent. The slogan 'Simply Press On' will always solve the problems of the human race.

My story of God was initially to seek help in finding the path, and everyone wanted that, even the guys who hung out in the church foyer on Sunday morning before church services, checking out the women.

SERETTA'S PASSING

In late 1992 I was living in Senegal and working with Jude in the city of Ziguinchor in the southern provinces of Senegal. A driver arrived from the capital with a message that I had to respond to an urgent telephone call from Staten Island, New York. I realized it had to be important because any landline phone calls to Africa at that time were very difficult.

When I got back to Dakar, the capital of Senegal, I placed a call to my sister Inez and she said that my mother, Seretta, was in St. Vincent's Hospital and she was not well; she wanted to go. I ask where she wanted to go, and Inez said, "She wants to die, Cleve. She has been in the hospital now for three days and she says she does not want to live any longer." Seretta was strong willed, always had been, and she would have it her way. I said, "Can you put her on?"

"No, she's in bed," said Inez. "She wants to see you, to talk to you, before she goes." Inez is matter of fact. Before she goes. Before she dies.

"OK," I said, "I'll come home as soon as possible, as soon as I can get a flight." A day later I was at my mother's bedside at St. Vincent's hospital. My sister said "Mom, Cleve is here." She said it several times. My mother opened her eyes and smiled at me. She said nothing but we connected silently. I held her limp hand. She tried to squeeze, and I felt a slight pressure. I was careful not to squeeze her bones with my huge hands, so I simply held her hand and I said "I'm here, I'm here." She did not respond. She closed her eyes as if she was asleep, and I realized that, at 92, Seretta would probably die.

We left by taxi, and Inez got out at her place, giving me the keys to the family home. The family home on Lockman Avenue was a shotgun-type house. Entering the old homestead was a bit like returning to the womb, only I was now a full-fledged adult. There were spirits in the house, and as I sat down I could hear the voices of my family members; my father, my mother, my sister, my brothers. I was not afraid but I realized that there were a lot of misfortunes that had lived here, entered these same rooms, a lot of human suffering and I'm sure Seretta had undergone and felt it intensely. How in the world did we all live in this house, where did we all sleep, how did we all live to be adults?

I wished that Jude were here.

I sat in the living room in a huge comfortable chair; my body unwinding and relaxing, and I looked around at the portraits placed smilingly around me. I experienced nothing and I realized, looking about, that Seretta had always had a home that was tidy, everything in its place, and I noticed then, under the huge bed that she had kept out of the public eye, shoeboxes. Of course, she had shoe problems. She had always been a firm supporter of Dr. Scholl's.

But there were many things on my mind. I had decisions to make; I didn't understand what I was supposed to do, but I knew there would be funeral arrangements. I couldn't leave things entirely to chance. I knew that I would have to contact the Billups Funeral Home. I was selfish, I guess, I simply wanted to return to Africa, to familiar places. I had to force myself into a kind of stoic calm. I didn't want to dig into my memory. It came.

I wondered if I would have the chutzpah to end my life as Seretta has described this day for many years. Would I rather have my life snuffed out immediately by a fatal heart attack, or hang around and linger in a hospital or a home with some slowpoke disease grinding away? Would I contract a cancer that would leave me suffering on the edge of life and death? Could I have this noble resignation that Seretta has to leave of her own volition?

I tried to rest. I turned on the TV, and there on the screen was a Black man, Rodney King, with a half dozen white policemen beating the shit out of him with long clubs and Tasers. I had more things to think about, but I watched, over and over again, the policemen beating him, waling him, kicking him; this vile nature, this human depravity raining down on the poor man. But I had to remain in the present, here on Staten Island.

Would cremation be better? It would be faster! But no, it wouldn't be proper. We needed the graveside religious affair; it was customary. We needed the ride to the cemetery in the custom limo, we needed the flowers, and we needed the officiating minister who didn't really know Seretta. I'd as soon dispense with the proprieties, but they're observed for the sake of any believers that show up. It was a necessary theatre.

While I was watching the TV I pulled out one of the shoeboxes under my mother's bed. Seretta had spent many years on her feet as a cook and a housekeeper for the Catholic priest at St. Michaels on the next block, Harbor Road. She always complained about corns and callouses and bunions. We had arch supports, cushions, pads, wedges, and liners, but I also knew that the shoeboxes under the bed were where Seretta kept her most important papers. There was no safe in the house, there were no locks and keys; there were just the Dr. Scholl's shoe boxes. They were innocent little boxes, but I open one and find the little green slips indicating how Seretta paid all of her bills. She would walk to the post office, pay the bill, get a receipt, and file the receipt away in her shoebox.

I would take the Bible and I would take with me some of the papers that I knew would become, at some point, important to me; the death notices, the birth notices, a lifetime of bits and pieces. I knew there was nothing else in the house that I would want.

It was only after being in the house during the few days of her burial, after speaking to some of the relatives, that I was able to savor the memories of better, kinder days in this house. I didn't have much time to look at what was in the boxes.

I wished Jude was here. I was always finding it difficult to make decisions and not have Jude here.

I would find more about my life and the life of my mother, in the shoeboxes and the Bible. I knew that she would want me to pray; I knew that she would want me to pray here, in this place, in this house. I knew that, and I would comply because there were spirits here. There were spirits, there was suffering here, in this house. I would simply do what I think she would have me do. If I were to open my mind and let my thoughts be free, I would have those spirits as my helpers. I would be a shaman of a sort, and they would carry me through the voyage. I would get through this; I would find a place to rest. I would gather my strengths, and eventually return to Africa

In one of the boxes that I pulled out from under the bed, the contents were carefully bound in rubber bands. There were postcards carefully put away, some letters, birthday cards, dozens of Christmas cards, death notices, family photos, and a number of the postal money orders which Seretta used to pay her bills.

In and among the postal money orders were $100 postal money order stubs paid to PTL. The PTL, I began to notice, was the Praise the Lord Club, and I looked at some of the PR from another box. There were a number of colorful photos and brief stories about a handsome looking couple: Jim Bakker with his hair carefully styled and a beautiful broad smile, and next to him his wife, Tammy Faye Bakker, a smiling young woman with a very small waist, a large bouffant hair do, and huge false eyelashes. I had to look very closely at what I was seeing. It was impossible for me at the time to find the motivation for what I was looking at.

I knew that Seretta would have us, the children, get a Christmas Club book at the bank, and put money in a Christmas Club each week or each month. It was money that was set aside for Christmas gifts. But this was something different. There were many pictures of buildings and there were written testimonials to the Praise the Lord Club. I felt at the time that if this was something that Seretta wanted to do and she was happy, it was her business; who could complain.

I knew nothing about Jim and Tammy Faye Bakker, but I would follow the press from time to time and at some point I realized that Jim and Tammy Faye were into a huge racket. I tried hard but failed to imagine my money going into the till of Jim and Tammy Faye. But this is Struggle Island and there is no monopoly on corruption here. I would follow the indictments of this gluttonous couple in the newspapers. Not only did they enrich themselves to buy Louis Vuitton bags and Rolex watches, personal hairdressers and barbers, they also used money to air condition their doghouses.

Jim and Tammy Faye Bakker were flashy, both sported ivory white teeth, but God seems to like flashy.

Jim Bakker was eventually indicted by a federal grand jury. He was tried for mail fraud, wire fraud, and conspiracy and he was sentenced to 45 years in federal prison.

I didn't really know where I stood. It really didn't concern me or make me feel angry toward Seretta or anyone. I felt she had been taken advantage of; she was sucked in like many other people. I just hoped that when I had joined the military and had my full military pay sent home to Seretta, none of it had found its way into the grubby coffers of Jim and Tammy Faye Bakker.

It was depressing for me to be back in the US with my mother in the hospital. My mother, a Black woman who had worked hard all her life, and given birth to a large family of eight surviving children. My father had built this shotgun styled house I was sitting in. I was finding more papers and all of the beautiful colorful literature from the PTL Club, and now I would watch the TV for hours on end to pick up the information about what was happening to a Black man in Los Angeles. Rodney King would survive, Seretta died in Saint Vincent's hospital a day later at age 92.

Leaving Staten Island was easy after the funeral, there were no more decisions to be made; my brothers and sisters would review the will. I went to the attorneys office on Port Richmond Avenue and signed the legal documents. I wanted nothing more than the shoe boxes. Leaving Struggle Island was not easy, it never was after being away, there were just too many ghosts here, never having time to read or write from the note books, I would leave my personal papers and the shoe boxes in the basement of a dear friend for safekeeping. I would get a few newspapers about the King beatings in California, board a plane at Kennedy Airport and return to Africa.

TO THE MEMORY OF MY PIOUS ANCESTORS

In June 24, 2006, I received a Certificate of Merit from the New York State Assembly in recognition of achievement that I, Cleve Overton, would be receiving this award, the Association's award, a Griot Award.

I had spent almost a decade in some countries in Africa. I met Senegalese Wolof griots; I listened to them, I sat at their feet for many hours, but Griots live in many parts of the African continent. I put these proclamations aside until I was asked a number of times why I was doing this. What difference would it make in the lives of anyone? I didn't know, but after becoming a Muslim and traveling to Saudi Arabia to the Hajj I would use the proclamations as it said - I think where would be some importance of being a Black man, an older Black man...I haven't found any griots on Staten Island, but I was given the title; I would use it.

I was also given a drawing of a griot, and the griots in North Africa were also marabous, religious people. The marabous and the griots were champions, fearless champions of history. The drawing sent to me was of a griot, a marabou, with a huge lion. The marabou was holding the great giant beast by a leather strap about it showing his superior strength. I would not attempt to walk through any of the streets of Staten Island with a lion or tiger.

We Black men have this warrior thing; we wear armor like we are under siege. After my work to find God I know the symptoms in other men and I say "Come. Take my hand and I will walk through the flames with you. We need each other."